Theories at-a-Glance

The tables in this book compare theories over a r[illegible] the ability to easily compare, contrast, and grasp [illegible] aspects of each theory. These tables also serve as invaluable resources that can be used to review the key concepts, philosophies, limitations, contributions to multicultural counseling, applications, techniques, and goals of all theories in this text.

The following chart provides a convenient guide to the tables in this text.

Overview of Focus Questions for the Theories

For the chapters dealing with the different theories, you will have a basic understanding of this book if you can answer the following questions as they apply to each of the eleven theories:

Who are the key figures (founder or founders) associated with the approach?

What are some of the basic assumptions underlying this approach?

What are a few of the key concepts that are essential to this theory?

What do you consider to be the most important goals of this therapy?

What is the role the therapeutic relationship plays in terms of therapy outcomes?

What are a few of the techniques from this therapy model that you would want to incorporate into your counseling practice?

What are some of the ways that this theory is applied to client populations, settings, and treatment of problems?

What do you see as the major strength of this theory from a diversity perspective?

What do you see as the major shortcoming of this theory from a diversity perspective?

What do you consider to be the most significant contribution of this approach?

What do you consider to be the most significant limitation of this approach?

THEORY AND PRACTICE OF COUNSELING AND PSYCHOTHERAPY

Tenth Edition

Gerald Corey

California State University, Fullerton
Diplomate in Counseling Psychology,
American Board of Professional Psychology

CENGAGE

Australia • Brazil • India • Mexico • Singapore • United Kingdom • United States

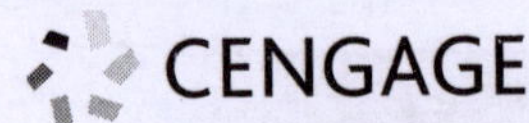

Theory and Practice of Counseling and Psychotherapy, Tenth Edition

Gerald Corey

ISBN-13: 978-93-5350-207-2
ISBN-10: 93-5350-207-1

Registered Office:
Cengage Learning India Private Limited
T-303, 3rd Floor
DAV Complex, Plot 3
Mayur Vihar Phase 1
Delhi-110091
Email: asia.infoindia@cengage.com

Cengage Learning is a leading provider of customized learning solutions with office locations around the globe, including Andover, Melbourne, Mexico City, Stamford (CT), Toronto, Hong Kong, New Delhi, Seoul, Singapore, and Tokyo. Locate your local office at:
www.cengage.com/global

Cengage Learning Products are represented in Canada by Nelson Education, Ltd.

For product information, visit our website at **www.cengage.co.in**

Printed in India
Sixth Indian Reprint 2022

To the founders and key figures of the theories presented in this book—with appreciation for their contributions to contemporary counseling practice.

ABOUT THE AUTHOR

GERALD COREY is Professor Emeritus of Human Services and Counseling at California State University at Fullerton. He received his doctorate in counseling from the University of Southern California. He is a Diplomate in Counseling Psychology, American Board of Professional Psychology; a licensed psychologist; and a National Certified Counselor. He is a Fellow of the American Psychological Association (Division 17, Counseling Psychology; and Division 49, Group Psychotherapy); a Fellow of the American Counseling Association; and a Fellow of the Association for Specialists in Group Work. He also holds memberships in the American Group Psychotherapy Association; the American Mental Health Counselors Association; the Association for Spiritual, Ethical, and Religious Values in Counseling; the Association for Counselor Education and Supervision; and the Western Association of Counselor Education and Supervision. Both Jerry and Marianne Corey received the Lifetime Achievement Award from the American Mental Health Counselors Association in 2011, and both of them received the Eminent Career Award from ASGW in 2001. Jerry was given the Outstanding Professor of the Year Award from California State University at Fullerton in 1991. He regularly teaches both undergraduate and graduate courses in group counseling and ethics in counseling. He is the author or coauthor of 15 textbooks in counseling currently in print, along with more than 60 journal articles and book chapters. Several of his books have been translated into other languages. *Theory and Practice of Counseling and Psychotherapy* has been translated into Arabic, Indonesian, Portuguese, Turkish, Korean, and Chinese. *Theory and Practice of Group Counseling* has been translated into Korean, Chinese, Spanish, and Russian. *Issues and Ethics in the Helping Professions* has been translated into Korean, Japanese, and Chinese.

In the past 40 years Jerry and Marianne Corey have conducted group counseling training workshops for mental health professionals at many universities in the United States as well as in Canada, Mexico, China, Hong Kong, Korea, Germany, Belgium, Scotland, England, and Ireland. In his leisure time, Jerry likes to travel, hike and bicycle in the mountains, and drive his 1931 Model A Ford. Marianne and Jerry have been married since 1964. They have two adult daughters, Heidi and Cindy, two granddaughters (Kyla and Keegan), and one grandson (Corey).

Recent publications by Jerry Corey, all with Cengage Learning, include:

- *Theory and Practice of Group Counseling*, Ninth Edition (and *Student Manual*) (2016)
- *Becoming a Helper*, Seventh Edition (2016, with Marianne Schneider Corey)
- *Issues and Ethics in the Helping Professions*, Ninth Edition (2015, with Marianne Schneider Corey, Cindy Corey, and Patrick Callanan)
- *Group Techniques*, Fourth Edition (2015, with Marianne Schneider Corey, Patrick Callanan, and J. Michael Russell)
- *Groups: Process and Practice*, Ninth Edition (2014, with Marianne Schneider Corey and Cindy Corey)

- *I Never Knew I Had a Choice*, Tenth Edition (2014, with Marianne Schneider Corey)
- *Case Approach to Counseling and Psychotherapy*, Eighth Edition (2013)
- *The Art of Integrative Counseling*, Third Edition (2013)

Jerry Corey is coauthor (with Barbara Herlihy) of *Boundary Issues in Counseling: Multiple Roles and Responsibilities*, Third Edition (2015) and *ACA Ethical Standards Casebook*, Seventh Edition (2015); he is coauthor (with Robert Haynes, Patrice Moulton, and Michelle Muratori) of *Clinical Supervision in the Helping Professions: A Practical Guide*, Second Edition (2010); he is the author of *Creating Your Professional Path: Lessons From My Journey* (2010). All four of these books are published by the American Counseling Association.

He has also made several educational DVD programs on various aspects of counseling practice: (1) *Ethics in Action: DVD and Workbook* (2015, with Marianne Schneider Corey and Robert Haynes); (2) *Groups in Action: Evolution and Challenges DVD and Workbook* (2014, with Marianne Schneider Corey and Robert Haynes); (3) *DVD for Theory and Practice of Counseling and Psychotherapy: The Case of Stan and Lecturettes* (2013); (4) *DVD for Integrative Counseling: The Case of Ruth and Lecturettes* (2013, with Robert Haynes); and (5) *DVD for Theory and Practice of Group Counseling* (2012). All of these programs are available through Cengage Learning.

Contents

Preface to Tenth Edition

This book is intended for counseling courses for undergraduate and graduate students in psychology, counselor education, human services, and the mental health professions. It surveys the major concepts and practices of the contemporary therapeutic systems and addresses some ethical and professional issues in counseling practice. The book aims to teach students to select wisely from various theories and techniques and to begin to develop a personal style of counseling.

I have found that students appreciate an overview of the divergent contemporary approaches to counseling and psychotherapy. They also consistently say that the first course in counseling means more to them when it deals with them personally. Therefore, I stress the practical applications of the material and encourage personal reflection. Using this book can be both a personal and an academic learning experience.

In this tenth edition, every effort has been made to retain the major qualities that students and professors have found useful in the previous editions: the succinct overview of the key concepts of each theory and their implications for practice, the straightforward and personal style, and the book's comprehensive scope. Care has been taken to present the theories in an accurate and fair way. I have attempted to be simple, clear, and concise. Because many students want suggestions for supplementary reading as they study each therapy approach, I have included an updated reading list at the end of each chapter and a list of references for each chapter at the end of the book.

This tenth edition updates the material and refines existing discussions. Part 1 deals with issues that are basic to the practice of counseling and psychotherapy. Chapter 1 puts the book into perspective, then students are introduced to the counselor—as a person and a professional—in Chapter 2. This chapter addresses a number of topics pertaining to the role of the counselor as a person and the therapeutic relationship. Chapter 3 introduces students to some key ethical issues in counseling practice, and several of the topics in this chapter have been updated and expanded. Expanded coverage is given to the ACA's 2014 *Code of Ethics*.

Part 2 is devoted to a consideration of 11 theories of counseling. Each of the theory chapters follows a common organizational pattern, and students can easily compare and contrast the various models. This pattern includes core topics such as key concepts, the therapeutic process, therapeutic techniques and procedures, multicultural perspectives, the theory applied to the case of Stan and new to this edition to the case of Gwen, and summary and evaluation. In this tenth edition, each of the chapters in Part 2 has been revised, updated, and expanded to reflect recent trends, and references have been updated as well. Revisions were based on the recommendations of experts in each theory, all of whom are listed in the Acknowledgments section. Attention was given to current trends and recent developments in the practice of each theoretical approach.

Each of the 11 theory chapters summarizes key points and evaluates the contributions, strengths, limitations, and applications of these theories. Special attention is given to evaluating each theory from a multicultural perspective as well, with a commentary on the strengths and shortcomings of the theory in working with diverse client populations. The consistent organization of the summary and evaluation sections makes comparing theories easier. Students are given recommendations regarding where to look for further training for all of the approaches in the *Where To Go From Here* sections at the end of the chapter.

In Part 3, Chapter 15 develops the notion that an integrative approach to counseling practice is in keeping with meeting the needs of diverse client populations in many different settings. Numerous tables and other integrating material help students compare and contrast the 11 approaches.

What's New in This Tenth Edition

Features of the tenth edition include *Learning Objectives* for all the theory chapters; *Self-Reflection and Discussion Questions* at the end of each theory chapter to facilitate thinking and interaction in class; and a new *Case of Gwen*, who is a composite of many clients, to complement the *Case of Stan* feature. Guest contributor Dr. Kellie Kirksey describes her way of working with Gwen from each of the theoretical perspectives.

Significant changes for the tenth edition for each of the theory chapters are outlined below:

Chapter 4 Psychoanalytic Therapy

- New material on countertransference, its role in psychoanalytic therapy, and guidelines for effectively dealing with countertransference
- Expanded discussion of brief psychodynamic therapy and its application

Chapter 5 Adlerian Therapy

- Revised material on the life tasks
- More emphasis on goals for the educational process of therapy
- More on the role of assessment and diagnosis
- New material on early recollections with concrete examples
- Many new examples to bring Adlerian concepts to life
- Revised discussion of reorientation and encouragement process
- Expanded discussion of Adlerian techniques

Chapter 6 Existential Therapy

- Revised material on existential anxiety and its implications for therapy
- Revised section on the client–therapist relationship
- Expanded discussion of tasks of the existential therapist

Chapter 7 Person-Centered Therapy

- Expanded discussion of clients as active self-healers
- Updated coverage of the core conditions of congruence, unconditional positive regard, and empathy
- More attention to the diversity of styles of therapists practicing person-centered therapy
- More emphasis on how the basic philosophy of the person-centered approach is appropriate for working with diverse client populations
- A new section on emotion-focused therapy, stressing the role of emotions as a route to change
- Revised section on motivational interviewing (person-centered approach with a twist)

Chapter 8 Gestalt Therapy

- Revised discussion of the role of experiments in Gestalt therapy and how they differ from techniques and structured exercises
- New emphasis on therapist presence, the role of dialogue in therapy, and the therapeutic relationship
- Expanded discussion of therapist authenticity and self-disclosure
- More attention to the contemporary relational approach to Gestalt practice

Chapter 9 Behavior Therapy

- Increased attention to the "third-generation" or "new wave" behavior therapies
- Updating of section on EMDR
- Expanded and updated discussion of the role of mindfulness and acceptance strategies in contemporary behavior therapy
- New and expanded material on mindfulness-based cognitive therapy and stress reduction
- Expanded and revised treatment of dialectical behavior therapy

Chapter 10 Cognitive Behavior Therapy

- Major reorganization and updating of the entire chapter
- Streamlining and updating of Albert Ellis's rational emotive behavior therapy
- Revised and expanded coverage of Aaron Beck's cognitive therapy
- Increased coverage of Judith Beck's role in the development of cognitive therapy
- New section on Christine Padesky's strength-based cognitive behavior therapy
- Increased attention on Donald Meichenbaum's influence in the development of CBT
- More clinical examples to illustrate key CBT techniques and concepts
- Expanded coverage of a comparison among the various CBT approaches

Chapter 11 Choice Theory/Reality Therapy

- Revision of the relationship of choice theory to reality therapy
- More practical examples of reality therapy practice

Chapter 12 Feminist Therapy

- Updated and expanded treatment of the principles of feminist therapy
- Increased attention given to cultural and social justice perspectives
- More emphasis on concepts of power, privilege, discrimination, and empowerment
- Expansion of relational-cultural theory and implications for practice
- Revised and expanded discussion on therapeutic techniques and strategies
- Revised material on strengths from a diversity perspective

Chapter 13 Postmodern Approaches

- Updated coverage on parallels between solution-focused brief therapy (SFBT) and positive psychology
- Broadened discussion of the key concepts of SFBT
- More emphasis on the client-as-expert in the therapy relationship in postmodern approaches
- More clinical examples to illustrate the use of SFBT techniques
- New material on the defining characteristics of brief therapy
- Increased emphasis on the collaborative nature of narrative therapy and SFBT
- Revision of narrative therapy section

Chapter 14 Family Systems Therapy

- Streamlined to focus mainly on an integrative approach to family therapy
- More on recent developments in family systems therapy
- More attention given to feminism, multiculturalism, and postmodern constructionism as applied to family therapy

Chapter 15 ("An Integrative Perspective") pulls together themes from all 11 theoretical orientations. This chapter represents a major revision of the discussion of the psychotherapy integration movement; updates of the various integrative approaches; revision of the section on integration of spirituality in counseling; added material on research demonstrating the therapeutic alliance; expanded discussion on the central role of the client in determining therapy outcomes; new section on feedback-informed treatment; and updated coverage of the conclusions from the research literature on the effectiveness of psychotherapy. New to this chapter are two cases (Stan and Gwen) that illustrate integrative approaches. Chapter 15 develops the notion that an integrative approach to counseling practice is in keeping with meeting the needs of diverse client populations in many different settings. Numerous tables and other integrating material help students compare and contrast the 11 approaches.

This text can be used in a flexible way. Some instructors will follow the sequencing of chapters in the book. Others will prefer to begin with the theory chapters (Part 2) and then deal later with the student's personal characteristics and ethical issues. The topics can be covered in whatever order makes the most sense. Readers are offered some suggestions for using this book in Chapter 1.

In this edition I have made every effort to incorporate those aspects that have worked best in the courses on counseling theory and practice that I teach. To help readers apply theory to practice, I have also revised the *Student Manual*, which is designed for experiential work. The *Student Manual for Theory and Practice of Counseling and Psychotherapy* still contains open-ended questions, many new cases for exploration and discussion, structured exercises, self-inventories, and a variety of activities that can be done both in class and out of class. The tenth edition features a structured overview, as well as a glossary, for each of the theories, and chapter quizzes for assessing the level of student mastery of basic concepts. New to this tenth edition of the *Student Manual* are experiential exercises for the *Case of Gwen* and questions raised by experts in each of the theory chapters. Each expert addresses the same six questions as applied to each of the given theories.

Case Approach to Counseling and Psychotherapy (Eighth Edition) features experts working with the case of Ruth from the various therapeutic approaches. The casebook, which is now available online, can supplement this book or stand alone.

Accompanying this tenth edition of the text and *Student Manual* are lecturettes on how I draw from key concepts and techniques from the various theories presented in the book. *The Art of Integrative Counseling* (Third Edition), which expands on the material in Chapter 15 of the textbook, also complements this book.

Also available is a revised and updated *Instructor's Resource Manual*, which includes suggestions for teaching the course, class activities to stimulate interest, PowerPoint presentations for all chapters, and a variety of test questions and a final examination.

Acknowledgments

The suggestions I received from the many readers of prior editions who took the time to complete the surveys have been most helpful in the revision process. Many other people have contributed ideas that have found their way into this tenth edition. I especially appreciate the time and efforts of those who participated in a prerevision review and offered constructive criticism and supportive commentaries, as well as those professors who have used this book and provided me with feedback that has been most useful in these revisions. Those who reviewed selected parts of the manuscript of the tenth edition are:

Jude Austin, doctoral student, University of Wyoming
Julius Austin, doctoral student, University of Wyoming
Mark E. Young, University of Central Florida
Robert Haynes, Borderline Productions
Beverly Palmer, California State University at Dominguez Hills
James Robert Bitter, East Tennessee State University
Patricia Robertson, East Tennessee State University
Jamie Bludworth, Arizona State University

Michelle Muratori, Johns Hopkins University
Jake Morris, Lipscomb University

Special thanks are extended to the chapter reviewers, who provided consultation and detailed critiques. Their insightful and valuable comments have generally been incorporated into this edition:

- Chapter 4 (Psychoanalytic Therapy): William Blau, Copper Mountain College, Joshua Tree, California
- Chapter 5 (Adlerian Therapy): Matt Englar-Carlson, California State University, Fullerton; Jon Carlson, Governors State University; Jon Sperry, Lynn University, Boca Raton. James Robert Bitter, East Tennessee State University, and I coauthored Chapter 5.
- Chapter 6 (Existential Therapy): Emmy van Deurzen, New School of Psychotherapy and Counselling, London, England, and University of Sheffield; J. Michael Russell of California State University, Fullerton; David N. Elkins, Graduate School of Education and Psychology, Pepperdine University; Bryan Farha, Oklahoma City College
- Chapter 7 (Person-Centered Therapy): Natalie Rogers, Person-Centered Expressive Arts Associates, Cotati, California; David N. Elkins, Graduate School of Education and Psychology, Pepperdine University; David Cain, California School of Professional Psychology at Alliant International University, San Diego
- Chapter 8 (Gestalt Therapy): Jon Frew, Private Practice, Vancouver, Washington, and Pacific University, Oregon; Lynne Jacobs, Pacific Gestalt Institute in Los Angeles; Gary Yontef, Pacific Gestalt Institute in Los Angeles; Jude Austin, doctoral student, University of Wyoming; Julius Austin, doctoral student, University of Wyoming
- Chapter 9 (Behavior Therapy): Sherry Cormier, West Virginia University; Frank M. Dattilio, Harvard Medical School, and the University of Pennsylvania School of Medicine; Ronald D. Siegel, Harvard Medical School
- Chapter 10 (Cognitive Behavior Therapy): Sherry Cormier, West Virginia University; Christine A. Padesky, Center for Cognitive Therapy at Huntington Beach, California; Frank M. Dattilio, Harvard Medical School, and the University of Pennsylvania School of Medicine; Beverly Palmer, California State University at Dominguez Hills; Jamie Bludworth, Arizona State University; Jude Austin, doctoral student, University of Wyoming; Julius Austin, doctoral student, University of Wyoming; Jon Sperry, Lynn University, Boca Raton; Debbie Joffe Ellis
- Chapter 11 (Choice Theory/Reality Therapy): Robert Wubbolding, Center for Reality Therapy, Cincinnati, Ohio
- Chapter 12 (Feminist Therapy): Carolyn Zerbe Enns, Cornell College; James Robert Bitter, East Tennessee State University; Patricia Robertson, East Tennessee State University; Elizabeth Kincade, Indiana University of Pennsylvania; Susan Rachael Seem, The College at Brockport, State University of New York; Kellie Kirksey, Cleveland Institute of Wellness; Amanda La Guardia of Sam

Houston State University. Barbara Herlihy, University of New Orleans, and I coauthored Chapter 12.

- Chapter 13 (Postmodern Approaches): John Winslade, California State University, San Bernardino; John Murphy, University of Central Arkansas
- Chapter 14 (Family Systems Therapy): James Robert Bitter, East Tennessee State University, and I co-authored Chapter 14.
- Chapter 15 (An Integrative Perspective): Scott D. Miller, The International Center for Clinical Excellence; Beverly Palmer, California State University at Dominguez Hills; Jude Austin, doctoral student, University of Wyoming; Julius Austin, doctoral student, University of Wyoming
- The Case of Gwen (all theory chapters) was written by Kellie Kirksey, Cleveland Clinic Center for Integrative Medicine

This book is the result of a team effort, which includes the combined efforts of a number of people at Cengage Learning. These people include Jon-David Hague, Product Director; Julie Martinez, Product Manager, Counseling, Human Services, and Social Work; Vernon Boes, Art Director, for his work on the interior design and cover of this book; Kyra Kane, Associate Content Developer, who coordinates the MindTap™ program and other supplementary materials for the book; Michelle Muratori, Johns Hopkins University, for her work on updating the *Instructor's Resource Manual* and assisting in developing other supplements; and Rita Jaramillo, Content Project Manager. Thanks to Ben Kolstad of Cenveo® Publisher Services, who coordinated the production of this book. Special recognition goes to Kay Mikel, the manuscript editor of this edition, whose exceptional editorial talents continue to keep this book reader friendly. I appreciate Susan Cunningham's work in creating and revising test items to accompany this text and in preparing the index. The efforts and dedication of all of these people certainly contribute to the high quality of this edition.

Gerald Corey

Introduction and Overview

1

LEARNING OBJECTIVES

1. Understand the author's philosophical stance.
2. Identify suggested ways to use this book.
3. Differentiate between each contemporary counseling model discussed in this book.
4. Identify key issues within the case of Stan.
5. Identify key issues within the case of Gwen.

Introduction

Counseling students can begin to acquire a counseling style tailored to their own personality by familiarizing themselves with the major approaches to therapeutic practice. This book surveys 11 approaches to counseling and psychotherapy, presenting the key concepts of each approach and discussing features such as the therapeutic process (including goals), the client–therapist relationship, and specific procedures used in the practice of counseling. This information will help you develop a balanced view of the major ideas of each of the theories and acquaint you with the practical techniques commonly employed by counselors who adhere to each approach. I encourage you to keep an open mind and to seriously consider both the unique contributions and the particular limitations of each therapeutic system presented in Part 2.

You cannot gain the knowledge and experience you need to synthesize various approaches by merely completing an introductory course in counseling theory. This process will take many years of study, training, and practical counseling experience. Nevertheless, I recommend a personal integration as a framework for the professional education of counselors. When students are presented with a single model and are expected to subscribe to it alone, their effectiveness will be limited when working with a diverse range of future clients.

An undisciplined mixture of approaches, however, can be an excuse for failing to develop a sound rationale for systematically adhering to certain concepts and to the techniques that are extensions of them. It is easy to pick and choose fragments from the various therapies because they support our biases and preconceptions. By studying the models presented in this book, you will have a better sense of how to integrate concepts and techniques from different approaches when defining your own personal synthesis and framework for counseling.

Each therapeutic approach has useful dimensions. It is not a matter of a theory being "right" or "wrong," as every theory offers a unique contribution to understanding human behavior and has unique implications for counseling practice. Accepting the validity of one model does not necessarily imply rejecting other models. There is a clear place for theoretical pluralism, especially in a society that is becoming increasingly diverse.

Although I suggest that you remain open to incorporating diverse approaches into your own personal synthesis—or integrative approach to counseling—let me caution that you can become overwhelmed and confused if you attempt to learn everything at once, especially if this is your introductory course in counseling theories. A case can be made for initially getting an overview of the major theoretical orientations, and then learning a particular approach by becoming steeped in that approach for some time, rather than superficially grasping many theoretical approaches. An integrative perspective is not developed in a random fashion; rather, it is an ongoing process that is well thought out. Successfully integrating concepts and techniques from diverse models requires years of reflective practice and a great deal of reading about the various theories. In Chapter 15 I discuss in more depth some ways to begin designing your integrative approach to counseling practice.

Visit CengageBrain.com or watch the DVD for the video program on Chapter 1, *Theory and Practice of Counseling and Psychotherapy: The Case of Stan and Lecturettes*. I suggest that you view the brief lecturette for each chapter in this book prior to reading the chapter.

Where I Stand

My philosophical orientation is strongly influenced by the existential approach. Because this approach does not prescribe a set of techniques and procedures, I draw techniques from the other models of therapy that are presented in this book. I particularly like to use role-playing techniques. When people reenact scenes from their lives, they tend to become more psychologically engaged than when they merely report anecdotes about themselves. I also incorporate many techniques derived from cognitive behavior therapy. LO1

The psychoanalytic emphasis on early psychosexual and psychosocial development is useful. Our past plays a crucial role in shaping our current personality and behavior. I challenge the deterministic notion that humans are the product of their early conditioning and, thus, are victims of their past. But I believe that an exploration of the past is often useful, particularly to the degree that the past continues to influence present-day emotional or behavioral difficulties.

I value the cognitive behavioral focus on how our thinking affects the way we feel and behave. These therapies also emphasize current behavior. Thinking and feeling are important dimensions, but it can be a mistake to overemphasize them and not explore how clients are behaving. What people are doing often provides a good clue to what they really want. I also like the emphasis on specific goals and on encouraging clients to formulate concrete aims for their own therapy sessions and in life.

More approaches have been developing methods that involve collaboration between therapist and client, making the therapeutic venture a shared responsibility. This collaborative relationship, coupled with teaching clients ways to use what they learn in therapy in their everyday lives, empowers clients to take an active stance in their world. It is imperative that clients be active, not only in their counseling sessions but in daily life as well. Homework, collaboratively designed by clients and therapists, can be a vehicle for assisting clients in putting into action what they are learning in therapy.

A related assumption of mine is that we can exercise increasing freedom to create our own future. Accepting personal responsibility does not imply that we can be anything we want to be. Social, environmental, cultural, and biological realities oftentimes limit our freedom of choice. Being able to choose must be considered in the sociopolitical contexts that exert pressure or create constraints; oppression is a reality that can restrict our ability to choose our future. We are also influenced by our social environment, and much of our behavior is a product of learning and conditioning. That being said, I believe an increased awareness of these contextual forces enables us to address these realities. It is crucial to learn how to cope with the external and internal forces that influence our decisions and behavior.

Feminist therapy has contributed an awareness of how environmental and social conditions contribute to the problems of women and men and how gender-role socialization leads to a lack of gender equality. Family therapy teaches us that it is not possible to understand the individual apart from the context of the system. Both family therapy and feminist therapy are based on the premise that to understand the individual it is essential to take into consideration the interpersonal dimensions and the sociocultural context rather than focusing primarily on the intrapsychic domain. This comprehensive approach to counseling goes beyond understanding our internal dynamics and addresses the environmental and systemic realities that influence us.

My philosophy of counseling challenges the assumption that therapy is exclusively aimed at "curing" psychological "ailments." Such a focus on the medical model restricts therapeutic practice because it stresses deficits rather than strengths. Instead, I agree with the postmodern approaches (see Chapter 13), which are grounded on the assumption that people have both internal and external resources to draw upon when constructing solutions to their problems. Therapists will view these individuals quite differently if they acknowledge that their clients possess competencies rather than pathologies. I view each individual as having resources and competencies that can be discovered and built upon in therapy.

Psychotherapy is a process of engagement between two people, both of whom are bound to change through the therapeutic venture. At its best, this is a collaborative process that involves both the therapist and the client in co-constructing solutions regarding life's tasks. Most of the theories described in this book emphasize the collaborative nature of the practice of psychotherapy.

Therapists are not in business to change clients, to give them quick advice, or to solve their problems for them. Instead, counselors facilitate healing through a process of genuine dialogue with their clients. The kind of person a therapist is remains the most critical factor affecting the client and promoting change. If practitioners possess wide knowledge, both theoretical and practical, yet lack human qualities of compassion, caring, good faith, honesty, presence, realness, and sensitivity, they are more like technicians. I believe that those who function exclusively as technicians do not make a significant difference in the lives of their clients. It is essential that counselors explore their own values, attitudes, and beliefs in depth and work to increase their own awareness. Throughout the book I encourage you to find ways to apply what you are reading to your personal life. Doing so will take you beyond a mere academic understanding of these theories.

With respect to mastering the techniques of counseling and applying them appropriately and effectively, it is my belief that you are your own very best technique. Your engagement with your clients is useful in moving the therapeutic process along. It is impossible to separate the techniques you use from your personality and the relationship you have with your clients.

Administering techniques to clients without regard for the relationship variables is ineffective. Techniques cannot substitute for the hard work it takes to develop a constructive client–therapist relationship. Although you can learn attitudes and skills and acquire certain knowledge about personality dynamics and the therapeutic process, much of effective therapy is the product of artistry. Counseling entails far more than becoming a skilled technician. It implies that you are able to establish and maintain a good working relationship with your clients, that you can draw on your own experiences and reactions, and that you can identify techniques suited to the needs of your clients.

As a counselor, you need to remain open to your own personal development and to address your personal problems. The most powerful ways for you to teach your clients is by the behavior you model and by the ways you connect with them. I suggest you experience a wide variety of techniques yourself *as a client*. Reading about a technique in a book is one thing; actually experiencing it from the vantage point of a client is quite another. If you have practiced mindfulness exercises, for example, you will have a much better sense for guiding clients in the practice of becoming increasingly mindful in daily life. If you have carried out real-life homework assignments as part of your own self-change program, you can increase your empathy for clients and their potential problems. Your own anxiety over self-disclosing and addressing personal concerns can be a most useful anchoring point as you work with the anxieties of your clients. The courage you display in your own personal therapy will help you appreciate how essential courage is for your clients.

Your personal characteristics are of primary importance in becoming a counselor, but it is not sufficient to be merely a good person with good intentions. To be effective, you also must have supervised experiences in counseling and sound knowledge of counseling theory and techniques. Further, it is essential to be well grounded in the various *theories of personality* and to learn how they are related to *theories of counseling*. Your conception of the person and the individual characteristics of your client affect the interventions you will make. Differences between you and your client may require modification of certain aspects of the theories. Some practitioners make the mistake of relying on one type of intervention (supportive, confrontational, information giving) for most clients with whom they work. In reality, different clients may respond better to one type of intervention than to another. Even during the course of an individual's therapy, different interventions may be needed at different times. Practitioners should acquire a broad base of counseling techniques that are suitable for individual clients rather than forcing clients to fit one approach to counseling.

Suggestions for Using the Book

Here are some specific recommendations on how to get the fullest value from **LO2** this book. The personal tone of the book invites you to relate what you are reading to your own experiences. As you read Chapter 2, "The Counselor: Person and Professional," begin the process of reflecting on your needs, motivations, values, and life experiences. Consider how you are likely to bring the person you are becoming into your professional work. You will assimilate much more knowledge about the various therapies if you make a conscious attempt to apply the key concepts and techniques of these theories to your own personal life. Chapter 2 helps you think about how to use yourself as your single most important therapeutic instrument, and it addresses a number of significant ethical issues in counseling practice.

Before you study each of the theories chapters, I suggest that you at least briefly read Chapter 15, which provides a comprehensive review of the key concepts from all 11 theories presented in this textbook. I try to show how an integration of these perspectives can form the basis for creating your own personal synthesis to counseling. In developing an integrative perspective, it is essential to think holistically. To understand human functioning, it is imperative to account for the physical, emotional, mental, social, cultural, political, and spiritual dimensions. If any one of these facets of human experience is neglected, a theory is limited in explaining how we think, feel, and act.

To provide you with a consistent framework for comparing and contrasting the various therapies, the 11 theory chapters share a common format. This format includes a few notes on the personal history of the founder or another key figure; a brief historical sketch showing how and why each theory developed at the time it did; a discussion of the approach's key concepts; an overview of the therapeutic process, including the therapist's role and client's work; therapeutic techniques and procedures; applications of the theory from a multicultural perspective; application of the theory to the cases of Stan and Gwen; a summary; a critique of the theory with emphasis on contributions and limitations; suggestions of how to continue your learning about each approach; and suggestions for further reading.

Refer to the Preface for a complete description of other resources that fit as a package and complement this textbook, including *Student Manual for Theory and Practice of Counseling and Psychotherapy* and *DVD for Integrative Counseling: The Case of Ruth and Lecturettes.* In addition, in *DVD for Theory and Practice of Counseling and Psychotherapy: The Case of Stan and Lecturettes* I demonstrate my way of counseling Stan from the various theoretical approaches in 13 sessions and present my perspective on the key concepts of each theory in a brief lecture, with emphasis on the practical application of the theory.

Overview of the Theory Chapters

I have selected 11 therapeutic approaches for this book. Table 1.1 presents **LO3** an overview of these approaches, which are explored in depth in Chapters 4 through 14. I have grouped these approaches into four general categories.

TABLE 1.1 Overview of Contemporary Counseling Models

Psychodynamic Approaches	
Psychoanalytic therapy	Founder: Sigmund Freud. A theory of personality development, a philosophy of human nature, and a method of psychotherapy that focuses on unconscious factors that motivate behavior. Attention is given to the events of the first six years of life as determinants of the later development of personality.
Adlerian therapy	Founder: Alfred Adler. Key Figure: Following Adler, Rudolf Dreikurs is credited with popularizing this approach in the United States. This is a growth model that stresses assuming responsibility, creating one's own destiny, and finding meaning and goals to create a purposeful life. Key concepts are used in most other current therapies.
Experiential and Relationship-Oriented Therapies	
Existential therapy	Key figures: Viktor Frankl, Rollo May, and Irvin Yalom. Reacting against the tendency to view therapy as a system of well-defined techniques, this model stresses building therapy on the basic conditions of human existence, such as choice, the freedom and responsibility to shape one's life, and self-determination. It focuses on the quality of the person-to-person therapeutic relationship.

Person-centered therapy	Founder: Carl Rogers; Key figure: Natalie Rogers. This approach was developed during the 1940s as a nondirective reaction against psychoanalysis. Based on a subjective view of human experiencing, it places faith in and gives responsibility to the client in dealing with problems and concerns.
Gestalt therapy	Founders: Fritz and Laura Perls; Key figures: Miriam and Erving Polster. An experiential therapy stressing awareness and integration; it grew as a reaction against analytic therapy. It integrates the functioning of body and mind and places emphasis on the therapeutic relationship.
Cognitive Behavioral Approaches	
Behavior therapy	Key figures: B. F. Skinner, and Albert Bandura. This approach applies the principles of learning to the resolution of specific behavioral problems. Results are subject to continual experimentation. The methods of this approach are always in the process of refinement. The mindfulness and acceptance-based approaches are rapidly gaining popularity.
Cognitive behavior therapy	Founders: Albert Ellis and A. T. Beck. Albert Ellis founded rational emotive behavior therapy, a highly didactic, cognitive, action-oriented model of therapy, and A. T. Beck founded cognitive therapy, which gives a primary role to thinking as it influences behavior. Judith Beck continues to develop CBT; Christine Padesky has developed strengths-based CBT; and Donald Meichenbaum, who helped develop cognitive behavior therapy, has made significant contributions to resilience as a factor in coping with trauma.
Choice theory/Reality therapy	Founder: William Glasser. Key figure: Robert Wubbolding. This short-term approach is based on choice theory and focuses on the client assuming responsibility in the present. Through the therapeutic process, the client is able to learn more effective ways of meeting her or his needs.
Systems and Postmodern Approaches	
Feminist therapy	This approach grew out of the efforts of many women, a few of whom are Jean Baker Miller, Carolyn Zerbe Enns, Oliva Espin, and Laura Brown. A central concept is the concern for the psychological oppression of women. Focusing on the constraints imposed by the sociopolitical status to which women have been relegated, this approach explores women's identity development, self-concept, goals and aspirations, and emotional well-being.
Postmodern approaches	A number of key figures are associated with the development of these various approaches to therapy. Steve de Shazer and Insoo Kim Berg are the cofounders of solution-focused brief therapy. Michael White and David Epston are the major figures associated with narrative therapy. Social constructionism, solution-focused brief therapy, and narrative therapy all assume that there is no single truth; rather, it is believed that reality is socially constructed through human interaction. These approaches maintain that the client is an expert in his or her own life.
Family systems therapy	A number of significant figures have been pioneers of the family systems approach, two of whom include Murray Bowen and Virginia Satir. This systemic approach is based on the assumption that the key to changing the individual is understanding and working with the family.

First are the *psychodynamic approaches. Psychoanalytic therapy* is based largely on insight, unconscious motivation, and reconstruction of the personality. The psychoanalytic model appears first because it has had a major influence on all of the formal systems of psychotherapy. Some of the therapeutic models are extensions of psychoanalysis, others are modifications of analytic concepts and procedures, and still others emerged as a reaction against psychoanalysis. Many theories of psychotherapy have borrowed and integrated principles and techniques from psychoanalytic approaches.

Adlerian therapy differs from psychoanalytic theory in many respects, but it can broadly be considered an analytic perspective. Adlerians focus on meaning, goals, purposeful behavior, conscious action, belonging, and social interest. Although Adlerian theory accounts for present behavior by studying childhood experiences, it does not focus on unconscious dynamics.

The second category comprises the *experiential and relationship-oriented therapies*: the existential approach, the person-centered approach, and Gestalt therapy. The *existential approach* stresses a concern for what it means to be fully human. It suggests certain themes that are part of the human condition, such as freedom and responsibility, anxiety, guilt, awareness of being finite, creating meaning in the world, and shaping one's future by making active choices. This approach is not a unified school of therapy with a clear theory and a systematic set of techniques. Rather, it is a philosophy of counseling that stresses the divergent methods of understanding the subjective world of the person. The *person-centered approach*, which is rooted in a humanistic philosophy, places emphasis on the basic attitudes of the therapist. It maintains that the quality of the client–therapist relationship is the prime determinant of the outcomes of the therapeutic process. Philosophically, this approach assumes that clients have the capacity for self-direction without active intervention and direction on the therapist's part. Another experiential approach is *Gestalt therapy*, which offers a range of experiments to help clients gain awareness of what they are experiencing in the here and now—that is, the present. In contrast to person-centered therapists, Gestalt therapists tend to take an active role, yet they follow the leads provided by their clients. These approaches tend to emphasize emotion as a route to bringing about change, and in a sense, they can be considered emotion-focused therapies.

Third are the *cognitive behavioral approaches*, sometimes known as the action-oriented therapies because they all emphasize translating insights into behavioral action. These approaches include choice theory/reality therapy, behavior therapy, rational emotive behavior therapy, and cognitive therapy. *Reality therapy* focuses on clients' current behavior and stresses developing clear plans for new behaviors. Like reality therapy, *behavior therapy* puts a premium on doing and on taking steps to make concrete changes. A current trend in behavior therapy is toward paying increased attention to cognitive factors as an important determinant of behavior. *Rational emotive behavior therapy* and *cognitive therapy* highlight the necessity of learning how to challenge inaccurate beliefs and automatic thoughts that lead to behavioral problems. These cognitive behavioral approaches are used to help people modify their inaccurate and self-defeating assumptions and to develop new patterns of acting.

The fourth general approach encompasses the *systems and postmodern perspectives*. Feminist therapy and family therapy are systems approaches, but they also share postmodern notions. The systems orientation stresses the importance of understanding individuals in the context of the surroundings that influence their development. To bring about individual change, it is essential to pay attention to how the individual's personality has been affected by his or her gender-role socialization, culture, family, and other systems.

The *postmodern approaches* include social constructionism, solution-focused brief therapy, and narrative therapy. These newer approaches challenge the basic assumptions of most of the traditional approaches by assuming that there is no single truth and that reality is socially constructed through human interaction. Both the postmodern and the systemic theories focus on how people produce their own lives in the context of systems, interactions, social conditioning, and discourse.

In my view, practitioners need to pay attention to what their clients are *thinking*, *feeling*, and *doing*, and a complete therapy system must address all three of these facets. Some of the therapies included here highlight the role that cognitive factors play in counseling. Others place emphasis on the experiential aspects of counseling and the role of feelings. Still others emphasize putting plans into action and learning by doing. Combining all of these dimensions provides the basis for a comprehensive therapy.

Introduction to the Case of Stan

You will learn a great deal by seeing a theory in action, preferably in a live demonstration or as part of experiential activities in which you function in the alternating roles of client and counselor. An online program (available in DVD format as well) demonstrates one or two techniques from each of the theories. As Stan's counselor, I show how I would apply some of the principles of each of the theories you are studying to Stan. Many of my students find this case history of the hypothetical client (Stan) helpful in understanding how various techniques are applied to the same person. Stan's case, which describes his life and struggles, is presented here to give you significant background material to draw from as you study the applications of the theories. Each of the 11 theory chapters in Part 2 includes a discussion of how a therapist with the orientation under discussion is likely to proceed with Stan. We examine the answers to questions such as these: LO4

- What themes in Stan's life merit special attention in therapy?
- What concepts would be useful to you in working with Stan on his problems?
- What are the general goals of Stan's therapy?
- What possible techniques and methods would best meet these goals?
- What are some characteristics of the relationship between Stan and his therapist?
- How might the therapist proceed?
- How might the therapist evaluate the process and treatment outcomes of therapy?

In Chapter 15 (which I recommend you read early) I explain how I would work with Stan, suggesting concepts and techniques I would draw on from many of the models (forming an integrative approach).

A single case illustrates both contrasts and parallels among the approaches. It also will help you understand the practical applications of the 11 models and provide a basis for integrating them. A summary of the intake interview with Stan, his autobiography, and some key themes in his life are presented next to provide a context for making sense of the way therapists with various theoretical orientations might work with Stan. Try to find attributes of each approach that you can incorporate into a personalized style of counseling.

Intake Interview and Stan's Autobiography

The setting is a community mental health agency where both individual and group counseling are available. Stan comes to counseling because of his drinking. He was convicted of driving under the influence, and the judge determined that he needed professional help. Stan recognizes that he does have problems, but he is not convinced that he is addicted to alcohol. Stan arrives for an intake interview and provides the counselor with this information:

> At the present time I work in construction. I like building houses, but probably won't stay in construction for the rest of my life. When it comes to my personal life, I've always had difficulty in getting along with people. I could be called a "loner." I like people in my life, but I don't seem to know how to stay close to people. It probably has a lot to do with why I drink. I'm not very good at making friends or getting close to people. Probably the reason I sometimes drink a bit too much is because I'm so scared when it comes to socializing. Even though I hate to admit it, when I drink, things are not quite so overwhelming. When I look at others, they seem to know the right things to say. Next to them I feel dumb. I'm afraid that people don't find me very interesting. I'd like to turn my life around, but I just don't know where to begin. That's why I went back to school. I'm a part-time college student majoring in psychology. I want to better myself. In one of my classes, Psychology of Personal Adjustment, we talked about ourselves and how people change. We also had to write an autobiographical paper.

That is the essence of Stan's introduction. The counselor says that she would like to read his autobiography. Stan hopes it will give her a better understanding of where he has been and where he would like to go. He brings her the autobiography, which reads as follows:

> Where am I currently in my life? At 35 I feel that I've wasted most of my life. I should be finished with college and into a career by now, but instead I'm only a junior. I can't afford to really commit myself to pursuing college full time because I need to work to support myself. Even though construction work is hard, I like the satisfaction I get when I look at what I have done.
>
> I want to get into a profession where I could work with people. Someday, I'm hoping to get a master's degree in counseling or in social work and eventually work as a counselor with kids who are in trouble. I know I was helped by someone who cared about me, and I would like to do the same for someone else.
>
> I have few friends and feel scared around most people. I feel good with kids. But I wonder if I'm smart enough to get through all the classes I'll need to become a counselor. One of my problems is that I frequently get drunk. This happens when I feel alone and when I'm scared of the intensity of my feelings. At first drinking seemed to help, but later on I felt awful. I have abused drugs in the past also.
>
> I feel overwhelmed and intimidated when I'm around attractive women. I feel cold, sweaty, and terribly nervous. I think they may be judging me and see me as not

much of a man. I'm afraid I just don't measure up to being a real *man*. When I am sexually intimate with a woman, I am anxious and preoccupied with what she is thinking about me.

I feel anxiety much of the time. I often feel as if I'm dying inside. I think about committing suicide, and I wonder who would care. I can see my family coming to my funeral feeling sorry for me. I feel guilty that I haven't worked up to my potential, that I've been a failure, that I've wasted much of my time, and that I let people down a lot. I get down on myself and wallow in guilt and feel *very depressed*. At times like this I feel hopeless and that I'd be better off dead. For all these reasons, I find it difficult to get close to anyone.

There are a few bright spots. I did put a lot of my shady past behind me, and did get into college. I like this determination in me—I *want* to change. I'm tired of feeling the way I do. I know that nobody is going to change my life for me. It's up to me to get what I want. Even though I feel scared at times, I like that I'm willing to take risks.

What was my past like? A major turning point for me was the confidence my supervisor had in me at the youth camp where I worked the past few summers. He helped me get my job, and he also encouraged me to go to college. He said he saw a lot of potential in me for being able to work well with young people. That was hard for me to believe, but his faith inspired me to begin to believe in myself. Another turning point was my marriage and divorce. This marriage didn't last long. It made me wonder about what kind of man I was! Joyce was a strong and dominant woman who kept repeating how worthless I was and how she did not want to be around me. We had sex only a few times, and most of the time I was not very good at it. That was hard to take. It made me afraid to get close to a woman. My parents should have divorced. They fought most of the time. My mother (Angie) constantly criticized my father (Frank Sr.). I saw him as weak and passive. He would *never* stand up to her. There were four of us kids. My parents compared me unfavorably with my older sister (Judy) and older brother (Frank Jr.). They were "perfect" children, successful honors' students. My younger brother (Karl) and I fought a lot. They spoiled him. It was all very hard for me.

In high school I started using drugs. I was thrown into a youth rehabilitation facility for stealing. Later I was expelled from regular school for fighting, and I landed in a continuation high school, where I went to school in the mornings and had afternoons for on-the-job training. I got into auto mechanics, was fairly successful, and even managed to keep myself employed for three years as a mechanic.

I can still remember my father asking me: "Why can't you be like your sister and brother? Why can't you do anything right?" And my mother treated me much the way she treated my father. She would say: "Why do you do so many things to hurt me? Why can't you grow up and be a man? Things are so much better around here when you're gone." I recall crying myself to sleep many nights, feeling terribly alone. There was no talk of religion in my house, nor was there any talk of sex. In fact, I find it hard to imagine my folks ever having sex.

Where would I like to be five years from now? What kind of person do I want to become? Most of all, I would like to start feeling better about myself. I would like to be able to stop drinking altogether and still feel good. I want to like myself much more than I do now. I hope I can learn to love at least a few other people, most of all, a woman. I want to lose my fear of women. I would like to feel equal with others and not always have to feel apologetic for my existence. I want to let go of my anxiety and guilt. I want to become a good counselor for kids. I'm not certain how I'll change or even what all the changes are I hope for. I do know that I want to be free of my self-destructive tendencies and learn how to trust people more. Perhaps when I begin to like myself more, I'll be able to trust that others will find something about me to like.

Effective therapists, regardless of their theoretical orientation, would pay attention to suicidal thoughts. In his autobiography Stan says, "I think about committing suicide." At times he doubts that he will ever change and wonders if he'd be "better off dead." Before embarking on the therapeutic journey, the therapist would need to make an assessment of Stan's current *ego strength* (or his ability to manage life realistically), which would include a discussion of his suicidal thoughts.

Overview of Some Key Themes in Stan's Life

A number of themes appear to represent core struggles in Stan's life. Here are some of the statements we can assume that he may make at various points in his therapy and themes that will be addressed from the theoretical perspectives in Chapters 4 through 15:

- Although I'd like to have people in my life, I just don't seem to know how to go about making friends or getting close to people.
- I'd like to turn my life around, but I have no sense of direction.
- I want to make a difference.
- I am afraid of failure.
- I know when I feel alone, scared, and overwhelmed, I drink heavily to feel better.
- I am afraid of women.
- Sometimes at night I feel a terrible anxiety and feel as if I'm dying.
- I often feel guilty that I've wasted my life, that I've failed, and that I've let people down. At times like this, I get depressed.
- I like it that I have determination and that I really want to change.
- I've never really felt loved or wanted by my parents.
- I'd like to get rid of my self-destructive tendencies and learn to trust people more.
- I put myself down a lot, but I'd like to feel better about myself.

In the chapters in Part 2, I write about how I would apply selected concepts and techniques of the particular theory in counseling Stan. In addition, in these chapters you are asked to think about how you would continue counseling Stan from each of these different perspectives. In doing so, refer to the introductory material given here and to Stan's autobiography as well. To make the case of Stan come alive for each theory, I highly recommend that you view and study the video program, *DVD for Theory and Practice of Counseling and Psychotherapy: The Case of Stan and Lecturettes.* In this video program I counsel Stan from each of the various theories and provide brief lectures that highlight each theory.

Introduction to the Case of Gwen

Meet Dr. Kellie Kirksey

I invited Dr. Kellie Kirksey to create a case ("Gwen") based on a composite of her clients over her many years of practice. Gwen's concerns are discussed as they relate to the theory featured in each chapter, and Dr. Kirksey demonstrates how she would work with Gwen using techniques that illustrate key concepts from the theory.

Kellie Kirksey

Kellie N. Kirksey

Kellie N. Kirksey, PhD, received her doctorate in Counselor Education and Psychology at The Ohio State University. She is a licensed clinical counselor, a certified rehabilitation counselor, and an approved clinical supervisor. She has practiced and taught in the counseling field for more than 25 years and has focused her work in the area of multicultural counseling, social justice, integrative counseling, and wellness. She was previously Associate Professor of Counselor Education at Malone University in Ohio where she taught practicum, internship, group counseling, theories, and cultural diversity. She is currently a Holistic Psychotherapist at the Cleveland Clinic Center for Integrative Medicine and focuses primarily on using holistic integrative methods such as hypnotherapy and meditation for health and wellness. She also has a part-time clinical practice in Ohio.

Dr. Kirksey is a contributor to Gerald Corey's *Case Approach to Counseling and Psychotherapy* text in which she works with Ruth from a spiritually focused integrative perspective. She enjoys exploring how wellness is achieved in other cultures and has given numerous workshops and presentations on wellness and self-care in North America, South Africa, Botswana, Hawaii, and Italy.

Background on the Case of Gwen

Gwen is a 56-year-old, married African American woman presenting with fibromyalgia, difficulty sleeping, and a history of anxiety and depression. She reports feeling stress and isolation on her job and is having a difficult time managing her multiple roles. Gwen is the oldest of five children, and after her parents' divorce, she took on the responsibility of caring for her younger siblings. Gwen has been married to Ron for 31 years and states they have ups and downs but basically their relationship is supportive. Ron is employed as a high school teacher and has always made the family a priority. They have three adult children, Brittany age 29, Lisa age 26, and Kevin age 23. Gwen has a master's degree in accounting and is employed at a large firm as a CPA. She reports being the only woman of color at her job. Because she is the only one speaking up for issues of diversity and racial equality at her workplace, she often feels isolated and tired. She does not have enough time to spend with friends or to do the things she once enjoyed because of her long work hours. Gwen also helps her adult children with their bills when needed and LO5 is the primary caretaker of her mother, who resides with her and is in the advanced stages of dementia.

This is Gwen's first time in formal counseling. She reports having gone to her pastor when she was feeling "down" in the past. Gwen also reports times of being sexually molested by an older cousin. She seeks counseling because she is having difficulty staying focused at work and is generally feeling sad and overwhelmed. Gwen also reports experiencing a great deal of anxiety. She states she is not suicidal but is "sick and tired of feeling sick and tired." Gwen summarizes her current situation by saying, "I realized the other day that I am tired of just existing and surviving. So here I am." Gwen was referred to Dr. Kirksey by the pastor of her church. Despite the many challenges in her life, Gwen says that her faith in God is strong and church has always been her place of refuge.

Intake Session

Gwen begins by saying she is ready to unload the stressors she has been holding inside. She states that she has held everything together for everyone far too long. During this initial session, I also address the relevant aspects of informed consent and begin an ongoing process of educating Gwen on how the therapeutic process works.

Gwen says she feels a heaviness in her heart, which is associated with all that is expected of her at work and with her family, what she has not accomplished, and where she is heading. I acknowledge this heaviness and ask her to start wherever she wants. Gwen states that she has not felt carefree since she was a young child before her parents' divorce. Her parents moved to the North from Georgia for work when she was 8 years old. Both of her parents were teachers and valued education. Her neighborhood and school were predominantly African American, and the community was close. In high school she was bussed across town to a predominately white school, and Gwen states she began to encounter what she felt were racist attitudes at this school. She reports:

> I felt different and excluded and this was reinforced by occasional name calling and subtle slights. That was one of the first times I remember feeling like I had to work twice as hard to get ahead and to be accepted in life. Throughout college I worked hard to be successful by pushing myself to achieve what people said I couldn't, but it seems that all my hard work has just worn me down.

A number of life concerns bring Gwen into counseling. A few of her concerns relate to her work. She experiences mounting tension on the job and, when she asserts her opinions, she is labeled as emotional and angry. The more tension she experiences at work, the less she engages at home. An additional concern is that her mother is slowly fading into another world due to dementia. Gwen states she is feeling terrible about herself and not even wanting to be around people anymore. Everything irritates her and she prefers to spend time by herself.

Gwen reports the following:

> I feel like a shell of a person. I am not depressed where I am wanting to kill myself. I just feel numb. There is no real point to doing this daily routine of waking, suffering through the day, and going to bed just to get up and do it all

> over again. My life is like a flat note with little joy. I don't go out; I don't have sex; and I am too tired to do anything. Nothing I do is good enough. I start projects, and then it's like they disappear. Nothing ever gets finished, and then I feel worse about myself. Sometimes I feel like I want to go into a cave and never come out. I feel like I will lose everything if I don't make some changes in my life. Everything looks good on the outside, but inside of me, I am on edge and need to do something different. My pastor and mentor tell me I am sabotaging myself. Usually, I get defensive and withdrawn, but this time, I want to get better and I am ready to do what it takes. I am done with feeling tired all the time and hiding from people. My goal is to live a more balanced life and to learn how to reduce my stress level.

The first step of our journey is to build a working alliance based on mutual respect. I let Gwen know that this is her time to use as she pleases, and that it is a safe and confidential space.

The Counselor: Person and Professional 2

LEARNING OBJECTIVES

1. Identify the characteristics of the counselor as a therapeutic person.
2. Understand the benefits of seeking personal counseling as a counselor.
3. Explain the concept of *bracketing* and what is involved in managing a counselor's personal values.
4. Explain how values relate to identifying goals in counseling.
5. Understand the role of diversity issues in the therapeutic relationship.
6. Describe what is involved in acquiring competency as a multicultural counselor.
7. Identify issues faced by beginning therapists.

Introduction

One of the most important instruments you have to work with as a counselor is yourself as a person. In preparing for counseling, you will acquire knowledge about the theories of personality and psychotherapy, learn assessment and intervention techniques, and discover the dynamics of human behavior. Such knowledge and skills are essential, but by themselves they are not sufficient for establishing and maintaining effective therapeutic relationships. To every therapy session we bring our human qualities and the experiences that have influenced us. In my judgment, this human dimension is one of the most powerful influences on the therapeutic process.

A good way to begin your study of contemporary counseling theories is by reflecting on the personal issues raised in this chapter. By remaining open to self-evaluation, you not only expand your awareness of self but also build the foundation for developing your abilities and skills as a professional. The theme of this chapter is that the *person* and the *professional* are intertwined facets that cannot be separated in reality. We know, clinically and scientifically, that the person of the therapist and the therapeutic relationship contribute to therapy outcome at least as much as the particular treatment method used (Duncan, Miller, Wampold, & Hubble, 2010; Elkins, 2016; Norcross, 2011).

Visit CengageBrain.com or watch the DVD for the video program on Chapter 2, *Theory and Practice of Counseling and Psychotherapy: The Case of Stan and Lecturettes*. I suggest that you view the brief lecture for each chapter prior to reading the chapter.

The Counselor as a Therapeutic Person

Counseling is an intimate form of learning, and it demands a practitioner who is willing to be an authentic person in the therapeutic relationship. It is within the context of such a person-to-person connection that the client experiences growth. If we hide behind the safety of our professional role, our clients will likely keep themselves hidden from us. If we strive for technical expertise alone, and leave our own reactions and self out of our work, the result is likely to be ineffective counseling. Our own genuineness can have a significant effect on our relationship with our clients. If we are willing to look at our lives and make the changes we want, we can model that process by the way we reveal ourselves and respond to our clients. If we are inauthentic, we will have difficulty establishing a working alliance with our clients. If we model authenticity by engaging in appropriate self-disclosure, our clients will tend to be honest with us as well. LO1

I believe that who the psychotherapist is directly relates to his or her ability to establish and maintain effective therapy relationships with clients. But what does the research reveal about the role of the counselor as a person and the therapeutic relationship on psychotherapy outcome? Abundant research indicates the centrality of the person of the therapist as a primary factor in successful therapy. The *person* of the psychotherapist is inextricably intertwined with the outcome of psychotherapy (see Elkins, 2016; Lambert, 2011; Norcross & Lambert, 2011; Norcross & Wampold, 2011). Clients place more value on the personality of the therapist than on the specific techniques used. Indeed, evidence-based psychotherapy relationships are critical to the psychotherapy endeavor.

Techniques themselves have limited importance in the therapeutic process. Wampold (2001) conducted a meta-analysis of many research studies on therapeutic effectiveness and found that the personal and interpersonal components are essential to effective psychotherapy, whereas techniques have relatively little effect on therapeutic outcome. The *contextual factors*—the alliance, the relationship, the personal and interpersonal skills of the therapist, client agency, and extra-therapeutic factors—are the primary determinants of therapeutic outcome. This research supports what humanistic psychologists have maintained for years: "It is not theories and techniques that heal the suffering client but the human dimension of therapy and the 'meetings' that occur between therapist and client as they work together" (Elkins, 2009, p. 82). In short, both the *therapy relationship* and the *therapy methods* used influence the outcomes of treatment, but it essential that the methods used support the therapeutic relationship being formed with the client.

Personal Characteristics of Effective Counselors

Particular personal qualities and characteristics of counselors are significant in creating a therapeutic alliance with clients. My views regarding these personal characteristics are supported by research on this topic (Norcross, 2011; Skovholt & Jennings, 2004; Sperry & Carlson, 2011). I do not expect any therapist to fully exemplify all the traits described in the list that follows. Rather, the willingness to struggle to become a more therapeutic person is the crucial variable. This list is intended to stimulate you to examine your own ideas about what kind of person can make a significant difference in the lives of others.

- *Effective therapists have an identity*. They know who they are, what they are capable of becoming, what they want out of life, and what is essential.
- *Effective therapists respect and appreciate themselves*. They can give and receive help and love out of their own sense of self-worth and strength. They feel adequate with others and allow others to feel powerful with them.
- *Effective therapists are open to change*. They exhibit a willingness and courage to leave the security of the known if they are not satisfied with the way they are. They make decisions about how they would like to change, and they work toward becoming the person they want to become.
- *Effective therapists make choices that are life oriented*. They are aware of early decisions they made about themselves, others, and the world. They are not the victims of these early decisions, and they are willing to revise them if necessary. They are committed to living fully rather than settling for mere existence.
- *Effective therapists are authentic, sincere, and honest*. They do not hide behind rigid roles or facades. Who they are in their personal life and in their professional work is congruent.
- *Effective therapists have a sense of humor*. They are able to put the events of life in perspective. They have not forgotten how to laugh, especially at their own foibles and contradictions.

- *Effective therapists make mistakes and are willing to admit them.* They do not dismiss their errors lightly, yet they do not choose to dwell on misery.
- *Effective therapists generally live in the present.* They are not riveted to the past, nor are they fixated on the future. They are able to experience and be present with others in the "now."
- *Effective therapists appreciate the influence of culture.* They are aware of the ways in which their own culture affects them, and they respect the diversity of values espoused by other cultures. They are sensitive to the unique differences arising out of social class, race, sexual orientation, and gender.
- *Effective therapists have a sincere interest in the welfare of others.* This concern is based on respect, care, trust, and a real valuing of others.
- *Effective therapists possess effective interpersonal skills.* They are capable of entering the world of others without getting lost in this world, and they strive to create collaborative relationships with others. They readily entertain another person's perspective and can work together toward consensual goals.
- *Effective therapists become deeply involved in their work and derive meaning from it.* They can accept the rewards flowing from their work, yet they are not slaves to their work.
- *Effective therapists are passionate.* They have the courage to pursue their dreams and passions, and they radiate a sense of energy.
- *Effective therapists are able to maintain healthy boundaries.* Although they strive to be fully present for their clients, they don't carry the problems of their clients around with them during leisure hours. They know how to say no, which enables them to maintain balance in their lives.

This picture of the characteristics of effective therapists might appear unrealistic. Who could be all those things? Certainly I do not fit this bill! Do not think of these personal characteristics from an all-or-nothing perspective; rather, consider them on a continuum. A given trait may be highly characteristic of you, at one extreme, or it may be very uncharacteristic of you, at the other extreme. I have presented this picture of the therapeutic person with the hope that you will examine it and develop your own concept of what personality traits you think are essential to strive for to promote your own personal growth. For a more detailed discussion of the person of the counselor and the role of the therapeutic relationship in outcomes of treatments, see *Psychotherapy Relationships That Work* (Norcross, 2011), *How Master Therapists Work: Exploring Change From the First Through the Last Session and Beyond* (Sperry & Carlson, 2011), and *Master Therapists: Exploring Expertise in Therapy and Counseling* (Skovholt & Jennings, 2004).

Personal Therapy for the Counselor

Discussion of the counselor as a therapeutic person raises another issue **LO2** debated in counselor education: Should people be required to participate in counseling or therapy before they become practitioners? My view is that counselors can benefit greatly from the experience of being clients at some time, a view that is supported by research. This experience can be obtained before your training, during it, or both, but I strongly support some form of self-exploration as vital preparation in learning to counsel others.

The vast majority of mental health professionals have experienced personal therapy, typically on several occasions (Geller, Norcross, & Orlinsky, 2005b). A review of research studies on the outcomes and impacts of the psychotherapist's own psychotherapy revealed that more than 90% of mental health professionals report satisfaction and positive outcomes from their own counseling experiences (Orlinsky, Norcross, Ronnestad, & Wiseman, 2005). Orlinsky and colleagues suggest that personal therapy contributes to the therapist's professional work in the following three ways: (1) as part of the therapist's training, personal therapy offers a model of therapeutic practice in which the trainee experiences the work of a more experienced therapist and learns experientially what is helpful or not helpful; (2) a beneficial experience in personal therapy can further enhance a therapist's interpersonal skills that are essential to skillfully practicing therapy; and (3) successful personal therapy can contribute to a therapist's ability to deal with the ongoing stresses associated with clinical work.

In his research on personal therapy for mental health professionals, Norcross (2005) states that lasting lessons practitioners learn from their personal therapy experiences pertain to interpersonal relationships and the dynamics of psychotherapy. Some of these lessons learned are the centrality of warmth, empathy, and the personal relationship; having a sense of what it is like to be a therapy client; valuing patience and tolerance; and appreciating the importance of learning how to deal with transference and countertransference. By participating in personal therapy, counselors can prevent their potential future countertransference from harming clients.

Through our work as therapists, we can expect to confront our own unexplored personal blocks such as loneliness, power, death, and intimate relationships. This does not mean that we need to be free of conflicts before we can counsel others, but we should be aware of what these conflicts are and how they are likely to affect us as persons and as counselors. For example, if we have great difficulty dealing with anger or conflict, we may not be able to assist clients who are dealing with anger or with relationships in conflict.

When I began counseling others, old wounds were opened and feelings I had not explored in depth came to the surface. It was difficult for me to encounter a client's depression because I had failed to come to terms with the way I had escaped from my own depression. I did my best to cheer up depressed clients by talking them out of what they were feeling, mainly because of my own inability to deal with such feelings. In the years I worked as a counselor in a university counseling center, I frequently wondered what I could do for my clients. I often had no idea what, if anything, my clients were getting from our sessions. I couldn't tell if they were getting better, staying the same, or getting worse. It was very important to me to note progress and see change in my clients. Because I did not see immediate results, I had many doubts about whether I could become an effective counselor. What I did not understand at the time was that my clients needed to struggle to find their own answers. To see my clients feel better quickly was *my need*, not theirs, for then I would know that I was helping them. It never occurred to me that clients often feel worse for a time as they give up their defenses and open themselves to their pain. My early experiences as a counselor showed me that I could benefit by participating in further personal therapy to better understand how my personal issues were affecting my professional work. I realized that periodic therapy, especially early in one's career, can be most useful.

Personal therapy can be instrumental in healing the healer. If student counselors are not actively involved in the pursuit of their own healing and growth, they will probably have considerable difficulty entering the world of a client. As counselors, can we take our clients any further than we have gone ourselves? If we are not committed personally to the value of examining our own life, how can we inspire clients to examine their lives? By becoming clients ourselves, we gain an experiential frame of reference with which to view ourselves. This provides a basis for understanding and compassion for our clients, for we can draw on our own memories of reaching impasses in our therapy, of both wanting to go farther and at the same time resisting change. Our own therapy can help us develop patience with our patients! We learn what it feels like to deal with anxieties that are aroused by self-disclosure and self-exploration and how to creatively facilitate deeper levels of self-exploration in clients. As we increase our self-awareness through our own therapy, we gain increased appreciation for the courage our clients display in their therapeutic journey. Gold and Hilsenroth (2009) studied graduate clinicians and found that those who had personal therapy felt more confident and were more in agreement with their clients on the goals and tasks of treatment than were those who did not experience personal therapy. They further found that graduate clinicians who had experienced personal therapy were able to develop strong agreement with their clients on the goals and tasks of treatment. Participating in a process of self-exploration can reduce the chances of assuming an attitude of arrogance or of being convinced that we are totally healed. Our own therapy helps us avoid assuming a stance of superiority over others and makes it less likely that we would treat people as objects to be pitied or disrespected. Indeed, experiencing counseling as a client is very different from merely reading about the counseling process.

For a comprehensive discussion of personal therapy for counselors, see *The Psychotherapist's Own Psychotherapy: Patient and Clinician Perspectives* (Geller, Norcross, & Orlinsky, 2005a).

The Counselor's Values and the Therapeutic Process

As alluded to in the previous section, the importance of self-exploration for counselors carries over to the values and beliefs we hold. My experience in teaching and supervising students of counseling shows me how crucial it is that students be aware of their values, of where and how they acquired them, and of how their values can influence their interventions with clients.

The Role of Values in Counseling

LO3

Our values are core beliefs that influence how we act, both in our personal and our professional lives. Personal values influence how we view counseling and the manner in which we interact with clients, including the way we conduct client assessments, our views of the goals of counseling, the interventions we choose, the topics we select for discussion in a counseling session, how we evaluate progress, and how we interpret clients' life situations.

Although total objectivity cannot be achieved, we can strive to avoid being encapsulated by our own worldview. We need to guard against the tendency to use our power to influence clients to accept our values; persuading clients to accept or adopt our value system is not a legitimate outcome of counseling. From my perspective, the counselor's role is to create a climate in which clients can examine their thoughts, feelings, and actions and to empower them to arrive at their own solutions to problems they face. The counseling task is to assist individuals in finding answers that are most congruent with their own values. It is not beneficial to provide advice or to give clients your answers to their questions about life.

You may not agree with certain of your clients' values, but you need to respect their right to hold divergent values from yours. This is especially true when counseling clients who have a different cultural background and perhaps do not share your own core cultural values. Your role is to provide a safe and inviting environment in which clients can explore the congruence between their values and their behavior. If clients acknowledge that what they are doing is not getting them what they want, it is appropriate to assist them in developing new ways of thinking and behaving to help them move closer to their goals. This is done with full respect for their right to decide which values they will use as a framework for living. Individuals seeking counseling need to clarify their own values and goals, make informed decisions, choose a course of action, and assume responsibility and accountability for the decisions they make.

Managing your personal values so that they do not contaminate the counseling process is referred to as "bracketing." Counselors are expected to set aside their personal beliefs and values when working with a wide range of clients (Kocet & Herlihy, 2014). Your core values may differ in many ways from the core values of your clients, and they will bring you a host of problems framed by their own worldview. Some clients may have felt rejected by others or suffered from discrimination, and they should not be exposed to further discrimination by counselors who refuse to render services to them because of differing values (Herlihy, Hermann, & Greden, 2014).

Counselors must have the ability to work with a range of clients with diverse worldviews and values. Counselors may impose their values either directly or indirectly. **Value imposition** refers to counselors directly attempting to define a client's values, attitudes, beliefs, and behaviors. It is unethical for counselors to impose their values in the therapeutic relationship. The American Counseling Association's (ACA, 2014) *Code of Ethics* is explicit regarding this matter:

> *Personal Values.* Counselors are aware of—and avoid imposing—their own values, attitudes, beliefs, and behaviors. Counselors respect the diversity of clients, trainees, and research participants and seek training in areas in which they are at risk of imposing their values onto clients, especially when the counselor's values are inconsistent with the client's goals or are discriminatory in nature. (Standard A.4.b.)

Value exploration is at the heart of why many counselor education programs encourage or require personal therapy for counselors in training. Your personal therapy sessions provide an opportunity for you to examine your beliefs and values and to explore your motivations for wanting to share your belief system.

Clients are in a vulnerable position and require understanding and support from a counselor rather than judgment. It can be burdensome for clients to be saddled with your disclosure of not being able to get beyond value differences. Clients may interpret this as a personal rejection and suffer harm as a result. Counseling is about working with clients within the framework of *their* value system. If you experience difficulties over conflicting personal values with clients, the ethical course of action is to seek supervision and learn ways to effectively manage these differences. The counseling process is not about your personal values; it is about the values and needs of your clients. Your task is to help clients explore and clarify their beliefs and apply their values to solving their problems (Herlihy & Corey, 2015d).

The Role of Values in Developing Therapeutic Goals

Who should establish the goals of counseling? Almost all theories are in agreement that it is largely the client's responsibility to decide upon goals, collaborating with the therapist as therapy proceeds. Counselors have general goals, which are reflected in their behavior during the therapy session, in their observations of the client's behavior, and in the interventions they make. The general goals of counselors must be congruent with the personal goals of the client. LO4

Setting goals is inextricably related to values. The client and the counselor need to explore what they hope to obtain from the counseling relationship, whether they can work with each other, and whether their goals are compatible. Even more important, it is essential that the counselor be able to understand, respect, and work within the framework of the client's world rather than forcing the client to fit into the therapist's scheme of values.

In my view, therapy ought to begin with an exploration of the client's expectations and goals. Clients initially tend to have vague ideas of what they expect from therapy. They may be seeking solutions to problems, they may want to stop hurting, they may want to change others so they can live with less anxiety, or they may seek to be different so that some significant persons in their lives will be more accepting of them. In some cases clients have no goals; they are in the therapist's office simply because they were sent for counseling by their parents, probation officer, or teacher.

So where can a counselor begin? The initial interview can be used most productively to focus on the client's goals or lack of them. The therapist may begin by asking any of these questions: "What do you expect from counseling? Why are you here? What do you want? What do you hope to leave with? How is what you are currently doing working for you? What aspects of yourself or your life situation would you most like to change?"

When a person seeks a counseling relationship with you, it is important to cooperatively discover what this person is expecting from the relationship. If you try to figure out in advance how to proceed with a client, you may be depriving the client of the opportunity to become an active partner in her or his own therapy. Why is this person coming in for counseling? It is the client's place to decide on the goals of therapy. It is important to keep this focus in mind so that the client's agenda is addressed rather than an agenda of your own.

Becoming an Effective Multicultural Counselor

Part of the process of becoming an effective counselor involves learning how to recognize diversity issues and shaping one's counseling practice to fit the client's worldview. It is an *ethical obligation* for counselors to develop sensitivity to cultural differences if they hope to make interventions that are consistent with the values of their clients. The therapist's role is to assist clients in making decisions that are congruent with their worldview, not to live by the therapist's values. LO5

Diversity in the therapeutic relationship is a two-way street. As a counselor, you bring your own heritage with you to your work, so you need to recognize the ways in which cultural conditioning has influenced the directions you take with your clients. Unless the social and cultural context of clients and counselors are taken into consideration, it is difficult to appreciate the nature of clients' struggles. Counseling students often hold values—such as making their own choices, expressing what they are feeling, being open and self-revealing, and striving for independence—that differ from the values of clients from different cultural backgrounds. Some clients may be very slow to disclose and have expectations about counseling that differ from those of therapist. Counselors need to become aware of how clients from diverse cultures may perceive them as therapists, as well as how clients may perceive the value of formal helping. It is the task of counselors to determine whether the assumptions they have made about the nature and functioning of therapy are appropriate for culturally diverse clients.

Clearly, effective counseling must take into account the impact of culture on the client's functioning, including the client's degree of acculturation. **Culture** is, quite simply, the values and behaviors shared by a group of individuals. It is important to realize that culture refers to more than ethnic or racial heritage; culture also includes factors such as age, gender, religion, sexual orientation, physical and mental ability, and socioeconomic status.

Acquiring Competencies in Multicultural Counseling

Effective counselors understand their own cultural conditioning, the cultural values of their clients, and the sociopolitical system of which they are a part. Acquiring this understanding begins with counselors' awareness of the cultural origins of any values, biases, and attitudes they may hold. Counselors from all cultural groups must examine their expectations, attitudes, biases, and assumptions about the counseling process and about persons from diverse groups. Recognizing our biases and prejudices takes courage because most of us do not want to acknowledge that we have cultural biases. Everyone has biases, but being unaware of the biased attitudes we hold is an obstacle to client care. It takes a concerted effort and vigilance to monitor our biases, attitudes, and values so that they do not interfere with establishing and maintaining successful counseling relationships. LO6

A major part of becoming a diversity-competent counselor involves challenging the idea that the values we hold are automatically true for others. We also need to understand how our values are likely to influence our practice with diverse clients who embrace different values. Furthermore, becoming a diversity-competent practitioner is not a destination that we arrive at once and for all; rather, it is an ongoing process, a journey we take with our clients.

Sue, Arredondo, and McDavis (1992) and Arredondo and her colleagues (1996) have developed a conceptual framework for competencies and standards in multicultural counseling. Their dimensions of competency involve three areas: (1) beliefs and attitudes, (2) knowledge, and (3) skills. For an in-depth treatment of multicultural counseling and therapy competence, refer to *Counseling the Culturally Diverse: Theory and Practice* (Sue & Sue, 2013).

Beliefs and Attitudes First, effective counselors have moved from being culturally unaware to ensuring that their personal biases, values, or problems will not interfere with their ability to work with clients who are culturally different from them. They believe cultural self-awareness and sensitivity to one's own cultural heritage are essential for any form of helping. Counselors are aware of their positive and negative emotional reactions toward people from other racial and ethnic groups that may prove detrimental to establishing collaborative helping relationships. They seek to examine and understand the world from the vantage point of their clients. They respect clients' religious and spiritual beliefs and values. They are comfortable with differences between themselves and others in terms of race, ethnicity, culture, and beliefs. Rather than maintaining that their cultural heritage is superior, they are able to accept and value cultural diversity. They realize that traditional theories and techniques may not be appropriate for all clients or for all problems. Culturally skilled counselors monitor their functioning through consultation, supervision, and further training or education.

Knowledge Second, culturally effective practitioners possess certain knowledge. They know specifically about their own racial and cultural heritage and how it affects them personally and professionally. Because they understand the dynamics of oppression, racism, discrimination, and stereotyping, they are in a position to detect their own racist attitudes, beliefs, and feelings. They understand the worldview of their clients, and they learn about their clients' cultural background. They do not impose their values and expectations on their clients from differing cultural backgrounds and avoid stereotyping clients. Culturally skilled counselors understand that external sociopolitical forces influence all groups, and they know how these forces operate with respect to the treatment of minorities. These practitioners are aware of the institutional barriers that prevent minorities from utilizing the mental health services available in their communities. They possess knowledge about the historical background, traditions, and values of the client populations with whom they work. They know about minority family structures, hierarchies, values, and beliefs. Furthermore, they are knowledgeable about community characteristics and resources. Those who are culturally skilled know how to help clients make use of indigenous support systems. In areas where they are lacking in knowledge, they seek resources to assist them. The greater their depth and breadth of knowledge of culturally diverse groups, the more likely they are to be effective practitioners.

Skills and Intervention Strategies Third, effective counselors have acquired certain skills in working with culturally diverse populations. Counselors take responsibility for educating their clients about the therapeutic process, including matters such as setting goals, appropriate expectations, legal rights, and the counselor's orientation.

Multicultural counseling is enhanced when practitioners use methods and strategies and define goals consistent with the life experiences and cultural values of their clients. Such practitioners modify and adapt their interventions to accommodate cultural differences. They do not force their clients to fit within one counseling approach, and they recognize that counseling techniques may be culture-bound. They are able to send and receive both verbal and nonverbal messages accurately and appropriately. They become actively involved with minority individuals outside the office (community events, celebrations, and neighborhood groups). They are willing to seek out educational, consultative, and training experiences to enhance their ability to work with culturally diverse client populations. They consult regularly with other multiculturally sensitive professionals regarding issues of culture to determine whether referral may be necessary.

Incorporating Culture in Counseling Practice

It is unrealistic to expect a counselor to know everything about the cultural background of a client, but some understanding of the client's cultural and ethnic background is essential. There is much to be said for letting clients teach counselors about relevant aspects of their culture. It is a good idea for counselors to ask clients to provide them with the information they will need to work effectively. Incorporating culture into the therapeutic process is not limited to working with clients from a certain ethnic or cultural background. It is critical that therapists take into account the worldview and background of *every* client. Failing to do this seriously restricts the potential impact of the therapeutic endeavor.

Counseling is by its very nature diverse in a multicultural society, so it is easy to see that there are no ideal therapeutic approaches. Instead, different theories have distinct features that have appeal for different cultural groups. Some theoretical approaches have limitations when applied to certain populations. Effective multicultural practice demands an open stance on the part of the practitioner, flexibility, and a willingness to modify strategies to fit the needs and the situation of the individual client. Practitioners who truly respect their clients will be aware of clients' hesitations and will not be too quick to misinterpret this behavior. Instead, they will patiently attempt to enter the world of their clients as much as they can. Although practitioners may not have had the same experiences as their clients, the empathy shown by counselors for the feelings and struggles of their clients is essential to good therapeutic outcomes. We are more often challenged by our differences than by our similarities to look at what we are doing.

Practical Guidelines in Addressing Culture If the counseling process is to be effective, it is essential that cultural concerns be addressed with all clients. Here are some guidelines that may increase your effectiveness when working with clients from diverse backgrounds:

- Learn more about how your own cultural background has influenced your thinking and behaving. Take steps to increase your understanding of other cultures.
- Identify your basic assumptions, especially as they apply to diversity in culture, ethnicity, race, gender, class, spirituality, religion, and

sexual orientation. Think about how your assumptions are likely to affect your professional practice.

- Examine where you obtained your knowledge about culture.
- Remain open to ongoing learning of how the various dimensions of culture may affect therapeutic work. Realize that this skill does not develop quickly or without effort.
- Be willing to identify and examine your own personal worldview and any prejudices you may hold about other racial/ethnic groups.
- Learn to pay attention to the common ground that exists among people of diverse backgrounds.
- Be flexible in applying the methods you use with clients. Don't be wedded to a specific technique if it is not appropriate for a given client.
- Remember that practicing from a multicultural perspective can make your job easier and can be rewarding for both you and your clients.

It takes time, study, and experience to become an effective multicultural counselor. Multicultural competence cannot be reduced simply to cultural awareness and sensitivity, to a body of knowledge, or to a specific set of skills. Instead, it requires a combination of all of these factors.

Issues Faced by Beginning Therapists

LO7

When you complete formal course work and begin helping clients, you will be challenged to integrate and to apply what you have learned. At that point, you are likely to have some real concerns about your adequacy as a person and as a professional. Beginning therapists typically face a number of common issues as they learn how to help others. Here are some useful guidelines to assist you in your reflection on what it takes to become an effective counselor.

Dealing With Anxiety

Most beginning counselors have ambivalent feelings when meeting their first clients. A certain level of anxiety demonstrates that you are aware of the uncertainties of the future with your clients and of your abilities to really be there for them. A willingness to recognize and deal with these anxieties, as opposed to denying them, is a positive sign. That we have self-doubts is normal; it is how we deal with them that matters. One way is to openly discuss our self-doubts with a supervisor and peers. The possibilities are rich for meaningful exchanges and for gaining support from fellow interns who probably have many of the same concerns and anxieties.

Being Yourself and Self-Disclosure

If you feel self-conscious and anxious when you begin counseling, you may have a tendency to be overly concerned with what the books say and with the mechanics of how to proceed. Inexperienced therapists too often fail to appreciate the values inherent in simply being themselves. If we are able to be ourselves in our therapeutic work, and appropriately disclose our reactions in counseling sessions, we increase the chances of being authentic. It is this level of genuineness and presence that enables us to connect with our clients and to establish an effective therapeutic relationship with them.

It is possible to err by going to extremes in two different directions. At one end are counselors who lose themselves in their fixed role and hide behind a professional facade. These counselors are so caught up in maintaining stereotyped role expectations that little of their personal self shows through. Counselors who adopt this behavior will likely remain anonymous to clients, and clients may perceive them as hiding behind a professional role.

At the other end of the spectrum is engaging in too much self-disclosure. Some counselors make the mistake of inappropriately burdening their clients with their spontaneous impressions about their clients. Judging the appropriate amount of self-disclosure can be a problem even for seasoned counselors, and it is often especially worrisome for new counselors. In determining the appropriateness of self-disclosure, consider *what* to reveal, *when* to reveal, and *how much* to reveal. It may be useful to mention something about ourselves from time to time, but we must be aware of our motivations for making ourselves known in this way. Assess the readiness of a client to hear these disclosures as well as the impact doing so might have on the client. Remain observant during any self-disclosure to get a sense of how the client is being affected by it.

The most productive form of self-disclosure is related to what is going on between the counselor and the client within the counseling session. The skill of immediacy involves revealing what we are thinking or feeling in the here and now with the client, but be careful to avoid pronouncing judgments about the client. When done in a timely way, sharing persistent reactions can facilitate therapeutic progress and improve the quality of our relationship with the client. Even when we are talking about reactions based on the therapeutic relationship, caution is necessary, and discretion and sensitivity are required in deciding what reactions we might share.

Avoiding Perfectionism

Perhaps one of the most common self-defeating beliefs with which we burden ourselves is that we must never make a mistake. Although we may well know *intellectually* that humans are not perfect, *emotionally* we often feel that there is little room for error. To be sure, you *will* make mistakes, whether you are a beginning or a seasoned therapist. If our energies are tied up presenting an image of perfection, this will affect our ability to be present for our clients. I tell students to question the notion that they should know everything and be perfectly skilled. I encourage them to share their mistakes or what they perceive as errors during their supervision meetings. Students willing to risk making mistakes in supervised learning situations and willing to reveal their self-doubts will find a direction that leads to growth.

Being Honest About Your Limitations

You cannot realistically expect to succeed with every client. It takes honesty to admit that you cannot work successfully with every client. It is important to learn *when* and *how* to make a referral for clients when your limitations prevent you from helping them. However, there is a delicate balance between learning your realistic limits and challenging what you sometimes think of as being "limits." Before deciding that you do not have the life experiences or the personal qualities to work with a given population, try working in a setting with a population you do not intend to specialize in. This can be done through diversified field placements or visits to agencies.

Understanding Silence

Silent moments during a therapeutic session may seem like silent hours to a beginning therapist, yet this silence can have many meanings. The client may be quietly thinking about some things that were discussed earlier or evaluating some insight just acquired. The client may be waiting for the therapist to take the lead and decide what to say next, or the therapist may be waiting for the client to do this. Either the client or the therapist may be distracted or preoccupied, or neither may have anything to say for the moment. The client and the therapist may be communicating without words. The silence may be refreshing, or the silence may be overwhelming. Perhaps the interaction has been on a surface level, and both persons have some fear or hesitancy about getting to a deeper level. When silence occurs, acknowledge and explore with your client the meaning of the silence.

Dealing With Demands From Clients

A major issue that puzzles many beginning counselors is how to deal with clients who seem to make constant demands. Because therapists feel they should extend themselves in being helpful, they often burden themselves with the unrealistic idea that they should give unselfishly, regardless of how great clients' demands may be. These demands may manifest themselves in a variety of ways. Clients may want to see you more often or for a longer period than you can provide. They may want to see you socially. Some clients may expect you to continually demonstrate how much you care or demand that you tell them what to do and how to solve a problem. One way of heading off these demands is to make your expectations and boundaries clear during the initial counseling sessions or in the disclosure statement.

Dealing With Clients Who Lack Commitment

Involuntary clients may be required by a court order to obtain therapy, and you may be challenged in your attempt to establish a working relationship with them. It is possible to do effective work with mandated clients, but practitioners must begin by openly discussing the nature of the relationship. Counselors who omit preparation and do not address clients' thoughts and feelings about coming to counseling are likely to encounter resistance. It is critical that therapists not promise what they cannot or will not deliver. It is good practice to make clear the limits of confidentiality as well as any other factors that may affect the course of therapy. In working with involuntary clients, it is especially important to prepare them for the process; doing so can go a long way toward increasing their cooperation and involvement.

Tolerating Ambiguity

Many beginning therapists experience the anxiety of not seeing immediate results. They ask themselves: "Am I really doing my client any good? Is the client perhaps getting worse?" I hope you will learn to tolerate the ambiguity of not knowing for sure whether your client is improving, at least during the initial sessions. Realize that oftentimes clients may seemingly "get worse" before they show therapeutic gains. Also, realize that the fruitful effects of the joint efforts of the therapist and the client may manifest themselves after the conclusion of therapy.

Becoming Aware of Your Countertransference

Working with clients can affect you in personal ways, and your own vulnerabilities and countertransference are bound to surface. If you are unaware of your personal dynamics, you are in danger of being overwhelmed by a client's emotional experiences. Beginning counselors need to learn how to "let clients go" and not carry around their problems until the next session. The most therapeutic thing is to be as fully present as we are able to be during the therapy hour, but to let clients assume the responsibility of their living and choosing outside of the session. If we become lost in clients' struggles and confusion, we cease being effective agents in helping them find solutions to their problems. If we accept responsibility for our clients' decisions, we are blocking rather than fostering their growth.

Countertransference, defined broadly, includes any of our projections that influence the way we perceive and react to a client. This phenomenon occurs when we are triggered into emotional reactivity, when we respond defensively, or when we lose our ability to be present in a relationship because our own issues become involved. Recognizing the manifestations of our countertransference reactions is an essential step in becoming competent counselors. Unless we are aware of our own conflicts, needs, assets, and liabilities, we can use the therapy hour more for our own purposes than for being available for our clients. Because it is not appropriate for us to use clients' time to work through our reactions to them, it is all the more important that we be willing to work on ourselves in our own sessions with another therapist, supervisor, or colleague. If we do not engage in this kind of self-exploration, we increase the danger of losing ourselves in our clients and using them to meet our unfulfilled needs.

The emotionally intense relationships we develop with clients can be expected to tap into our own unresolved problem areas. Our clients' stories and pain are bound to have an impact on us; we will be affected by their stories and can express compassion and empathy. However, we have to realize that it is their pain and not carry it *for* them lest we become overwhelmed by their life stories and thus render ourselves ineffective in working with them. Although we cannot completely free ourselves from any traces of countertransference or ever fully resolve all personal conflicts from the past, we can become aware of ways these realities influence our professional work. Our personal therapy can be instrumental in enabling us to recognize and manage our countertransference reactions. (This topic is explored in more depth in Chapter 4.)

Developing a Sense of Humor

Therapy is a responsible endeavor, but it need not be deadly serious. Both clients and counselors can enrich a relationship through humor. What a welcome relief when we can admit that pain is not our exclusive domain. It is important to recognize that laughter or humor does not mean that clients are not respected or work is not being accomplished. There are times, of course, when laughter is used to cover up anxiety or to escape from the experience of facing threatening material. The therapist needs to distinguish between humor that distracts and humor that enhances the situation.

Sharing Responsibility With the Client

You might struggle with finding the optimum balance in sharing responsibility with your clients. One mistake is to assume full responsibility for the direction and outcomes of therapy. This will lead to taking from your clients their rightful responsibility of making their own decisions. It could aiso increase the likelihood of your early burnout. Another mistake is for you to refuse to accept the responsibility for making accurate assessments and designing appropriate treatment plans for your clients. How responsibility will be shared should be addressed early in the course of counseling. It is your responsibility to discuss specific matters such as length and overall duration of the sessions, confidentiality, general goals, and methods used to achieve goals. (Informed consent is discussed in Chapter 3.)

It is important to be alert to your clients' efforts to get you to assume responsibility for directing their lives. Many clients seek a "magic answer" as a way of escaping the anxiety of making their own decisions. It is not your role to assume responsibility for directing your clients' lives. Collaboratively designing contracts and homework assignments with your clients can be instrumental in your clients' increasingly finding direction within themselves. Perhaps the best measure of our effectiveness as counselors is the degree to which clients are able to say to us, "I appreciate what you have been to me, and because of your faith in me, and what you have taught me, I am confident that I can go it alone." Eventually, if we are effective, we will be out of business!

Declining to Give Advice

Quite often clients who are suffering come to a therapy session seeking and even demanding advice. They want more than direction; they want a wise counselor to make a decision or resolve a problem for them. However, counseling should not be confused with dispensing information. Therapists help clients discover their own solutions and recognize their own freedom to act. Even if we, as therapists, were able to resolve clients' struggles for them, we would be fostering their dependence on us. They would continually need to seek our counsel for every new twist in their difficulties. Our task is to help clients make independent choices and accept the consequences of their choices. The habitual practice of giving advice does not work toward this end.

Defining Your Role as a Counselor

One of your challenges as a counselor will be to define and clarify your professional role. As you read about the various theoretical orientations, you will discover the many different roles of counselors that are related to the various theories. As a counselor, you will likely be expected to function with a diverse range of roles.

From my perspective, the central function of counseling is to help clients recognize their own strengths, discover what is preventing them from using their resources, and clarify what kind of life they want to live. Counseling is a process by which clients are invited to look honestly at their behavior and make certain decisions about how they want to modify the quality of their life. In this framework counselors provide support and warmth, yet care enough to challenge clients so that they will be able to take the actions necessary to bring about significant change.

You will need to consider that the professional roles you assume are likely to be dependent on factors such as the client populations with whom you are working, the specific therapeutic services you are providing, the particular stage of counseling, and the setting in which you work. Your role will not be defined once and for all. You will have to reassess the nature of your professional commitments and redefine your role at various times.

Learning to Use Techniques Appropriately

When you are at an impasse with a client, you may have a tendency to look for a technique to get the sessions moving. Ideally, therapeutic techniques should evolve from the therapeutic relationship and the material presented, and they should enhance the client's awareness or suggest possibilities for experimenting with new behavior. It is imperative that you know the theoretical rationale for each technique you use, and you need to be aware that the techniques are appropriate for the goals of therapy. This does not mean that you need to restrict yourself to drawing on procedures within a single model; quite the contrary. However, it is important to avoid using techniques in a hit-or-miss fashion, to fill time, to meet your own needs, or to get things moving. Your methods need to be thoughtfully chosen as a way to help clients make therapeutic progress.

Developing Your Own Counseling Style

Be aware of any tendency to copy the style of a supervisor, therapist, or some other model. There is no one way to conduct therapy, and wide variations in approach can be effective. You will inhibit your potential effectiveness in reaching others if you attempt to imitate another therapist's style or if you fit most of your behavior during the session into the Procrustean bed of some expert's theory. Your counseling style will be influenced by your teachers, therapists, and supervisors, but don't blur your potential uniqueness by trying to imitate them. I advocate borrowing from others, yet, at the same time, doing it in a way that is distinctive to you.

Maintaining Your Vitality as a Person and as a Professional

Ultimately, your single most important instrument is the person you are, and your most powerful technique is your ability to model aliveness and realness. It is of paramount importance that we take care of ourselves, for how can we take care of others if we are not taking care of ourselves? We need to work at dealing with those factors that threaten to drain life from us and render us helpless. I encourage you to consider how you can apply the theories you will be studying to enhance your life from both a personal and a professional standpoint.

Learn to look within yourself to determine what choices you are making (and not making) to keep yourself vital. If you are aware of the factors that sap your vitality as a person, you are in a better position to prevent the condition known as *professional burnout*. You have considerable control over whether you become burned out or not. You cannot always control stressful events, but you do have a great deal of control over how you interpret and react to these events. It is important to realize that you cannot continue to give and give while getting little in return. There is a price to pay for always being available and for assuming responsibility over the lives and destinies of others. Become attuned to the subtle signs of burnout rather than waiting for a full-blown condition of emotional and physical exhaustion to set in. You would be wise to develop your own strategy for keeping yourself alive personally and professionally.

Self-monitoring is a crucial first step in self-care. If you make an honest inventory of how well you are taking care of yourself in specific domains, you will have a framework for deciding what you may want to change. By making periodic assessments of the direction of your own life, you can determine whether you are living the way you want to live. If not, decide what you are willing to actually *do* to *make* changes occur. By being in tune with yourself, by having the experience of centeredness and solidness, and by feeling a sense of personal power, you have the foundation for integrating your life experiences with your professional experiences. Such an awareness can provide the basis for retaining your physical and psychological vitality and for being an effective professional.

As counseling professionals, we tend to be caring people who are good at taking care of others, but often we do not treat ourselves with the same level of care. Self-care is not a luxury; it is an ethical mandate. If we neglect to care for ourselves, our clients will not be getting the best of us. If we are physically drained and psychologically depleted, we will not have much to give to those with whom we work. It is not possible to provide nourishment to our clients if we are not nourishing ourselves.

Mental health professionals often comment that they do not have time to take care of themselves. My question to them is, "Can you afford *not* to take care of yourself?" To successfully meet the demands of our professional work, we must take care of ourselves physically, psychologically, intellectually, socially, and spiritually. Ideally, our self-care should mirror the care we provide for others. If we hope to have the vitality and stamina required to stay focused on our professional goals, we need to incorporate a wellness perspective into our daily living. Wellness is the result of our conscious commitment to a way of life that leads to zest, peace, vitality, and happiness.

Wellness and self-care are being given increased attention in professional journals and at professional conferences. When reading about self-care and wellness, reflect on what you can do to put what you know into action. If you are interested in learning more about therapist self-care, I highly recommend *Leaving It at the Office: A Guide to Psychotherapist Self-Care* (Norcross & Guy, 2007) and *Empathy Fatigue: Healing the Mind, Body, and Spirit of Professional Counselors* (Stebnicki, 2008). For more on the topic of the counselor as a person and as a professional, see *Creating Your Professional Path: Lessons From My Journey* (Corey, 2010).

Summary

One of the basic issues in the counseling profession concerns the significance of the counselor as a person in the therapeutic relationship. In your professional work, you are asking people to take an honest look at their lives and to make choices concerning how they want to change, so it is critical that you do this in your own life. Ask yourself questions such as "What do I personally have to offer others who are struggling to find their way?" and "Am I doing in my own life what I may be urging others to do?"

You can acquire an extensive theoretical and practical knowledge and can make that knowledge available to your clients. But to every therapeutic session you also bring yourself as a person. If you are to promote change in your clients, you need to be open to change in your own life. This willingness to attempt to live in accordance with what you teach and thus to be a positive model for your clients is what makes you a "therapeutic person."

Ethical Issues in Counseling Practice 3

LEARNING OBJECTIVES

1. Understand mandatory, aspirational, and positive ethics.
2. Identify characteristics and procedural steps of ethical decision making.
3. Understand the right of informed consent.
4. Articulate the dimensions of confidentiality (privacy, privileged communications, and exceptions).
5. Become familiar with the ethical and legal aspects of using technology.
6. Identify the major exceptions to confidentiality.
7. Understand ethical issues from a multicultural perspective.
8. Recognize when it is necessary to modify techniques with diverse clients.
9. Identify some key ethical issues in assessment and diagnosis.
10. Understand how ethnic and cultural factors can influence assessment and diagnosis.
11. Compare arguments for and against evidence-based practice.
12. Describe ethical issues related to multiple relationships in counseling practice.
13. Understand various perspectives on multiple relationships.
14. Explain the differences between a boundary crossing and a boundary violation.
15. Understand how to manage boundaries and risks associated with using social media.
16. Explain what is involved in becoming an ethical counselor.

Introduction

This chapter introduces some of the ethical principles and issues that will be **LO1** a basic part of your professional practice. I hope to stimulate your thinking about the importance of ethical practice so you will have a sound foundation for making **ethical decisions**. Topics addressed include balancing clients' needs against your own needs, ways of making good ethical decisions, educating clients about their rights, parameters of confidentiality, ethical concerns in counseling diverse client populations, ethical issues involving diagnosis, evidence-based practice, and dealing with multiple relationships and managing boundaries.

Students sometimes think of ethics merely as a list of rules and prohibitions that result in sanctions and malpractice actions if practitioners do not follow them. You will learn that being an ethical practitioners is far more complex than a set of rules. **Mandatory ethics** involves a level of ethical functioning at the minimum level of professional practice. In contrast, **aspirational ethics** focuses on doing what is in the best interests of clients. Functioning at the aspirational level involves the highest standards of thinking and conduct. Aspirational practice requires counselors to do more than simply meet the letter of the ethics code. It entails understanding the spirit of the code and the principles on which the code is based. *Fear-based ethics* does not constitute sound ethical practice. Ethics is more than a list of things to avoid for fear of punishment. Strive to work toward *concern-based ethics*, and think about how you can become the best practitioner possible (Corey, Corey, Corey, & Callanan, 2015). **Positive ethics** is an approach taken by practitioners who want to do their best for clients rather than simply meet minimum standards to stay out of trouble (Knapp & VandeCreek, 2006).

Visit CengageBrain.com or watch the DVD for the video program on Chapter 3, *Theory and Practice of Counseling and Psychotherapy: The Case of Stan and Lecturettes*. I suggest that you view the brief lecture for each chapter prior to reading the chapter.

Putting Clients' Needs Before Your Own

As counselors we cannot always keep our personal needs completely separate from our relationships with clients. Ethically, it is essential that we become aware of our own needs, areas of unfinished business, potential personal problems, and especially our sources of countertransference. We need to realize how such factors could interfere with effectively and ethically serving our clients.

Our professional relationships with our clients exist for their benefit. A useful question to frequently ask yourself is this: "Whose needs are being met in this relationship, my client's or my own?" It takes considerable professional maturity to make an honest appraisal of how your behavior affects your clients. It is not unethical for us to meet our personal needs through our professional work, but it is essential that these needs be kept in perspective. An ethical problem exists when we meet our needs, in either obvious or subtle ways, at the expense of our clients' needs. It is crucial that we avoid exploiting or harming clients.

We all have certain blind spots and distortions of reality. As helping professionals, we must actively work toward expanding our self-awareness and learn to recognize our areas of prejudice and vulnerability. If we are aware of our personal problems and are willing to work through them, there is less chance that we will project them onto clients. If certain problem areas surface and old conflicts become reactivated, we have an ethical obligation to do whatever it takes to avoid harming our clients.

We must also examine other, less obviously harmful personal needs that can get in the way of creating growth-producing relationships, such as the need for control and power; the inordinate need to be nurturing; the need to change others in the direction of our own values; the need for feeling adequate, particularly when it becomes overly important that the client confirm our competence; and the need to be respected and appreciated. It is crucial that we do not meet our needs at the expense of our clients. For an expanded discussion of this topic, see M. Corey and Corey (2016, chap. 1).

Ethical Decision Making

LO2

The ready-made answers to ethical dilemmas provided by professional organizations typically contain only broad guidelines for responsible practice. In practice, you will have to apply the ethics codes of your profession to the many practical problems you face. Professionals are expected to exercise prudent judgment when it comes to interpreting and applying ethical principles to specific situations. Although you are responsible for making ethical decisions, you do not have to do so alone. Learn about the resources available to you. Consult with colleagues, keep yourself informed about laws affecting your practice, keep up to date in your specialty field, stay abreast of developments in ethical practice, reflect on the impact your values have on your practice, and be willing to engage in honest self-examination. You should also be aware of the consequences of practicing in ways that are not sanctioned by organizations of which you are a member or the state in which you are licensed to practice.

The Role of Ethics Codes as a Catalyst for Improving Practice

Professional codes of ethics serve a number of purposes. They educate counseling practitioners and the general public about the responsibilities of the profession. They provide a basis for accountability, and protect clients from unethical practices. Perhaps most important, ethics codes provide a basis for reflecting on and improving your professional practice. Self-monitoring is a better route for professionals to take than being policed by an outside agency (Herlihy & Corey, 2015a).

From my perspective, an unfortunate recent trend is for ethics codes to increasingly take on legalistic, rule-based dimensions. Being an ethical practitioner involves far more than following a list of rules. Practitioners anxious to avoid any litigation may gear their practices mainly toward fulfilling legal minimums. If we are too concerned with being sued, it is unlikely that we will be very creative or effective in our work. It makes sense to be aware of the legal aspects of practice and to know and practice risk-management strategies, but we should not lose sight of what is best for our clients. One of the best ways to prevent being sued for malpractice is to demonstrate respect for clients, keep client welfare as a central concern, and practice within the framework of professional codes.

No code of ethics can delineate what would be the appropriate or best course of action in each problematic situation a professional will face. In my view, ethics codes are best used as guidelines to formulate sound reasoning and serve practitioners in making the best judgments possible. A number of professional organizations and their websites are listed near the end of the chapter; each has its own code of ethics, which you can access through its website. Compare your professional organization's code of ethics to several others to understand their similarities and differences.

Some Steps in Making Ethical Decisions

Most models for ethical decision making focus on the application of principles to ethical dilemmas. My colleagues and I have identified a series of procedural steps to help you think through ethical problems when using these principles (see Corey, Corey, Corey, & Callanan, 2015):

- Identify the problem or dilemma. Gather information that will shed light on the nature of the problem. This will help you decide whether the problem is mainly ethical, legal, professional, clinical, or moral.
- Identify the potential issues. Evaluate the rights, responsibilities, and welfare of all those who are involved in the situation.
- Look at the relevant ethics codes for general guidance on the matter. Consider whether your own values and ethics are consistent with or in conflict with the relevant guidelines.
- Consider the applicable laws and regulations, and determine how they may have a bearing on an ethical dilemma.
- Seek consultation from more than one source to obtain various perspectives on the dilemma, and document in the client's record the suggestions you received from this consultation.
- Brainstorm various possible courses of action. Continue discussing options with other professionals. Include the client in this process of considering options for action. Again, document the nature of this discussion with your client.
- Enumerate the consequences of various decisions, and reflect on the implications of each course of action for your client.
- Decide on what appears to be the best possible course of action. Once the course of action has been implemented, follow up to evaluate the outcomes and to determine whether further action is necessary. Document the reasons for the actions you took as well as your evaluation measures.

In reasoning through any ethical dilemma, there is rarely just one course of action to follow, and practitioners may make different decisions. The more subtle the ethical dilemma, the more complex and demanding the decision-making process.

Professional maturity implies that you are open to questioning and discussing your quandaries with colleagues. In seeking consultation, it is generally possible to protect the identity of your client and still get useful input that is critical to making sound ethical decisions. Because ethics codes do not make decisions for you, it is a good practice to demonstrate a willingness to explore various aspects of a problem, raise questions, discuss ethical concerns with others, and continually clarify your values and examine your motivations. To the degree that it is possible, include the client in all phases of the ethical decision-making process. Again, it is essential to document how you included your client as well as the steps you took to ensure ethical practice.

The Right of Informed Consent

Regardless of your theoretical framework, informed consent is an ethical and legal requirement that is an integral part of the therapeutic process. It also establishes a basic foundation for creating a working alliance and a collaborative partnership between the client and the therapist. **Informed consent** involves the right of clients to be informed about their therapy and to make autonomous decisions pertaining to it. Providing clients with information they need to make informed choices tends to promote the active cooperation of clients in their counseling plan. By educating your clients about their rights and responsibilities, you are both empowering them and building a trusting relationship with them. Seen in this light, informed consent is something far broader than simply making sure clients sign the appropriate forms. It is a positive approach that helps clients become active partners and true collaborators in their therapy. LO3

Some aspects of the informed consent process include the general goals of counseling, the responsibilities of the counselor toward the client, the responsibilities of clients, limitations of and exceptions to confidentiality, legal and ethical parameters that could define the relationship, the qualifications and background of the practitioner, the fees involved, the services the client can expect, and the approximate length of the therapeutic process. Further areas might include the benefits of counseling, the risks involved, and the possibility that the client's case will be discussed with the therapist's colleagues or supervisors.

There are a host of ways to violate a client's privacy through the inappropriate use of various forms of modern-day technology. Most of us have become accustomed to relying on technology, and we need to give careful thought to the subtle ways client privacy can be compromised. As a part of the informed consent process, it is wise to discuss the potential privacy problems of using a wide range of technology and to take preventive measures to protect both you and your clients. For example, clients and counselors should carefully consider privacy issues before agreeing to send e-mail messages to clients' workplace or home. A good policy is to limit e-mail exchanges to basic information such as appointment times.

Educating the client begins with the initial counseling session, and this process will continue for the duration of counseling. The challenge of fulfilling the spirit of informed consent is to strike a balance between giving clients too much information and giving them too little. For example, it is too late to tell minors that you intend to consult with their parents *after* they have disclosed that they are considering an abortion. Young clients have a right to know about the limitations of confidentiality before they make such highly personal disclosures. Clients can be overwhelmed, however, if counselors go into too much detail initially about the interventions they are likely to make. It takes both intuition and skill for practitioners to strike a balance.

Informed consent in counseling can be provided in written form, orally, or some combination of both. If it is done orally, therapists must make an entry in the client's clinical record documenting the nature and extent of informed consent (Nagy, 2011). It is a good idea to provide basic information about the therapy process in writing, as well as to discuss with clients topics that will enable them to get the maximum benefit from their counseling experience. Written information protects both clients and therapists and enables clients to think about the information and bring up questions at the following session. For a more complete discussion of informed consent and client rights, see *Issues and Ethics in the Helping Professions* (Corey, Corey, Corey, & Callanan, 2015, chap. 5), *The Counselor and the Law: A Guide to Legal and Ethical Practice* (Wheeler & Bertram, 2015, chap. 2), *Ethical, Legal, and Professional Issues in Counseling* (Remley & Herlihy, 2016), and *Essential Ethics for Psychologists* (Nagy, 2011, chap. 5).

Dimensions of Confidentiality

LO4

Confidentiality and privileged communication are two related but somewhat different concepts. Both of these concepts are rooted in a client's right to privacy. **Confidentiality** is an *ethical concept*, and in most states it is the legal duty of therapists not to disclose information about a client. **Privileged communication** is a *legal concept* that protects clients from having their confidential communications revealed in court without their permission (Herlihy & Corey, 2015a). All states have enacted into law some form of psychotherapist–client privilege, but the specifics of this privilege vary from state to state. These laws ensure that disclosures clients make in therapy will be protected from exposure by therapists in legal proceedings. Generally speaking, the legal concept of privileged communication does *not* apply to group counseling, couples counseling, family therapy, child and adolescent therapy, or whenever there are more than two people in the room.

Confidentiality is central to developing a trusting and productive client–therapist relationship. Because no genuine therapy can occur unless clients trust in the privacy of their revelations to their therapists, professionals have the responsibility to define the degree of confidentiality that can be promised. Counselors have an ethical and legal responsibility to discuss the nature and purpose of confidentiality with their clients early in the counseling process. In addition, clients have a right to know that their therapist may be discussing certain details of the relationship with a supervisor or a colleague.

Ethical Concerns with the Use of Technology

LO5

Issues pertaining to confidentiality and privacy can become more complicated when technology is involved. Section H of the *ACA Code of Ethics* (2014) contains a new set of standards with regard to the use of technology, relationships established through computer-mediated communication, and social media as a delivery platform. Major subsections address competency to provide services and the laws associated with distance counseling, components of informed consent and security (confidentiality and its limitations), client verification, the distance counseling relationship (access, accessibility, and professional boundaries), maintenance of records, accessibility of websites, and the use of social media (Jencius, 2015).

Exceptions to Confidentiality and Privileged Communication

Although most counselors agree on the essential value of confidentiality, they realize that other obligations may override this pledge. There are times when confidential information must be divulged, and there are many instances in which keeping or breaking confidentiality becomes a cloudy issue. In determining when to breach confidentiality, therapists must consider the requirements of the law, the institution in which they work, and the clientele they serve. Because these circumstances are frequently not clearly defined by accepted ethics codes, counselors must exercise professional judgment. LO6

Whenever counselors are not clear about their obligations regarding confidentiality or privileged communication, it is critical to seek consultation and to document these discussions. Remley and Herlihy (2016) identify at least 15 exceptions to confidentiality and privileged communication. There is a legal requirement to break confidentiality in cases involving child abuse, abuse of the elderly, abuse of dependent adults, and danger to self or others. All mental health practitioners and interns need to be aware of their duty to report in these situations and to know the limitations of confidentiality. Here are some other circumstances in which information must legally be reported by counselors:

- When the therapist believes a client under the age of 16 is the victim of incest, rape, child abuse, or some other crime
- When the therapist determines that the client needs hospitalization
- When information is made an issue in a court action
- When clients request that their records be released to them or to a third party

In general, the counselor's primary obligation is to protect client disclosures as a vital part of the therapeutic relationship. Informing clients about the limits of confidentiality does not necessarily inhibit successful counseling.

For a more complete discussion of confidentiality, see *Issues and Ethics in the Helping Professions* (Corey, Corey, Corey, & Callanan, 2015, chap. 6), *Essential Ethics for Psychologists* (Nagy, 2011, chap. 6), *The Counselor and the Law: A Guide to Legal and Ethical Practice* (Wheeler & Bertram, 2015, chap. 5), and *Ethical, Legal, and Professional Issues in Counseling* (Remley & Herlihy, 2016, chap. 5).

Ethical Issues From a Multicultural Perspective

Ethical practice requires that we take the client's cultural context into account in counseling practice. In this section we look at how it is possible for practitioners to practice unethically if they do not address cultural differences in counseling practice. LO7

Are Current Theories Adequate in Working With Culturally Diverse Populations?

I believe current theories can be, and need to be, expanded to include a multicultural perspective. Assumptions made about mental health, optimum human development, the nature of psychopathology, and the nature of effective treatment may have little relevance for some clients. For traditional theories to be relevant in a multicultural and diverse society, they must incorporate an interactive person-in-the-environment focus. That is, individuals are best understood by taking into consideration salient cultural and environmental variables. It is essential for therapists to create therapeutic strategies that are congruent with the range of values and behaviors that are characteristic of a pluralistic society.

Is Counseling Culture-Bound?

Historically, therapists have relied on Western therapeutic models to guide their practice and to conceptualize problems that clients present in mental health settings. Western models of counseling have some limitations when applied to special populations and cultural groups such as Asian and Pacific Islanders, Latinos, Native Americans, and African Americans. Multicultural writers have asserted that theories of counseling and psychotherapy represent different worldviews, each with its own values, biases, and assumptions about human behavior. Some of these approaches may not be applicable to clients from different racial, ethnic, and cultural backgrounds. Methods often need to be modified when working with clients from diverse cultural backgrounds. **LO8**

Contemporary therapy approaches are grounded on a core set of values, which are neither value-neutral nor applicable to all cultures. For example, the values of individual choice and autonomy are not universal. In some cultures the key values are collectivist, and primary consideration is given to what is good for the group. Regardless of the therapist's orientation, it is crucial to listen to clients and determine why they are seeking help and how best to deliver the help that is appropriate for them. Competent therapists understand themselves as social and cultural beings and possess at least a minimum level of knowledge and skill that they can bring to bear on any counseling situation. These practitioners understand what their clients need and avoid forcing clients into a preconceived mold.

Cultural diversity is a fact of life in our world. To the extent that counselors are focused on the values of the dominant culture and insensitive to variations among groups and individuals, they are at risk for practicing unethically (Barnett & Johnson, 2015). Counselors need to understand and accept clients who have a different set of assumptions about life, and they need to be alert to the possibility of imposing their own worldview. In working with clients from different cultural backgrounds and life experiences, it is important that counselors resist making value judgments for them. It is essential to be mindful of diversity and social justice issues if we are to practice ethically and effectively (Chung & Bemak, 2012; Lee, 2015).

Focusing on Both Individual and Environmental Factors

A theoretical orientation provides practitioners with a map to guide them in a productive direction with their clients. It is hoped that the theory orients them but does not control what they attend to in the therapeutic venture. Counselors who operate from a multicultural framework also have certain assumptions and a focus that guides their practice. They view individuals in the context of the family and the culture, and their aim is to facilitate social action that will lead to change within the client's community rather than merely increasing the individual's insight. Both multicultural practitioners and feminist therapists maintain that therapeutic practice will be effective only to the extent that interventions are tailored toward social action aimed at changing those factors that are creating the client's problem rather than blaming the client for his or her condition (Chung & Bemak, 2012). These topics are developed in more detail in later chapters.

An adequate theory of counseling *does* deal with the social and cultural factors of an individual's problems. However, there is something to be said for helping clients deal with their response to environmental realities. Counselors may well be at a loss in trying to bring about social change when they are sitting with a client who is in pain because of social injustice. By using techniques from many of the traditional therapies, counselors can help clients increase their awareness of their options in dealing with barriers and struggles. However, it is essential to focus on both individual and social factors if change is to occur, as the feminist, postmodern, and family systems approaches to therapy teach us. Indeed, the person-in-the-environment perspective acknowledges this interactive reality. For a more detailed treatment of the ethical issues in multicultural counseling, see Chung and Bemak (2012), Corey, Corey, Corey, and Callanan (2015, chap. 4), and Lee (2013).

Ethical Issues in the Assessment Process

Both clinical and ethical issues are associated with the use of assessment and diagnostic procedures. As you will see when you study the various theories of counseling, some approaches place heavy emphasis on the role of assessment as a prelude to the treatment process; other approaches find assessment less useful in this regard. LO9

The Role of Assessment and Diagnosis in Counseling

Assessment and diagnosis are integrally related to the practice of counseling and psychotherapy, and both are often viewed as essential for planning treatment. For some approaches, a comprehensive assessment of the client is the initial step in the therapeutic process. The rationale is that specific counseling goals cannot be formulated and appropriate treatment strategies cannot be designed until a client's past and present functioning is understood. Regardless of their theoretical orientation, therapists need to engage in assessment, which is generally an ongoing part of the therapeutic process. This assessment may be subject to revision as the clinician gathers further data during therapy sessions. Some practitioners consider *assessment* as a part of the process that leads to a *formal diagnosis*.

Assessment consists of evaluating the relevant factors in a client's life to identify themes for further exploration in the counseling process. **Diagnosis**, which is sometimes part of the assessment process, consists of identifying a specific mental disorder based on a pattern of symptoms. Both assessment and diagnosis can be understood as providing direction for the treatment process.

Diagnosis may include an explanation of the causes of the client's difficulties, an account of how these problems developed over time, a classification of any disorders, a specification of preferred treatment procedure, and an estimate of the chances for a successful resolution. The purpose of diagnosis in counseling and psychotherapy is to identify disruptions in a client's present behavior and lifestyle. Once problem areas are clearly identified, the counselor and client are able to establish the goals of the therapy process, and then a treatment plan can be tailored to the unique needs of the client. A diagnosis provides a working hypothesis that guides the practitioner in understanding the client. The therapy sessions provide useful clues about the nature of the client's problems. Thus diagnosis begins with the intake interview and continues throughout the duration of therapy.

The classic book for guiding practitioners in making diagnostic assessments is the fifth edition of the American Psychiatric Association's (2013) *Diagnostic and Statistical Manual of Mental Disorders* (also known as the *DSM-5*). Clinicians who work in community mental health agencies, private practice, and other human service settings are generally expected to assess client problems within this framework. This manual advises practitioners that it represents only an initial step in a comprehensive evaluation and that it is necessary to gain information about the person being evaluated beyond that required for a *DSM-5* diagnosis.

Sme clinicians view diagnosis as central to the counseling process, but others view it as unnecessary, as a detriment, or as discriminatory against ethnic minorities and women. As you will see when you study the therapeutic models in this book, some approaches do not use diagnosis as a precursor to treatment.

Considering Ethnic and Cultural Factors in Assessment and Diagnosis LO10

A danger of the diagnostic approach is the possible failure of counselors to consider ethnic and cultural factors in certain patterns of behavior. The *DSM-5* emphasizes the importance of being aware of unintentional bias and keeping an open mind to the presence of distinctive ethnic and cultural patterns that could influence the diagnostic process. Unless cultural variables are considered, some clients may be subjected to erroneous diagnoses. Certain behaviors and personality styles may be labeled neurotic or deviant simply because they are not characteristic of the dominant culture. Counselors who work with diverse client populations may erroneously conclude that a client is repressed, inhibited, passive, and unmotivated, all of which are seen as undesirable by Western standards.

The *DSM-5* is based on a medical model of mental illness that defines problems as residing with the individual rather than in society. It does not take into account the political, economic, social, and cultural factors in the lives of clients, which may play a significant role in the problems of clients. The DSM system tends to pathologize clients, perpetuating the oppression of clients from diverse groups (Remley & Herlihy, 2016). Barnett and Johnson (2015) suggest that practitioners give careful consideration before rendering a diagnosis and take into consideration the realities of discrimination, oppression, and racism in society and in the mental health disciplines.

Assessment and Diagnosis From Various Theoretical Perspectives The theory from which you operate influences your thinking about the use of a diagnostic framework in your therapeutic practice. Many practitioners who use the cognitive behavioral approaches and the medical model place heavy emphasis on the role of assessment as a prelude to the treatment process. The rationale is that specific therapy goals cannot be designed until a clear picture emerges of the client's past and present functioning. In addition, progress, change, improvement, or success may be difficult to evaluate without an initial assessment. Counselors who base their practice on the relationship-oriented approaches tend to view the process of assessment and diagnosis as external to the immediacy of the client–counselor relationship, impeding their understanding of the subjective world of the client. As you will see in Chapter 12, feminist therapists contend that traditional diagnostic practices are often oppressive and that such practices are based on a White, male-centered, Western notion of mental health and mental illness. Both the feminist perspective and the postmodern approaches (Chapter 13) charge that these diagnoses ignore societal contexts. Therapists with a feminist, social constructionist, solution-focused, or narrative therapy orientation challenge many *DSM-5* diagnoses. However, these practitioners do make assessments and draw conclusions about client problems and strengths. Regardless of the particular theory espoused by a therapist, both clinical and ethical issues are associated with the use of assessment procedures and possibly a diagnosis as part of a treatment plan.

A Commentary on Assessment and Diagnosis Most practitioners and many writers in the field consider assessment and diagnosis to be a continuing process that focuses on understanding the client. The collaborative perspective that involves the client as an active participant in the therapy process implies that both the therapist and the client are engaged in a search-and-discovery process from the first session to the last. Even though some practitioners may avoid formal diagnostic procedures and terminology, making tentative hypotheses and sharing them with clients throughout the process is a form of ongoing diagnosis. This perspective on assessment and diagnosis is consistent with the principles of feminist therapy, an approach that is critical of traditional diagnostic procedures.

Ethical dilemmas may be created when diagnosis is done strictly for insurance purposes, which often entails arbitrarily assigning a client to a diagnostic classification. However, it is a clinical, legal, and ethical obligation of therapists to screen clients for life-threatening problems such as organic disorders, schizophrenia, bipolar disorder, and suicidal types of depression. Students need to learn the clinical skills necessary to do this type of screening, which is a form of diagnostic thinking.

It is essential to assess the whole person, which includes assessing dimensions of mind, body, and spirit. Therapists need to take into account the biological processes as possible underlying factors of psychological symptoms and work closely with physicians. Clients' values can be instrumental resources in the search for solutions to their problems, and spiritual and religious values often illuminate client concerns.

For a more detailed discussion of assessment and diagnosis in counseling practice as it is applied to a single case, consult *Case Approach to Counseling and Psychotherapy* (Corey, 2013b), in which theorists from 12 different theoretical orientations share their diagnostic perspectives on the case of Ruth. For a comprehensive review of the changes in the *DSM-5*, see *DSM-5 Learning Companion for Counselors* (Dailey, Gill, Karl, & Minton, 2014).

Ethical Aspects of Evidence-Based Practice

LO11

Mental health practitioners are faced with the task of choosing the best interventions with a particular client. For many practitioners this choice is based on their theoretical orientation. In recent years, however, a shift has occurred toward promoting the use of specific interventions for specific problems or diagnoses based on empirically supported treatments (APA Presidential Task Force on Evidence-based Practice, 2006; Cukrowicz et al., 2005; Deegear & Lawson, 2003; Edwards, Dattilio, & Bromley, 2004).

This trend toward specific, empirically supported treatment is referred to as **evidence-based practice (EBP):** "the integration of the best available research with clinical expertise in the context of patient characteristics, culture, and preferences" (APA Presidential Task Force on Evidence-based Practice, 2006, p. 273). Increasingly, those practitioners who work in a behavioral health care system must cope with the challenges associated with evidence-based practice. Norcross, Hogan, and Koocher (2008) advocate for inclusive evidence-based practices that incorporate the three pillars of EBP: (1) looking for the best available research, (2) relying on clinical expertise, and (3) taking into consideration the client's characteristics, culture, and preferences.

Many aspects of treatment—the therapy relationship, the therapist's personality and therapeutic style, the client, and environmental factors—are vital contributors to the success of psychotherapy. Evidence-based practices tend to emphasize only one of these aspects—interventions based on the best available research. The central aim of evidence-based practice is to require psychotherapists to base their practice on techniques that have empirical evidence to support their efficacy. Research studies empirically analyze the most effective and efficient treatments, which then can be widely implemented in clinical practice (Norcross, Beutler, & Levant, 2006).

In many mental health settings, clinicians are pressured to use interventions that are both brief and standardized. In such settings, treatments are operationalized by reliance on a treatment manual that identifies what is to be done in each therapy session and how many sessions will be required (Edwards et al., 2004). Many practitioners believe this approach is mechanistic and does not take into full consideration the relational dimensions of the psychotherapy process and individual variability. Indeed, relying exclusively on standardized treatments for specific problems may raise another set of ethical concerns because the reliability and validity of these empirically based techniques is questionable.

Human change is complex and difficult to measure beyond such a simplistic level that the change may be meaningless. Furthermore, not all clients come to therapy with clearly defined psychological disorders. Many clients have existential concerns that do not fit with any diagnostic category and do not lend themselves to clearly specified symptom-based outcomes. EBP may have something to offer mental health professionals who work with individuals with specific emotional, cognitive, and behavioral disorders, but it does not have a great deal to offer practitioners working with individuals who want to pursue more meaning and fulfillment in their lives.

Norcross and his colleagues (2006) contend that the call for accountability in mental health care is here to stay and that all mental health professionals are challenged by the mandate to demonstrate the efficiency, efficacy, and safety of the services they provide. They emphasize that the overarching goal of EBP is to enhance the effectiveness of client services and to improve public health and warn that mental health professionals need to take a proactive stance to make sure this goal is kept in focus. They realize there is potential for misuse and abuse by third-party payers who could selectively use research findings as cost-containment measures rather than ways of improving the quality of services delivered.

For further reading on the topic of evidence-based practice, I recommend *Clinician's Guide to Evidence-based Practice* (Norcross et al., 2008).

Managing Multiple Relationships in Counseling Practice

Dual or multiple relationships, either sexual or nonsexual, occur when counselors assume two (or more) roles simultaneously or sequentially with a client. This may involve assuming more than one professional role or combining professional and nonprofessional roles. The term *multiple relationship* is more often used than the term *dual relationship* because of the complexities involved in these relationships, but both terms appear in various professional codes of ethics, and the ACA (2014) uses the term *nonprofessional relationships*. In this section I use the broader term of *multiple relationships* to encompass both dual relationships and nonprofessional relationships. LO12

When clinicians blend their professional relationship with another kind of relationship with a client, ethical concerns must be considered. Many forms of nonprofessional interactions or nonsexual multiple relationships pose a challenge to practitioners. Some examples of *nonsexual* dual or multiple relationships are combining the roles of teacher and therapist or of supervisor and therapist; bartering for goods or therapeutic services; borrowing money from a client; providing therapy to a friend, an employee, or a relative; engaging in a social relationship with a client; accepting an expensive gift from a client; or going into a business venture with a client. Some multiple relationships are clearly exploitative and do serious harm both to the client and to the professional. For example, becoming emotionally or sexually involved with a *current* client is clearly unethical, unprofessional, and illegal. Sexual involvement with a *former* client is unwise, can be exploitative, and is generally considered unethical.

Because nonsexual multiple relationships are necessarily complex and multidimensional, there are few simple and absolute answers to resolve them. It is not always possible to play a single role in your work as a counselor, nor is it always desirable. You may have to deal with managing multiple roles, regardless of the setting in which you work or the client population you serve. It is a wise practice to give careful thought to the complexities of multiple roles and relationships before embroiling yourself in ethically questionable situations.

Ethical reasoning and judgment come into play when ethics codes are applied to specific situations. The *ACA Code of Ethics* (ACA, 2014) makes it clear that counseling professionals must learn how to *manage* multiple roles and responsibilities in an ethical way. This entails dealing effectively with the power differential that is inherent in counseling relationships and training relationships, balancing boundary issues, addressing nonprofessional relationships, and striving to avoid using power in ways that might cause harm to clients, students, or supervisees (Herlihy & Corey, 2015b).

Although multiple relationships do carry inherent risks, it is a mistake to conclude that these relationships are always unethical and necessarily lead to harm and exploitation. Some of these relationships can be beneficial to clients if they are implemented thoughtfully and with integrity (Zur, 2007). An excellent resource on the ethical and clinical dimensions of multiple relationships is *Boundaries in Psychotherapy: Ethical and Clinical Explorations* (Zur, 2007).

Perspectives on Multiple Relationships

What makes multiple relationships so problematic? Herlihy and Corey **LO13** (2015b) contend that some of the problematic aspects of engaging in multiple relationships are that they are pervasive; they can be difficult to recognize; they are unavoidable at times; they are potentially harmful, but not necessarily always harmful; they can be beneficial; and they are the subject of conflicting advice from various experts. A review of the literature reveals that dual and multiple relationships are hotly debated. Except for sexual intimacy with current clients, which is unequivocally unethical, there is not much consensus regarding the appropriate way to deal with multiple relationships.

Some of the codes of the professional organizations advise against forming multiple relationships, mainly because of the potential for misusing power, exploiting the client, and impairing objectivity. When multiple relationships exploit clients, or have significant potential to harm clients, they are unethical. The ethics codes do not mandate avoidance of all such relationships, however; nor do the codes imply that nonsexual multiple relationships are unethical. The current focus of ethics codes is to remain alert to the possibilities of harm to clients and to develop safeguard to protect clients. Although codes can provide some general guidelines, good judgment, the willingness to reflect on one's practices, and being aware of one's motivations are critical dimensions of an ethical practitioner. It bears repeating that multiple relationship issues cannot be resolved with ethics codes alone; counselors must think through all of the ethical and clinical dimensions involved in a wide range of boundary concerns.

A consensus of many writers is that multiple relationships are inevitable and unavoidable in some situations and that a global prohibition is not a realistic answer. Because interpersonal boundaries are not static but undergo redefinition over time, the challenge for practitioners is to learn how to manage boundary fluctuations and to deal effectively with overlapping roles (Herlihy & Corey, 2015b). One key to learning how to manage multiple relationships is to think of ways to minimize the risks involved.

Ways of Minimizing Risk In determining whether to proceed with a multiple relationship, it is critical to consider whether the potential benefit to the client of such a relationship outweighs its potential harm. Some relationships may have more potential benefits to clients than potential risks. It is your responsibility to develop safeguards aimed at reducing the potential for negative consequences. Herlihy and Corey (2015b) identify the following guidelines:

- Set healthy boundaries early in the therapeutic relationship. Informed consent is essential from the beginning and throughout the therapy process.

- Involve clients in ongoing discussions and in the decision-making process, and document your discussions. Discuss with your clients what you expect of them and what they can expect of you.
- Consult with fellow professionals as a way to maintain objectivity and identify unanticipated difficulties. Realize that you don't need to make a decision alone.
- When multiple relationships are potentially problematic, or when the risk for harm is high, it is always wise to work under supervision. Document the nature of this supervision and any actions you take in your records.
- Self-monitoring is critical throughout the process. Ask yourself whose needs are being met and examine your motivations for considering becoming involved in a dual or multiple relationship.

In working through a multiple relationship concern, it is best to begin by ascertaining whether such a relationship can be avoided. Nagy (2011) points out that multiple relationships cannot always be avoided, especially in small towns. Nor should every multiple relationship be considered unethical. However, when a therapist's objectivity and competence are compromised, the therapist may find that personal needs surface and diminish the quality of the therapist's professional work. Sometimes nonprofessional interactions are avoidable and your involvement would put the client needlessly at risk. In other cases multiple relationships are unavoidable. One way of dealing with any potential problems is to adopt a policy of completely avoiding any kind of nonprofessional interaction. As a general guideline, Nagy (2011) recommends avoiding multiple relationships to the extent this is possible. Therapists should document precautions taken to protect clients when such relationships are unavoidable. Another alternative is to deal with each dilemma as it develops, making full use of informed consent and at the same time seeking consultation and supervision in dealing with the situation. This second alternative includes a professional requirement for self-monitoring. It is one of the hallmarks of professionalism to be willing to grapple with these ethical complexities of day-to-day practice.

Establishing Personal and Professional Boundaries Establishing and maintaining consistent yet flexible boundaries is necessary if you are to effectively counsel clients. If you have difficulty establishing and maintaining boundaries in your personal life, you are likely to find that you will have difficulty when it comes to managing boundaries in your professional life. Developing appropriate and effective boundaries in your counseling practice is the first step to learning how to manage multiple relationships. There is a relationship between developing appropriate boundaries in the personal and professional realms. If you are successful in establishing boundaries in various aspects of your personal life, you have a good foundation for creating sound boundaries with clients. LO14

One important aspect of maintaining appropriate professional boundaries is to recognize boundary crossings and prevent them from becoming boundary violations. A **boundary crossing** is a departure from a commonly accepted practice that could *potentially* benefit a client. For example, attending the wedding of a client may be extending a boundary, but it could be beneficial for the client. In contrast, a **boundary violation** is a serious breach that harms the client and is therefore unethical. A boundary violation is a boundary crossing that takes the practitioner out of the professional role, generally involves exploitation, and results in harm to a client (Gutheil & Brodsky, 2008). Flexible boundaries can be useful in the counseling process when applied ethically. Some boundary crossings pose no ethical problems and may enhance the counseling relationship. Other boundary crossings may lead to a pattern of blurred professional roles and become problematic.

Social Media and Boundaries It is not unusual for a counselor to **LO15** receive a "friend request" from a client or former client. Facebook and other social media sites raise many ethical concerns for counselors regarding boundaries, dual relationships, confidentiality, and privacy. One possibility is to set up two distinct Facebook pages, one for professional use and the other for personal use. Spotts-De Lazzer (2012) believes practitioners will have to translate and maintain traditional ethics when it comes to social media and offers these recommendations:

- Limit what is shared online.
- Include clear and thorough social networking policies as part of the informed consent process.
- Regularly update protective settings because social media providers often change their privacy rules.

As social media use continues to spread, the *ACA Code of Ethics* (2014) emphasizes the need for counselors to develop a social media policy and to include that in their informed consent discussions. The virtual relationship between counselor and client and how counselors can safely maintain a virtual presence are emphasized in ACA's revised code (Jencius, 2015).

Becoming an Ethical Counselor

Knowing and following your profession's code of ethics is part of being an **LO16** ethical practitioner, but these codes do not make decisions for you. As you become involved in counseling, you will find that interpreting the ethical guidelines of your professional organization and applying them to particular situations demand the utmost ethical sensitivity. Even responsible practitioners differ over how to apply established ethical principles to specific situations. In your professional work you will deal with questions that do not always have obvious answers. You will have to assume responsibility for deciding how to act in ways that will further the best interests of your clients.

Throughout your professional life you will need to reexamine the ethical questions raised in this chapter. You can benefit from both formal and informal opportunities to discuss ethical dilemmas during your training program. Even if you resolve some ethical matters while completing a graduate program, there is no guarantee that these matters have been settled once and for all. These topics are bound to take on new dimensions as you gain more experience. Oftentimes students burden themselves unnecessarily with the expectation that they should resolve all potential

ethical problem areas before they begin to practice. Throug life, seek consultation from trusted colleagues and supervisor ethical dilemma. Ethical decision making is an evolutionar you to be continually open and self-reflective. Becoming ar not a final destination but a journey that will continue throu

Summary

It is essential that you learn a process for thinking about and dealing with ethical dilemmas, keeping in mind that most ethical issues are complex and defy simple solutions. A sign of good faith is your willingness to share your struggles with colleagues. Such consultation can be helpful in clarifying issues by giving you another perspective on a situation. New issues are constantly surfacing, and positive ethics demands periodic reflection and an openness to change on the part of the practitioner.

If there is one fundamental question that can serve to tie together all the issues discussed in this chapter, it is this: "Who has the right to counsel another person?" This question can be the focal point of your reflection on ethical and professional issues. It also can be the basis of your self-examination each day that you meet with clients. Continue to ask yourself: "What makes me think I have a right to counsel others?" "What do I have to offer the people I'm counseling?" "Am I doing in my own life what I'm encouraging my clients to do?" At times you may feel that you have no ethical right to counsel others, perhaps because your own life isn't always the model you would like it to be for your clients. More important than resolving all of life's issues is knowing what kinds of questions to ask and remaining open to reflection.

This chapter has introduced you to a number of ethical issues that you are bound to face at some point in your counseling practice. I hope your interest has been piqued and that you will want to learn more. For further reading on this important topic, choose some of the books listed in the Recommended Supplementary Readings section for further study.

Where to Go From Here

The following professional organizations provide helpful information about what each group has to offer, including the code of ethics for the organization.

American Association for Marriage and Family Therapy (AAMFT)	www.aamft.org
American Counseling Association (ACA)	www.counseling.org
American Mental Health Counselors Association (AMHCA)	www.amhca.org
American Music Therapy Association	www.musictherapy.org
American Psychological Association (APA)	www.apa.org

American School Counselor Association (ASCA)	www.schoolcounselor.org
Commission on Rehabilitation Counselor Certification (CRCC)	www.crccertification.com
National Association of Alcohol and Drug Abuse Counselors (NAADAC)	www.naadac.org
National Association of Social Workers (NASW)	www.socialworkers.org
National Organization for Human Services (NOHS)	www.nationalhumanservices.org

Recommended Supplementary Readings for Part 1

The Counselor and the Law: A Guide to Legal and Ethical Practice (Wheeler & Bertram, 2015) offers a comprehensive overview of the law as it pertains to counseling practice. It highlights ethical and legal responsibilities of counselors and identifies risk-management strategies.

Leaving It at the Office: A Guide to Psychotherapist Self-Care (Norcross & Guy, 2007) addresses 12 self-care strategies that are supported by empirical evidence. The authors develop the position that self-care is personally essential and professionally ethical. This is one of the most useful books on therapist self-care and on prevention of burnout.

Psychotherapy Relationships That Work: Evidence-Based Responsiveness (Norcross, 2011) is a comprehensive treatment of the effective elements of the therapy relationship. Many different contributors address ways of tailoring the therapy relationship to individual clients. Implications from research for effective clinical practice are presented.

Ethics Desk Reference for Counselors (Barnett & Johnson, 2015) is a practical guide to understand and applying the *ACA Code of Ethics*. It is a reference that is easy to read, interesting, and has appeal for both students and practitioners.

ACA Ethical Standards Casebook (Herlihy & Corey, 2015a) contains a variety of useful cases that are geared to the *ACA Code of Ethics*. The examples illustrate and clarify the meaning and intent of the standards.

Boundary Issues in Counseling: Multiple Roles and Responsibilities (Herlihy & Corey, 2015b) puts the multiple relationship controversy into perspective. The book focuses on dual relationships in a variety of work settings.

Boundaries in Psychotherapy: Ethical and Clinical Explorations (Zur, 2007) examines the complex nature of boundaries in professional practice by offering a decision-making process to help practitioners deal with a range of topics such as gifts, nonsexual touch, home visits, bartering, and therapist self-disclosure.

Issues and Ethics in the Helping Professions (Corey, Corey, Corey, & Callanan, 2015) is devoted entirely to the issues that were introduced briefly in Chapter 3. Designed to involve readers in a personal and active way, many open-ended cases are presented to help readers formulate their own thoughts on a wide range of ethical issues.

Becoming a Helper (M. Corey & Corey, 2016) expands on issues dealing with the personal and professional lives of helpers and ethical issues in counseling practice.

Ethics in Action: DVD and Workbook (Corey, Corey, & Haynes, 2015) is a self-instructional program divided into three parts: (1) ethical decision making, (2) values and the helping relationship, and (3) boundary issues and multiple relationships. The program includes video clips of vignettes demonstrating ethical situations aimed at stimulating discussion.

Student Manual for Theory and Practice of Counseling and Psychotherapy (Corey, 2017) is designed to help you integrate theory with practice and to make the concepts covered in this book come alive. It consists of self-inventories, overview summaries of the theories, a glossary of key concepts, study questions, issues and questions for personal application, activities and exercises, comprehension checks and quizzes, and case examples. The manual is fully coordinated with the textbook to make it a personal study guide.

The Art of Integrative Counseling (Corey, 2013a) presents concepts and techniques from the various theories of counseling and provides guidelines for readers in developing their own approach to counseling practice.

Case Approach to Counseling and Psychotherapy (Corey, 2013b) provides case applications of how each of the theories presented in this book works in action. A hypothetical client, Ruth, experiences counseling from all of the therapeutic vantage points.

DVD for Theory and Practice of Counseling and Psychotherapy: The Case of Stan and Lecturettes (Corey, 2013) is an interactive self-study tool that consists of two programs. Part 1 includes 13 sessions in which Gerald Corey counsels Stan using a few selected techniques from each theory. Part 2 consists of brief lectures by the author for each chapter in *Theory and Practice of Counseling and Psychotherapy*. Both programs emphasize the practical applications of the various theories.

DVD for Integrative Counseling: The Case of Ruth and Lecturettes (Corey & Haynes, 2013) is an interactive, self-study tool that contains video segments and interactive questions designed to teach students ways of working with a client (Ruth) by drawing concepts and techniques from diverse theoretical approaches. The topics in this video program parallel the topics in *The Art of Integrative Counseling.*

Creating Your Professional Path: Lessons From My Journey (Corey, 2010) is a personal book that deals with a range of topics pertaining to the counselor as a person and as a professional. In addition to the author's discussion of his personal and professional journey, 18 contributors share their personal stories regarding turning points in their lives and lessons they learned.

[illegible] [illegible] [illegible] [illegible] of [illegible] [illegible] [illegible] [illegible] [illegible] [illegible]

Psychoanalytic Therapy 4

LEARNING OBJECTIVES

1. Understand the Freudian deterministic view of human nature.
2. Identify the differences between the id, ego, and superego.
3. Explain how ego-defense mechanisms help individuals cope with anxiety.
4. Understand the influence of early childhood development on an individual's present problems.
5. Identify the main differences between classical psychoanalysts and ego psychology theorists.
6. Explain the rationale for the analyst maintaining an anonymous role in classical psychoanalysis.
7. Identify what is expected of clients who participate in traditional (classical) psychoanalysis.
8. Explain the role of transference and countertransference in the therapy process.
9. Define these techniques commonly used in psychoanalytic practice: maintaining the analytic framework, free association, interpretation, dream analysis, and analysis and interpretation of resistance and transference.
10. Understand the application of psychodynamic concepts to group therapy.
11. Describe unique characteristics of the Jungian perspective on personality development.
12. Describe these contemporary trends in psychoanalytically oriented therapy: object-relations theory, self psychology, and relational psychoanalysis.
13. Identify some of the strengths and the shortcomings of psychoanalysis from a multicultural perspective.
14. Describe some of the main contributions and limitations of psychodynamic therapy.

SIGMUND FREUD (1856–1939) was the firstborn in a Viennese family of three boys and five girls. His father, like many others of his time and place, was very authoritarian. Freud's family background is a factor to consider in understanding the development of his theory.

Print Collector/Getty Images

Sigmund Freud

Even though Freud's family had limited finances and was forced to live in a crowded apartment, his parents made every effort to foster his obvious intellectual capacities. Freud had many interests, but his career choices were restricted because of his Jewish heritage. He finally settled on medicine. Only four years after earning his medical degree from the University of Vienna at the age of 26, he attained a prestigious position there as a lecturer.

Freud devoted most of his life to formulating and extending his theory of psychoanalysis. Interestingly, the most creative phase of his life corresponded to a period when he was experiencing severe emotional problems of his own. During his early 40s, Freud had numerous psychosomatic disorders, as well as exaggerated fears of dying and other phobias, and was involved in the difficult task of self-analysis. By exploring the meaning of his own dreams, he gained insights into the dynamics of personality development. He first examined his childhood memories and came to realize the intense hostility he had felt for his father. He also recalled his childhood sexual feelings for his mother, who was attractive, loving, and protective. He then clinically formulated his theory as he observed his patients work through their own problems in analysis.

Freud had very little tolerance for colleagues who diverged from his psychoanalytic doctrines. He attempted to keep control over the movement by expelling those who dared to disagree. Carl Jung and Alfred Adler, for example, worked closely with Freud, but each founded his own therapeutic school after repeated disagreements with Freud on theoretical and clinical issues.

Freud was highly creative and productive, frequently putting in 18-hour days. His collected works fill 24 volumes. Freud's productivity remained at this prolific level until late in his life when he contracted cancer of the jaw. During his last two decades, he underwent 33 operations and was in almost constant pain. He died in London in 1939.

As the originator of psychoanalysis, Freud distinguished himself as an intellectual giant. He pioneered new techniques for understanding human behavior, and his efforts resulted in the most comprehensive theory of personality and psychotherapy ever developed.

Introduction

Freud's views continue to influence contemporary practice. Many of his basic concepts are still part of the foundation on which other theorists build and develop their ideas. Indeed, most of the theories of counseling and psychotherapy discussed in this book have been influenced by psychoanalytic principles and techniques. Some of these therapeutic approaches extended the psychoanalytic model, others modified its concepts and procedures, and others emerged as a reaction against it.

Freud's psychoanalytic system is a model of personality development and an approach to psychotherapy. He gave psychotherapy a new look and new horizons, calling attention to psychodynamic factors that motivate behavior, focusing on the role of the unconscious, and developing the first therapeutic procedures for understanding and modifying the structure of one's basic character. Freud's theory is a benchmark against which many other theories are measured.

I begin with discussion of the basic psychoanalytic concepts and practices that originated with Freud, then provide a glimpse of a few of the diverse approaches that fall well within his legacy. We are in an era of theoretical pluralism in psychoanalytic theory today and can no longer speak of *the* psychoanalytic theory of treatment (Wolitzky, 2011b). Both psychoanalysis and its more flexible variant, psychoanalytically oriented psychotherapy, are discussed in this chapter. In addition, I summarize Erik Erikson's theory of psychosocial development, which extends Freudian theory in several ways, and give brief attention to Carl Jung's approach. Finally, we look at contemporary psychoanalytic approaches: object-relations theory, self psychology, and the relational model of psychoanalysis. These contemporary theories are variations on psychoanalytic theory that entail modification or abandonment of Freud's drive theory but take Freud's theories as their point of departure (Wolitzky, 2011b). Although deviating significantly from traditional Freudian psychoanalysis, these approaches retain the emphasis on unconscious processes, the role of transference and countertransference, the existence of ego defenses and internal conflicts, and the importance of early life experiences (McWilliams, 2016).

Visit CengageBrain.com or watch the DVD for the video program on Chapter 4, *Theory and Practice of Counseling and Psychotherapy: The Case of Stan and Lecturettes*. I suggest that you view the brief lecture for each chapter prior to reading the chapter.

Key Concepts

View of Human Nature

LO1

The Freudian view of human nature is basically deterministic. According to Freud, our behavior is determined by irrational forces, unconscious motivations, and biological and instinctual drives as these evolve through key psychosexual stages in the first six years of life.

Instincts are central to the Freudian approach. Although he originally used the term **libido** to refer to sexual energy, he later broadened it to include the energy of all the **life instincts**. These instincts serve the purpose of the survival of the individual and the human race; they are oriented toward growth, development, and creativity. Libido, then, should be understood as a source of motivation that encompasses sexual energy but goes beyond it. Freud includes all pleasurable acts in his concept of the life instincts; he sees the goal of much of life as gaining pleasure and avoiding pain.

Freud also postulates **death instincts**, which account for the aggressive drive. At times, people manifest through their behavior an unconscious wish to die or to hurt themselves or others. Managing this aggressive drive is a major challenge to the human race. In Freud's view, both sexual and aggressive drives are powerful determinants of why people act as they do.

Structure of Personality

LO2

According to the Freudian psychoanalytic view, the personality consists of three systems: the id, the ego, and the superego. These are names for psychological structures and should not be thought of as manikins that separately operate the personality; one's personality functions as a whole rather than as three discrete segments. The **id** is roughly all the untamed drives or impulses that might be likened to the biological component. The **ego** attempts to organize and mediate between the id and the reality of dangers posed by the id's impulses. One way to protect ourselves from the dangers of our own drives is to establish a **superego**, which is the internalized social component, largely rooted in what the person imagines to be the expectations of parental figures. Because the point of taking in these imagined expectations is to protect ourselves from our own impulses, the superego may be more punitive and demanding than the person's parents really were. Actions of the ego may or may not be conscious. For example, defenses typically are not conscious. Because ego and consciousness are not the same, the slogan for psychoanalysis has shifted from "making the unconscious conscious" to "where there was id, let there be ego."

From the orthodox Freudian perspective, humans are viewed as energy systems. The dynamics of personality consist of the ways in which psychic energy is distributed to the id, ego, and superego. Because the amount of energy is limited, one system gains control over the available energy at the expense of the other two systems. Behavior is determined by this psychic energy.

The ID The **id** is the original system of personality; at birth a person is all id. The id is the primary source of psychic energy and the seat of the instincts. It lacks organization and is blind, demanding, and insistent. A cauldron of seething excitement, the id cannot tolerate tension, and it functions to discharge tension immediately. Ruled by the **pleasure principle**, which is aimed at reducing tension, avoiding pain, and gaining pleasure, the id is illogical, amoral, and driven to satisfy instinctual needs. The id never matures, remaining the spoiled brat of personality. It does not think but only wishes or acts. The id is largely unconscious, or out of awareness.

The Ego The **ego** has contact with the external world of reality. It is the "executive" that governs, controls, and regulates the personality. As a "traffic cop," it mediates between the instincts and the surrounding environment. The ego controls consciousness and exercises censorship. Ruled by the **reality principle**, the ego does realistic and logical thinking and formulates plans of action for satisfying needs. The ego, as the seat of intelligence and rationality, checks and controls the blind impulses of the id. Whereas the id knows only subjective reality, the ego distinguishes between mental images and things in the external world.

The Superego The **superego** is the judicial branch of personality. It includes a person's moral code, the main concern being whether an action is good or bad, right or wrong. It represents the ideal rather than the real and strives not for pleasure but for perfection. The superego represents the traditional values and ideals of society as they are handed down from parents to children. It functions to inhibit the id impulses, to persuade the ego to substitute moralistic goals for realistic ones, and to strive for perfection. As the internalization of the standards of parents and society, the superego is related to psychological rewards and punishments. The rewards are feelings of pride and self-love; the punishments are feelings of guilt and inferiority.

Consciousness and the Unconscious

Perhaps Freud's greatest contributions are his concepts of the unconscious and of the levels of consciousness, which are the keys to understanding behavior and the problems of personality. The unconscious cannot be studied directly but is inferred from behavior. Clinical evidence for postulating the unconscious includes the following: (1) dreams, which are symbolic representations of unconscious needs, wishes, and conflicts; (2) slips of the tongue and forgetting, for example, a familiar name; (3) posthypnotic suggestions; (4) material derived from free-association techniques; (5) material derived from projective techniques; and (6) the symbolic content of psychotic symptoms.

For Freud, consciousness is a thin slice of the total mind. Like the greater part of the iceberg that lies below the surface of the water, the larger part of the mind exists below the surface of awareness. The **unconscious** stores all experiences, memories, and repressed material. Needs and motivations that are inaccessible—that is, out of awareness—are also outside the sphere of conscious control. Most psychological functioning exists in the out-of-awareness realm. The aim of psychoanalytic therapy is to make the unconscious motives conscious, for only then can an individual exercise choice. Understanding the role of the unconscious is central to grasping the essence of the psychoanalytic model of behavior.

Unconscious processes are at the root of all forms of neurotic symptoms and behaviors. From this perspective, a "cure" is based on uncovering the meaning of symptoms, the causes of behavior, and the repressed materials that interfere with healthy functioning. It is to be noted, however, that intellectual insight alone does not resolve the symptom. The client's need to cling to old patterns (repetition) must be confronted by working through transference distortions, a process discussed later in this chapter.

Anxiety

Also essential to the psychoanalytic approach is its concept of anxiety. **Anxiety** is a feeling of dread that results from repressed feelings, memories, desires, and experiences that emerge to the surface of awareness. It can be considered as a state of tension that motivates us to do something. It develops out of a conflict among the id, ego, and superego over control of the available psychic energy. The function of anxiety is to warn of impending danger.

There are three kinds of anxiety: reality, neurotic, and moral. **Reality anxiety** is the fear of danger from the external world, and the level of such anxiety is proportionate to the degree of real threat. Neurotic and moral anxieties are evoked by threats to the "balance of power" within the person. They signal to the ego that unless appropriate measures are taken the danger may increase until the ego is overthrown. **Neurotic anxiety** is the fear that the instincts will get out of hand and cause the person to do something for which she or he will be punished. **Moral anxiety** is the fear of one's own conscience. People with a well-developed conscience tend to feel guilty when they do something contrary to their moral code. When the ego cannot control anxiety by rational and direct methods, it relies on indirect ones—namely, ego-defense behavior.

Ego-Defense Mechanisms

Ego-defense mechanisms help the individual cope with anxiety and prevent the ego from being overwhelmed. Rather than being pathological, ego defenses LO3 are normal behaviors that can have adaptive value provided they do not become a style of life that enables the individual to avoid facing reality. The defenses employed depend on the individual's level of development and degree of anxiety. Defense mechanisms have two characteristics in common: (1) they either deny or distort reality, and (2) they operate on an unconscious level. Table 4.1 provides brief descriptions of some common ego defenses.

TABLE 4.1 Ego-Defense Mechanisms

	Defense	Uses for Behavior
Repression	Threatening or painful thoughts and feelings are excluded from awareness.	One of the most important Freudian processes, it is the basis of many other ego defenses and of neurotic disorders. Freud explained repression as an involuntary removal of something from consciousness. It is assumed that most of the painful events of the first five or six years of life are buried, yet these events do influence later behavior.
Denial	"Closing one's eyes" to the existence of a threatening aspect of reality.	Denial of reality is perhaps the simplest of all self-defense mechanisms. It is a way of distorting what the individual thinks, feels, or perceives in a traumatic situation. This mechanism is similar to repression, yet it generally operates at preconscious and conscious levels.
Reaction formation	Actively expressing the opposite impulse when confronted with a threatening impulse.	By developing conscious attitudes and behaviors that are diametrically opposed to disturbing desires, people do not have to face the anxiety that would result if they were to recognize these dimensions of themselves. Individuals may conceal hate with a facade of love, be extremely nice when they harbor negative reactions, or mask cruelty with excessive kindness.
Projection	Attributing to others one's own unacceptable desires and impulses.	This is a mechanism of self-deception. Lustful, aggressive, or other impulses are seen as being possessed by "those people out there, but not by me."
Displacement	Directing energy toward another object or person when the original object or person is inaccessible.	Displacement is a way of coping with anxiety that involves discharging impulses by shifting from a threatening object to a "safer target." For example, the meek man who feels intimidated by his boss comes home and unloads inappropriate hostility onto his children.
Rationalization	Manufacturing "good" reasons to explain away a bruised ego.	Rationalization helps justify specific behaviors, and it aids in softening the blow connected with disappointments. When people do not get positions they have applied for in their work, they think of logical reasons they did not succeed, and they sometimes attempt to convince themselves that they really did not want the position anyway.

Sublimation	Diverting sexual or aggressive energy into other channels.	Energy is usually diverted into socially acceptable and sometimes even admirable channels. For example, aggressive impulses can be channeled into athletic activities, so that the person finds a way of expressing aggressive feelings and, as an added bonus, is often praised.
Regression	Going back to an earlier phase of development when there were fewer demands.	In the face of severe stress or extreme challenge, individuals may attempt to cope with their anxiety by clinging to immature and inappropriate behaviors. For example, children who are frightened in school may indulge in infantile behavior such as weeping, excessive dependence, thumb-sucking, hiding, or clinging to the teacher.
Introjection	Taking in and "swallowing" the values and standards of others.	Positive forms of introjection include incorporation of parental values or the attributes and values of the therapist (assuming that these are not merely uncritically accepted). One negative example is that in concentration camps some of the prisoners dealt with overwhelming anxiety by accepting the values of the enemy through identification with the aggressor.
Identification	Identifying with successful causes, organizations, or people in the hope that you will be perceived as worthwhile.	Identification can enhance self-worth and protect one from a sense of being a failure. This is part of the developmental process by which children learn gender-role behaviors, but it can also be a defensive reaction when used by people who feel basically inferior.
Compensation	Masking perceived weaknesses or developing certain positive traits to make up for limitations.	This mechanism can have direct adjustive value, and it can also be an attempt by the person to say "Don't see the ways in which I am inferior, but see me in my accomplishments."

Development of Personality

Importance of Early Development A significant contribution of the LO4 psychoanalytic model is delineation of the stages of psychosexual and psychosocial stages of development from birth through adulthood. The **psychosexual stages** refer to the Freudian chronological phases of development, beginning in infancy.

Freud postulated three early stages of development that often bring people to counseling when not appropriately resolved. First is the **oral stage**, which deals with the inability to trust oneself and others, resulting in the fear of loving and forming close relationships and low self-esteem. Next, is the **anal stage**, which deals with the inability to recognize and express anger, leading to the denial of one's own power as a person and the lack of a sense of autonomy. Third, is the **phallic stage**, which deals with the inability to fully accept one's sexuality and sexual feelings, and also to difficulty in accepting oneself as a man or woman. According to the Freudian psychoanalytic view, these three areas of personal and social development—love and trust, dealing with negative feelings, and developing a positive acceptance of sexuality—are all grounded in the first six years of life. This period is the foundation on which later personality development is built. When a child's needs are not adequately met during these stages of development, an individual may become fixated at that stage and behave in psychologically immature ways later on in life.

Erikson's Psychosocial Perspective The developmental stages postulated **LO5** by Freud have been expanded by other theorists. Erik Erikson's (1963) psychosocial perspective on personality development is especially significant. Erikson built on Freud's ideas and extended his theory by stressing the psychosocial aspects of development beyond early childhood. The **psychosocial stages** refer to Erikson's basic psychological and social tasks, which individuals need to master at intervals from infancy through old age. This stage perspective provides the counselor with the conceptual tools for understanding key developmental tasks characteristic of the various stages of life. Erikson's theory of development holds that psychosexual growth and psychosocial growth take place together, and that at each stage of life we face the task of establishing equilibrium between ourselves and our social world. He describes development in terms of the entire life span, divided by specific crises to be resolved. According to Erikson, a **crisis** is equivalent to a turning point in life when we have the potential to move forward or to regress. At these turning points, we can either resolve our conflicts or fail to master the developmental task. To a large extent, our life is the result of the choices we make at each of these stages.

Erikson is often credited with bringing an emphasis on social factors to contemporary psychoanalysis. **Classical psychoanalysis** is grounded on **id psychology**, and it holds that instincts and intrapsychic conflicts are the basic factors shaping personality development (both normal and abnormal). **Contemporary psychoanalysis** tends to be based on **ego psychology**, which does not deny the role of intrapsychic conflicts but emphasizes the striving of the ego for mastery and competence throughout the human life span. Ego psychology therapists assist clients in gaining awareness of their defenses and help them develop better ways of coping with these defenses (McWilliams, 2016). Ego psychology deals with both the early and the later developmental stages, for the assumption is that current problems cannot simply be reduced to repetitions of unconscious conflicts from early childhood. The stages of adolescence, mid-adulthood, and later adulthood all involve particular crises that must be addressed. As one's past has meaning in terms of the future, there is continuity in development, reflected by stages of growth; each stage is related to the other stages.

Viewing an individual's development from a combined perspective that includes both psychosexual and psychosocial factors is useful. Erikson believed Freud did not go far enough in explaining the ego's place in development and did not give enough attention to social influences throughout the life span. A comparison of Freud's psychosexual view and Erikson's psychosocial view of the stages of development is presented in Table 4.2.

Counseling Implications By taking a combined psychosexual and psychosocial perspective, counselors have a helpful conceptual framework for understanding developmental issues as they appear in therapy. The key needs and developmental tasks, along with the challenges inherent at each stage of life, provide a model for

TABLE 4.2 Comparison of Freud's Psychosexual Stages and Erikson's Psychosocial Stages

Period of Life	Freud	Erikson
First year of life	*Oral stage* Sucking at mother's breasts satisfies need for food and pleasure. Infant needs to get basic nurturing, or later feelings of greediness and acquisitiveness may develop. Oral fixations result from deprivation of oral gratification in infancy. Later personality problems can include mistrust of others, rejecting others; love, and fear of or inability to form intimate relationships.	*Infancy: Trust versus mistrust* If significant others provide for basic physical and emotional needs, infant develops a sense of trust. If basic needs are not met, an attitude of mistrust toward the world, especially toward interpersonal relationships, is the result.
Ages 1-3	*Anal stage* Anal zone becomes of major significance in formation of personality. Main developmental tasks include learning independence, accepting personal power, and learning to express negative feelings such as rage and aggression. Parental discipline patterns and attitudes have significant consequences for child's later personality development.	*Early childhood: Autonomy versus shame and doubt* A time for developing autonomy. Basic struggle is between a sense of self-reliance and a sense of self-doubt. Child needs to explore and experiment, to make mistakes, and to test limits. If parents promote dependency, child's autonomy is inhibited and capacity to deal with world successfully is hampered.
Ages 3-6	*Phallic stage* Basic conflict centers on unconscious incestuous desires that child develops for parent of opposite sex and that, because of their threatening nature, are repressed. Male phallic stage, known as *Oedipus complex,* involves mother as love object for boy. Female phallic stage, known as *Electra complex,* involves girl's striving for father's love and approval. How parents respond, verbally and nonverbally, to child's emerging sexuality has an impact on sexual attitudes and feelings that child develops.	*Preschool age: Initiative versus guilt* Basic task is to achieve a sense of competence and initiative. If children are given freedom to select personally meaningful activities, they tend to develop a positive view of self and follow through with their projects. If they are not allowed to make their own decisions, they tend to develop guilt over taking initiative. They then refrain from taking an active stance and allow others to choose for them.
Ages 6-12	*Latency stage* After the torment of sexual impulses of preceding years, this period is relatively quiescent. Sexual interests are replaced by interests in school, playmates, sports, and a range of new activities. This is a time of socialization as child turns outward and forms relationships with others.	*School age: Industry versus inferiority* Child needs to expand understanding of world, continue to develop appropriate gender-role identity, and learn the basic skills required for school success. Basic task is to achieve a sense of industry, which refers to setting and attaining personal goals. Failure to do so results in a sense of inadequacy.
Ages 12-18	*Genital stage* Old themes of phallic stage are revived. This stage begins with puberty and lasts until senility sets in. Even though there are societal restrictions and taboos, adolescents can deal with sexual energy by investing it in various socially acceptable activities such as forming friendships, engaging in art or in sports, and preparing for a career.	*Adolescence: Identity versus role confusion* A time of transition between childhood and adulthood. A time for testing limits, for breaking dependent ties, and for establishing a new identity. Major conflicts center on clarification of self-identity, life goals, and life's meaning. Failure to achieve a sense of identity results in role confusion.

(continued)

TABLE 4.2 Comparison of Freud's Psychosexual Stages and Erikson's Psychosocial Stages (continued)

Period of Life	Freud	Erikson
Ages 18-35	*Genital stage continues* Core characteristic of mature adult is the freedom "to love and to work." This move toward adulthood involves freedom from parental influence and capacity to care for others.	*Young adulthood: Intimacy versus isolation.* Developmental task at this time is to form intimate relationships. Failure to achieve intimacy can lead to alienation and isolation.
Ages 35-60	*Genital stage continues*	*Middle age: Generativity versus stagnation.* There is a need to go beyond self and family and be involved in helping the next generation. This is a time of adjusting to the discrepancy between one's dream and one's actual accomplishments. Failure to achieve a sense of productivity often leads to psychological stagnation.
Ages 60+	*Genital stage continues*	*Later life: Integrity versus despair* If one looks back on life with few regrets and feels personally worthwhile, ego integrity results. Failure to achieve ego integrity can lead to feelings of despair, hopelessness, guilt, resentment, and self-rejection.

understanding some of the core conflicts clients explore in their therapy sessions. Questions such as these can give direction to the therapeutic process:

- What are some major developmental tasks at each stage in life, and how are these tasks related to counseling?
- What themes give continuity to this individual's life?
- What are some universal concerns of people at various points in life? How can people be challenged to make life-affirming choices at these points?
- What is the relationship between an individual's current problems and significant events from earlier years?
- What choices were made at critical periods, and how did the person deal with these various crises?
- What are the sociocultural factors influencing development that need to be understood if therapy is to be comprehensive?

Psychosocial theory gives special weight to childhood and adolescent factors that are significant in later stages of development while recognizing that the later stages also have their significant crises. Themes and threads can be found running throughout clients' lives.

The Therapeutic Process

Therapeutic Goals

The ultimate goal of psychoanalytic treatment is to increase adaptive functioning, which involves the reduction of symptoms and the resolution of conflicts

(Wolitzky, 2011a). Two goals of Freudian psychoanalytic therapy are to make the unconscious conscious and to strengthen the ego so that behavior is based more on reality and less on instinctual cravings or irrational guilt. Successful analysis is believed to result in significant modification of the individual's personality and character structure. Therapeutic methods are used to bring out unconscious material. Then childhood experiences are reconstructed, discussed, interpreted, and analyzed. It is clear that the process is not limited to solving problems and learning new behaviors. Rather, there is a deeper probing into the past to develop the level of self-understanding that is assumed to be necessary for a change in character. Psychoanalytic therapy is oriented toward achieving insight, but not just an intellectual understanding; it is essential that the feelings and memories associated with this self-understanding be experienced.

Therapist's Function and Role

LO6

In classical psychoanalysis, analysts typically assume an anonymous nonjudgmental stance, which is sometimes called the "**blank-screen" approach**. They avoid self-disclosure and maintain a sense of neutrality to foster a **transference relationship**, in which their clients will make *projections* onto them. This transference relationship is a cornerstone of psychoanalysis and "refers to the transfer of feelings originally experienced in an early relationship to other important people in a person's present environment" (Luborsky, O'Reilly-Landry, & Arlow, 2011, p. 18). If therapists say little about themselves and rarely share their personal reactions, the assumption is that whatever the client feels toward them will largely be the product of feelings associated with other significant figures from the past. These projections, which have their origins in unfinished and repressed situations, are considered "grist for the mill," and their analysis is the very essence of therapeutic work.

One of the central functions of analysis is to help clients acquire the freedom to love, work, and play. Other functions include assisting clients in achieving self-awareness, honesty, and more effective personal relationships; in dealing with anxiety in a realistic way; and in gaining control over impulsive and irrational behavior. Establishing a therapeutic alliance is a primary treatment goal, and repairing any damaged alliance is essential if therapy is to progress (McWilliams, 2014). The empathic attunement to the client facilitates the analyst's appreciation of the client's intrapsychic world (Wolitzky, 2011b). Particular attention is given to the client's resistances. The analyst listens in a respectful, open-minded way and decides when to make appropriate interpretations; tact and timing are essential for effective interpretations (McWilliams, 2014). A major function of interpretation is to accelerate the process of uncovering unconscious material. The psychoanalytic therapist pays attention to both what is spoken and what is unspoken, listens for gaps and inconsistencies in the client's story, infers the meaning of reported dreams and free associations, and remains sensitive to clues concerning the client's feelings toward the therapist.

Organizing these therapeutic processes within the context of understanding personality structure and psychodynamics enables the analyst to formulate the nature of the client's problems. One of the central functions of the analyst is to teach clients the meaning of these processes (through interpretation) so that they are able to achieve insight into their problems, increase their awareness of ways to change, and thus gain more control over their lives. A primary aim of psychodynamic approaches is to foster the capacity of clients to solve their own problems.

The process of psychoanalytic therapy is somewhat like putting the pieces of a puzzle together. Whether clients change depends considerably more on their readiness to change than on the accuracy of the therapist's interpretations. If the therapist pushes the client too rapidly or offers ill-timed interpretations, therapy will not be effective. Change occurs through the process of reworking old patterns so that clients might become freer to act in new ways (Luborsky et al., 2011).

Client's Experience in Therapy

Clients interested in **classical psychoanalysis** must be willing to commit themselves to an intensive, long-term therapy process. After some face-to-face sessions with the analyst, clients lie on a couch and engage in **free association;** that is, they try to say whatever comes to mind without self-censorship. This process of free association is known as the "fundamental rule." Clients report their feelings, experiences, associations, memories, and fantasies to the analyst. Lying on the couch encourages deep, uncensored reflections and reduces the stimuli that might interfere with getting in touch with internal conflicts and productions. It also reduces the ability of clients to "read" their analyst's face for reactions, which fosters the projections characteristic of a transference. LO7

The client in psychoanalysis experiences a unique relationship with the analyst. The client is free to express any idea or feeling, no matter how irresponsible, scandalous, politically incorrect, selfish, or infantile. The analyst remains nonjudgmental, listening carefully and asking questions and making interpretations as the analysis progresses. This structure encourages the client to loosen defense mechanisms and "regress," experiencing a less rigid level of adjustment that allows for positive therapeutic growth but also involves some vulnerability. It is a responsibility of the analyst to keep the analytic situation safe for the client, so the analyst is *not* free to engage in spontaneous self-expression. Every intervention by the therapist is made to further the client's progress. In classical analysis, therapeutic neutrality and anonymity are valued by the analyst, and holding a consistent setting or "frame" plays a large part in this analytic technique. Therapeutic change requires an extended period of "working through" old patterns in the safety of the therapeutic relationship.

Psychodynamic therapy emerged as a way of shortening and simplifying the lengthy process of classical psychoanalysis (Luborsky et al., 2011). Many psychoanalytically oriented practitioners, or psychodynamic therapists (as distinct from analysts), do not use all the techniques associated with classical analysis. However, psychodynamic therapists do remain alert to transference manifestations, explore the meaning of clients' dreams, explore both the past and the present, offer interpretations for defenses and resistance, and are concerned with unconscious material. Traditional analytic therapists make more frequent interpretations of transferences and engage in fewer supportive interventions than do psychodynamic therapists (Wolitzky, 2011a).

Clients in psychoanalytic therapy make a commitment with the therapist to stick with the procedures of an intensive therapeutic process. They agree to talk because their verbal productions are the heart of psychoanalytic therapy. They are typically asked not to make any radical changes in their lifestyle during the period of analysis, such as getting a divorce or quitting their job. The reason for avoiding making such changes pertains to the therapeutic process that oftentimes is unsettling and also associated with loosening of defenses. These restrictions are less relevant to psychoanalytic psychotherapy than to classical psychoanalysis. Psychoanalytic psychotherapy typically involves fewer sessions per week, the sessions are usually face to face, and the therapist is supportive; hence, there is less therapeutic "regression."

Psychoanalytic clients are ready to terminate their sessions when they and their analyst mutually agree that they have resolved those symptoms and core conflicts that were amenable to resolution, have clarified and accepted their remaining emotional problems, have understood the historical roots of their difficulties, have mastery of core themes, have insight into how their environment affects them and how they affect the environment, have achieved reduced defensiveness, and can integrate their awareness of past problems with their present relationships. Wolitzky (2011a) lists other optimal criteria for termination, including the reduction of transference, accomplishing the main goals of therapy, an acceptance of the futility of certain strivings and childhood fantasies, an increased capacity for love and work, achieving more stable coping patterns, and a self-analytic capacity. Successful analysis answers a client's "why" questions regarding his or her life. Curtis and Hirsch (2011) suggest that termination tends to bring up intense feelings of attachment, separation, and loss. Thus a termination date is set well enough in advance to talk about these feelings and about what the client learned in psychotherapy. Therapists assist clients in clarifying what they have done to bring about changes.

Relationship Between Therapist and Client

LO8

There are some differences between how the therapeutic relationship is conceptualized by classical analysis and contemporary relational analysis. The classical analyst stands outside the relationship, comments on it, and offers insight-producing interpretations. In contemporary relational psychoanalysis, the therapist does not strive for an objective stance. Contemporary psychodynamic therapists focus as much on here-and-now transference as on earlier reenactment. By bringing the past into the present relationship, a new understanding of the past can unfold (Wolitzky, 2011a). Contemporary psychodynamic therapists view their emotional communication with clients as a useful way to gain information and create connection. Analytic therapy focuses on feelings, perceptions, and action that are happening in the moment in the therapy sessions (Luborsky et al., 2011; McWilliams, 2014; Wolitzky, 2011a, 2011b). The therapeutic relationship is central to increasing client self-awareness, self-understanding, and exploration (Barber, Muran, McCarthy, & Keefe, 2013). Current findings of interpersonal neurobiology lend strong support for the effectiveness of the psychoanalytic relationship when treating clients who have suffered interpersonal trauma and neglect (Schore, 2014).

Transference and countertransference are central to understanding psychodynamic therapy. A significant aspect of the therapeutic relationship is manifested through transference reactions. **Transference** is the client's unconscious shifting to the analyst of feelings, attitudes, and fantasies (both positive and negative) that are reactions to significant others in the client's past. Transference involves the unconscious repetition of the past in the present. "It reflects the deep patterning of old experiences in relationships as they emerge in current life" (Luborsky et al., 2011, p. 47). A client often has a mixture of positive and negative feelings and reactions to a therapist. When these feelings become conscious and are transferred to the therapist, clients can understand and resolve past "unfinished business." As therapy progresses, childhood feelings and conflicts begin to surface from the depths of the unconscious, and clients regress emotionally. Transference takes place when clients resurrect these early intense conflicts relating to love, sexuality, hostility, anxiety, and resentment; bring them into the present; reexperience them; and attach them to the therapist. For example, clients may transfer unresolved feelings toward a stern and unloving father to the therapist, who, in their eyes, becomes stern and unloving. Angry feelings are the product of negative transference, but clients also may develop a positive transference and, for example, fall in love with the therapist, wish to be adopted, or in many other ways seek the love, acceptance, and approval of an all-powerful therapist. In short, the therapist becomes a current substitute for significant others.

If therapy is to produce change, the transference relationship must be worked through. The **working-through** process consists of repetitive and elaborate explorations of unconscious material and defenses, most of which originated in early childhood. Clients learn to accept their defensive structures and recognize how they may have served a purpose in the past (Rutan, Stone, & Shay, 2014). This results in a resolution of old patterns and enables clients to make new choices. Effective therapy requires that the client develop a relationship with the therapist in the present that is a corrective and integrative experience.

Clients have many opportunities to see the variety of ways in which their core conflicts and core defenses are manifested in their daily life. It is assumed that for clients to become psychologically independent they must not only become aware of this unconscious material but also achieve some level of freedom from behavior motivated by infantile strivings, such as the need for total love and acceptance from parental figures. If this demanding phase of the therapeutic relationship is not properly worked through, clients simply transfer their infantile wishes for universal love and acceptance to other figures. It is precisely in the client–therapist relationship that the manifestation of these childhood motivations becomes apparent.

Regardless of the length of psychoanalytic therapy, traces of our childhood needs and traumas will never be completely erased. Infantile conflicts may not be fully resolved, even though many aspects of transference are worked through with a therapist. We may need to struggle at times throughout our life with feelings that we project onto others as well as with unrealistic demands that we expect others to fulfill. In this sense we experience transference with many people, and our past is always a vital part of the person we are presently becoming.

It is a mistake to assume that all feelings clients have toward their therapists are manifestations of transference. Many of these reactions may have a reality base, and clients' feelings may well be directed to the here-and-now style the therapist exhibits. Not every positive response (such as liking the therapist) should be labeled "positive transference." Conversely, a client's anger toward the therapist may be a function of the therapist's behavior; it is a mistake to label all negative reactions as signs of "negative transference."

The notion of never becoming completely free of past experiences has significant implications for therapists who become intimately involved in the unresolved conflicts of their clients. Even if the conflicts of therapists have surfaced to awareness, and even if therapists have dealt with these personal issues in their own intensive therapy, they may still project distortions onto clients. Therapists' countertransference reactions are inevitable because all therapists have unresolved conflicts and personal vulnerabilities that are activated through their professional work. From a traditional psychoanalytic perspective, **countertransference** is viewed as a phenomenon that occurs when there is inappropriate affect, when therapists respond in irrational ways, or when they lose their objectivity in a relationship because their own conflicts are triggered. Countertransference consists of a therapist's unconscious emotional responses to a client based on the therapist's own past, resulting in a distorted perception of the client's behavior (Rutan et al., 2014). Over the years this traditional view of countertransference has broadened to include all of the therapist's reactions, not only to the client's transference, but to all aspects of the client's personality and behavior. In this broader perspective, countertransference involves the therapist's total emotional response to a client and may include withdrawal, anger, love, annoyance, powerlessness, avoidance, overidentification, control, or sadness. In today's psychoanalytic practice, countertransference is manifested in the form of subtle nonverbal, tonal, and attitudinal actions that inevitably affect clients, either consciously or unconsciously (Curtis & Hirsch, 2011; Wolitzky, 2011b).

To avoid misunderstanding and overidentification with clients, the analytic approach requires therapists to undergo their own analytic psychotherapy. McWilliams (2014) emphasizes how important it is for therapists to access and understand their unconscious and suggests that a key outcome of therapy is humility, which provides a good foundation for creating authentic, egalitarian, and healing connections with clients. Personal therapy and clinical supervision for therapists can be helpful in better understanding how internal reactions influence the therapy process and how to use these countertransference reactions to benefit the work of therapy (Hayes, Gelso, & Hummel, 2011).

Not all countertransference reactions are detrimental to therapeutic progress. Indeed, countertransference reactions are often the strongest source of data for understanding the world of the client and for self-understanding on the therapist's part. For example, a therapist who notes a countertransference mood of irritability may learn something about a client's pattern of being demanding, which can be explored in therapy. Viewed in this more positive way, countertransference can become a key avenue for helping the client gain self-understanding. Most research on countertransference has dealt with its deleterious effects, but Hayes (2004) suggests it would be useful to undertake systematic study of the potential therapeutic benefits of countertransference.

Psychoanalytic therapists vary in the manner in which they use their observations of countertransference. In some instances the feelings may be shared with the client, but traditional analytic therapists strive to minimize their expression of countertransference while silently learning from its inevitable occurrence. The ability of therapists to gain self-understanding and to establish appropriate boundaries with clients is critical in managing and effectively using their countertransference reactions (Hayes et al., 2011).

It is of paramount importance that therapists develop some level of objectivity and not react defensively and subjectively in the face of anger, love, adulation, criticism, and other intense feelings expressed by their clients. If psychotherapists become aware of a strong aversion to certain types of clients, a strong attraction to other types of clients, psychosomatic reactions that occur at definite times in therapeutic relationships, and the like, it is imperative for them to seek professional consultation, clinical supervision, or enter their own therapy for a time to work out these personal issues that stand in the way of their being effective therapists.

Through the client–therapist relationship, clients acquire insights into the workings of their unconscious processes. Awareness of and insights into repressed material are the bases of the analytic growth process. Clients come to understand the association between their past experiences and their current behavior. The psychoanalytic approach assumes that without this dynamic self-understanding there can be no substantial personality change or resolution of present conflicts.

Application: Therapeutic Techniques and Procedures

This section deals with the techniques most commonly used by psychoanalytically oriented therapists. It also includes a section on the applications of the psychoanalytic approach to group counseling. Psychoanalytic or psychodynamic therapy differs from traditional psychoanalysis in these ways: LO9

- The therapy has more to limited objectives than restructuring one's personality.
- The therapist is less likely to use the couch.
- There are fewer sessions each week.
- There is more frequent use of supportive interventions such as reassurance, expressions of empathy and support, and suggestions.
- There is more emphasis on the here-and-now relationship between therapist and client.
- There is more latitude for therapist self-disclosure without "polluting the transference."
- Less emphasis is given to the therapist's neutrality.
- There is a focus on mutual transference and countertransference enactments.
- The focus is more on pressing practical concerns than on working with fantasy material.

The techniques of psychoanalytic therapy are aimed at increasing awareness, fostering insights into the client's behavior, and understanding the meanings of symptoms. The therapy proceeds from the client's talk to catharsis (or expression of emotion), to insight, to working through unconscious material. This work is done to attain the goals of intellectual and emotional understanding and reeducation, which, it is hoped, will lead to personality change. The six basic techniques of psychoanalytic therapy are (1) maintaining the analytic framework, (2) free association, (3) interpretation, (4) dream analysis, (5) analysis of resistance, and (6) analysis of transference. See *Case Approach to Counseling and Psychotherapy* (Corey, 2013, chap. 2) for an illustration by Dr. William Blau, a psychoanalytically oriented therapist, of some treatment techniques in the case of Ruth.

Maintaining the Analytic Framework

The psychoanalytic process stresses maintaining a particular framework aimed at accomplishing the goals of this type of therapy. **Maintaining the analytic framework** refers to a whole range of procedural and stylistic factors, such as the analyst's relative anonymity, maintaining neutrality and objectivity, the regularity and consistency of meetings, starting and ending the sessions on time, clarity on fees, and basic boundary issues such as the avoidance of advice giving or imposition of the therapist's values (Curtis & Hirsch, 2011). One of the most powerful features of psychoanalytically oriented therapy is that the consistent framework is itself a therapeutic factor, comparable on an emotional level to the regular feeding of an infant. Analysts attempt to minimize departures from this consistent pattern (such as vacations, changes in fees, or changes in the meeting environment). Where departures are unavoidable, these will often be the focus of interpretations.

Free Association

Free association is a central technique in psychoanalytic therapy, and it plays a key role in the process of maintaining the analytic framework. In **free association**, clients are encouraged to say whatever comes to mind, regardless of how painful, silly, trivial, illogical, or irrelevant it may seem. In essence, clients try to flow with any feelings or thoughts by reporting them immediately without censorship. As the analytic work progresses, most clients will occasionally depart from this basic rule, and these resistances will be interpreted by the therapist when it is timely to do so.

Free association is one of the basic tools used to open the doors to unconscious wishes, fantasies, conflicts, and motivations. This technique often leads to some recollection of past experiences and, at times, a catharsis or release of intense feelings that have been blocked. This release is not seen as crucial in itself, however. During the free-association process, the therapist's task is to identify the repressed material that is locked in the unconscious. The sequence of associations guides the therapist in understanding the connections clients make among events. Blockings or disruptions in associations serve as cues to anxiety-arousing material. The therapist interprets the material to clients, guiding them toward increased insight into the underlying dynamics.

As analytic therapists listen to their clients' free associations, they hear not only the surface content but also the hidden meaning. Nothing the client says is taken at face value. For example, a slip of the tongue can suggest that an expressed emotion is accompanied by a conflicting affect. Areas that clients do not talk about are as significant as the areas they do discuss.

Interpretation

Interpretation consists of the analyst's pointing out, explaining, and even teaching the client the meanings of behavior that is manifested in dreams, free association, resistances, defenses, and the therapeutic relationship itself. The functions of interpretations are to enable the ego to assimilate new material and to speed up the process of uncovering further unconscious material. Interpretation is grounded in the therapist's assessment of the client's personality and of the factors in the client's past that contributed to his or her difficulties. Under contemporary definitions, interpretation includes identifying, clarifying, and translating the client's material. Relational psychoanalytic therapists present possible meanings associated with a client's thoughts, feelings, or events as a hypothesis rather than a truth about a client's inner world (Curtis & Hirsch, 2011). Interpretations are provided in a collaborative manner to help clients make sense of their lives and to expand their consciousness.

The therapist uses the client's reactions as a gauge in determining a client's readiness to make an interpretation. It is important that interpretations be appropriately timed because the client will reject therapist interpretations that are poorly timed. A general rule is that interpretation should be presented when the phenomenon to be interpreted is close to conscious awareness. In other words, the therapist should interpret material that the client has not yet seen but is capable of tolerating and incorporating. Another general rule is that interpretation should start from the surface and go only as deep as the client is able to go.

Dream Analysis

Dream analysis is an important procedure for uncovering unconscious material and giving the client insight into some areas of unresolved problems. During sleep, defenses are lowered and repressed feelings surface. Freud sees dreams as the "royal road to the unconscious," for in them one's unconscious wishes, needs, and fears are expressed. Some motivations are so unacceptable to the person that they are expressed in disguised or symbolic form rather than being revealed directly.

Dreams have two levels of content: latent content and manifest content. **Latent content** consists of hidden, symbolic, and unconscious motives, wishes, and fears. Because they are so painful and threatening, the unconscious sexual and aggressive impulses that make up latent content are transformed into the more acceptable **manifest content**, which is the dream as it appears to the dreamer. The process by which the latent content of a dream is transformed into the less threatening manifest content is called **dream work**. The therapist's task is to uncover disguised meanings by studying the symbols in the manifest content of the dream.

During the session, therapists may ask clients to free associate to some aspect of the manifest content of a dream for the purpose of uncovering the latent meanings. Therapists participate in the process by exploring clients' associations with them. Interpreting the meanings of the dream elements helps clients unlock the repression that has kept the material from consciousness and relate the new insight to their present struggles. Dreams may serve as a pathway to repressed material, but dreams also provide an understanding of clients' current functioning. Relational psychoanalytic therapists are particularly interested in the connection of dreams to clients' lives. The dream is viewed as a significant message to clients to examine something that could be problematic if left unexamined (Curtis & Hirsch, 2011).

Analysis and Interpretation of Resistance

Resistance, a concept fundamental to the practice of psychoanalysis, is anything that works against the progress of therapy and prevents the client from producing previously unconscious material. Specifically, resistance is the client's reluctance to bring to the surface of awareness unconscious material that has been repressed. Resistance refers to any idea, attitude, feeling, or action (conscious or unconscious) that fosters the status quo and gets in the way of change. During free association or association to dreams, the client may evidence an unwillingness to relate certain thoughts, feelings, and experiences. Freud viewed resistance as an unconscious dynamic that people use to defend against the intolerable anxiety and pain that would arise if they were to become aware of their repressed impulses and feelings.

As a defense against anxiety, resistance operates specifically in psychoanalytic therapy to prevent clients and therapists from succeeding in their joint effort to gain insights into the dynamics of the unconscious. An assumption of analytic treatment is that clients wish both to change and to remain embedded in their old world. Clients tend to cling to their familiar patterns, regardless of how painful they may be. Therapists need to create a safe climate so clients can recognize resistance and explore it in therapy (Curtis & Hirsch, 2011; McWilliams, 2014; Wolitzky, 2011a). Because resistance blocks threatening material from entering awareness, analytic therapists point it out, but Safran and Kriss (2014) caution therapists to avoid framing resistance in a way that implies that the client is not cooperating with the treatment. Therapists' interpretations help clients become aware of the reasons for the resistance so they can deal with them. As a general rule, therapists point out and interpret the most obvious resistances to lessen the possibility of clients' rejecting the interpretation and to increase the chance that they will begin to look at their resistive behavior.

Resistances are not just something to be overcome. Because they are representative of usual defensive approaches in daily life, they need to be recognized as devices that defend against anxiety but that interfere with the ability to accept change that could lead to experiencing a more gratifying life. It is crucial that therapists respect the resistances of clients and assist them in working therapeutically with their defenses. When handled properly, exploring resistance can be an extremely valuable tool in understanding the client.

Analysis and Interpretation of Transference

As was mentioned earlier, transference manifests itself in the therapeutic process when earlier relationships contribute to clients distorting the present with the therapist. The transference situation is considered valuable because its manifestations provide clients with the opportunity to reexperience a variety of feelings that would otherwise be inaccessible. Through the relationship with the therapist, clients express feelings, beliefs, and desires that they have buried in their unconscious.

Interpreting transference is a route to elucidating the client's intrapsychic life (Wolitzky, 2011b). Through this interpretation, clients can recognize how they are repeating the same dynamic patterns in their relationships with the therapist, with significant figures from the past, and in present relationships with significant others. Through appropriate interpretations and working through of these current expressions of early feelings, clients are able to become aware of and to gradually change some of their long-standing patterns of behavior. Analytically oriented therapists consider the process of exploring and interpreting transference feelings as the core of the therapeutic process because it is aimed at achieving increased awareness and personality change.

The analysis of transference is a central technique in both classical psychoanalysis and psychoanalytically oriented therapy, for it allows clients to achieve here-and-now insight into the influence of the past on their present functioning. Interpretation of the transference relationship enables clients to work through old conflicts that are keeping them fixated and retarding their emotional growth. In essence, the effects of early relationships are counteracted by working through a similar emotional conflict in the current therapeutic relationship. An example of utilizing transference is given in a later section on the case of Stan.

Application to Group Counseling

The psychodynamic model offers a conceptual framework for understanding the history of the members of a group and a way of thinking about how their past is affecting them now in the group and in their everyday lives. Group leaders can *think* psychoanalytically, even if they do not use many psychoanalytic techniques. Regardless of their theoretical orientation, it is well for group therapists to understand such psychoanalytic phenomena as transference, countertransference, resistance, and the use of ego-defense mechanisms as reactions to anxiety. **LO10**

Transference and countertransference have significant implications for the practice of group counseling and therapy. Group work may re-create early life situations that continue to affect the client. In most groups, individuals elicit a range of feelings such as attraction, anger, competition, and avoidance. These transference feelings may resemble those that members experienced toward significant people in their past. Members will most likely find symbolic mothers, fathers, siblings, and lovers in their group. Group participants frequently compete for the attention of the leader—a situation reminiscent of earlier times when they had to vie for their parents' attention with their brothers and sisters. This rivalry can be explored in a group as a way of gaining increased awareness of how the participants dealt with competition as children and how their past success or lack of it affects their present interactions with others. A basic tenet of psychodynamic therapy groups is the notion that group participants, through their interactions within the group, re-create their social situation, implying that the group becomes a microcosm of their everyday lives (Rutan et al., 2014). Groups can provide a dynamic understanding of how people function in out-of-group situations. Projections onto the leader and onto other members are valuable clues to unresolved conflicts within the person that can be identified, explored, and worked through in the group.

The group therapist also has reactions to members and is affected by members' reactions. Countertransference can be a useful tool for the group therapist to understand the dynamics that might be operating in a group. However, group leaders need to be alert to signs of unresolved internal conflicts that could interfere with effective group functioning and create a situation in which members are used to satisfy the leaders' own unfulfilled needs. If, for example, a group leader has an extreme need to be liked and approved of, the leader might behave in ways to get members' approval and confirmation, resulting in behaviors primarily designed to please the group members and ensure their continued support.

Group therapists need to exercise vigilance lest they misuse their power by turning the group into a forum for pushing clients to adjust by conforming to the dominant cultural values at the expense of losing their own worldview and cultural identity. Group practitioners also need to be aware of their own potential biases. The concept of countertransference can be expanded to include unacknowledged bias and prejudices that may be conveyed unintentionally through the techniques used by group therapists.

For a more extensive discussion of the psychoanalytic approach to group counseling, refer to *Theory and Practice of Group Counseling* (Corey, 2016, chap. 6). *Psychodynamic Group Psychotherapy* (Rutan et al., 2014) also provides an excellent discussion of this subject.

Jung's Perspective on the Development of Personality

At one time Freud referred to Carl Jung as his spiritual heir, but Jung eventually developed a theory of personality that was markedly different from Freudian psychoanalysis. Jung's **analytical psychology** is an elaborate explanation of human nature that combines ideas from history, mythology, anthropology, and religion (Schultz & Schultz, 2013). Jung made monumental contributions to our deep understanding of the human personality and personal development, particularly during middle age. LO11

Jung's pioneering work places central importance on the psychological changes that are associated with midlife. He maintained that at midlife we need to let go of many of the values and behaviors that guided the first half of our life and confront our unconscious. We can best do this by paying attention to the messages of our dreams and by engaging in creative activities such as writing or painting. The task facing us during the midlife period is to be less influenced by rational thought and to instead give expression to these unconscious forces and integrate them into our conscious life (Schultz & Schultz, 2013).

Jung learned a great deal from his own midlife crisis. At age 81 he wrote about his recollections in his autobiography, *Memories, Dreams, Reflections* (1961), in which he also identified some of his major contributions. Jung made a choice to focus on the unconscious realm in his personal life, which influenced the development of his theory of personality. However, he had a very different conception of the unconscious than did Freud. Jung was a colleague of Freud's and valued many of his contributions, but Jung eventually came to the point of not being able to support some of Freud's basic concepts, especially his theory of sexuality. Jung (1961) recalled Freud's words to him: "My dear Jung, promise me never to abandon the sexual theory. This is the most essential thing of all. You see, we must make a dogma of it, an unshakable bulwark" (p. 150). Jung became convinced that he could no longer collaborate with Freud because he believed Freud placed his own authority over truth. Freud had little tolerance for theoreticians such as Jung and Adler who dared to challenge his theories. Although Jung had a lot to lose professionally by withdrawing from Freud, he saw no other choice. He subsequently developed a spiritual approach that places great emphasis on being impelled to find meaning in life in contrast to being driven by the psychological and biological forces described by Freud.

Jung maintained that we are not merely shaped by past events (Freudian determinism), but that we are influenced by our future as well as our past. Part of the nature of humans is to be constantly developing, growing, and moving toward a balanced and complete level of development. For Jung, our present personality is shaped both by who and what we have been and also by what we aspire to be in the future. His theory is based on the assumption that humans tend to move toward the fulfillment or realization of all of their capabilities. Achieving **individuation**—the harmonious integration of the conscious and unconscious aspects of personality—is an innate and primary goal. For Jung, we have both constructive and destructive forces, and to become integrated, it is essential to accept our dark side, or **shadow**, with its primitive impulses such as selfishness and greed. Acceptance of our shadow does not imply being dominated by this dimension of our being, but simply recognizing that this is a part of our nature.

Jung taught that many dreams contain messages from the deepest layer of the unconscious, which he described as the source of creativity. Jung referred to the **collective unconscious** as "the deepest and least accessible level of the psyche," which contains the accumulation of inherited experiences of human and prehuman species (as cited in Schultz & Schultz, 2013, p. 95). Jung saw a connection between each person's personality and the past, not only childhood events but also the history of the species. This means that some dreams may deal with an individual's relationship to a larger whole such as the family, universal humanity, or generations over time. The images of universal experiences contained in the collective unconscious are called **archetypes**. Among the most important archetypes are the persona, the anima and animus, and the shadow. The **persona** is a mask, or public face, that we wear to protect ourselves. The **animus** and the **anima** represent both the biological and psychological aspects of masculinity and femininity, which are thought to coexist in both sexes. The **shadow** has the deepest roots and is the most dangerous and powerful of the archetypes. It represents our dark side, the thoughts, feelings, and actions that we tend to disown by projecting them outward. In a dream all of these parts can be considered manifestations of who and what we are.

Jung agreed with Freud that dreams provide a pathway into the unconscious, but he differed from Freud on their functions. Jung wrote that dreams have two purposes. They are prospective; that is, they help people prepare themselves for the experiences and events they anticipate in the near future. They also serve a compensatory function, working to bring about a balance between opposites within the person. They compensate for the overdevelopment of one facet of the individual's personality (Schultz & Schultz, 2013).

Jung viewed dreams more as an attempt to express than as an attempt to repress and disguise. Dreams are a creative effort of the dreamer in struggling with contradiction, complexity, and confusion. The aim of the dream is resolution and integration. According to Jung, each part of the dream can be understood as some projected quality of the dreamer. His method of interpretation draws on a series of dreams obtained from a person, during the course of which the meaning gradually unfolds. If you are interested in further reading, I suggest *Memories, Dreams, Reflections* (Jung, 1961) and *Living With Paradox: An Introduction to Jungian Psychology* (Harris, 1996).

Contemporary Trends: Object-Relations Theory, Self Psychology, and Relational Psychoanalysis

Psychoanalytic theory continues to evolve. Freud emphasized intrapsychic **LO12** conflicts pertaining to the gratification of basic needs. Writers in the neo-Freudian school moved away from this orthodox position and contributed to the growth and expansion of the psychoanalytic movement by incorporating the cultural and social influences on personality. **Ego psychology** is part of classical psychoanalysis with the emphasis placed on the vocabulary of id, ego, and superego, and on Anna Freud's identification of defense mechanisms. She spent most of her professional life adapting psychoanalysis to children and adolescents. Erikson expanded this perspective by emphasizing psychosocial development throughout the life span.

Psychoanalytic theory has evolved, undergoing a number of reformulations over the years (McWilliams, 2016). Today psychoanalytic theory is comprised of a variety of schools, including the classical perspective, ego psychology, object relations and interpersonal psychoanalysis, self psychology, and relational psychoanalysis. Rutan, Stone, and Shay (2014) note some commonalities between these psychoanalytic perspectives: "All presuppose a supportive, warm, but neutral and fairly unobtrusive therapist who strives to create a safe, supportive, and therapeutic relationship" (p. 73).

Object-relations theory encompasses the work of a number of rather different psychoanalytic theorists who are especially concerned with investigating attachment and separation. Their emphasize is how our relationships with other people are affected by the way we have internalized our experiences of others and set up representations of others within ourselves. Object relations are interpersonal relationships as these are represented intrapsychically, and as they influence our interactions with the people around us. The term *object* was used by Freud to refer to that which satisfies a need, or to the significant person or thing that is the object, or target, of one's feelings or drives. It is used interchangeably with the term *other* to refer to an important person to whom the child, and later the adult, becomes attached. Rather than being individuals with separate identities, others are perceived by an infant as objects for gratifying needs. Object-relations theories have diverged from orthodox psychoanalysis. However, some theorists, most notably Otto Kernberg, attempt to integrate the increasingly varied ideas that characterize this school of thought within a classical psychoanalytic framework (St. Clair, 2004).

Traditional psychoanalysis assumes that the analyst can discover and name the intrapersonal "truth" about individual clients. As psychoanalytic theory has evolved, the approach has more fully considered the unconscious influence of other people. **Self psychology**, which grew out of the work of Heinz Kohut (1971), emphasizes how we use interpersonal relationships (self objects) to develop our own sense of self. Kohut emphasized nonjudgmental acceptance, empathy, and authenticity. Kohut and other self psychologists put empathy in the forefront of psychoanalytic healing and choose interventions based on them being genuinely empathically attuned to clients (McWilliams, 2016).

The **relational model** is based on the assumption that therapy is an interactive process between client and therapist. Whether called intersubjective, interpersonal, or relational, a number of contemporary psychoanalytic approaches are based on the exploration of the complex conscious and unconscious dynamics at play with respect to both therapist and client. The relational movement ushered in a new emphasis on a more egalitarian therapeutic style (McWilliams, 2016). Relational analysts put value on *not knowing* and approach clients with genuine curiosity. Therapists expect to participate in mutual enactments, or repetition of themes from the client's life that evoke themes of their own.

From the time of Freud to the late 20th century, the power between analyst and patient was unequal. Contemporary relational theorists have challenged what they consider to be the authoritarian nature of the traditional psychoanalytic relationship and replaced it with a more egalitarian model. The task of relational analysis is to explore each client's life in a creative way, customized to the therapist and client working together in a particular culture at a particular moment in time.

Mitchell (1988, 2000) has written extensively about these new conceptualizations of the analytic relationship. He integrates developmental theory, attachment theory, systems theory, and interpersonal theory to demonstrate the profound ways in which we seek attachments with others, especially early caregivers. Interpersonal analysts believe that countertransference provides an important source of information about the client's character and dynamics. Mitchell adds to this object-relations position a cultural dimension, noting that the caregiver's qualities reflect the particular culture in which the person lives. We are all deeply embedded within our cultures. Different cultures maintain different values, so there can be no objective psychic truths. Our internal (unconscious) structures are all relational and relative. This is in stark contrast to the Freudian notion of universal biological drives that could be said to function in every human.

Summary of Stages of Development

Most contemporary psychoanalytic theories center on predictable developmental sequences in which the early experiences of the self shift in relation to an expanding awareness of others. Once self-other patterns are established, it is assumed they influence later interpersonal relationships. Specifically, people search for relationships that match the patterns established by their earlier experiences. People who are either overly dependent or overly detached, for example, can be repeating patterns of relating they established with their mother when they were toddlers (Hedges, 1983). These newer theories provide insight into how an individual's inner world can cause difficulties in living in the everyday world of people and relationships (St. Clair, 2004).

Margaret Mahler (1968) had a central influence on contemporary object-relations theory. A pediatrician who emphasized the observation of children, she viewed the resolution of the Oedipus complex during Freud's proposed phallic stage as less critical than the child's progression from a symbiotic relationship with a maternal figure toward separation and individuation. Her studies focus on the interactions between the child and the mother in the first thee years of life. Mahler conceptualizes the development of the self somewhat differently from the traditional Freudian psychosexual stages. Her belief is that the individual begins in a state of psychological fusion with the mother and progresses gradually to separation. The unfinished crises and residues of the earlier state of fusion, as well as the process of separating and individuating, have a profound influence on later relationships. Object relations of later life build on the child's search for a reconnection with the mother (St. Clair, 2004). Psychological development can be thought of as the evolution of the way in which individuals separate and differentiate themselves from others.

Mahler calls the first three or four weeks of life *normal infantile autism*. Here the infant is presumed to be responding more to states of physiological tension than to psychological processes. Mahler believes the infant is unable to differentiate itself from its mother in many respects at this age. According to Melanie Klein (1975), another major contributor to the object-relations perspective, the infant perceives parts—breasts, face, hands, and mouth—rather than a unified self. In this undifferentiated state there is no whole self, and there are no whole objects. When adults show the most extreme lack of psychological organization and sense of self, they may be thought of as returning to this most primitive infantile stage. Subsequent infant research by Daniel Stern (1985) has challenged this aspect of Mahler's theory, maintaining that infants are interested in others practically from birth.

Mahler's next phase, called *symbiosis,* is recognizable by the 3rd month and extends roughly through the 8th month. At this age the infant has a pronounced dependency on the mother. She (or the primary caregiver) is clearly a partner and not just an interchangeable part. The infant seems to expect a very high degree of emotional attunement with its mother.

The *separation–individuation* process begins in the 4th or 5th month. During this time the child moves away from symbiotic forms of relating. The child experiences separation from significant others yet still turns to them for a sense of confirmation and comfort. The child may demonstrate ambivalence, torn between enjoying separate states of independence and dependence. The toddler who proudly steps away from the parents and then runs back to be swept up in approving arms illustrates some of the main issues of this period (Hedges, 1983, p. 109). Others are looked to as approving mirrors for the child's developing sense of self; optimally, these relationships can provide a healthy self-esteem.

Children who do not experience the opportunity to differentiate, and those who lack the opportunity to idealize others while also taking pride in themselves, may later suffer from *narcissistic* character disorders and problems of self-esteem. The **narcissistic personality** is characterized by a grandiose and exaggerated sense of self-importance and an exploitive attitude toward others, which serve the function of masking a frail self-concept. Such individuals seek attention and admiration from others. They unrealistically exaggerate their accomplishments, and they have a tendency toward extreme self-absorption. Kernberg (1975) characterizes narcissistic people as focusing on themselves in their interactions with others, having a great need to be admired, possessing shallow affect, and being exploitive and, at times, parasitic in their relationships with others. Kohut (1971) characterizes such people as perceiving threats to their self-esteem and as having feelings of emptiness and deadness.

"Borderline" conditions are also rooted in the period of separation-individuation. People with a **borderline personality disorder** have moved into the separation process but have been thwarted by parental rejection of their individuation. In other words, a crisis ensues when the child does develop beyond the stage of symbiosis, but the parents are unable to tolerate this beginning individuation and withdraw emotional support. Borderline people are characterized by instability, irritability, self-destructive acts, impulsive anger, and extreme mood shifts. They typically experience extended periods of disillusionment, punctuated by occasional euphoria. Kernberg (1975) describes the syndrome as including a lack of clear identity, a lack of deep understanding of other people, poor impulse control, and the inability to tolerate anxiety.

Mahler's final subphase in the separation-individuation process involves a move toward constancy of self and object. This development is typically pronounced by the 36th month (Hedges, 1983). By now others are more fully seen as separate from the self. Ideally, children can begin to relate without being overwhelmed with fears of losing their sense of individuality, and they may enter into the later psychosexual and psychosocial stages with a firm foundation of selfhood. Borderline and narcissistic disorders seem to be rooted in traumas and developmental disturbances during the separation-individuation phase. However, the full manifestations of the personality and behavioral symptoms tend to develop in early adulthood.

This chapter permits only a glimpse of the newer formulations in psychoanalytic theory. If you would like to pursue this emerging approach, good overviews can be found in Mitchell (1988, 2000), Mitchell and Black (1995), and Wolitzky (2011b).

Treating Borderline and Narcissistic Disorders Some of the most powerful tools for understanding borderline and narcissistic personality disorders have emerged from the psychoanalytic models. Among the most significant theorists in this area are Kernberg (1975, 1976, 1997; Kernberg, Yeomans, Clarkin, & Levy, 2008), Kohut (1971, 1977, 1984), and Masterson (1976). A great deal of psychoanalytic writing deals with the nature and treatment of borderline and narcissistic personality disorders and sheds new light on the understanding of these disorders. Kohut (1984) maintains that people are their healthiest and best when they can feel both independence and attachment, taking joy in themselves and also being able to idealize others. Mature adults feel a basic security grounded in a sense of freedom, self-sufficiency, and self-esteem; they are not compulsively dependent on others but also do not have to fear closeness. If you are interested in learning more about treating individuals with borderline personality disorders from an object-relations perspective, see *Psychotherapy for Borderline Personality* (Clarkin, Yeomans, & Kernberg, 2006).

Some Directions of Contemporary Psychodynamic Therapy

Strupp (1992) maintains that the various contemporary modifications of psychoanalysis have infused psychodynamic psychotherapy with renewed vitality and vigor. Although long-term analytic therapy will remain a luxury for most people in our society, Strupp sees a growing trend toward short-term treatments for specific disorders, limited goals, and containment of costs. Some of the directions in psychodynamic theory and practice that Strupp identifies are summarized here:

- Increased attention is being given to disturbances during childhood and adolescence.
- The emphasis on treatment has shifted to dealing therapeutically with chronic personality disorders, borderline conditions, and narcissistic personality disorders. There is also a movement toward devising specific treatments for specific disorders.
- Increased attention is being paid to establishing a good therapeutic alliance early in therapy. A collaborative working relationship is now viewed as a key factor in a positive therapeutic outcome.
- There is a renewed interest in the development of briefer forms of psychodynamic therapy, largely due to societal pressures for accountability and cost-effectiveness.

Strupp's assessment of the current scene and his predictions for the future have been quite accurate.

The Trend Toward Brief, Time-Limited Psychodynamic Therapy Many psychoanalytically oriented therapists are adapting their work to a time-limited framework while retaining their original focus on depth and the inner life. These therapists support the use of briefer therapy when this is indicated by the client's needs rather than by arbitrary limits set by a managed care system. Although there are different approaches to brief psychodynamic therapy, Prochaska and Norcross (2014) believe they all share these common characteristics:

- Work within the framework of time-limited therapy.
- Target a specific interpersonal problem and goals during the initial session.
- Assume a less neutral therapeutic stance than is true of traditional analytic approaches.
- Establish a strong working alliance early in the therapy.
- Use interpretation relatively early in the therapy relationship.

Messer and Warren (2001) describe **brief psychodynamic therapy (BPT)** as a promising approach. This adaptation applies the principles of psychodynamic theory and therapy to treating selective disorders within a preestablished time limit of, generally, 10 to 25 sessions. BPT uses key psychodynamic concepts such as the enduring impact of psychosexual, psychosocial, and object-relational stages of development; the existence of unconscious processes and resistance; the usefulness of interpretation; the importance of the working alliance; and reenactment of the client's past emotional issues in relation to the therapist.

Most forms of the time-limited dynamic approach call upon the therapist to assume an active and directive role in quickly formulating a therapeutic focus, such as a central theme or problem area that guides the work (Levenson, 2010). Some possible goals of this approach might include conflict resolution, greater access to feelings, increasing choice possibilities, improving interpersonal relationships, and symptom remission. Levenson emphasizes that the aim of time-limited dynamic therapy is not to bring about a cure but to foster changes in behavior, thinking, and feeling. This is accomplished by using the client–therapist relationship as a way to understand how the person interacts in the world. It is assumed that clients interact with the therapist in the same dysfunctional ways they interact with significant others.

McWilliams (2014, 2016) acknowledges the pressures psychoanalytic practitioners face in creating short-term treatments that focus on unconscious processes, especially as they are manifested and influenced in the therapeutic relationship. Brief dynamic therapy tends to emphasize a client's strengths, competencies, and resources in dealing with real-life issues. Levenson (2010) notes that a major modification of the psychoanalytic technique is the emphasis on the here and now of the client's life rather than exploring the there and then of childhood.

BPT is an opportunity to begin the process of change, which continues long after therapy is terminated. Short-term treatments are based on conceptual approaches similar to those of long-term therapy, but the techniques used are different. Rather than asking clients to free associate, practitioners ask questions, are more direct and confrontive, and deal quickly with transference issues (Sharf, 2016). Levenson (2010) acknowledges that the interactive, directive, focused, and self-disclosing strategies of brief psychodynamic therapy are not suited for all clients or all therapists. This approach is generally not suitable for individuals with severe characterological disorders or for those with severe depression. BPT is more appropriate for people who are neurotic, motivated, and focused (Sharf, 2016).

By the end of brief therapy, clients tend to have acquired a richer range of interactions with others, and they continue to have opportunities to practice functional behaviors in daily life. At some future time, clients may have a need for additional therapy sessions to address different concerns. Instead of thinking of time-limited dynamic psychotherapy as a definitive intervention, it is best to view this approach as offering multiple, brief therapy experiences over an individual's life span.

If you want to learn more about time-limited dynamic therapy, I recommend *Brief Dynamic Therapy* (Levenson, 2010).

Psychoanalytic Therapy From a Multicultural Perspective

Strengths From a Diversity Perspective

LO13

Psychoanalytically oriented therapy can be made appropriate for culturally diverse populations if techniques are modified to fit the settings in which a therapist practices. All of us have a background of childhood experiences and have addressed developmental crises throughout our lives. Erikson's psychosocial approach, with its emphasis on critical issues in stages of development, has particular application to clients from diverse cultures. Erikson has made significant contributions to how social and cultural factors affect people in many cultures over the life span (Sharf, 2016). Therapists can help their clients review environmental situations at the various critical turning points in their lives to determine how certain events have affected them either positively or negatively.

Psychotherapists need to recognize and confront their own potential sources of bias and how countertransference could be conveyed unintentionally through their interventions. To the credit of the psychoanalytic approach, it stresses the value of intensive psychotherapy as part of the training of therapists. This helps therapists become aware of their own sources of countertransference, including their biases, prejudices, and racial or ethnic stereotypes.

Shortcomings From a Diversity Perspective

Traditional psychoanalytic approaches are costly, and psychoanalytic therapy is generally perceived as being based on upper- and middle-class values. All clients do not share these values, and for many the cost of treatment is prohibitive. Another shortcoming pertains to the ambiguity inherent in most psychoanalytic approaches. This can be problematic for clients from cultures who expect direction from a professional. For example, many Asian American clients may prefer a more structured, directive, problem-oriented approach to counseling and may not continue therapy if a nondirective or unstructured approach is employed. Furthermore, intrapsychic analysis may be in direct conflict with some clients' social framework and environmental perspective. Psychoanalytic therapy is generally more concerned with long-term personality reconstruction than with short-term problems of living.

Many writers on social justice counseling emphasize how important it is to consider possible external sources of clients' problems, especially if clients have experienced an oppressive environment. The psychoanalytic approach can be criticized for failing to adequately address the social, cultural, and political factors that result in an individual's problems. If there is not a balance between the external and internal perspectives, clients may feel responsible for their condition. However, the nonjudgmental stance that is a cornerstone of the psychoanalytic tradition may ameliorate any tendency to blame the client.

There are likely to be some difficulties in applying a psychoanalytic approach with low-income clients. If these clients seek professional help, they are generally dealing with a crisis situation and want to finding solutions to concrete problems, or at least some direction in addressing survival needs pertaining to housing, employment, and child care. This does not imply that low-income clients are unable to profit from analytic therapy; rather, this particular orientation could be more beneficial *after* more pressing issues and concerns have been resolved.

Psychoanalytic Therapy Applied to the Case of Stan

In each of the theory chapters, the case of Stan is used to demonstrate the practical applications of the theory in question. Refer to the last section of Chapter 1, where Stan's biography is given, to refresh your memory of his central concerns.

The psychoanalytic approach focuses on the unconscious psychodynamics of Stan's behavior. Considerable attention is given to material that he has repressed. At the extreme, Stan demonstrated a self-destructive tendency, which is a way of inflicting punishment on himself. Instead of directing his hostility toward his parents and siblings, he turned it inward. Stan's preoccupation with drinking could be hypothesized as evidence of an oral fixation. Because he never received love and acceptance during his early childhood, he is still suffering from this deprivation and continues to desperately search for approval and acceptance from others. Stan's gender-role identification was fraught with difficulties. He learned the basis of female–male relationships through his early experiences with his parents. What he saw was fighting, bickering, and discounting. His father was the weak one who always lost, and his mother was the strong, domineering force who could and did hurt men. Stan generalized his fear of his mother to all women. It could be further hypothesized that the woman he married was similar to his mother, both of whom reinforced his feelings of impotence.

The opportunity to develop a transference relationship and work through it is the core of the therapy process. Stan will eventually relate to me, as his therapist, as he did to his father, and this process will be a valuable means of gaining insight into the origin of Stan's difficulties in relating to others. The analytic process stresses an intensive exploration of Stan's past. Stan devotes much therapy time to reliving and exploring his early past. As he talks, he gains increased understanding of the dynamics of his behavior. He begins to see connections between his present problems and early experiences in his childhood. Stan explores memories of relationships with his siblings and with his mother and father and also explores how he has generalized his view of women and men from his view of these family members. It is expected that he will reexperience old feelings and uncover buried feelings related to traumatic events. From another perspective, apart from whatever conscious insight Stan may acquire, the goal is for him to have a more integrated self, where feelings split off as foreign (the id) become more a part of what he is comfortable with (the ego). In Stan's relationship with me, his old feelings can have different outcomes from his past experiences with significant others and can result in deep personality growth.

I am likely to explore some of these questions with Stan: "What did you do when you felt unloved?" "As a child, what did you do with your negative feelings?" "As a child, could you express your anger, hurt, and fears?" "What effects did your relationship with your mother and father have on you?" "What did this teach you about women and about men?" Brought into the here and now of the transference relationship, I might ask, "When have you felt anything like you felt with your parents?"

The analytic process focuses on key influences in Stan's developmental years, sometimes explicitly, sometimes in terms of how those earlier events are being relived in the present analytic relationship. As he comes to understand how he has been shaped by these past experiences, Stan is increasingly able to exert control over his present functioning. Many of Stan's fears become conscious, and then his energy does not have to remain fixed on defending himself from unconscious feelings. Instead, he can make new decisions about his current life. He can do this only if he works through the transference relationship, however, for the depth of his endeavors in therapy largely determine the depth and extent of his personality changes.

If I am operating from a contemporary object-relations psychoanalytic orientation, my focus may well be on Stan's developmental sequences. Particular attention is paid to understanding his current behavior in the world as largely a repetition of one of his earlier developmental phases. Because of his dependency, it is useful in understanding his behavior to see that he is now repeating patterns that he formed with his mother during his infancy. Viewed from this perspective, Stan has not accomplished the task of separation and individuation. He is still "stuck" in the symbiotic phase on some levels. He is unable to obtain his confirmation of worth from himself, and he has not resolved the dependence–independence struggle. Looking at his behavior from the viewpoint of self psychology can shed light on his difficulties in forming intimate relationships.

Follow-Up: You Continue as Stan's Therapist

With each of the 11 theoretical orientations, you will be encouraged to try your hand at applying the principles and techniques you have just studied in the chapter to working with Stan from that particular perspective. The information presented about Stan from each of these theory chapters will provide you with some ideas of how you might continue working with him if he were referred to you. Do your best to stay within the general spirit of each theory by identifying specific concepts you would draw from and techniques that you might use in helping Stan explore the struggles he identifies.

Questions for Reflection

- How much interest would you have in Stan's early childhood? What are some ways you'd help him see patterns between his childhood issues and his current problems?
- Consider the transference relationship that is likely to be established between you and Stan. How might you react to his making you into a significant person in his life?
- In working with Stan, what countertransference issues might arise for you?
- What resistances and defenses might you predict in your work with Stan? From a psychoanalytic perspective, how would you interpret and work with this resistance?
- Which of the various forms of psychoanalytic therapy—classical, relational, or object relations—would you be most inclined to apply in working with Stan?

Visit CengageBrain.com or watch the DVD for *Theory and Practice of Counseling and Psychotherapy: The Case of Stan and Lecturettes*, Session 1 (an initial session with Stan) and Session 2 (on psychoanalytic therapy), for a demonstration of my approach to counseling Stan from this perspective. The first session consists of the intake and assessment process. The second session focuses on Stan's resistance and dealing with transference.

Psychoanalytic Therapy Applied to the Case of Gwen*

In each of the theory chapters, the case of Gwen is used to demonstrate the practical applications of that theoretical approach. Refer to the last section of Chapter 1, where Gwen's background information and intake session are presented, to refresh your memory of her central concerns.

Gwen show's up late for her appointment and states she is feeling frustrated with a work project she is behind on.

Gwen: I feel like I am on the edge of falling apart, like nothing is going right and everyone is looking at me like I'm a failure. I am just sad and unable to put the pieces together. I am behind on everything ... and I am scared I will lose it all.

I listen to Gwen with the goal of allowing her to connect to what lies beneath the surface of her strong emotions. As a psychoanalytic therapist, I believe the genesis of psychological problems are rooted in the unconscious mind. Issues brought into session often stem from unresolved childhood conflicts and trauma. Childhood pain and suffering is not necessarily rooted in an extreme or horrific event; children may repress memories of any negative emotional event.

My initial goal is to help Gwen see how her early history is affecting her current habits, feelings, and behaviors. Once Gwen is able to bring the unconscious material to a conscious level, she can better understand her triggers and recurrent emotional conflicts. In making unconscious material conscious, Gwen can recognize the origins of her behavior, explore some of these patterns, work through early experiences, release dysfunctional behaviors, and begin relating to life from a position of greater clarity and strength.

Gwen continues discussing her frustrations with work and begins to cry. I help Gwen achieve a more relaxed state so she can bypass the conscious mind and find out what is happening at an unconscious level. My intervention is not the typical free association of traditional psychoanalysis but rather guided association based on familiar emotions.

Therapist: Sit back and relax for a moment. Go back to one of the very first times in life when you felt this same or a similar feeling of frustration. Let yourself go back in time, back to when you were a little girl and you had the sense that nothing was going right and that things were falling apart.

[*I prompt Gwen*].

You feel yourself getting younger and younger. When you are there, tell me how old you are, who is there with you, and describe the situation.

*Dr. Kellie Kirksey writes about her ways of thinking and practicing from a psychoanalytic perspective and applies this model to Gwen.

I watch as Gwen's facial expression begins to change. After a few minutes she begins to speak.

Gwen: I am 5 years old, and I am sitting at the kitchen table crying. I have on a pink dress, and the front of my dress is dirty. My mother had told me to wait for her in the car. Instead of waiting in the car, I started playing in the backyard and got dirty. She hit my legs, and I just cried and cried. She yelled and told me that I always mess everything up. All I wanted to do was to play. I never got to play, I just wanted to kick the ball around and have some fun.

Gwen continues to cry as she tells me about herself as a little girl. I ask her to go to another time in her childhood when she had that same feeling of frustration.

Gwen: I am 12 years old, and I am upstairs in my parent's room. My little sister had set the bed on fire, and my parents are blaming me because I was supposed to be watching her. I tell them that I was watching her. I keep telling them that it is not my fault, but they don't listen to me. They put me on punishment for two months, and I overhear them say that I never do anything right.

Therapist: What did that little girl need in those situations?

Gwen: I needed understanding, and someone to tell me it was going to be OK. I needed love, even though I was not the perfect little girl.

I ask Gwen to reflect on what decision she made at that time as a little girl. Gwen pauses and then replies.

Gwen: I decided I had to be perfect in order to be loved.

I ask Gwen to reflect on how often this early decision affects her life now. She sits quietly for a while and then comments that she often feels like that little girl. Gwen is surprised by the feelings and insights that have surfaced.

Gwen: I had not thought about those early times in ages. I can't believe those situations still bother me. I had not realized that.

In that moment Gwen recognizes the power of the unconscious and how bringing the unconscious material to the surface can serve as a healing force in her life. I tell Gwen that as an adult she is now able to give that little girl aspects of herself: love, acceptance, and attention.

Gwen tells me that loving the little girl aspects of her sounds a bit strange, but she is open to being gentler with herself—just as she wanted her parents to be easier on her and love her as she was.

Gwen: I never imagined that those spankings and getting yelled at stuck with me all these years. So now I see that everything seems to be connected, and all that I have ever experienced is still affecting me today. Wow! I have to go home and sit with all of this.

As Gwen leaves my office, I tell her to pay attention to her dreams and keep a dream journal for the next week so we can continue to explore the unconscious material through the symbols in her dreams. Gwen smiles and says she had no idea therapy would be like this. I remind her that psychoanalytically oriented therapy is a long journey and that she is not alone.

It is important for me to be aware of transference (Gwen's unconscious reactions to me). My awareness of transference can facilitate Gwen's deepening connection to her past. It is also important for me to be aware of countertransference (my unconscious reactions to Gwen). As Gwen spoke of getting spanked as a child, I could relate to her pain and felt her sadness. I could have told countless stories of pain inflicted upon me during my childhood, but it is not my session. However, I can use my countertransference in a productive way by deepening my therapeutic relationship with Gwen and showing empathy for the hurt child that she was. I examine the feelings and sensations that came up for me in the session, and I challenge myself to seek supervision or peer consultation when necessary to avoid engaging in behavior that is not therapeutically beneficial.

Questions for Reflection

- What interventions did the therapist make to help Gwen begin to see how her early experiences have an impact on her present behavior?
- What therapeutic value do you see in facilitating Gwen's exploration of early childhood pain?
- If you were counseling Gwen, what potential countertransference issues might surface for you?

Summary and Evaluation

Summary

Some major concepts of psychoanalytic theory include the dynamics of the unconscious and its influence on behavior, the role of anxiety, an understanding of transference and countertransference, and the development of personality at various stages in the life cycle. LO14

Erikson broadened Freud's developmental perspective by including psychosocial trends. In his model, each of the eight stages of human development is characterized by a crisis, or turning point. We can either master the developmental task or fail to resolve the core struggle (Table 4.2 compares Freud's and Erikson's views on the developmental stages).

Psychoanalytic therapy consists largely of using methods to bring out unconscious material that can be worked through. It focuses primarily on childhood experiences, which are discussed, reconstructed, interpreted, and analyzed. The assumption is that this exploration of the past, which is typically accomplished by working through the transference relationship with the therapist, is necessary for character change. The most important techniques typically employed in psychoanalytic practice are maintaining the analytic framework, free association, interpretation, dream analysis, analysis of resistance, and analysis of transference.

Unlike Freudian theory, Jungian theory is not reductionist. Jung viewed humans positively and focused on individuation, the capacity of humans to move toward wholeness and self-realization. To become what they are capable of becoming, individuals must explore the unconscious aspects of their personality, both the personal unconscious and the collective unconscious. In Jungian analytical therapy, the therapist assists the client in tapping his or her inner wisdom. The goal of therapy is not merely the resolution of immediate problems but the transformation of personality.

The contemporary trends in psychoanalytic theory are reflected in these general areas: ego psychology, object-relations interpersonal approaches, self psychology, and relational approaches. Ego psychology does not deny the role of intrapsychic conflicts but emphasizes the striving of the ego for mastery and competence throughout the human life span. The object-relations approaches are based on the notion that at birth there is no differentiation between others and self and that others represent objects of need gratification for infants. Separation–individuation is achieved over time. When this process is successful, others are perceived as both separate and related. Self psychology focuses on the nature of the therapeutic relationship, using empathy as a main tool. The relational approaches emphasize what evolves through the client–therapist relationship.

Contributions of the Classical Psychoanalytic Approach

I believe therapists can broaden their understanding of clients' struggles by appreciating Freud's many significant contributions. It must be emphasized that competent use of psychoanalytic techniques requires training beyond what most therapists are given in their training program. The psychoanalytic approach provides practitioners with a conceptual framework for looking at behavior and for understanding the origins and functions of symptoms. Applying the psychoanalytic point of view to therapy practice is particularly useful in (1) understanding resistances that take the form of canceling appointments, fleeing from therapy prematurely, and refusing to look at oneself; (2) understanding that unfinished business can be worked through, so that clients can provide a new ending to some of the events that have restricted them emotionally; (3) understanding the value and role of transference; and (4) understanding how the overuse of ego defenses, both in the counseling relationship and in daily life, can keep clients from functioning effectively.

Although there is little to be gained from blaming the past for the way a person is now or from dwelling on the past, considering the early history of a client is often useful in understanding and working with a client's current situation. The client can use this awareness in making significant changes in the present and in future directions. Even though you may not agree with all of the premises of the classical psychoanalytic position, you can still draw on many of the psychoanalytic concepts as a framework for understanding your clients and for helping them achieve a deeper understanding of the roots of their conflicts.

Contributions of Contemporary Psychoanalytic Approaches

If the psychoanalytic (or psychodynamic) approach is considered in a broader context than is true of classical psychoanalysis, it becomes a more powerful and useful model for understanding human behavior. Although I find Freud's psychosexual concepts of value, adding Erikson's emphasis on psychosocial factors gives a more complete picture of the critical turning points at each stage of development. Integrating these two perspectives is, in my view, most useful for understanding key themes in the development of personality. Erikson's developmental schema does not avoid the psychosexual issues and stages postulated by Freud; rather, Erikson extends the stages of psychosexual development throughout life. His perspective integrates psychosexual and psychosocial concepts without diminishing the importance of either.

Therapists who work from a developmental perspective are able to see continuity in life and to see certain directions their clients have taken. This perspective gives a broader picture of an individual's struggle, and clients are able to discover some significant connections among the various life stages.

The contemporary trends in psychoanalytic thinking contribute to the understanding of how our current behavior in the world is largely a repetition of patterns set during one of the early phases of development. Object-relations theory helps us see the ways in which clients interacted with significant others in the past and how they are superimposing these early experiences on present relationships. For the many clients in therapy who are struggling with issues such as separation and individuation, intimacy, dependence versus independence, and identity, these newer formulations can provide a framework for understanding how and where aspects of development have been fixated. They have significant implications for many areas of human interaction such as intimate relationships, the family and child rearing, and the therapeutic relationship.

In my opinion, it is possible to use key concepts of a psychodynamic framework to provide structure and direction to a counseling practice and at the same time to draw on other therapeutic techniques. I find value in the contributions of those writers who have built on the basic ideas of Freud and have added an emphasis on the social and cultural dimensions affecting personality development. In contemporary psychoanalytic practice, more latitude is given to the therapist in using techniques. The newer psychoanalytic theorists have enhanced, extended, and refocused classical analytic techniques. They are concentrating on the development of the ego, are paying attention to the social and cultural factors that influence the differentiation of an individual from others, and are giving new meaning to the relational dimensions of therapy.

Several meta-analyses have found that the quality of the therapeutic relationship and the therapeutic alliance are critical to the outcomes of analytic therapy, and research attests to the overall helpfulness of psychoanalytic treatments. McWilliams (2014) admits that psychoanalytic therapies are difficult to investigate through randomized controlled trials because they are more complex, individualized, and unstructured than many other therapy approaches. However, the professional community needs to appreciate the value of process research, qualitative research, case studies, and accumulated clinical wisdom. McWilliams cites some literature on evidence-based psychodynamic therapy and adds that literature is emerging that supports the efficacy of psychodynamic therapies. There is also extensive empirical literature on attachment, emotion, defenses, personality, and other areas that support the theoretical models and clinical experiences of psychoanalytic therapists.

Although contemporary psychodynamic approaches diverge considerably in many respects from the original Freudian emphasis on drives, the basic Freudian concepts of unconscious motivation, the influence of early development, transference, countertransference, and resistance are still central to the newer psychodynamic approaches. These concepts are of major importance in therapy and can be incorporated into therapeutic practices based on various theoretical approaches.

Limitations and Criticisms of Psychoanalytic Approaches

There are a number of practical limitations of psychoanalytic therapy. Considering factors such as time, expense, and availability of trained psychoanalytic therapists, the practical applications of many psychoanalytic techniques are limited. This is especially true of methods such as free association on the couch, dream analysis, and extensive analysis of the transference relationship. A factor limiting the practical application of classical psychoanalysis is that many severely disturbed clients lack the level of ego strength needed for this treatment.

A major limitation of traditional psychoanalytic therapy is the relatively long time commitment required to accomplish analytic goals. Contemporary psychoanalytically oriented therapists are interested in their clients' past, but they intertwine that understanding with the present and with future goals. The emergence of brief, time-limited psychodynamic therapy is a partial response to the criticism of lengthy therapy. Psychodynamic psychotherapy evolved from traditional analysis to address the need for treatment that was not so lengthy and involved (Luborsky et al., 2011).

A potential limitation of the psychoanalytic approach is the anonymous role assumed by some therapists. This stance can be justified on theoretical grounds, but in therapy situations other than classical psychoanalysis this stance is unduly restrictive. The newer formulations of psychoanalytic practice place considerable emphasis on the interaction between therapist and client in the here and now, and therapists can decide when and what to disclose to clients. Yalom (2003) suggests that appropriate therapist self-disclosure tends to enhance therapy outcomes. Rather than adopting a blank screen, he believes it is more productive to strive to understand the past as a way of shedding light on the dynamics of the present therapist–client relationship. This is in keeping with the spirit of the relational analytic approach, which emphasizes the here-and-now interaction between therapist and client.

From a feminist perspective there are distinct limitations to a number of Freudian concepts, especially the Oedipus and Electra complexes. In her review of feminist counseling and therapy, Enns (1993) also notes that the object-relations approach has been criticized for its emphasis on the role of the mother–child relationship in determining later interpersonal functioning. The approach gives great responsibility to mothers for deficiencies and distortions in development. Fathers are conspicuously absent from the hypothesis about patterns of early development; only mothers are blamed for inadequate parenting. Linehan's (1993a, 1993b, 2015) dialectical behavior therapy (DBT), addressed in some detail in Chapter 9, is an eclectic approach that avoids mother bashing while accepting the notion that the borderline client experienced a childhood environment that was "invalidating" (Linehan, 1993a, pp. 49–52).

Luborsky, O'Reilly-Landry, and Arlow (2011) note that psychoanalytic therapies have been criticized for being irrelevant to contemporary culture and being appropriate only to an elite, highly educated clientele. To this criticism, they counter with the following statement: "Psychoanalysis is a continually evolving field that has been revised and altered by psychoanalytic theorists and clinicians ever since its origin. This evolution began with Freud himself, who often rethought and substantially revised his own ideas" (p. 27).

Self-Reflection and Discussion Questions

1. What are a few key concepts of the relational psychoanalytic approach that you would be most likely integrate into your counseling practice?
2. Psychoanalytic therapists pay particular attention to early childhood experiences and the past as crucial determinants of present behavior. What are your thoughts about this emphasis? How does this concept apply to your life?
3. Transference can allow clients to explore the parallels between their past and present experience and to acquire a new understanding of their dynamics. What value would you place on exploring transference with a client?
4. What are some aspects of the psychoanalytic approach that you think could be applied to brief therapy or time-limited therapy?
5. What is one topic area that has the potential to trigger countertransference for you? How can you identify your countertransference reactions? How can you best manage your countertransference as a therapist?

Where to Go From Here

If this chapter has provided the impetus for you to learn more about the psychoanalytic approach or the contemporary offshoots of psychoanalysis, you might consider selecting a few books from the Recommended Supplementary Readings listed at the end of the chapter.

If you are using the *DVD for Integrative Counseling: The Case of Ruth and Lecturettes*, refer to Session 10 ("Transference and Countertransference") and compare what I've written here with how I deal with transference and countertransference.

DVDs from the American Psychological Association's Systems of Psychotherapy Video Series that address the psychoanalytic approaches discussed in this chapter include:

McWilliams, N. (2007). *Psychoanalytic Therapy*

Safran, J. (2008). *Relational Psychotherapy*

Safran, J. (2010). *Psychoanalytic Therapy Over Time*

Wachtel, P. (2008). *Integrative Relational Psychotherapy*

Levenson, H. (2009). *Brief Dynamic Therapy Over Time*

Psychotherapy.net (www.Psychotherapy.net) is a comprehensive resource for students and professionals, offering videos and interviews with renowned psychoanalysts such as Otto Kernberg and Nancy McWilliams. New articles, interviews, blogs, and videos are published monthly. Two from 2011 by Otto Kernberg are:

Otto Kernberg: Live Case Consultation

Psychoanalytic Psychotherapy for Personality Disorders: An Interview with Otto Kernberg, MD

Various colleges and universities offer special workshops or short courses through continuing education on topics such as therapeutic considerations in working with borderline and narcissistic personalities. These workshops could give you a new perspective on the range of applications of contemporary psychoanalytic therapy. For further information about training programs, workshops, and graduate programs in various states, contact:

American Psychoanalytic Association
www.apsa.org

Recommended Supplementary Readings

Psychodynamic Group Psychotherapy (Rutan, Stone, & Shay, 2014) presents a comprehensive discussion of various facets of psychodynamic group therapy. Among the topics addressed are the stages of group development, the role of the group therapist, therapeutic factors accounting for change, working with difficult groups and difficult group members, and time-limited psychodynamic groups.

Brief Dynamic Therapy (Levenson, 2010) describes a model of psychodynamic therapy that fits the reality of time-limited therapy and outlines the steps toward clinical work that is both focused and deep. The book deals with how psychoanalytic concepts and techniques can be modified to suit the needs of many clients who cannot participate in long-term therapy.

Psychodynamic Psychiatry in Clinical Practice (Gabbard, 2005) offers an excellent account of various psychoanalytic perspectives on borderline and narcissistic disorders.

[illegible]

[illegible]

[illegible]

[illegible]

[illegible]

[illegible]

[illegible]

[illegible]

[illegible]

[illegible]

[illegible]

[illegible]

[illegible]

Adlerian Therapy 5

LEARNING OBJECTIVES

1. Describe these key concepts of the Adlerian approach: purposeful and goal-oriented behavior, inferiority and superiority, subjective view of reality, unity of personality, lifestyle, and encouragement.
2. Explain the meaning of social interest and how this is a foundational concept of the Adlerian approach.
3. Define the life tasks and explain the implications for therapy practice.
4. Describe how Adlerians view birth order and the implications of sibling relationships.
5. Understand the role of the family constellation and early recollections in a lifestyle assessment.
6. Explain how the relationship between therapist and client is viewed from the Adlerian perspective.
7. Describe the four phases of the Adlerian therapeutic process.
8. Identify what is involved in a thorough assessment of an individual.
9. Explain how Adlerians view the role of interpretation in the therapy process.
10. Describe what is involved in the reorientation and reeducation process.
11. Describe areas in which the Adlerian approach can be applied.
12. Identify the strengths and limitations of Adlerian therapy from a diversity perspective.
13. Understand the unique contributions of this approach to the development of other counseling approaches.
14. Identify at least one criticism of the Adlerian approach.

Alfred Adler

ALFRED ADLER (1870–1937) grew up in a Vienna family of six boys and two girls. His younger brother died at a very young age in the bed next to Alfred. Adler's early childhood was not a happy time; he was sickly and very much aware of death. At age 4 he almost died of pneumonia, and he heard the doctor tell his father that "Alfred is lost." Adler associated this time with his decision to become a physician. Because he was ill so much during the first few years of his life, Adler was pampered by his mother. He developed a trusting relationship with his father but did not feel very close to his mother. He was extremely jealous of his older brother, Sigmund, which led to a strained relationship between the two during childhood and adolescence. When we consider Adler's strained relationship with Sigmund Freud, we cannot help but suspect that patterns from his early family constellation were repeated in this relationship.

Adler's early childhood experiences had an impact on the formation of his theory. Adler shaped his own life rather than leaving it to fate. Adler was always considered bright, but he did just enough to get by in school until one day he realized that a math teacher did not know the answer to a question he had posed. Adler waited until the best students had given it a try, and then he raised his hand and stood up. People laughed at him, but he came up with the right answer. After that he began to apply himself, and he rose to the top of his class. He went on to study medicine at the University of Vienna, entering private practice as an ophthalmologist, and then shifting to general medicine. He eventually specialized in neurology and psychiatry, and he had a keen interest in incurable childhood diseases.

Adler experienced anti-Semitism and the horrors of World War I. Those experiences, and the sociopolitical context of the time, contributed to his emphasis on humanism and the need for people to work together. He was acutely aware of the impact of context and culture on the human personality, and his theory emanated from this awareness.

Adler had a passionate concern for the common person and was outspoken about child-rearing practices, school reforms, and prejudices that resulted in conflict. He spoke and wrote in simple, nontechnical language and advocated for children at risk, women's rights, the equality of the sexes, adult education, community mental health, family counseling, and brief therapy (Watts, 2012). Adler's (1927/1959) *Understanding Human Nature* was the first major psychology book to sell hundreds of thousands of copies in the United States. After serving in World War I as a medical officer, Adler created 32 child guidance clinics in the Vienna public schools and began training teachers, social workers, physicians, and other professionals. He pioneered the practice of teaching professionals through live demonstrations with parents and children before large audiences, now called "open-forum" family counseling. The clinics he founded grew in number and in popularity, and he was indefatigable in lecturing and demonstrating his work.

Although Adler had an overcrowded work schedule most of his professional life, he still took some time to sing, enjoy music, and be with friends. In the mid-1920s he began lecturing in the United States, and he later made frequent visits and tours. He ignored the warning of his friends to slow down, and on May 28, 1937, while taking a walk before a scheduled lecture in Aberdeen, Scotland, Adler collapsed and died of heart failure.

If you have an interest in learning more about Adler's life, see Edward Hoffman's (1996) excellent biography, *The Drive for Self*. For more on Adler's writings and their meaning in modern society, see Jon Carlson and Michael Maniacci's (2012) edited book, *Alfred Adler Revisited*.

JON D. CARLSON (b. 1945) grew up in a Chicago suburb and was the youngest of four children. As the youngest child at home and at school, he struggled with inferiority. According to Adler, youngest children strive to belong to the adult world and overachieve, and Carlson fit that pattern. As a youngster he had asthma and serious allergies that often kept him housebound, but he eventually "out grew" the breathing issues and *compensated* by becoming a competitive distance runner and university coach, earning several national awards. He has authored or edited more than 60 books and 300 professional training videos and has more than 60,000 hours of clinical practice. He earned two doctoral degrees in counseling and clinical psychology, as well as the prestigious Certificate of Psychotherapy from the Adler School in Chicago. Presently, Jon Carlson holds the position of Distinguished Professor of Adlerian Psychology at Adler University in Chicago. Carlson received lifetime contribution awards from the APA, ACA, and NASAP and was named a "Living Legend in Counseling" by the ACA in 2004.

Jon Carlson

Jon D. Carlson

Carlson believes professional counselors and psychotherapists should be models of mental health and authentic in all that they do and say, whether inside the consulting room or out. "I take pride in having been married to Laura for five decades and having good relationships with all five of our children. I served for over 30 years as a school counselor/psychologist in our neighborhood public school. I have practiced as couples and family therapist and have participated on the faculty of the Evolution of Psychotherapy Conference demonstrating psychotherapy from an Adlerian perspective."

Carlson doubts that even Adler himself would be an Adlerian today. In Carlson's work as editor of the *Journal of Individual Psychology* and keynote speaker at several Adlerian conferences, he has encouraged professionals to go "on beyond Adler" and integrate Adler's ideas with the many other valuable approaches available in contemporary psychotherapy and counseling.

JAMES ROBERT BITTER (b. 1947), coauthor of this chapter, is one of the leading contemporary figures in Adlerian therapy. He grew up in Wenatchee, Washington, the oldest of two children, both adopted. While still in high school, Manford Sonstegard, a student and colleague of Rudolf Dreikurs, started a family education center in his town. Sonstegard would later become Bitter's mentor, teaching him how to be an effective counselor.

James Bitter

James Robert Bitter

Bitter's mother died of cancer when he was 14 years old, and he felt he was largely on his own in high school and college. An underachiever in everything, after his sophomore year in college, a friend challenged him to approach learning seriously and take charge of his life. Bitter began to achieve in both academic work and extracurricular activities.

Introduced to Adlerian family counseling in the1970s by Professor Tom Edgar, Bitter and other students at Idaho State University opened the first family education center in Idaho. Bitter received a master's degree and a doctorate at Idaho State University, then took a job at the West Virginia College of Graduate Studies in a counseling program chaired by Manford Sonstegard. Over the next 13 years, together they taught courses, ran workshops and conferences, wrote papers and edited a journal, and developed an Adlerian model for group counseling (Sonstegard & Bitter, 2004).

After a month-long training session led by Virginia Satir in 1979, Bitter became part of Satir's AVANTA Network. For the next nine years, Bitter helped lead Satir's training sessions. In 1987, Satir came to California State University at Fullerton to help Bitter initiate a new era in the counseling program there. At Fullerton Bitter met Jerry Corey, who encouraged Bitter to contribute to this book as well as to write his own books, one of which is *Theory and Practice of Family Therapy and Counseling* (Bitter, 2014). This collaboration and friendship with Corey has continued for more than a quarter of a century. Bitter will serve as president of the North American Society of Adlerian Psychology (NASAP) in 2017 and 2018.

Bitter is an Adlerian integrationist, like his friend Jon Carlson. He integrates ideas gathered from other people, but his foundation remains in the systemic therapeutic practice of Adlerian psychology. Bitter believes Adler's emphasis on the importance of *community feeling* and acting with *social interest* are what guarantees mental health and helps people overcome inferiority feelings and know that they have a place in the world. Bitter brings his philosophy and practical experience to the discussion of Adlerian theory and practice in this chapter.

Introduction

Along with Freud and Jung, Alfred Adler was a major contributor to the initial development of the psychodynamic approach to therapy. After a decade of collaboration, Freud and Adler parted company, with Freud declaring that Adler was a heretic who had deserted him. Adler resigned as president of the Vienna Psychoanalytic Society in 1911 and founded the Society for Individual Psychology in 1912. Freud then asserted that it was not possible to support Adlerian concepts and still remain in good standing as a psychoanalyst.

Later, a number of other psychoanalysts deviated from Freud's orthodox position. These Freudian revisionists—including Karen Horney, Erich Fromm, and Harry Stack Sullivan—agreed that relational, social, and cultural factors were of great significance in shaping personality. Even though these three therapists are typically called neo-Freudians, it would be more appropriate, as Heinz Ansbacher (1979) has suggested, to refer to them as neo-Adlerians because they moved away from Freud's biological and deterministic point of view and toward Adler's social-psychological and teleological (or goal-oriented) view of human nature.

Adler stresses the unity of personality, contending that people can only be understood as integrated and complete beings. This view also espouses the purposeful nature of behavior, emphasizing that where we have come from is not as important as where we are striving to go. Adler saw people as both the creators and the creations of their own lives; that is, people develop a unique style of living that is both a movement toward and an expression of their selected goals. In this sense, we create ourselves rather than merely being shaped by our childhood experiences.

After Adler's death in 1937, Rudolf Dreikurs was the most significant figure in bringing Adlerian psychology to the United States, especially as its principles applied to education, parenting, individual and group therapy, and family counseling. Dreikurs is credited with giving impetus to the idea of child guidance centers and to training professionals to work with a wide range of clients (Terner & Pew, 1978).

Visit CengageBrain.com or watch the DVD for the video program on Chapter 5, *Theory and Practice of Counseling and Psychotherapy: The Case of Stan and Lecturettes*. I suggest that you view the brief lecture for each chapter prior to reading the chapter.

Key Concepts

View of Human Nature

LO1

Adler abandoned Freud's basic theories because he believed Freud was excessively narrow in his emphasis on biological and instinctual determination. Adler believed that the individual begins to form an approach to life somewhere in the first six years of living. He focused on the person's past as perceived in the present and how an individual's interpretation of early events continued to influence that person's present behavior. According to Adler, humans are motivated primarily by social relatedness rather than by sexual urges; behavior is purposeful and goal-directed; and consciousness, more than unconsciousness, is the focus of therapy. Adler stressed choice and responsibility, meaning in life, and the striving for success, completion, and perfection. Adler and Freud created very different theories, even though both men grew up in the same city in the same era and were educated as physicians at the same university. Their individual and distinct childhood experiences, their personal struggles, and the populations with whom they worked were key factors in the development of their particular views of human nature (Schultz & Schultz, 2013).

Adler's theory starts with a consideration of inferiority feelings, which he saw as a normal condition of all people and as a source of all human striving. Rather than being considered a sign of weakness or abnormality, **inferiority feelings** can be the wellspring of creativity. They motivate us to strive for mastery, success (superiority), and completion. We are driven to overcome our sense of inferiority and to strive for increasingly higher levels of development (Ansbacher & Ansbacher, 1956/1964). Indeed, at around 6 years of age our fictional vision of ourselves as perfect or complete begins to form into a life goal. The life goal unifies the personality and becomes the source of human motivation; every striving and every effort to overcome inferiority is now in line with this goal.

From the Adlerian perspective, human behavior is neither determined by heredity nor environment. Instead, we have the capacity to interpret, influence, and create events. Adler asserted that genetics and heredity are not as important as what we choose to do with the abilities and limitations we possess. Freud viewed people as being fixed by their early experiences, whereas Adler believed people could change through social learning. Although Adlerians reject a deterministic stance, they do not go to the other extreme and maintain that individuals can become whatever they want to be. Adlerians recognize that biological and environmental conditions limit our capacity to choose and to create.

Adlerians put the focus on reeducating individuals and reshaping society. Adler was the forerunner of a subjective approach to psychology that focuses on internal determinants of behavior such as values, beliefs, attitudes, goals, interests, and the individual perception of reality. He was a pioneer of an approach that is holistic, social, goal oriented, systemic, and humanistic. Adler was the first systemic therapist: he maintained that it is essential to understand people within the systems in which they live.

Subjective Perception of Reality

Adlerians attempt to view the world from the client's subjective frame of reference, an orientation described as **phenomenological**. Paying attention to the individual way in which people perceive their world, referred to as "subjective reality," includes the individual's perceptions, thoughts, feelings, values, beliefs, convictions, and conclusions. Behavior is understood from the vantage point of this subjective perspective. From the Adlerian perspective, objective reality is less important than how we interpret reality and the meanings we attach to what we experience.

Unity and Patterns of Human Personality

Adler chose the name **Individual Psychology** (from the Latin, *individuum*, meaning indivisible) for his theoretical approach because he wanted to avoid Freud's reductionist divisions such as ego, id, and superego. For Adler, Individual Psychology meant *indivisible* psychology. Adler emphasized the unity and indivisibility of the person and stressed understanding the whole person in the context of his or her life—how all dimensions of a person are interconnected components, and how all of these components are unified by the individual's movement toward a life goal. This **holistic concept** implies that we cannot be understood in parts; rather, all aspects of ourselves must be understood in relationship to the socially embedded contexts of family, culture, school, and work (Carlson & Johnson, 2016). We are social, creative, decision-making beings who act with purpose and cannot be fully known outside the contexts that have meaning in our lives (Sherman & Dinkmeyer, 1987).

The human personality becomes unified through development of a life goal. An individual's thoughts, feelings, beliefs, convictions, attitudes, character, and actions are expressions of his or her uniqueness, and all reflect a plan of life that allows for movement toward a self-selected life goal. An implication of this *holistic view of personality* is that the client is an integral part of a social system. There is more emphasis on interpersonal relationships than on the individual's internal psychodynamics.

Behavior as Purposeful and Goal Oriented Individual Psychology assumes that all human behavior has a purpose, and this purposefulness is the cornerstone of Adler's theory. Adler replaced deterministic explanations with teleological (purposive, goal-oriented) ones. A basic assumption of Individual Psychology is that we can only think, feel, and act in relation to our goal; we can be fully understood only in light of knowing the purposes and goals toward which we are striving. Although Adlerians are interested in the future, they do not minimize the importance of past influences. They assume that most decisions are based on the person's experiences, on the present situation, and on the direction in which the person is moving—with the latter being the most important. They look for continuity by paying attention to themes running through a person's life.

Adler was influenced by the philosopher Hans Vaihinger (1965), who noted that people often live by fictions (or views of how the world should be). People form cognitive assumptions (or fictions) that serve as a map of the world. Many Adlerians use the term **fictional finalism** to refer to an imagined life goal that guides a person's behavior. It should be noted, however, that Adler ceased using this term and replaced it with "guiding self-ideal" and "goal of perfection" to account for our striving toward superiority or perfection. Adler's concept of *striving for perfection* implies striving for greater competence, not only for oneself but for the common good of others (Bitter, 2012; Watts, 2012). Very early in life, we begin to envision what we might be like if we were successful, complete, whole, or perfect. Applied to human motivation, a guiding self-ideal might be expressed in this way: "Only when I am perfect can I be secure" or "Only when I am important can I be accepted." The guiding self-ideal represents an individual's image of a goal of perfection, for which he or she strives in any given situation. Because of our subjective final goal, we have the creative power to choose what we will accept as truth, how we will behave, and how we will interpret events.

Striving for Significance and Superiority Adler stressed that the recognition of inferiority feelings and the consequent striving for perfection or mastery are innate (Ansbacher & Ansbacher, 1979); they are two sides of the same coin. To understand human behavior, it is essential to grasp the ideas of basic inferiority and compensation. From our earliest years, we need adults to care for us, but this is not a negative factor in life. According to Adler, the moment we experience inferiority, we are pulled by the striving for superiority. For example, when the toddler learns to walk or grab a crayon, there is often an accompanying triumphant smile or shout. This victory over inferiority is a step on the path of striving for superiority. Adler maintained that the goal of success pulls people forward toward mastery and enables them to overcome obstacles.

The goal of superiority contributes to the development of human community. However, it is important to note that "superiority," as used by Adler, does not necessarily mean superiority over others. Rather, it means moving from a perceived lower (or minus) position to a perceived better (or plus) position in relation to oneself. People cope with feelings of helplessness by striving for competence, self-mastery, and perfection. They can seek to change a weakness into a strength, for example, or strive to excel in one area to compensate for defects in other areas. The unique ways in which people develop a style of striving for competence is what constitutes individuality or lifestyle. The manner in which Adler reacted to his childhood and adolescent experiences of loss, rejection, and poor academic grades is a living example of this aspect of his theory.

Lifestyle The movement from a felt minus to a desired plus results in the development of a life goal, which in turn unifies the personality and the individual's core beliefs and assumptions. These core beliefs and assumptions guide each person's movement through life and organize his or her reality, giving meaning to life events. Adler called this life movement the individual's "lifestyle." Synonyms for this term include "plan of life," "style of life," "strategy for living," and "road map of life." **Lifestyle**, often described as our perceptions regarding self, others, and the world, includes the connecting themes and rules of interaction that give meaning to our actions. It is the characteristic way we think, act, feel, perceive, and live (Carlson & Johnson, 2016).

Adler saw us as actors, creators, and artists. Understanding one's lifestyle is somewhat like understanding the style of a composer: "We can begin wherever we choose: every expression will lead us in the same direction—toward the one motive, the one melody, around which the personality is built" (Adler, as cited in Ansbacher & Ansbacher, 1956/1964, p. 332).

People are viewed as adopting a proactive, rather than a reactive, approach to their social environment. Although events in the environment influence the development of personality, such events are not the causes of what people become; rather, it is our interpretation of these events that shape personality. Faulty interpretations may lead to mistaken notions in our private logic, which will significantly influence present behavior. Once we become aware of the patterns and continuity of our life, we are in a position to modify those faulty assumptions and make basic changes. We can reframe childhood experiences and *consciously* create a new style of living.

Social Interest and Community Feeling

Social interest and community feeling (*Gemeinschaftsgefühl*) are probably **LO2** Adler's most significant and distinctive concepts (Ansbacher, 1992). These terms refer to individuals' awareness of being part of the human community and to individuals' attitudes in dealing with the social world.

Social interest is the action line of one's community feeling, and it involves being as concerned about others as one is about oneself. This concept involves the capacity to cooperate and contribute to something bigger than oneself (Milliren & Clemmer, 2006). Social interest requires that we have enough contact with the present to make a move toward a meaningful future, that we are willing to give and to take, and that we develop our capacity for contributing to the welfare of others and strive for the betterment of humanity.

The socialization process associated with social interest begins in childhood and involves helping children find a place in society and acquire a sense of belonging (Kefir, 1981). While Adler considered social interest to be innate, he also believed that it must be learned, developed, and used. Adler equated social interest with a sense of identification and empathy with others: "to see with the eyes of another, to hear with the ears of another, to feel with the heart of another" (as cited in Ansbacher & Ansbacher, 1979, p. 42; also see Clark, 2007). For Adlerians, social interest is the central indicator of mental health. Those with social interest tend to direct their striving toward the healthy and socially useful side of life. As social interest develops, feelings of inferiority and alienation diminish. People express social interest through shared activity, cooperation, participation in the common good, and mutual respect (Carlson & Johnson, 2016).

Individual Psychology rests on a central belief that our happiness and success are largely related to this social connectedness. Because we are embedded in a society, and indeed in the whole of humanity, we cannot be understood in isolation from that social context. We are primarily motivated by a desire to belong. **Community feeling** embodies the feeling of being connected to all of humanity—past, present, and future—and to being involved in making the world a better place. Community feeling entails the evolutionary need to belong, and it manifests itself in courage, empathy, caring, compassion, engagement, and cooperation (Bitter, 2012). Those who lack this community feeling become discouraged and end up on the useless side of life. We seek a place in the family and in society to fulfill basic needs for security, acceptance, and worthiness. Many of the problems we experience are related to the fear of not being accepted by the groups we value. If our sense of belonging is not fulfilled, anxiety is the result. Only when we feel united with others are we able to act with courage in facing and dealing with our problems (Adler, 1938/1964).

The Life Tasks

Adler taught that we must successfully master three universal life tasks: LO3 building friendships (social task), establishing intimacy (love–marriage task), and contributing to society (occupational task). All people need to address these tasks, regardless of age, gender, time in history, culture, or nationality. Each of these tasks requires the development of psychological capacities for *friendship* and *belonging*, for *contribution* and *self-worth*, and for *cooperation* (Bitter, 2007). These basic life tasks are so fundamental that impairment in any one of them is often an indicator of a psychological disorder (American Psychiatric Association, 2013). Our personality is the result of stances we have taken in relation to the life tasks we face (Bitter, 2012). More often than not, when people seek therapy, it is because they are struggling unsuccessfully to meet one or more of these life tasks. The aim of therapy is to encourage clients to develop increased social interest and to modify their lifestyle so they can more effectively navigate each of these life tasks (Carlson & Johnson, 2016).

Most people get into difficulty when they lack courage and seek to avoid the demands posed by these life tasks. Adler (1929/1969) introduced "The Question" as a means of determining which life task a problem or symptom might be helping the person avoid. In its original form, the question asked was "*What would you do if you were quite well?*" (p. 201). If the person answered that he would complete his examinations at school if not for his anxiety, Adler knew that the anxiety was needed for the person to avoid the possibility of failure.

Birth Order and Sibling Relationships

LO4

The Adlerian approach is unique in giving special attention to the relationships between siblings and the psychological birth position in one's family. Adler identified five psychological positions, or vantage points, from which children tend to view life: oldest, second of only two, middle, youngest, and only. **Birth order** is not a deterministic concept but does increase an individual's probability of having a certain set of experiences. Actual birth order is less important than the individual's interpretation, or the psychological position of the child's place in the family. For example, the second born child (out of four) might experience the family from the psychological position of a youngest child if there is a 10-year gap before the next youngest child is born. And the third child might have the experience of a youngest child for her first 10 years of life. Because Adlerians view most human problems as social in nature, they emphasize relationships within the family as our earliest and, perhaps, our most influential social system.

Adler (1931/1958) observed that many people wonder why children in the same family often differ so widely, and he pointed out that it is a fallacy to assume that children of the same family are formed in the same environment. Although siblings share aspects in common in the family constellation, the psychological situation of each child is different from that of the others due to birth order. The following description of the influence of birth order is based on Ansbacher and Ansbacher (1964), Dreikurs (1953), and Adler (1931/1958).

1. The *oldest child* generally receives a good deal of attention, and during the time she is the only child, she is typically somewhat spoiled as the center of attention. She tends to be dependable and hard working and strives to keep ahead. When a new brother or sister arrives on the scene, however, she finds herself ousted from her favored position. She is no longer unique or special. She may readily believe that the newcomer (or intruder) will rob her of the love to which she is accustomed. Most often, she reasserts her position by becoming a model child, bossing younger children, and exhibiting a high achievement drive.
2. The *second child* of only two is in a different position. From the time she is born, she shares the attention with another child. The typical second child behaves as if she was in a race and is generally under full steam at all times. It is as though this second child were in training to surpass the older brother or sister. This competitive struggle between the first

two children influences the later course of their lives. The younger child develops a knack for finding out the elder child's weak spots and proceeds to win praise from both parents and teachers by achieving successes where the older sibling has failed. If one is talented in a given area, the other strives for recognition by developing other abilities. The second-born is often opposite to the firstborn.

3. The *middle child* often feels squeezed out. This child may become convinced of the unfairness of life and feel cheated. This person may assume a "poor me" attitude and can become a problem child. However, especially in families characterized by conflict, the middle child may become the switchboard and the peacemaker, the person who holds things together. If there are four children in a family, the second child will often feel like a middle child and the third will be more easygoing, more social, and may align with the firstborn.
4. The *youngest child* is always the baby of the family and tends to be the most pampered one. Because of being pampered or spoiled, he may develop helplessness into an art form and become expert at putting others in his service. Youngest children tend to go their own way, often developing in ways no others in the family have attempted and may outshine everyone.
5. The *only child* has a problem of her own. Although she shares some of the characteristics of the oldest child (for example, a high achievement drive), she may not learn to share or cooperate with other children. She will learn to deal with adults well, as they make up her original familial world. Often, the only child is pampered by her parents and may become dependently tied to one or both of them. She may want to have center stage all of the time, and if her position is challenged, she will feel it is unfair.

Birth order and the interpretation of one's position in the family have a great deal to do with how adults interact in the world. Individuals acquire a certain style of relating to others in childhood and form a definite picture of themselves that they carry into their adult interactions. In Adlerian therapy, working with family dynamics, especially relationships among siblings, assumes a key role, but Adlerians do not dogmatically adopt the descriptions of birth order. It is important to avoid stereotyping individuals, but certain personality trends that began in childhood as a result of sibling rivalry can influence individuals throughout life.

The Therapeutic Process

Therapeutic Goals

Adlerian counseling and therapy rests on a collaborative arrangement between the client and the counselor. In general, the therapeutic process includes forming a relationship based on mutual respect; a holistic *psychological investigation* or lifestyle assessment; and disclosing *mistaken goals* and *faulty assumptions* within the person's style of living. This is followed by a reeducation or reorientation of the client toward

the useful side of life. The main aim of therapy is to develop the client's sense of belonging and to assist in the adoption of behaviors and processes characterized by community feeling and social interest. This is accomplished by increasing the client's self-awareness and challenging and modifying his or her fundamental premises, life goals, and basic concepts (Dreikurs, 1967, 1997).

Adlerians favor the growth model of personality, with an emphasis on strengths and well-being, rather than a pathology-based medical model. The emphasis is on health and prevention, not remediation. Adlerian theory is an optimistic perspective that views people as creative, unique, capable, and responsible (Watts, 2012, 2015). Rather than being stuck in some kind of pathology, Adlerians contend that clients are often discouraged. The therapeutic process focuses on providing information, teaching, guiding, and offering encouragement to discouraged clients. Encouragement is the most powerful method available for changing a person's beliefs, for it helps clients build self-confidence and stimulates courage. Courage is the willingness to act *even when fearful* in ways that are consistent with social interest. Fear and courage go hand in hand; without fear, there would be no need for courage. The loss of courage, or discouragement, results in mistaken and dysfunctional behavior. Discouraged people tend to act only in line with their perceived self-interest, which often is associated with a lack of social interest.

Adlerian counselors provide clients with an opportunity to view things from a different perspective, yet it is up to the clients to decide whether to accept an alternative perspective. Adlerians work collaboratively with clients to help them reach their self-defined goals. Adlerians educate clients in new ways of looking at themselves, others, and life. Through the process of providing clients with a new "cognitive map," a fundamental understanding of the purpose of their behavior, counselors assist them in changing their perceptions. Maniacci, Sackett-Maniacci, and Mosak (2014) identify these goals for the educational process of therapy:

- Fostering social interest by helping clients connect with their responsibility to their community
- Helping clients overcome feelings of discouragement and inferiority
- Modifying clients' lifestyle in the direction of becoming more adaptive, flexible, and social
- Changing faulty motivation
- Encouraging equality and acceptance of self and others
- Helping people to become contributing members of the world community

Therapist's Function and Role

Adlerian therapists realize that clients can become discouraged and function **LO5** ineffectively because of mistaken beliefs, faulty values, and useless or self-absorbed goals. Adlerians operate on the assumption that clients will feel and behave better once they discover and correct their basic mistakes. Therapists tend to look for major mistakes in thinking and valuing such as mistrust, selfishness, unrealistic ambitions, and lack of confidence. In addition to examining basic mistakes, Adlerian therapists often help clients identify and explore their core fears, such as being imperfect, being vulnerable, being disapproved of, or suffering from past regrets (Carlson & Englar-Carlson, 2013).

A major task for the therapist is to make a comprehensive assessment of the client's functioning. Therapists often gather information about the individual's style of living by means of a questionnaire on the client's **family constellation**, which includes parents, siblings, and others living in the home, life tasks, and early recollections. This is a time when the assessment of birth order might be appropriate. When summarized and interpreted, this questionnaire renders the individual's life story to this point in time. From this information on the family constellation, the therapist is able to get a perspective on the client's major areas of success and failure, how the client pursues life goals, and the critical influences that have had a bearing on the role the client has assumed in the world. These influences include the cultural context and the sociopolitical reality in which the client lives (Carlson & Englar-Carlson, 2013).

The counselor also uses early recollections as an assessment procedure. **Early recollections** (ERs) are defined as "stories of events that a person *says* occurred [one time] before he or she was 10 years of age" (Mosak & Di Pietro, 2006, p. 1). ERs are *specific* incidents that clients recall, along with the feelings and thoughts that accompanied these childhood incidents. These recollections are quite useful in getting a better understanding of the client (Clark, 2002). After these early recollections are summarized and interpreted, the therapist identifies some of the major successes and mistakes in the client's life. The aim is to provide a point of departure for the therapeutic venture. ERs are particularly useful as a functional assessment device because they indicate what clients do and how they think in both adaptive and maladaptive ways (Mosak & Di Pietro, 2006). The process of gathering early memories is part of what is called a **lifestyle assessment**, which involves learning to understand the goals and motivations of the client. When this process is completed, the therapist and the client have targets for therapy.

Client's Experience in Therapy

How do clients maintain their lifestyle, and why do they resist changing it? A person's style of living serves the individual by staying stable and constant. In other words, it is predictable. It is, however, also resistant to change throughout most of one's life. Generally, people fail to change because they do not recognize the errors in their thinking or the purposes of their behaviors, do not know what to do differently, and are fearful of leaving old patterns for new and unpredictable outcomes. Thus, even though their ways of thinking and behaving are not successful, they tend to cling to familiar patterns (Sweeney, 2009). Clients in Adlerian counseling focus their work on desired outcomes and a resilient lifestyle that can provide a new blueprint for their actions.

In therapy, clients explore what Adlerians call **private logic**, the concepts about self, others, and life that constitutes the philosophy on which an individual's lifestyle is based. Private logic involves our convictions and beliefs that get in the way of social interest and that do not facilitate useful, constructive belonging (Carlson, Watts, & Maniacci, 2006). Clients' problems arise because the conclusions based on their private logic often do not conform to the requirements of social living. The heart of therapy is helping clients to discover the purposes of behaviors or symptoms and the basic mistakes associated with their personal coping. Learning how to correct faulty assumptions and conclusions is central to therapy.

To provide a concrete example, think of a chronically depressed middle-aged man who begins therapy. After a lifestyle assessment is completed, these basic mistakes are identified:

- He has convinced himself that nobody could really care about him.
- He rejects people before they have a chance to reject him.
- He is harshly critical of himself, expecting perfection.
- He has expectations that things will rarely work out well.
- He burdens himself with guilt because he is convinced he is letting everyone down.

Even though this man may have developed these mistaken beliefs about himself and life when he was young, he is still clinging to them as rules for living. His expectations, most of which are pessimistic, tend to be fulfilled because on some level he is seeking to validate his beliefs. Indeed, his depression will eventually serve the purpose of helping him avoid contact with others, a life task at which he expects to fail. In therapy, this man will learn how to challenge the structure of his private logic. In his case the syllogism goes as follows:

- "I am basically unlovable."
- "The world is filled with people who are likely to be rejecting."
- "Therefore, I must keep to myself so I won't be hurt."

This person holds onto several basic mistakes, and his private logic offers a psychological focus for treatment. A central theme or convictions in this client's life might be: "I must control everything in my life." "I must be perfect in everything I do."

It is easy to see how depression might follow from this thinking, but Adlerians also know that the depression serves as an excuse for this man's retreat from life. It is important for the therapist to listen for the underlying purposes of this client's behavior. He has isolated himself from any community feeling, so his social interest is low. Adlerians see feelings as being aligned with thinking and as the fuel for behaving. First we think, then we feel, and then we act. Because emotions and cognitions serve a purpose, a good deal of therapy time is spent in discovering and understanding this purpose and in reorienting the client toward effective ways of being. Because the client is not perceived by the therapist to be mentally ill or emotionally disturbed, but as mainly discouraged, the therapist will offer the client encouragement so that change is possible. Through the therapeutic process, the client will discover that he or she has resources and options to draw on in dealing with significant life issues and life tasks.

Relationship Between Therapist and Client

Adlerians consider a good client–therapist relationship to be one between LO6
equals that is based on cooperation, mutual trust, respect, confidence, collaboration, and alignment of goals. They place special value on the counselor's modeling of communication and acting in good faith. From the beginning of therapy, the

relationship is a collaborative one, characterized by two persons working equally toward specific, agreed-upon goals. Adlerian therapists strive to establish and maintain an egalitarian therapeutic alliance and a person-to-person relationship with their clients. Developing a strong therapeutic relationship is essential to successful outcomes. Dinkmeyer and Sperry (2000) maintain that at the outset of therapy clients should begin to formulate a plan, or contract, detailing what they want, how they plan to get where they are heading, what is preventing them from successfully attaining their goals, how they can change nonproductive behavior into constructive behavior, and how they can make full use of their assets in achieving their purposes. This therapeutic contract sets forth the goals of the therapeutic process and specifies the responsibilities of both therapist and client. Developing a contract is not a requirement of Adlerian therapy, but a contract can bring a tight focus to therapy.

Application: Therapeutic Techniques and Procedures

Adlerian counseling is structured around four central objectives that correspond to the four phases of the therapeutic process (Dreikurs, 1967). LO7

1. Establish the proper therapeutic relationship.
2. Explore the psychological dynamics operating in the client (an assessment).
3. Encourage the development of self-understanding (insight into purpose).
4. Help the client make new choices (reorientation and reeducation).

These phases are not linear and do not progress in rigid steps; rather, they can best be understood as a weaving that leads to a tapestry. Dreikurs (1997) incorporated these phases into what he called *minor psychotherapy* in the context and service of holistic medicine. His approach to therapy has been elaborated in what is now called **Adlerian brief therapy**, or ABT (Bitter, Christensen, Hawes, & Nicoll, 1998). This way of working is discussed in the following sections.

Phase 1: Establish the Relationship

The Adlerian practitioner works in a collaborative way with clients, and this relationship is based on a sense of interest that grows into caring, involvement, and friendship. Therapeutic progress is possible only when there is an alignment of clearly defined goals between therapist and client. The counseling process, to be effective, must deal with the personal issues the client recognizes as significant and is willing to explore and change. The therapeutic efficacy in the later phases of Adlerian therapy is predicated upon the development and continuation of a solid therapeutic relationship during this first phase of therapy (Watts, 2015).

Adlerian therapists focus on making person-to-person contact with clients rather than starting with "the problem." Clients' concerns surface rather quickly in therapy, but the initial focus should be on the person, not the problem. One way to create effective contact is for counselors to help clients become aware of their assets and strengths rather than dealing continually with their deficits and liabilities. During the initial phase, a positive relationship is created by listening, responding, demonstrating respect for clients' capacity to understand purpose and seek change, and exhibiting hope and caring. When clients enter therapy, they typically have a diminished sense of self-worth and self-respect. They lack faith in their ability to cope with the tasks of life, and they often feel discouraged. Therapists provide support, which is an antidote to despair and discouragement. For some people, therapy may be one of the few times in which they have truly experienced a caring human relationship.

Adlerians pay more attention to the subjective experiences of the client than they do to using techniques. During the initial phase of counseling, the therapist works to understand the client's identity and experience of the world. Techniques are fitted to the needs of each client and may include attending and listening with empathy, following the subjective experience of the client as closely as possible, identifying and clarifying goals, and suggesting initial hunches about purpose in client's symptoms, actions, and interactions. Adlerian counselors are generally active, especially during the initial sessions. They provide structure and assist clients in defining personal goals, conduct psychological assessments, and offer interpretations (Carlson et al., 2006). Adlerians attempt to grasp both the verbal and nonverbal messages of the client; they want to access the core patterns in the client's life. If the client feels deeply understood and accepted, the client is likely to focus on what he or she wants from therapy and thus establish goals. At this stage the counselor's function is to provide a wide-angle perspective that will eventually help the client view his or her world differently.

Phase 2: Assessing the Individual's Psychological Dynamics

LO8

The aim of the second phase of Adlerian counseling is to get a deeper understanding of an individual's lifestyle. During this assessment phase, the focus is on understanding the client's identity and how that identity relates to the world at large. This assessment phase proceeds from two interview forms: the *subjective interview* and the *objective interview* (Dreikurs, 1997). In the **subjective interview**, the counselor helps the client tell his or her life story as completely as possible. This process is facilitated by a generous use of empathic listening and responding. Active listening, however, is not enough. The subjective interview must follow from a sense of wonder, fascination, and interest. What the client says will spark an interest in the counselor and lead, naturally, to the next most significant question or inquiry about the client and his or her life story. Indeed, the best subjective interviews treat clients as experts in their own lives, allowing clients to feel completely heard. Throughout the subjective interview, the Adlerian counselor is listening for clues to the purposive aspects of the client's coping and approaches to life. "The subjective interview should extract patterns in the person's life, develop hypotheses about what works for the person, and determine what accounts for the various concerns in the client's life" (Bitter et al., 1998, p. 98). Toward the end of this part of the interview, Adlerian brief therapists ask, "Is there anything else you think I should know to understand you and your concerns?"

An initial assessment of the purpose that symptoms, actions, or difficulties serve in a person's life can be gained from Dreikurs (1997) revision of "The Question." Adlerians often end a subjective interview by asking, "How would your life be different, and what would you be *doing* differently, if you did not have this symptom or problem?" Adlerians use this question to help with differential diagnosis. More often, the symptoms or problems experienced by the client help the client avoid something that is perceived as necessary but from which the person wishes to retreat, usually a life task: "If it weren't for my depression, I would get out more and see my friends." Such a statement betrays the client's concern about the possibility of being a good friend or being welcomed by his or her friends. "I need to get married, but how can I with these panic attacks?" indicates the person's worry about being a partner in a marriage. Depression can serve as the client's solution when faced with problems in relationships. If a client reports that nothing would be different, especially with physical symptoms, Adlerians suspect that the problem may be organic and require medical intervention.

The **objective interview** seeks to discover information about (a) how problems in the client's life began; (b) any precipitating events; (c) a medical history, including current and past medications; (d) a social history; (e) the reasons the client chose therapy at this time; (f) the person's coping with life tasks; and (g) a lifestyle assessment. Based on interview approaches developed by Adler and Dreikurs, the lifestyle assessment starts with an investigation of the person's family constellation and early childhood history (Powers & Griffith, 2012a; Shulman & Mosak, 1988). Counselors also interpret the person's early memories, seeking to understand the meaning that she or he has attached to life experiences. They operate on the assumption that it is the interpretations people develop about themselves, others, the world, and life that govern what they do. Lifestyle assessment seeks to develop a holistic narrative of the person's life, to make sense of the way the person copes with life tasks, and to uncover the private interpretations and logic involved in that coping. For example, if Jenny has lived most of her life in a critical environment, and now she believes she must be perfect to avoid even the appearance of failure, the assessment process will highlight the restricted living that flows from this perspective. Another example is Ramon who grew up as a child of undocumented immigrants. He lived most of his life in fear of his environment, and he tried to remain invisible and was wary of trusting others. Now he struggles to connect with peers and to maintain a committed relationship. The assessment process explores how his lifestyle is inconsistent with his stated goals of wanting connection.

The Family Constellation Adler considered the family of origin as having a central impact on an individual's personality. Adler suggested that it was through the family constellation that each person forms his or her unique view of self, others, and life. Factors such as cultural and familial values, gender-role expectations, and the nature of interpersonal relationships are all influenced by a child's observation of the interactional patterns within the family. Adlerian assessment relies heavily on an exploration of the client's **family constellation**, including the client's evaluation of conditions that prevailed in the family when the person was a young child (family atmosphere), birth order, parental relationship and family values, and extended family and culture. Some of these questions are almost always explored:

- Who was the favorite child?
- What was your father's relationship with the children? Your mother's?

- Which child was most like your father? Your mother? In what respects?
- Who among the siblings was most different from you? In what ways?
- Who among the siblings was most like you? In what ways?
- What were you like as a child?
- How did your parents get along? In what did they both agree? How did they handle disagreements? How did they discipline the children?

An investigation of family constellation is far more comprehensive than these few questions, but these questions give an idea of the type of information the counselor is seeking. The questions are always tailored to the individual client with the goal of eliciting the client's perceptions of self and others, of development, and of the experiences that have affected that development.

Early Recollections As you will recall from the section on the therapist's functions and role, another assessment procedure used by Adlerians is to ask the client to provide his or her earliest memories, including the age of the person at the time of the remembered events and the feelings or reactions associated with the recollections. Early recollections are one-time occurrences, usually before the age of 10, that can be pictured by the client in clear detail. Early recollections are a series of small mysteries that can be woven together into a tapestry that leads to an understanding of how we view ourselves, how we see the world, what our life goals are, what motivates us, what we value and believe in, and what we anticipate for our future (Clark, 2002; Mosak & Di Pietro, 2006). Adler reasoned that out of the millions of early memories we might have we select those special memories that project the essential convictions and even the basic mistakes of our lives. To a large extent, what we selectively attend to from the past is reflective of what we believe, how we behave in the present, and our anticipation of the future (Watts, 2015).

Early memories cast light on the "story of our life" because they represent metaphors for our current views. From the thousands of experiences we have before the age of 10, we tend to remember only 6 to 12 memories. By understanding why we retain these memories and what they tell us about how we see ourselves, others, and life in the present, it is possible to get a clear sense of our mistaken notions, present attitudes, social interests, and possible future behavior. Early recollections are specific instances that clients tell therapists, and they are very useful in understanding those who are sharing a story (Mosak & Di Pietro, 2006). Exploring early recollections involves discovering how mistaken notions based on faulty goals and values continue to create problems in a client's life. Early recollections serve an organizing function in understanding the purposefulness of behavior, the style of life, striving for superiority, holism, and birth order (Clark, 2012).

To tap such recollections, the counselor might proceed as follows: "I would like to hear about your early memories. Think back to when you were very young, as early as you can remember (before the age of 10), and *tell me something that happened one time.* Be sure to recall something you remember, not something you were told about by others." After receiving each memory, the counselor might also ask: "What part stands out to you? What was the most vivid part of your early memory? If you played the whole memory like a movie and stopped it at one frame, what would be happening? Putting yourself in that moment, what are you feeling? What's your reaction?" Three memories are usually considered a minimum to assess a pattern, and some counselors ask for as many as a dozen memories.

Adlerian therapists use early recollections as a projective technique (Clark, 2002; Hays, 2013) and to (a) assess the client's convictions about self, others, life, and ethics; (b) assess the client's stance in relation to the counseling session and the counseling relationship; (c) verify the client's coping patterns; and (d) assess individual strengths, assets, and interfering ideas (Bitter et al., 1998, p. 99). In interpreting these early recollections, Adlerians may consider questions such as these:

- What part does the client take in the memory? Is the client an observer or a participant?
- Who else is in the memory? What position do others take in relation to the client?
- What are the dominant themes and overall patterns of the memories?
- What feelings are expressed in the memories?
- Why does the client choose to remember this event? What is the client trying to convey?

Let's try this out. Here are three memory stories and some guesses about what these memories might mean.

Memory 1: "I was 4 years old. We were staying at grandma and grandpa's house. I got to sleep in the attic, and it had a neat hole from which I could spy on the adults below. I could see and hear them, but they could not see me. I love being sneaky.

Interpretation: I like to (a) be on top of things; (b) know what's going on—even if it's none of my business; and (c) I like to be an observer.

Memory 2: I am 8 years old. It is summer. My father wants to take me with him to a baseball game, but I am not around. I am off playing where I should not be, and my mom can't find me. I miss out on going with my dad. I cry when I am told, and I am sad.

Interpretation: If I do things I am not supposed to do, even if I am having fun, I might miss out on something even more fun.

Memory 3: I am in the second or third grade, maybe 8 or 9. I am asked to come to the blackboard and work out a problem. I remember how to do it mostly. I get almost to the end, but I cannot complete it. Someone else has to come up and complete it, and I miss out on getting to the right answer. I am watching Gary Snitley complete the problem, and I am disappointed that I didn't remember it.

Interpretation: There is always someone out there who is smarter than me. If I am going to do something and get credit for it, I better do it all and do it right the first time; there is no room for error.

Can you match these tentative interpretations with the details offered in each memory story?

Integration and Summary Once material has been gathered from both subjective and objective interviews with the client, integrated summaries of the data are developed. Different summaries are prepared for different clients, but common ones are a narrative summary of the person's subjective experience and life story; a summary of family constellation and developmental data; a summary of early recollections, personal strengths or assets, and interfering ideas; and a summary of coping strategies. The summaries are presented to the client and discussed in the session, with the client and the counselor together refining specific points. This information provides the client with the chance to discuss specific topics and to raise questions.

The Student Manual that accompanies this textbook includes a concrete example of the lifestyle assessment as it is applied to the case of Stan. In *Case Approach to Counseling and Psychotherapy* (Corey, 2013, chap. 3), Drs. Jim Bitter and Bill Nicoll present a lifestyle assessment of another hypothetical client, Ruth.

Phase 3: Encourage Self-Understanding and Insight

During this third phase, Adlerian therapists interpret the findings of the assessment as an avenue for promoting self-understanding and insight. When Adlerians speak of insight, they are referring to an understanding of the motivations that operate in a client's life. Self-understanding is only possible when hidden purposes and goals of behavior are made conscious. Adlerians consider insight as a special form of awareness that facilitates a meaningful understanding within the therapeutic relationship and acts as a foundation for change. Insight without action is not enough. Insight is a means to an end, and not an end in itself. People can make rapid and significant changes without much insight. LO9

Disclosure and well-timed interpretations are techniques that facilitate the process of gaining insight. **Interpretation** deals with clients' underlying motives for behaving the way they do in the here and now. Adlerian disclosures and interpretations are concerned with creating awareness of one's direction in life, one's goals and purposes, one's private logic and how it works, and one's current behavior.

Adlerian interpretations are suggestions presented tentatively in the form of open-ended questions that can be explored in the sessions. They are hunches or guesses, and they often begin with phrases such as "I could be wrong, but I am wondering if ... ," "Could it be that ... ," or "Is it possible that ..." Because interpretations are presented in this manner, clients are not led to defend themselves, and they feel free to discuss and even argue with the counselor's hunches and impressions. Through this process, both counselor and client eventually come to understand the client's motivations, the ways in which these motivations are now contributing to the maintenance of the problem, and what the client can do to correct the situation. During this phase of therapy, the counselor helps the client understand the limitations of the style of life the client has chosen.

Phase 4: Reorientation and Reeducation

The final stage of the therapeutic process is the action-oriented phase known as reorientation and reeducation: putting insights into practice. This phase focuses on helping clients discover a new and more functional perspective. Clients are both encouraged and challenged to develop the courage to take risks and make LO10 changes in their life. During this phase, clients can choose to adopt a new style of life based on the insights they gained in the earlier phases of therapy. More commonly, clients figure out how to reorient their current style of living to the useful side of life, increasing their community feeling and social interest. The useful side involves a sense of belonging and being valued, having an interest in others and their welfare, courage, the acceptance of imperfection, confidence, a sense of humor, a willingness to contribute, and an outgoing friendliness. The useless side of life is characterized by self-absorption, withdrawal from life tasks, self-protection, or acts against one's fellow human beings. People acting on the useless side of life become less functional and are more susceptible to psychopathology. Adlerian therapy stands in opposition to self-depreciation, isolation, and retreat, and it seeks to help clients gain courage and to connect to strengths within themselves, to others, and to life.

Reorientation involves shifting rules of interaction, process, and motivation. These shifts are facilitated through changes in awareness, which often occur during the therapy session and which are transformed into action outside of the therapy office (Bitter & Nicoll, 2004). In addition, especially at this phase of therapy, Adlerians focus on reeducation (see the section Therapeutic Goals). Throughout this phase, no intervention is more important than encouragement.

The Encouragement Process Encouragement is the most distinctive Adlerian procedure, and it is central to all phases of counseling and therapy. It is especially important as people consider change in their lives. **Encouragement** literally means "to build courage." Encouragement is a process of increasing the courage needed for a person to face difficulties in life (Carlson & Englar-Carlson, 2013). Courage develops when people become aware of their strengths, when they feel they belong and are not alone, and when they have a sense of hope and can see new possibilities for themselves and their daily living. Therapists help clients focus on their resources and strengths and to have faith that they can make life changes, even though life can be difficult. Milliren, Evans, and Newbauer (2007) consider encouragement key in promoting and activating social interest. They add that encouragement is the universal therapeutic intervention for Adlerian counselors, that it is a fundamental attitude, or way of being, rather than a technique. Because clients often do not recognize or accept their positive qualities, strengths, or internal resources, one of the counselor's main tasks is to help them do so.

Adlerians believe discouragement is the basic condition that prevents people from functioning, and they see encouragement as the antidote. As a part of the encouragement process, Adlerians use a variety of relational, cognitive, behavioral, emotional, and experiential techniques to help clients identify and challenge self-defeating cognitions, generate perceptional alternatives, and make use of assets, strengths, and resources (Ansbacher & Ansbacher, 1964; Watts, 2015).

Encouragement takes many forms, depending on the phase of the counseling process. In the relationship phase, encouragement results from the mutual respect the counselor seeks to engender. Here is an opening intervention focusing on encouragement:

Client: I almost didn't come . . .

Counselor: . . . but you did.

Client: Yes, but I just don't know. Maybe it would have been better just to end it all, not even bother.

Counselor: So you are in a lot of pain, even thinking about ending it all, but still you came. That took a lot of courage, How did you manage to summon that courage and then act on it?

In the assessment phase, which is partially designed to illuminate personal strengths, clients are encouraged to recognize that they are in charge of their own lives and can make different choices based on new understandings.

During reorientation, encouragement comes when new possibilities are generated and when clients are acknowledged and affirmed for taking positive steps to change their lives for the better. This later intervention focused on encouragement has a triumphant tone:

Counselor: Let me see if I understand this. You were in a familiar family setting. Your father was berating you about a minor difference of opinion, really trying to push your buttons, and you managed not only to stay calm but also offered to help him sort some materials in his office. You must feel so proud of yourself, triumphant even. What a transformation of your normal interactions.

Client: Yes, and I even walked away feeling I had made a difference in his life. I did not lose my temper. I did not strike back. I actually just heard him in a different way, knew he needed to feel right and important, and when I let that happen, everything changed between us.

Counselor: You even know the steps that got you there.

Client: Yes, I do.

Counselor: Achieving a change in long-held family patterns is one of the hardest things to attain. You have a right to feel delighted.

Change and the Search for New Possibilities During the reorientation phase of counseling, clients make decisions and modify their goals. They are encouraged to act *as if* they were the people they want to be, which can serve to challenge self-limiting assumptions. Clients are asked to *catch themselves* in the process of repeating old patterns that have led to ineffective behavior (Watts, 2015). Commitment is an essential part of reorientation. If clients hope to change, they must be willing to set tasks for themselves in everyday life and do something specific about their problems. In this way, clients translate their new insights into concrete actions. Bitter and Nicoll (2004) emphasize that real change happens between sessions, and not in therapy itself. They state that arriving at a strategy for change is an important first step, and stress that it takes courage and encouragement for clients to apply what they have learned in therapy to daily living.

This action-oriented phase is a time for solving problems and making decisions. The counselor and the client consider possible alternatives and their consequences, evaluate how these alternatives will meet the client's goals, and decide on a specific course of action. The best alternatives and new possibilities are those generated by the client, and the counselor must offer the client a great deal of support and encouragement during this stage of the process.

Making a Difference Adlerian therapists seek to make a difference in the lives of their clients. That difference may be manifested by a change in behavior or attitude or perception. Adlerians use many different techniques to promote change, some of which have become common interventions in other therapeutic models. Techniques that go by the names of immediacy, advice, humor, silence, paradoxical intention, acting as if, catching oneself, the push-button technique, externalization, reauthoring, avoiding the traps, confrontation, use of stories and fables, early recollection analysis, lifestyle assessment, encouraging, task setting and commitment, giving homework, and terminating and summarizing have all been used (Carlson & Johnson, 2016; Carlson et al., 2006; Dinkmeyer & Sperry, 2000; Disque & Bitter, 1998; Mozdzierz, Peluso, & Lisiecki, 2009). Contemporary Adlerian practitioners are diverse in their styles of counseling (Maniacci, 2012; Watts, 2015), and they can creatively employ a wide range of other techniques, as long as these methods are philosophically consistent with the basic theoretical premises of Adlerian psychology. Adlerians are pragmatic when it comes to using techniques that are appropriate for a given client. In general, however, Adlerian practitioners focus on motivation modification more than behavior change and encourage clients to make holistic changes on the useful side of living.

All therapy is a cooperative effort, and making a difference depends on the therapist's ability to win the client's cooperation. Let's focus on one technique traditionally associated with Adlerian counseling to see what it looks like in action. Harold Mosak, a highly respected therapist, uses the *push-button technique* with clients who know they are depressed but feel that the depression controls them and that nothing can be done. The goal of this technique is to help clients become aware of their role in contributing to their unpleasant feelings. Typically, clients are asked to re-create an unpleasant memory, which is then followed by recalling a pleasant memory (Watts, 2015).

Counselor: I am sure we can end your depression rather easily. Let's start with what you really need to do with your life [*the set up*].

Client: Wait a minute. If you can get rid of my depression easily, let's do it.

Counselor: Well, OK. You will have to close your eyes. I want you to think about the worst, most awful thing that has happened to you recently. When you have it in mind, I want you to raise your right hand. [*The client pauses for a few moments and then raises his hand.*] Now, I would like you to add the feeling you feel when you think about this horrible part of your life. [*Taking the client's right hand, the counselor presses the index finger onto the client's leg.*] We will call this your depression button.

Now, I want you to think about the best thing that has happened to you or could happen to you or you would love to have happen to you. Raise your left hand when you know what that is.

Client: I can't really think of anything.

Counselor: You may have to go back to an earlier time to remember a really good time that you would like to have in your life now, but I know you can do it. [*A minute later the man raises his left hand.*] Now, add the feeling you have thinking about that happy time. [*Taking the client's left hand, the counselor presses the index finger onto the client's other leg.*]

So you have a depression button on your right leg, and you can push it and think about everything horrible, awful, or worse, and feel depressed. Or you can push the happy button on the other leg, think about wonderful things or events or people, and feel happy. If you come in next week and tell me you have felt depressed, I will simply ask you why you decided to push the depression button rather than the happy button.

The push-button technique recognizes that "control" is a major theme in depression, and this intervention is designed to help the client regain a sense of control over the negative feelings that seem overwhelming. An effective way of using this technique may be to give the client, especially a child or an adolescent, an actual push-button to carry in his or her pocket as a physical reminder.

Areas of Application

Adler anticipated the future direction of the helping professions by calling **LO11** upon therapists to become social activists and by addressing the prevention and remediation of social conditions that were contrary to social interest and resulted in human problems. Adler's own experiences of discrimination and the influence of social inequality are well represented in his writings. Adler's pioneering efforts on prevention services in mental health led him to increasingly advocate for the role of Individual Psychology in schools and families. Because Individual Psychology is based on a growth model, not a medical model, it is applicable to such varied spheres of life as child guidance; parent–child counseling; couples counseling; family counseling and therapy; group counseling and therapy; individual counseling with children, adolescents, and adults; cultural conflicts; correctional and rehabilitation counseling; and mental health institutions. Adler's basic ideas have been incorporated into the practices of school psychology, school counseling, the community mental health movement, and parent education. Adlerian principles have been widely applied to substance abuse programs, social problems to combat poverty and crime, problems of the aged, school systems, religion, and business. Adlerian ideas also have had widespread international application and acceptance (see Fall and Winter 2012 special issues of the *Journal of Individual Psychology* for international perspectives on Individual Psychology).

Application to Family Counseling With its emphasis on the family constellation, holism, and the freedom of the therapist to improvise, Adler's approach contributed to the foundation of the family therapy perspective. Adlerians working with families focus on the family atmosphere, the family constellation, and the interactive goals of each member (Bitter, 2014). The family atmosphere is the climate characterizing the relationship between the parents and their attitudes toward life, gender roles, decision making, competition, cooperation, dealing with conflict, responsibility, and so forth. This atmosphere, including the role models the parents provide, influences the children as they grow up. The therapeutic process seeks to increase awareness of the interaction of the individuals within the family system. Those who practice Adlerian family therapy strive to understand the goals, beliefs, and behaviors of each family member and the family as an entity in its own right.

Application to Group Counseling Adler and his coworkers used a group approach in their child guidance centers in Vienna as early as 1921 (Dreikurs, 1969). Dreikurs extended and popularized Adler's work with groups and used group psychotherapy in his private practice for more than 40 years. Although Dreikurs introduced group therapy into his psychiatric practice as a way to save time, he quickly discovered some unique characteristics of groups that made them an effective way of helping people change. Inferiority feelings can be challenged and counteracted effectively in groups, and the mistaken concepts and values that are at the root of social and emotional problems can be deeply influenced because the group is a value-forming agent (Sonstegard & Bitter, 2004).

The rationale for Adlerian group counseling is based on the premise that our problems are mainly of a social nature. The group provides the social context in which members can develop a sense of belonging, social connectedness, and community. Sonstegard and Bitter (2004) write that group participants come to see that many of their problems are interpersonal in nature, that their behavior has social meaning, and that their goals can best be understood in the framework of social purposes. Group counseling is particularly helpful in promoting social interest. A core therapeutic factor is the role of altruism, which is the process of helping others in the group. The process of developing group cohesion parallels social interest (promoting the social welfare, in this case of the group) and community feeling (feeling connected and closer to the group itself), which are primary goals of Adlerian therapy. For example, in a men's group, one of the core goals is often helping discouraged and isolated men feel useful to others (building altruism) and connected to fellow men. While this group process is building, group members are also building their social interest by feeling connected to something bigger than themselves.

The use of early recollections is a unique feature of Adlerian group counseling. As mentioned earlier, from a series of early memories, individuals can get a clear sense of their mistaken notions, current attitudes, social interests, and possible future behavior. Through the mutual sharing of these early recollections, members develop a sense of connection with one another, and group cohesion is increased. The group becomes an agent of change because of the improved interpersonal relationships among members and the emergence of hope.

Especially valuable is the way Adlerian group counselors implement action strategies at each of the group sessions and especially during the reorientation stage when new decisions are made and goals are modified. To challenge self-limiting assumptions, members are encouraged to act *as if* they were the persons they want to be. They are asked to "catch themselves" in the process of repeating old patterns that have led to ineffective or self-defeating behavior. The members come to appreciate that if they hope to change, they need to set tasks for themselves, apply group lessons to daily life, and take steps in finding solutions to their problems. This final stage is characterized by group leaders and members working together to challenge erroneous beliefs about self, life, and others. During this stage, members are considering alternative beliefs, behaviors, and attitudes.

Adlerian group counseling can be considered a brief approach to treatment. The core characteristics associated with brief group therapy include rapid establishment of a strong therapeutic alliance, clear problem focus and goal alignment, rapid assessment, emphasis on active and directive therapeutic interventions, a focus on strengths and abilities of clients, an optimistic view of change, a focus on both the present and the future, and an emphasis on tailoring treatment to the unique needs of clients in the most time-efficient manner possible (Carlson et al., 2006).

Adlerian brief group therapy is addressed by Sonstegard, Bitter, Pelonis-Peneros, and Nicoll (2001). For more on the Adlerian approach to group counseling, refer to *Theory and Practice of Group Counseling* (Corey, 2016, chap. 7) and Sonstegard and Bitter (2004).

Adlerian Therapy From a Multicultural Perspective

Strengths From a Diversity Perspective

Carlson and Englar-Carlson (2013) believe that Adlerian theory is well suited to counseling diverse populations and doing social justice work. They state that Adlerian therapy not only focuses acutely on multicultural and social justice issues but is "alive, well, and poised to address the concerns of a contemporary global society" (p. 94). **LO12**

Although the Adlerian approach is called Individual Psychology, its focus is on the person in a social context. Clients are encouraged to define themselves within their social environments and to understand how those environments influence their lifestyle and health. Adlerians allow broad concepts of age, ethnicity, lifestyle, sexual/affectional orientations, and gender differences to emerge in therapy, and these issues are then addressed (Carlson & Englar-Carlson, 2013). The therapeutic process is grounded within a client's culture and worldview rather than attempting to fit clients into preconceived models.

In their analysis of the various theoretical approaches to counseling, Arciniega and Newlon (2003) state that Adlerian theory holds a great deal of promise for addressing diversity issues. They note a number of characteristics of Adlerian theory that are congruent with the values of many racial, cultural, and ethnic groups, including the emphasis on understanding the individual in a familial and sociocultural context; the role of social interest and contributing to others; and the focus on belonging and the collective spirit. Cultures that stress the welfare of the social group and emphasize the role of the family will find the basic assumptions of Adlerian psychology to be consistent with their values.

Adlerian therapists tend to focus on cooperation and socially oriented values as opposed to competitive and individualistic values. This makes the Adlerian approach well-suited for our increasingly multicultural and pluralistic society.

Native American clients, for example, tend to value cooperation over competition. One such client told a story about a group of boys who were in a race. When one boy got ahead of the others, he would slow down and allow the others to catch up, and they all made it to the finish line at the same time. Although the coach tried to explain that the point of the race was for an individual to finish first, these boys were socialized to work together cooperatively as a group. Adlerian therapy is easily adaptable to cultural values that emphasize community.

Adlerian practitioners are not wedded to any particular set of procedures and may apply a range of cognitive and action-oriented techniques to helping clients explore their practical problems in a cultural context. Adlerians are conscious of the value of adapting their techniques to each client's situation, but most of them do conduct a lifestyle assessment that is heavily focused on the structure and dynamics within the client's family. Because of their cultural background, many clients have been conditioned to respect their family heritage and to appreciate the impact of their family on their own personal development. It is essential that counselors be sensitive to the conflicting feelings and struggles of their clients. If counselors demonstrate an understanding of these cultural values, it is likely that these clients will be receptive to an exploration of their lifestyle. Such an exploration will involve a detailed discussion of their own place within their family.

It should be noted that Adlerians investigate culture in much the same way that they approach birth order and family atmosphere. Culture is a vantage point from which life is experienced and interpreted; it is also a background of values, history, convictions, beliefs, customs, and expectations that must be addressed by the individual. Culture provides a way of grasping the subjective and experiential perspective of an individual. Although culture influences each person, it is expressed within each individual differently, according to the perception, evaluation, and interpretation of culture that the person holds. Adlerians find in different cultures opportunities for viewing the self, others, and the world in multidimensional ways.

Shortcomings From a Diversity Perspective

As is true of most Western models, the Adlerian approach tends to focus on the self as the locus of change and responsibility. Because other cultures may have different conceptions, this primary emphasis on changing the autonomous self may be problematic for many clients. Assumptions about the Western nuclear family are built into the Adlerian concepts of birth order and family constellation. For people brought up in extended family contexts, some of these ideas may be less relevant or at least may need to be reconfigured.

Adlerian theory has some potential drawbacks for clients from those cultures who are not interested in exploring past childhood experiences, early memories, family experiences, and dreams. This approach also has limited effectiveness with clients who do not understand the purpose of exploring the details of a lifestyle analysis when dealing with life's current problems (Arciniega & Newlon, 2003). In addition, the culture of some clients may contribute to their viewing the counselor as the "expert" and expecting that the counselor will provide them with solutions to their problems. For these clients, the role of the Adlerian therapist may pose problems because Adlerian therapists are not experts in solving other people's problems.

Instead, they view it as their function to collaboratively teach people alternative methods of coping with life concerns.

Many clients who have pressing problems are likely to be hesitant to discuss areas of their lives that they may not see as connected to the struggles that bring them into therapy. Individuals may believe that it is inappropriate to reveal family information. On this point Carlson and Carlson (2000) suggest that a therapist's sensitivity and understanding of a client's culturally constructed beliefs about disclosing family information are critical. If the therapist is able to demonstrate an understanding of a client's cultural values, it is likely that this person will be more open to the assessment and treatment process.

Adlerian Therapy Applied to the Case of Stan

The basic aims of an Adlerian therapist working with Stan are fourfold and correspond to the four stages of counseling: (1) establishing and maintaining a good working relationship with Stan, (2) exploring Stan's dynamics, (3) encouraging Stan to develop insight and understanding, and (4) helping Stan see new alternatives and make new choices.

To develop mutual trust and respect, I pay close attention to Stan's subjective experience and attempt to get a sense of how he has reacted to the turning points in his life. During the initial session, Stan reacts to me as the expert who has the answers. He is convinced that when he makes decisions he generally ends up regretting the results. Stan approaches me out of desperation. Because I view counseling as a relationship between equals, I initially focus on his feeling of being unequal to most other people. A good place to begin is exploring his feelings of inferiority, which he says he feels in most situations. The goals of counseling are developed mutually, and I avoid deciding for Stan what his goals should be. I also resist giving Stan the simple formula he is requesting.

I prepare a lifestyle assessment based on a questionnaire that taps information about Stan's early years, especially his experiences in his family. (See the *Student Manual for Theory and Practice of Counseling and Psychotherapy* [Corey, 2017] for a complete description of this lifestyle assessment form as it is applied to Stan.) This assessment includes a determination of whether he poses a danger to himself because Stan did mention suicidal ideation. During the assessment phase, which might take a few sessions, I explore with Stan his social relationships, his relationships with members of his family, his work responsibilities, his role as a man, and his feelings about himself. I place considerable emphasis on Stan's goals in life and his priorities. I do not pay a great deal of attention to his past, except to show him the consistency between his past and present as he moves toward the future.

As an Adlerian counselor, I place value on exploring early recollections as a source of understanding his goals, motivations, and values. I ask Stan to report his earliest memories.

Stan: I was about 6, I went to school, and I was scared of the other kids and the teacher. When I came home, I cried and told my mother I didn't want to go back to school. She yelled at me and called me a baby. After that I felt horrible and even more scared.

Another of Stan's early recollections was at age 8:

Stan: My family was visiting my grandparents. I was playing outside, and some neighborhood kid hit me for no reason. We started fighting, and my mother came out and scolded me for being such a rough kid. She wouldn't believe me when I told her he started the fight. I felt angry and hurt that she didn't believe me.

Based on these early recollections, I suggest that Stan sees life as frightening and unpredictably hostile and that he feels he cannot count on women; they are likely to be harsh, unbelieving, and uncaring.

Having gathered the data based on the lifestyle assessment about his family constellation and his early recollections, I assist Stan in the process of summarizing and interpreting this information. I give particular attention to identifying basic mistakes, which are faulty conclusions about life and self-defeating perceptions. Here are some of the mistaken conclusions Stan has reached:

- "I must not get close to people, because they will surely hurt me."
- "Because my own parents didn't want me and didn't love me, I'll never be desired or loved by anybody."
- "If only I could become perfect, maybe people would acknowledge and accept me."
- "Being a man means not showing emotions."

The information I summarize and interpret leads to insight and increased self-understanding on Stan's part. He gains increased awareness of his need to control his world so that he can keep painful feelings in check. He sees more clearly some of the ways he tries to gain control over his pain: through the use of alcohol, avoiding interpersonal situations that are threatening, and being unwilling to count on others for psychological support. Through continued emphasis on his beliefs, goals, and intentions, Stan comes to see how his private logic is inaccurate. In his case, a syllogism for his style of life can be explained in this way: (1) "I am unloved, insignificant, and do not count"; (2) "The world is a threatening place to be, and life is unfair"; (3) "Therefore, I must find ways to protect myself and be safe." During this phase of the process, I make interpretations centering on his lifestyle, his current direction, his goals and purposes, and how his private logic works. Of course, Stan is expected to carry out homework assignments that assist him in translating his insights into new behavior. In this way he is an active participant in his therapy.

In the reorientation phase of therapy, Stan and I work together to consider alternative attitudes, beliefs, and actions. By now Stan sees that he does not have to be locked into past patterns, feels encouraged, and realizes that he has the power to change his life. He accepts that he will not change merely by gaining insights and knows that he will have to make use of these insights by carrying out an action-oriented plan. Stan begins to feel that he can create a new life for himself and not remain the victim of circumstances.

Questions for Reflection

- What are some ways you would attempt to establish a relationship with Stan based on trust and mutual respect? Can you imagine any difficulties in developing this relationship with him?
- What aspects of Stan's lifestyle particularly interest you? In counseling him, how would these be explored?
- The Adlerian therapist identified four of Stan's mistaken conclusions. Can you identify with any of these basic mistakes? If so, do you think this would help or hinder your therapeutic effectiveness with him?
- How might Stan's cultural identity and context be assessed, and what might be the relationship to his presenting concerns?
- How might you assist Stan in discovering his social interest and going beyond a preoccupation with his own problems?
- What strengths and resources in Stan might you draw on to support his determination and commitment to change?

See the *DVD for Theory and Practice of Counseling and Psychotherapy: The Case of Stan and Lecturettes* (Session 3 on Adlerian therapy) for a demonstration of my approach to counseling Stan by focusing on his early recollections.

Adlerian Therapy Applied to the Case of Gwen*

As the eldest child, Gwen learned early on that she was responsible not only for herself but for all those in need around her as well. She often sacrificed her own desires in an effort to please of others. She knows how to stand up for herself, but too often takes on the role of helper and loses her sense of personal meaning and identity.

*Dr. Kellie Kirksey writes about her ways of thinking and practicing from an Adlerian perspective and applying this model to Gwen.

Gwen: I have played by everyone's rules for so long, and now I am just tired. I just can't seem to win.

Therapist: If I were facing everything you are facing, I too would be tired and sad ... and sometimes irritated.

I want to normalize Gwen's experience because I know all too well that being an African American woman juggling multiple roles carries with it additional stresses and burdens.

Therapist: Is it safe to say that your life feels out of control?

Gwen: Yes. I can't remember the last time I felt I was really in the driver's seat.

Therapist: So, let's see. You take care of your spouse, your mother, and check in on your siblings—which, by the way, you have been doing since you were a child. Even though your children are gone, you still listen to their needs on a regular basis and help out in any way that you can. You seldom if ever see your friends (no time), and you cannot seem to concentrate on your work enough to feel productive. Did I understand you correctly?

Gwen: Yes. You got it all.

Therapist: I am not even sure I am close to getting it all, because all of that is enough to overload anyone.

Gwen: Yes, I am totally overloaded. I have to handle all of this, get things done, and get life back to normal. But I just can't get focused.

Therapist: Yes. There is so much. You get distracted; you start running without knowing where you are going; you worry; and the cycle continues.

Gwen: I just have so many problems.

Therapist: What would you be doing with your life if you did not have all of these problems in your life? How would your life be different? [*Asking "The Question."*]

Gwen: That's just it: I don't know anymore. Well, I wouldn't feel so depressed anymore. I would hope for a better life with my husband and friends, but I don't even know if that is possible.

Gwen comes to the next session looking somewhat more relaxed than at our first session. I ask her what accounts for this, and she says that really everything is about the same, but she felt understood at the last session, so she has some hope. I thank her for telling me and congratulate her on the courage she has shown in coming to therapy.

Therapist: Gwen, I would like to get to know you a little better, to have a sense of what you have learned from life. Would it be OK if I ask you about some important parts of your life so far?

Gwen: Yes, of course.

During this session, I begin to ask Gwen about the story of her life, using the tools Adlerians include in a lifestyle assessment. I ask about her family constellation, including descriptions of and the relationship between her parents. I ask which of her siblings was most different from her and in what way? Which one was like her and in what way? And what was she like as a child? In each of these descriptions, Gwen tells me about the early meaning she attached to her family life. During this discussion she tells me about being molested as a child by an older cousin and her determination to protect her siblings from a similar fate.

In the next session, Gwen tells me about her developmental history, addressing each one of Adler's three tasks of life. She has always been a person who had just a few close friends, and she tends to take charge. "I guess some of my friends think I am a bit bossy. I know my sister does for sure, and she is still my best friend." Gwen has always worked, first in the home, and then increasingly out in the world. She had her first real job when she was 14, having lied about her age, so she could work at a neighborhood restaurant. She has always taken care of other people, even while going to college—and now, even while she has heavy demands at her work. Her husband is a community activist. Ron is the only man with whom she has ever been in love. She feels they are growing apart, but they handle it by both staying busy. It is easy to hear in her stories how responsible for others she feels, how exhausted she must be, and how much of herself gets lost in the daily struggles.

Therapist: The struggles you mention are hard enough by themselves. But you also mentioned dealing with experiences of racism and sexism. Can you tell me about some of the particular challenges you have had to face as an African American woman?

I, too, am an African American woman, but I cannot assume that my own experiences are similar to hers. I have to hear what meaning she personally associates with race and gender, which are additional tasks of life she must address every day of her existence. I want to know what her biggest challenge is as a member of her culture as well as her greatest strength and points of cultural pride.

Toward the end of the session, I ask Gwen to prepare a list of early recollections for our next session. I ask her to remember six or more stories that happened before she was 8 years old. I want her to think of the event like a moving picture and stop it at a single frame: What is happening in that frame, and what is she feeling? What is her reaction to what happened? If this were a newspaper story, what would be the headline? These memories will most likely confirm what I am already learning about Gwen, and they will help me identify the convictions and beliefs, some of which may be faulty, that guide her life.

Lifestyle assessment is a way of investigating the client's unique approach to the life tasks of love, friendship, and work. It is filled with meaning and identity and convictions and beliefs. It also contains the traits that make up the individual's internal resources, the motivations for both feelings and behaviors, and the foundation for where life might develop from here. The golden rule of Individual Psychology is that "everything can be different." What difference does Gwen want to make in her life now?

Questions for Reflection

- What are your thoughts about asking Gwen to identify some of her early recollections? Is this kind of ancient history really important in how an individual develops a lifestyle? Why do we remember these things?
- Gwen wants more suggestions from her therapist. If you were her therapist, how would you intervene with her when she wants more direction from you?
- Encouragement is a foundational technique of Adlerian therapy. Can you identify any encouraging behaviors by the therapist? What value do you place on encouragement? What is the difference between encouragement and praise?
- How interested would you be in getting information from Gwen about issues of race and culture?
- What additional Adlerian technique would you use if you were counseling Gwen? What would your aim be in making this intervention?

Summary and Evaluation

Summary

Adler was far ahead of his time, and most contemporary therapies have incorporated at least some of his ideas. Individual Psychology assumes that people are motivated by social factors; are responsible for their own thoughts, feelings, and actions; are the creators of their own lives, as opposed to being helpless victims; and are impelled by purposes and goals, looking more toward the future than back to the past.

The basic goal of the Adlerian approach is to help clients identify and change their mistaken beliefs about self, others, and life and thus to participate more fully in a social world. Clients are not viewed as psychologically sick, but as discouraged. The therapeutic process helps individuals become aware of their patterns and make some basic changes in their style of living, which lead to changes in the way they feel and behave. The role of the family in the development of the individual is emphasized. Therapy is a cooperative venture that challenges clients to translate their insights into action in the real world. Contemporary Adlerian theory is an integrative approach, combining cognitive, constructivist, existential, psychodynamic, relational, and systems perspectives. Some of these common characteristics include an emphasis on establishing a respectful client–therapist relationship, an emphasis on clients' strengths and resources, and an optimistic and future orientation.

Contributions of the Adlerian Approach

A strength of the Adlerian approach is its flexibility and its integrative nature. **LO13** Adlerian therapists are resourceful and flexible in drawing on many methods, which can be applied to a diverse range of clients in a variety of settings and formats. They tend to be theoretically consistent and technically eclectic (Watts, 2015). Therapists are mainly concerned with doing what is in the best interests of clients rather than squeezing clients into one theoretical framework (Carlson et al., 2006).

Another contribution of the Adlerian approach is that it is suited to brief, time-limited therapy. Adler was a proponent of time-limited therapy, and the techniques used by many contemporary brief therapeutic approaches are very similar to interventions created by or commonly used by Adlerian practitioners (Carlson et al., 2006). Adlerian therapy and contemporary brief therapy have in common a number of characteristics, including quickly establishing a strong therapeutic alliance, a clear problem focus and goal alignment, rapid assessment and application to treatment, an emphasis on active and directive intervention, a psychoeducational focus, a present and future orientation, a focus on clients' strengths and abilities and an optimistic expectation of change, and a time sensitivity that tailors treatment to the unique needs of the client (Carlson et al., 2006; Hoyt, 2015). According to Mosak and Di Pietro (2006), early recollections are a significant assessment intervention in brief therapy. They claim that early recollections are often useful in minimizing the number of therapy sessions. This procedure takes little time to administer and interpret and provides a direction for therapists to pursue.

Bitter and Nicoll (2000) identify five characteristics that form the basis for an integrative framework in brief therapy: time limitation, focus, counselor directiveness, symptoms as solutions, and the assignment of behavioral tasks. Bringing a time-limitation process to therapy conveys to clients the expectation that change will occur in a short period of time. When the number of sessions is specified, both client and therapist are motivated to stay focused on desired outcomes and to work as efficiently as possible. Because there is no assurance that a future session will occur, brief therapists tend to ask themselves this question: "If I had only one session to be useful in this person's life, what would I want to accomplish?" (p. 38).

It is difficult to overestimate the contributions of Adler to contemporary therapeutic practice. In many ways, I believe Adler's influence on current practice is greater than that of Freud. Many of Adler's ideas were revolutionary and far ahead of his time. His influence went beyond counseling individuals, extending into the community mental health movement (Ansbacher, 1974). Abraham Maslow, Viktor Frankl, Rollo May, Paul Watzlawick, Karen Horney, Erich Fromm, Aaron T. Beck, and Albert Ellis have all acknowledged their debt to Adler. Both Frankl and May see him as a forerunner of the existential movement because of his position that human beings are free to choose and are entirely responsible for what they make of themselves. This view also makes him a forerunner of the subjective approach to psychology, which focuses on the internal determinants of behavior: values, beliefs, attitudes, goals, interests, personal meanings, subjective perceptions of reality, and strivings toward self-realization. Bitter (2008; Bitter, Robertson, Healey, & Cole, 2009) has drawn attention to the link between Adlerian thinking and feminist therapy approaches.

One of Adler's most important contributions was his influence on other therapy systems. Many of his basic ideas have found their way into most of the other psychological schools, a few of which include existential therapy, cognitive behavior therapy, rational emotive behavior therapy, reality therapy, solution-focused brief therapy, feminist therapy, and family therapy. Adlerian psychology is a phenomenological, holistic, optimistic, and socially embedded theory based on basic assumptions that have been woven into various theories of counseling (Carlson & Johnson, 2016; Maniacci et al., 2014). In many respects, Adler seems to have paved the way for current developments in both the cognitive and constructivist therapies (Watts, 2012, 2015). Adlerians' basic premise is that if clients can change their thinking, then they can change their feelings and behavior. A study of contemporary counseling theories reveals that many of Adler's notions have reappeared in these modern approaches with different nomenclature, and often without giving Adler the credit that is due to him (Watts, 2015). One example of this is found in the emergence of the positive psychology movement, which calls for an increased study of hope, courage, contentment, happiness, well-being, perseverance, resilience, tolerance, and personal resources. Adler clearly addressed major themes associated with positive psychology long before this approach appeared on the therapeutic scene (Watts, 2012). It is clear that there are significant linkages between Adlerian theory and most of the present-day theories, especially those that view the person as purposive, self-determining, and striving for growth. Carlson and Englar-Carlson (2013) assert that Adlerians face the challenge of continuing to develop their approach so that it meets the needs of contemporary global society: "Whereas Adlerian ideas are alive in other theoretical approaches, there is a question about whether Adlerian theory as a stand-alone approach is viable in the long term" (p. 124). With so many Adlerian concepts co-opted by other models, these authors believe that for the Adlerian model to survive and thrive it will be necessary to find ways to strive for significance.

Limitations and Criticisms of the Adlerian Approach

Adler had to choose between devoting his time to formalizing his theory **LO14** and teaching others the basic concepts of Individual Psychology. He placed practicing therapy and teaching before organizing and presenting a well-defined and systematic theory. Many of Adler's ideas are vague and general, which makes it difficult to conduct research on some concepts (Carlson & Johnson, 2016). His written presentations are often difficult to follow, and many of them are transcripts of lectures he gave. Adler's global reach was unprecedented, but he did not attend to the way his work was translated. Although he was brilliant in many ways, he was not scholarly (Maniacci, 2012).

Self-Reflection and Discussion Questions

1. What are some of your earliest memories? Identify one specific early memory and reflect on the significance this early recollection has for you. What value do you see in the Adlerian technique of having individuals recall their earliest memories?

2. Adlerians contend that each of us has a unique lifestyle, or personality, that starts to develop in early childhood to compensate for and overcome some perceived inferiority. How does this key concept apply to you? In what ways have you felt inferior in the past, and how have you dealt with it? Do you see any potential connection between your struggle with basic inferiority and your accomplishments?
3. From an Adlerian perspective, individuals are best understood by looking at their future strivings. How are your goals influencing what you are doing now? How do you think your past has influenced your future goals? In what ways can you apply this purposive, goal-oriented approach in your work as a therapist?
4. Adlerians emphasize the family constellation. Reflect on what it was like for you to grow up in your family. How would you characterize your relationship with each of your siblings? What did you learn about yourself and others through your early family experiences?
5. Social interest is a central concept in the Adlerian approach. What value do you place on social interest in your own life? In what ways do you think you could assist your clients in developing their social interest?

Where to Go From Here

Visit CengageBrain.com or watch the *DVD for Integrative Counseling: The Case of Ruth and Lecturettes*, Session 6 ("Cognitive Focus in Counseling"), which illustrates Ruth's striving to live up to expectations and measure up to perfectionist standards. In this therapy session with Ruth, you will see how I draw upon cognitive concepts and apply them in practice.

Free Podcasts for ACA Members

You can download ACA Podcasts (prerecorded interviews) by going to www.counseling.org and clicking on the Resource button, and then the Podcast Series. For Chapter 5, look for Podcast 11, Adlerian Therapy, by Dr. Jon Carlson.

Other Resources

Videos from Psychotherapy.net demonstrate Adlerian therapy with adults, families, and children and are available to students and professionals at www.Psychotherapy.net. New articles, interviews, blogs, therapy cartoons, and videos are published monthly. For this chapter, see the following:

Carlson, J. (1997). *Adlerian Therapy* (Psychotherapy with the Experts Series)

Carlson, J. (2001). *Adlerian Parent Consultation* (Child Therapy with the Experts Series)

Kottman, T. (2001). *Adlerian Play Therapy* (Child Therapy with the Experts Series)

Two other videos that depict Adlerian therapy with a real client are available from the American Psychological Association (http://www.apa.org/pubs/videos/index.aspx). One shows an example of brief Adlerian therapy, and the other shows six sessions of the working with the same client over time:

Carlson, J. D. (2005). *Adlerian Therapy* (Systems of Psychotherapy series)

Carlson, J. D. (2006). *Psychotherapy Over Time* (Psychotherapy in Six Sessions video series)

If your thinking is allied with the Adlerian approach, consider seeking training in Individual Psychology or becoming a member of the North American Society of Adlerian Psychology (NASAP). To obtain information on NASAP and a list of Adlerian organizations and institutes, contact:

North American Society of Adlerian Psychology (NASAP)
www.alfredadler.org

The society publishes a newsletter and a quarterly journal and maintains a list of institutes, training programs, and workshops in Adlerian psychology. The *Journal of Individual Psychology* presents current scholarly and professional research. Columns on counseling, education, and parent and family education are regular features. Information about subscriptions is available by contacting the society.

If you are interested in pursuing training, postgraduate study, continuing education, or a degree, contact NASAP for a list of Adlerian organizations and institutes. A few training institutes are listed here:

Adler School of Professional Psychology
www.adler.edu

Adlerian Training Institute, Inc.
www.adleriantraining.com

International Committee of Adlerian Summer Schools and Institutes
www.icassi.net

Recommended Supplementary Readings

Adlerian Therapy: Theory and Practice (Carlson, Watts, & Maniacci, 2006) clearly presents a comprehensive overview of Adlerian therapy in contemporary practice. There are chapters on the therapeutic relationship, brief individual therapy, brief couples therapy, group therapy, play therapy, and consultation. A list of available Adlerian intervention videos is provided.

Alfred Adler Revisited (Carlson & Maniacci, 2012) represents some of Adler's most important writings placed into contemporary contexts by many of today's leading Adlerian scholars and practitioners.

Adlerian Counseling and Psychotherapy: A Practitioner's Approach (Sweeney, 2009) is one of the most comprehensive books written on the wide range of Adlerian applications to therapy and wellness.

Early Recollections: Interpretative Method and Application (Mosak & Di Pietro, 2006) is an extensive review of the use of early recollections as a way to understand an individual's dynamics and behavioral style. This book addresses the theory, research, and clinical applications of early recollections.

The Key to Psychotherapy: Understanding the Self-created Individual (Powers & Griffith, 2012a) is a useful source of information for doing a lifestyle assessment. Separate chapters deal with interview techniques, lifestyle assessment, early recollections, the family constellation, and methods of summarizing and interpreting information.

Existential Therapy 6

LEARNING OBJECTIVES

1. Identify the major themes that characterize existential philosophy and therapy.
2. Compare the unique contributions of some prominent existential thinkers and therapists.
3. Examine the key concepts and basic assumptions underlying this approach, including self-awareness, freedom and responsibility, intimacy and isolation, meaning in life, death anxiety, and authenticity.
4. Identify the therapeutic goals of existential therapy.
5. Understand the unique emphasis placed on the therapeutic relationship.
6. Describe the three phases of existential counseling.
7. Understand the applications of this approach to brief therapy.
8. Identify the applications of this approach to group counseling.
9. Describe ways in which the existential approach is and is not well suited to multicultural counseling.
10. Evaluate the contributions and limitations of the existential approach.

Viktor Frankl

VIKTOR FRANKL (1905–1997) was born and educated in Vienna. He founded the Youth Advisement Centers there in 1928 and directed them until 1938. From 1942 to 1945 Frankl was a prisoner in the Nazi concentration camps at Auschwitz and Dachau, where his parents, brother, wife, and children died. He vividly remembered his horrible experiences in these camps, but he did not allow them to dampen his love and enthusiasm for life. He traveled all around the world, giving lectures in Europe, Latin America, Southeast Asia, and the United States.

Frankl received his MD in 1930 and his PhD in philosophy in 1949, both from the University of Vienna. He became an associate professor at the University of Vienna and later was a distinguished speaker at the United States International University in San Diego. He was a visiting professor at Harvard, Stanford, and Southern Methodist universities. Frankl's works have been translated into more than 20 languages, and his ideas continue to have a major impact on the development of existential therapy. His compelling book *Man's Search for Meaning* (1963) has been a best-seller around the world.

Although Frankl had begun to develop an existential approach to clinical practice before his grim years in the Nazi death camps, his experiences there confirmed his views. Frankl (1963) observed and personally experienced the truths expressed by existential philosophers and writers who hold that we have choices in every situation. Even in terrible circumstances, he believed, we could preserve a vestige of spiritual freedom and independence of mind. He learned experientially that everything could be taken from a person except one thing: "the last of human freedoms—to choose one's attitude in any given set of circumstances, to choose one's own way" (p. 104). Frankl believed that the essence of being human lies in searching for meaning and purpose. We can discover this meaning through our actions and deeds, by experiencing a value (such as love or achievements), and by suffering.

Frankl was deeply influenced by Freud, but he disagreed with the rigidity of Freud's psychoanalytic system and became a student of Alfred Adler. Reacting against most of Freud's deterministic notions, Frankl developed his own theory and practice of psychotherapy, which emphasized the concepts of freedom, responsibility, meaning, and the search for values. He established his international reputation as the founder of what has been called "The Third School of Viennese Psychoanalysis," the other two being Sigmund Freud's psychoanalysis and Alfred Adler's Individual Psychology.

Frankl was a central figure in developing existential therapy in Europe and in bringing it to the United States. He was fond of quoting Nietzsche: "He who has a *why* to live for can bear with almost any *how*" (as cited in Frankl, 1963, pp. 121, 164). Frankl contended that those words could be the motto for all psychotherapeutic practice. Another quotation from Nietzsche seems to capture the essence of Frankl's own experience and writings: "That which does not kill me, makes me stronger" (as cited in Frankl, 1963, p. 130).

Frankl developed **logotherapy**, which means "therapy through meaning." Frankl's philosophical model sheds light on what it means to be fully alive. The central themes running through his works are *life has meaning*, under all circumstances; the central motivation for living is the *will to meaning*; we have the *freedom to find meaning* in all that we think; and we must *integrate body, mind, and spirit* to be fully alive. Frankl's writings reflect the theme that the modern person has the means to live, but often has no meaning to live for.

I have selected Frankl as one of the key figures of the existential approach because of the dramatic way in which his theories were tested by the tragedies of his life. His life was an illustration of his theory, for he lived what his theory espouses.

ROLLO MAY (1909–1994) first lived in Ohio and then moved to Michigan as a young child along with his five brothers and a sister. He remembered his home life as being unhappy, a situation that contributed to his interest in psychology and counseling. In his personal life, May struggled with his own existential concerns and the failure of two marriages.

Hulton Archive/Getty Images

Rollo May

May graduated from Oberlin College in 1930 and then went to Greece as a teacher. During his summers in Greece he traveled to Vienna to study with Alfred Adler. After receiving a degree in theology from Union Theological Seminary, May decided that the best way to reach out and help people was through psychology instead of theology. He completed his doctorate in clinical psychology at Columbia University and started a private practice in New York; he also became a supervisory training analyst for the William Alanson Institute.

While May was pursuing his doctoral program, he came down with tuberculosis, which resulted in a two year stay in a sanitarium. During his recovery period, May spent much time learning firsthand about the nature of anxiety. He also spent time reading, and he studied the works of Søren Kierkegaard, which was the catalyst for May recognizing the existential dimensions of anxiety and resulted in him writing *The Meaning of Anxiety* (1950). His popular book *Love and Will* (1969) reflects his own personal struggles with love and intimate relationships and mirrors Western society's questioning of its values pertaining to sex and marriage.

The greatest personal influence on Rollo May was the existential theologian Paul Tillich (author of *The Courage to Be*, 1952), who became his mentor and a personal friend. The two spent much time together discussing philosophical, religious, and psychological topics. May was deeply influenced by the existential philosophers, by the concepts of Freudian psychology, and by many aspects of Alfred Adler's Individual Psychology. Most of May's writings reflect a concern with the nature of human experience, such as recognizing and dealing with power, accepting freedom and responsibility, and discovering one's identity. He draws from his rich knowledge based on the classics and his existential perspective.

May's writings have had a significant impact on existentially oriented practitioners, and his writings helped translate key existential concepts into psychotherapeutic practice in the United States and Europe. May believed psychotherapy should be aimed at helping people discover the meaning of their lives and should be concerned with the problems of *being* rather than with problem solving. It takes courage to "be," and our choices determine the kind of person we become. Questions of being include learning to deal with issues such as sex and intimacy, growing old, facing death, and taking action in the world. According to May, the real challenge is for people to be able to live in a world where they are alone and where they will eventually have to face death. It is the task of therapists to help individuals find ways to contribute to the betterment of the society in which they live.

IRVIN YALOM (b. 1931) was born of parents who immigrated from Russia shortly after World War I. During his early childhood, Yalom lived in the inner city of Washington, D.C., in a poor neighborhood. Life on the streets was perilous, and Yalom took refuge indoors reading novels and other works. Twice a week he made the hazardous bicycle trek to the library to stock up on reading supplies. He found an alternative and satisfying world in reading fiction, which was a source of inspiration and wisdom to him. Early in his life he decided that writing a novel was the very finest thing a person could do, and subsequently he has written several teaching novels.

Gerald Corey

Irvin Yalom

Irvin Yalom is Professor Emeritus of Psychiatry at the Stanford University School of Medicine. A psychiatrist and author, Yalom has been a major figure in the field of group psychotherapy since publication in 1970 of his influential book *The Theory and Practice of Group*

Psychotherapy (1970/2005b), which has been translated into 12 languages and is currently in its fifth edition. His pioneering work, *Existential Psychotherapy*, written in 1980, is a classic and authoritative textbook on existential therapy. A contemporary existential therapist in the United States, Yalom acknowledges the contributions of both European and American psychologists and psychiatrists to the development of existential thinking and practice. Drawing on his clinical experience and on empirical research, philosophy, and literature, Yalom developed an existential approach to psychotherapy that addresses four "givens of existence," or ultimate human concerns: freedom and responsibility, existential isolation, meaninglessness, and death. These existential themes deal with the client's existence, or being-in-the-world. Yalom believes the vast majority of experienced therapists, regardless of their theoretical orientation, address these core existential themes. How we address these existential themes greatly influences the design and quality of our lives.

Psychotherapy has been endlessly intriguing for Yalom, who has approached all of his patients with a sense of wonderment at the stories they reveal. He believes that a different therapy must be designed for each client because each has a unique story. He advocates using the here and now of the therapeutic relationship to explore the client's interpersonal world, and believes the therapist must be transparent, especially regarding his or her experience of the client. His basic philosophy is existential and interpersonal, which he applies to both individual and group therapy.

Irvin Yalom has authored many stories and novels related to psychotherapy, including *Love's Executioner* (1987), *When Nietzsche Wept* (1992), *Lying on the Couch* (1997), *Momma and the Meaning of Life* (2000), and *The Schopenhauer Cure* (2005a). His 2008 nonfiction book, *Staring at the Sun: Overcoming the Terror of Death*, is a treatise on the role of death anxiety in psychotherapy, illustrating how death and the meaning of life are foundational themes associated with in-depth therapeutic work. Yalom's works, translated into more than 20 languages, have been widely read by therapists and laypeople alike.

Introduction

Existential therapy is more a way of thinking, or an attitude about psychotherapy, than a particular style of practicing psychotherapy. It is neither an independent or separate school of therapy, nor is it a clearly defined model with specific techniques. Existential therapy can best be described as a *philosophical approach* that influences a counselor's therapeutic practice. **LO1**

> Existential psychotherapy is an attitude toward human suffering and has no manual. It asks deep questions about the nature of the human being and the nature of anxiety, despair, grief, loneliness, isolation, and anomie. It also deals centrally with the questions of meaning, creativity, and love. (Yalom & Josselson, 2014, p. 265)

Existential therapy focuses on exploring themes such as mortality, meaning, freedom, responsibility, anxiety, and aloneness as these relate to a person's current struggle. The goal of existential therapy is to assist clients in their exploration of the existential "givens of life," how these are sometimes ignored or denied, and how addressing them can ultimately lead to a deeper, more reflective and meaningful existence. Clients are invited to reflect on life, to recognize their range of alternatives, and to decide among them. Existential therapy is grounded on the assumption that we are free and therefore responsible for our choices and actions. We are the authors of our lives, and we design the pathways we follow. This chapter addresses some of the existential concepts and themes that have significant implications for the existentially oriented practitioner.

A basic existential premise is that we are not victims of circumstance because, to a large extent, we are what we choose to be. Once clients begin the process of recognizing the ways in which they have passively accepted circumstances and surrendered control, they can start down a path of consciously shaping their own lives. The first step in the therapeutic journey is for clients to accept responsibility. As Yalom (2003) puts it, "Once individuals recognize their role in creating their own life predicament, they also realize that they, and only they, have the power to change that situation" (p. 141). The aim of existential therapy is to invite clients to explore their values and beliefs and take action that grows out of this honest appraisal of their life's purpose. The therapist's basic task is to encourage clients to consider what they are most serious about so they can pursue a direction in life (Deurzen, 2012).

Visit CengageBrain.com or watch the DVD for the video program on Chapter 6, *Theory and Practice of Counseling and Psychotherapy: The Case of Stan and Lecturettes*. I suggest that you view the brief lecture for each chapter prior to reading the chapter.

Historical Background in Philosophy and Existentialism

Many streams of thought contributed to the existential therapy movement **LO2** in the 1940s and 1950s, and it arose spontaneously in different parts of Europe and among different schools of psychology and psychiatry. Many Europeans found that their lives had been devastated by World War II, and they struggled with existential issues including feelings of isolation, alienation, and meaninglessness. Early writers focused on the individual's experience of being alone in the world and facing the anxiety of this situation. The European existential perspective focused on human limitations and the tragic dimensions of life (Sharp & Bugental, 2001).

The thinking of existential psychologists and psychiatrists was influenced by a number of philosophers and writers during the 19th century. To understand the philosophical underpinnings of modern existential psychotherapy, one must have some awareness of the cultural, philosophical, and religious writings of Søren Kierkegaard, Friedrich Nietzsche, Martin Heidegger, Jean-Paul Sartre, and Martin Buber. These major figures of existentialism and existential phenomenology provided the basis for the formation of existential therapy. Ludwig Binswanger and Medard Boss were also early existential psychoanalysts who contributed key ideas to existential psychotherapy. Acknowledging the influence of these early philosophers, Yalom found that each contributed significant themes that guided his own thinking:

- From Kierkegaard: creative anxiety, despair, fear and dread, guilt, and nothingness
- From Nietzsche: death, suicide, and will

- From Heidegger: authentic being, caring, death, guilt, individual responsibility, and isolation
- From Sartre: meaninglessness, responsibility, and choice
- From Buber: interpersonal relationships, I/Thou perspective in therapy, and self-transcendence

Søren Kierkegaard (1813–1855) A Danish philosopher and Christian theologian, Kierkegaard was particularly concerned with *angst*—a Danish and German word whose meaning lies between the English words *dread* and *anxiety*—and he addressed the role of anxiety and uncertainty in life. Existential anxiety is associated with making basic decisions about how we want to live, and it is not pathological. Kierkegaard believed that anxiety is the school in which we are educated to be a self. Without the experience of angst, we may go through life as sleepwalkers. But many of us, especially in adolescence, are awakened into real life by a terrible uneasiness. Life is one contingency after another, with no guarantees beyond the certainty of death. This is by no means a comfortable state, but it is necessary to our becoming human. Kierkegaard believed that "the sickness unto death" arises when we are not true to ourselves. What is needed is the willingness to risk a leap of faith in making choices. Becoming human is a *project*, and our task is not so much to discover who we are as to *create* ourselves.

Friedrich Nietzsche (1844–1900) The German philosopher Nietzsche is the iconoclastic counterpart to Kierkegaard, expressing a revolutionary approach to the self, to ethics, and to society. Like Kierkegaard, he emphasized the importance of subjectivity. Nietzsche set out to prove that the ancient definition of humans as *rational* was entirely misleading. We are far more creatures of will than we are impersonal intellects. But where Kierkegaard emphasized the "subjective truth" of an intense concern with God, Nietzsche located values within the individual's "will to power." We give up an honest acknowledgment of this source of value when society invites us to rationalize powerlessness by advocating other worldly concerns. If, like sheep, we acquiesce in "herd morality," we will be nothing but mediocrities. But if we release ourselves by giving free rein to our will to power, we will tap our potentiality for creativity and originality. Kierkegaard and Nietzsche, with their pioneering analyses of anxiety, depression, subjectivity, and the authentic self, together are generally considered to be the originators of the existential perspective (Sharp & Bugental, 2001).

Martin Heidegger (1889–1976) Heidegger's phenomenological existentialism reminds us that we exist "in the world" and should not try to think of ourselves as beings apart from the world into which we are thrown. The way we fill our everyday life with superficial conversation and routine shows that we often assume we are going to live forever and can afford to waste day after day. Our moods and feelings (including anxiety about death) are a way of understanding whether we are living authentically or whether we are inauthentically constructing our life around the expectations of others. When we translate this wisdom from vague feeling to explicit awareness, we may develop a more positive resolve about how we want to be. Phenomenological existentialism, as presented by Heidegger, provides a view of human history that does not focus on past events but motivates individuals to look forward to "authentic experiences" that are yet to come.

Martin Buber (1878–1965) Leaving Germany to live in the new state of Israel, Buber took a less individualistic stand than most of the other existentialists. He said that we humans live in a kind of *betweenness*; that is, there is never just an *I*, but always an *other*. The *I*, the person who is the agent, changes depending on whether the other is an *it* or a *Thou*. But sometimes we make the serious mistake of reducing another person to the status of a mere object, in which case the relationship becomes *I/it*. Although Buber recognizes that of necessity we must have many *I/it* interactions (in everyday life), we are seriously limited if we live only in the world of the *I/it*. Buber stresses the importance of *presence*, which has three functions: (1) it enables true *I/Thou* relationships; (2) it allows for meaning to exist in a situation; and (3) it enables an individual to be responsible in the here and now (Gould, 1993). In a famous dialogue with Carl Rogers, Buber argued that the therapist and the client could never be on the same footing because the latter comes to the former for help. When the relationship is fully mutual, we have become "dialogic," a fully human condition.

Ludwig Binswanger (1881–1966) An existential analyst, Binswanger proposed a holistic model of self that addresses the relationship between the person and his or her environment. He used a phenomenological approach to explore significant features of the self, including choice, freedom, and caring. He based his existential approach largely on the ideas of Heidegger and accepted Heidegger's notion that we are "thrown into the world." However, this "thrown-ness" does not release us from the responsibility of our choices and for planning for the future (Gould, 1993). **Existential analysis** (*Daseinanalysis*) emphasizes the subjective and spiritual dimensions of human existence. Binswanger (1975) contended that crises in therapy were typically major choice points for the client. Although he originally looked to psychoanalytic theory to shed light on psychosis, he moved toward an existential view of his patients. This perspective enabled him to understand the worldview and immediate experience of his patients, as well as the meaning of their behavior, as opposed to superimposing his view as a therapist on their experience and behavior.

Medard Boss (1903–1991) Both Binswanger and Boss were early existential psychoanalysts and significant figures in the development of existential psychotherapy. They talked of *dasein*, or *being-in-the-world*, which pertains to our ability to reflect on life events and attribute meaning to these events. They believed the therapist must enter the client's subjective world without presuppositions that would get in the way of this experiential understanding. Both Binswanger and Boss were significantly influenced by Heidegger's seminal work, *Being and Time* (1962), which provided a broad basis for understanding the individual (May, 1958). Boss was deeply influenced by Freudian psychoanalysis, but even more so by Heidegger. Boss's major professional interest was applying Heidegger's philosophical notions to therapeutic practice, and he was especially concerned with integrating Freud's methods with Heidegger's concepts, as described in his book *Daseinanalysis and Psychoanalysis* (1963).

Jean-Paul Sartre (1905–1980) A philosopher and novelist, Sartre was convinced, in part by his years in the French Resistance in World War II, that humans are even more free than earlier existentialists had believed. The existence of a space—nothingness—between the whole of our past and the *now* frees us to choose what we will. Our values are what we choose. The failure to acknowledge our freedom and choices results in emotional problems. This freedom is hard to face, so we tend to invent an excuse by saying, "I can't change now because of my past conditioning." Sartre called excuses "bad faith." No matter what we have been, we can make choices now and become something quite different. We are condemned to be free. To choose is to become committed; this is the responsibility that is the other side of freedom. Sartre's view was that at every moment, by our actions, we are choosing who we are being. Our existence is never fixed or finished. Every one of our actions represents a fresh choice. When we attempt to pin down who we are, we engage in self-deception (Russell, 2007).

Key Figures in Contemporary Existential Psychotherapy

Viktor Frankl, Rollo May, and Irvin Yalom (featured at the beginning of the chapter) created their existential approaches to psychotherapy from their strong backgrounds in both existential and humanistic psychology. James Bugental has also made major contributions to the development of existential therapy in the United States, and Emmy van Deurzen continues to influence the practice of existential therapy in Great Britain.

James Bugental (1915–2008) James Bugental (1987) wrote about **life-changing psychotherapy**, which is the effort to help clients examine how they have answered life's existential questions and to invite them to revise their answers so they can live more authentically. Bugental coined the term "existential-humanistic" psychotherapy, and he was a leading spokesman for this approach. His philosophical and therapeutic approach included a curiosity and focus that moved him away from the traditional therapeutic milieu of labeling and diagnosing clients. His work emphasized the cultivation of both client and therapist *presence*. He developed interventions to assist the client in deepening inner exploration, or *searching*. The therapist's primary task involved helping clients make new discoveries about themselves in the living moment, as opposed to merely *talking about* themselves.

Central to Bugental's approach is his view of *resistance*, which from an existential-humanistic perspective is not resistance to therapy *per se* but rather to being fully present both during the therapy hour and in life. Resistance is seen as part of the *self-and-world construct*—how a person understands his or her being and relationship to the world at large. Forms of resistance include intellectualizing, being argumentative, always seeking to please, and any other life-limiting pattern. As resistance emerges in the therapy sessions, the therapist repeatedly notes, or "tags," the resistance so the client increases his or her awareness and ultimately has an increased range of choices.

Bugental's theory and practice emphasized the distinction between therapeutic process and content. He became known for being a masterful teacher and psychotherapist, primarily because he lived his work. He was an existentialist at heart, which made him a great model and mentor, not only for clients but also for students and professionals. In his workshops, he developed many exercises to help therapists refine and practice their skills. He frequently brought his interventions to life with live demonstrations, which emphasized therapeutic work taking place in the moment, impromptu *here-and-now* dialogue, and exploring in the context of self as client or therapist. Bugental's (1987) classic text, *The Art of the Psychotherapist,* is widely recognized for deconstructing the therapy process and moving beyond theory and generalizations to show what actually occurs moment-to-moment in the therapeutic encounter. *Psychotherapy Isn't What You Think* (Bugental, 1999) is the last book he wrote before he died in 2008, at the age of 93.

British Contribution to Existential Therapy Emmy van Deurzen, a key contributor to British existential psychology, is a philosopher, psychotherapist, and counseling psychologist. Deurzen has earned a worldwide reputation in existential psychotherapy through her many books and her role in teaching and training. Deurzen (2012) states that existential therapy is not designed to "cure" people of illness in the tradition of the medical model because people are not sick but are "sick of life or clumsy at living" (p. 30). Deurzen's (2014) psychotherapy practice has taught her that individuals have incredible resilience and intelligence in overcoming their problems once they commit themselves to a self-searching process. Her therapy clients find meaning in their past hardships rather than experiencing these difficulties as defining them in old patterns. Her clients are able to recognize the contradictions and paradoxes of life and to face their troubles and solve dilemmas. They also discover what is most important in life.

Deurzen is the cofounder of the New School of Psychotherapy and Counselling, which is developing academic and training programs. In the past decades the existential approach has spread rapidly in Britain and is now an alternative to traditional methods (Deurzen, 2002, 2012). For a description of the historical context and development of existential therapy in Britain, see Deurzen (2002), Deurzen and Adams (2011), and Cooper (2003); for an excellent overview of the theory and practice of existential therapy, see Deurzen (2012) and Schneider and Krug (2010). For information on the New School in Britain, see the Other Resources section at the end of this chapter.

Key Concepts

View of Human Nature

The crucial significance of the existential movement is that it reacts against **LO3** the tendency to identify therapy with a set of techniques. Instead, it bases therapeutic practice on an understanding of what it means to be human. The existential movement stands for respect for the person, for exploring new aspects of human behavior, and for divergent methods of understanding people. It uses numerous approaches to therapy based on its assumptions about human nature.

The **existential tradition** seeks a balance between recognizing the limits and tragic dimensions of human existence on one hand and the possibilities and opportunities of human life on the other hand. It grew out of a desire to help people engage the dilemmas of contemporary life, such as isolation, alienation, and meaninglessness. The current focus of the existential approach is on the individual's experience of being in the world alone and facing the anxiety of this isolation. "No relationship can eliminate existential isolation, but aloneness can be shared in such a way that love compensates for its pain" (Yalom & Josselson, 2014, p. 281).

The existential view of human nature is captured, in part, by the notion that the significance of our existence is never fixed once and for all; rather, we continually re-create ourselves through our projects. Humans are in a constant state of transition, emerging, evolving, and becoming in response to the tensions, contradictions, and conflicts in our lives. Being a person implies that we are discovering and making sense of our existence. We continually question ourselves, others, and the world. Although the specific questions we raise vary in accordance with our developmental stage in life, the fundamental themes do not vary. We pose the same questions philosophers have pondered throughout Western history: "Who am I?" "What can I know?" "What ought I to do?" "What can I hope for?" "Where am I going?"

The basic dimensions of the human condition, according to the existential approach, include (1) the capacity for self-awareness; (2) freedom and responsibility; (3) creating one's identity and establishing meaningful relationships with others; (4) the search for meaning, purpose, values, and goals; (5) anxiety as a condition of living; and (6) awareness of death and nonbeing. I develop these propositions in the following sections by summarizing themes that emerge in the writings of existential philosophers and psychotherapists, and I also discuss the implications for counseling practice of each of these propositions.

Proposition 1: The Capacity for Self-Awareness

Freedom, choice, and responsibility constitute the foundation of self-awareness. The greater our awareness, the greater our possibilities for freedom (see Proposition 2). We increase our capacity to live fully as we expand our awareness in the following areas:

- We are finite and do not have unlimited time to do what we want in life.
- We have the potential to take action or not to act; inaction is a decision.
- We choose our actions, and therefore we can partially create our own destiny.
- Meaning is the product of discovering how we are "thrown" or situated in the world and then, through commitment, living creatively.
- As we increase our awareness of the choices available to us, we also increase our sense of responsibility for the consequences of these choices.
- We are subject to loneliness, meaninglessness, emptiness, guilt, and isolation.
- We are basically alone, yet we have an opportunity to relate to other beings.

We can choose either to expand or to restrict our consciousness. Because self-awareness is at the root of most other human capacities, the decision to expand it is fundamental to human growth. Here are some areas of emerging awareness that individuals may experience in the counseling process:

- They see how they are trading the security of dependence for the anxieties that accompany choosing for themselves.
- They begin to see that their identity is anchored in someone else's definition of them; that is, they are seeking approval and confirmation of their being in others instead of looking to themselves for affirmation.
- They learn that in many ways they are keeping themselves prisoner by some of their past decisions, and they realize that they can make new decisions.
- They learn that although they cannot change certain events in their lives they can change the way they view and react to these events.
- They learn that they are not condemned to a future similar to the past, for they can learn from their past and thereby reshape their future.
- They realize that they are so preoccupied with suffering, death, and dying that they are not appreciating living.
- They are able to accept their limitations yet still feel worthwhile, for they understand that they do not need to be perfect to feel worthy.
- They come to realize that they are failing to live in the present moment because of preoccupation with the past, planning for the future, or trying to do too many things at once.

Increasing self-awareness—which includes awareness of alternatives, motivations, factors influencing the person, and personal goals—is an aim of all counseling. Clients need to learn that a price must be paid for increased awareness. As we become more aware, it is more difficult to "go home again." Ignorance of our condition may have brought contentment along with a feeling of partial deadness, but as we open the doors in our world, we can expect more turmoil as well as the potential for more fulfillment.

Proposition 2: Freedom and Responsibility

A characteristic existential theme is that people are free to choose among alternatives and therefore play a large role in shaping their own destiny. Schneider and Krug (2010) write that existential therapy embraces three values: (1) the *freedom to become* within the context of natural and self-imposed limitations; (2) the *capacity to reflect* on the meaning of our choices; and (3) the *capacity to act* on the choices we make. Although we do not choose the circumstances into which we are born, we create our own destiny by the choices we make. Sartre claims we are constantly confronted with the choice of what kind of person we are becoming, and to exist is never to be finished with this kind of choosing. Living an authentic existence requires that we assume responsibility for our choices (Ruben & Lichtanski, 2015).

A central existential concept is that although we long for freedom we often try to escape from our freedom by defining ourselves as a fixed or static entity (Russell, 2007). Jean-Paul Sartre (1971) refers to this as the **inauthenticity** of not accepting personal responsibility. We can then avoid choosing and instead make excuses such as these: "Since that's the way I'm made, I couldn't help what I did" or "Naturally I'm this way, because I grew up in a dysfunctional family." An inauthentic mode of existence consists of lacking awareness of personal responsibility for our lives and passively assuming that our existence is largely controlled by external forces.

Freedom implies that we are responsible for our lives, for our actions, and for our failures to take action. From Sartre's perspective, people are condemned to freedom. He calls for a *commitment* to choosing for ourselves. **Existential guilt** is being aware of having evaded a commitment, or having chosen not to choose. This guilt is a condition that grows out of a sense of incompleteness, or a realization that we are not what we might have become. Guilt may be a sign that we have failed to rise to the challenge of our anxiety and that we have tried to evade it by not doing what we know is possible for us to do (Deurzen, 2012). This condition is not viewed as neurotic, nor is it seen as a symptom that needs to be cured. Existential guilt can be a powerful source of motivation toward transformation and living authentically (Ruben & Lichtanski, 2015). The existential therapist explores this guilt to see what clients can learn about the ways in which they are living their life. This guilt also results from allowing others to define us or to make our choices for us. Sartre said, "We are our choices." **Authenticity** implies that we are living by being true to our own evaluation of what is a valuable existence for ourselves; it is the courage to be who we are. One of the aims of existential therapy is to help people face up to the difficulties of life with courage rather than avoiding life's struggles (Deurzen & Adams, 2011).

For existentialists, then, being free and being human are identical. Freedom and responsibility go hand in hand. We are the authors of our lives in the sense that we create our destiny, our life situation, and our problems (Russell, 1978). Assuming responsibility is a basic condition for change. Clients who refuse to accept responsibility by persistently blaming others for their problems are not likely to profit from therapy.

Frankl (1978) also links freedom with responsibility. He suggested that the Statue of Liberty on the East Coast should be balanced with a Statue of Responsibility on the West Coast. His basic premise is that freedom is bound by certain limitations. We are not free from conditions, but we are free to take a stand against these restrictions. Ultimately, these conditions are subject to our decisions, which means we are responsible.

The therapist assists clients in discovering how they are avoiding freedom and encourages them to learn to risk using it. Not to do so is to cripple clients and make them dependent on the therapist. Therapists have the task of teaching clients that they can explicitly accept that they have choices, even though they may have devoted most of their life to evading them. Those who are in therapy often have mixed feelings when it comes to choice. As Russell (2007) puts it: "We resent it when we don't have choices, but we get anxious when we do! Existentialism is all about broadening the vision of our choices" (p. 111).

People often seek psychotherapy because they feel that they have lost control of how they are living. They may look to the counselor to direct them, give them advice, or produce magical cures. They may also need to be heard and understood. Two central tasks of the therapist are inviting clients to recognize how they have allowed others to decide for them and encouraging them to take steps toward choosing for themselves. In inviting clients to explore other ways of being that are more fulfilling than their present restricted existence, some existential counselors ask, "Although you have lived in a certain pattern, now that you recognize the price of some of your ways, are you willing to consider creating new patterns?" Others may have a vested interest in keeping the client in an old pattern, so the initiative for changing it will have to come from the client.

Cultural factors need to be taken into account in assisting clients in the process of examining their choices. A person who is struggling with feeling limited by her family situation can be invited to look at her part in this process and values that are a part of her culture. For example, Meta, a Norwegian American, is working to attain a professional identity as a social worker, but her family thinks she is being selfish and neglecting her primary duties. The family is likely to exert pressure on her to give up her personal interests in favor of what they feel is best for the welfare of the entire family. Meta may feel trapped in the situation and see no way out unless she rejects what her family wants. In cases such as this, it is useful to explore the client's underlying values and to help her determine whether her values are working for her and for her family. Clients such as Meta have the challenge of weighing values and balancing behaviors between two cultures. Ultimately, Meta must decide in what ways she might change her situation, and she needs to assess values based on her culture. The existential therapist will invite Meta to begin to explore what she *can* do and to realize that she can be authentic in spite of pressures on her by her situation. According to Vontress (2013), we can be authentic in any society, whether we are a part of an individualistic or collectivistic society.

It is essential to respect the purpose that people have in mind when they initiate therapy. If we pay careful attention to what our clients tell us about what they want, we can operate within an existential framework. We can encourage individuals to weigh the alternatives and to explore the consequences of what they are doing with their lives. Although oppressive forces may be severely limiting the quality of their lives, we can help people see that they are not solely the victims of circumstances beyond their control. Even though we sometimes cannot control things that happen to us, we have complete control over how we choose to perceive and handle them. Although our freedom *to act* is limited by external reality, our freedom *to be* relates to our internal reality. At the same time that people are learning how to change their external environment, they can be challenged to look within themselves to recognize their own contributions to their problems. Through the therapy experience, clients may be able to discover new courses of action that will lead to a change in their situation.

Proposition 3: Striving for Identity and Relationship to Others

People are concerned about preserving their uniqueness and centeredness, yet at the same time they have an interest in going outside of themselves to relate to other beings and to nature. Each of us would like to discover a self or, to put it more authentically, to create our personal identity. This is not an automatic process, and creating an identity takes courage. As relational beings, we also strive for connectedness with others. Many existential writers discuss loneliness, uprootedness, and alienation, which can be seen as the failure to develop ties with others and with nature.

The trouble with so many of us is that we have sought directions, answers, values, and beliefs from the important people in our world. Rather than trusting ourselves to search within and find our own answers to the conflicts in our life, we sell out by becoming what others expect of us. Our being becomes rooted in their expectations, and we become strangers to ourselves.

The Courage to Be Paul Tillich (1886–1965), a leading Protestant theologian of the 20th century, believed awareness of our finite nature gives us an appreciation of ultimate concerns. It takes courage to discover the true "ground of our being" and to use its power to transcend those aspects of nonbeing that would destroy us (Tillich, 1952). Courage entails the will to move forward in spite of anxiety-producing situations, such as facing our death (May, 1975). We struggle to discover, to create, and to maintain the core deep within our being. One of the greatest fears of clients is that they will discover that there is no core, no self, no substance, and that they are merely reflections of everyone's expectations of them. A client may say, "My fear is that I'll discover I'm nobody, that there really is nothing to me. I'll find out that I'm an empty shell, hollow inside, and nothing will exist if I shed my masks." If clients demonstrate the courage to confront these fears, they might well leave therapy with an increased tolerance for the uncertainty of life. By assisting clients in facing the fear that their lives or selves are empty and meaningless, therapists can help clients to *create* a self that has meaning and substance that *they have chosen*.

Existential therapists may begin by asking their clients to allow themselves to intensify the feeling that they are nothing more than the sum of others' expectations and that they are merely the introjects of parents and parent substitutes. How do they feel now? Are they condemned to stay this way forever? Is there a way out? Can they create a self if they find that they are without one? Where can they begin? Once clients have demonstrated the courage to recognize this fear, to put it into words and share it, it does not seem so overwhelming. I find that it is best to begin work by inviting clients to accept the ways in which they have lived outside themselves and to explore ways in which they are out of contact with themselves.

The Experience of Aloneness The existentialists postulate that part of the human condition is the experience of aloneness. But they add that we can derive strength from the experience of looking to ourselves and sensing our separation. The sense of isolation comes when we recognize that we cannot depend on anyone else for our own confirmation; that is, we alone must give a sense of meaning to life, and we alone must decide how we will live. If we are unable to tolerate ourselves when we are alone, how can we expect anyone else to be enriched by our company? Before we can have any solid relationship with another, we must have a relationship with ourselves. We are challenged to learn to listen to ourselves. We have to be able to stand alone before we can truly stand beside another.

The Experience of Relatedness We humans depend on relationships with others. We want to be significant in another's world, and we want to feel that another's presence is important in our world. When we are able to stand alone and tap into our own strength, our relationships with others are based on our fulfillment, not our deprivation. If we feel personally deprived, however, we can expect little but a clinging and symbiotic relationship with someone else.

Perhaps one of the functions of therapy is to help clients distinguish between a neurotically dependent attachment to another and a life-affirming relationship in which both persons are enhanced. The therapist can challenge clients to examine what they get from their relationships, how they avoid intimate contact, how they prevent themselves from having equal relationships, and how they might create therapeutic, healthy, and mature human relationships. Existential therapists speak of intersubjectivity, which is the fact of our interrelatedness with others and the need for us to struggle with this in a creative way.

Struggling With Our Identity Because of our fear of dealing with our aloneness, Farha (1994) points out that some of us get caught up in ritualistic behavior patterns that cement us to an image or identity we acquired in early childhood. We become trapped in a *doing mode* to avoid the experience of being. Part of the therapeutic journey consists of the therapist challenging clients to begin to examine the ways in which they have lost touch with their identity, especially by letting others design their life for them. The therapy process itself is often frightening for clients when they realize that they have surrendered their freedom to others and that in the therapy relationship they will have to assume their freedom again. By refusing to give easy solutions or answers, existential therapists confront clients with the reality that they alone must find their own answers.

Proposition 4: The Search for Meaning

A distinctly human characteristic is the struggle for a sense of significance and purpose in life. In my experience the underlying conflicts that bring people into counseling and therapy are centered in these existential questions: "Why am I here?" "What do I want from life?" "What gives my life purpose?" "Where is the source of meaning for me in life?"

Existential therapy can provide the conceptual framework for helping clients challenge the meaning in their lives. Questions that the therapist might ask are, "Do you like the direction of your life?" "Are you pleased with what you now are and what you are becoming?" "If you are confused about who you are and what you want for yourself, what are you doing to get some clarity?"

The Problem of Discarding Old Values One of the problems in therapy is that clients may discard traditional (and imposed) values without creating other, suitable ones to replace them. What does the therapist do when clients no longer cling to values that they never really challenged or internalized and now experience a vacuum? Clients may report that they feel like a boat without a rudder. They seek new guidelines and values that are appropriate for the newly discovered facets of themselves, and yet for a time they are without them. One of the tasks of the therapeutic process is to help clients create a value system based on a way of living that is consistent with their way of being.

The therapist's job is to trust in the capacity of clients to eventually create an internally derived value system that provides the foundation for a meaningful life. They will no doubt flounder for a time and experience anxiety as a result of the absence of clear-cut values. The therapist's trust is important in helping clients trust their own capacity to create a new source of values.

Meaninglessness According to Frankl (1963), the central human concern is to discover meaning that will give one's life direction. Frankl's life experiences and his clinical work led him to the conclusion that a lack of meaning is the major source of existential stress and anxiety in modern times. He views **existential neurosis** as the experience of meaninglessness. When the world we live in seems meaningless, we may wonder whether it is worth it to continue struggling or even living. Faced with the prospect of our mortality, we might ask, "Is there any point to what I do now, since I will eventually die? Will what I do be forgotten when I am gone? Given the fact of mortality, why should I busy myself with anything?" A man in one of my groups captured precisely the idea of personal significance when he said, "I feel like another page in a book that has been turned quickly, and nobody bothered to read the page." Frankl believes that such a feeling of meaninglessness is the major existential neurosis of modern life.

Meaninglessness in life can lead to emptiness and hollowness, or a condition that Frankl calls the **existential vacuum**. This condition is often experienced when people do not busy themselves with routine or with work. Because there is no preordained design for living, people are faced with the task of creating their own meaning. At times people who feel trapped by the emptiness of life withdraw from the struggle of creating a life with purpose. Experiencing meaninglessness and establishing values that are part of a meaningful life are issues that become the heart of counseling.

Creating New Meaning **Logotherapy** is designed to help clients find meaning in life. The therapist's function is not to tell clients what their particular meaning in life should be but to point out that they can create meaning even in suffering (Frankl, 1978). This view holds that human suffering (the tragic and negative aspects of life) can be turned into human achievement by the stand an individual takes when faced with it. Frankl also contends that people who confront pain, guilt, despair, and death can effectively deal with their despair and thus triumph.

Yet meaning is not something that we can directly search for and obtain. Paradoxically, the more rationally we seek it, the more likely we are to miss it. Meaning is created out of an individual's engagement with what is valued, and this commitment provides the purpose that makes life worthwhile (Deurzen, 2012). I like the way Vontress (2013) captures the idea that meaning in life is an ongoing process we struggle with throughout our life: "What provides meaning one day may not provide meaning the next, and what has been meaningful to a person throughout life may be meaningless when a person is on his or her deathbed" (p. 147).

Proposition 5: Anxiety as a Condition of Living

Anxiety arises from one's personal strivings to survive and to maintain and assert one's being, and the feelings anxiety generates are an inevitable aspect of the human condition. **Existential anxiety** is the unavoidable result of being confronted with the "givens of existence"—death, freedom, choice, isolation, and meaninglessness (Vontress, 2013; Yalom, 1980; Yalom & Josselson, 2014). Existential anxiety arises as we recognize the realities of our mortality, our confrontation with pain and suffering, our need to struggle for survival, and our basic fallibility. We experience this anxiety as we become increasingly aware of our freedom and the consequences of accepting or rejecting that freedom. In fact, when we make a decision that involves reconstruction of our life, the accompanying anxiety can be a signal that we are ready for personal change and can be a stimulus for growth. If we learn to listen to the subtle messages of anxiety, we can dare to take the steps necessary to change the direction of our lives.

Existential therapists differentiate between normal and neurotic anxiety, and they see anxiety as a potential source of growth. **Normal anxiety** is an appropriate response to an event being faced. Accepting freedom and the responsibility for making decisions and life choices, searching for meaning, and facing mortality can be frightening. This kind of anxiety does not have to be repressed, and it can be a powerful motivational force toward change and growth (Ruben & Lichtanski, 2015). From the existential viewpoint, normal anxiety is an invitation to freedom. "Anxiety is a teacher, not an obstacle or something to be removed or avoided" (Deurzen & Adams, 2011, p. 24).

Failure to move through anxiety results in **neurotic anxiety**, which is anxiety about concrete things that is out of proportion to the situation. Neurotic anxiety is typically out of awareness, and it tends to immobilize the person. Being psychologically healthy entails living with as little neurotic anxiety as possible, while accepting and struggling with the unavoidable existential anxiety that is a part of living.

Many people who seek counseling want solutions that will enable them to eliminate anxiety. Creating the illusion that there is security in life may help us cope with the unknown, yet we know on some level that we are deceiving ourselves. Deurzen (2012) believes that existential anxiety is part of living with awareness and being fully alive. In fact, the courage to live fully entails accepting the reality of death and the anxiety associated with uncertainty. Facing existential anxiety involves viewing life as an adventure rather than hiding behind imagined securities that seem to offer protection. Opening up to new life means opening up to anxiety. We pay a steep price when we short-circuit anxiety.

The existential therapist can help clients recognize that learning how to tolerate ambiguity and uncertainty and how to live without props can be a necessary phase in the journey from dependence to autonomy. The therapist and client can explore the possibility that although breaking away from crippling patterns and building new ways of living will be fraught with anxiety for a while, anxiety will diminish as the client experiences more satisfaction with newer ways of being. When a client becomes more self-confident, the anxiety that results from an expectation of catastrophe is likely to decrease.

Proposition 6: Awareness of Death and Nonbeing

The existentialist does not view death negatively but holds that awareness of death as a basic human condition gives significance to living. A distinguishing human characteristic is the ability to grasp the reality of the future and the inevitability of death. It is necessary to think about death if we are to think significantly about life. Death should not be considered a threat; death provides the motivation for us to take advantage of appreciating the present moment. Instead of being frozen by the fear of death, reflecting on the reality of death can teach us how to live fully.

Deurzen and Adams (2011) write: "Life is a taskmaster, while death is a master teacher" (p. 105). If we defend ourselves against the reality of our eventual death, life becomes insipid and meaningless. But if we realize that we are mortal, we know that we do not have an eternity to complete our projects and that the present is crucial. Our awareness of death is the source of zest for life and creativity. Death and life are interdependent, and though physical death destroys us, the idea of death saves us (Yalom, 1980, 2003).

Yalom (2008) recommends that therapists talk directly to clients about the reality of death. He believes the fear of death percolates beneath the surface and haunts us throughout life. Death is a visitor in the therapeutic process, and Yalom believes that ignoring its presence sends the message that death is too overwhelming to explore. Confronting this fear can be the factor that helps us transform an inauthentic mode of living into a more authentic one. Accepting the reality of our personal death can result in a major shift in the way we live in the world (Yalom & Josselson, 2014). We can turn our fear of death into a positive force when we accept the reality of our mortality. In *Staring at the Sun: Overcoming the Terror of Death*, Yalom (2008) develops the idea that confronting death enables us to live in a more compassionate way.

One focus in existential therapy is on exploring the degree to which clients are doing the things they value. Without being morbidly preoccupied by the ever-present threat of nonbeing, clients can develop a healthy awareness of death as a way to evaluate how well they are living and what changes they want to make in their lives. Those who fear death also fear life. When we emotionally accept the reality of our eventual death, we realize more clearly that our actions do count, that we do have choices, and that we must accept the ultimate responsibility for how well we are living (Corey & Corey, 2014).

The Therapeutic Process

Therapeutic Goals

Existential therapy is best considered as an invitation to clients to recognize the ways in which they are not living fully authentic lives and to make choices that will lead to their becoming what they are capable of being. An aim of therapy is to assist clients in moving toward authenticity and learning to recognize when they are deceiving themselves (Deurzen, 2012). The existential orientation holds that there is no escape from freedom as we will always be held responsible. We can relinquish our freedom, however, which is the ultimate inauthenticity. Existential therapy aims at helping clients face anxiety and engage in action that is based on the authentic purpose of creating a worthy existence. Authenticity involves claiming authorship—taking responsibility for our actions and the way we are living (Deurzen & Adams, 2011). LO4

May (1981) contends that people come to therapy with the self-serving illusion that they are inwardly enslaved and that someone else (the therapist) can free them. Existential therapists are mainly concerned about helping people to reclaim and reown their lives. The task of existential therapy is to teach clients to listen to what they already know about themselves, even though they may not be attending to what they know. Schneider and Krug (2010) identify four essential aims of existential-humanistic therapy: (1) to help clients become more present to both themselves and others; (2) to assist clients in identifying ways they block themselves from fuller presence; (3) to challenge clients to assume responsibility for designing their present lives; and (4) to encourage clients to choose more expanded ways of being in their daily lives.

Increased awareness is the central goal of existential therapy, which allows clients to discover that alternative possibilities exist where none were recognized before. Clients come to realize that they are able to make changes in their way of being in the world.

Therapist's Function and Role

Existential therapists are primarily concerned with understanding the subjective world of clients to help them come to new understandings and options. Existential therapists are especially concerned about clients avoiding responsibility; they consistently invite clients to accept personal responsibility. When clients complain about the predicaments they are in and blame others, the therapist is likely to ask them how they contributed to their situation.

Therapists with an existential orientation usually deal with people who have what could be called a **restricted existence**. These clients have a limited awareness of themselves and are often vague about the nature of their problems. They may see few, if any, options for dealing with life situations, and they tend to feel trapped, helpless, and stuck. One of the therapist's functions is to assist clients in seeing the ways in which they constrict their awareness and the cost of such constrictions (Bugental, 1997). The therapist may hold up a mirror, so to speak, so that clients can gradually engage in self-confrontation. In this way clients can see how they became the way they are and how they might enlarge the way they live. Once clients are aware of factors in their past and of stifling modes of their present existence, they can begin to accept responsibility for changing their future.

Existential practitioners may make use of techniques that originate from diverse theoretical orientations, yet no set of techniques is considered essential. The therapeutic journey is creative and uncertain and different for each client. Russell (2007) captures this notion well when he writes: "There is no one right way to do therapy, and certainly no rigid doctrine for existentially rooted techniques. What is crucial is that you create your own authentic way of being attuned to your clients" (p. 123). Existential therapists encourage experimentation not only within the therapy office but also outside of the therapy setting, based on the belief that life outside therapy is what counts. Practitioners often ask clients to reflect on or write about problematic events they encounter in daily life (Schneider, 2011).

Client's Experience in Therapy

Clients in existential therapy are clearly encouraged to assume responsibility for how they are currently choosing to be in their world. Effective therapy does not stop with this awareness itself, for the therapist encourages clients to take action on the basis of the insights they develop through the therapeutic process. Experimentation with new ways of behaving in the outside world is necessary if clients are to change. Further, clients must be active in the therapeutic process, for during the sessions they must decide what fears, guilt feelings, and anxieties they will explore.

Merely deciding to enter psychotherapy is itself a frightening prospect for most people. The experience of opening the doors to oneself can be frightening, exciting, joyful, depressing, or a combination of all of these. As clients wedge open the closed doors, they also begin to loosen the deterministic shackles that have kept them psychologically bound. Gradually, they become aware of what they have been and who they are now, and they are better able to decide what kind of future they want. Through the process of their therapy, individuals can explore alternatives for making their visions real.

When clients plead helplessness and attempt to convince themselves that they are powerless, May (1981) reminds them that their journey toward freedom began by putting one foot in front of the other to get to his office. As narrow as their range of freedom may be, individuals can begin building and augmenting that range by taking small steps. The therapeutic journey that opens up new horizons is poetically described by Deurzen (2010):

> Embarking on our existential journey requires us to be prepared to be touched and shaken by what we find on the way and to not be afraid to discover our own limitations and weaknesses, uncertainties and doubts. It is only with such an attitude of openness and wonder that we can encounter the impenetrable everyday mysteries, which take us beyond our own preoccupations and sorrows and which by confronting us with death, make us rediscover life. (p. 5)

Another aspect of the experience of being a client in existential therapy is confronting ultimate concerns rather than coping with immediate problems. Rather than being solution-oriented, existential therapy is aimed toward removing roadblocks to meaningful living and helping clients assume responsibility for their actions (Yalom & Josselson, 2014). Existential therapists assist people in facing life with courage, hope, and a willingness to find meaning in life. Deurzen and Adams (2011) maintain that a therapist must resonate with the client's experience and struggle to face life honestly. This capacity for resonance must be honed constantly, and it requires the therapist to be fully present with the client and take part in the therapeutic encounter in a fully engaged manner.

Relationship Between Therapist and Client

Existential therapists give central prominence to their relationship with the **LO5** client. The relationship is important in itself because the quality of this person-to-person encounter in the therapeutic situation is the stimulus for positive change. Attention is given to the client's immediate, ongoing experience, especially what is going on in the interaction between the therapist and the client. Therapy is viewed as a social microcosm in the sense that the interpersonal and existential problems of the client will become apparent in the here and now of the therapy relationship (Yalom & Josselson, 2014).

Therapists with an existential orientation believe their basic attitudes toward the client and their own personal characteristics of honesty, integrity, and courage are what they have to offer. Therapy is a journey taken by therapist and client that delves deeply into the world as perceived and experienced by the client. But this type of quest demands that therapists also be in contact with their own phenomenological world. Existential therapy is a voyage into self-discovery and a journey of life-discovery for both client and therapist (Deurzen, 2010; Yalom & Josselson, 2014).

Buber's (1970) conception of the *I/Thou* relationship has significant implications here. His understanding of the self is based on two fundamental relationships: the *I/it* and the *I/Thou*. The *I/it* is the relation to time and space, which is a necessary starting place for the self. The *I/Thou* is the relationship essential for connecting the self to the spirit and, in so doing, to achieve true dialogue. This form of relationship is the paradigm of the fully human self, the achievement of which is the goal of Buber's existential philosophy. Relating in an *I/Thou* fashion means that there is direct, mutual, and present interaction. Rather than prizing therapeutic objectivity and professional distance, existential therapists strive to create caring and intimate relationships with clients.

The core of the therapeutic relationship is respect, which implies faith in clients' potential to cope authentically with their troubles and in their ability to discover alternative ways of being. Existential therapists share their reactions to clients with genuine concern and empathy as one way of deepening the therapeutic relationship. Therapists invite clients to grow by modeling authentic behavior. If therapists keep themselves hidden during the therapeutic session or if they engage in inauthentic behavior, clients will also remain guarded and persist in their inauthentic ways.

Bugental (1987) emphasizes the crucial role the *presence* of the therapist plays in the therapeutic relationship. In his view many therapists and therapeutic systems overlook its fundamental importance. He contends that therapists are too often so concerned with the content of what is being said that they are not aware of the distance between themselves and their clients. Schneider (2011) believes that the therapist's presence is both a condition and a goal of therapeutic change. Presence serves the dual functions of reconnecting people to their pain and to attuning them to the opportunities to transform their pain.

Application: Therapeutic Techniques and Procedures

The existential approach is unlike most other therapies in that it is not technique-oriented. Although existentially oriented therapists may incorporate many techniques from other models, these interventions are made within the context of striving to understand the subjective world of the client. The interventions existential practitioners employ are based on philosophical views about the nature of human existence. These practitioners prefer description, understanding, and exploration of the client's subjective reality, as opposed to diagnosis, treatment, and prognosis (Deurzen, 2002). "Existential therapists prefer to be thought of as philosophical companions, not as people who repair psyches" (Vontress, 2013, p. 150). Yalom and Josselson (2014) describe existential therapists as "fellow travelers" who are willing to make themselves known through appropriate self-disclosure. It is not theories and techniques that heal but the encounter that occurs between client and therapist as they work together (Elkins, 2007, 2016). Existential therapists are free to draw from techniques that flow from many other orientations, but they have a set of assumptions and attitudes that guide their interventions with clients. See *Case Approach to Counseling and Psychotherapy* (Corey, 2013, chap. 4) for an illustration of how Dr. J. Michael Russell works in an existential way with some key themes in the case of Ruth.

A primary ground rule of existential work is the openness to the individual creativity of the therapist and the client. Existential therapists need to adapt their interventions to their own personality and style, as well as being sensitive to what each client requires. The main guideline is that the existential practitioner's interventions are responsive to the uniqueness of each client (Deurzen, 2010).

Deurzen (2012) believes that the starting point for existential work is for practitioners to clarify their views on life and living. She stresses the importance of therapists reaching sufficient depth and openness in their own lives to venture into clients' murky waters without getting lost. The nature of existential work is assisting people in the process of living with greater expertise and ease. Deurzen (2010) identifies how therapists make a difference with clients: "We help them to get better at reflecting on their situation, deal with their dilemma, face their predicament and think for themselves" (p. 236). Deurzen reminds us that existential therapy is a collaborative adventure in which both client and therapist will be transformed if they allow themselves to be touched by life. When the deepest self of the therapist meets the deepest part of the client, the counseling process is at its best. Therapy is a creative, evolving process of discovery that can be conceptualized in three general phases.

Phases of Existential Counseling

During the initial phase of counseling, therapists assist clients in identifying and clarifying their assumptions about the world. Clients are invited to define and question the ways in which they perceive and make sense of their existence. They examine their values, beliefs, and assumptions to determine their validity. This is a difficult task for many clients because they may initially present their problems as resulting almost entirely from external causes. They may focus on what other people "make them feel" or on how others are largely responsible for their actions or inaction. The counselor teaches them how to reflect on their own existence and to examine their role in creating their problems in living. **LO6**

During the middle phase of existential counseling, clients are assisted in more fully examining the source and authority of their present value system. This process of self-exploration typically leads to new insights and some restructuring of values and attitudes. Individuals get a better idea of what kind of life they consider worthy to live and develop a clearer sense of their internal valuing process.

The final phase of existential counseling focuses on helping people take what they are learning about themselves and put it into action. Transformation is not limited to what takes place during the therapy hour. The therapeutic hour is a small contribution to a person's renewed engagement with life, or a rehearsal for life (Deurzen, 2002). The aim of therapy is to enable clients to discover ways of implementing their examined and internalized values in a concrete way between sessions and after therapy has terminated. Clients typically discover their strengths and find ways to put them to the service of living a purposeful existence.

Clients Appropriate for Existential Counseling

Existential practice has been applied in a variety of settings and with a diverse population of clients, including those with substance abuse issues, ethnic and racial minorities, gay and lesbian clients, and psychiatric inpatients (Schneider, 2011). A strength of the perspective is its focus on available choices and pathways toward personal growth. For people who are coping with developmental crises, experiencing grief and loss, confronting death, or facing a major life decision, existential therapy is especially appropriate. Some examples of these critical turning points that mark passages from one stage of life into another are the struggle for identity in adolescence, coping with possible disappointments in middle age, adjusting to children leaving home, coping with failures in marriage and work, and dealing with increased physical limitations as one ages. These developmental challenges involve both dangers and opportunities. Uncertainty, anxiety, and struggling with decisions are all part of this process.

Deurzen (2002) suggests that this form of therapy is most appropriate for clients who are committed to dealing with their problems about living, for people who feel alienated from the current expectations of society, or for those who are searching for meaning in their lives. It tends to work well with people who are at a crossroads and who question the state of affairs in the world and are willing to challenge the status quo. It can be useful for people who are on the edge of existence, such as those who are dying or contemplating suicide, who are working through a developmental or situational crisis, who feel that they no longer belong in their surroundings, or who are starting a new phase of life.

Application to Brief Therapy

The existential approach can focus clients on significant areas such as assuming personal responsibility, making a commitment to deciding and acting, and expanding their awareness of their current situation. It is possible for a time-limited approach to serve as a catalyst for clients to become actively and fully involved in each of their therapy sessions. Sharp and Bugental (2001) maintain that short-term applications of the existential approach require more structuring and clearly defined and less ambitious goals. At the termination of short-term therapy, it is important for individuals to evaluate what they have accomplished and what issues may need to be addressed later. It is essential that both therapist and client determine that short-term work is appropriate, and that beneficial outcomes are likely. LO7

Application to Group Counseling

An existential group can be described as people making a commitment to a lifelong journey of self-exploration with these goals: (1) enabling members to become honest with themselves, (2) widening their perspectives on themselves and the world around them, and (3) clarifying what gives meaning to their present and LO8 future life (Deurzen, 2002). An open attitude toward life is essential, as is the willingness to explore unknown territory. Recurring universal themes evolve in many groups that challenge members to seriously explore existential concerns such as the ability to choose a path in life, freedom and anxiety, how to live a meaningful life in the face of the reality of death, and how to establish authentic and mutual relationships (Leszcz, 2015). The heart of the work in an existential group is reducing avoidance of universal existential concerns because not addressing these themes diminishes one's engagement with life. The group leader is generally more of a participant-observer who engages as an informed fellow traveler rather than as an aloof sage. Leszcz (2015) notes that the leader engages in appropriate self-disclosure and transparency, gives feedback, and shares his or her reactions within the group. Leader disclosures center on the members' interests rather than on the leader's needs or interests.

The existential group provides the optimal conditions for therapeutic work on responsibility. The members are responsible for the way they behave in the group, and this provides a mirror for how they are likely to act in the world. A group represents a microcosm of the world in which participants live and function. A group can be instrumental in helping members see how some of the self-constricting patterns they manifest in the group parallel patterns in their everyday life. Over time the interpersonal and existential problems of the participants become evident in the here-and-now interactions within the group (Yalom & Josselson, 2014). Through feedback, members learn to view themselves through others' eyes, and they learn the ways in which their behavior affects others. Building on what members learn about their interpersonal functioning in the group, they can take increased responsibility for making changes in everyday life. The group experience provides the opportunity to participants to relate to others in meaningful ways, to learn to be themselves in the company of other people, and to establish rewarding, nourishing relationships.

In existential group counseling, members come to terms with the paradoxes of existence: that life can be undone by death, that success is precarious, that we are determined to be free, that we are responsible for a world we did not choose, that we must make choices in the face of doubt and uncertainty. Members experience anxiety when they recognize the realities of the human condition, including pain and suffering, the need to struggle for survival, and their basic fallibility. Clients learn that there are no ultimate answers for ultimate concerns. Through the support that is within a group, participants are able to tap the strength needed to create an internally derived value system that is consistent with their way of being.

A group provides a powerful context to look at oneself, and to consider what choices might be more authentically one's own. Members can openly share their fears related to living in unfulfilling ways and come to recognize how they have compromised their integrity. Members can gradually discover ways in which they have lost their direction and can begin to be more true to themselves. The group becomes a place where people can be together in deeply meaningful ways. Members learn that it is not in others that they find the answers to questions about significance and purpose in life. Existential group leaders help members live in authentic ways and refrain from prescribing simple solutions. For a more detailed discussion of the existential approach to group counseling, see Corey (2016, chap. 9).

Existential Therapy From a Multicultural Perspective

Strengths From a Diversity Perspective

Because the existential approach does not dictate a particular way of viewing or relating to reality, and because of its broad perspective, this approach is highly relevant in working in a multicultural context (Deurzen, 2012). Vontress and colleagues (1999) write about the existential foundation of cross-cultural counseling: "Existential counseling is probably the most useful approach to helping clients of all cultures find meaning and harmony in their lives, because it focuses on the sober issues each of us must inevitably face: love, anxiety, suffering, and death" (p. 32). These are the human experiences that transcend the boundaries that separate cultures. LO9

Existential therapy emphasizes presence, the I/Thou relationship, and courage. As such, it can be effectively applied with diverse client populations with a range of specific problems and in a wide array of settings (Schneider, 2008, 2011; Schneider & Krug, 2010). Schneider's (2008) "existential-integrative" model of practice coordinates a variety of therapeutic modes within an overarching existential or experiential framework. Vontress (2013) believes existential therapy is especially useful in working with culturally diverse populations because of its focus on universality, or the similarities we all share. He encourages counselors-in-training to focus on the universal commonalities of clients first and secondarily on areas of differences. In working with cultural diversity, it is essential to recognize how we are both alike and different.

The existential focus on subjective experience, or phenomenology, is a strength from a multicultural perspective. Another strength consists of inviting clients to examine the degree to which their behavior is being influenced by social and cultural conditioning. Clients can be challenged to look at the price they are paying for the decisions they have made. Although it is true that some clients may not feel a sense of freedom, their freedom can be increased if they recognize the social limits they are facing. Their freedom can be hindered by institutions and limited by their family. In fact, it may be difficult to separate individual freedom from the context of their family structure.

There is wide-ranging international interest in the existential approach. Several Scandinavian societies, an East European society (encompassing Estonia, Latvia, Lithuania, Russia, Ukraine, and Belarus), and Mexican and South American societies are thriving. In addition, an Internet course, SEPTIMUS, is taught in Ireland, Iceland, Sweden, Poland, Czech Republic, Romania, Italy, Portugal, Austria, France, Belgium, the United Kingdom, Israel, and Australia. Most recently, the First International East-West Existential Psychology conference was held in Nanjing, China, with representatives from the United States, Korea, and Japan. The International Collaborative of Existential Counsellors and Psychotherapists (ICECAP) meets online and hosts international conferences as well. The existential movement in the United Kingdom is thriving, and several doctoral programs are offered. These international developments confirm that existential therapy has wide appeal for diverse populations in many parts of the world.

Shortcomings From a Diversity Perspective

For those who hold a systemic perspective, the existentialists can be criticized on the grounds that they are excessively individualistic and ignore the social factors that cause human problems. However, with the advent of the "existential-integrative" model of practice (Schneider, 2008), this situation is beginning to change. According to Schneider (2011), existential practitioners are not only concerned with facilitating individual change but with promoting an in-depth inquiry that has implications for social change: "One cannot simply heal individuals to the neglect of the social context within which they are thrust. To be a responsible practitioner, one must develop a vision of responsible social change alongside and in coordination with one's vision of individual transformation" (p. 281).

Some individuals who seek counseling may operate on the assumption that they have very little choice because environmental circumstances severely restrict their ability to influence the direction of their lives. Even if they change internally, they see little hope that the external realities of racism, discrimination, and oppression will change. They are likely to experience a deep sense of frustration and feelings of powerlessness when it comes to making changes outside of themselves. As you will see in Chapter 12, feminist therapists maintain that therapeutic practice will be effective only to the extent that therapists intervene with some form of social action to change those factors that are creating clients' problems. In working with people of color who come from the barrio or ghetto, for example, it is important to engage their survival issues. If a counselor too quickly puts across the message to these clients that they have a choice in making their lives better, they may feel patronized and misunderstood. These real-life concerns can provide a good focus for counseling, assuming the therapist is willing to deal with them.

A potential problem within existential theory is that it is highly focused on the philosophical assumption of self-determination, which may not take into account the complex factors that many people who have been oppressed must deal with. In many cultures it is not possible to talk about the self and self-determination apart from the context of the social network and environmental conditions. However, a case can be made for the existential approach being instrumental in enabling clients to make conscious choices when it comes to the values they live by. Existential therapists do not push autonomy apart from a client's culture. They do assist clients in critically evaluating the source of their values and making a choice rather than uncritically accepting the values of their culture and family.

Many clients expect a structured and problem-oriented approach to counseling that is not found in the conventional existential approach. Although clients may feel better if they have an opportunity to talk and to be understood, they are likely to expect the counselor to do something to bring about a change in their life situation. A major task for the counselor who practices from an existential perspective is to provide enough concrete direction for these clients without taking the responsibility away from them.

Existential Therapy Applied to the Case of Stan

As an existentially oriented therapist, I counsel Stan with the assumption that he has the capacity to increase his self-awareness and decide for himself the future direction of his life. I want him to realize more than anything else that he does not have to be the victim of his past conditioning but can be the architect in redesigning his future. He can free himself of his deterministic shackles and accept the responsibility that comes with directing his own life. This approach emphasizes the importance of my understanding of Stan's world, primarily by establishing an authentic relationship as a means to a fuller degree of self-understanding.

Stan is demonstrating what Sartre would call "bad faith" by not accepting personal responsibility. I confront Stan with the ways in which he is attempting to escape from his freedom through alcohol and drugs. Eventually, I challenge Stan's passivity. I reaffirm that he is now entirely responsible for his life, for his actions, and for his failure to take action. I do this in a supportive yet firm manner.

I do not see Stan's anxiety as something negative, but as a vital part of living with uncertainty and freedom. Because there are no guarantees and because the individual is ultimately alone, Stan can expect to experience some degree of healthy anxiety, aloneness, guilt, and even despair. These conditions are not neurotic in themselves, but the way in which Stan orients himself and copes with these conditions is critical.

Stan sometimes talks about his suicidal feelings. Certainly, I investigate further to determine if he poses an immediate threat to himself. In addition to this assessment to determine lethality, I view his thoughts of "being better off dead" as symbolic. Could it be that Stan feels he is dying as a person? Is Stan using his human potential? Is he choosing a way of merely existing instead of affirming life? Is Stan mainly trying to elicit sympathy from his family? I invite Stan to explore the meaning and purpose in his life. Is there any reason for him to want to continue living? What are some of the projects that enrich his life? What can he do to find a sense of purpose that will make him feel more significant and alive?

Stan needs to accept the reality that he may at times feel alone. Choosing for oneself and living from one's own center accentuates the experience of aloneness. He is not, however, condemned to a life of isolation, alienation from others, and loneliness. I hope to help Stan discover his own centeredness and live by the values he chooses and creates for himself. By doing so, Stan can become a more substantial person and come to appreciate himself more. When he does, the chances are lessened that he will have a need to secure approval from others, particularly his parents and parental substitutes. Instead of forming a dependent relationship, Stan could choose to relate to others out of his strength. Only then would there be the possibility of overcoming his feelings of separateness and isolation.

Questions for Reflection

- If Stan resisted your attempts to help him see that he is responsible for the direction of his life, how might you intervene?
- Stan experiences a great deal of anxiety. From an existential perspective, how do you view his anxiety? How might you work with his anxiety in helpful ways?
- If Stan talks with you about suicide as a response to despair and a life without meaning, how would you respond?

Visit CengageBrain.com or watch the DVD for the video program *Theory and Practice of Counseling and Psychotherapy: The Case of Stan and Lecturettes*, Session 4 (existential therapy), for a demonstration of my approach to counseling Stan from this perspective. This session focuses on the themes of death and the meaning of life.

Existential Therapy Applied to the Case of Gwen*

In working with Gwen from an existential approach, I want to be a witness to her subjective experience of the world and assist her in exploring powerful life themes such as meaning making, the inevitability of death, freedom, choice, and responsibility. It is important for me to hear and understand the concerns Gwen brings to this session. As Gwen walks into my office, I observe her rounded shoulders and feel the heaviness of her emotions.

Therapist: Tell me what you are experiencing [*phenomenological inquiry*].

Gwen: I feel overwhelmed, shut down, sad, and exhausted.

Therapist: The feelings you describe sound similar to your feelings when you first began counseling: numbness, feeling like your life is a flat note with little joy.

Gwen: Yes! I am tired of the violence. I am tired of young black men that look like my son losing their lives. This has got to stop. Something has to change in our country, and I don't mean on the surface. Something has really got to change.

Therapist: I hear you.

Gwen: I can't even sleep at night. I am trying not to watch the news because young people dying seems like an everyday occurrence. It's not fair. Life cut short by ignorance and injustice. When I haven't heard from my children in a while, I get a hole in the pit of my stomach. I am just sick thinking I will lose my child.

I am focused on being present for Gwen as she grapples with these challenging existential themes in her life. I listen to Gwen's personal stories of racism and injustice and her search for meaning. She describes her anxiety as being like a fog that is always there and that no one can do anything about. Her sense of helplessness and fear of death for her son is real. I assist Gwen in seeing that she has options in how she confronts experiences of injustice and unfairness as they occur in her life. As Gwen explores and expresses her anxieties and fears, she begins to realize she has the power and freedom to create meaning from the circumstances that arise in her life. Even those events and experiences that bring her pain can assist her in taking more control of her circumstances and living in a more vital manner.

Gwen: Worrying keeps me up much of the night. I end up feeling scared and depressed, and then I get into this whole spiral where everything feels wrong. Life is so fragile and can be cut short in a blink.

Therapist: It seems as though you have come to the realization that we are finite and that time is limited, and that's frightening and anxiety producing.

Gwen: I feel helpless. I fear for my son's life and feel like there is nothing I can do to protect him.

Therapist: With these intense feelings of helplessness, fear, and anxiety, how do you even get through your day?

Gwen: I have been through a lot and I have survived. Even though I have my fears, I surprise myself and bounce back eventually. At the end of the day, it's my faith and the knowledge that I am making a difference in the world by passing my faith on to my children that helps me move forward.

As an existential practitioner, I share with Gwen that anxiety is a natural part of life and that death awareness is a powerful force that can assist us in living a fuller existence. In our awareness of our own mortality, we can decide to take charge of our life and make choices that enhance our existence. Gwen begins to see that her experience of anxiety may be a key to informing her of exactly how she might begin to do things differently in her life.

*Dr. Kellie Kirksey writes about her ways of thinking and practicing from an existential perspective and applying this model to Gwen.

As our session comes to a close, I remind Gwen of the powerful themes that surfaced in her session and her ability to identify as a strong, spiritual, resilient woman. I support her decision to journal more of her thoughts and feelings about what gives meaning and joy to her life and how she can make a difference in these challenging times.

Questions for Reflection

- What existential questions is Gwen facing in her life?
- How would you experience being in the room with Gwen during this session? What may surface for you as you sit with her?
- How can awareness of the fragility of life be a catalyst for making decisions about how to live more fully? Have you ever lost someone close to you? What decisions did you make?
- Gwen has talked about her loneliness and isolation, which are part of the human condition. How do you think an existential approach can help Gwen deal with this issue?

Summary and Evaluation

Summary

Existential therapists believe we all are capable of self-awareness, which is the distinctive capacity that allows us to reflect and to decide. With this awareness we become free beings who are responsible for choosing the way we live, and we influence our own destiny. This awareness of freedom and responsibility gives rise to existential anxiety, which is another basic human characteristic. Whether we like it or not, we are free, even though we may seek to avoid reflecting on this freedom. The knowledge that we must choose, even though the outcome is not certain, leads to anxiety. This anxiety is heightened when we reflect on the reality that we are mortal. Facing the inevitable prospect of eventual death gives the present moment significance, for we become aware that we do not have forever to accomplish our projects. As humans we are unique in that we strive toward fashioning purposes and values that give meaning to living. Whatever meaning our life has is developed through freedom and a commitment to make choices in the face of uncertainty.

Existential therapy places central prominence on the person-to-person relationship. It assumes that client growth occurs through this genuine encounter. It is not the techniques a therapist uses that make a therapeutic difference; rather, it is the quality of the client–therapist relationship that heals (Elkins, 2016). It is essential that therapists reach sufficient depth and openness in their own lives to allow them to venture into their clients' subjective world without losing their own sense of identity. Presence is both a condition for therapy to occur and a goal of therapy. Existential therapists strive to be authentic and self-disclosing in their therapy work. Because this approach focuses on the goals of therapy, basic conditions of being human, and therapy as a shared journey, practitioners are not bound by specific techniques. Although existential therapists may apply techniques from other orientations, their interventions are guided by a philosophical framework about what it means to be human.

Contributions of the Existential Approach

The existential approach has helped bring the person back into central **LO10** focus. It concentrates on the central facts of human existence: self-consciousness and our consequent freedom. To the existentialist goes the credit for providing a new view of death as a positive force, not a morbid prospect to fear, for death gives life meaning. Existentialists have contributed a new dimension to the understanding of anxiety, guilt, frustration, loneliness, and alienation.

I particularly appreciate the way Deurzen (2012) views the existential practitioner as a mentor and fellow traveler who encourages people to reflect upon the problems they encounter in living. What clients need is "some assistance in surveying the terrain and in deciding on the right route so that they can again find their way" (p. 30). The existential approach encourages people to live life by their own standards and values.

One of the major contributions of the existential approach is its emphasis on the human quality of the therapeutic relationship. This aspect lessens the chances of dehumanizing psychotherapy by making it a mechanical process. Existential counselors reject the notions of therapeutic objectivity and professional distance, viewing them as being unhelpful.

I very much value the existential emphasis on freedom and responsibility and the person's capacity to redesign his or her life by choosing with awareness. This perspective provides a sound philosophical base on which to build a personal and unique therapeutic style because it addresses itself to the core struggles of the contemporary person.

Contributions to the Integration of Psychotherapies From my perspective, the key concepts of the existential approach can be integrated into most therapeutic schools. Regardless of a therapist's orientation, the foundation for practice can be based on existential themes. Existential psychotherapy continues to have an enduring impact on a variety of psychological practices. "Indeed, existential psychotherapy is in the ironic position of being one of the most widely influential yet least officially embraced orientations on the professional scene" (Schneider, 2008, p. 1).

A key contribution is the possibility of a creative integration of the conceptual propositions of existential therapy with many other therapeutic orientations (Bugental & Bracke, 1992; Schneider, 2008, 2011; Schneider & Krug, 2010). One example of such a creative integration is provided by Dattilio (2002), who integrates cognitive behavioral techniques with the themes of an existential approach. As a cognitive behavior therapist and author, Dattilio maintains that he directs much of his efforts to "helping clients make a deep existential shift—to a new understanding of the world" (p. 75). He uses techniques such as restructuring of belief systems, relaxation methods, and a variety of cognitive and behavioral strategies, but he does so within an existential framework that can begin the process of real-life transformation. Many of his clients suffer from panic attacks or depression. Dattilio often explores with these people existential themes of meaning, guilt, hopelessness, anxiety—and at the same time he provides them with cognitive behavioral tools to cope with the problems of daily living. In short, he grounds symptomatic treatment in an existential approach.

Some people have argued that the new trend toward positive psychology is similar to the existential approach, but this rests on a superficial comparison of these two approaches. Existential therapists favor intensity and passionate experience, including that of happiness, but they equally value the darker side of human nature and would encourage clients to learn to value both sides of their experience (Deurzen, 2009).

Limitations and Criticisms of the Existential Approach

A major criticism often aimed at this approach is that it lacks a systematic statement of the principles and practices of psychotherapy. Some practitioners have trouble with what they perceive as its mystical language and concepts. Some therapists who claim adherence to an existential orientation describe their therapeutic style in vague and global terms such as *self-actualization, dialogic encounter, authenticity*, and *being in the world*. This particular use of language causes confusion at times and makes it difficult to conduct research on the process or outcomes of existential therapy.

Both beginning and advanced practitioners who are not of a philosophical turn of mind tend to find many of the existential concepts lofty and elusive. As we have seen, this approach places primary emphasis on a subjective understanding of the world of clients. It is assumed that techniques follow understanding. The fact that few techniques are generated by this approach makes it essential for practitioners to develop their own innovative procedures or to borrow from other schools of therapy. For counselors who believe they need a specific set of techniques to counsel effectively, this approach has limitations (Vontress, 2013).

Practitioners who prefer a counseling practice based on research contend that the concepts should be empirically sound, that definitions should be operational, that the hypotheses should be testable, and that therapeutic practice should be based on the results of research into both the process and outcomes of counseling. Certainly, the notions of manualized therapy and evidence-based practice are not part of the existential perspective because every psychotherapy experience is unique (Walsh & McElwain, 2002). According to Cooper (2003), existential practitioners generally reject the idea that the therapeutic process can be measured and evaluated in quantitative and empirical ways. Although existential practices are generally upheld in recent research on therapeutic effectiveness (see Elkins, 2009), few studies directly evaluate and examine the existential approach. To a large extent, existential therapy makes use of techniques from other theories, which makes it difficult to apply research to thiss approach to study its effectiveness (Sharf, 2016).

According to Deurzen (2002), the main limitation of this approach is that of the level of maturity, life experience, and intensive training required of practitioners. Existential therapists need to be wise and capable of profound and wide-ranging understanding of what it means to be human. Authenticity is a cardinal characteristic of a competent existential practitioner, which is certainly more involved than mastering a body of knowledge and acquiring technical skills. Russell (2007) puts this notion nicely: "Authenticity means being able to sign your own name on your work and your life. It means you will want to take responsibility for creating your own way of being a therapist" (p. 123).

Self-Reflection and Discussion Questions

1. Identify at least one turning point in your life. What decision did you make at this time, and how has this influenced the person you are today?
2. What does existential anxiety mean to you? How do you deal with this kind of anxiety in your life?
3. Existential therapy provides a philosophy and a framework for psychotherapy, but few techniques. How can you have an existential orientation and at the same time incorporate techniques from other therapy models?
4. Existential themes have relevance for working with a range of clients with a variety of problems in various settings. What one existential theme do you believe is a key issue for many people today?
5. How would you work with a client who has little interest in exploring existential themes and asks for advice on how to deal with some concrete problem?

Where to Go From Here

Refer to the *DVD for Integrative Counseling: The Case of Ruth and Lecturettes*, Session 11 ("Understanding How the Past Influences the Present and the Future"), for a demonstration of ways I utilize existential notions in counseling Ruth. We engage in a role play where Ruth becomes the voice of her church and I take on a new role as Ruth—one in which I have been willing to challenge certain beliefs from church. This segment illustrates how I assist Ruth in finding new values. In Session 12 ("Working Toward Decisions and Behavioral Changes") I challenge Ruth to make new decisions, which is also an existential concept.

Free Podcasts for ACA Members

You can download ACA Podcasts (prerecorded interviews) at www.counseling.org; click on the Resource button and then the Podcast Series. For Chapter 6, Existential Therapy, look for Podcast 14 by Dr. Gerald Corey.

Other Resources

The American Psychological Association offers a DVD by K. J. Schneider (2009) titled *Existential-Humanistic Therapy* in their Systems of Psychotherapy Video Series.

Psychotherapy.net is a comprehensive resource for students and professionals that offers videos and interviews on existential therapy featuring Irvin Yalom, James Bugental, and Rollo May. New video and editorial content is made available monthly. DVDs relevant to this chapter are available at www.psychotherapy.net and include the following:

Bugental, J. F. T. (1995). *Existential-Humanistic Psychotherapy in Action*

Bugental, J. (1997). *Existential-Humanistic Psychotherapy* (Psychotherapy with the Experts Series)

Bugental, J. (2008). *James Bugental: Live Case Consultation*

May, R. (2007). *Rollo May on Existential Psychotherapy*

Yalom, I. (2002). *The Gift of Therapy: A Conversation with Irvin Yalom, MD*

Yalom, I. (2006). *Irvin Yalom: Live Case Consultation*

Yalom, I. (2011). *Confronting Death and Other Existential Issues in Psychotherapy*

If you are interesting in further information on Irvin Yalom, check out his website.

Irvin Yalon
www.yalom.com

The Existential-Humanistic Institute's (EHI) primary focus is training; the institute offers courses and, in conjunction with Saybrook University, a new certificate program in existential-humanistic therapy and theory. A secondary focus is community building. EHI was formed as a nonprofit organization under the auspices of the Pacific Institute in 1997 and provides a home for those mental health professionals, scholars, and students who seek in-depth training in existential-humanistic theory and practice. EHI's year-long certificate program offers graduate and postgraduate students an opportunity to gain a basic foundation in the theory and practice of existential-humanistic therapy. EHI offers courses on the principles of existential-humanistic practice and case seminars in existential-humanistic theory and practice. Most of EHI's instructors have studied extensively with such masters as James Bugental, Irvin Yalom, and Rollo May, and are, like Kirk Schneider and Orah Krug, acknowledged leaders of the existential-humanistic movement today.

The Existential-Humanistic Institute
www.ehinstitute.org

The Society for Existential Analysis is a professional organization devoted to exploring issues pertaining to an existential/phenomenological approach to counseling and therapy. Membership is open to anyone interested in this approach and includes students, trainees, psychotherapists, philosophers, psychiatrists, counselors, and psychologists. Members receive a regular newsletter and an annual copy of the *Journal of the Society for Existential Analysis*. The society provides a list of existentially oriented psychotherapists for referral purposes The School of Psychotherapy and Counselling at Regent's University in London offers an advanced diploma in existential psychotherapy as well as short courses in the field. Additional Information is available at www.dilemmas.org.

Society for Existential Analysis
www.existentialanalysis.co.uk/

The International Society for Existential Psychotherapy and Counselling was created in London in July 2006 and was renamed International Collaborative of Existential Counselors and Psychotherapists soon after (www.icecap.org.uk). It brings together the existing national societies as well as providing a forum for the development and accreditation of the approach.

International Society for Existential Psychotherapy and Counselling
www.existentialpsychotherapy.net

SEPTIMUS is an Internet-based course taught in Ireland, Iceland, Sweden, Poland, Czech Republic, Romania, Italy, Portugal, Austria, Belgium, France, Israel, Australia, and the United Kingdom. Additional Information is available at www.psychotherapytraining.net.

Psychotherapy Training on the Net: SEPTIMUS
www.septimus.info

The New School of Psychotherapy and Counselling (NSPC) now offers two doctoral programs: one in existential psychotherapy and one in existential counselling psychology. NSPC offers intensive courses for distance learners (worldwide student body) including e-learning.

New School of Psychotherapy and Counselling
www.nspc.org.uk

Recommended Supplementary Readings

Everyday Mysteries: A Handbook of Existential Psychotherapy (Deurzen, 2010) provides a framework for practicing counseling from an existential perspective. The author puts into clear perspective topics such as anxiety, authentic living, clarifying one's worldview, determining values, discovering meaning, and coming to terms with life.

Existential Counselling and Psychotherapy in Practice (Deurzen, 2012) offers an excellent presentation of the theory and practice of existential therapy based on the European tradition. The author provides a framework for addressing problems in living rather than techniques for working with clients.

Skills in Existential Counselling and Psychotherapy (Deurzen & Adams, 2011) is a clearly written book that explains the existential attitude, highlights the importance of the person of the therapist, and describes the process of existential therapy. This is a superb resource that provides a basis for understanding how to apply existential notions to therapeutic practice.

Existential Therapies (Cooper, 2003) provides a useful and clear introduction to the existential therapies. There are separate chapters on logotherapy, the British school of existential analysis, the American existential-humanistic approach, dimensions of existential therapeutic practice, and brief existential therapies.

Existential Psychotherapy (Yalom, 1980) is a superb treatment of the ultimate human concerns of death, freedom, isolation, and meaninglessness as these issues relate to therapy. This book has depth and clarity, and it is rich with clinical examples that illustrate existential themes.

Existential-Humanistic Therapy (Schneider & Krug, 2010) is a clear presentation of the theory and practice of existential-humanistic therapy. This approach incorporates techniques from other contemporary therapeutic approaches.

Existential-Integrative Psychotherapy: Guideposts to the Core of Practice (Schneider, 2008) is an edited book that offers recent and future trends in existential-integrative therapy and case illustrations of this model.

I Never Knew I Had a Choice (Corey & Corey, 2014) is a self-help book written from an existential perspective. Topics include our struggle to achieve autonomy; the meaning of loneliness, death, and loss; and how we choose our values and philosophy of life.

Person-Centered Therapy

7

LEARNING OBJECTIVES

1. Examine the evolution of person-centered therapy over time.
2. Describe the main thrust of emotion-focused therapy.
3. Differentiate the contributions of Carl Rogers and Abraham Maslow to humanistic psychology.
4. Understand the role of the therapist's attitudes in the therapy process.
5. Describe the ways that empathy, unconditional positive regard, and genuineness are fundamental to the process and outcome of therapy.
6. Identify the personal characteristics of therapists that are essential for clients' progress.
7. Examine the application of the person-centered approach to crisis intervention.
8. Understand the unique characteristics of person-centered expressive arts and how it is based on person-centered philosophy.
9. Examine the key concepts and principles of motivational interviewing and the stages of change.
10. Recognize the contributions and shortcomings of the person-centered approach to understanding and working with clients from diverse cultures.
11. Identify the contributions and limitations of the person-centered approach.

Carl Rogers

CARL ROGERS (1902–1987), a major spokesperson for humanistic psychology, led a life that reflected the ideas he developed for half a century. He showed a questioning stance, a deep openness to change, and the courage to forge into unknown territory both as a person and as a professional. In writing about his early years, Rogers (1961) recalled his family atmosphere as characterized by close and warm relationships but also by strict religious standards. Play was discouraged, and the virtues of the Protestant ethic were extolled. His boyhood was somewhat lonely, and he pursued scholarly interests instead of social ones. Rogers was an introverted person, and he spent a lot of time reading and engaging in imaginative activity and reflection. During his college years his interests and academic major changed from agriculture to history, then to religion, and finally to clinical psychology.

Rogers held academic positions in various fields, including education, social work, counseling, psychotherapy, group therapy, peace, and interpersonal relations, and he earned recognition around the world for originating and developing the humanistic movement in psychotherapy. His foundational ideas, especially the central role of the client–therapist relationship as a means to growth and change, have been incorporated in many other theoretical approaches. Rogers's ideas continue to have far-reaching effects on the field of psychotherapy (Cain, 2010).

It is difficult to overestimate the significance of Rogers's contributions to clinical and counseling psychology. He was a courageous pioneer who "was about 50 years ahead of his time and has been waiting for us to catch up" (Elkins, 2009, p. 20). Often called the "father of psychotherapy research," Rogers was the first to study the counseling process in depth by analyzing the transcripts of actual therapy sessions, and he was the first clinician to conduct major studies on psychotherapy using quantitative methods. He was the first to formulate a comprehensive theory of personality and psychotherapy grounded in empirical research, and he contributed to developing a theory of psychotherapy that focused on the strengths and resources of individuals. He was not afraid to take a strong position and challenged the status quo throughout his professional career.

During the last 15 years of his life, Rogers applied the person-centered approach to world peace by training policymakers, leaders, and groups in conflict. Perhaps his greatest passion was directed toward the reduction of interracial tensions and the effort to achieve world peace, for which he was nominated for the Nobel Peace Prize.

For a detailed video presentation of the life and works of Carl Rogers, see *Carl Rogers: A Daughter's Tribute* (N. Rogers, 2002), which is described at the end of this chapter. For an in-depth look at this remarkable man and his work, see *Carl Rogers: The Quiet Revolutionary* (Rogers & Russell, 2002) and *The Life and Work of Carl Rogers* (Kirschenbaum, 2009).

Natalie Rogers

NATALIE ROGERS (b. 1928) is a pioneer in the field of person-centered expressive arts therapy. She expanded on her father's (Carl Rogers) theory of creativity by using the expressive arts to enhance personal growth for individuals and groups. **Person-centered expressive arts therapy** employs a variety of forms—movement, painting, sculpting, music, writing, and improvisation—in a supportive setting to facilitate growth and healing. It extends person-centered theory by helping individuals access their feelings through creative expressions. N. Rogers has developed the concept of the **Creative Connection**®—a process whereby the client or group member is invited to access inner feelings through an uninterrupted sequence of movement, sound, visual art, and journal writing. As the client moves through this process, hidden or unconscious aspects of self are discovered, and these insights are shared with the therapist.

N. Rogers's work evolved from what she felt was lacking in her father's theory. As a woman growing up in an era when females were meant to be accommodating to men, she eventually discovered her underlying anger at being a second-class citizen. Her art was one vehicle to express and gain insight into this injustice. She also expressed her anger at her father because he was unknowingly a part of the patriarchal system. He was surprised but open to learning. After hearing about the role he and other men played in holding women back, he changed many of his ways of being and writing.

Today, at 87 years of age, N. Rogers continues to find ways to bring meaning to her personal and professional life. During the past 10 years she taught and facilitated workshops in the United States, England, Hong Kong, Latin America, Russia, and South Korea. She continues to participate in teaching the six-week expressive arts certificate program at Sofia University in northern California. See the resources section at the end of this chapter if you are interested in training in the person-centered approach to expressive arts therapy.

Introduction

Of all the pioneers who have founded a therapeutic approach, for me Carl Rogers stands out as one of the most influential figures in revolutionizing the direction of counseling theory and practice. Rogers has become known as a "quiet revolutionary" who both contributed to theory development and whose influence continues to shape counseling practice today (see Cain, 2010; Kirschenbaum, 2009; Rogers & Russell, 2002).

The person-centered approach shares many concepts and values with the existential perspective presented in Chapter 6. Rogers's basic assumptions are that people are essentially trustworthy, that they have a vast potential for understanding themselves and resolving their own problems without direct intervention on the therapist's part, and that they are capable of self-directed growth if they are involved in a specific kind of therapeutic relationship. From the beginning, Rogers emphasized the attitudes and personal characteristics of the therapist and the quality of the client–therapist relationship as the prime determinants of the outcome of the therapeutic process. He consistently relegated to a secondary position matters such as the therapist's knowledge of theory and techniques. This belief in the client's capacity for self-healing is in contrast with many theories that view the therapist's techniques as the most powerful agents that lead to change (Bohart & Tallman, 2010). Clearly, Rogers revolutionized the field of psychotherapy by proposing a theory that centered on the client as the primary agent for constructive self-change (Bohart & Tallman, 2010; Bozarth, Zimring, & Tausch, 2002; Elkins, 2016).

Contemporary person-centered therapy is the result of an evolutionary process that continues to remain open to change and refinement (see Cain, 2010; Cain & Seeman, 2002). Rogers did not present the person-centered theory as a fixed and completed approach to therapy. He hoped that others would view his theory as a set of tentative principles relating to how the therapy process develops, not as dogma. Rogers expected his model to evolve and was open and receptive to change.

Visit CengageBrain.com or watch the DVD for the video program on Chapter 7, *Theory and Practice of Counseling and Psychotherapy: The Case of Stan and Lecturettes*. I suggest that you view the brief lecture for each chapter prior to reading the chapter.

Four Periods of Development of the Approach

In tracing the major turning points in Rogers's approach, Zimring and LO1 Raskin (1992) and Bozarth, Zimring, and Tausch (2002) have identified four periods of development. In the first period, during the 1940s, Rogers developed what was known as *nondirective counseling,* which provided a powerful and revolutionary alternative to the directive and interpretive approaches to therapy then being practiced. While he was a professor at Ohio State University, Rogers (1942) published *Counseling and Psychotherapy: Newer Concepts in Practice,* which described the philosophy and practice of nondirective counseling. Rogers's theory emphasized the counselor's creation of a permissive and nondirective climate. When he challenged the basic assumption that "the counselor knows best," he realized this radical idea would affect the power dynamics and politics of the counseling profession, and indeed it caused a great furor (Elkins, 2009).

Rogers also challenged the validity of commonly accepted therapeutic procedures such as advice, suggestion, direction, persuasion, teaching, diagnosis, and interpretation. Based on his conviction that diagnostic concepts and procedures were inadequate, prejudicial, and often misused, Rogers omitted them from his approach. Nondirective counselors avoided sharing a great deal about themselves with clients and instead focused mainly on reflecting and clarifying the clients' verbal communications and intended meanings.

In the second period, during the 1950s, Rogers (1951) renamed his approach *client-centered therapy,* which reflected his emphasis on the *client* rather than on nondirective methods. In addition, he started the Counseling Center at the University of Chicago. This period was characterized by a shift from clarification of feelings to a focus on the phenomenological world of the client. Rogers assumed that the best vantage point for understanding how people behave was from their own internal frame of reference. He focused more explicitly on the actualizing tendency as the basic motivational force that leads to client change.

The third period, which began in the late 1950s and extended into the 1970s, addressed the necessary and sufficient conditions of therapy. Rogers (1957) set forth a hypothesis that resulted in three decades of research. A significant publication was *On Becoming a Person* (C. Rogers, 1961), which addressed the nature of "becoming the self that one truly is," an idea he borrowed from Kierkegaard. Rogers published this work during the time that he held joint appointments in the departments of psychology and psychiatry at the University of Wisconsin. In this book he described the process of "becoming one's experience," which is characterized by an openness to experience, a trust in one's experience, an internal locus of evaluation, and the willingness to be in process. During the 1950s and 1960s, Rogers and his associates continued to test the underlying hypotheses of the client-centered approach by conducting extensive research on both the process and the outcomes of psychotherapy. He was interested in how people best progress in psychotherapy, and he studied the qualities of the client–therapist relationship as a catalyst leading to personality change.

Rogers and his associates at the University of Chicago conducted research to identify the ingredients in psychotherapy that account for therapeutic change. The client-centered approach emphasized the role of the therapist as a facilitator of growth and honored the inherent power of the client. Research findings consistently supported this approach, confirming that therapeutic change is due to personal and interpersonal factors rather than to specific techniques for curing specific disorders (Elkins, 2016). On the basis of this research, the approach was further refined and expanded (C. Rogers, 1961). For example, client-centered philosophy was applied to education and was called *student-centered teaching* (C. Rogers & Freiberg, 1994). The approach was also applied to encounter groups (C. Rogers, 1970).

The fourth phase, during the 1980s and the 1990s, was marked by considerable expansion to education, couples and families, industry, groups, conflict resolution, politics, and the search for world peace. Because of Rogers's ever-widening scope of influence, including his interest in how people obtain, possess, share, or surrender power and control over others and themselves, his theory became known as the *person-centered approach*. This shift in terms reflected the broadening application of the approach. Although the person-centered approach has been applied mainly to individual and group counseling, important areas of further application include education, family life, leadership and administration, organizational development, health care, cross-cultural and interracial activity, and international relations. During the 1980s Rogers directed his efforts toward applying the person-centered approach to politics, especially to efforts related to the achievement of world peace.

In a comprehensive review of the research on person-centered therapy over a period of 60 years, Bozarth, Zimring, and Tausch (2002) concluded the following:

- In the earliest years of the approach, the client rather than the therapist determined the direction and goals of therapy and the therapist's role was to help the client clarify feelings. This style of nondirective therapy was associated with increased understanding, greater self-exploration, and improved self-concepts.
- Later a shift from clarification of feelings to a focus on the client's lived experiences took place.
- As person-centered therapy developed further, research centered on the core conditions assumed to be both necessary and sufficient for successful therapy. The attitude of the therapist—an empathic understanding of the client's world and the ability to communicate a non-judgmental stance to the client—along with the therapist's genuineness were found to be basic to a successful therapy outcome.
- The main source of successful psychotherapy is the client. The therapist's attention to the client's frame of reference fosters the client's utilization of inner and outer resources.

Emotion-Focused Therapy

Emotion-focused therapy (EFT) emerged as a person-centered "approach informed by understanding the role of emotion in human functioning and psychotherapeutic change" (Greenberg, 2014, p. 15). Leslie Greenberg, a prominent figure in the development of this integrative approach, states that EFT is designed to help clients increase their awareness of their emotions and make productive use of them. Like person-centered therapists, emotion-focused therapists establish a therapeutic LO2 relationship based on the core therapeutic conditions. Once the therapeutic alliance is created, however, the EFT practitioner actively works with emotions using a range of experiential techniques to strengthen the self, regulate affect, and create new meaning. New narratives can be created that disrupt maladaptive past emotional schemas, which provides opportunities for positive emotional experiencing (McDonald, 2015).

EFT strategies focus on two major tasks: (1) help clients with too little emotion access their emotions, and (2) help clients who experience too much emotion contain their emotions (Greenberg, 2014). Many traditional therapies emphasize conscious understanding and cognitive and behavioral change, but they often neglect the foundational role of emotional change. A main goal of EFT is to help individuals access and process emotions to construct new ways of being. This approach has a good deal to offer with respect to teaching us about the role of emotion in personal change and how emotional change can be a primary pathway to cognitive and behavioral change (Greenberg, 2014).

EFT emphasizes the importance of awareness, acceptance, and understanding the visceral experience of emotion. Greenberg (2014) believes that our emotions cannot be change merely by talking about them, understanding their origins, or by modifying our beliefs. Clients are encouraged to identify, experience, accept, express, explore, transform, and manage their emotions. The act of experiencing feelings and replacing old feelings with new positive feelings offers a corrective emotional experience. "One changes emotions by accepting and experiencing them, by opposing them with different emotions to transform them, and by reflecting on them to create new narrative meaning" (p. 18).

Both psychoanalytic and cognitive behavioral approaches are increasingly focusing on emotions and are rapidly assimilating many aspects of EFT. Gestalt therapy has always emphasized experiencing and exploring emotions. McDonald (2015) reports that a strength of EFT is that it is an empirically validated brief therapeutic approach with demonstrated effectiveness in treating anxiety, intimate partner violence, eating disorders, and trauma. EFT is being applied to counseling individuals, groups, couples, families, and in working in diverse cultural contexts.

The theory and practice of EFT are only briefly discussed in this chapter. For an in-depth discussion of the principles and techniques involved in the practice of EFT, see Greenberg (2011), *Emotion-Focused Therapy*.

Existentialism and Humanism

In the 1960s and 1970s there was a growing interest among counselors in a "third force" in therapy as an alternative to the psychoanalytic and behavioral approaches. Under this heading fall existential therapy (Chapter 6), person-centered therapy (Chapter 7), Gestalt therapy (Chapter 8), and certain other experiential and relationship-oriented approaches.

The connections between the terms *existentialism* and *humanism* have tended to be confusing for students and theorists alike. The two viewpoints have much in common, yet there also are significant philosophical differences between them. They share a respect for the client's subjective experience, the uniqueness and individuality of each client, and a trust in the capacity of the client to make positive and constructive conscious choices. They have in common an emphasis on concepts such as freedom, choice, values, personal responsibility, autonomy, purpose, and meaning. Both approaches place little value on the role of techniques in the therapeutic process and emphasize instead the importance of genuine encounter.

They differ in that existentialists take the position that we are faced with the anxiety of choosing to create an identity in a world that lacks intrinsic meaning. Existentialists tend to acknowledge the stark realities of human experience, and their writings often focus on death, anxiety, meaninglessness, and isolation. The humanists, in contrast, take the somewhat less anxiety-evoking and more optimistic view that each of us has a natural potential that we can actualize and through which we can find meaning. Many contemporary existential therapists refer to themselves as *existential-humanistic* practitioners, indicating that their roots are in existential philosophy but that they have incorporated many aspects of North American humanistic psychotherapies (Cain, 2002a; Schneider & Krug, 2010).

As will become evident in this chapter, the existential and person-centered approaches have parallel concepts with regard to the client–therapist relationship being at the core of therapy. The phenomenological emphasis that is basic to the existentialist approach is also fundamental to person-centered theory. Both approaches focus on the client's perceptions and call for the therapist to be fully present with the client so that it is possible to understand the client's subjective world, and they both emphasize the client's capacity for self-awareness and self-healing. The therapist aims to provide the client with a safe, responsive, and caring relationship to facilitate self-exploration, growth, and healing (Watson, Goldman, & Greenberg, 2011).

Abraham Maslow's Contributions to Humanistic Psychology

LO3

Abraham Maslow (1970) was a pioneer in the development of humanistic psychology and was influential in furthering the understanding of self-actualizing individuals. Many of Carl Rogers's ideas, especially on the positive aspects of being human and the fully functioning person, are influenced by Maslow's basic philosophy. Maslow criticized Freudian psychology for what he saw as its preoccupation with the sick and dark side of human nature. Maslow believed too much research was being conducted on anxiety, hostility, and neuroses and too little into joy, creativity, and self-fulfillment. Self-actualization was the central theme of the work of Abraham Maslow (1968, 1970, 1971). The *positive psychology* movement that recently has come into prominence shares many concepts on the healthy side of human existence with the humanistic approach.

Maslow studied what he called "self-actualizing people" and found that they differed in important ways from so-called normal individuals. The core characteristics of self-actualizing people are self-awareness, freedom, basic honesty and caring, and trust and autonomy. Other characteristics of self-actualizing individuals include a capacity to welcome uncertainty in their lives, acceptance of themselves and others, spontaneity and creativity, a need for privacy and solitude, autonomy, a capacity for deep and intense interpersonal relationships, a genuine caring for others, an inner-directedness (as opposed to the tendency to live by others' expectations), the absence of artificial dichotomies within themselves (such as work/play, love/hate, and weak/strong), and a sense of humor (Maslow, 1970). All of these personal characteristics are compatible with the person-centered philosophy.

Maslow postulated a *hierarchy of needs* as a source of motivation, with the most basic needs being physiological needs. If we are hungry and thirsty, our attention is riveted on meeting these basic needs. Next are the safety needs, which include a sense of security and stability. Once our physical and safety needs are fulfilled, we become concerned with meeting our needs for belonging and love, followed by our need for esteem, both from self and others. We are able to strive toward self-actualization only after these four basic needs are met. The key factor determining which need is dominant at a given time is the degree to which those below it are satisfied.

The Vision of Humanistic Philosophy The underlying vision of humanistic philosophy is captured by the metaphor of how an acorn, if provided with the appropriate conditions, will "automatically" grow in positive ways, pushed naturally toward its actualization as an oak. In contrast, for many existentialists there is nothing that we "are," no internal "nature" we can count on. We are faced at every moment with a choice about what to make of this condition. Maslow's emphasis on the healthy side of being human and the emphasis on joy, creativity, and self-fulfillment are part of the person-centered philosophy. The humanistic philosophy on which the person-centered approach rests is expressed in attitudes and behaviors that create a growth-producing climate. According to Rogers (1986b), when this philosophy is lived, it helps people develop their capacities and stimulates constructive change in others. Individuals are empowered, and they are able to use this power for personal and social transformation.

Key Concepts

View of Human Nature

A common theme originating in Rogers's early writing and continuing to permeate all of his works is a basic sense of trust in the client's ability to move forward in a constructive manner if conditions fostering growth are present. His professional experience taught him that if one is able to get to the core of an individual, one finds a trustworthy, positive center (C. Rogers, 1987a). In keeping with the philosophy of humanistic psychology, Rogers firmly maintained that people are trustworthy, resourceful, capable of self-understanding and self-direction, able to make constructive changes, and able to live effective and productive lives. When therapists are able to experience and communicate their realness, support, caring, and nonjudgmental understanding, significant changes in the client are most likely to occur.

Rogers maintained that three therapist attributes create a growth-promoting climate in which individuals can move forward and become what they are capable of becoming: (1) *congruence* (genuineness, or realness), (2) *unconditional positive regard* (acceptance and caring), and (3) *accurate empathic understanding* (an ability to deeply grasp the subjective world of another person). According to Rogers, if therapists communicate these attitudes, those being helped will become less defensive and more open to themselves and their world, and they will behave in prosocial and constructive ways.

The **actualizing tendency** is a directional process of striving toward realization, fulfillment, autonomy, and self-determination. This natural inclination of humans is based on Maslow's (1970) studies of self-actualizing people, and it has significant implications for the practice of therapy. Because of the belief that the individual has an inherent capacity to move away from maladjustment and toward psychological health and growth, the therapist places the primary responsibility on the client. The person-centered approach rejects the role of the therapist as the authority who knows best and of the passive client who depends on the therapist's expertise. Therapy is rooted in the client's capacity for awareness and self-directed change in attitudes and behavior.

The person-centered approach emphasizes clients' abilities to engage their own resources to act in their world with others. Clients can move forward in constructive directions and successfully deal with obstacles (both from within themselves and outside of themselves) that are blocking their growth. By promoting self-awareness and self-reflection, clients learn to exercise choice. Humanistic therapists emphasize a discovery-oriented approach in which clients are the experts on their own inner experience (Watson et al., 2011), and they encourage clients to make changes that will lead to living fully and authentically, with the realization that this kind of existence demands a continuing struggle.

The Therapeutic Process

Therapeutic Goals

Rogers did not believe the goal of therapy was merely to solve problems. Rather, the goal is to assist clients in achieving a greater degree of independence and integration so they can better cope with problems as they identify them. Before clients are able to work toward that goal, they must first get behind the masks they wear, which they develop through the process of socialization. Clients come to recognize that they have lost contact with themselves by using facades. In a climate of safety in the therapeutic session, they also come to realize that there are more authentic ways of being. The therapist does not choose specific goals for the client. The cornerstone of person-centered theory is the view that clients in a relationship with a facilitating therapist have the capacity to define and clarify their own goals. Person-centered therapists are in agreement on the matter of not setting goals for *what* clients need to change, yet they differ on the matter of *how* to best help clients achieve their own goals and to find their own answers (Bohart & Watson, 2011).

Therapist's Function and Role

The role of person-centered therapists is rooted in their ways of being and attitudes, not in techniques designed to get the client to "do something." Research on person-centered therapy indicates that the attitude of therapists, rather than their knowledge, theories, or techniques, facilitate personality change in clients (C. Rogers, 1961). Basically, therapists use themselves as an instrument of change by encountering clients on a person-to-person level. In examining the human elements of psychotherapy, Elkins (2016) concludes that the human dimensions are more powerful determinants of therapeutic effectiveness than theories or techniques. It is the therapist's attitude and belief in the inner resources of the client that creates the therapeutic climate for growth (Bozarth et al., 2002). LO4

Person-centered theory holds that the therapist's function is to be present and accessible to clients and to focus on their immediate experience. First and foremost, the therapist must be willing to be real in the relationship with clients. By being congruent, accepting, and empathic, the therapist is a catalyst for change. Instead of viewing clients in preconceived diagnostic categories, the therapist meets them on a moment-to-moment experiential basis and enters their world. Through the therapist's attitude of genuine caring, respect, acceptance, support, and understanding, clients are able to loosen their defenses and rigid perceptions and move to a higher level of personal functioning. When these therapist attitudes are present, clients then have the necessary freedom to explore areas of their life that were either denied to awareness or distorted.

Client's Experience in Therapy

Therapeutic change depends on clients' perceptions both of their own experience in therapy and of the counselor's basic attitudes. If the counselor creates a climate conducive to self-exploration, clients have the opportunity to explore the full range of their experience, which includes their feelings, beliefs, behavior, and worldview. What follows is a general sketch of clients' experiences in therapy.

Clients come to the counselor in a state of incongruence; that is, a discrepancy exists between their self-perception and their experience in reality. For example, Leon, a college student, may see himself as a future physician, yet his below-average grades could exclude him from medical school. The discrepancy between how Leon sees himself (self-concept) or how he would *like* to view himself (ideal self-concept) and the reality of his poor academic performance may result in anxiety and personal vulnerability, which can provide the necessary motivation to enter therapy. Leon must perceive that a problem exists or, at least, that he is uncomfortable enough with his present psychological adjustment to want to explore possibilities for change.

One reason clients seek therapy is a feeling of basic helplessness, powerlessness, and an inability to make decisions or effectively direct their own lives. They may hope to find "the way" through the guidance of the therapist. Within the person-centered framework, however, clients soon learn that they can be responsible for themselves in the relationship and that they can learn to be more free by using the relationship to gain greater self-understanding.

As counseling progresses, clients are able to explore a wider range of beliefs and feelings. They can express their fears, anxiety, guilt, shame, hatred, anger, and other emotions that they had deemed too negative to accept and incorporate into their self-structure. With therapy, people distort less and move to a greater acceptance and integration of conflicting and confusing feelings. They increasingly discover aspects within themselves that had been kept hidden. As clients feel understood and accepted, they become less defensive and become more open to their experience. Because they feel safer and are less vulnerable, they become more realistic, perceive others with greater accuracy, and become better able to understand and accept others. Individuals in therapy come to appreciate themselves more as they are, and their behavior shows more flexibility and creativity. They become less concerned about meeting others' expectations, and thus begin to behave in ways that are truer to themselves. These individuals direct their own lives instead of looking outside of themselves for answers. They move in the direction of being more in contact with what they are experiencing at the present moment, less bound by the past, less determined, freer to make decisions, and increasingly trusting in themselves to manage their own lives. In short, their experience in therapy is like throwing off the self-imposed shackles that had kept them in a psychological prison. With increased freedom, they tend to become more mature psychologically and move toward increased self-actualization.

Person-centered therapy is grounded on the assumption that clients create their own self-growth and are active self-healers (Bohart & Tallman, 1999, 2010; Bohart & Wade, 2013; Bohart & Watson, 2011). The therapy relationship provides a supportive structure within which clients' self-healing capacities are activated. What clients value most is being understood and accepted, which results in creating a safe place to explore feelings, thoughts, behaviors, and experiences; clients also value support for trying out new behaviors (Bohart & Tallman, 2010).

Relationship Between Therapist and Client

Rogers (1957) based his hypothesis of the "necessary and sufficient conditions for therapeutic personality change" on the quality of the relationship: "If I can provide a certain type of relationship, the other person will discover within himself or herself the capacity to use that relationship for growth and change, and personal development will occur" (C. Rogers, 1961, p. 33). Rogers (1967) hypothesized further that "significant positive personality change does not occur except in a relationship" (p. 73). Rogers's hypothesis was formulated on the basis of many years of his professional experience, and it remains basically unchanged to this day. LO5

1. Two persons are in psychological contact.
2. The first, whom we shall term the client, is in a state of incongruence, being vulnerable or anxious.
3. The second person, whom we term the therapist, is congruent (real or genuine) in the relationship, and this congruence is perceived by the client.
4. The therapist experiences unconditional positive regard for the client.
5. The therapist experiences an empathic understanding of the client's internal frame of reference and endeavors to communicate this experience to the client.
6. The communication to the client of the therapist's empathic understanding and unconditional positive regard is to a minimal degree achieved. (as cited in Cain 2002a, p. 20)

Rogers hypothesized that no other conditions were necessary. If the **therapeutic core conditions** exist over some period of time, constructive personality change will occur. The core conditions do not vary according to client type. Further, they are both necessary *and* sufficient for therapeutic change to occur.

From Rogers's perspective, the client–therapist relationship is characterized by equality. Therapists do not keep their knowledge a secret or attempt to mystify the therapeutic process. The process of change in the client depends to a large degree on the quality of this equal relationship. As clients experience the therapist listening in an accepting way to them, they gradually learn how to listen acceptingly to themselves. As they find the therapist caring for and valuing them (even the aspects that have been hidden and regarded as negative), clients begin to develop worth and value in themselves. As they experience the realness of the therapist, clients drop many of their pretenses and become real with both themselves and the therapist.

This humanistic approach is perhaps best characterized as a *way of being* and as a *shared journey* in which therapist and client reveal their humanness and participate in a growth experience. The therapist can be a relational guide on this journey because he or she is usually more psychologically experienced in this role than the client. Therapists are invested in broadening their own life experiences and are willing to do what it takes to deepen their self-knowledge.

Rogers admitted that his theory was strikingly provocative and radical. His formulation has generated considerable controversy, for he maintained that many conditions other therapists commonly regard as necessary for effective psychotherapy were nonessential. The core therapist conditions of congruence, unconditional positive regard, and accurate empathic understanding subsequently have been embraced by many therapeutic schools as essential in facilitating therapeutic change. These core qualities of therapists, along with the therapist's presence, work holistically to create a safe environment for learning (Cain, 2010). Regardless of theoretical orientation, most therapists strive to listen fully and empathically to clients, especially during the initial stages of therapy. We now turn to a detailed discussion of how these core conditions are an integral part of the therapeutic relationship.

Congruence, or Genuineness **Congruence** implies that therapists are real; that is, they are genuine, integrated, and authentic during the therapy hour. They are without a false front, their inner experience and outer expression of that experience match, and they can openly express feelings, thoughts, reactions, and attitudes that are present in the relationship with the client. This communication is done with careful reflection and considered judgment on the therapist's part (Kolden, Klein, Wang, & Austin, 2011).

Through authenticity the therapist serves as a model of a human being struggling toward greater realness. Being congruent might necessitate expressing a range of feelings including anger, frustration, liking, concern, and annoyance. This does not mean that therapists should impulsively share all their reactions, for self-disclosure must be appropriate, well timed, and have a constructive therapeutic intent. Counselors can try too hard to be genuine; sharing because they think it will be good for the client, without being genuinely moved to express something regarded as personal, can be incongruent. Person-centered therapy stresses that counseling will be inhibited if the counselor feels one way about the client but acts in a different way. For example, if the practitioner dislikes or disapproves of the client but feigns acceptance, therapy will be impaired. Cain (2010) stresses that therapists need to be attuned to the emerging needs of the client and to respond in ways that are in the best interests of the individual. If therapists keep this in mind, they are likely to make sound therapeutic decisions most of the time.

Rogers's concept of congruence does not imply that only a fully self-actualized therapist can be effective in counseling. Because therapists are human, they cannot be expected to be fully authentic. Congruence exists on a continuum from highly congruent to very incongruent. This is true of all three characteristics.

Unconditional Positive Regard and Acceptance The second attitude therapists need to communicate is deep and genuine caring for the client as a person. **Unconditional positive regard** can best be achieved through empathic identification with the client (Farber & Doolin, 2011). The caring is nonpossessive and is not contaminated by evaluation or judgment of the client's feelings, thoughts, and behavior as good or bad. Therapists value and warmly accept clients without placing stipulations on their acceptance. It is not an attitude of "I'll accept you when…"; rather, it is one of "I'll accept you as you are." Therapists communicate through their behavior that they value their clients as they are and that clients are free to have feelings and experiences.

According to Rogers's (1977) research, the greater the degree of caring, prizing, accepting, and valuing of the client in a nonpossessive way, the greater the chance that therapy will be successful. He also makes it clear that it is not possible for therapists to genuinely feel acceptance and unconditional caring at all times. However, if therapists have little respect for their clients, or an active dislike or disgust, it is not likely that the therapeutic work will be fruitful. If therapists' caring stems from their own need to be liked and appreciated, constructive change in the client is inhibited. This notion of positive regard has implications for all therapists, regardless of their theoretical orientation (Farber & Doolin, 2011).

Accurate Empathic Understanding One of the main tasks of the therapist is to understand clients' experience and feelings sensitively and accurately as they are revealed in the moment-to-moment interaction during the therapy session. The therapist strives to sense clients' subjective experience, particularly in the here and now. The aim is to encourage clients to get closer to themselves, to feel more deeply and intensely, and to recognize and resolve the incongruity that exists within them.

Empathy is a deep and subjective understanding of the client *with* the client. Empathy is not sympathy, or feeling sorry for a client. Therapists are able to share the client's subjective world by drawing from their own experiences that may be similar to the client's feelings. Yet therapists must not lose their own separateness. Rogers asserts that when therapists can grasp the client's private world as the client sees and feels it—without losing the separateness of their own identity—constructive change is likely to occur. Empathy, particularly emotionally focused empathy, helps clients (1) pay attention to and value their experiencing, (2) process their experience both cognitively and bodily, (3) view prior experiences in new ways, and (4) increase their confidence in making choices and in pursuing a course of action (Cain, 2010).

Clark (2010) describes an integral model of empathy in the counseling process that is based on three ways of knowing: (1) *subjective empathy* enables practitioners to experience what it is like to be the client; (2) *interpersonal empathy* pertains to understanding a client's internal frame of reference and conveying a sense of the private meanings to the person; and (3) *objective empathy* relies on knowledge sources outside of a client's frame of reference. By using a multiple-perspective model of empathy, counselors have a broader way to understand clients.

Accurate empathy is the cornerstone of the person-centered approach, and it is a necessary ingredient of any effective therapy (Cain, 2010). **Accurate empathic understanding** implies that the therapist will sense clients' feelings *as if* they were his or her own without becoming lost in those feelings. It is a way for therapists to hear the meanings expressed by their clients that often lie at the edge of their awareness. A primary means of determining whether an individual experiences a therapist's empathy is to secure feedback from the client (Norcross, 2010).

According to Watson (2002), full empathy entails understanding the meaning and feeling of a client's experiencing. It is like grasping "what it is like to be you." Empathy is an active ingredient of change that facilitates clients' cognitive processes and emotional self-regulation. Watson's comprehensive review of the research literature on therapeutic empathy has consistently demonstrated that therapist empathy is the most potent predictor of client progress in therapy. Empathy is an essential component of successful therapy in every therapeutic modality.

Clients' perceptions of feeling understood by their therapists relate favorably to outcome. Empathic therapists strive to discover the meaning of the client's experience, understand the overall goals of the client, and tailor their responses to the particular client. Effective empathy is grounded in authentic caring for the client (Elliott, Bohart, Watson, & Greenberg, 2011).

Application: Therapeutic Techniques and Procedures

Early Emphasis on Reflection of Feelings

Rogers's original emphasis was on grasping the world of the client and reflecting this understanding. As his view of psychotherapy developed, however, his focus shifted away from an absolutist, nondirective stance and emphasized the therapist's relationship with the client. Many followers of Rogers simply imitated his reflective style, and client-centered therapy has often been identified primarily with the technique of reflection despite Rogers's contention that the therapist's relational attitudes and fundamental ways of being with the client constitute the heart of the change process. Rogers and other contributors to the development of the person-centered approach have been critical of the stereotypic view that this approach is basically a simple restatement of what the client just said.

Evolution of Person-Centered Methods

LO6

Contemporary person-centered therapy is the result of an evolutionary process of more than 70 years, and it continues to remain open to change and refinement. One of Rogers's main contributions to the counseling field is the notion that the quality of the therapeutic relationship, as opposed to administering techniques, is the primary agent of growth in the client. The therapist's ability to establish a strong connection with clients is *the* critical factor determining successful counseling outcomes.

No techniques are basic to the practice of person-centered therapy; "being with" clients and entering imaginatively into their world of perceptions and feelings is sufficient for facilitating a process of change. Person-centered therapists are not prohibited from suggesting techniques, but *how* these suggestions are presented is crucial. Some clients do better with more direction, whereas others do better in a nondirective climate (Cain, 2010). What is essential for clients' progress is the therapist's **presence**—being completely attentive to and immersed in the client as well as in the client's expressed concerns (Cain, 2010). Qualities and skills such as listening, accepting, respecting, understanding, and responding must be honest expressions by the therapist. Techniques may be suggested when doing so fosters the process of client and therapist being together in an empathic way. Techniques are not attempts at "doing anything" to a client (Bohart & Watson, 2011).

Rogers expected person-centered therapy to continue to evolve and supported others in breaking new ground. One of the main ways in which person-centered therapy has evolved is the diversity, innovation, and individualization in practice. There is no longer one way of practicing person-centered therapy (Cain, 2010), and there has been increased latitude for therapists to share their reactions, to confront clients in a caring way, and to participate more actively and fully in the therapeutic process (Bozarth et al., 2002). **Immediacy**, or addressing what is going on between the client and therapist, is highly valued in this approach. This development encourages the use of a wider variety of methods and allows for considerable diversity in personal style among person-centered therapists. The shift toward genuineness enables person-centered therapists both to practice in more flexible and integrative ways that suit their personalities and to have greater flexibility in tailoring the counseling relationship to suit different clients (Bohart & Watson, 2011).

Cain (2010, 2013) believes it is essential for therapists to adapt their therapeutic style to accommodate the unique needs of each client. Person-centered therapists have the freedom to use a variety of responses and methods to assist their clients; a guiding question therapists need to ask is, "Does it fit?" Cain contends that, ideally, therapists will continually monitor whether what they are doing fits, especially whether their therapeutic style is compatible with their clients' way of viewing and understanding their problems. For an illustration of how Dr. David Cain works with the case of Ruth in a person-centered style, see *Case Approach to Counseling and Psychotherapy* (Corey, 2013, chap. 5).

Today, those who practice a person-centered approach work in diverse ways that reflect both advances in theory and practice and a plethora of personal styles. This is appropriate and fortunate, for none of us can emulate the style of Carl Rogers and still be true to ourselves. If we strive to model our style after Rogers, and if that style does not fit for us, we are not being ourselves and we are not being fully congruent.

The Role of Assessment

Assessment is frequently viewed as a prerequisite to the treatment process. Many mental health agencies use a variety of assessment procedures, including diagnostic screening, identification of clients' strengths and liabilities, and various tests. Person-centered therapists generally do not find traditional assessment and diagnosis to be useful because these procedures encourage an external and expert perspective on the client (Bohart & Watson, 2011). What matters is not how the counselor assesses the client but the client's self-assessment. From a person-centered perspective, the best source of knowledge about the client is the individual client. Rogers saw therapy as co-assessment, whereby the therapist and the client engage in a continuous process of self-understanding.

Assessment seems to be gaining in importance in short-term treatments in most counseling agencies, and it is imperative that clients be involved in a collaborative process in making decisions that are central to their therapy. Today it may not be a question of whether to incorporate assessment into therapeutic practice but of *how* to involve clients as fully as possible in their assessment and treatment process.

Application of the Philosophy of the Person-Centered Approach

The person-centered approach has been applied to working with individuals, groups, and families. Bozrath, Zimring, and Tausch (2002) cite studies done through the 1990s that revealed the effectiveness of person-centered therapy with a wide range of client problems including anxiety disorders, alcoholism, psychosomatic problems, agoraphobia, interpersonal difficulties, depression, cancer, and personality disorders. Person-centered therapy has been shown to be as viable as the more goal-oriented therapies. Furthermore, outcome research conducted in the 1990s revealed that effective therapy is based on the client–therapist relationship in combination with the inner and external resources of the client (Duncan, Miller, Wampold, & Hubble, 2010).

The person-centered approach has been applied extensively in training both professionals and paraprofessionals who work with people in a variety of settings. This approach emphasizes staying with clients as opposed to getting ahead of them with interpretations. People without advanced psychological education are able to benefit by translating the therapeutic conditions of genuineness, empathic understanding, and unconditional positive regard into both their personal and professional lives. Learning to listen to oneself with acceptance is a valuable life skill that enables individuals to be their own therapists. The basic concepts are straightforward and easy to comprehend, and they encourage locating power in the person rather than fostering an authoritarian structure in which control and power are denied to the person. These core skills also provide an essential foundation for virtually all of the other therapy systems covered in this book. If counselors are lacking in these relationship and communication skills, they will not be effective in carrying out a treatment program for their clients.

The person-centered approach demands a great deal of the therapist. An effective person-centered therapist must be an astute listener who is grounded, centered, genuine, respectful, caring, present, focused, patient, and accepting in a way that involves maturity. Without a person-centered *way of being*, mere application of skills is likely to be hollow. Natalie Rogers (2011) points out that the person-centered approach is a way of being that is easy to understand intellectually but is very difficult to put into practice. She continues to find the core conditions of genuineness, positive regard, and empathy most important in developing trust, safety, and growth in a group.

Application to Crisis Intervention

The person-centered approach is especially applicable in crisis intervention **LO7** such as an unwanted pregnancy, an illness, a disastrous event, or the loss of a loved one. People in the helping professions (nursing, medicine, education, the ministry) are often first on the scene in a variety of crises, and they can do much if the basic attitudes described in this chapter are present. When people are in crisis, one of the first steps is to give them an opportunity to fully express themselves. Sensitive listening, hearing, and understanding are essential at this point. Being heard and understood helps ground people in crises, helps to calm them in the midst of turmoil, and enables them to think more clearly and make better decisions. Although a person's crisis is not likely to be resolved by one or two contacts with a helper, such contacts can pave the way for being open to receiving help later. If the person in crisis does not feel understood and accepted, he or she may lose hope of "returning to normal" and may not seek help in the future. Genuine support, caring, and nonpossessive warmth can go a long way in building bridges that can motivate people to *do* something to work through and resolve a crisis. Communicating a deep sense of understanding should always precede other more problem-solving interventions.

In crisis situations person-centered therapists may need to provide more structure and direction than would be the case for clients who are not experiencing a crisis. Suggestions, guidance, and even direction may be called for if clients are not able to function effectively. For example, it may be necessary to take action to hospitalize a suicidal client to protect this person from self-harm.

Application to Group Counseling

The person-centered approach emphasizes the unique role of the group counselor as a facilitator rather than a leader. The primary function of the facilitator is to create a safe and healing climate—a place where the group members can interact in honest and meaningful ways. In this climate members become more appreciative and trusting of themselves as they are and are able to move toward self-direction and empowerment. The facilitator's way of being can create a productive climate within a group:

> Facilitators cannot make participants trust the group process. Facilitators earn trust by being respectful, caring, and even loving. Being an effective group facilitator has much to do with one's "way of being." No method or technique can evoke trust unless the facilitator herself has a capacity to be fully present, considerate, caring, authentic, and responsive. This includes the ability to challenge people constructively. (N. Rogers, 2011, p. 57)

With the presence of the facilitator and the support of other members, participants realize that they do not have to experience the struggles of change alone and that groups as collective entities have their own source of transformation.

Carl Rogers (1970) clearly believed that groups tend to move forward if the facilitator exhibits a deep sense of trust in the members and refrains from using techniques or exercises to get a group moving. Facilitators should avoid making interpretive comments or group process observations because such comments are apt to make the group self-conscious and slow the process down. Group process observations should come from members, a view that is consistent with Rogers's philosophy of placing the responsibility for the direction of the group on the members. Instead of leading the members toward specific goals, the group facilitator assists members in developing attitudes and behaviors of genuineness, acceptance, and empathy, which enables the members to interact with each other in therapeutic ways to find their own sense of direction as a group.

Regardless of a group leader's theoretical orientation, the core conditions that have been described here are highly applicable to any leader's style of group facilitation. Only when the leader is able to create a person-centered climate will movement take place within a group. All of the theories discussed in this book depend on the quality of the therapeutic relationship as a foundation. As you will see, the cognitive behavioral approaches to group work also emphasize creating a working alliance and collaborative relationships. Indeed, most effective approaches to group work share key elements of a person-centered philosophy. For a more detailed treatment of person-centered group counseling, see Corey (2016, chap. 10). Also see Natalie Rogers's book (2011), *The Creative Connection for Groups: Person-Centered Expressive Arts for Healing and Social Change.*

Person-Centered Expressive Arts Therapy*

Natalie Rogers (1993, 2011) expanded on her father's (C. Rogers, 1961) theory of creativity using the expressive arts to enhance personal growth for individuals and groups. N. Rogers's approach, known as **expressive arts therapy**, extends the person-centered approach to spontaneous creative expression, which symbolizes deep and sometimes inaccessible feelings and emotional states. Counselors trained in person-centered expressive arts offer their clients the opportunity to create movement, visual art, journal writing, sound, and music to express their feelings and gain insight from these activities. LO8

Principles of Expressive Arts Therapy

Expressive arts therapy uses various artistic forms—movement, drawing, painting, sculpting, music, writing, and improvisation—toward the end of growth, healing, and self-discovery. This is a multimodal approach integrating mind, body, emotions, and inner spiritual resources. Methods of expressive arts therapy are based on humanistic principles but give fuller form to Carl Rogers's notions of creativity. These principles include the following (N. Rogers, 1993):

- All people have an innate ability to be creative.
- The creative process is transformative and healing. The healing aspects involve activities such as meditation, movement, art, music, and journal writing.
- Personal growth and higher states of consciousness are achieved through self-awareness, self-understanding, and insight.

*Much of the material in this section is based on key ideas that are more fully developed in *The Creative Connection: Expressive Arts as Healing* (N. Rogers, 1993) and *The Creative Connection for Groups: Person-Centered Expressive Arts for Healing and Social Change* (N. Rogers, 2011). This section was written in close collaboration with Natalie Rogers.

- Self-awareness, understanding, and insight are achieved by delving into our feelings of grief, anger, pain, fear, joy, and ecstasy.
- Our feelings and emotions are an energy source that can be channeled into the expressive arts to be released and transformed.
- The expressive arts lead us into the unconscious, thereby enabling us to express previously unknown facets of ourselves and bring to light new information and awareness.
- One art form stimulates and nurtures the other, bringing us to an inner core or essence that is our life energy.
- A connection exists between our life force—our inner core, or soul—and the essence of all beings.
- As we journey inward to discover our essence or wholeness, we discover our relatedness to the outer world, and the inner and outer become one.

The various art modes interrelate in what Natalie Rogers calls the "creative connection." When we move, it affects how we write or paint. When we write or paint, it affects how we feel and think.

Natalie Rogers's approach is based on a person-centered theory of individual and group process. The same conditions that Carl Rogers and his colleagues found basic to fostering a facilitative client–counselor relationship also help support creativity. Personal growth takes place in a safe, supportive environment created by counselors or facilitators who are genuine, warm, empathic, open, honest, congruent, and caring—qualities that are best learned by first being experienced. Taking time to reflect on and evaluate these experiences allows for personal integration at many levels—intellectual, emotional, physical, and spiritual.

Creativity and Offering Stimulating Experiences

According to Natalie Rogers, this deep faith in the individual's innate drive to become fully oneself is basic to the work in person-centered expressive arts. Individuals have a tremendous capacity for self-healing through creativity if given the proper environment. When one feels appreciated, trusted, and given support to use individuality to develop a plan, create a project, write a paper, or to be authentic, the challenge is exciting, stimulating, and gives a sense of personal expansion. N. Rogers believes the tendency to actualize and become one's full potential, including innate creativity, is undervalued, discounted, and frequently squashed in our society. Traditional educational institutions tend to promote conformity rather than original thinking and the creative process.

Person-centered expressive arts therapy utilizes the arts for spontaneous creative expression that symbolizes deep and sometimes inaccessible feelings and emotional states. The conditions that foster creativity require acceptance of the individual, a nonjudgmental setting, empathy, psychological freedom, and availability of stimulating and challenging experiences. With this type of environment in place, the facilitative internal conditions of the client are encouraged and inspired. The client experiences a nondefensive openness and an internal locus of evaluation that receives but is not overly concerned with the reactions of others. N. Rogers (1993) believes that we cheat ourselves out of a fulfilling and joyous source of creativity if we cling to the idea that an artist is the only one who can enter the realm of creativity. Art is not only for the few who develop a talent or master a medium. We all can use various art forms to facilitate self-expression and personal growth.

Motivational Interviewing

LO9

Motivational Interviewing (MI) is a humanistic, client-centered, psychosocial, and modestly directive counseling approach developed by William R. Miller and Stephen Rollnick in the early 1980s. The clinical and research applications of this evidenced-based practice have received increased attention in recent years, and MI has been shown to be effective as a relatively brief intervention (Corbett, 2016; Dean, 2015). Motivational interviewing is based on humanistic principles, has many basic similarities with person-centered therapy, and expands the traditional person-centered approach.

Motivational interviewing was initially designed as a brief intervention for problem drinking, but more recently this approach has been applied to a wide range of clinical problems including substance abuse, compulsive gambling, eating disorders, anxiety disorders, depression, suicidality, chronic disease management, and health behavior change practices (Arkowitz & Miller, 2008; Arkowitz & Westra, 2009). MI stresses client self-responsibility and promotes an invitational style for working cooperatively with clients to generate alternative solutions to behavioral problems. MI provides multiple ways to address the impasses clients often experience during the change process. Both MI and person-centered practitioners believe in the client's abilities, strengths, resources, and competencies. The underlying assumption is that clients want to be healthy and desire positive change.

The MI Spirit

MI is rooted in the philosophy of person-centered therapy, but with a "twist." Unlike the nondirective and unstructured person-centered approach, MI is deliberately directive while staying within the client's frame of reference. The primary goal is to reduce client ambivalence about change and increase the client's own motivation for change. Miller and Rollnick (2013) believe that "MI is about arranging conversations so that people talk themselves into change, based on their own values and interests" (p. 4). It is essential that therapists function within the spirit of MI—that is, within the relational context of therapy—rather than simply applying the strategies of the approach. The attitudes and skills in MI are based on a person-centered philosophy and include using open-ended questions, employing reflective listening, creating a safe climate, affirming and supporting the client, expressing empathy, responding to resistance in a nonconfrontational manner, guiding a discussion of ambivalence, summarizing and linking at the end of sessions, and eliciting and reinforcing "change talk" (Dean, 2015). MI therapists avoid arguing with clients and reframe resistance as a healthy response. MI therapists do not view clients as opponents to be defeated but as allies who play a major role in their present and future success. Practitioners assist clients in becoming their own advocates for change and the primary agents of change in their lives.

In both person-centered therapy and MI, the counselor provides the conditions for growth and change by communicating attitudes of accurate empathy and unconditional positive regard. In MI, the therapeutic relationship is as important in achieving successful outcomes as the specific theoretical model or school of psychotherapy from which the therapist operates (Miller & Rollnick, 2013). Both MI and person-centered therapy are based on the premise that individuals have within themselves the capacity to generate an intrinsic motivation to change. Responsibility for change rests with clients, not with the counselor, and therapist and client share a sense of hope and optimism that change is possible. Once clients believe that they have the capacity to change and heal, new possibilities open up for them.

The Basic Principles of Motivational Interviewing

Miller and Rollnick (2013) formulated five basic principles of MI:

1. Therapists strive to experience the world from the client's perspective without judgment or criticism. MI emphasizes reflective listening, which is a way for practitioners to better understand the subjective world of clients. Expressing empathy is foundational in creating a safe climate for clients to explore their ambivalence for change. When clients are slow to change, they likely have compelling reasons to remain as they are as well as having reasons to change.
2. MI is designed to evoke and explore both discrepancies and ambivalence. Counselors reflect discrepancies between the behaviors and values of clients to increase the motivation to change. Counselors pay particular attention to clients' arguments for changing compared to their arguments for not changing. Therapists elicit and reinforce change talk by employing specific strategies to strengthen discussion about change. Clinicians encourage clients to determine whether change will occur, and if so, what kinds of changes will occur and when.
3. Reluctance to change is viewed as an expected part of the therapeutic process. Although individuals may see advantages to making life changes, they also may have many concerns and fears about changing. People who seek therapy are often ambivalent about change, and their motivation may ebb and flow during the course of therapy. MI therapists assume a respectful view of resistance and work therapeutically with any reluctance or caution on the part of clients. MI practitioners avoid disagreeing with, arguing with, or persuading clients because this only entrenches resistance. Instead, therapists roll with the resistance, which tends to reduce clients' defensiveness (Corbett, 2016).
4. Practitioners support clients' self-efficacy, mainly by encouraging them to use their own resources to take necessary actions that can lead to success in changing. MI clinicians strive to enhance client agency about change and emphasize the right and inherent ability of clients to formulate their own personal goals and to make their own decisions. MI focuses on present and future conditions and empowers clients to find ways to achieve their goals.

5. When clients show signs of readiness to change through decreased resistance to change and increased talk about change, a critical phase of MI begins. In this stage, clients may express a desire and ability to change, show an interest in questions about change, experiment with making changes between sessions, and envision a future picture of how their life will be different once the desired changes have been made. At this time therapists shift their focus toward strengthening clients' commitments to change and helping them implement a change plan.

The Stages of Change

The stages of change model assumes that people progress through a series of five identifiable stages in the counseling process. In the *precontemplation stage*, there is no intention of changing a behavior pattern in the near future. In the *contemplation stage*, people are aware of a problem and are considering overcoming it, but they have not yet made a commitment to take action to bring about the change. In the *preparation stage*, individuals intend to take action immediately and report some small behavioral changes. In the *action stage*, individuals are taking steps to modify their behavior to solve their problems. During the *maintenance stage*, people work to consolidate their gains and prevent relapse.

People do not pass neatly through these five stages in linear fashion, and a client's readiness can fluctuate throughout the change process. If change is initially unsuccessful, individuals may return to an earlier stage (Prochaska & Norcross, 2014). MI therapists strive to match specific interventions with whatever stage of change clients are experiencing. If there is a mismatch between process and stage, movement through the stage will be impeded and is likely to be manifested in reluctant behavior. When clients demonstrate any form of reluctance or resistance, this could be due to a therapist's misjudgment of a client's readiness to change.

Motivational interviewing is but one example of how therapeutic strategies have been developed based on the foundational principles and philosophy of the person-centered approach. Indeed, most of the therapeutic models illustrate how the core therapeutic conditions are necessary aspects leading to client change. Where many therapeutic approaches, including motivational interviewing, diverge from traditional person-centered therapy is the assumption that the therapeutic factors are both necessary *and sufficient* in bringing about change. Many other models employ specific intervention strategies to address specific concerns clients bring to therapy.

Person-Centered Therapy From a Multicultural Perspective

Strengths From a Diversity Perspective

One of the strengths of the person-centered approach is its impact on the field of human relations with diverse cultural groups. Person-centered philosophy and practice can now be studied in several European countries, South America, LO10 and Japan. Here are some examples of ways in which this approach has been incorporated in various countries and cultures:

- In several European countries person-centered concepts have had a significant impact on the practice of counseling as well as on education, cross-cultural communication, and reduction of racial and political tensions. In the 1980s Carl Rogers (1987b) elaborated on a theory of reducing tension among antagonistic groups that he began developing in 1948.
- In the 1970s Rogers and his associates began conducting workshops promoting cross-cultural communication. Well into the 1980s he led large workshops in many parts of the world. International encounter groups have provided participants with multicultural experiences.
- Japan, Australia, South America, Mexico, and the United Kingdom have all been receptive to person-centered concepts and have adapted these practices to fit their cultures.
- Shortly before his death, Rogers conducted intensive workshops with professionals in the former Soviet Union.

There is no doubt that Carl Rogers has had a global impact. His work has reached more than 30 countries, and his writings have been translated into 12 languages. The emphasis on core conditions makes the person-centered approach useful in understanding diverse worldviews. The underlying philosophy of person-centered therapy is grounded on the importance of hearing the deeper messages of a client. Empathy, being present, and respecting the values of clients are essential attitudes and skills in counseling culturally diverse clients. Although person-centered therapists are aware of diversity factors, they do not make initial assumptions about individuals (Cain, 2010, 2013). Therapists realize that each client's journey is unique and take steps to tailor their methods to fit the individual.

Several writers consider person-centered therapy as being ideally suited to clients in a diverse world. Bohart and Watson (2011) claim that the person-centered philosophy is particularly appropriate for working with diverse client populations because the counselor does not assume the role of expert who is going to impose a "right way of being" on the client. Instead, the therapist is a "fellow explorer" who attempts to understand the client's phenomenological world in an interested, accepting, and open way and checks with the client to confirm that the therapist's perceptions are accurate. Motivational interviewing, which is based on the philosophy of person-centered therapy, is a culturally sensitive approach that can be effective across population domains, including gender, age, ethnicity, and sexual orientation (Levensky, Kersh, Cavasos, & Brooks, 2008).

Shortcomings From a Diversity Perspective

Although the person-centered approach has made significant contributions to counseling people from diverse social, political, and cultural backgrounds, there are some shortcomings to practicing exclusively within this framework. Many clients who come to community mental health clinics or who are involved in outpatient treatment want more structure than this approach provides. Some clients seek professional help to deal with a crisis, to alleviate emotional problems, or to learn coping skills in dealing with everyday problems. These clients often expect counselors to provide guidance or give advice and can be put off by this unstructured approach.

A second shortcoming of the person-centered approach is that it is difficult to translate the core therapeutic conditions into actual practice in certain cultures. Communication of these core conditions must be consistent with the client's cultural framework. Consider, for example, the expression of therapist congruence and empathy. Clients accustomed to indirect communication may not be comfortable with direct expressions of empathy or self-disclosure on the therapist's part.

A third shortcoming in applying the person-centered approach with clients from diverse cultures pertains to the fact that this approach extols the value of an *internal* locus of evaluation. The humanistic foundation of person-centered therapy emphasizes dimensions such as self-awareness, freedom, autonomy, self-acceptance, inner-directedness, and self-actualization. Cain (2010) points out that "persons from collectivistic cultures are oriented less toward self-actualization and more toward intimacy, connection, and harmony with others and toward what is best for the community and the common good" (p. 143). The focus on development of individual autonomy and personal growth may be viewed as being selfish in a culture that stresses the common good.

Consider Lupe, a Latina client who values the interests of her family over her self-interests. From a person-centered perspective she could be viewed as being in danger of "losing her own identity" by being primarily concerned with her role in taking care of others in the family. Rather than pushing her to make her personal wants a priority, the counselor will explore Lupe's cultural values and her level of commitment to these values in working with her. It would be inappropriate for the counselor to communicate a vision of the kind of woman she should be. (This topic is discussed more extensively in Chapter 12.)

Despite these shortcomings, the person-centered approach offers many opportunities for working with clients from diverse cultures. There is great diversity among any group of people, and there is room for a variety of therapeutic styles. Counseling a culturally different client may require more activity and structuring than is usually the case in a person-centered framework, but the potential positive impact of a counselor who responds empathically to a culturally different client cannot be overestimated.

Person-Centered Therapy Applied to the Case of Stan

Stan's autobiography indicates that he has a sense of what he wants for his life. As a person-centered therapist, I rely on his self-report of the way he views himself rather than on a formal assessment and diagnosis. My concern is with understanding him from his internal frame of reference. Stan has stated goals that are meaningful for him. He is motivated to change and seems to have sufficient anxiety to work toward these desired changes. I have faith in Stan's ability to find his own way, and I trust that he has the necessary resources for reaching his therapy goals. I encourage Stan to speak freely about the discrepancy between the person he sees himself as being and the person he would like to become; about his feelings of being a failure, being inadequate; about his fears and uncertainties; and about his hopelessness at times. I attempt to create an atmosphere of freedom and security that will encourage Stan to explore the threatening aspects of his self-concept.

Stan has a low evaluation of his self-worth. Although he finds it difficult to believe that others really like him, he wants to feel loved. He says, "I hope I can learn to love at least a few people, most of all, women." He wants to feel equal to others and not have to apologize for his existence, yet most of the time he feels inferior. By creating a supportive, trusting, and encouraging atmosphere, I can help Stan learn to be more accepting of himself, with both his strengths and limitations. He has the opportunity to openly express his fears of women, of not being able to work with people, and of feeling inadequate and stupid. He can explore how he feels judged by his parents and by authorities. He has an opportunity to express his guilt—that is, his feelings that he has not lived up to his parents' expectations and that he has let them and himself down. He can also relate his feelings of hurt over not having ever felt loved and wanted. He can express the loneliness and isolation that he so often feels, as well as the need to numb these feelings with alcohol or drugs.

Stan is no longer totally alone, for he is taking the risk of letting me into his private world of feelings. Stan gradually gets a sharper focus on his experiencing and is able to clarify his own feelings and attitudes. He sees that he has the capacity to make his own decisions. In short, our therapeutic relationship frees him from his self-defeating ways. Because of the caring and faith he experiences from me in our relationship, Stan is able to increase his own faith and confidence in himself.

My empathy assists Stan in hearing himself and accessing himself at a deeper level. Stan gradually becomes more sensitive to his own internal messages and less dependent on confirmation from others around him. As a result of the therapeutic venture, Stan discovers that there is someone in his life whom he can depend on—himself.

Questions for Reflection

- How would you respond to Stan's deep feelings of self-doubt? Could you enter his frame of reference and respond in an empathic manner that lets Stan know you hear his pain and struggle without needing to give advice or suggestions?
- How would you describe Stan's deeper struggles? What sense do you have of his world?
- To what extent do you think that the relationship you would develop with Stan would help him move forward in a positive direction? What, if anything, might get in your way—either with him or in yourself—in establishing a therapeutic relationship?

Visit CengageBrain.com or watch the DVD for the video program *Theory and Practice of Counseling and Psychotherapy: The Case of Stan and Lecturettes*, Session 5 (person-centered therapy), for a demonstration of my approach to counseling Stan from this perspective. This session focuses on exploring the immediacy of our relationship and assisting Stan in finding his own way.

Person-Centered Therapy Applied to the Case of Gwen*

Gwen arrives for this session moving quite slowly. She reports having been in pain for the past few days. I asked her to describe the pain in her body, and she explains that it is a full body achiness.

Gwen: I can't sleep through the night, and I feel tired all day long. I try to push through the achiness, but sometimes I just want to sit down and not get up.

Therapist: Tell me more about this feeling.

Gwen: I don't mean sit down and die, I mean sit down and take a break from life for a while. I have just been feeling down and stressed.

To gain a better understanding of how Gwen's pain has affected her week, I administer a brief rating

*Dr. Kellie Kirksey writes about her ways of thinking and practicing from a person-centered perspective and applying this model to Gwen.

scale at the beginning of this session. The Outcome Rating Scale (ORS) is a short questionnaire developed by Scott D. Miller that assesses how well a person has been doing (individually, interpersonally, socially, and overall well-being) during the last week. I explain that the ORS will give us a quick look at her current level of functioning and feeling. The ORS can also help Gwen see which particular areas of her life hold the most stress for her. Gwen marks the form quickly, and the results indicate that personal well-being and interpersonal relationships are her most significant areas of challenge. This assessment provides a starting point for discussing how our therapeutic relationship is contributing to her overall well-being.

Therapist: Gwen, I hope that information is helpful for you. Where would you like to start today?

Gwen: I need to work on the personal well-being issues. I just want to unwind and relax a little before I go back into my busy day. I get so tired of running around so much. I seem to live in an "overwhelm" mode. I am ready to retire that way of living. I could use some balance in my life. I know that's why I have been feeling so achy. It's the stress I have been carrying. I can feel the tension.

Therapist: Would you like to say more about the sense of "overwhelm" you mentioned?

Gwen: I am always juggling between getting my own house in order and putting out fires with my mom's health team or insurance. I work hard at my job, and then I come home and need to get my own house in order. I am stretched in too many directions, and at the end of the day I still feel like I am on call and can't turn my mind off. I lay down at night and feel all my responsibilities whirling around in my mind. Sometimes I just cover my head and hope that everything will go away and I can at least have some peace at night. I know nothing will disappear from my list until I take it off and that I have to make an effort to find space for relaxation in my life.

Therapist: Hearing you explain what "overwhelm mode" looks like for you gets my heart rate up [*immediacy*]. Although you know that many of your responsibilities will not diminish, you would like to find some way of dealing with them and find more peace in your life.

Gwen: Yes, but I don't know where to begin. I can't seem to find time for relaxation.

Therapist: It sounds like you feel unsure about where to start and whether you'll find time for yourself at all. I am wondering when you feel somewhat relaxed.

Gwen: I feel best when I'm caught up with all my projects at work and have some time for myself. I like it when I have crossed some things off my list of things to do. I used to reward myself with a spa day when I finished a big project. I haven't done that in ages.

Therapist: As you talk about this time, I can see how excited you are about crossing things off your list and having time for yourself. That's when you really feel good about yourself—when you're accomplishing things yet you realize you need to take care of yourself too.

Gwen: Before I became the caregiver for my mom, I used to get to the gym about three days a week. I loved doing dancing and yoga! It really made a difference in my stress level. Working out just fell by the wayside as my life got busier.

Therapist: That must be exhausting; you take care of your mom, husband, grown kids, colleagues, and everyone else. Yet I hear that you are not taking care of yourself. How satisfied are you about meeting your own needs right now?

Gwen: Not at all. I have totally abandoned myself. I am feeling worn down.

Therapist: Tell me more about being worn down.

Gwen: I guess saying I am worn down is a bit extreme [*Gwen is smiling*]. My body is definitely telling me to slow down and focus on me for a change.

Therapist: So one side is telling you that you can't keep up this pace and you need to take care of yourself, and the other side is saying, "Gwen, you need to handle everything that's being thrown at you."

Gwen: That sounds right. It's been a while since I actually paid attention to myself. I feel sad saying that out loud. I know I want to do something different. Even if it's a small something!

Therapist: You are disappointed in yourself for not recognizing that you need a break, and yet you seem determined to make some small change now. Can you identify what you might begin to do differently?

Gwen: I want to make myself a priority. I can start taking my breaks at work again and use that time to take care of me. I used to do some stretching at my desk and walk around the building. It was actually fun: we would do a pedometer challenge at work. It was good. I don't know why I let all of that go. I just started putting everyone and everything in front of me. We even have a lunch time dance class I could go to. I forgot how happy doing those little things used to make me feel.

Therapist: It sounds like you regret that some of those activities aren't in you life. What would it look like to make yourself a priority in some small way?

Gwen: I guess I could find 15 minutes to do something for myself. I could even go get my hair done. Maybe a break in my regular routine would be helpful. It's been forever since I treated myself.

Therapist: With you changing your lifestyle, I want to make sure you do it safely. I suggest you ask your primary care physician about a physical examination to determine any possible reasons for the pain and physical symptoms you are experiencing.

Gwen: That is a good idea, and I will follow up on that suggestion.

Therapist: Before you leave, I want to give you the Session Rating Scale (SRS). All you have to do is rate today's session based on four items: our relationship, goals and topics, therapeutic approach, and overall view of our time today. It's similar to the form you filled out at the beginning of session.

Gwen takes a moment to fill out the form and passes it back with marks reflecting that she felt heard and that we talked about what she wanted to discuss. She also marked that there was something missing from the session, which gave us an opportunity to identify what might be missing for her. Using the ORS and the SRS is a good way to get Gwen's feedback on her own progress and her perception of the value of the therapy session. As a therapist, I invite this feedback and see it as a useful way of getting Gwen's perspective. In collaboration with Gwen, I strive to make adjustments in my work with her based on her feedback. Gwen then says a few words about how she is feeling.

Gwen: I am definitely not as tense as I was when I first came in. I needed to get some things off of my chest. I would have liked more suggestions from you on what I need to do next. I know you don't have the magic answer, but sometimes that's just what I want.

Therapist: Thanks for your honest feedback. The goal is for you to be the director of this session and of your life. As you lead the way, your own answers will surface to assist you in resolving some of your challenges. In today's session you clearly identified areas of stress, and then you reconnected with activities that brought you peace and relaxation in the past. You were able to find your answers within yourself.

Person-centered therapy is a collaborative journey driven by what the client brings into the session. I followed the lead provided by Gwen of what was troubling her and attempted to work within the framework of what she said she wanted. At each step along the way, I show empathy and compassion for her challenges as she works to rebuild self-trust and reconnect to her own sense of personal power and value.

Questions for Reflection

- What are your thoughts about soliciting client feedback using rating scales such as the ORS and the SRS?
- Gwen wants more suggestions from her therapist. If you were her therapist, how would you intervene with her when she wants more direction from you?
- How does person-centered therapy fit with who you are as a person? Would you be comfortable in mostly identifying the client's underlying messages as the therapist did in this session?
- Frequently person-centered therapists identify conflicts or the competing sides of an issue. Where did the therapist do this in her dialogue with Gwen?

Summary and Evaluation

Summary

Person-centered therapy is based on a philosophy of human nature that postulates an innate striving for self-actualization. Carl Rogers's view of human nature is phenomenological; that is, we structure ourselves according to our perceptions of reality. We are motivated to actualize ourselves in the reality that we perceive.

Rogers's theory rests on the assumption that clients can understand the factors in their lives that are causing them to be distressed. They also have the capacity for self-direction and constructive personal change. Change will occur if a congruent therapist makes psychological contact with a client in a state of anxiety or incongruence. It is essential for the therapist to establish a relationship the client perceives as genuine, accepting, and understanding. Therapeutic counseling is based on an I/Thou, or person-to-person, relationship in the safety and acceptance of which clients drop their defenses and come to accept and integrate aspects that they have denied or distorted. The person-centered approach emphasizes this personal relationship between client and therapist; the therapist's attitudes are more critical than are knowledge, theory, or techniques employed. In the context of this relationship, clients unleash their growth potential and become more of the person they are capable of becoming. An abundance of research supports the notion that the human elements of psychotherapy (client factors, therapist effects, and the therapeutic alliance) are far more important than models and techniques in the effectiveness and outcomes of therapy (Elkins, 2016).

This approach places primary responsibility for the direction of therapy on the client. In the therapeutic context, individuals have the opportunity to decide for themselves and come to terms with their own personal power. The underlying assumption is that no one knows the client better than the client; in short, the client is viewed as an expert on his or her own life (Cain, 2010). The general goals of therapy are becoming more open to experience, achieving self-trust, developing an internal source of evaluation, and being willing to continue growing. Specific goals are not suggested for clients; rather, clients choose their own values and goals. Current applications of the theory emphasize more active participation by the therapist than was the case earlier. Counselors are now encouraged to be fully involved as persons in the therapeutic relationship. More latitude is allowed for therapists to express their reactions and feelings as they are appropriate to what is occurring in therapy. Person-centered practitioners are willing to be transparent about persistent feelings that exist in their relationships with clients (Watson et al., 2011). It is the therapist's job to adapt and accommodate in a manner that works best for each client, which means being flexible in the application of methods in the counseling process (Cain, 2010).

Contributions of the Person-Centered Approach

When Carl Rogers founded nondirective counseling more than 70 years **LO11** ago, there were very few other therapeutic models. The longevity of this approach is certainly a factor to consider in assessing its influence. Rogers had, and his theory continues to have, a major impact on the field of counseling and psychotherapy.

When he introduced his revolutionary ideas in the 1940s, he provided a powerful and radical alternative to psychoanalysis and to the directive approaches then practiced. Rogers was a pioneer in shifting the therapeutic focus from an emphasis on technique and reliance on therapist authority to that of the power of the therapeutic relationship.

Kirschenbaum (2009) contends that the scope and influence of Rogers's work has continued well beyond his death; the person-centered approach is alive, well, and expanding. Today there is not one version of person-centered therapy, but a number of continuously evolving person-centered psychotherapies (Cain, 2010). Although few psychotherapists claim to have an exclusive person-centered theoretical orientation, the philosophy and principles of this approach permeate the practice of most therapists. Other schools of therapy are increasingly recognizing the centrality of the therapeutic relationship as a route to therapeutic change.

Person-centered therapy is strongly represented in Europe, and there is continuing interest in this approach in both South America and the Far East. The person-centered approach has established a firm foothold in British universities, and some of the most in-depth training of person-centered counselors is taking place in the United Kingdom today (N. Rogers, 2011).

As we have seen, Natalie Rogers has made a significant contribution to the application of the person-centered approach by incorporating the expressive arts as a medium to facilitate healing and social change, primarily in a group setting. She has been instrumental in the evolution of the person-centered approach using nonverbal methods to enable individuals to heal and to develop. Many individuals who have difficulty expressing themselves verbally can find new possibilities for self-expression through nonverbal channels and through the expressive arts (N. Rogers, 2011). Cain (2010) believes "Natalie Rogers's expressive arts therapy represents a major innovation in practice and helped open the way for other person-centered therapists to expand the variety and range of practice" (p. 60).

Emphasis on Research One of Carl Rogers's contributions to the field of psychotherapy was his willingness to state his concepts as testable hypotheses and to submit them to research. He literally opened the field to research. He was truly a pioneer in his insistence on subjecting the transcripts of therapy sessions to critical examination and applying research technology to counselor–client dialogues. According to Cain (2010), an enormous body of research, conducted over a period of 70 years, supports the effectiveness of the person-centered approach. This research is ongoing in many parts of the world and continues to expand and refine our understanding of what constitutes effective psychotherapy. Cain (2010) concludes, "person centered therapy is as vital and effective as it has ever been and continues to develop in ways that will make it increasingly so in the years to come" (p. 169).

Even his critics give Rogers credit for having conducted and inspired others to conduct extensive studies of counseling process and outcome. Rogers presented a challenge to psychology to design new models of scientific investigation capable of dealing with the inner, subjective experiences of the person. His theories of therapy and personality change have had a tremendous heuristic effect, and though much controversy surrounds this approach, his work has challenged practitioners and theoreticians to examine their own therapeutic styles and beliefs.

Limitations and Criticisms of the Person-Centered Approach

Although I applaud person-centered therapists for their willingness to subject their hypotheses and procedures to empirical scrutiny, some researchers have been critical of the methodological errors contained in some of these studies. Accusations of scientific shortcomings involve using control subjects who are not candidates for therapy, failing to use an untreated control group, failing to account for placebo effects, reliance on self-reports as a major way to assess the outcomes of therapy, and using inappropriate statistical procedures. In all fairness, these accusations apply to the research on many other therapeutic approaches as well.

There is a similar limitation shared by both the person-centered and existential (experiential) approaches. Neither of these therapeutic modalities emphasizes the role of techniques aimed at bringing about change in clients' behavior. Proponents of psychotherapy manuals, or manualized treatment methods for specific disorders, find serious limitations in the experiential approaches due to their lack of attention to proven techniques and strategies. Those who call for accountability as defined by evidence-based practices within the field of mental health also are quite critical of the experiential approaches.

I do not believe manualized treatment methods can be considered the gold standard in psychotherapy, however. There is good research demonstrating that techniques account for only 15% of client outcome (see Duncan et al., 2010), whereas contextual factors have powerful effects on what happens in therapy (Elkins, 2009, 2012, 2016). Research points to relational and client factors as the main predictors of effective therapy. Furthermore, the evaluation of evidence-based practices has been broadened to include best available research; the expertise of the clinician; and client characteristics, culture, and preferences (see Norcross, Hogan, & Koocher, 2008).

A potential limitation of the person-centered approach is that some students-in-training and practitioners with this orientation may have a tendency to be very supportive of clients without being challenging. Out of their misunderstanding of the basic concepts of the approach, some have limited the range of their responses and counseling styles mainly to reflections and empathic listening. Although there is value in accurately and deeply hearing a client and in reflecting and communicating understanding, counseling entails more than this. I believe that the therapeutic core conditions are *necessary* for therapy to succeed, yet I do not see them as being *sufficient* conditions for change for all clients at all times. From my perspective, these basic attitudes are the foundation on which counselors must then build the *skills* of therapeutic intervention. Motivational interviewing rests on the therapeutic core conditions, for example, but MI employs a range of strategies that enables clients to develop action plans leading to change.

A related challenge for counselors using this approach is to truly support clients in finding their own way. Counselors sometimes experience difficulty in allowing clients to decide their own specific goals in therapy. It is easy to give lip service to the concept of clients' finding their own way, but it takes considerable respect for clients and faith on the therapist's part to encourage clients to listen to themselves and follow their own directions, particularly when they make choices that are not what the therapist hoped for.

More than any other quality, the therapist's genuineness determines the power of the therapeutic relationship. If therapists submerge their unique identity and style in a passive and nondirective manner, they are not likely to affect clients in powerful ways. Therapist authenticity and congruence are so vital to this approach that those who practice within this framework must feel natural in doing so and must find a way to express their own reactions to clients. If not, a real possibility is that person-centered therapy will be reduced to a bland, safe, and ineffectual approach.

Self-Reflection and Discussion Questions

1. To what degree do you believe clients have the ability to understand and resolve their own problems without a great deal of advice or suggestions from a therapist?
2. This therapy approach places considerable importance on congruence (realness or genuineness) on the part of the therapist. How confident are you that you will be able to be genuine in your interaction with your clients?
3. The therapeutic relationship is given prominence in this theory. What kind of relationship do you hope to create with your clients? Identify the characteristics you deem most important.
4. Empathy is a core ingredient in person-centered therapy. What do you think you can do to increase your ability to develop empathy toward a client who you perceive of as being difficult?
5. How would it be for you to practice by relying on a minimum of techniques and instead staying tuned into a client's moment-by-moment experience?

Where to Go From Here

In the *DVD for Integrative Counseling: The Case of Ruth and Lecturettes*, you will see a concrete illustration of how I view the therapeutic relationship as the foundation for our work together. Refer especially to Session 1 ("Beginning of Counseling"), Session 2 ("The Therapeutic Relationship"), and Session 3 ("Establishing Therapeutic Goals") for a demonstration of how I apply principles from the person-centered approach to my work with Ruth.

Free Podcasts for ACA Members

You can download ACA Podcasts (prerecorded interviews) by going to www.counseling.org; click on the Resource button and then select the Podcast Series. For Chapter 7, Carl Rogers and the Person-Centered Approach, look for Podcast 7 by Dr. Howard Kirschenbaum.

Other Resources

The American Psychological Association offers the following DVDs in their Psychotherapy Video Series:

Greenberg, L. S. (2010). *Emotion-Focused Therapy Over Time*

Cain, D. J. (2010). *Person-Centered Therapy Over Time*

Psychotherapy.net is a comprehensive resource for students and professionals that offers videos and interviews featuring Natalie Rogers, Rollo May, and more. New articles, interviews, blogs, therapy cartoons, and videos are published monthly. DVDs relevant to this chapter are available at www.psychotherapy.net and include the following:

Rogers, N. (1997). *Person-Centered Expressive Arts Therapy*

May, R. (2007). *Rollo May on Existential Psychotherapy*

The Association for the Development of the Person-Centered Approach (ADPCA) is an interdisciplinary and international organization that consists of a network of individuals who support the development and application of the person-centered approach. Membership includes a subscription to the *Person-Centered Journal*, the association's newsletter, a membership directory, and information about the annual meeting. ADPCA also provides information about continuing education and supervision and training in the person-centered approach. For information about the *Person-Centered Journal*, contact the editor (Jon Rose).

Association for the Development of the Person-Centered Approach, Inc.
www.adpca.org

The Association for Humanistic Psychology (AHP) is devoted to promoting personal integrity, creative learning, and active responsibility in embracing the challenges of being human in these times. Information about the *Journal of Humanistic Psychology* is available from the Association for Humanistic Psychology or at the publisher's website.

Association for Humanistic Psychology
www.ahpweb.org

Division 32 of APA, Society for Humanistic Psychology, represents a constellation of "humanistic psychologies" that includes the earlier Rogerian, transpersonal, and existential orientations as well as recently developing perspectives. Division 32 seeks to contribute to psychotherapy, education, theory, research, epistemological diversity, cultural diversity, organization, management, social responsibility, and change. The division has been at the forefront in the development of qualitative research methodologies. The Society for Humanistic Psychology offers journal access to *The Humanistic Psychologist*. Information about membership, conferences, and journals is available from the website of Division 32.

Society for Humanistic Psychology
www.societyforhumanisticpsychology.com/

The Carl Rogers CD-ROM is a visually beautiful and lasting archive of the life and works of the founder of humanistic psychology. It includes excerpts from his 16 books, over 120 photographs spanning his lifetime, and award-winning video footage of two encounter groups and Carl's early counseling sessions. It is an essential resource for students, teachers, libraries, and universities. It is a profound tribute to one of the most important thinkers, influential psychologists, and peace activists of the 20th century. Developed for Natalie Rogers, PhD, by Mindgarden Media, Inc.

Carl Rogers: A Daughter's Tribute
www.nrogers.com

The Center for Studies of the Person (CSP) offers workshops, training seminars, experiential small groups, residential workshops, and sharing of learning in community meetings.

Center for Studies of the Person
www.centerfortheperson.org

For training in expressive art therapy, join Natalie Rogers, Sue Ann Herron, and Terri Goslin-Jones in their course, "Expressive Arts for Healing and Social Change: A Person-Centered Approach" at Sofia University. This 16-unit certificate program requires six weeks of study spread over two years at a retreat center north of San Francisco. The expressive arts within a person-centered counseling framework program includes counseling demonstrations, practice counseling sessions, readings, discussions, papers, and a creative project to teach experiential and theoretical methods.

Training in the Person-Centered Approach to Expressive Arts
www.nrogers.com

Sofia University
www.sofia.edu/

Recommended Supplementary Readings

On Becoming a Person (C. Rogers, 1961) is one of the best primary sources for further reading on person-centered therapy. This classic book is a collection of Rogers's articles on the process of psychotherapy, its outcomes, the therapeutic relationship, education, family life, communication, and the nature of the healthy person.

A Way of Being (C. Rogers, 1980) contains a series of writings on Rogers's personal experiences and perspectives, as well as chapters on the foundations and applications of the person-centered approach.

The Creative Connection: Expressive Arts as Healing (N. Rogers, 1993) is a practical, spirited book lavishly illustrated with color and action photos and filled with fresh ideas to stimulate creativity, self-expression, healing, and transformation. Natalie Rogers combines the philosophy of her father with the expressive arts to enhance communication between client and therapist.

The Life and Work of Carl Rogers (Kirschenbaum, 2009) is a definitive biography of Carl Rogers that follows his life from his early childhood through his death. This book illustrates the legacy of Carl Rogers and shows his enormous influence on the field of counseling and psychotherapy.

Person-Centered Psychotherapies (Cain, 2010) contains a clear discussion of person-centered theory, the therapeutic process, evaluation of the approach, and future developments.

Humanistic Psychology: A Clinical Manifesto (Elkins, 2009) offers an insightful critique of the medical model of psychotherapy and the myth of empirically supported treatments. The author calls for a relationship-based approach to psychotherapy that can provide both individual and social transformation.

Gestalt Therapy

8

LEARNING OBJECTIVES

1. Understand the evolution of this approach from the pioneering work of Fritz Perls to contemporary relational approaches.
2. Define the philosophy and basic assumptions underlying Gestalt theory and therapy.
3. Identify these key concepts of the approach: here and now, awareness, dealing with unfinished business, contact and resistance to contact, body language, and the role of experiments in therapy.
4. Describe how the I/Thou relationship is central to the use of experiments in the therapy process.
5. Understand the role of confrontation in contemporary relational Gestalt therapy.
6. Explain these standard Gestalt therapy interventions: role playing, future projection, making the rounds, staying with the feeling, working with dreams, and creating experiments based on here-and-now awareness.
7. Understand the application of Gestalt therapy to group counseling.
8. Describe the practice of Gestalt therapy from a multicultural perspective.
9. Evaluate the contributions, strengths, and limitations of the Gestalt approach.

ERVING POLSTER (b. 1922) is still professionally active and gives presentations, therapy demonstrations, and workshops. He is regularly featured at the Evolution of Psychotherapy conference and the Brief Therapy conference. Erving Polster writes the following about his connection with Gestalt Therapy:*

Erving Polster

Erving Polster

> I first became aware of Gestalt Therapy in 1953 when I attended a workshop in Cleveland with Frederick Perls. He was masterful in the therapy sessions he conducted with those of us who attended the workshop. Two aspects of the experience stand out for me. One was the combination of simplicity and power in both his concepts and his therapeutic work. The second was the surprising public nature of the personal explorations. This openness was revelatory in a process that had been steeped in privacy. Yet this freedom seemed both natural and daring, an enchanting exemplification of the drama of living.
>
> These explorations led to the formation of the Gestalt Institute of Cleveland, where I was faculty chairman from 1956 to 1973. The courses I created there composed a point of view that became the foundation of *Gestalt Therapy Integrated: Contours of Theory and Practice* (1973), a book coauthored with my wife, Miriam. We moved to San Diego in 1973 and opened the Gestalt Training Center. People came there for 25 years from all over the world for extensive training work with us. Those were exciting and productive days, and Miriam and I had the pleasure of our partnership in developing our ideas and our training programs.
>
> Some years later, I wrote *Every Person's Life Is Worth a Novel* (1987b) and *A Population of Selves: A Therapeutic Exploration of Personality Diversity* (1995) and coauthored an anthology of Miriam's and my writings titled *From the Radical Center: The Heart of Gestalt Therapy* (1999). Miriam died in 2001, at which point we had both been retired for two years. After she died, I came out of retirement and began to explore a new theme, advocating the advancement of psychotherapy principles from a private office procedure into a communal application. I have written one book about this, *Uncommon Ground* (2006), and am currently completing another book, *A Life Focus Revolution: The Mind's Answer to the Speed of Living.*

*I invited Erving Polster to write his biography in the first person and his wife Miriam's biography, which he kindly accepted. My gratitude to Erv for providing these sketches of the Polsters' contributions to the development of Gestalt therapy.

MIRIAM POLSTER (1924–2001) earned her undergraduate degree in music. She was trained as a classical vocalist and a performer of operatic music. Her artistic gifts remained with her throughout her personal and professional life. M. Polster led workshops in which music served as a framework for assisting clients in exploring personal experiences.

Miriam Polster

Miriam Polster

She was a strong advocate of the relational dimension of Gestalt therapy, a counterpoint to the skewed stereotype of it as confrontational and technically narrow. The freshness of her perspectives, the clarity of her language, and the excitement evoked by her radiance all served to raise the charismatic potential of the therapist who entered into the realm of simple fascination with the way people lived their lives. The long arc of her influence was drawn by a feminine candor and conversational mutuality that achieved its strength through presence and intelligence more than through forcefulness; of relationship more than through manipulation; of optimism more than metallic rationalism; and, at last, of a wisdom-based tension that created a natural progression of experience.

Gestalt Therapy Integrated: Contours of Theory and Practice (1973), coauthored with her husband, Erving Polster, is considered a classic and a benchmark in the evolution of Gestalt therapy. In *Eve's Daughters: The Forbidden Heroism of Women* (1992), M. Polster painted an eye-opening picture of the contributions and the character of women in our society. She spelled out the historical role of women and their special heroic contributions to social progress. However, she went further than their overlooked heroism by also postulating a picture of heroism itself. She brightened the concept by reminding us of the heroism that is a part of everyday living. This interweaving of *women's* heroism with the *heroism of everyday life* accented the value of women's potential for effecting new social norms. Women's heroism had been taken for granted and was relegated to the background of social importance. M. Polster tied this social expansion of feminine heroism, often part of their ministrations in the world of everyday living, to an enlivened understanding of the subtle role of ordinary heroism of people at large.

Introduction

Gestalt therapy is an existential, phenomenological, and process-based approach created on the premise that individuals must be understood in the context of their ongoing relationship with the environment. Awareness, choice, and responsibility are cornerstones of practice. The initial goal is for clients to expand their *awareness* of what they are experiencing in the present moment. Through this awareness, change automatically occurs. The approach is *phenomenological* because it focuses on the client's perceptions of reality and *existential* because it is grounded in the notion that people are always in the process of becoming, remaking, and rediscovering themselves. As an existential approach, Gestalt therapy gives special attention to existence as individuals experience it and affirms the human capacity for growth and healing through interpersonal contact and insight (Yontef, 1995). In a nutshell, this approach focuses on the here and now, the *what* and *how* of experiencing, the authenticity of the therapist, active dialogic inquiry and exploration, and the I/Thou of relating (Brown, 2007; Resnick, 2015; Wheeler & Axelsson, 2015; Yontef & Jacobs, 2014). LO1

Fritz Perls was the main originator and developer of Gestalt therapy. Although Perls was influenced by psychoanalytic concepts, he took issue with Freud's theory on a number of grounds. Whereas Freud's view of human beings is basically mechanistic, Perls stressed a holistic approach to personality. Freud focused on repressed intrapsychic conflicts from early childhood, whereas Perls valued examining the present situation. The Gestalt approach focuses much more on process than on content. This process involves Gestalt therapists putting themselves as fully as possible into the experience of the client without judgment, analyzing, or interpreting, while concurrently holding a sense of one's individual, independent presence. Therapists devise experiments designed to increase clients' awareness of *what* they are doing and *how* they are doing it moment to moment. Perls asserted that *how* individuals behave in the present moment is far more crucial to self-understanding than *why* they behave as they do. Awareness usually involves insight and sometimes introspection, but Gestalt therapists consider it to be much more than either. A defining characteristic of awareness is paying attention to the flow of your experience and being in contact with what you are doing when you are doing it (Resnick, 2015).

Self-acceptance, knowledge of the environment, responsibility for choices, and the ability to make contact with their **field** (a dynamic system of interrelationships) and the people in it are important awareness processes and goals, all of which are based on a here-and-now experiencing that is always changing. Clients are expected to do their own seeing, feeling, sensing, and interpreting, as opposed to waiting passively for the therapist to provide them with insights and answers.

Contemporary relational Gestalt therapy stresses dialogue and the I/Thou relationship between client and therapist. Therapists emphasize the therapeutic relationship and work collaboratively with clients in a search for understanding (Wheeler & Axelsson, 2015; Yontef & Schulz, 2013). Following the lead of Laura Perls and the "Cleveland school" when Erving and Miriam Polster and Joseph Zinker were on the faculty in the 1960s and 1970s, this model includes more support and increased sensitivity and compassion in therapy than the confrontational and dramatic style of Fritz Perls (Yontef, 1999). The majority of today's Gestalt therapists emphasizes support, acceptance, empathy, respect, and dialogue as well as confrontation.

Gestalt therapy is lively and promotes direct experiencing rather than the abstractness of talking about situations. Gestalt therapy is an experiential approach in that clients come to grips with what and how they are thinking, feeling, and doing as they interact with the therapist. Gestalt practitioners value being fully present during the therapeutic encounter with the belief that growth occurs out of genuine contact between client and therapist.

Visit CengageBrain.com or watch the DVD for the video program on Chapter 8, *Theory and Practice of Counseling and Psychotherapy: The Case of Stan and Lecturettes*. I suggest that you view the brief lecture for each chapter prior to reading the chapter.

Key Concepts

View of Human Nature

LO2

The Gestalt view of human nature is rooted in existential philosophy, phenomenology, and field theory. Genuine knowledge is the product of what is immediately evident in the experience of the perceiver. Therapy aims at awareness and contact with the environment, which consists of both the external and internal worlds. The quality of contact with aspects of the external world (for example, other people) and the internal world (for example, parts of the self that are disowned) are monitored. The process of "reowning" parts of oneself that have been disowned and the unification process proceed step by step until clients can carry on with their own personal growth. By becoming aware, clients become able to make informed choices and thus to live a more meaningful existence.

Due to this view of human nature, Fritz Perls (1969a) practiced Gestalt therapy paternalistically. Clients have to grow up, stand on their own two feet, and "deal with their life problems themselves" (p. 225). Perls's style of doing therapy involved two personal agendas: moving the client from environmental support to self-support and reintegrating the disowned parts of one's personality. His conception of human nature and these two agendas set the stage for a variety of techniques and for his confrontational style of conducting therapy. He was a master at intentionally frustrating clients to enhance their awareness.

A basic assumption of Gestalt therapy is that individuals have the capacity to self-regulate when they are aware of what is happening in and around them.

Therapy provides the setting and opportunity for that awareness to be supported and restored. The therapist is attentive to the client's present experience and trusts in the process, thereby assisting the client in moving toward increased awareness, contact, and integration (Brown, 2007).

The Gestalt theory of change posits that the more we work at becoming who or what we are not, the more we remain the same. Fritz's good friend and psychiatrist colleague Arnie Beisser (1970) suggested that authentic change occurs more from being who we are than from trying to be who we are not. Beisser called this simple tenet the **paradoxical theory of change**. We are constantly moving between who we "should be" and who we "are." Gestalt therapists ask clients to invest themselves fully in their current condition rather than striving to become who they should be. Gestalt therapists believe people change and grow when they experience who they really are in the world (Yontef & Schulz, 2013).

Some Principles of Gestalt Therapy Theory

Several basic principles underlying the theory of Gestalt therapy are briefly described in this section: holism, field theory, the figure-formation process, and organismic self-regulation. Other key concepts of Gestalt therapy are developed in more detail in the sections that follow. LO3

Holism *Gestalt* is a German word meaning a whole or completion, or a form that cannot be separated into parts without losing its essence. All of nature is seen as a unified and coherent whole, and the whole is different from the sum of its parts. Because Gestalt therapists are interested in the whole person, they place no superior value on a particular aspect of the individual. Gestalt practice attends to a client's thoughts, feelings, behaviors, body, memories, and dreams.

Field Theory Gestalt therapy is based on **field theory**, which, simply put, asserts that the organism must be seen in its environment, or in its context, as part of the constantly changing field. Gestalt therapists pay attention to and explore what is occurring at the boundary between the person and the environment. Emphasis may be on a **figure** (those aspects of the individual's experience that are most salient at any moment) or the **ground** (those aspects of the client's presentation that are often out of his or her awareness). Cues to this background can be found on the surface through physical gestures, tone of voice, demeanor, and other nonverbal content. This is often referred to by Gestalt therapists as "attending to the obvious," while paying attention to how the parts fit together, how the individual makes contact with the environment, and integration.

The Figure-Formation Process Derived from the study of visual perception by a group of Gestalt psychologists, the **figure-formation process** tracks how the individual organizes experience from moment to moment as some aspect of the environmental field emerges from the background and becomes the focal point of the individual's attention and interest. For example, imagine seeing a woman on a hill in the distance. You do not see her clearly but receive an overall impression of this figure: a Gestalt. As you move closer, you gain more awareness of this figure and she becomes increasingly clear and more detailed: you see her face and the way she buttons her blouse. In the figure-formation process, contemporary Gestalt therapists facilitate the client's movement toward and away from this figure of interest. The dominant needs of the individual at a given moment influence this process (Frew, 1997).

Organismic Self-Regulation The figure-formation process is intertwined with the principle of **organismic self-regulation**, a process by which equilibrium is "disturbed" by the emergence of a need, a sensation, or an interest. Organisms will do their best to regulate themselves, given their own capabilities and the resources of their environment (Latner, 1986). Individuals can take actions and make contacts to restore equilibrium or to contribute to growth and change. What emerges in therapeutic work is what is of interest to the client or what the client needs to gain equilibrium or to change. Gestalt therapists direct the client's awareness to the figures that emerge from the background during a therapy session and use the figure-formation process as a guide for the focus of therapeutic work.

Contact and Resistances to Contact

In Gestalt therapy contact is necessary if change and growth are to occur. **Contact** is made by seeing, hearing, smelling, touching, and moving. Effective contact means interacting with nature and with other people without losing one's sense of individuality. Prerequisites for good contact are clear awareness, full energy, and the ability to express oneself. Contact between therapist and client are key to Gestalt therapy practice (Yontef & Schulz, 2013; Zinker, 1978). Miriam Polster (1987) claimed that contact is the lifeblood of growth. It is the continually renewed creative adjustment of individuals to their environment. It entails zest, imagination, and creativity. There are only moments of this type of contact, so it is most accurate to think of levels of contact rather than a final state to achieve. After a contact experience, there is typically a withdrawal to integrate what has been learned. Gestalt therapists talk about the two functions of boundaries: to connect and to separate. Both contact and withdrawal are necessary and important to healthy functioning.

Gestalt therapists also focus on interruptions, disturbances, and resistances to contact, which were developed as coping processes but often end up preventing us from experiencing the present in a full and real way. Resistances are typically adopted out of our awareness and, when they function in a chronic way, can contribute to dysfunctional behavior. Because resistances are developed as a means of coping with life situations, they possess positive qualities as well as problematic ones, and many contemporary Gestalt therapists refer to them as "contact boundary phenomena." Polster and Polster (1973) describe five different kinds of contact boundary disturbances: introjection, projection, retroflection, deflection, and confluence.

Introjection is the tendency to uncritically accept others' beliefs and standards without assimilating them to make them congruent with who we are. These introjects remain alien to us because we have not analyzed and restructured them. When we introject, we passively incorporate what the environment provides rather than clearly identifying what we want or need. If we remain in this stage, our energy is bound up in taking things as we find them and believing that authorities know what is best for us rather than working for things ourselves.

Projection is the reverse of introjection. In projection we disown certain aspects of ourselves by assigning them to the environment. Those attributes of our personality that are inconsistent with our self-image are disowned and put onto, assigned to, and seen in other people; thus, blaming others for lots of our problems. By seeing in others the very qualities that we refuse to acknowledge in ourselves, we avoid taking responsibility for our own feelings and the person who we are, and this keeps us powerless to initiate change. People who use projection as a pattern tend to feel that they are victims of circumstances, and they believe that people have hidden meanings behind what they say.

Retroflection consists of turning back onto ourselves what we would like to do to someone else or doing to ourselves what we would like someone else to do to or for us. This process is principally an interruption of the action phase in the cycle of experience and typically involves a fair amount of anxiety. People who rely on retroflection tend to inhibit themselves from taking action out of fear of embarrassment, guilt, and resentment. People who self-mutilate or who injure themselves, for example, are often directing aggression inward out of fear of directing it toward others. Depression and psychosomatic complaints are often created by retroflecting. Typically, these maladaptive styles of functioning are adopted outside of our awareness; part of the process of Gestalt therapy is to help us discover a self-regulatory system so that we can deal realistically with the world.

Deflection is the process of distraction or veering off, so that it is difficult to maintain a sustained sense of contact. We attempt to diffuse or defuse contact through the overuse of humor, abstract generalizations, and questions rather than statements (Frew, 1986). When we deflect, we speak through and for others, beating around the bush rather than being direct and engaging the environment in an inconsistent and inconsequential basis, which results in emotional depletion.

Confluence involves blurring the differentiation between the self and the environment. As we strive to blend in and get along with everyone, there is no clear demarcation between internal experience and outer reality. Confluence in relationships involves the absence of conflicts, slowness to anger, and a belief that all parties experience the same feelings and thoughts we do. This style of contact is characteristic of clients who have a high need to be accepted and liked, thus finding enmeshment comfortable. This condition makes genuine contact extremely difficult. A therapist might assist clients who use this channel of resistance by asking questions such as: "What are you doing now?" "What are you experiencing at this moment?" "What do you want right now?"

Terms such as *interruptions in contact* or *boundary disturbance* refer to the characteristic styles people employ in their attempts to control their environment through one of these channels of resistance. The premise in Gestalt therapy is that contact is both normal and healthy, and clients are encouraged to become increasingly aware of their dominant style of blocking contact and their use of resistance. Today's Gestalt therapists readily attend to how clients interrupt contact, approaching the interruptive styles with respect and taking each style seriously, knowing that it has served an important function in the past. It is important to explore what the resistance does for clients: what it protects them from, and what it keeps them from experiencing.

The Now

One of the main contributions of the Gestalt approach is its emphasis on learning to appreciate and fully experience the present moment. Focusing on the past and the future can be a way to avoid coming to terms with the present. Polster and Polster (1973) developed the thesis that "power is in the present." It is a common tendency for clients to invest their energies in bemoaning their past mistakes and ruminating about how life could and should have been different or engaging in endless resolutions and plans for the future. As clients direct their energy toward what was or what might have been or live in fantasy about the future, the power of the present diminishes.

Phenomenological inquiry involves paying attention to what is occurring now. Most people can stay in the present for only a short time and are inclined to find ways of interrupting the flow of the present. Instead of experiencing their feelings in the here and now, clients often *talk about* their feelings, almost as if their feelings were detached from their present experiencing. One of the aims of Gestalt therapy is to help clients to become increasingly aware of their present experience.

To help the client make contact with the present moment, Gestalt therapists ask "what" and "how" questions, but rarely ask "why" questions. To promote "now" awareness, the therapist encourages a dialogue in the present tense by asking questions like these: "What is happening now?" "What is going on now?" "What are you experiencing as you sit there and attempt to talk?" "What is your awareness at this moment?" "How are you experiencing your fear?" "How are you attempting to withdraw at this moment?" "How is it for you to be with me in this room now?" Phenomenological inquiry also involves suspending any preconceived ideas, assumptions, or interpretations concerning the meaning of a client's experience.

For example, if Josephine begins to talk about sadness, pain, or confusion, the Gestalt therapist invites her to experience her sadness, pain, or confusion *now*. As she attends to the present experience, the therapist gauges how much anxiety or discomfort is present and chooses further interventions accordingly. The therapist might choose not to comment as Josephine moves away from the present moment, only to extend another invitation several minutes later. If a feeling emerges, the therapist might suggest an experiment that would help Josephine to increase her awareness of the feeling, such as exploring where and how she experiences it. Likewise, if a thought or idea emerges, introducing an experiment can help her delve into the thought, explore it more fully, and consider its effects and possible ramifications.

Gestalt therapists recognize that the past will make regular appearances in the present moment, usually because of some lack of completion of that past experience. When the past seems to have a significant bearing on clients' present attitudes or behavior, it is dealt with by bringing it into the present as much as possible. When clients speak about their past, the therapist may ask them to reenact it as though they were living it now. The therapist directs clients to "bring the fantasy here" or "tell me the dream as though you were having it now," striving to help them relive what they experienced earlier. For example, rather than talking about a past childhood trauma with her father, a client becomes the hurt child and talks directly to her father in fantasy, or by imagining him being present in the room in an empty chair.

Unfinished Business

When figures emerge from the background but are not completed and resolved, individuals are left with **unfinished business**, which can be manifested in unexpressed feelings such as resentment, rage, hatred, pain, anxiety, grief, guilt, and abandonment. Unacknowledged feelings create unnecessary emotional debris that clutters present-centered awareness. Because the feelings are not fully experienced in awareness, they linger in the background and are carried into present life in ways that interfere with effective contact with oneself and others: "These incomplete directions *do seek* completion and when they get powerful enough, the individual is beset with preoccupation, compulsive behavior, wariness, oppressive energy and much self-defeating behavior" (Polster & Polster, 1973, p. 36). Unfinished business persists until the individual faces and deals with the unexpressed feelings. The effects of unfinished business often show up in some blockage within the body, and the therapist's task is to assist clients in exploring these bodily expressions. Gestalt therapists emphasize paying attention to the bodily experience on the assumption that if feelings are unexpressed they tend to result in some physical sensations or problems.

The **impasse**, or stuck point, occurs when external support is not available or the customary way of being does not work. The therapist's task is to accompany clients in experiencing the impasse without rescuing or frustrating them. The counselor assists clients by providing situations that encourage them to fully experience their condition of being stuck. By completely experiencing the impasse, they are able to get into contact with their frustrations and accept whatever is rather than wishing they were different. Gestalt therapy is based on the notion that individuals have a striving toward actualization and growth and that if they accept all aspects of themselves without judging these dimensions they can begin to think, feel, and act differently.

Energy and Blocks to Energy

When energy is blocked, in may result in unfinished business (Conyne, 2015). In Gestalt therapy special attention is given to where energy is located, how it is used, and how it can be blocked. Blocked energy is another form of defensive behavior. It can be manifested by tension in some part of the body, by posture, by keeping one's body tight and closed, by not breathing deeply, by looking away from people when speaking to avoid contact, by choking off sensations, by numbing feelings, and by speaking with a restricted voice, to mention only a few.

Clients may not be aware of their energy or where it is located, and they may experience it in a negative way. One of the tasks of the therapist is to help clients find the focus of interrupted energy, identify the ways in which they are blocking energy, and transform this blocked energy into more adaptive behaviors. Clients can be encouraged to recognize how their resistance is being expressed in their body. Rather than trying to rid themselves of certain bodily symptoms, clients can be encouraged to delve fully into tension states and bodily symptoms. For example, by allowing themselves to exaggerate their tight mouth and shaking legs, they can discover for themselves how they are diverting energy and keeping themselves from a full expression of aliveness.

The Therapeutic Process

Therapeutic Goals

Gestalt therapy does not ascribe to a "goal-oriented" methodology per se, but therapists clearly attend to a basic goal—namely, assisting the client to attain greater awareness, and with it, greater choice. Awareness includes knowing the environment, knowing oneself, accepting oneself, and being able to make contact. Increased and enriched awareness, by itself, is seen as curative. Without awareness clients do not possess the tools for personality change. With awareness they have the capacity to face, accept, and integrate denied parts as well as to fully experience their subjectivity. Through becoming aware of these denied parts and working toward owning their experience, clients can become integrated, or whole. When clients stay with their awareness, important unfinished business will emerge and can be dealt with in therapy. The Gestalt approach helps clients note their own awareness process so that they can be responsible and can selectively and discriminatingly make choices. Awareness emerges within the context of a genuine meeting (contact) between client and therapist.

The existential view (see Chapter 6) is that we are continually engaged in a process of remaking and discovering ourselves. We do not have a static identity, but discover new facets of our being as we face new challenges. Gestalt therapy is basically an existential encounter out of which clients tend to move in certain directions. Through a creative involvement in Gestalt process, Zinker (1978) expects clients will do the following:

- Move toward increased awareness of themselves
- Gradually assume ownership of their experience (as opposed to making others responsible for what they are thinking, feeling, and doing)
- Develop skills and acquire values that will allow them to satisfy their needs without violating the rights of others
- Become more aware of all of their senses
- Learn to accept responsibility for what they do, including accepting the consequences of their actions
- Be able to ask for and get help from others and be able to give to others

Therapist's Function and Role

The therapist's job is to invite clients into an active partnership where they can learn about themselves by adopting an experimental attitude toward life in which they try out new behaviors and notice what happens (Perls, Hefferline, & Goodman, 1951). Gestalt therapists use active methods and personal engagement with clients to increase their awareness, freedom, and self-direction rather than directing them toward preset goals (Yontef & Jacobs, 2014).

Contemporary Gestalt practitioners view clients as the experts on their own experience and encourage them to attend to their sensory awareness in the present moment. Gestalt therapists value self-discovery and assume that clients can discover for themselves the ways in which they block or interrupt their awareness and experience (Watson, Goldman, & Greenberg, 2011). Yontef (1993) stresses that although the therapist functions as a guide and a catalyst, presents experiments, and shares observations, the basic work of therapy is done by the client. Yontef maintains that the therapist's task is to create a climate in which clients are likely to try out new ways of being and behaving. Gestalt therapists do not force change on clients through confrontation. Instead, they work within a context of I/Thou dialogue in a here-and-now framework.

An important function of Gestalt therapists is paying attention to clients' body language. These nonverbal cues provide rich information as they often represent feelings of which the client is unaware. The therapist needs to be alert for gaps in attention and awareness and for incongruities between verbalizations and what clients are doing with their bodies. Therapists might direct clients to speak for and become their gestures or body parts by asking, "What do your eyes say?" "If your hands could speak at this moment, what would they say?" "Can you carry on a conversation between your right and left hands?" Clients may verbally express anger and at the same time smile. Or they may say they are in pain and at the same time laugh. Therapists can ask clients to become aware of what their laughter might mean. Laughter may mask feelings of anger or pain, and therapists can facilitate clients' work in discovering what it could mean for them.

In addition to calling attention to clients' nonverbal language, the Gestalt therapist places emphasis on the relationship between language patterns and personality. Clients' speech patterns are often an expression of their feelings, thoughts, and attitudes. The Gestalt approach focuses on overt speaking habits as a way to increase clients' awareness of themselves, especially by asking them to notice whether their words are congruent with what they are experiencing or instead are distancing them from their emotions.

Language can both describe and conceal. By focusing on language, clients are able to increase their awareness of what they are experiencing in the present moment and of how they are avoiding coming into contact with this here-and-now experience. Here are some examples of the aspects of language that Gestalt therapists might focus on:

- *"It" talk.* When clients say "it" instead of "I," they are using depersonalizing language. The counselor may ask them to substitute personal pronouns for impersonal ones so that they will assume an increased sense of responsibility. For example, if a client says, "It is difficult to make friends," he could be asked to restate this by making an "I" statement: "I have trouble making friends."
- *"You" talk.* Global and impersonal language tends to keep the person hidden. The therapist often points out generalized uses of "you" and invites the client to experiment with substituting "I" when this is what is meant.
- *Questions.* Questions have a tendency to keep the questioner hidden, safe, and unknown. Gestalt therapists often ask clients to experiment with changing their questions into statements. In making personal statements, clients begin to assume responsibility for what they say. They may become aware of how they are keeping themselves mysterious through a barrage of questions and how this serves to prevent them from making declarations that express themselves.

- *Language that denies power*. Some clients have a tendency to deny their personal power by adding qualifiers or disclaimers to their statements. The therapist may also point out to clients how certain qualifiers subtract from their effectiveness. Experimenting with omitting qualifiers such as "maybe," "perhaps," "sort of," "I guess," "possibly," and "I suppose" can help clients change ambivalent messages into clear and direct statements. Likewise, when clients say "I can't," they are really implying "I won't." Encouraging clients to substitute "won't" for "can't" often assists them in owning and accepting their power by taking responsibility for their decisions. The therapist must be careful in intervening so that clients do not feel that everything they say is subject to scrutiny. The therapist hopes to foster awareness of what is really being expressed through words, not to scrutinize behavior.
- *Listening to clients' metaphors*. In his workshops, Erv Polster (1995) emphasizes the importance of a therapist learning how to listen to the metaphors of clients. By tuning into metaphors, the therapist gets rich clues to clients' internal struggles. Examples of metaphors that can be amplified include client statements such as "It's hard for me to spill my guts in here." "At times I feel that I don't have a leg to stand on." "I feel like I have a hole in my soul." "I need to be prepared in case someone blasts me." "I felt ripped to shreds after you confronted me last week." "After this session, I feel as though I've been put through a meat grinder." Beneath the metaphor may lie a suppressed internal dialogue that represents critical unfinished business or reactions to a present interaction. For example, to the client who says she feels that she has been put through a meat grinder, the therapist could ask: "What is your experience of being ground meat?" or "Who is doing the grinding?" It is essential to encourage this client to say more about what she is experiencing. The art of therapy consists of assisting clients in translating the meaning of their metaphors so that they can be dealt with in therapy.
- *Listening for language that uncovers a story*. Polster (1995) also teaches the value of what he calls "fleshing out a flash." He reports that clients often use language that is elusive yet gives significant clues to a story that illustrates their life struggles. Effective therapists learn to pick out a small part of what someone says and then to focus on and develop this element. Clients are likely to slide over pregnant phrases, but the alert therapist can ask questions that will help them flesh out their story line. It is essential for therapists to pay attention to what is fascinating about the person who is sitting before them and get that person to tell a story.

In a workshop I observed Erv Polster's magnificent style in challenging a person (Joe) who had volunteered for a demonstration of an individual session. Although Joe had a fascinating story to reveal about a particular facet of his life, he was presenting himself in a lifeless manner, and the energy was going flat. Eventually, Polster asked him, "Are you keeping my interest right now? Does it matter to you whether I am engaged with you?" Joe looked shocked, but he soon got the point. He accepted

Polster's challenge to make sure that he not only kept the therapist interested but also presented himself in a way to keep those in the audience interested. It was clear that Polster was directing Joe's attention to a process of *how* he was expressing his feelings and life experiences rather than being concerned with *what* he was talking about.

Polster believes storytelling is not always a form of resistance. Instead, it can be the heart of the therapeutic process. He maintains that people are storytelling beings. The therapist's task is to assist clients in telling their story in a lively way. Polster (1987b) believes many people come to therapy to change the titles of their stories rather than to transform their life stories.

Client's Experience in Therapy

The general orientation of Gestalt therapy is toward **dialogue**, an engagement between people who each bring their unique experiences to that meeting (Yontef & Schulz, 2013). Traditional Gestalt therapists assumed that clients must be confronted about how they avoid accepting responsibility, but the dialogic attitude that characterizes contemporary Gestalt therapy creates the ground for a meeting place between client and therapist. Other issues that can become the focal point of therapy include the client–therapist relationship and the similarities in the ways clients relate to the therapist and to others in their environment.

Gestalt therapists do not make interpretations that explain the dynamics of an individual's behavior or tell a client why he or she is acting in a certain way because they are not the experts on the client's experience. Clients in Gestalt therapy are active participants who make their own interpretations and meanings. It is they who increase awareness and decide what they will or will not do with their personal meaning.

Miriam Polster (1987) described a three-stage integration sequence that characterizes client growth in therapy. The first part of this sequence consists of *discovery*. Clients are likely to reach a new realization about themselves or to acquire a novel view of an old situation, or they may take a new look at some significant person in their lives. Such discoveries often come as a surprise to them.

The second stage of the integration sequence is *accommodation*, which involves clients' recognizing that they have a choice. Clients begin by trying out new behaviors in the supportive environment of the therapy office, and then they expand their awareness of the world. Making new choices is often done awkwardly, but with therapeutic support clients can gain skill in coping with difficult situations. Clients are likely to participate in out-of-office experiments, which can be discussed in the next therapy session.

The third stage of the integration sequence is *assimilation*, which involves clients' learning how to influence their environment. At this phase clients feel capable of dealing with the surprises they encounter in everyday living. They are now beginning to do more than passively accept the environment. Behavior at this stage may include taking a stand on a critical issue. Eventually, clients develop confidence in their ability to improve and improvise. Improvisation is the confidence that comes from knowledge and skills. Clients are able to make choices that will result in getting what they want. The therapist points out that something has been accomplished and acknowledges the changes that have taken place within the client. At this phase clients have learned what they can do to maximize their chances of getting what is needed from their environment.

Relationship Between Therapist and Client

As an existential brand of therapy, Gestalt practice involves a person-to-person relationship between therapist and client. Therapists are responsible for the quality of their presence, for knowing themselves and the client, and for remaining open to the client. They are also responsible for establishing and maintaining a therapeutic atmosphere that will foster a spirit of work on the client's part. It is important that therapists allow themselves to be affected by their clients and that they actively share their own present perceptions and experiences as they encounter clients in the here and now. However, therapists need to be thoughtful about *when* and *what* to share. When a difficulty in a client's life is being enacted in the therapeutic relationship, the therapist invites the client to explore this issue (Wheeler & Axelsson, 2015).

Gestalt therapists not only allow their clients to be who they are but also remain themselves and do not get lost in a role. Therapists are expected to encounter clients with honest and immediate reactions, and therapists share their personal experience and stories in relevant and appropriate ways. Further, they give feedback that allows clients to develop an awareness of what they are actually doing. Brown (2007) suggests that therapists share their reactions with clients, yet she also stresses the importance of demonstrating an attitude of respect, acceptance, present-centeredness, and presence.

A number of writers have given central importance to the I/Thou relationship and the quality of the therapist's presence, as opposed to emphasizing technical skills. They warn of the dangers of becoming technique-bound and losing sight of their own being as they engage with the client. Contemporary relational Gestalt therapy has moved beyond earlier (traditional) therapeutic practices. Creating a relationship (or alliance) is not a prelude to therapy but is at the heart of Gestalt therapy. The therapist's attitudes and behavior and the relationship that is established are what really count (Brown, 2007; Frew, 2013; Melnick & Nevis, 2005; E. Polster, 1987a, 1987b; M. Polster, 1987; Resnick, 2015; Wheeler & Axelsson, 2015; Yontef & Jacobs, 2014).

Many contemporary Gestalt therapists place increasing emphasis on factors such as presence, authentic dialogue, gentleness, more direct self-expression by the therapist, decreased use of stereotypic exercises, and greater trust in the client's experiencing. Laura Perls (1976) stressed the notion that the person of the therapist is more important than using techniques. She says, "There are as many styles as there are therapists and clients who discover themselves and each other and together invent their relationship" (p. 223). A current trend in Gestalt practice is toward greater emphasis on the client–therapist relationship, and therapists who operate from this orientation are able to establish a present-centered, nonjudgmental dialogue that allows clients to deepen their awareness and to make contact with another person (Jacobs, 1989; Wheeler & Axelsson, 2015).

Polster and Polster (1973) emphasize the importance of therapists knowing themselves and being therapeutic instruments. Like artists who need to be in touch with what they are painting, therapists are artistic participants in the creation of new life. The Polsters implore therapists to use their own experiences as essential ingredients in the therapy process. According to them, therapists are more than mere responders or catalysts. If they are to make effective contact with clients, therapists must be in tune with both their clients and themselves. Therapy is a two-way engagement that changes both the client and the therapist. If therapists are not sensitively tuned to their own qualities of tenderness, toughness, and compassion and to their reactions to the client, they become technicians. Experiments should be aimed at awareness, not at simple solutions to a client's problem.

Application: Therapeutic Techniques and Procedures

The Experiment in Gestalt Therapy

Although the Gestalt approach is concerned with the obvious, its simplicity should not be taken to mean that the therapist's job is easy. Developing a variety of interventions is simple, but employing these methods in a mechanical fashion allows clients to continue inauthentic living. If clients are to become authentic, they need contact with an authentic therapist. Gestalt therapy methodology is tailored to the needs of clients, and experiments are typically presented in an invitational manner. Dr. Jon Frew, a Gestalt therapist, demonstrates Gestalt interventions applied to the case of Ruth in *Case Approach to Counseling and Psychotherapy* (Corey, 2013, chap. 6).

Before discussing the variety of Gestalt methods you could include in your repertoire of counseling procedures, it is helpful to differentiate between *exercises* (or techniques) and *experiments*. **Exercises** are ready-made techniques that are sometimes used to make something happen in a therapy session or to achieve a goal. They can be catalysts for individual work or for promoting interaction among members of a therapy group. **Experiments**, in contrast, grow out of the interaction between client and therapist, and they emerge within this dialogic process. They can be considered the very cornerstone of experiential learning. Frew (2013) defines the experiment "as a method that shifts the focus of counseling from talking about a topic to an activity that will heighten the client's awareness and understanding through experience" (p. 238). According to Melnick and Nevis (2005), experiments have been confused with techniques: "A technique is a performed experiment with specific learning goals. . . . An experiment, on the other hand, flows directly from psychotherapy theory and is crafted to fit the individual as he or she exists in the here and now" (p. 108).

In Gestalt therapy, an experiment is an intervention and active technique that facilitates the collaborative exploration of a client's experience (Brownell, 2016; Yontef & Schulz, 2013). Experiments give people a chance to be systematic in learning by doing and are best thought of as ways of exploring a client's experiential world. Clients explore their awareness process and discover how their thinking, feeling, sensing, and behaving either works for them or does not (Yontef & Schulz, 2013). "The goal [of an experiment] is always learning–slowing down and deepening experience in the service of new understanding and new possibilities for more flexible and effective response" (Wheeler & Axelsson, 2015, p. 40). Experiences are a key part of the ongoing dialogue between client and therapist, not a method to fix the client or to make the therapy process more exciting (Yontef & Schulz, 2013).

The experiment is fundamental to Gestalt therapy. Zinker (1978) sees therapy sessions as a series of experiments, which are the avenues for clients to learn experientially. What is learned from an experiment is a surprise to both the client and the therapist because an experiment is an intentional entry into novel experience aimed at discovery. The most dynamic experiments emerge uniquely from the work between client and therapist (Brownell, 2016). Gestalt experiments are a creative adventure and a way in which clients can express themselves behaviorally. Experiments are spontaneous, one-of-a-kind, and relevant to a particular moment and a particular development of a figure-formation process. They are not designed to achieve a particular goal but occur in the context of a moment-to-moment contacting process between therapist and client. Polster (1995) indicates that experiments are designed by the therapist and evolve from the theme already developing through therapeutic engagement, such as the client's report of needs, dreams, fantasies, and body awareness. Experimentation is an attitude inherent in all Gestalt therapy; it is a collaborative process with full participation of the client. Clients test an experiment to determine what does and does not fit for them through their own awareness (Yontef, 1993, 1995).

Miriam Polster (1987) says that an experiment is a way to bring out some kind of internal conflict by making this struggle an actual process. It is aimed at facilitating a client's ability to work through the stuck points of his or her life. Experiments encourage spontaneity and inventiveness by bringing the possibilities for action directly into the therapy session. By dramatizing or playing out problem situations or relationships in the relative safety of the therapy context, clients increase their range of flexibility of behavior. According to M. Polster, Gestalt experiments can take many forms: imagining a threatening future encounter; setting up a dialogue between a client and some significant person in his or her life; dramatizing the memory of a painful event; reliving a particularly profound early experience in the present; assuming the identity of one's mother or father through role playing; focusing on gestures, posture, and other nonverbal signs of inner expression; or carrying on a dialogue between two conflicting aspects within the person. Clients may experience the feelings associated with their conflicts as experiments bring struggles to life by inviting clients to enact them in the present. It is crucial that experiments be tailored to each individual and used in a timely and appropriate manner; they also need to be carried out in a context that offers a balance between support and risk. Sensitivity and careful attention on the therapist's part are essential so that clients are "neither blasted into experiences that are too threatening nor allowed to stay in safe but infertile territory" (M. Polster & Polster, 1990, p. 104).

If students-in-training limit their understanding of Gestalt therapy to simply reading about the approach, Gestalt methods are likely to seem abstract and the notion of experiments may seem strange. Asking clients to "become" an object in one of their dreams, for instance, may seem silly and pointless. It is important for counselors to *personally* experience the power of Gestalt experiments and to feel comfortable suggesting them to clients. In this regard, it can be most useful for trainees to personally experience Gestalt methods as a client.

Preparing Clients for Gestalt Experiments

LO4 It is essential that counselors establish a relationship with their clients, so that the clients will feel trusting enough to participate in the learning that can result from Gestalt experiments. Clients will get more from Gestalt experiments if they are oriented and prepared for them. Through a trusting relationship with the therapist, clients are likely to recognize their resistance and allow themselves to participate in these experiments.

If clients are to cooperate, counselors must avoid directing them in a commanding fashion to carry out an experiment. Typically, I ask clients if they are willing to try out an experiment to see what they might learn from it. I also tell clients that they can stop when they choose to, so the power is with them. Clients at times say that they feel silly or self-conscious or that the task feels artificial or unreal. At such times I am likely to respond by asking, "Are you willing to give it a try and see what happens?" The *way* in which clients resist doing an experiment reveals a great deal about their personality and their way of being in the world. Gestalt therapists expect and respect the emergence of reluctance and meet clients wherever they are. Gestalt experiments work best when the therapist is respectful of the client's cultural background and has a solid working alliance with the person. Clients with a long history of containing their feelings may be reluctant to participate in experiments that are likely to bring their emotions to the surface.

Contemporary Gestalt therapy places much less emphasis on resistance than the early version of Gestalt therapy. Although it is possible to look at "resistance to awareness" and "resistance to contact," the idea of resistance is viewed as unnecessary by some Gestalt therapists. Frew (2013) argues that the notion of resistance is completely foreign to the theory and practice of Gestalt therapy and suggests that resistance is a term frequently used for clients who are not doing what the therapist wants them to do. Polster and Polster (1976) suggest that it is best for therapists to observe what is actually and presently happening rather than trying to make something happen. This gets away from the notion that clients are resisting and thus behaving wrongly. According to the Polsters, change occurs through contact and awareness—one does not have to try to change. Maurer (2005) writes about "appreciating resistance" as a creative adjustment to a situation rather than something to overcome. Maurer claims that we need to respect resistance, take it seriously, and view it as "the energy" and not "the enemy."

It is well to remember that Gestalt experiments are designed to expand clients' awareness and to help them try out new modes of behavior. Within the safety of the therapeutic situation, clients are given opportunities and encouraged to "try on" a new behavior. An experimental attitude in the therapeutic process involves the client's input and allows what emerges between client and therapist to guide the direction of the therapy (Yontef & Schulz, 2013). This heightens the awareness of a particular aspect of functioning, which leads to increased self-understanding (Breshgold, 1989; Yontef, 1995). Experiments are only means to the end of helping people become more aware and making changes they most desire.

The Role of Confrontation

LO5

Students are sometimes put off by their perception that a Gestalt counselor's style is direct and confrontational. I tell my students that it is a mistake to equate the practice of any theory with its founder. In the workshops that Fritz Perls gave, people often found him harshly confrontational and saw him as meeting his own needs through showmanship. Yontef (1993) refers to the traditional Perlsian style as a "boom-boom-boom therapy" characterized by theatrics, abrasive confrontation, and intense catharsis. Yontef (1993, 1999) is critical of the anti-intellectual, individualistic, dramatic, and confrontational flavor that characterized traditional Gestalt therapy in the "anything goes environment" of the 1960s and 1970s.

The contemporary practice of Gestalt therapy has progressed beyond this style. According to Yontef (1999), contemporary relational Gestalt therapy has evolved to include more support and increased kindness and compassion in therapy. This approach "combines sustained empathic inquiry with crisp, clear, and relevant awareness focusing" (p. 10). Perls practiced a highly confrontational approach as a way to deal with avoidance, but this technique-focused style of working has given way to a more dialogue-centered methodology today (Bowman, 2005; Frew, 2013; Yontef & Jacobs, 2014; Yontef & Schulz, 2013).

In contemporary Gestalt therapy, **confrontation** is set up in a way that *invites* clients to examine their behaviors, attitudes, and thoughts. Therapists can encourage clients to look at certain incongruities, especially gaps between their verbal and nonverbal expression. Further, confrontation does not have to be aimed at weaknesses or negative traits; clients can be challenged to recognize how they are blocking their strengths.

Therapists who care enough to make demands on their clients are telling them, in effect, that they could be in fuller contact with themselves and others. Ultimately, however, clients must decide for themselves if they want to accept this invitation to learn more about themselves. This caveat needs to be kept in mind with all of the experiments that are to be described.

Gestalt Therapy Interventions

LO6

Exercises are preplanned activities that can be used to elicit emotion, produce action, or achieve a specific goal. Experiments, in contrast, are spontaneously created to fit what is happening in the therapeutic process and can be useful tools to help clients gain fuller awareness, experience internal conflicts, resolve inconsistencies and dichotomies, and work through impasses that prevent completion of unfinished business (Conyne, 2015). Some therapists operate on the erroneous assumption that the practice of Gestalt therapy consists of a bag of techniques that define the therapy, but as Resnick (2015) states, techniques and exercises are the least important part of Gestalt therapy.

The techniques described here neither define Gestalt therapy nor are they a necessary part of Gestalt practice. When used at their best, these interventions fit the therapeutic situation and highlight whatever the client is experiencing. The following material is based on Levitsky and Perls (1970), with my own suggestions added for implementing these methods.

The Internal Dialogue Exercise One goal of Gestalt therapy is to bring about integrated functioning and acceptance of aspects of one's personality that have been disowned and denied. Gestalt therapists pay close attention to splits in personality function. A main division is between the "top dog" and the "underdog," and therapy often focuses on the war between the two.

The top dog is righteous, authoritarian, moralistic, demanding, bossy, and manipulative. This is the "critical parent" that badgers with "shoulds" and "oughts" and manipulates with threats of catastrophe. The underdog manipulates by playing the role of victim: by being defensive, apologetic, helpless, and weak and by feigning powerlessness. This is the passive side, the one without responsibility, and the one that finds excuses.

The top dog and the underdog are engaged in a constant struggle for control. The struggle helps to explain why one's resolutions and promises often go unfulfilled and why one's procrastination persists. The tyrannical top dog demands that one be thus-and-so, whereas the underdog defiantly plays the role of disobedient child. As a result of this struggle for control, the individual becomes fragmented into controller and controlled. The civil war between the two sides continues, with both sides fighting for their existence.

The conflict between the two opposing poles in the personality is rooted in the mechanism of introjection, which involves incorporating aspects of others, usually parents, into one's personality. It is essential that clients become aware of their introjects, especially the toxic introjects that poison the person and prevent personality integration.

The Empty-Chair Technique Jacob Moreno, the founder of psychodrama, originated the empty-chair technique, which was later incorporated into Gestalt therapy by Perls. The **empty chair** is a vehicle for the technique of role reversal, which is useful in bringing into consciousness the fantasies of what the "other" might be thinking or feeling. Essentially, this is a role-playing technique in which all the parts are played by the client. In this way the introjects can surface, and the client can experience the conflict more fully. There are many applications for this technique. One of the more important uses is to explore what another person in one's social network might be feeling, and what that person's more realistic predicament might be.

Using two chairs, the therapist asks the client to sit in one chair and be fully the top dog and then shift to the other chair and become the underdog. The dialogue can continue between both sides of the client. The conflict can be resolved by the client's acceptance and integration of both sides. This exercise helps clients get in touch with a feeling or a side of themselves that they may be denying; rather than merely talking about a conflicted feeling, they intensify the feeling and experience it fully. Further, by helping clients realize that the feeling is a very real part of themselves, the intervention discourages clients from disassociating the feeling. The goal of this exercise is to promote a higher level of integration between the polarities and conflicts that exist in everyone. The aim is not to rid oneself of certain traits but to learn to accept and live with the polarities.

Future Projection Technique In future projection, an anticipated event is brought into the present moment and acted out. This technique, often associated with psychodrama, is designed to help clients express and clarify concerns they have about the future. These concerns may include wishes and hopes, dreaded fears of tomorrow, or goals that provide some direction to life. A client creates a future time and place with selected people, brings this event into the present, and gets a new perspective on a problem. Clients may act out either a version of the way they hope a given situation will ideally unfold or their version of a feared outcome. Once clients clarify their hopes for a particular outcome, they are in a better position to take specific steps that will enable them to achieve the future they desire.

Making the Rounds Making the rounds is a Gestalt exercise that involves asking a person in a group to go up to others in the group and either speak to or do something with each person. The purpose is to confront, to risk, to disclose the self, to experiment with new behavior, and to grow and change. I have experimented with "making the rounds" when I sensed that a participant needed to face each person in the group with some theme. For example, a group member might say: "I've been sitting here for a long time wanting to participate but holding back because I'm afraid of trusting people in here. And besides, I don't think I'm worth the time of the group anyway." I might counter with "Are you willing to do something right now to get yourself more invested and to begin to work on gaining trust and self-confidence?" If the person answers affirmatively, my suggestion could well be, "Go around to each person and finish this sentence: 'I don't trust you because . . .'." Any number of exercises could be invented to help individuals involve themselves and choose to work on the things that keep them frozen in fear.

Some other related illustrations and examples that I find appropriate for the making-the-rounds intervention are reflected in clients' comments such as these: "I would like to reach out to people more often." "Nobody in here seems to care very much." "I'd like to make contact with you, but I'm afraid of being rejected [or accepted]." "It's hard for me to accept compliments; I always discount good things people say to me."

The Reversal Exercise Certain symptoms and behaviors often represent reversals of underlying or latent impulses. Thus, the therapist could ask a person who claims to suffer from severe inhibitions and excessive timidity to play the role of an exhibitionist. I remember a client in one of our therapy groups who had difficulty being anything but sugary sweet. I asked her to reverse her typical style and be as negative as she could be. The reversal worked well; soon she was playing her part with real gusto, and later she was able to recognize and accept her "negative side" as well as her "positive side."

The theory underlying the reversal technique is that clients take the plunge into the very thing that is fraught with anxiety and make contact with those parts of themselves that have been submerged and denied. This technique can help clients begin to accept certain personal attributes that they have tried to deny.

The Rehearsal Exercise Oftentimes we get stuck rehearsing silently to ourselves so that we will gain acceptance. When it comes to the performance, we experience stage fright, or anxiety, because we fear that we will not play our role well. Internal rehearsal consumes much energy and frequently inhibits our spontaneity and willingness to experiment with new behavior. When clients share their rehearsals out loud with a therapist, they become more aware of the many preparatory means they use in bolstering their social roles. They also become increasingly aware of how they try to meet the expectations of others, of the degree to which they want to be approved, accepted, and liked, and of the extent to which they go to attain acceptance.

The Exaggeration Exercise One aim of Gestalt therapy is for clients to become more aware of the subtle signals and cues they are sending through body language. Movements, postures, and gestures may communicate significant meanings, yet the cues may be incomplete. In this exercise the person is asked to exaggerate the movement or gesture repeatedly, which usually intensifies the feeling attached to the behavior and makes the inner meaning clearer. Some examples of behaviors that lend themselves to the exaggeration technique are trembling (shaking hands, legs), slouched posture and bent shoulders, clenched fists, tight frowning, facial grimacing, crossed arms, and so forth. If a client reports that his or her legs are shaking, the therapist may ask the client to stand up and exaggerate the shaking. Then the therapist may ask the client to put words to the shaking limbs.

Staying With the Feeling Most people want to escape from fearful stimuli and avoid unpleasant feelings. At key moments when clients refer to a feeling or a mood that is unpleasant and from which they have a great desire to flee, the therapist may urge clients to stay with their feeling and encourage them to go deeper into the feeling or behavior they wish to avoid. Facing and experiencing feelings not only takes courage but also is a mark of a willingness to endure the pain necessary for unblocking and making way for newer levels of growth. A strong therapeutic relationship built on trust and nonjudgmental acceptance fosters the safety needed for clients to stay with these unpleasant feelings.

The Gestalt Approach to Dream Work In psychoanalysis dreams are interpreted, intellectual insight is stressed, and free association is used to explore the unconscious meanings of dreams. The Gestalt approach does not interpret and analyze dreams. Instead, the intent is to bring dreams back to life and relive them as though they were happening now. The dream is acted out in the present, and the dreamer becomes a part of his or her dream. The suggested format for working with dreams includes making a list of all the details of the dream, remembering each person, event, and mood in it, and then becoming each of these parts by transforming oneself, acting as fully as possible and inventing dialogue. Each part of the dream is assumed to be a projection of the self, and the client creates scripts for encounters between the various characters or parts. All of the different parts of a dream are expressions of the client's own contradictory and inconsistent sides. By engaging in a dialogue between these opposing sides, the client gradually becomes more aware of the range of his or her own feelings.

Perls's concept of projection is central in his theory of dream formation; every person and every object in the dream represents a projected aspect of the dreamer. Perls (1969a) suggested that "we start with the impossible assumption that whatever we believe we see in another person or in the world is nothing but a projection"

(p. 67). Recognizing the senses and understanding projections go hand in hand. Clients do not think about or analyze the dream but use it as a script and experiment with the dialogue among the various parts of the dream. Because clients can act out a fight between opposing sides, eventually they can appreciate and accept their inner differences and integrate the opposing forces. Freud called the dream the royal road to the unconscious, but to Perls dreams are the "royal road to integration" (p. 66).

According to Perls, the dream is the most spontaneous expression of the existence of the human being. It represents an unfinished situation, but every dream also contains an existential message regarding oneself and one's current struggle. Everything can be found in dreams if all the parts are understood and assimilated; dreams serve as an excellent way to discover personality voids by revealing missing parts and clients' methods of avoidance. Perls asserts that if dreams are properly worked with, the existential message becomes clearer. If people do not remember dreams, they may be refusing to face what is wrong with their life. At the very least, the Gestalt counselor asks clients to talk to their missing dreams. For example, as directed by her therapist, a client reported the following dream in the present tense, as though she were still dreaming:

> I have three monkeys in a cage. One big monkey and two little ones! I feel very attached to these monkeys, although they are creating a lot of chaos in a cage that is divided into three separate spaces. They are fighting with one another—the big monkey is fighting with the little monkey. They are getting out of the cage, and they are clinging onto me. I feel like pushing them away from me. I feel totally overwhelmed by the chaos that they are creating around me. I turn to my mother and tell her that I need help, that I can no longer handle these monkeys because they are driving me crazy. I feel very sad and very tired, and I feel discouraged. I am walking away from the cage, thinking that I really love these monkeys, yet I have to get rid of them. I am telling myself that I am like everybody else. I get pets, and then when things get rough, I want to get rid of them. I am trying very hard to find a solution to keeping these monkeys and not allowing them to have such a terrible effect on me. Before I wake up from my dream, I am making the decision to put each monkey in a separate cage, and maybe that is the way to keep them.

The therapist then asked his client, Brenda, to "become" different parts of her dream. Thus, she became the cage, and she became and had a dialogue with each monkey, and then she became her mother, and so forth. One of the most powerful aspects of this technique was Brenda's reporting her dream as though it were still happening. She quickly perceived that her dream expressed a struggle she was having with her husband and her two children. From her dialogue work, Brenda discovered that she both appreciated and resented her family. She learned that she needed to let them know about her feelings and that together they might work on improving an intensely difficult lifestyle. She did not need an interpretation from her therapist to understand the clear message of her dream.

Application to Group Counseling

As a therapeutic orientation based on field theory, Gestalt therapy is well **LO7** suited for a group context. A main goal of the Gestalt group is to heighten awareness and self-regulation through interactions with one another and the group itself (Conyne, 2015). Gestalt therapy encourages direct experience and actions as opposed to merely *talking about* conflicts, problems, and feelings. If members have anxieties pertaining to some future event, they can enact these future concerns in the present. This here-and-now focus enlivens the group and assists members in vividly exploring their concerns. Moving from *talking about* to action is often done by the use of experiments in a group. Gestalt therapy employs a rich variety of interventions designed to intensify what group members are directly experiencing in the present moment for the purpose of leading to increased awareness. Gestalt group therapists attend to matters such as verbal and nonverbal language, postures, voice, interpersonal interactions, and group processes (Conyne, 2015).

When one member is the focus of work, other members can be used to enhance an individual's work. Through the skill of linking, the group leader can bring a number of members into the exploration of a problem. I prefer an interactive style of Gestalt group work and find that bringing in an interpersonal dimension maximizes the therapeutic potency within the group. I do not like to introduce a technique to promote something happening within a group; rather, I tend to invite members to try out different behavioral styles as a way to heighten what a given member might be experiencing at the moment. A group format provides a context for a great deal of creativity in using interventions and designing experiments. These experiments need to be tailored to each group member and used in a timely manner; they also need to be carried out in a context that offers a balance between support and risk. Experiments, at their best, evolve from what is going on within individual members and what is happening in the group at the moment.

Although Gestalt group leaders encourage members to heighten their awareness and attend to their interpersonal style of relating, leaders tend to take an active role in creating experiments to help members tap their resources. Gestalt leaders are actively engaged with the members, and leaders frequently engage in self-disclosure as a way to enhance relationships and create a sense of mutuality within the group. Gestalt leaders are especially concerned with awareness, contact, and experimentation (Yontef & Jacobs, 2014).

If members experience the group as being a safe place, they will be inclined to move into the unknown and challenge themselves. To increase the chances that members will benefit from Gestalt methods, group leaders need to communicate the general purpose of these interventions and create an experimental climate. Leaders are not trying to push an agenda; rather, members are free to try something new and determine for themselves the outcomes of an experiment.

In training workshops in group counseling that Marianne Schneider Corey and I conducted in Korea, the Gestalt approach was well accepted. Group members were very open and willing to share themselves emotionally once a climate of safety was created. Adopting the stance of phenomenological inquiry, we strive to avoid making assumptions about the members of a group, and we are careful not to impose our worldviews or values on them. Instead, we approach clients with respect, interest, compassion, and presence. We work collaboratively with our clients to discover how to best help them resolve the difficulties they experience internally, interpersonally, and in the context of their social environment. Although it is unrealistic to think you need to know everything about different cultures, it is essential to bring an attitude of respect and appreciation for differences to your work in diverse cultural environments around the world. With these attitudes we found that we were able to use many Gestalt interventions with Korean people in a group training context. In some ways this is not surprising because in Korea there is an emphasis on collectivistic values, and group work fits well into the Korean culture.

For a more detailed account of Gestalt therapy in groups, see Feder and Frew (2008), Feder (2006), and Corey (2016, chap. 11).

Gestalt Therapy From a Multicultural Perspective

Strengths From a Diversity Perspective

LO8

There are opportunities to creatively use Gestalt methods with culturally diverse populations if interventions are timed appropriately and used flexibly. Frew (2013) notes that contemporary Gestalt therapy can be a useful and effective approach with clients from diverse backgrounds because it takes the clients' context into account. One of the advantages of drawing on Gestalt experiments is that they can be tailored to fit the unique way in which an individual perceives and interprets his or her culture. Although most therapists have preconceptions, Gestalt therapists strive to approach each client in an open way. By bracketing their own values, Gestalt therapists remaining receptive to how clients' realities differ from their own. They do this by checking out their biases and views in dialogue with the client. This is particularly important in working with individuals from other cultures.

Fernbacher and Plummer (2005) stress the importance of assisting Gestalt therapy trainees in developing their own awareness and contend: "to undertake work across cultures from a Gestalt perspective, it is essential that we explore our own cultural selves . . . to make contact and encourage contact in and with others, we need to know about ourselves" (p. 131).

Gestalt therapy is particularly effective in helping people integrate the polarities within themselves. Many bicultural clients experience an ongoing struggle to reconcile what appears to be diverse aspects of the two cultures in which they live. In one of my weeklong groups, a dynamic piece of work was done by a woman with European roots. Her struggle consisted of integrating her American side with her experiences in Germany as a child. I suggested that she "bring her family into this group" by talking to selected members in the group as though they were members of her family. I invited her to imagine that she was 8 years old and that she could now say to her parents and siblings things that she had never expressed. She was asked to speak in German (because this was her primary language as a child). The combined factors of her trust in the group, her willingness to re-create an early scene by reliving it in the present moment, and her symbolic work with fantasy helped her achieve a significant breakthrough. She was able to put a new ending to an old and unfinished situation through her participation in this Gestalt experiment.

There are many opportunities to apply Gestalt experiments in creative ways with diverse client populations. In cultures where indirect speech is the norm, nonverbal behaviors may emphasize the unspoken content of verbal communication. These clients may express themselves nonverbally more expressively than they do with words. Gestalt therapists typically ask clients to focus on their gestures, facial expressions, and what they are experiencing within their own body. They attempt to fully understand the background of their clients' culture. They are concerned about which aspects of this background become central or figural for their clients and what meaning clients place on these figures.

Shortcomings From a Diversity Perspective

To a greater extent than is true of most other approaches, there are some potential problems in too quickly utilizing Gestalt experiments with some clients. Gestalt methods can lead to a high level of intense feelings. This focus on affect has clear limitations with those clients who have been culturally conditioned to be emotionally reserved and to avoid openly expressing feelings. As mentioned earlier, some individuals believe expressing feelings openly is a sign of weakness and a display of one's vulnerability. Therapists who operate on the assumption that catharsis is necessary for any change to occur are likely to find certain clients becoming increasingly reluctant to participate in experiments, and such clients may prematurely terminate counseling. Other individuals have strong cultural injunctions prohibiting them from directly expressing their emotions to their parents (such as "Never show your parents that you are angry at them" or "Strive for peace and harmony, and avoid conflicts"). I recall a client from India who was asked by his counselor to "bring your father into the room." The client was very reluctant to even symbolically tell his father of his disappointment with their relationship. In his culture the accepted way to deal with his father was to use his uncle as a go-between, and it was considered highly inappropriate to express any negative feelings toward his father. The client later said that he would have felt very guilty if he had symbolically told his father what he sometimes thought and felt.

Gestalt therapists who have truly integrated their approach are sensitive enough to practice in a flexible way. They consider the client's cultural framework and are able to adapt methods that are likely to be well received. They strive to help clients experience themselves as fully as possible in the present, yet they are not rigidly bound by dictates, nor do they routinely intervene whenever clients stray from the present. Sensitively staying in contact with a client's flow of experiencing entails the ability to focus on the person and not on the mechanical use of techniques for a certain effect.

Gestalt Therapy Applied to the Case of Stan

Gestalt-oriented therapy focuses on the unfinished business Stan has with his parents, siblings, and ex-wife. It appears that this unfinished business consists mainly of feelings of resentment, and Stan turns this resentment on himself. His present life situation is spotlighted, but he may also need to reexperience past feelings that could be interfering with his present attempts to develop intimacy with others.

Although the focus is on Stan's present behavior, I guide him toward becoming aware of how he is carrying old baggage around and how it interferes with his life today. My task is to assist him in re-creating the context in which he made *creative adjustments* during his childhood years that are no longer serving him well. One of his cardinal introjections was, "I'm stupid, and it would be better if I did not exist."

Stan has been influenced by cultural messages that he has accepted. I am interested in exploring his cultural background, including his values and the values characteristic of his culture. With this focus, I assist Stan in identifying some of the following cultural introjections: "Don't talk about your family with strangers, and don't hang your dirty linen in public." "Don't confront your parents because they deserve respect." "Don't be too concerned about yourself." "Don't show your vulnerabilities; hide your feelings and weaknesses." I invite Stan to examine those introjections to assess their utility in his present circumstances. Although he can decide to retain those aspects of his culture that he prizes, he is in a position to modify or reject other cultural expectations. Of course, this will be done when these issues emerge in the foreground of his work.

I ask Stan to attend to what he becomes aware of as the session begins: "What are you experiencing as we are getting started today?" As I encourage Stan to tune in to his present experience and selectively make observations, a number of figures will emerge. The goal is to focus on a figure of interest, one that seems to hold the most energy or relevance for Stan. When a figure is identified, my task is to deepen Stan's awareness of this thought, feeling, body sensation, or insight through related experiments.

In typical Gestalt fashion, Stan deals with his present struggles within the context of our relationship and through experimentation. One possible experiment would involve Stan becoming some of those individuals who told him how to think, feel, and behave as a child. He can then become the child that he was and respond to them from the place where he feels the most confusion or pain. He experiences in new ways the feelings that accompany his beliefs about himself, and he comes to a deeper appreciation of how his feelings and thoughts influence what he is doing today.

Stan has learned to hide his emotions rather than to reveal them. Understanding this about him, we explore his objections and concerns about "getting into feelings." The figure of interest now is his hesitation to experience or express emotion. Although I have no agenda to get Stan to experience his feelings at this point, it is important for him to increase his awareness of his reluctance and to explore the meaning it holds for him.

If Stan decides that he wants to experience his emotions rather than deny them, I ask: "What are you aware of now having said what you did?" Stan says that he can't get his ex-wife out of his mind. He tells me about the pain he feels over that relationship and how he is frightened of getting involved again lest he be hurt again. I continue to ask him to focus inward and get a sense of what stands out for him at this very moment. Stan replies: "I'm hurt and angry over all the pain that I've allowed her to inflict on me." I ask him to imagine himself in earlier scenes with his ex-wife, as though the painful situation were occurring in the here and now. He symbolically relives and reexperiences the situation by talking "directly" to his wife. By expressing his resentments and hurts directly, Stan can begin to complete some unfinished business that is interfering with his current functioning. By participating in this experiment, Stan is attaining more awareness of what he is now doing and how he keeps himself locked into his past.

Questions for Reflection

- How might you begin a session with Stan? Would you suggest a direction he should pursue? Would you wait for him to initiate work? Would you ask him to continue from where he left off in the previous session? Would you attend to whatever theme or issue becomes figural to him?
- What unfinished business can you identify in Stan's case? Does any of his experience of being stuck remind you of yourself? How might you work with Stan if he did bring up your own unfinished business?
- What kind of an experiment might you propose to assist Stan in learning more about his hesitation and reluctance to access and express his feelings?
- Stan participated in an experiment to deal with pain, resentment, and hurt over situations with his ex-wife. How might you have worked with the material Stan brought up? What kind of experiment might you design? How would you decide what kind of experiment to create?
- How might you work with Stan's cultural messages? Would you be able to respect his cultural values and still encourage him to make an assessment of some of the ways in which his culture is affecting him today?

Visit CengageBrain.com or watch the DVD for the video program on Chapter 8, *Theory and Practice of Counseling and Psychotherapy: The Case of Stan and Lecturettes*, Session 6 (Gestalt therapy), for a demonstration of my approach to counseling Stan from this perspective. This session consists of Stan exploring one of his dreams in Gestalt fashion.

Gestalt Therapy Applied to the Case of Gwen*

From a Gestalt perspective, I am interested in assisting Gwen in becoming more aware of herself as a whole person in the here and now. My job is to hold a mirror up and help her see herself with greater clarity. I notice that Gwen has a slight limp as she walks into my office. I ask about her limp, and Gwen tells me she has had a great deal of pain in her left hip for the past week. She explains that she has had trouble with her hip before and that an MRI revealed negative results. She goes on to say that it may be due to their old mattress.

Therapist: Describe exactly where the pain is and what the sensations feel like.

Gwen: Well, it feels uncomfortable in the crease of my hip, and it's a dull sore feeling.

Therapist: Describe the texture and color of the feeling in your hip [*asking her to make contact with her bodily sensations*].

Gwen: The pain is prickly, gray, and heavy [*she begins to connect with her body in the moment*].

Therapist: What is that hip saying to you?

Gwen: This seems a bit strange, and I must admit I am uncomfortable in giving my hip a voice.

Therapist: Although it may seem strange, I hope you will give it a try to see what you might learn from doing this. You can always stop when you think that doing this is not helpful.

Gwen: OK, this is uncomfortable, but I will give it a try [*she has trust in our relationship*]. This hip is moaning and groaning!

Therapist: [*An experiment may increase this connection.*] This may feel a little weird, but try to become your hip and exaggerate how your hip is feeling.

Gwen: [*Begins to groan and whimper and tears come to her eyes*] I am so tired of the mountain of things I have to do and never getting anywhere. I feel like a fallen tree in the forest. I have fallen and no one knows I am there and it is up to me to get up and get going again.

In her daily life Gwen typically holds back her true feelings. She is used to suppressing her irritations and even her triumphs. Because she was frequently ignored as a child, she feels that her thoughts and emotions don't really matter. Her role at work is to solve problems, and at home she is the caretaker of everyone. She rarely allows herself to be vulnerable or fully human. Gwen sees herself as "in charge" and seldom gives herself a moment to pause or catch her breath.

Gwen: I know that basically I have a good life, I just rush past the good stuff and forget to stop and really appreciate all the blessings. I can get so caught up in what I have not done or what feels wrong, but I can't really complain. I know this hip is telling me to slow down and enjoy more of my life. I don't have to be that fallen tree, I just need to ask for the support I really need [*her body has shifted and she seems more relaxed in her chair*].

Therapist: Bring your attention back to your hip. What does it feel like now?

Gwen: It feels better now. It might be OK to slow down. It might even be OK to take myself off of some of these committees I am on. [*Laughing*] Maybe my hip just needs to sit on a beach somewhere or at least slow down enough to have some fun.

Therapist: It is important for you to stop for a moment and check in with your body. We hold our emotions in our bodies. It's important to take time out to listen to what the sensations in our body may be telling us.

As Gwen's awareness increases, she is beginning to realize some of her past ways of functioning are no longer serving her and she can begin to do something differently. It is my hope that Gwen can now see the

*Dr. Kellie Kirksey writes about her ways of thinking and practicing from a Gestalt therapy perspective and applying this model to Gwen.

connection between her unexpressed emotions and the discomfort in her physical body. Gestalt therapy gives Gwen the opportunity to focus on what is happening in her mind and body in the present moment and on how an expression of emotions can lead to a release in her physical body. Gestalt therapy can assist Gwen in becoming more aware of herself as a whole person. She can begin to challenge unfinished business that has enabled her to experience success in her career but has also resulted in her feeling overwhelmed and filled with anxiety.

Questions for Reflection

- What is the importance of exploring bodily sensations and physical symptoms with Gwen?
- What therapeutic value do you see in asking Gwen to "become her hip" and speak from it?
- What are your reactions to the way that the therapist introduced the idea to Gwen of carrying out an experiment?
- How might you have experienced doing this experiment if you were in Gwen's position?

Summary and Evaluation

Summary

Gestalt therapy is an experiential approach that stresses present awareness and the quality of contact between the individual and the environment. The major focus is on assisting the client to become aware of how behaviors that were once part of creatively adjusting to past environments may be interfering with effective functioning and living in the present. The goal of the approach is, first and foremost, to gain awareness.

Another therapeutic aim is to assist clients in exploring how they make contact with elements of their environment. Change occurs through the heightened awareness of "what is." Because the Gestalt therapist has no agenda beyond assisting clients to increase their awareness, there is no need to label a client's behavior as "resistance." Instead, the therapist simply follows this new process as it emerges. The therapist has faith that self-regulation is a naturally unfolding process that does not have to be controlled (Breshgold, 1989). Awareness is a key requirement for the restoration of self-regulation within the person's environment (Resnick, 2015). With expanded awareness, clients are able to reconcile polarities and dichotomies within themselves and proceed toward the reintegration of all aspects of themselves.

The therapist works with the client to identify the figures, or most salient aspects of the individual–environmental field, as they emerge from the background. The Gestalt therapist believes each client is capable of self-regulating if those figures are engaged and resolved so others can replace them. The role of the Gestalt therapist is to help clients identify the most pressing issues, needs, and interests and to design experiments that sharpen those figures or that explore resistances to contact and awareness. Gestalt therapists are encouraged to be appropriately self-disclosing, both about their here-and-now reactions in the therapy hour and about their personal experiences, when doing so will facilitate the therapeutic process (Yontef & Jacobs, 2014; Zahm, 1998).

Contributions of Gestalt Therapy

LO9

One contribution of Gestalt therapy is the exciting way in which the past is dealt with in a lively manner by bringing relevant aspects into the present. Therapists challenge clients in creative ways to become aware of and work with issues that are obstructing current functioning. Further, paying attention to the obvious verbal and nonverbal leads provided by clients is a useful way to approach a counseling session. Through the skillful and sensitive use of Gestalt interventions, practitioners can assist clients in heightening their present-centered awareness of what they are thinking and feeling as well as what they are doing.

Gestalt methods bring conflicts and human struggles to life. Gestalt therapy is a creative approach that uses experiments to move clients from talk to action and experience. The creative and spontaneous use of active experiments is a pathway to experiential learning. The focus is on growth and enhancement rather than being a system of techniques to treat disorders, which reflects an early Gestalt motto, "You don't have to be sick to get better." Clients are provided with a wide range of tools—in the form of Gestalt experiments—for discovering new facets of themselves and making decisions about changing their course of living.

The Gestalt approach to working with dreams is a unique pathway for people to increase their awareness of key themes in their lives. By seeing each aspect of a dream as a projection of themselves, clients are able to bring the dream to life, to interpret its personal meaning, and to assume responsibility for it.

Gestalt therapy is a holistic approach that values each aspect of the individual's experience equally. Therapists allow the figure-formation process to guide them. They do not approach clients with a preconceived set of biases or a set agenda. Instead, they place emphasis on what occurs at the boundary between the individual and the environment. Therapists do not try to move the client anywhere. The main goal is to increase the client's awareness of "what is." Instead of trying to make something happen, the therapist's role is assisting the client to increase awareness that will allow reidentification with the part of the self from which he or she is alienated.

A key strength of Gestalt therapy is the attempt to integrate theory, practice, and research. Although Gestalt therapy was light on empirical research for several years, it has come more into vogue recently. Two books show potential for influencing future research: *Handbook for Theory, Research and Practice in Gestalt Therapy* (Brownell, 2008); and *Becoming a Practitioner Researcher: A Gestalt Approach to Holistic Inquiry* (Barber, 2006). Strumpfel and Goldman (2002) note that both process and outcome studies have advanced the theory and practice of Gestalt therapy, and they summarize a number of significant findings based on outcome research:

- Outcome studies have demonstrated Gestalt therapy to be equal to or greater than other therapies for various disorders.
- More recent studies have shown that Gestalt therapy has a beneficial impact with personality disturbances, psychosomatic problems, and substance addictions.
- The effects of Gestalt therapy tend to be stable in follow-up studies one to three years after termination of treatment.
- Gestalt therapy has demonstrated effectiveness in treating a variety of psychological disorders.

Limitations and Criticisms of Gestalt Therapy

Most of my criticisms of Gestalt therapy pertain to the traditional version, or the style of Fritz Perls, which emphasized confrontation and de-emphasized the cognitive factors of personality. This style of Gestalt therapy placed more attention on using techniques to confront clients and getting them to experience their feelings. Contemporary Gestalt therapy has come a long way, and more attention is being given to theoretical instruction, theoretical exposition, and cognitive factors in general (Yontef, 1993, 1995).

In Gestalt therapy clients clarify their thinking, explore beliefs, and put meaning to experiences they are reliving in therapy. Clients assume an active role in participating in experiments, and they learn experientially. The emphasis is on *facilitating* the clients' own process of self-discovery and learning. This experiential and self-directed learning process is based on the fundamental belief in organismic self-regulation, which implies that clients arrive at their own truths through awareness and improved contact with the environment. It seems to me, however, that clients can engage in self-discovery and at the same time benefit from appropriate teaching by the therapist. In addition to the benefits of experiential learning, clients can profit from timely and useful information, and a psychoeducational focus can enhance the learning process.

Contemporary Gestalt practice places a high value on the contact and dialogue between therapist and client. For Gestalt therapy to be effective, the therapist must have a high level of personal development. Being aware of one's own needs and seeing that they do not interfere with the client's process, being present in the moment, and being willing to be nondefensive and self-revealing all demand a lot of the therapist. There is a danger that therapists who are inadequately trained will be primarily concerned with impressing clients.

Some Cautions Typically, Gestalt therapists are highly active and exhibit sensitivity, timing, inventiveness, empathy, and respect for the client (Zinker, 1978). If therapists lack these qualities, their experiments can easily boomerang. Some therapists employ Gestalt techniques without having a sound theoretical rationale. Inept therapists may use powerful techniques to stir up feelings and open up problems clients have kept from full awareness only to abandon the clients once they have managed to have a dramatic catharsis. Such a failure to stay with clients and help them work through what they have experienced and bring some closure to the experience can be detrimental and could be considered as unethical practice.

Effective practitioners of Gestalt therapy require a strong general clinical background and training, not only in the theory and practice of Gestalt therapy but also in personality theory, psychopathology, and knowledge of psychodynamics (Yontef & Jacobs, 2014). Competent practitioners need to have engaged in their own personal therapy and to have had advanced clinical training and supervised experience. Such therapists have learned to blend a phenomenological and dialogic approach, which is inherently respectful to the client, with well-timed experiments.

Self-Reflection and Discussion Questions

1. What are some advantages you can see in asking clients to bring any problems or concerns they are experiencing into the here and now?
2. The ability of a therapist to be present during the therapy session is central in Gestalt therapy practice. Can you think of some challenges you are likely to face in being fully present for your clients? How can you deal with these challenges?
3. What do you understand as the difference between an experiment and an exercise or technique in Gestalt therapy?
4. Energy and blocks to energy are given prominence in Gestalt therapy. What are some ideas you have for working with a client's energy without making interpretations for the client?
5. Imagine yourself as a client with a Gestalt therapist. What do you think this experience would be like for you?

Where to Go From Here

Visit CengageBrain.com or watch the DVD for *Integrative Counseling: The Case of Ruth and Lecturettes*, Session 7 (Emotive Focus in Counseling), in which I demonstrate how I create experiments to heighten Ruth's awareness. In my version of Gestalt work with Ruth, I watch for cues from Ruth about what she is experiencing in the here and now. By attending to what she is expressing both verbally and nonverbally, I am able to suggest experiments during our sessions. In this particular session I employ a Gestalt experiment, asking Ruth to talk to me as if I were her husband, John. During this experiment, Ruth becomes quite emotional. You will see ways of exploring emotional material and integrating this work into a cognitive framework as well.

Other Resources

Psychotherapy.net is a comprehensive resource for students and professionals that offers videos demonstrating Gestalt therapy with adults and children. New articles, interviews, blogs, therapy cartoons, and videos are published monthly. DVDs relevant to this chapter are available at www.psychotherapy.net and include the following:

Oaklander, V. (2001). *Gestalt Therapy with Children* (Child Therapy with the Experts Series)

Polster, I. (1997). *Psychotherapy With the Unmotivated Patient*

Training Programs and Associations

If you are interested in furthering your knowledge and skill in the area of Gestalt therapy, you might consider pursuing Gestalt training, which would include attending workshops, seeking out personal therapy from a Gestalt therapist, and enrolling in a Gestalt training program that would involve reading, practice, and supervision.

A comprehensive list of these resources, along with their websites is available in the Appendixes of Woldt and Toman's textbook (2005). Some of the most prominent training programs and associations are listed here.

Gestalt Institute of Cleveland. Inc.
www.gestaltcleveland.org

Pacific Gestalt Institute
www.gestalttherapy.org

Gestalt Center for Psychotherapy and Training
www.gestaltnyc.org

Gestalt International Study Center
www.GISC.org

Gestalt Therapy Training Center Northwest
www.gttcnw.org

Gestalt Associates Training, Los Angeles
www.gatla.org

The most prominent professional associations for Gestalt therapy that hold international conferences follow.

Association for the Advancement of Gestalt Therapy (AAGT)
www.AAGT.org

European Association for Gestalt Therapy (EAGT)
www.EAGT.org

Gestalt Australia New Zealand
www.ganz.org.au

Gestalt Review
www.gestaltreview.com

British Gestalt Journal
www.britishgestaltjournal.com

The *Gestalt Directory* includes information about Gestalt practitioners and training programs throughout the world and is available free of charge upon request to the Center for Gestalt Development, Inc. The center also has many books, audiotapes, and videotapes available that deal with Gestalt practice.

The Center for Gestalt Development, Inc.
www.gestalt.org

Recommended Supplementary Readings

Gestalt Therapy Verbatim (Perls, 1969a) provides a firsthand account of the way Fritz Perls worked. It contains many verbatim transcripts of workshop demonstrations.

Gestalt Therapy (Wheeler & Axelsson, 2015) offers an excellent introduction to the theory, evolution, research, and practice of Gestalt therapy. The book is based on principles that encourage an active, present-focused, relational stance on the therapist's part.

Gestalt Therapy: History, Theory, and Practice (Woldt & Toman, 2005) introduces the historical underpinnings and key concepts of Gestalt therapy and features applications of those concepts to therapeutic practice. This is a significant publication in the field of Gestalt therapy that contains pedagogical learning activities and experiments, review questions, and photographs of all contributors.

Gestalt Therapy Integrated: Contours of Theory and Practice (E. Polster & Polster, 1973) is a classic in the field and an excellent source for those who want a more advanced and theoretical treatment of this model.

Behavior Therapy 9

LEARNING OBJECTIVES

1. Identify the key figures associated with the development of behavior therapy.
2. Differentiate the four developmental areas of behavior therapy: classical conditioning, operant conditioning, social cognitive theory, and cognitive behavior therapy.
3. Evaluate the central characteristics and assumptions that unite the diverse field of behavior therapy.
4. Understand how the function and role of the therapist affects the therapy process.
5. Describe the role of the client–therapist relationship in the behavioral approaches.
6. Identify the diverse array of behavioral techniques and procedures and how they fit within the evidence-based practice movement.
7. Describe the key concepts of EMDR, its main applications, and the effectiveness of this approach.
8. Describe the basic elements of social skills training.
9. Understand and explain the main steps involved in self-management programs.
10. Identify the key concepts of the four major approaches of the mindfulness and acceptance-based behavior therapies.
11. Examine the application of behavioral principles and techniques to brief interventions and to group counseling.
12. Understand the advantages and shortcomings of behavior therapy in working with culturally diverse clients.
13. Discuss the evaluation of contemporary behavior therapy.

B. F. SKINNER (1904–1990) reported that he was brought up in a warm, stable family environment.* As he was growing up, Skinner was greatly interested in building all sorts of things, an interest that followed him throughout his professional life. He received his PhD in psychology from Harvard University in 1931 and eventually returned to Harvard after teaching in several universities. He had two daughters, one of whom is an educational psychologist and the other an artist.

AP Images

B. F. Skinner

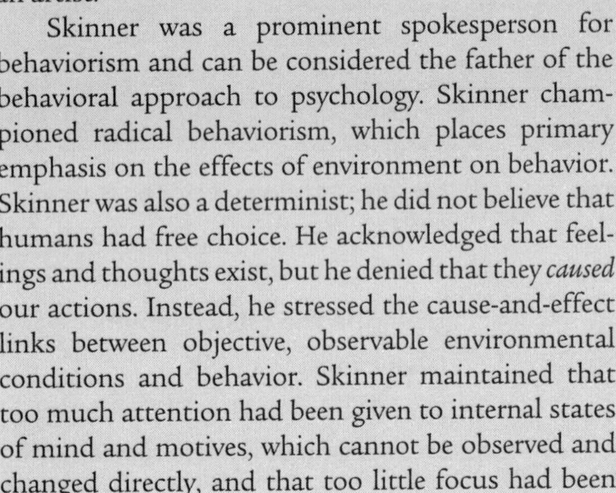

Skinner was a prominent spokesperson for behaviorism and can be considered the father of the behavioral approach to psychology. Skinner championed radical behaviorism, which places primary emphasis on the effects of environment on behavior. Skinner was also a determinist; he did not believe that humans had free choice. He acknowledged that feelings and thoughts exist, but he denied that they *caused* our actions. Instead, he stressed the cause-and-effect links between objective, observable environmental conditions and behavior. Skinner maintained that too much attention had been given to internal states of mind and motives, which cannot be observed and changed directly, and that too little focus had been given to environmental factors that can be directly observed and changed. He was extremely interested in the concept of reinforcement, which he applied to his own life. For example, after working for many hours, he would go into his constructed cocoon (like a tent), put on headphones, and listen to classical music (Frank Dattilio, personal communication, September 24, 2010).

Most of Skinner's work was of an experimental nature in the laboratory, but others have applied his ideas to teaching, managing human problems, and social planning. *Science and Human Behavior* (Skinner, 1953) best illustrates how Skinner thought behavioral concepts could be applied to every domain of human behavior. In *Walden II* (1948) Skinner describes a utopian community in which his ideas, derived from the laboratory, are applied to social issues. His 1971 book, *Beyond Freedom and Dignity*, addressed the need for drastic changes if our society was to survive. Skinner believed that science and technology held the promise for a better future.

*This biography is based largely on Nye's (2000) discussion of B. F. Skinner's radical behaviorism.

ALBERT BANDURA (b. 1925) was born in a small town in northern Alberta, Canada; he was the youngest of six children in a family of Eastern European descent.* Bandura spent his elementary and high school years in the one school in town, which was short of teachers and resources. These meager educational resources proved to be an asset rather than a liability as Bandura early on learned the skills of self-directedness, which would later become one of his research themes. He earned his PhD in clinical psychology from the University of Iowa in 1952, and a year later he joined the faculty at Stanford University. Bandura and his colleagues did pioneering work in the area of social modeling and demonstrated that modeling is a powerful process that explains diverse forms of learning (see Bandura 1971a, 1971b; Bandura & Walters, 1963). In his research programs at Stanford University, Bandura and his colleagues explored social learning theory and the prominent role of observational learning and social modeling in human motivation, thought, and action. By the mid-1980s Bandura had renamed his theoretical approach *social cognitive theory*, which shed light on how we function as self-organizing, proactive, self-reflective, and self-regulating beings (see Bandura, 1986). This notion that we are not simply reactive organisms shaped by environmental forces or driven by inner impulses represented a dramatic shift in the development of behavior therapy. Bandura broadened the scope of behavior therapy by exploring the inner cognitive-affective forces that motivate human behavior.

Courtesy, Dr. Albert Bandura, StanfordUniversity, Palo Alto, CA

Albert Bandura

There are some existential qualities inherent in Bandura's social cognitive theory. Bandura has produced a wealth of empirical evidence that demonstrates the life choices we have in all aspects of our lives. In *Self-Efficacy: The Exercise of Control* (Bandura, 1997), Bandura shows the comprehensive applications of his theory of self-efficacy to areas such as human development, psychology, psychiatry, education, medicine and health, athletics, business, social and political change, and international affairs.

Bandura has concentrated on four areas of research: (1) the power of psychological modeling in shaping thought, emotion, and action; (2) the mechanisms of human agency, or the ways people influence their own motivation and behavior through choice; (3) people's perceptions of their efficacy to exercise influence over the events that affect their lives; and (4) how stress reactions and depressions are caused. Bandura has created one of the few mega-theories that still thrive in the 21st century. He has shown that people need a sense of self-efficacy and resilience to create a successful life and to meet the inevitable obstacles and adversities they encounter.

Bandura has written nine books, many of which have been translated into various languages. In 2004 he received the Outstanding Lifetime Contribution to Psychology Award from the American Psychological Association. He still makes time for hiking, opera, being with his family, and wine tasting in the Napa and Sonoma valleys.

*This biography is based largely on Panjares's (2004) discussion of Bandura's life and work.

Introduction

Behavior therapy practitioners focus on directly observable behavior, current determinants of behavior, learning experiences that promote change, tailoring treatment strategies to individual clients, and rigorous assessment and evaluation. Behavior therapy has been used to treat a wide range of psychological disorders with specific client populations. Anxiety disorders, depression, posttraumatic stress disorder, substance abuse, eating and weight disorders, sexual problems, pain management, and hypertension have all been successfully treated using this approach (Wilson, 2011). Behavioral procedures are used in the fields of developmental disabilities, mental illness, education and special education, community psychology, clinical psychology, rehabilitation, business, self-management, sports psychology, health-related behaviors, medicine, and gerontology (Miltenberger, 2012; Wilson, 2011).

Historical Background

The behavioral approach had its origin in the 1950s and early 1960s, and it LO1 was a radical departure from the dominant psychoanalytic perspective. The behavior therapy movement differed from other therapeutic approaches in its application of principles of classical and operant conditioning (which will be explained shortly) to the treatment of a variety of problem behaviors. Today, it is difficult to find a consensus on the definition of behavior therapy because the field has grown, become more complex, and is marked by a diversity of views. Contemporary behavior therapy is no longer limited to treatments based on traditional learning theory (Antony & Roemer, 2011b), and it increasingly overlaps with other theoretical approaches (Antony, 2014). Behavior therapists now use a variety of evidence-based techniques in their practices, including cognitive therapy, social skills training, relaxation training, and mindfulness strategies—all discussed in this chapter. The following historical sketch of behavior therapy is largely based on Spiegler (2016).

Traditional behavior therapy arose simultaneously in the United States, South Africa, and Great Britain in the 1950s. In spite of harsh criticism and resistance from psychoanalytic psychotherapists, the approach has survived. Its focus was on demonstrating that behavioral conditioning techniques were effective and were a viable alternative to psychoanalytic therapy.

In the 1960s Albert Bandura developed social learning theory, which combined classical and operant conditioning with observational learning. Bandura made cognition a legitimate focus for behavior therapy. During the 1960s a number of *cognitive behavioral approaches* sprang up, which focus on cognitive representations of the environment rather than on characteristics of the objective environment.

Contemporary behavior therapy emerged as a major force in psychology during the 1970s, and it had a significant impact on education, psychology, psychotherapy, psychiatry, and social work. Behavioral techniques were expanded to provide solutions for business, industry, and child-rearing problems as well. Behavior therapy techniques were viewed as the treatment of choice for many psychological problems.

The 1980s were characterized by a search for new horizons in concepts and methods that went beyond traditional learning theory. Behavior therapists continued to subject their methods to empirical scrutiny and to consider the impact of the practice of therapy on both their clients and the larger society. Increased attention was given to the role of emotions in therapeutic change, as well as to the role of biological factors in psychological disorders. Two of the most significant developments in the field were (1) the continued emergence of cognitive behavior therapy as a major force and (2) the application of behavioral techniques to the prevention and treatment of health-related disorders.

By the late 1990s the Association for Behavioral and Cognitive Therapies (ABCT) (formerly known as the Association for Advancement of Behavior Therapy) claimed a membership of about 4,500. Currently, ABCT includes approximately 6,000 mental health professionals and students who are interested in empirically based behavior therapy or cognitive behavior therapy. This name change and description reveals the current thinking of integrating behavioral and cognitive therapies.

By the early 2000s, the behavioral tradition had broadened considerably, which involved enlarging the scope of research and practice. This newest development, sometimes known as the "third generation" or "third wave" of behavior therapy, includes dialectical behavior therapy (DBT), mindfulness-based stress reduction (MBSR), mindfulness-based cognitive therapy (MBCT), and acceptance and commitment therapy (ACT). Behavior therapies are among the most widely used treatment interventions for psychological and behavioral problems today (Antony, 2014).

Visit CengageBrain.com or watch the DVD for the video program on Chapter 9, *Theory and Practice of Counseling and Psychotherapy: The Case of Stan and Lecturettes*. I suggest that you view the brief lecture for each chapter prior to reading the chapter.

Four Areas of Development

LO2

Contemporary behavior therapy can be understood by considering four major areas of development: (1) classical conditioning, (2) operant conditioning, (3) social-cognitive theory, and (4) cognitive behavior therapy.

Classical conditioning (respondent conditioning) refers to what happens prior to learning that creates a response through pairing. A key figure in this area is Ivan Pavlov who illustrated classical conditioning through experiments with dogs. Placing food in a dog's mouth leads to salivation, which is respondent behavior. When food is repeatedly presented with some originally neutral stimulus (something that does not elicit a particular response), such as the sound of a bell, the dog will eventually salivate to the sound of the bell alone. However, if a bell is sounded repeatedly but not paired again with food, the salivation response will eventually diminish and become extinct. An example of a procedure that is based on the classical conditioning model is Joseph Wolpe's systematic desensitization, which is described later in this chapter. This technique illustrates how principles of learning derived from the experimental laboratory can be applied clinically. Desensitization can be applied to people who, through classical conditioning, developed an intense fear of flying after having a frightening experience while flying.

Technically one can develop an intense fear of flying without having a frightening experience personally. For example, someone may see visual images of a plane crashing off the coast of Brazil and develop a fear of flying even though that person has never flown anywhere. Some researchers hold a different view and believe that fear of flying may be due primarily to claustrophobia (Frank Dattilio, personal communication, September 24, 2010).

Most of the significant responses we make in everyday life are examples of operant behaviors, such as reading, writing, driving a car, and eating with utensils. **Operant conditioning** involves a type of learning in which behaviors are influenced mainly by the consequences that follow them. If the environmental changes brought about by the behavior are reinforcing—that is, if they provide some reward to the organism or eliminate aversive stimuli—the chances are increased that the behavior will occur again. If the environmental changes produce no reinforcement or produce aversive stimuli, the chances are lessened that the behavior will recur. Positive and negative reinforcement, punishment, and extinction techniques, described later in this chapter, illustrate how operant conditioning in applied settings can be instrumental in developing prosocial and adaptive behaviors. Operant techniques are used by behavioral practitioners in parent education programs and with weight management programs.

The behaviorists of both the classical and operant conditioning models excluded any reference to mediational concepts, such as the role of thinking processes, attitudes, and values. This focus is perhaps due to a reaction against the insight-oriented psychodynamic approaches. The **social learning approach** (or the *social-cognitive* approach) developed by Albert Bandura and Richard Walters (1963) is interactional, interdisciplinary, and multimodal (Bandura, 1977, 1982). *Social-cognitive theory* involves a triadic reciprocal interaction among the environment, personal factors (beliefs, preferences, expectations, self-perceptions, and interpretations), and individual behavior. In the social-cognitive approach, the environmental events on behavior are mainly determined by cognitive processes governing how environmental influences are perceived by an individual and how these events are interpreted. A basic assumption is that people are capable of self-directed behavior change and that the person is the agent of change. For Bandura (1982, 1997), *self-efficacy* is the individual's belief or expectation that he or she can master a situation and bring about desired change. An example of social learning is ways people can develop effective social skills after they are in contact with other people who effectively model interpersonal skills.

Cognitive behavior therapy (CBT) represents the mainstream of contemporary behavior therapy and is a popular theoretical orientation among psychologists. Cognitive behavioral therapy operates on the assumption that what people believe influences how they act and feel. Since the early 1970s, the behavioral movement has conceded a legitimate place to thinking, even to the extent of giving cognitive factors a central role in understanding and treating emotional and behavioral problems. By the mid-1970s, *cognitive behavior therapy* had replaced *behavior therapy* as the accepted designation, and the field began emphasizing the interaction among affective, behavioral, and cognitive dimensions.

Contemporary behavior therapy has much in common with cognitive behavior therapy in which the mechanism of change is both cognitive (modifying thoughts to change behaviors) and behavioral (altering external factors that lead to behavior change; Follette & Callaghan, 2011). Social skills training, cognitive therapy, stress management training, mindfulness, and acceptance-based practices all represent the cognitive behavioral tradition. This chapter goes beyond the traditional behavioral perspective and deals mainly with applied aspects of this model. Chapter 10 is devoted to the cognitive behavioral approaches, which focus on changing clients' cognitions (thoughts and beliefs) that maintain psychological problems.

Key Concepts

Current Trend in Behavior Therapy

Contemporary behavior therapy is grounded on a scientific view of human behavior that accommodates a systematic and structured approach to counseling. The current trend in behavior therapy is toward developing procedures that give control to clients and thus increase their range of freedom. Behavior therapy aims to increase people's skills so that they have more options for responding. By overcoming debilitating behaviors that restrict choices, people are freer to select from possibilities that were not available to them earlier, which increases individual freedom.

Basic Characteristics and Assumptions

Seven key characteristics define behavior therapy and its assumptions. One LO3 defining characteristic is that behavior therapy is based on the principles and procedures of the scientific method. Experimentally derived principles of learning are systematically applied to help people change their maladaptive behaviors. The distinguishing characteristic of behavioral practitioners is their systematic adherence to precision and to empirical evaluation. Behavior therapists state treatment goals in concrete objective terms to make replication of their interventions possible. Treatment goals are agreed upon by the client and the therapist. Throughout the course of therapy, the therapist assesses problem behaviors and the conditions that are maintaining them. Evaluation methods are used to discern the effectiveness of both assessment and treatment procedures. Therapeutic techniques employed must have demonstrated effectiveness. In short, behavioral concepts and procedures are stated explicitly, tested empirically within a conceptual framework, and revised continually.

Behavior is not limited to overt actions a person engages in that we can observe, however; behavior also includes internal processes such as cognitions, images, beliefs, and emotions. The key characteristic of a behavior is that it is something that can be *operationally defined*.

Behavior therapy deals with the client's current problems and the factors influencing them today rather than analyzing possible historical determinants. Emphasis is on specific factors that influence present functioning and what factors can be used to modify performance. Behavior therapists look to the current environmental events that maintain problem behaviors and help clients produce behavior change by changing environmental events, through a process called *functional assessment*, or what Wolpe (1990) referred to as a "behavioral analysis." Behavior therapy recognizes the importance of the individual, the individual's environment, and the interaction between the person and the environment in facilitating change.

Clients involved in behavior therapy are expected to assume an active role by engaging in specific actions to deal with their problems. Rather than simply talking about their condition, clients are required to *do* something to bring about change. Clients monitor their behaviors both during and outside the therapy sessions, learn and practice coping skills, and role-play new behavior. Therapeutic tasks that clients carry out in daily life, or homework assignments, are a basic part of this approach. Behavior therapy is an action-oriented and an educational approach, and learning is viewed as being at the core of therapy. Clients learn new and adaptive behaviors to replace old and maladaptive behaviors.

This approach assumes that change can take place without insight into underlying dynamics and without understanding the origins of a psychological problem. Behavior therapists operate on the premise that changes in behavior can occur prior to or simultaneously with understanding of oneself, and that behavioral changes may well lead to an increased level of self-understanding. Although it is true that insight and understanding about the contingencies that exacerbate one's problems can supply motivation to change, knowing that one has a problem and knowing *how* to change it are two different things (Martell, 2007).

Assessment is an ongoing process of observation and self-monitoring that focuses on the current determinants of behavior, including identifying the problem and evaluating the change. Assessment informs the treatment process and involves attending to the culture of clients as part of their social environments, including social support networks relating to target behaviors. Critical to behavioral approaches is the careful assessment and evaluation of the interventions used to determine whether the behavior change resulted from the procedure.

Behavioral treatment interventions are individually tailored to specific problems experienced by the client. Several therapy techniques may be used to treat an individual client's problems. An important question that serves as a guide for this choice is, "*What* treatment, by *whom*, is the most effective for *this* individual with *that* specific problem and under *which* set of circumstances?" (Paul, 1967, p. 111).

The Therapeutic Process

Therapeutic Goals

Goals occupy a place of central importance in behavior therapy. The general goals of behavior therapy are to increase personal choice and to create new conditions for learning. The client, with the help of the therapist, defines specific treatment goals at the outset of the therapeutic process. Although assessment and treatment occur together, a formal assessment takes place prior to treatment to determine behaviors that are targets of change. Continual assessment throughout therapy determines the degree to which identified goals are being met. It is important to devise a way to measure progress toward goals based on empirical validation.

Contemporary behavior therapy stresses clients' active role in formulating specific measurable goals. Goals must be clear, concrete, understood, and agreed on by the client and the counselor. The counselor and client discuss the behaviors associated with the goals, the circumstances required for change, the nature of subgoals, and a plan of action to work toward these goals. This process of determining therapeutic goals entails a negotiation between client and counselor that results in a contract that guides the course of therapy. Behavior therapists and clients alter goals throughout the therapeutic process as needed.

Therapist's Function and Role

Behavior therapists conduct a thorough **functional assessment** (or **behavioral analysis**) to identify the maintaining conditions by systematically gathering information about situational antecedents (A), the dimensions of the problem behavior (B), and the consequences (C) of the problem. This is known as the **ABC model**, and the goal of a functional assessment of a client's behavior is to understand the ABC sequence. This model of behavior suggests that *behavior* (B) is influenced by some particular events that precede it, called *antecedents* (A), and by certain events that follow it, called *consequences* (C). **Antecedent events** cue or elicit a certain behavior. For example, with a client who has trouble going to sleep, listening to a relaxation tape may serve as a cue for sleep induction. Turning off the lights and removing the television from the bedroom may elicit sleep behaviors as well. **Consequences** are events that maintain a behavior in some way, either by increasing or decreasing it. For example, a client may be more likely to return to counseling after the counselor offers verbal praise or encouragement for having come in or for having completed some homework. A client may be less likely to return if the counselor is consistently late to sessions. In doing a **behavioral assessment interview**, the therapist's task is to identify the particular antecedent and consequent events that influence, or are functionally related to, an individual's behavior (Cormier, Nurius, & Osborn, 2013). LO4

Behaviorally oriented practitioners tend to be active and directive and to function as consultants and problem solvers. They rely heavily on empirical evidence about the efficacy of the techniques they apply to particular problems. Behavioral practitioners must have skills in selecting and applying treatment methods. They pay close attention to the clues given by clients, and they are willing to follow their clinical hunches. Behavior therapists use some techniques common to other approaches, such as summarizing, reflection, clarification, and open-ended questioning. Behavior therapists are directive and often offer suggestions (Antony, 2014), but they may perform these other functions as well (Miltenberger, 2012; Speigler, 2016):

- The therapist strives to understand the function of client behaviors, including how certain behaviors originated and how they are sustained. With this understanding, the therapist formulates initial treatment goals and designs and implements a treatment plan to accomplish these goals.
- The behavioral clinician uses strategies that have research support for use with a particular kind of problem. These evidence-based strategies promote generalization and maintenance of behavior change. A number of these strategies are described later in this chapter.
- The clinician evaluates the success of the change plan by measuring progress toward the goals throughout the duration of treatment. Outcome measures are given to the client at the beginning of treatment (called a baseline) and collected again periodically during and after treatment to determine whether the strategy and treatment plan are working. If not, adjustments are made in the strategies being used.
- Follow-up assessments are conducted to evaluate whether the changes are durable over time. Clients learn how to identify and cope with potential setbacks and acquire behavioral and cognitive coping skills to maintain changes and to prevent relapses.

Let's examine how a behavior therapist might perform these functions. A client comes to therapy to reduce her anxiety, which is preventing her from leaving the house. The therapist is likely to begin with a specific analysis of the nature of her anxiety. The therapist will ask how she experiences the anxiety of leaving her house, including what she actually *does* in these situations. Systematically, the therapist gathers information about this anxiety. When did the problem begin? In what situations does it arise? What does she do at these times? What are her feelings and thoughts in these situations? Who is present when she experiences anxiety? What does she do to reduce the anxiety? How do her present fears interfere with living effectively? After this assessment, specific behavioral goals are developed, and strategies such as relaxation training, systematic desensitization, and exposure therapy are designed to help the client reduce her anxiety to a manageable level. The therapist will get a commitment from the client to work toward the specified goals, and the two of them will evaluate the client's progress toward meeting these goals throughout the duration of therapy.

For a description of applying a behavioral approach to the assessment and treatment of an individual client, see Dr. Sherry Cormier's behavioral interventions with Ruth in *Case Approach to Counseling and Psychotherapy* (Corey, 2013, chap. 7).

Client's Experience in Therapy

One of the unique contributions of behavior therapy is that it provides the therapist with a well-defined system of procedures to employ. Both therapist and client have clearly defined roles, and the importance of client awareness and participation in the therapeutic process is stressed. Behavior therapy is characterized by an active role for both therapist and client. A large part of the therapist's role is to teach concrete skills through the provision of instructions, modeling, and performance feedback. The client engages in behavioral rehearsal with feedback until skills are well learned and generally receives active homework assignments (such as self-monitoring of problem behaviors) to complete between therapy sessions. Behavior clinicians emphasize that changes clients make in therapy need to be translated into their daily lives.

It is important for clients to be motivated to change, and they are expected to cooperate in carrying out therapeutic activities, both during therapy sessions and in everyday life. If clients are not involved in this way, the chances are slim that therapy will be successful. Motivational interviewing (see Chapter 7), which honors the client's resistance in such a way that his or her motivation to change is increased over time, is a behavioral strategy that has considerable empirical support (Miller & Rollnick, 2013).

Clients are encouraged to experiment for the purpose of enlarging their repertoire of adaptive behaviors. Counseling is not complete unless actions follow verbalizations. Behavioral practitioners make the assumption that it is only when the transfer of changes is made from the sessions to everyday life that the effects of therapy can be considered successful. Clients are as aware as the therapist is regarding when the goals have been accomplished and when it is appropriate to terminate treatment. It is clear that clients are expected to do more than merely gather insights; they need to be willing to make changes and to continue implementing new behavior once formal treatment has ended.

Relationship Between Therapist and Client

Behavioral practitioners have increasingly recognized the role of the therapeutic relationship and therapist behavior as critical factors related to the process and outcome of treatment. As you will recall, the experiential therapies (existential therapy, person-centered therapy, and Gestalt therapy) place primary emphasis on the nature of the engagement between counselor and client. Today most behavioral practitioners stress the value of establishing a collaborative working relationship with clients but contend that warmth, empathy, authenticity, permissiveness, and acceptance are necessary, *but not sufficient*, for behavior change to occur. The client–therapist relationship is a foundation on which behavioral strategies are built to help clients change in the direction they wish. LO5

Application: Therapeutic Techniques and Procedures

A strength of the behavioral approaches is the development of specific therapeutic procedures that must be shown to be effective through objective means. The results of behavioral interventions become clear because therapists receive continual direct feedback from their clients. A hallmark of the behavioral approaches is that the therapeutic techniques are empirically supported and evidence-based practice is highly valued. Behavior therapy has been shown to be effective with many different populations and for a wide array of disorders. Behavioral techniques can easily be incorporated in other approaches as well. LO6

The therapeutic procedures used by behavior therapists are specifically designed for a particular client rather than being randomly selected from a "bag of techniques." Therapists are often quite creative in their interventions. In the following sections I describe a range of behavioral techniques available to the practitioner: applied behavioral analysis, relaxation training, systematic desensitization, exposure therapies, eye movement desensitization and reprocessing, social skills training, self-management programs, multimodal therapy, and mindfulness and acceptance-based approaches. These techniques do not encompass the full spectrum of behavioral procedures, but they do represent a sample of the approaches used in the practice of contemporary behavior therapy.

Applied Behavioral Analysis: Operant Conditioning Techniques

This section describes a few key principles of operant conditioning: positive reinforcement, negative reinforcement, extinction, positive punishment, and negative punishment. For a detailed treatment of the wide range of operant conditioning methods that are part of contemporary behavior modification, I recommend Miltenberger (2012) and Speigler (2016).

The most important contribution of applied behavior analysis is that it offers a functional approach to understanding clients' problems and addresses these problems by changing antecedents and consequences (the ABC model). Behaviorists believe we respond in predictable ways because of the gains we experience (positive reinforcement) or because of the need to escape or avoid unpleasant consequences (negative reinforcement). Once clients' goals have been assessed, specific behaviors are targeted. The goal of reinforcement, whether positive or negative, is to increase the target behavior. **Positive reinforcement** involves the *addition* of something of value to the individual (such as praise, attention, money, or food) as a consequence of certain behavior. The stimulus that follows the behavior is the positive reinforcer. For example, a child earns excellent grades and is praised for studying by her parents. If she values this praise, it is likely that she will have an investment in studying in the future. When the goal of a program is to decrease or eliminate undesirable behaviors, positive reinforcement is often used to increase the frequency of more desirable behaviors, which replace undesirable behaviors. In the above example, the parental praise functions as the positive reinforcer and makes it more likely that the child will maintain or even increase the frequency of studying and earning good grades. Note that if a child did *not* value parental praise, this would not serve as a reinforcer. The reinforcer is not defined by the form or substance that it takes but rather by the *function* it serves: namely, to maintain or increase the frequency of a desired behavior.

Negative reinforcement involves the *escape* from or the avoidance of aversive (unpleasant) stimuli. The individual is motivated to exhibit a desired behavior to avoid the unpleasant condition. For example, a friend of mine does not appreciate waking up to the shrill sound of an alarm clock. She has trained herself to wake up a few minutes before the alarm sounds to avoid the aversive stimulus of the alarm buzzer.

Another operant method of changing behavior is **extinction**, which refers to withholding reinforcement from a previously reinforced response. In applied settings, extinction can be used for behaviors that have been maintained by positive reinforcement or negative reinforcement. For example, in the case of children who display temper tantrums, parents often reinforce this behavior by the attention they give to it. An approach to dealing with problematic behavior is to eliminate the connection between a certain behavior (tantrums) and positive reinforcement (attention). In this example, if the parent ignores the child's tantrum-related behaviors, these behaviors will decrease or be eliminated through the *extinction process*. It should be noted that extinction might well have negative side effects, such as anger and aggression. Also note that during the extinction process unwanted behaviors may increase temporarily before they begin to decrease. Extinction can reduce or eliminate certain behaviors, but extinction does not replace those responses that have been extinguished.

Another way behavior is controlled is through **punishment**, sometimes referred to as aversive control, in which the consequences of a certain behavior result in a decrease of that behavior. The goal of reinforcement is to *increase target behavior*, but the goal of punishment is to *decrease target behavior*. Miltenberger (2012) describes two kinds of punishment that may occur as a consequence of behavior: positive punishment and negative punishment. In **positive punishment** an aversive stimulus is *added* after the behavior to decrease the frequency of a behavior (such as a time-out procedure with a child who is displaying misbehavior).

In **negative punishment** a reinforcing stimulus is *removed* following the behavior to decrease the frequency of a target behavior (such as deducting money from a worker's salary for missing time at work, or taking television time away from a child for misbehavior). In both kinds of punishment, the behavior is less likely to occur in the future. These four operant procedures form the basis of behavior therapy programs for parent skills training and are also used in the self-management procedures that are discussed later in this chapter.

Some behavioral practitioners are opposed to using aversive control or punishment and recommended substituting positive reinforcement. The key principle in the applied behavior analysis approach is to use the least aversive means possible to change behavior, and positive reinforcement is known to be the most powerful change agent. It is essential that reinforcement be used as a way to develop appropriate behaviors that replace the behaviors that are suppressed.

Progressive Muscle Relaxation

Progressive muscle relaxation has become increasingly popular as a method of teaching people to cope with the stresses produced by daily living. It is aimed at achieving muscle and mental relaxation and is easily learned. After clients learn the basics of relaxation procedures, it is essential that they practice these exercises daily to obtain maximum results.

Jacobson (1938) is credited with initially developing the progressive muscle relaxation procedure. It has since been refined and modified, and relaxation procedures are frequently used in combination with a number of other behavioral techniques. Progressive muscle relaxation involves several components. Clients are given a set of instructions that teaches them to relax. They assume a passive and relaxed position in a quiet environment while alternately contracting and relaxing muscles. This progressive muscle relaxation is explicitly taught to the client by the therapist. Deep and regular breathing also is associated with producing relaxation. At the same time clients learn to mentally "let go," perhaps by focusing on pleasant thoughts or images. Clients are instructed to actually feel and experience the tension building up, to notice their muscles getting tighter and study this tension, and to hold and fully experience the tension. It is useful for clients to experience the difference between a tense and a relaxed state. The client is then taught how to relax all the muscles while visualizing the various parts of the body, with emphasis on the facial muscles. The arm muscles are relaxed first, followed by the head, the neck and shoulders, the back, abdomen, and thorax, and then the lower limbs. Relaxation becomes a well-learned response, which can become a habitual pattern if practiced daily for about 25 minutes each day.

Relaxation procedures have been applied to a variety of clinical problems, either as a separate technique or in conjunction with related methods. The most common use has been with problems related to stress and anxiety, which are often manifested in psychosomatic symptoms. Relaxation training has benefits in areas such as preparing patients for surgery, teaching clients how to cope with chronic pain, and reducing the frequency of migraine attacks (Ferguson & Sgambati, 2008). Some other ailments for which progressive muscle relaxation is helpful include asthma, headache, hypertension, insomnia, irritable bowel syndrome, and panic disorder (Cormier et al., 2013).

For an exercise of the phases of the progressive muscle relaxation procedure that you can apply to yourself, see *Student Manual for Theory and Practice of Counseling and Psychotherapy* (Corey, 2017). For a more detailed discussion of progressive muscle relaxation, see Ferguson and Sgambati (2008).

Systematic Desensitization

Systematic desensitization, which is based on the principle of classical conditioning, is a basic behavioral procedure developed by Joseph Wolpe, one of the pioneers of behavior therapy. Clients imagine successively more anxiety-arousing situations at the same time that they engage in a behavior that competes with anxiety. Gradually, or systematically, clients become less sensitive (desensitized) to the anxiety-arousing situation. This procedure can be considered a form of exposure therapy because clients are required to expose themselves to anxiety-arousing images as a way to reduce anxiety.

Systematic desensitization is an empirically researched behavior therapy procedure that is time consuming, yet it is clearly effective and efficient in reducing maladaptive anxiety and treating anxiety-related disorders, particularly in the area of specific phobias (Cormier et al., 2013; Spiegler, 2016). Before implementing the desensitization procedure, the therapist conducts an initial interview to identify specific information about the anxiety and to gather relevant background information about the client. This interview, which may last several sessions, gives the therapist a good understanding of who the client is. The therapist questions the client about the particular circumstances that elicit the conditioned fears. For instance, under what circumstances does the client feel anxious? If the client is anxious in social situations, does the anxiety vary with the number of people present? Is the client more anxious with women or men? The client is asked to begin a self-monitoring process consisting of observing and recording situations during the week that elicit anxiety responses. Some therapists also administer a questionnaire to gather additional data about situations leading to anxiety.

If the decision is made to use the desensitization procedure, the therapist gives the client a rationale for the procedure and briefly describes what is involved. A three-step process is carried out in the desensitization process: (1) relaxation training, (2) development of a graduated anxiety hierarchy, and (3) systematic desensitization through presentation of hierarchy items while the client is in a deeply relaxed state (Head & Gross, 2008).

The first step is *progressive muscle relaxation*, which were described earlier. The therapist uses a quiet, soft, and pleasant voice to teach progressive muscular relaxation. The client is asked to create imagery of previously relaxing situations, such as sitting by a lake or wandering through a beautiful field. It is important that the client reach a state of calm and peacefulness. The client is instructed to practice relaxation both as a part of the desensitization procedure and also outside the session on a daily basis.

The therapist then works with the client to develop an *anxiety hierarchy* for each of the identified areas. Stimuli that elicit anxiety in a particular area are analyzed, such as rejection, jealousy, criticism, disapproval, or any phobia. The therapist constructs a ranked list of situations that elicit increasing degrees of anxiety or avoidance. The hierarchy is arranged in order from the most anxiety-provoking situation the client can imagine down to the situation that evokes the least anxiety. If it has been determined that the client has anxiety related to fear of rejection, for example, the highest anxiety-producing situation might be rejection by the spouse, next, rejection by a close friend, and then rejection by a coworker. The least disturbing situation might be a stranger's indifference toward the client at a party.

Desensitization does not begin until several sessions after the initial interview has been completed. Enough time is allowed for clients to learn relaxation in therapy sessions, to practice it at home, and to construct their anxiety hierarchy. The desensitization process begins with the client reaching complete relaxation with eyes closed. A neutral scene is presented, and the client is asked to imagine it. If the client remains relaxed, he or she is asked to imagine the least anxiety-arousing scene on the hierarchy of situations that has been developed. The therapist moves progressively up the hierarchy until the client signals that he or she is experiencing anxiety, at which time the scene is terminated. Relaxation is then induced again, and the scene is reintroduced again until little anxiety is experienced to it. Treatment ends when the client is able to remain in a relaxed state while imagining the scene that was formerly the most disturbing and anxiety-producing. The core of systematic desensitization is repeated exposure in the imagination to anxiety-evoking situations without experiencing any negative consequences.

Homework and follow-up are essential components of successful desensitization. Clients are encouraged to practice selected relaxation procedures daily, at which time they visualize scenes completed in the previous session. Gradually, they can expose themselves to daily-life situations as a further way to manage their anxieties. Clients tend to benefit the most when they have a variety of ways to cope with anxiety-arousing situations that they can continue to use once therapy has ended (Head & Gross, 2008).

Systematic desensitization is among the most empirically supported therapy methods available, especially for the treatment of anxiety. Not only does systematic desensitization have a good track record in dealing with fears, it also has been used to treat a variety of conditions including anger, asthmatic attacks, insomnia, motion sickness, nightmares, and sleepwalking (Spiegler, 2016). Systematic desensitization is often acceptable to clients because they are gradually and symbolically exposed to anxiety-evoking situations. For a more detailed discussion of systematic desensitization, see Head and Gross (2008), Speigler (2016), and Cormier et al. (2013).

In Vivo Exposure and Flooding

Exposure therapies are designed to treat fears and other negative emotional responses by introducing clients, under carefully controlled conditions, to the situations that contributed to such problems. Exposure is a key process in treating a wide range of problems associated with fear and anxiety. Exposure therapy involves systematic confrontation with a feared stimulus, either through imagination or *in vivo* (live). Imaginal exposure can be used prior to implementing in vivo exposure when a client's fears are so severe that the client is unable to participate in live exposure (Hazlett-Stevens & Craske, 2008). Whatever route is used, exposure involves contact by clients with what they find fearful. Desensitization is one type of exposure therapy, but there are others. Two variations of traditional systematic desensitization are *in vivo exposure* and *flooding.*

In Vivo Exposure In vivo exposure involves client exposure to the actual anxiety-evoking events rather than simply imagining these situations. Live exposure has been a cornerstone of behavior therapy for decades. Hazlett-Stevens and Craske (2008) describe the key elements of the process of in vivo exposure. Typically, treatment begins with a functional analysis of objects or situations a person avoids or fears. Together, the therapist and the client generate a hierarchy of situations for the client to encounter in ascending order of difficulty. In vivo exposure involves repeated systematic exposure to fear items, beginning from the bottom of the hierarchy. Clients engage in a brief, graduated series of exposures to feared events. As is the case with systematic desensitization, clients learn responses incompatible with anxiety, such as responses involving muscle relaxation. Clients are encouraged eventually to experience their full fear response during exposure without engaging in avoidance. Between therapy sessions, clients carry out self-directed exposure exercises. Clients' progress with home practice is reviewed, and the therapist provides feedback on how the client could deal with any difficulties encountered.

In some cases the therapist may accompany clients as they encounter feared situations. For example, a therapist could go with clients in an elevator if they had phobias of using elevators. Of course, when this kind of out-of-office procedure is used, matters of safety and appropriate ethical boundaries are always considered. People who have extreme fears of certain animals could be exposed to these animals in real life in a safe setting with a therapist. Self-managed in vivo exposure–a procedure in which clients expose themselves to anxiety-evoking events on their own–is an alternative when it is not practical for a therapist to be with clients in real-life situations.

Flooding Another form of exposure therapy is flooding, which refers to either in vivo or imaginal exposure to anxiety-evoking stimuli for a prolonged period of time. As is characteristic of all exposure therapies, even though the client experiences anxiety during the exposure, the feared consequences do not occur.

In vivo flooding consists of intense and prolonged exposure to the actual anxiety-producing stimuli. Remaining exposed to feared stimuli for a prolonged period without engaging in any anxiety-reducing behaviors allows the anxiety to decrease on its own. Generally, highly fearful clients tend to curb their anxiety through the use of maladaptive behaviors. In flooding, clients are prevented from engaging in their usual maladaptive responses to anxiety-arousing situations. In vivo flooding tends to reduce anxiety rapidly.

Imaginal flooding is based on similar principles and follows the same procedures except the exposure occurs in the client's imagination instead of in daily life. An advantage of using imaginal flooding over in vivo flooding is that there are no restrictions on the nature of the anxiety-arousing situations that can be treated. In vivo exposure to actual traumatic events (airplane crash, rape, fire, flood) is often not possible nor is it appropriate for both ethical and practical reasons. Imaginal flooding can re-create the circumstances of the trauma in a way that does not bring about adverse consequences to the client. Survivors of an airplane crash, for example, may suffer from a range of debilitating symptoms. They are likely to have nightmares and flashbacks to the disaster; they may avoid travel by air or have anxiety about travel by any means; and they probably have a variety of distressing symptoms such as guilt, anxiety, and depression. In vivo and imaginal exposure, as well as flooding, are frequently used in the behavioral treatment for anxiety-related disorders, specific phobia, social phobia, panic disorder, obsessive-compulsive disorder, posttraumatic stress disorder, and agoraphobia (Hazlett-Stevens & Craske, 2008).

Because of the discomfort associated with prolonged and intense exposure, some clients may not elect these exposure treatments. It is important for the behavior therapist to work with the client to create motivation and readiness for exposure. From an ethical perspective, clients should have adequate information about prolonged and intense exposure therapy before agreeing to participate. It is important that they understand that anxiety will be induced as a way to reduce it. Clients need to make informed decisions after considering the pros and cons of subjecting themselves to temporarily stressful aspects of treatment. Clients should be informed that they can terminate exposure if they experience a high level of anxiety.

The repeated success of exposure therapy in treating various disorders has resulted in exposure being used as a part of most behavioral treatments for anxiety disorders. Spiegler (2016) notes that exposure therapies are among the most potent behavioral procedures available for anxiety-related disorders, and they can have long-lasting effects. However, he adds, using exposure as a single treatment procedure is not always sufficient. In cases involving severe and multifaceted disorders, more than one behavioral intervention is often required. This is especially true with posttraumatic stress disorders. Increasingly, imaginal and in vivo exposure are being used in combination, which fits with the trend in behavior therapy to use treatment packages as a way to enhance the effectiveness of therapy.

Eye Movement Desensitization and Reprocessing

Eye movement desensitization and reprocessing (EMDR) is a form of LO7 exposure therapy that entails assessment and preparation, imaginal flooding, and cognitive restructuring in the treatment of individuals with traumatic memories. According to Shapiro and Solomon (2015), "EMDR is an integrative psychotherapeutic approach that conceptualizes current mental health problems as emanating from past experiences that have been maladaptively stored neurophysiologically as unprocessed memories" (p. 303). The treatment involves the use of rapid, rhythmic eye movements and other bilateral stimulation to treat clients who have experienced traumatic stress. "EMDR comprises eight phases and a three-pronged methodology to identify and process (1) memories of past adverse life experiences that underlie present problems, (2) current situations that elicit disturbance, and (3) needed skills that will provide positive memory templates to guide the client's future behavior" (p. 389). Developed by Francine Shapiro (2001), this therapeutic procedure draws from a wide range of behavioral interventions. Designed to assist clients in dealing with posttraumatic stress disorders, EMDR has been applied to a variety of populations including children, couples, sexual abuse victims, combat veterans, victims of crime, rape survivors, accident victims, and individuals dealing with anxiety, panic, depression, grief, addictions, and phobias.

Shapiro (2001) emphasizes the importance of the safety and welfare of the client when using this approach. EMDR may appear simple to some, but the ethical use of the procedure demands training and clinical supervision, as is true of using exposure therapies in general. Because of the powerful reactions from clients, it is essential that practitioners know how to safely and effectively manage these occurrences. Therapists should not use this procedure unless they receive proper training and supervision from an authorized EMDR instructor. A more complete discussion of this behavioral procedure can be found in Shapiro (2001, 2002a).

There is some controversy over whether the eye movements themselves create change or whether cognitive techniques paired with eye movements act as change agents. The role of lateral eye movements has yet to be clearly demonstrated, and some evidence indicates that the eye movement component may not be integral to the treatment (Prochaska & Norcross, 2014; Speigler, 2016). In a review of controlled studies of EMDR in the treatment of trauma, Shapiro (2002b) reports that EMDR clearly outperforms no treatment and achieves similar or superior results to other methods of treating trauma. Shapiro and Solomon (2015) state that extensive research has validated EMDR and randomized trials have confirmed that EMDR is both effective and efficient. Twelve sessions with combat veterans resulted in the elimination of PTSD diagnosis in more than 77% of the cases. When it comes to the overall effectiveness of EMDR, Prochaska and Norcross (2014) note that "in its 25-year history, EMDR has garnered more controlled research than any other method used to treat trauma" (p. 210). In writing about the future of EMDR, Prochaska and Norcross make several predictions: increasing numbers of practitioners will receive training in EMDR; outcome research will shed light on EMDR's effectiveness compared to other current therapies for trauma; and further research and practice will provide a sense of its effectiveness with disorders beyond posttraumatic stress disorder.

Social Skills Training

Social skills training is a broad category that deals with an individual's ability to interact effectively with others in various social situations; it is used to help clients develop and achieve skills in interpersonal competence. *Social skills* involve being able to communicate with others in a way that is both appropriate and effective. Individuals who experience psychosocial problems that are partly caused by interpersonal difficulties are good candidates for social skills training. Typically, social skills training involves various behavioral techniques such as psychoeducation, modeling, behavior rehearsal, and feedback (Antony & Roemer, 2011b). Social skills training is effective in treating psychosocial problems by increasing clients' interpersonal skills (Kress & Henry, 2015; Segrin, 2008). Some of the desirable aspects of social skills training are that it has a very broad base of applicability and that it can easily be tailored to suit the particular needs of individual clients. LO8

Key elements of social skills training include assessment, direct instruction and coaching, modeling, role playing, and homework assignments (Segrin 2008). Clients learn information that they can apply to various interpersonal situations, and skills are modeled for them so they can actually see how skills can be used. A key step involves clients putting into action the information they are acquiring. Individuals actively practice desired behaviors through role playing. Feedback and reinforcement assist clients in conceptualizing and using a new set of social skills that enables them to communicate more effectively. If clients are able to correct their problematic behaviors in practice situations, they can then apply these new skills in daily life (Kress & Henry, 2015). A follow-up phase is critical for clients in establishing a range of effective behaviors that can be applied to many social situations.

A few examples of evidence-based applications of social skills training include alcohol/substance abuse, attention-deficit/hyperactivity disorder, bullying, social anxiety, emotional and behavioral problems in children, behavioral treatment for couples, and depression (Antony & Roemer, 2011b; Segrin, 2008). A popular variation of social skills training is *anger management training,* which is designed for individuals who have trouble with aggressive behavior.

Self-Management Programs and Self-Directed Behavior

For some time there has been a trend toward "giving psychology away." This involves psychologists being willing to share their knowledge so that "consumers" can increasingly lead self-directed lives and not be dependent on experts to deal with their problems. Psychologists who share this perspective are primarily concerned with teaching people the skills they will need to manage their own lives effectively. An advantage of self-management techniques is that treatment can be extended to consumers in ways that cannot be done with traditional approaches to therapy. Another advantage is that costs are minimal. Because clients have a direct role in their own treatment, techniques aimed at self-change tend to increase involvement and commitment to their treatment. LO9

The basic idea of self-management assessments and interventions is that change can be brought about by teaching people to use coping skills in problematic situations. **Self-management** strategies include teaching clients how to select realistic goals, how to translate these goals into target behaviors, how to create an action plan for change, and ways to self-monitor and evaluate their actions (Kress & Henry 2015). Generalization and maintenance of the outcomes are enhanced by encouraging clients to accept the responsibility for carrying out these strategies in daily life.

In self-management programs people make decisions concerning specific behaviors they want to control or change. People frequently discover that a major reason they do not attain their goals is the lack of certain skills or unrealistic expectations of change. Hope can be a therapeutic factor that leads to change, but unrealistic hope can pave the way for a pattern of failures in a self-change program. A self-directed approach can provide the guidelines for change and a realistic plan that will lead to change.

If you want to succeed in such a program, a careful analysis of the context of the behavior pattern is essential, and you must be willing to follow some basic steps such as these provided by Watson and Tharp (2014):

1. *Selecting goals.* Goals should be established one at a time, and they should be measurable, attainable, positive, and significant for you. It is essential that expectations be realistic.
2. *Translating goals into target behaviors.* Identify behaviors targeted for change. Once targets for change are selected, anticipate obstacles and think of ways to negotiate them.
3. *Self-monitoring.* Deliberately and systematically observe your own behavior, and keep a *behavioral diary* in which you record your actions, thoughts, and feelings along with comments about the relevant antecedent cues and consequences. This diary can help you identify what you need to change.
4. *Working out a plan for change.* A good plan involves substituting new thoughts and behaviors for ineffective thoughts and behaviors. Devise an action program to bring about actual changes that are in line with your goals. Various plans for the same goal can be designed, each of which can be effective. Some type of self-reinforcement system is necessary in this plan because reinforcement is the cornerstone of modern behavior therapy. Discover and select reinforcers to use until the new behaviors have been implemented in everyday life. Practice the new behaviors you want to acquire or refine, and take steps to ensure that the gains made will be maintained.
5. *Evaluating an action plan.* Evaluate the plan for change to determine whether goals are being achieved, and adjust and revise the plan as other ways to meet goals are learned. Be willing to adjust your plan as conditions change. Evaluation is an ongoing process rather than a one-time occurrence, and self-change is a lifelong practice.

Self-management strategies have been successfully applied to many populations and problems, a few of which include coping with panic attacks, reducing perfectionism, helping children to cope with fear of the dark, increasing creative productivity, managing anxiety in social situations, encouraging speaking in front of a class, increasing exercise, reducing conflict with coworkers, improving study habits, control of smoking, and dealing with depression (Watson & Tharp, 2014). Research on self-management has been conducted in a wide variety of health problems, a few of which include arthritis, asthma, cancer, cardiac disease, substance abuse, diabetes, headaches, vision loss, depression, nutrition, and self-health care (Cormier et al., 2013).

Multimodal Therapy: Clinical Behavior Therapy

Multimodal therapy is a comprehensive, systematic, holistic approach to behavior therapy developed by the late Arnold Lazarus (1989,1997, 2005, 2008a), a key pioneer in clinical behavior therapy. Multimodal therapy is grounded in social cognitive learning theory. The assessment process is multimodal, yet the treatment is cognitive behavioral and draws upon empirically supported methods. It is an open system that encourages *technical eclecticism* in that it applies diverse behavioral techniques from a variety of theories to a wide range of problems. Whenever possible, multimodal therapists strive to incorporate empirically supported and evidence-based treatments in their practice (Lazarus & Lazarus, 2015). This approach serves as a major link between some behavioral principles and the cognitive behavioral approach that has largely replaced traditional behavioral therapy.

Multimodal therapists borrow techniques from many other therapy systems, but Lazarus and Lazarus (2015) point out that these techniques are never used in a shotgun manner: "a rag-tag combination of techniques without a sound rationale will likely result only in syncretistic confusion" (p. 682). Multimodal therapists take great pains to determine precisely what relationship and what treatment strategies will work best with each client and under which particular circumstances. The underlying assumption of this approach is that because individuals are troubled by a variety of specific problems it is appropriate that a multitude of treatment strategies be used in bringing about change. Therapeutic flexibility and versatility, along with breadth over depth, are highly valued, and multimodal therapists are constantly adjusting their procedures to achieve the client's goals. Therapists need to decide when and how to be challenging or supportive and how to adapt their relationship style to the needs of the client. The therapeutic relationship is the soil that enables techniques to take root, and multimodal therapists recognize that a good working alliance is a cornerstone in the foundation of effective therapeutic practice (Lazarus & Lazarus, 2015). Multimodal therapists tend to be very active during therapist sessions, functioning as trainers, educators, consultants, coaches, and role models. They provide information, instruction, and feedback as well as modeling assertive behaviors. They offer suggestions, positive reinforcements, and are appropriately self-disclosing.

For an illustration of how Dr. Lazarus applies the BASIC I.D. assessment model to the case of Ruth, along with examples of various techniques he uses, see *Case Approach to Counseling and Psychotherapy* (Corey, 2013, chap. 7).

Mindfulness and Acceptance-Based Approaches

LO10

The third generation (or "third wave") of behavior therapy emphasizes considerations that were considered off limits for behavior therapists until recently, including mindfulness, acceptance, the therapeutic relationship, spirituality, values, meditation, being in the present moment, and emotional expression (Hayes, Follette, & Linehan, 2004; Herbert & Forman, 2011). Third-generation behavior therapies center around five interrelated core themes: (1) an expanded view of psychological health, (2) a broad view of acceptable outcomes in therapy, (3) acceptance, (4) mindfulness, and (5) creating a life worth living (Speigler, 2016).

Mindfulness is "the awareness that emerges through having attention on purpose, in the present moment, and nonjudgmentally, to the unfolding of experience moment by moment" (Kabat-Zinn, 2003, p. 145). In mindfulness practice, clients train themselves to intentionally focus on their "present experience with acceptance" (Siegel, 2010, p. 27) and develop an attitude of curiosity and compassion toward present experience.

Mindfulness shows promise across a broad range of clinical problems, including the treatment of depression, anxiety disorders, relationship problems, substance abuse, and psychophysiological disorders (Germer, Siegel, & Fulton, 2013). It is useful in treating posttraumatic stress disorder among military veterans. Through mindfulness exercises, veterans may be better able to observe repetitive negative thinking and prevent extensive engagement with maladaptive ruminative processes (Vujanovic, Niles, Pietrefesa, Schmertz, & Potter, 2011). Many therapeutic approaches are incorporating mindfulness and meditation, as well as other contemplative practices, in the counseling process, and this trend seems likely to continue (Worthington, 2011).

Acceptance is a process involving receiving one's present experience without judgment or preference, but with curiosity and kindness, and striving for full awareness of the present moment (Germer, 2013). Acceptance is an alternative way of responding to our internal experience. By replacing judgment, criticism, and avoidance with acceptance, the likely result is increased adaptive functioning (Antony & Roemer, 2011b). Mindfulness and acceptance approaches are also good avenues for the integration of spirituality in the counseling process.

For an extensive discussion of mindfulness and acceptance, see *Acceptance and Mindfulness in Cognitive Behavior Therapy: Understanding and Applying the New Therapies* (Herbert & Forman, 2011).

Recent developments in the cognitive behavioral tradition include four major approaches: (1) *dialectical behavior therapy*, which has become a recognized treatment for borderline personality disorder (Linehan, 1993a, 1993b, 2015); (2) *mindfulness-based stress reduction*, an 8- to 10-week group program that applies mindfulness techniques to coping with stress and promoting physical and psychological health (Kabat-Zinn, 1990, 2003); (3) *mindfulness-based cognitive therapy*, aimed primarily at treating depression (Segal, Williams, & Teasdale, 2013); and (4) *acceptance and commitment therapy*, which encourages clients to accept unpleasant sensations rather than attempting to control or change them (Hayes, Strosahl, & Houts, 2005; Hayes, Strosahl, & Wilson, 2011). All four of these approaches use mindfulness strategies that have been subjected to empirical scrutiny, a hallmark of the behavioral tradition.

Dialectical Behavior Therapy (DBT) Dialectical behavior therapy was originally developed to treat chronically suicidal individuals diagnosed with borderline personality disorder (BPD), and it is now recognized as a major psychological treatment for this population. Formulated by Linehan (1993a, 1993b, 2015), who was motivated to alleviate emotional suffering for those miserable enough to consider suicide, DBT has been proven effective in treating a wide range of disorders, including substance dependence, depression, posttraumatic stress disorder (PTSD), eating disorders, suicidal behavior, and nonsuicidal self-injury (Linehan, 2015).

DBT is a promising blend of behavioral and psychoanalytic techniques for treating borderline personality disorders. Like analytic therapy, DBT emphasizes the importance of the psychotherapeutic relationship, validation of the client, the etiologic importance of the client having experienced an "invalidating environment" as a child, and confrontation of resistance. DBT treatment includes both acceptance- and change-oriented strategies. Mindfulness procedures are taught to develop an attitude of acceptance (Fishman, Rego, & Muller, 2011; Kuo & Fitzpatrick, 2015). The treatment program is geared toward helping clients make changes in their behavior and environment while communicating acceptance of their current state (Kuo & Fitzpatrick, 2015; Robins & Rosenthal, 2011). To help clients who have particular problems with emotional regulation, DBT teaches clients to recognize and accept the existence of simultaneous, opposing forces. By acknowledging this fundamental dialectic relationship—such as not wanting to engage in a certain behavior, yet knowing they have to engage in the behavior if they want to achieve a desired goal—clients can learn to integrate the opposing notions of acceptance and change, and the therapist can teach clients how to regulate their emotions and behaviors.

DBT skills training is not a "quick fix" approach. It generally involves a minimum of one year of treatment and includes both individual therapy and skills training done in a group. DBT is an empirically supported intervention that employs behavioral and cognitive behavioral techniques, including a form of exposure therapy in which the client learns to tolerate painful emotions without enacting self-destructive behaviors. DBT draws upon Zen teachings and practices to integrate mindfulness and acceptance-based techniques in therapy (Kuo & Fitzpatrick, 2015). Some of the Zen Buddhist principles and practices include being aware of the present moment, seeing reality without distortion, accepting reality without judgment, letting go of attachments that result in suffering, developing a greater degree of acceptance of self and others, and entering fully into present activities without separating oneself from ongoing events and interactions (Robins & Rosenthal, 2011).

DBT promotes a structured, predictable therapeutic environment. The goals are tailored to each individual. Therapists assist clients in using whatever skills they possess or are learning to navigate crises more effectively and to address problem behaviors (Robins & Rosenthal, 2011). Skills are taught in four modules: mindfulness, interpersonal effectiveness, emotional regulation, and distress tolerance (Kuo & Fitzpatrick, 2015).

Mindfulness is a fundamental skill in DBT that teaches individuals to be aware of and accept the world as it is and to respond to each moment effectively. Through mindfulness, clients learn to embrace and tolerate the intense emotions they experience when facing distressing situations. *Interpersonal effectiveness* teaches clients to ask for what they need and how to say "no" while maintaining self-respect and relationships with others. This skill entails increasing the chances that a client's goals will be met, while at the same time not damaging the relationship. *Emotional regulation* includes identifying emotions, identifying obstacles to changing emotions, reducing vulnerability, and increasing positive emotions. Clients learn the benefits of regulating emotions such as anger, depression, and anxiety. *Distress tolerance* is aimed at helping individuals to calmly recognizing emotions associated with negative situations without becoming overwhelmed by these situations. Clients learn how to tolerate pain or discomfort skillfully.

DBT helps individuals acquire, strengthen, and generalize the skills they learn in therapy to their daily environments (Kuo & Fitzpatrick, 2015). Because DBT places heavy emphasis on didactic instruction and teaching mindfulness skills, therapists must obtain training to become competent in applying these skills and be able to model specific strategies and attitudes for clients. Therapists who want to employ mindfulness strategies must also have personal understanding of these interventions to be able to effectively use them with clients.

For a more detailed review of DBT, see *DBT Skills Training Manual* (Linehan, 2015), which includes instructions for orienting clients to DBT and explains how to use many skills in DBT. Another useful resource for a more detailed discussion of DBT is Robins and Rosenthal (2011).

Mindfulness-Based Stress Reduction (MBSR) Jon Kabat-Zinn, at the University of Massachusetts, developed MBSR in 1979 to see if it was possible to create a training program to relieve medical patients of stress, pain, illness, and other forms of suffering. The eight-week structured group program involves training people in mindfulness meditation, and today instructors are often not mental health clinicians. Originally designed to help people increase their responsibility for their own well-being and to actively develop inner resources for treating their physical health concerns (Kabat-Zinn, 2003), MBSR is not a form of psychotherapy per se, but it can be an adjunct to therapy.

The essence of mindfulness-based stress reduction (MBSR) consists of the notion that much of our distress and suffering results from continually wanting things to be different from how they actually are (Salmon, Sephton, & Dreeben, 2011). MBSR assists people in learning how to live more fully in the present rather than ruminating about the past or being overly concerned about the future. MBSR does not actively teach cognitive modification techniques, nor does it label certain cognitions as "dysfunctional," because this is not consistent with the nonjudgmental attitude one strives to cultivate in mindfulness practice.

The approach adopted in the MBSR program is to develop the capacity for sustained directed attention through formal and informal meditation practice. There is a heavy emphasis on experiential learning and the process of client self-discovery (Dimidjian & Linehan, 2008). In formal practice, skills taught include sitting meditation and mindful yoga, which are aimed at cultivating mindfulness. The program includes a body scan meditation, which helps clients to observe all the sensations in their body. Clients are encouraged to bring mindfulness into all of their daily activities, and this informal practice includes being mindful when standing, walking, eating, and doing chores. Those who are involved in the program are encouraged to practice formal mindfulness meditation for 45 minutes daily.

The MBSR program is designed to teach participants to relate to external and internal sources of stress in constructive ways, and an ongoing commitment to cultivate and practice its principles in each moment is required. Acquiring a mindful way of being is not a simple behavioral technique but is more like an art form that individuals develop over time as they deepen their focus through disciplined practice. Kabat-Zinn (2003) makes it clear that mindfulness is not about getting anywhere or fixing anything: "It is an invitation to allow oneself to be where one already is and to know the inner and outer landscape of the direct experience in each moment" (p. 148).

MBSR programs are offered in hospitals, clinics, schools, workplaces, corporate offices, law schools, prisons, and inner-city health centers (Kabat-Zinn, 2003). MBSR has many clinical applications, and it is expected that the approach will evolve to address a range of negative psychological states, such as anxiety, stress, and depression. This approach has many applications in the area of health and wellness and in promoting healthy lifestyle changes. Numerous research reviews and meta-analyses indicate that mindfulness, acceptance, and compassion-based treatments are effective in promoting physical and psychological health (Germer, 2013). One of these studies suggests that MBSR training may lead to changes in the brain that result in people being able to better cope with negative emotional reactions under stress (as cited in Kabat-Zinn, 2003).

Kabat-Zinn's (1990, 1994) books offer a comprehensive treatment of MBSR, and they did a great deal to popularize the program he developed. An excellent resource for a more detailed treatment of MBSR is Salmon, Sephton, and Dreeben (2011).

Mindfulness-Based Cognitive Therapy (MBCT) This program is a comprehensive integration of the principles and skills of mindfulness applied to the treatment of depression (Segal et al., 2013). MBCT is an eight-week group treatment program of two-hour weekly sessions adapted from Kabat-Zinn's (1990, 2003) mindfulness-based stress reduction program. The program integrates techniques from MBSR with teaching cognitive behavioral skills to clients. The primary aim is to change clients' awareness of and relation to their negative thoughts. Participants are taught how to respond in skillful and intentional ways to their automatic negative thought patterns (Hammond, 2015).

Segal, Williams, and Teasdale (2013) describe kindness and self-compassion as essential components of MBCT. Mindfulness is a way of developing **self-compassion**, which is a form of self-care when facing difficult situations. Mindfulness practices focus on moment-to-moment experiencing and assist clients in developing an attitude of open awareness and acceptance of what is rather than being self-critical. When we acknowledge our shortcomings without critical judgment, we can begin to treat ourselves with **kindness**. We can intentionally activate goodwill toward ourselves and others while experiencing emotions such as anger, anxiety, and depression. Research has shown that self-compassion is positively associated with emotional well-being and decreased levels of anxiety and depression (Morgan, Morgan, & Germer, 2013; Neff, 2012). Other research findings on the association between self-compassion and emotional well-being have been reported by Neff (2012):

- Self-compassionate people recognize when they are suffering, yet they are kind toward themselves in these moments.
- Self-compassion is associated with greater wisdom and emotional intelligence.
- Self-compassion is associated with feelings of life satisfaction and connection to others.
- Self-compassionate individuals tend to experience increased happiness, optimism, curiosity, and positive emotions.
- Self-compassion engenders compassion toward others.

Morgan, Morgan, and Germer (2013) report that there is ample evidence that mindfulness meditation enhances the ability to pay attention in a concentrated and sustained manner. Being able to attend to present experiencing is a route to developing compassion toward oneself and expressing compassion toward others. Mindfulness is something that is *caught* more than something that is *taught*. The attitude and behavior of the instructor/facilitator of the MBCT group are critical in helping participants acquire an accepting way of being and discarding self-critical and judgmental habits.

Segal, Williams, and Teasdale (2013) describe the essence of eight sessions in the MBCT program:

- Therapy begins by identifying negative automatic thinking of people experiencing depression and by introducing some basic mindfulness practices.
- In the second session, participants learn about the reactions they have to life experiences and learn more about mindfulness practices. Clients learn the importance of kindness and self-compassion, both to self and to others.
- The third session is focused on gathering the scattered mind; participants learn breathing techniques and focus their attention on their present experiencing. Clients learn how to anchor thoughts with a focus on the breath while allowing experience to unfold.
- In session four, the emphasis is on learning to experience the moment without becoming attached to outcomes; participants practice sitting meditation and mindful walking.
- The fifth session teaches participants how to accept their experiencing without holding on; participants learn the value of allowing and letting be.
- Session six is used to describe thoughts as "merely thoughts"; clients learn that they do not have to act on their thoughts. They can tell themselves, "I am not my thoughts" and "Thoughts are not facts."
- In session seven, participants learn how to take care of themselves and to develop an action plan to deal with the threat of relapse.
- Session eight focuses on maintaining and extending new learning; clients learn how to generalize their mindfulness practices to daily life.

MBCT emphasizes experiential learning, in-session practice, learning from feedback, completing homework assignments, and applying what is learned in the program to challenging situations encountered outside of the sessions. The brevity of MBCT makes this approach an efficient and cost-effective treatment. For a more detailed review of MBCT, see *Mindfulness-Based Cognitive Therapy for Depression* (Segal et al., 2013).

Acceptance and Commitment Therapy (ACT) Another mindfulness-based approach is *acceptance and commitment therapy* (Hayes et al., 2005, 2011). ACT is a unique empirically based psychological intervention that uses acceptance and mindfulness strategies, together with commitment and behavior change strategies, to increase psychological flexibility. ACT involves fully accepting present experience and mindfully letting go of obstacles. In this approach "acceptance is not merely tolerance–rather it is the active nonjudgmental embracing of experience in the here and now" (Hayes, 2004, p. 32). Acceptance is a stance or posture from which to conduct therapy and from which a client can conduct life that provides an alternative to contemporary forms of cognitive behavioral therapy. In contrast to the cognitive behavioral approaches discussed in Chapter 10, in which dysfunctional thoughts are identified and challenged, in ACT there is little emphasis on changing the content of a client's thoughts. Hayes has found that confronting maladaptive cognitions strengthens rather than reduces these cognitions. Instead, the emphasis is on *acceptance* (nonjudgmental awareness) of cognitions. The goal is for individuals to become aware of and examine their thoughts. Clients learn how to change their relationship to their thoughts. They learn how to accept yet not identify with thoughts and feelings they may have been trying to deny.

Values are a basic part of the therapeutic process, and the work of ACT depends on what an individual wants and values. Client and therapist work together to identify personal values in areas such as work, relationships, spirituality, and well-being (Batten & Cairrochi, 2015). ACT practitioners might ask clients, "What do you want your life to stand for?" Therapy involves assisting clients to choose values they want to live by, designing specific goals, and taking steps to achieve their goals (Speigler, 2016).

A commitment to action is essential, and clients are asked to make mindful decisions about what they are willing to do to live a valued and meaningful life. Concrete homework and behavioral exercises as two ways clients can commit to action. For example, one form of homework asks clients to write down life goals or things they value in various aspects of their lives. Clients learn to allow experience to come and go while they pursue a meaningful life.

ACT is an effective form of therapy that continues to influence the practice of behavior therapy. Germer (2013) suggests "mindfulness appears to be drawing clinical theory, research, and practice closer together, and helping to integrate the private and professional lives of therapists" (p. 13). ACT emphasizes common processes across clinical disorders, which makes it easier to learn basic treatment skills. Practitioners can then implement basic principles in diverse and creative ways. ACT has been empirically shown to be effective in the treatment of a variety of disorders, including substance abuse, depression, anxiety, phobias, posttraumatic stress disorder, and chronic pain (Batten & Cairrochi, 2015).

For an in-depth discussion of the role of mindfulness in psychotherapeutic practice, four highly recommended books are *Acceptance and Mindfulness in Cognitive Behavior Therapy: Understanding and Applying the New Therapies* (Herbert & Forman, 2011), *Mindfulness and Acceptance: Expanding the Cognitive-Behavioral Tradition* (Hayes et al., 2004), *Mindfulness and Psychotherapy* (Germer et al., 2013), and *Wisdom and Compassion in Psychotherapy: Deepening Mindfulness in Clinical Practice*, (Germer & Siegel, 2012).

Application to Group Counseling

Behavioral group therapy incorporates classical behavior therapy treatment **LO11** principles rooted in classical conditioning, operant conditioning, and social learning theory. The focus of a behavioral group is on teaching, modeling, and applying scientific principles to target specific behaviors for change (Kress & Henry, 2015).

Group-based behavioral approaches emphasize teaching clients self-management skills and a range of new coping behaviors, as well as how to restructure their thoughts. Clients can learn to use these techniques to control their lives, deal effectively with present and future problems, and function well after they complete their group experience. Many groups are designed primarily to increase the client's degree of control and freedom in specific aspects of daily life.

Group leaders who function within a behavioral framework may develop techniques from various theoretical viewpoints. Behavioral practitioners make use of a brief, active, directive, structured, collaborative, psychoeducational model of therapy that relies on empirical validation of its concepts and techniques. The leader follows the progress of group members through the ongoing collection of data *before, during,* and *after* all interventions. Such an approach provides both the group leader and the members with continuous feedback about therapeutic progress. Today, many groups in community agencies demand this kind of accountability.

Behavioral group therapy has some unique characteristics that set it apart from most of the other group approaches. A distinguishing characteristic of behavioral practitioners is their systematic adherence to specification and measurement. The specific unique characteristics of behavioral group therapy include (1) conducting a behavioral assessment, (2) precisely spelling out collaborative treatment goals, (3) formulating a specific treatment procedure appropriate to a particular problem, and (4) objectively evaluating the outcomes of therapy. Behavior therapists tend to utilize short-term, time-limited interventions aimed at efficiently and effectively solving problems and assisting members in developing new skills.

Behavioral group leaders assume the role of teacher and encourage members to learn and practice skills in the group that they can apply to everyday living. Group leaders typically assume an active, directive, and supportive role in the group and apply their knowledge of behavioral principles and skills to the resolution of problems. They model active participation and collaboration by their involvement with members in creating an agenda, designing homework, and teaching skills and new behaviors. Leaders carefully observe and assess behavior to determine the conditions that are related to certain problems and the conditions that will facilitate change. Members in behavioral groups identify specific skills that they lack or would like to enhance. Assertiveness and social skills training fit well into a group format. Relaxation procedures, behavioral rehearsal, modeling, coaching, meditation, and mindfulness techniques are often incorporated in behavioral groups. The experience of being mindful is expanded in the group setting where people meditate and are still in the presence of others. Most of the other techniques described earlier in this chapter can be applied to group work.

Today, most behavior therapy groups blend cognitive and behavioral concepts and techniques, with few having a strictly behavioral focus (Kress & Henry, 2015). There are many different types of groups with a behavioral twist, or groups that blend both behavioral and cognitive methods for specific populations. Structured groups, with a psychoeducational focus, are especially popular in various settings today. At least four general approaches can be applied to the practice of behavioral groups: (1) social skills training groups, (2) psychoeducational groups with specific themes, (3) stress management groups, and (4) mindfulness and acceptance-based behavior therapy in groups.

For a more detailed discussion of cognitive behavioral approaches to groups, see Corey (2016, chap. 13).

Behavior Therapy From a Multicultural Perspective

Strengths From a Diversity Perspective

Behavior therapy has some clear advantages over many other theories in counseling culturally diverse clients. Because of their cultural and ethnic backgrounds, some clients hold values that are contrary to the free expression of feelings and the sharing of personal concerns. Behavioral counseling does not generally place emphasis on experiencing catharsis. Rather, it stresses changing specific behaviors and developing problem-solving skills. Some potential strengths of the behavioral approaches in working with diverse client populations include its specificity, task orientation, focus on objectivity, focus on cognition and behavior, action orientation, dealing with the present more than the past, emphasis on brief interventions, teaching coping strategies, and problem-solving orientation. The attention given to transfer of learning and the principles and strategies for maintaining new behavior in daily life are crucial. Clients who are looking for action plans and specific behavioral change are likely to cooperate with this approach because they can see that it offers them concrete methods for dealing with their problems of living. LO12

Behavior therapy focuses on environmental conditions that contribute to a client's problems. Social and political influences can play a significant role in the lives of people of color through discriminatory practices and economic problems, and the behavioral approach takes into consideration the social and cultural dimensions of the client's life. Behavior therapy is based on an experimental analysis of behavior in the client's own social environment and gives special attention to a number of specific conditions: the client's cultural conception of problem behaviors, establishing specific therapeutic goals, arranging conditions to increase the client's expectation of successful therapeutic outcomes, and employing appropriate social influence agents (Tanaka-Matsumi, Higginbotham, & Chang, 2002). The foundation of ethical practice involves a therapist's familiarity with the client's culture, as well as the competent application of this knowledge in formulating assessment, diagnostic, and treatment strategies.

The behavioral approach has moved beyond treating clients for a specific symptom or behavioral problem. Instead, it stresses a thorough assessment of the person's life circumstances to ascertain not only what conditions give rise to the client's problems but also whether the target behavior is amenable to change and whether such a change is likely to lead to a significant improvement in the client's total life situation.

In designing a change program for clients from diverse backgrounds, effective behavioral practitioners conduct a functional analysis of the problem situation. This assessment includes the cultural context in which the problem behavior occurs, the consequences both to the client and to the client's sociocultural environment, the resources within the environment that can promote change, and the impact that change is likely to have on others in the client's social surroundings. Assessment methods should be chosen with the client's cultural background in mind (Spiegler, 2016; Tanaka-Matsumi et al., 2002). Counselors must be knowledgeable as well as open and sensitive to issues such as these: What is considered normal and abnormal behavior in the client's culture? What are the client's culturally based conceptions of his or her problems? What is the potential role of spirituality or religion in the client's life? What kind of information about the client is essential in making an accurate assessment?

Shortcomings From a Diversity Perspective

Although behavior therapy is sensitive to differences among clients in a broad sense, behavior therapists need to become more responsive to *specific* issues pertaining to all forms of diversity. Because race, gender, ethnicity, and sexual orientation are critical variables that influence the process and outcome of therapy, it is essential that behavior therapists pay careful attention to these factors and address social justice issues as they arise in a client's therapy.

Some behavioral counselors may focus on using a variety of techniques in narrowly treating specific behavioral problems. Instead of viewing clients in the context of their sociocultural environment, these practitioners concentrate too much on problems within the individual. In doing so they may overlook significant issues in the lives of clients. Such practitioners are not likely to bring about beneficial changes for their clients.

The fact that behavioral interventions often work well raises an interesting issue in multicultural counseling. When clients make significant personal changes, it is very likely that others in their environment will react to them differently. Before deciding too quickly on goals for therapy, the counselor and client need to discuss the complexity inherent in change. It is essential for therapists to conduct a thorough assessment of the interpersonal and cultural dimensions of the problem. Clients should be helped in assessing the possible consequences of some of their newly acquired social skills. Once goals are determined and therapy is under way, clients should have opportunities to talk about the problems they encounter as they bring new skills and behaviors into their home and work settings.

Behavior Therapy Applied to the Case of Stan

In Stan's case many specific and interrelated problems can be identified through an assessment process. *Behaviorally*, he is defensive, avoids eye contact, speaks hesitantly, uses alcohol excessively, has a poor sleep pattern, and displays various avoidance behaviors in social and interpersonal situations. In the *emotional* area, Stan has a number of specific problems, some of which include anxiety, panic attacks, depression, fear of criticism and rejection, feeling worthless and stupid, and feeling isolated and alienated. He experiences a range of physiological complaints such as dizziness, heart palpitations, and headaches. *Cognitively*, he worries about death and dying, has many self-defeating thoughts and beliefs, is governed by categorical imperatives ("shoulds," "oughts," "musts"), engages in fatalistic thinking, and compares himself negatively with others. In the *interpersonal* area, Stan is unassertive, has an unsatisfactory relationship with his parents, has few friends, is afraid of contact with women and fears intimacy, and feels socially inferior.

After completing this assessment, I focus on helping Stan define the specific areas where he would like to make changes. Before developing a treatment plan, I assist Stan in understanding the purposes of his behavior. I then educate Stan about how the therapy sessions (and his work outside of the sessions) can help him reach his goals. Early during treatment I help Stan translate some of his general goals into concrete and measurable ones. When Stan says, "I want to feel better about myself," I help him define more specific goals. When he says, "I want to get rid of my inferiority complex," I reply: "What exactly do you mean by this? What are some situations in which you feel inferior? What do you actually do that leads to feelings of inferiority?" Stan's concrete aims include his desire to function without drugs or alcohol. I suggest that he keep a record of when he drinks and what events lead to drinking. My hope is that Stan will establish goals that are based on positive markers, not negative goals. Instead of focusing on what Stan would like to get rid of, I am more interested in what he would like to acquire and develop.

Stan indicates that he does not want to feel apologetic for his existence. I introduce behavioral skills training because he has trouble talking with his boss and coworkers. I demonstrate specific skills that he can use in approaching them more directly and confidently. This procedure includes modeling, role playing, and behavior rehearsal. He then tries more effective behaviors with me as I play the role of the boss. I give him feedback on how strong or apologetic he seemed.

Imaginal exposure and systematic desensitization are appropriate in working with Stan's fear of failing. Before using these procedures, I explain the procedure to Stan and get his informed consent. Stan first learns relaxation procedures during the sessions and then practices them daily at home. Next, he lists his specific fears relating to failure, and he then generates a hierarchy of fear items. Stan identifies his greatest fear as fear of dating and interacting with women. The least fearful situation he identifies is being with a female student for whom he does not feel an attraction. I first do some systematic desensitization on Stan's hierarchy. Stan begins repeated, systematic exposure to items that he finds frightening, beginning at the bottom of the fear hierarchy. He continues with repeated exposure to the next fear hierarchy item when exposure to the previous item generates only mild fear. Part of the process involves exposure exercises for practice in various situations away from the therapy office.

The goal of therapy is to help Stan modify the behavior that results in his feelings of guilt and anxiety. By learning more appropriate coping behaviors, eliminating unrealistic anxiety and guilt, and acquiring more adaptive responses, Stan's presenting symptoms decrease, and he reports a greater degree of satisfaction.

Questions for Reflection

- How would you collaboratively work with Stan in identifying specific behavioral goals to give a direction to your therapy?
- What behavioral techniques might be most appropriate in helping Stan with his problems?
- Stan indicates that he does not want to feel apologetic for his existence. How might you help him translate this wish into a specific behavioral goal? What behavioral techniques might you draw on in helping him in this area?
- What homework assignments are you likely to suggest for Stan?

Visit CengageBrain.com or watch the DVD for the video program *Theory and Practice of Counseling and Psychotherapy: The Case of Stan and Lecturettes*, Session 7 (behavior therapy), for a demonstration of my approach to counseling Stan from this perspective. This session involves collaboratively working on homework and behavior rehearsals to experiment with assertive behavior.

Behavior Therapy Applied to the Case of Gwen*

In daily life, Gwen has a tendency to try to get everything done without enlisting the support of others. In our previous session, she decided on a goal of asking for support from others both at home and at work. We engaged in behavioral rehearsals in which Gwen practiced asking someone for support. Gwen found this difficult, but she hesitantly said she was willing to try out these new behaviors. Her homework was to

*Dr. Kellie Kirksey writes about her ways of thinking and practicing from a behavior therapy perspective and applying this model to Gwen.

ask for help both at work and at home. Gwen is late for our session, and when she arrives she looks tired and defeated.

Gwen: Sorry I am late. I left work early to take my mother to the doctor, and the appointment ran longer than I expected.

Therapist: I am pleased you were able to make it, but our session will be shorter. Last week you talked about feeling disconnected from your husband. We agreed that asking him for assistance and sharing your daily life with him might help you communicate with each other. What have you done this week to get support and share more at home?

Gwen: I expressed to colleagues that I needed help when completing some tasks at work, but I fell back into the same pattern of silence when at home with Ron.

Therapist: Tell me more about falling back into the same pattern of silence.

Gwen: I wanted to ask Ron to help with my mom, but ultimately I feel like she is my mom and my responsibility. He sees what I am doing and could offer to pitch in.

Therapist: You seemed eager to express your need for support to Ron, but then something stopped you. What do you think caused you to stop? [*Using the A-B-C model*]

Gwen: I hate to ask. It is my responsibility. I think I am the only one who can do it. I would feel like I was putting a burden on Ron's shoulders if I asked for help.

Therapist: You must feel an overwhelming amount of pressure being solely responsible for so much.

Gwen: Yes, it is hard to make sense of it all.

Therapist: Let me see if I understand. It sounds as though taking care of your mom is your sole responsibility and not Ron's [*antecedent*]. You do not want to feel like a burden to Ron, so you stop yourself from asking for support [*behavior*].

Gwen: Yes, when I get home I want to talk, but I do not want to become a burden on someone I love. So I just withdraw into myself [*consequence*].

Assessment is a large part of behavioral therapy, and reviewing homework assignments helps us to see if our approach is effective. Although Gwen was aware of her pattern of silence at home, she was not able to modify her behavior and express her feelings to her husband.

I decide to introduce Gwen to the concept of mindfulness to help her stop the automatic behaviors that have kept her feeling stressed and overwhelmed. Gwen has difficulty being in the present moment, and she could profit from slowing down and engaging in self-care activities. Mindfulness practice can bring increased peace and calm into her life and quiet the constant chatter in her mind. I want to give Gwen some simple tools she can use and practice at home.

Therapist: Gwen, take a moment to sit quietly. Let your thoughts flow away and concentrate your attention on the present moment. How are you feeling? [*She begins to notice bodily sensations*] Gwen please bring your awareness to the top of your head and slowly begin to scan your entire body for any sensations of tension or tightness. What are you noticing?

Gwen: I am aware of tightness in my chest. It feels like a ball of stress.

Therapist: Focus all of your attention on the sensation in your chest. As you consciously tell yourself to relax, simply notice the sensations without judging them. How are you feeling?

Gwen: It's a little strange, but I feel more at ease than when I first walked in the door.

Therapist: Do you think you can practice this mindfulness at home this week and focus on what you want to bring into your life?

Gwen: I do want to communicate better with my husband and be able to ask him for support. I feel much more relaxed here now, and I would like to try to feel that at home too. Calming myself and staying in the moment is a new experience for me.

Therapist: You have a good start on learning how mindfulness feels; let's see how much progress you can make at home as you practice this week.

Gwen: OK, I feel less stressed when I slow down and try to relax in the moment. I am going to practice this every day during the week. [*Goal-setting is an important part of behavior therapy*]

I encourage Gwen to practice paying attention to her behaviors and to consider using mindfulness practice as a way of refocusing on what she wants to bring into her life. It is my hope that her mindfulness practice will lead to an overall reduction in stress and increased presence and connection in her life.

Questions for Reflection

- What could be the consequence(s) if Gwen does not change her behavior?
- What kind of homework might you suggest to Gwen?
- What kind of mindfulness practices would you like to incorporate into your daily life?

Summary and Evaluation

Summary

LO13

Behavior therapy is diverse with respect not only to basic concepts but also to techniques that can be applied in coping with specific problems with a wide range of clients. The behavioral movement includes four major areas of development: classical conditioning, operant conditioning, social-cognitive theory, and increasing attention to the cognitive factors influencing behavior (see Chapter 10). Third-generation behavior therapies are recent developments in the field, and they include mindfulness and acceptance-based behavior therapies. A unique characteristic of all forms of behavior therapy is its strict reliance on the principles of the scientific method. Concepts and procedures are stated explicitly, tested empirically, and revised continually. Treatment and assessment are interrelated and occur simultaneously. Research is considered to be a basic aspect of the approach, and therapeutic techniques are continually refined.

A cornerstone of behavior therapy is identifying specific goals at the outset of the therapeutic process. In helping clients achieve their goals, behavior therapists typically assume an active and directive role. Although the client generally determines *what* behavior will be changed, the therapist typically determines *how* this behavior can best be modified. In designing a treatment plan, behavior therapists employ techniques and procedures from a wide variety of therapeutic systems and apply them to the unique needs of each client.

Contemporary behavior therapy places emphasis on the interplay between the individual and the environment. Behavioral strategies can be used to attain both individual goals and societal goals. Because cognitive factors have a place in the practice of behavior therapy, techniques from this approach can be used to attain humanistic ends. It is clear that bridges can connect humanistic and behavioral therapies, especially with the current focus of attention on self-management and the incorporation of mindfulness and acceptance-based approaches into behavioral practice. Mindfulness practices rely on experiential learning and client discovery rather than on didactic instruction. Mindfulness is a way of being that takes ongoing effort to develop and refine (Kabat-Zinn, 2003). Self-compassion is a foundational part of the new wave of behavior therapies and is linked to an increased sense of well-being. These newer approaches represent a blend of Eastern practices and Western methodology. Contemporary behavior therapy has broadened from a narrow focus on dealing with simple problems to addressing complex aspects of personal functioning.

Contributions of Behavior Therapy

Behavior therapy challenges us to reconsider our global approach to counseling. Some may assume they know what a client means by the statement, "I feel unloved; life has no meaning." A humanist might nod in acceptance to such a statement, but the behaviorist may respond with: "Who specifically do you feel is not loving you?" "What is going on in your life to make you think it has no meaning?" "What are some specific things you might be doing that contribute to the state you are in?" "What would you most like to change?" A key strength of behavior therapy is its precision in specifying goals, target behaviors, and procedures. The specificity of the behavioral approaches helps clients translate unclear goals into concrete plans of action, and it helps both the counselor and the client to keep these plans clearly in focus. Ledley, Marx, and Heimberg (2010) state that therapists can help clients learn about the contingencies that maintain their problematic thoughts and behaviors and then teach them ways to make the changes they want. Techniques such as role playing, relaxation procedures, behavioral rehearsal, coaching, guided practice, modeling, feedback, learning by successive approximations, mindfulness skills, and homework assignments can be included in any therapist's repertoire, regardless of theoretical orientation.

An advantage behavior therapists have is the wide variety of specific behavioral techniques at their disposal. Because behavior therapy stresses *doing*, as opposed to merely talking about problems and gathering insights, practitioners use many behavioral strategies to assist clients in formulating a plan of action for changing behavior. The basic therapeutic conditions stressed by person-centered therapists—active listening, accurate empathy, positive regard, genuineness, respect, acceptance, and immediacy—need to be integrated in a behavioral framework.

A major contribution of behavior therapy is its emphasis on research into and assessment of treatment outcomes. It is up to practitioners to demonstrate that therapy is working. If progress is not being made, therapists look carefully at the original analysis and treatment plan. Of all the therapies presented in this book, this approach and its techniques have been subjected to the most empirical research. Behavioral practitioners are put to the test of identifying specific interventions that have been demonstrated to be effective.

Evidence-based therapies (EBT) are a hallmark of both behavior therapy and cognitive behavior therapy. To their credit, behavior therapists are willing to examine the effectiveness of their procedures in terms of the generalizability, meaningfulness, and durability of change. Most studies show that behavior therapy methods are more effective than no treatment. Moreover, a number of behavioral and cognitive behavioral procedures are currently the best treatment strategies available for depression, obsessive-compulsive disorder, panic disorder, social phobia, hypochondriasis, generalized anxiety disorder, posttraumatic stress disorder, eating disorders, borderline personality disorder, bipolar disorder, and childhood disorders (Hollon & DiGiuseppe, 2011).

The new generation of mindfulness and acceptance-based therapies has shifted behavior therapy from treating simple and discrete problems to a more complex and complete psychotherapy that is based in behavioral principles (Prochaska & Norcross, 2014). Prochaska and Norcross confidently predict an increase and expansion of the third-wave therapies in the next decade and state that these approaches will likely "become firmly established within the ever-expanding, evidence-based context of cognitive-behavioral therapy" (p. 314).

A strength of the behavioral approaches is the emphasis on ethical accountability. Behavior therapy is ethically neutral in that it does not dictate whose behavior or what behavior should be changed. At least in cases of voluntary counseling, the behavioral practitioner only specifies *how* to change those behaviors the client targets for change. Clients have a good deal of control and freedom in deciding *what* the goals of therapy will be. A collaborative therapist–client relationship is an essential aspect of behavior therapy. Because clients are active in selecting goals and procedures in the therapy process and are applying what they are learning in therapy to daily life, the chance that they will become the target of unethical behavior is decreased (Speigler, 2016).

Limitations and Criticisms of Behavior Therapy

Behavior therapy has been criticized for a variety of reasons. Let's examine four common criticisms and misconceptions people often have about behavior therapy, together with my reactions.

Behavior therapy may change behaviors, but it does not change feelings. Some critics argue that feelings must change before behavior can change. Behavioral practitioners hold that empirical evidence has not shown that feelings must be changed first, and behavioral clinicians do in actual practice deal with feelings as an overall part of the treatment process. A general criticism of both the behavioral and the cognitive approaches is that clients are not encouraged to experience their emotions. In concentrating on how clients are behaving or thinking, some behavior therapists tend to play down the working through of emotional issues. Generally, I favor initially focusing on what clients are feeling and then working with the behavioral and cognitive dimensions. When clients' feelings are engaged, this seems to me to be a good point of departure. I can still tie a discussion of what clients are feeling with how this is affecting their behavior, and I can later inquire about their cognitions.

Behavior therapy does not provide insight. If this assertion is indeed true, behavior therapists would probably respond that insight is not a necessary requisite for behavior change. Follette and Callaghan (2011) state that contemporary behavior therapists tend to be leery of the role of insight in favor of alterable, controllable, causal variables. It is possible for therapy to proceed without a client knowing how change is taking place. Although change may be taking place, clients often cannot explain precisely why. Furthermore, insights may result after clients make a change in behavior. Behavioral shifts often lead to a change in understanding or to insight, which may lead to emotional changes as well.

Behavior therapy treats symptoms rather than causes. The psychoanalytic assumption is that early traumatic events are at the root of present dysfunction. Behavior therapists may acknowledge that deviant responses have historical origins, but they contend that history is less important in the maintenance of current problems than environmental events such as antecedents and consequences. However, behavior therapists emphasize changing current environmental circumstances to change behavior.

Related to this criticism is the notion that unless historical causes of present behavior are therapeutically explored new symptoms will soon take the place of those that were "cured." Behaviorists rebut this assertion on both theoretical and empirical grounds. They contend that behavior therapy directly changes the maintaining conditions of problem behaviors (symptoms), thereby indirectly changing the problem behaviors. Furthermore, they assert that there is no empirical evidence that symptom substitution occurs after behavior therapy has successfully eliminated unwanted behavior because they have changed the conditions that give rise to those behaviors (Spiegler, 2016).

Behavior therapy involves control and social influence by the therapist. All therapists have a power relationship with the client and thus therapy involves social influence; the ethical issue relates to the therapist's degree of awareness of this influence and how it is addressed in therapy. Behavior therapy recognizes the importance of making the social influence process explicit, and it emphasizes client-oriented behavioral goals. Therapy progress is continually assessed and treatment is modified to ensure that the client's goals are being met.

Behavior therapists address ethical issues by stating that therapy is basically a psychoeducational process. At the outset of behavior therapy, clients learn about the nature of counseling, the procedures that may be employed, and the benefits and risks. Clients are given information about the specific therapy procedures appropriate for their particular problems. To some extent, they also participate in the choice of techniques that will be used in dealing with their problems. With this information clients become informed, genuine partners in the therapeutic venture.

The literature in the field of behavior therapy is so extensive and diverse that it is not possible in one brief survey chapter to present a comprehensive, in-depth discussion of behavioral concepts and techniques. Examining some of the suggested readings at the end of this chapter will further your knowledge of this complex approach.

Self-Reflection and Discussion Questions

1. Behavior therapists use a brief, active, directive, collaborative, present-focused, didactic, psychoeducational model of therapy that relies on empirical validation of its concepts and techniques. What do you see as the main strengths and limitations of this focus?

2. What are some unique characteristics common to all of the behavioral therapies? How do you see these therapies as being able to apply to a setting in which you might work?
3. The third-generation behavioral approaches involve mindfulness and acceptance-based concepts. What aspects of these concepts would you most want to incorporate in your work with clients?
4. How can you apply mindfulness techniques in your daily life? What value do you place on becoming more mindful?
5. What are some of the behavioral interventions that you can see yourself applying to your personal life? What specific behavioral techniques do you most want to incorporate into your counseling practice?

Where to Go From Here

Visit CengageBrain,com or watch the DVD program *Integrative Counseling: The Case of Ruth and Lecturettes*, Session 8 ("Behavioral Focus in Counseling"), in which I demonstrate a behavioral way to assist Ruth in developing an exercise program. It is crucial that Ruth makes her own decisions about specific behavioral goals she wants to pursue. This applies to my attempts to work with her in developing methods of relaxation, increasing her self-efficacy, and designing an exercise plan.

Other Resources

DVDs offered by the American Psychological Association that are relevant to this chapter include the following:

Antony, M. M. (2009). *Behavioral Therapy Over Time* (APA Psychotherapy Video Series)

Hayes, S. C. (2011). *Acceptance and Commitment Therapy* (Systems of Psychotherapy Video Series)

Psychotherapy.net is a comprehensive resource for students and professionals that offers videos and interviews on behavior therapy. New video and editorial content is made available monthly. DVDs relevant to this chapter are available at www.psychotherapy.net and include the following:

Stuart, R. (1998). *Behavioral Couples Therapy* (Couples Therapy With the Experts Series)

If you have an interest in further training in behavior therapy, the Association for Behavioral and Cognitive Therapies (ABCT) is an excellent resource. ABCT (formerly AABT) is a membership organization of more than 4,500 mental health professionals and students who are interested in behavior therapy, cognitive behavior therapy, behavioral assessment, and applied behavioral analysis. Members receive discounts on all ABCT publications, some of which are:

- *Directory of Graduate Training in Behavior Therapy and Experimental-Clinical Psychology* is an excellent source for students and job seekers who want information on programs with an emphasis on behavioral training.

- *Directory of Psychology Internships: Programs Offering Behavioral Training* describes training programs having a behavioral component.
- *Behavior Therapy* is an international quarterly journal focusing on original experimental and clinical research, theory, and practice.
- *Cognitive and Behavioral Practice* is a quarterly journal that features clinically oriented articles.

Full and associate memberships are $199 and include one journal subscription (to either *Behavior Therapy* or *Cognitive and Behavioral Practice*) and a subscription to the *Behavior Therapist* (a newsletter with feature articles, training updates, and association news). Membership also includes reduced registration and continuing education course fees for ABCT's annual convention held in November, which features workshops, master clinician programs, symposia, and other educational presentations. Student memberships are $49.

Association for Behavioral and Cognitive Therapies
www.abct.org

Mindfulness and Acceptance-Based Approaches

If you are interested in finding out more about mindfulness and acceptance-based programs and resources for the newer therapies, explore some of these websites:

Institute for Meditation and Psychotherapy
www.meditationandpsychotherapy.org

Mindfulness-Based Stress Reduction
www.umassmed.edu/cfm

Dialectical Behavior Therapy
www.behavioraltech.com

Acceptance and Commitment Therapy
www.acceptanceandcommitmenttherapy.com

Self-Compassion Resources
www.self-compassion.org

Recommended Supplementary Readings

Behavior Therapy (Antony & Roemer, 2011a) offers a useful and updated overview of behavior therapy.

Contemporary Behavior Therapy (Spiegler, 2016) is a comprehensive discussion of basic principles and applications of the behavior therapies. It is an excellent text that is based on research.

Interviewing and Change Strategies for Helpers (Cormier, Nurius, & Osborn, 2013) is a comprehensive and clearly written textbook dealing with training experiences and skill development. This book offers practitioners a wealth of material on a variety of topics, such as assessment procedures, selection of goals, development of appropriate treatment programs, and methods of evaluating outcomes.

Mindfulness and Psychotherapy (Germer, Siegel, & Fulton, 2013) is a practical introduction to mindfulness and its clinical applications. This edited work addresses the basics of mindfulness meditation, the centrality of the therapeutic relationship, and ways that cultivating mindfulness can enhance acceptance and empathy.

Wisdom and Compassion in Psychotherapy: Deepening Mindfulness in Clinical Practice (Germer & Siegel, 2012) is an edited book that expands on the message that we need to treat ourselves as we would want other to treat us. There are some excellent contributed chapters that discuss the meaning of wisdom and demonstrate the clinical applications inherent in blending Western psychotherapy and Buddhist psychology.

Sitting Together: Essential Skills for Mindfulness-Based Psychotherapy (Pollak, Pedulla, & Siegel, 2014) is a very useful resource for introducing mindfulness into the practice of psychotherapy. This clearly written book features practical meditation exercises that can enhance the therapy process and demonstrates the power of mindful presence for therapists and their clients.

Mindfulness-Based Cognitive Therapy for Depression (Segal, W lliams, & Teasdale, 2013) is an excellent resource for those who are interested in learning about the fundamentals and clinical applications of mindfulness-based cognitive therapy, especially in working with depression.

Acceptance and Mindfulness in Cognitive Behavior Therapy: Understanding and Applying the New Therapies (Herbert & Forman, 2011) is one of the best resources for discussion of new developments in behavior therapy and future trends.

The Mindfulness Solution: Everyday Practices for Everyday Problems (Siegel, 2010) is an outstanding practical guide in applying mindfulness practices to living a meaningful life, as well as a guide for practitioners who wish to teach clients how to use mindfulness in meeting life's challenges. This is a well-written book that highlights applications to personal and professional areas.

Cognitive Behavior Therapy

10

LEARNING OBJECTIVES

1. Identify common attributes shared by all cognitive behavior approaches.
2. Describe how the A-B-C model is a way of understanding the interaction among feelings, thoughts, and behavior.
3. Understand how cognitive methods can be applied to change thinking and behavior.
4. Understand the unique contributions of Aaron Beck to the development of cognitive therapy.
5. Identify the basic principles of cognitive therapy.
6. Describe the basic principles of strengths-based CBT.
7. Understand Meichenbaum's three-phase process of behavior change.
8. Describe the key concepts and phases of Meichenbaum's stress inoculation training.
9. Identify the strengths and limitations of cognitive behavior therapy from a multicultural perspective.
10. Differentiate REBT from CT with respect to how faulty beliefs are explored in therapy.
11. Know some of the main differences in how Ellis, Beck, Padesky, and Meichenbaum apply CBT in practice.

Introduction

LO1 As you saw in Chapter 9, traditional behavior therapy has broadened and largely moved in the direction of cognitive behavior therapy. Several of the more prominent cognitive behavioral approaches are featured in this chapter, including Albert Ellis's rational emotive behavior therapy (REBT), Aaron T. Beck and Judith Beck's cognitive therapy (CT), Christine Padesky's strengths-based CBT (SB-CBT), and Donald Meichenbaum's cognitive behavior therapy. These approaches all fall under the general umbrella of cognitive behavior therapies (CBT).

All of the cognitive behavioral approaches share the same basic characteristics and assumptions as traditional behavior therapy (see Chapter 9). Although the approaches are quite diverse, they do share these attributes: (1) a collaborative relationship between client and therapist, (2) the premise that psychological distress is often maintained by cognitive processes, (3) a focus on changing cognitions to produce desired changes in affect and behavior, (4) a present-centered, time-limited focus, (5) an active and directive stance by the therapist, and (6) an educational treatment focusing on specific and structured target problems (A. Beck & Weishaar, 2014). In addition, both cognitive therapy and the cognitive behavioral therapies are based on a structured psychoeducational model, make use of homework, place responsibility on the client to assume an active role both during and outside therapy sessions, emphasize developing a strong therapeutic alliance, and draw from a variety of cognitive and behavioral strategies to bring about change. Therapists help clients examine how they understand themselves and their world and suggest ways clients can experiment with new ways of behaving (Dienes, Torres-Harding, Reinecke, Freeman, & Sauer, 2011).

To a large degree, both cognitive therapy and cognitive behavior therapy are based on the assumption that beliefs, behaviors, emotions, and physical reactions are all reciprocally linked. Changes in one area lead to changes in the other areas. A change in beliefs is not the only target of therapy, but enduring changes usually require a change in beliefs. CBT therapists apply behavioral techniques such as operant conditioning, modeling, and behavioral rehearsal to the more subjective processes of thinking and internal dialogue. In addition, therapists help clients actively test their beliefs in therapy, on paper, and through behavioral experiments. Cognitive therapy and the cognitive behavioral approaches include a variety of behavioral strategies (discussed in Chapter 9) as well as cognitive strategies as a part of their integrative repertoire.

Visit CengageBrain.com or watch the DVD video program on Chapter 10, *Theory and Practice of Counseling and Psychotherapy: The Case of Stan and Lecturettes*. I suggest that you view the brief lecture for each chapter prior to reading the chapter.

Albert Ellis's Rational Emotive Behavior Therapy

Introduction

Rational emotive behavior therapy (REBT) was the first of the cognitive behavior therapies, and today it continues to be a major cognitive behavioral approach. REBT has a great deal in common with the therapies that are oriented toward

Albert Ellis

ALBERT ELLIS (1913–2007) was born in Pittsburgh but escaped to the wilds of New York at the age of 4 and lived there (except for a year in New Jersey) for the rest of his life. He was hospitalized nine times as a child, mainly with nephritis, and developed renal glycosuria at the age of 19 and diabetes at the age of 40. Despite his many physical challenges, he lived an unusually robust, active, and energetic life until his death at age 93. As he put it, "I am busy spreading the gospel according to St. Albert."

Realizing that he could counsel people skillfully and that he greatly enjoyed doing so, Ellis decided to become a psychologist. Believing psychoanalysis to be the deepest form of psychotherapy, Ellis was analyzed and supervised by a training analyst. He then practiced psychoanalytically oriented psychotherapy, but eventually he became disillusioned with the slow progress of his clients. He observed that they improved more quickly once they changed their ways of thinking about themselves and their problems. Early in 1955 he developed an approach to psychotherapy he called rational therapy and later rational emotive therapy, and which is now known as rational emotive behavior therapy (REBT). Ellis has rightly been referred to as the grandfather of cognitive behavior therapy.

To some extent Ellis developed his approach as a method of dealing with his own problems during his youth. At one point in his life, for example, he had exaggerated fears of speaking in public. During his adolescence he was extremely shy around young women. At age 19 he forced himself to talk to 100 different women in the Bronx Botanical Gardens over a period of one month. Although he never managed to get a date from these brief encounters, he does report that he desensitized himself to his fear of rejection by women. By applying rational and behavioral methods, he managed to conquer some of his strongest emotional blocks (A. Ellis, 1994, 1997).

People who heard Ellis lecture often commented on his abrasive, humorous, and flamboyant style. In his workshops it seemed that he took delight in giving vent to his eccentric side, such as peppering his speech with four-letter words. He greatly enjoyed his work and teaching REBT, which was his passion and primary commitment in life. He gave workshops wherever he went in his travels and had proclaimed, "I wouldn't go to the Taj Mahal unless they asked me to do a workshop there!"

Ellis married Australian psychologist Debbie Joffe in November 2004, whom he has called "the greatest love of my life" (A. Ellis, 2008). They shared the same life goals and ideals, and they worked as a team presenting workshops. If you are interested in learning more about the life and work of Albert Ellis, I recommend two of his books: *Rational Emotive Behavior Therapy: It Works for Me—It Can Work for You* (A. Ellis, 2004a) and *All Out! An Autobiography* (A. Ellis, 2010).

cognition and behavior as it also emphasizes thinking, assessing, deciding, analyzing, and doing. A basic assumption of REBT is that people contribute to their own psychological problems, as well as to specific symptoms, by the rigid and extreme beliefs they hold about events and situations. REBT is based on the assumption that cognitions, emotions, and behaviors interact significantly and have a reciprocal cause-and-effect relationship. REBT has consistently emphasized all three of these modalities and their interactions, thus qualifying it as a holistic and integrative approach (A. Ellis & Ellis, 2011, 2014; D. Ellis, 2014).

Although REBT is generally conceded to be the parent of today's cognitive behavioral approaches, it was preceded by earlier schools of thought. Ellis gave credit to Alfred Adler as an influential precursor of REBT, and Karen Horney's (1950) ideas on the "tyranny of the shoulds" are apparent in the conceptual framework of REBT. Ellis also acknowledged his debt to some of the Eastern philosophies and the ancient Greeks, especially the Stoic philosopher Epictetus, who said around 2,000 years ago:

"People are disturbed not by events, but by the views which they take of them" (as cited in A. Ellis, 2001a, p. 16). Ellis's reformulation of Epictetus's dictum can be stated as, "People disturb themselves as a result of the rigid and extreme beliefs they hold about events more than the events themselves."

REBT's basic hypothesis is that our emotions are mainly created from our beliefs, which influence the evaluations and interpretations we make and fuel the reactions we have to life situations. Through the therapeutic process, clients are taught skills that give them the tools to identify and dispute irrational beliefs that have been acquired and self-constructed and are now maintained by self-indoctrination. They learn how to replace such detrimental ways of thinking with effective and rational cognitions, and as a result they change their emotional experience and their reactions to situations. The therapeutic process allows clients to apply REBT principles for change not only to a particular presenting problem but also to many other problems in life or future problems they might encounter.

A large part of the therapy is seen as an *educational process*. The therapist functions in many ways like teacher, collaborating with the client on homework assignments and introducing strategies for constructive thinking. The client is the learner who then practices these new skills in everyday life.

Key Concepts

View of Emotional Disturbance

REBT is based on the premise that we learn irrational beliefs from significant others during childhood and then re-create these irrational beliefs throughout our lifetime. We actively reinforce our self-defeating beliefs through the processes of autosuggestion and self-repetition, and we then behave in ways that are consistent with these beliefs. Hence, it is largely our own repetition of early-indoctrinated irrational beliefs, rather than a parent's repetition, that keeps dysfunctional attitudes alive and operative within us.

Ellis asserted that blame can be at the core of many emotional disturbances. If we want to become psychologically healthy, we had better stop blaming ourselves and others and learn to fully and unconditionally accept ourselves despite our imperfections. Ellis (A. Ellis & Blau, 1998; A. Ellis & Harper, 1997; A. Ellis & Ellis, 2011) hypothesizes that we have strong tendencies to transform our desires and preferences into dogmatic "shoulds," "musts," "oughts," demands, and commands. When we are feeling disturbed, it is a good idea to look to our hidden dogmatic "musts" and absolutist "shoulds." Such demands create disruptive feelings and dysfunctional behaviors (A. Ellis, 2001a, 2004a).

Here are *three basics musts* (or irrational beliefs) we internalize that inevitably lead to self-defeat (A. Ellis & Ellis, 2011):

1. "I must do well and be loved and approved by others."
2. "Other people must treat me fairly, kindly, and well."
3. "The world and my living conditions must be comfortable, gratifying, and just, providing me with all that I want in life."

We have a strong tendency to make and keep ourselves emotionally disturbed by internalizing and perpetuating self-defeating beliefs such as these, which is one reason it is a real challenge to achieve and maintain good psychological health (A. Ellis, 2001a, 2001b).

A-B-C Framework

LO2

The A-B-C framework is central to REBT theory and practice. This model provides a useful tool for understanding the client's feelings, thoughts, events, and behavior (A. Ellis & Ellis, 2011). ***A*** is the existence of an activating event or adversity, or an inference about an event by an individual. ***C*** is the emotional and behavioral consequence or reaction of the individual; the reaction can be either healthy or unhealthy. A (the activating event) does not cause C (the emotional consequence). Instead, ***B***, which is the person's belief about A, largely creates C, the emotional reaction.

If a person experiences depression after a divorce, for example, it may not be the divorce itself that causes the depressive reaction, nor his inference that he has failed, but the person's *beliefs* about his divorce or about his failure (D. Ellis, 2014). Ellis maintains that the beliefs about the rejection and failure (at point B) are what mainly cause the depression (at point C)—not the actual event of the divorce or the person's inference of failure (at point A). Believing that human beings are largely responsible for creating their own emotional reactions and disturbances, and showing people how they can change their irrational beliefs that directly "cause" their disturbed emotional consequences, is at the heart of REBT (A. Ellis & Ellis, 2011; A. Ellis & Harper, 1997).

After A, B, and C comes ***D*** (disputing). Essentially, D encompasses methods that help clients challenge their irrational beliefs. There are three components of this disputing process: detecting, debating, and discriminating. Clients learn to *discriminate* irrational (self-defeating) beliefs from rational (self-helping) beliefs (A. Ellis & Ellis, 2011). Once they can *detect* irrational beliefs, particularly absolutistic "shoulds" and "musts," "awfulizing," and "self-downing," clients *debate* dysfunctional beliefs by logically, empirically, and pragmatically questioning them. Clients are asked to vigorously argue themselves out of believing and acting on irrational beliefs. Although REBT uses many other cognitive, emotive, and behavioral methods to help clients minimize their irrational beliefs, it emphasizes the process of vigorously disputing (D) such beliefs both during therapy sessions and in everyday life. Following that, clients are encouraged to develop ***E***, a new effective philosophy, which also has a practical side. A new and effective belief system consists of replacing unhealthy irrational thoughts with healthy rational ones. "Homework" can enhance and maintain these therapeutic gains and personal insights.

The Therapeutic Process

Therapeutic Goals

The many roads taken in rational emotive behavior therapy lead toward the destination of clients minimizing their emotional disturbances and self-defeating behaviors by acquiring a more realistic, workable, and compassionate philosophy of life.

The therapeutic process of REBT involves a collaborative effort between therapist and client to choose realistic and life-enhancing therapeutic goals. The therapist's task is to help clients differentiate between realistic and unrealistic goals and also between self-defeating and life-enhancing goals. A basic aim is to teach clients how to change their dysfunctional emotions and behaviors into healthy ones. According to Ellis and Ellis (2011) another goal of REBT is to assist clients in the process of achieving *unconditional self-acceptance* (USA), *unconditional other-acceptance* (UOA), and *unconditional life-acceptance* (ULA). As clients become more able to accept themselves, they are more likely to unconditionally accept others and to accept life as it is. A famous saying of Ellis (A. Ellis & Ellis, 2011) is: "Life has inevitable suffering as well as pleasure. By realistically thinking, feeling, and acting to enjoy what you can, and unangrily and unwhiningly accepting painful aspects that cannot be changed, you open yourself to much joy" (p. 48).

Therapist's Function and Role

The therapist has specific tasks, and the first step is to show clients how they have incorporated many irrational absolute "shoulds," "oughts," and "musts" into their thinking. The therapist disputes clients' irrational beliefs and encourages clients to engage in activities that will counter their self-defeating beliefs by replacing their rigid "musts" with preferences.

A second step in the therapeutic process is to demonstrate how clients are keeping their emotional disturbances active by continuing to think illogically and unrealistically. In other words, when clients keep reindoctrinating themselves, they create their own psychological problems. Ellis reminds us that we are responsible for our own emotional destiny (A. Ellis, 2004b, 2010).

To get beyond mere recognition of irrational thoughts, the therapist takes a third step—helping clients change their thinking and minimize their irrational ideas. Although it may be unlikely that we can entirely eliminate the tendency to think irrationally, we can make ongoing efforts to reduce the frequency of such thinking. The therapist encourages clients to identify the irrational beliefs they have unquestioningly accepted, demonstrates how they are continuing to indoctrinate themselves with these beliefs, and reminds them that change is possible with persistent effort.

The fourth step in the therapeutic process is to strongly encourage clients to develop a rational philosophy of life so that in the future they can avoid hurting themselves again by believing other irrational beliefs. Tackling only specific problems or symptoms can give no assurance that new disabling fears will not emerge. It is desirable, then, for the therapist to dispute the core irrational thinking and to teach clients how to substitute rational beliefs and healthy behaviors for irrational beliefs and self-defeating behaviors.

Client's Experience in Therapy

The therapeutic process largely focuses on clients' experiences in the present. Like the person-centered and existential approaches to therapy, REBT emphasizes here-and-now experiences and clients' present ability to change the patterns of thinking and emoting that they constructed earlier. The therapist may not devote much time to exploring clients' early history and making connections between their past and present behavior unless doing so will aid the therapeutic process. REBT differs from many other therapeutic approaches in that it does not place much value on free association, working with dreams, or dealing with transference phenomena. Ellis and Ellis (2014) maintain that transference is not encouraged, and when it does occur, the therapist is likely to confront it because it is generally based on the client's dire need to be liked and approved of by the therapist. Any unhealthy neediness clients display can be counterproductive and foster dependence on approval from the therapist.

Clients are encouraged to actively work outside therapy sessions. By carrying out behavioral homework assignments, clients become increasingly proficient at minimizing irrational thinking and disturbances in feeling and behaving. **Homework** is carefully designed and agreed upon and is aimed at getting clients to carry out productive actions that contribute to emotional and attitudinal change. These assignments are checked in later sessions, and clients continue to focus on learning effective ways to dispute self-defeating thinking. Toward the end of therapy, clients review their progress, make plans, and identify strategies to prevent, or cope with, any new challenges as they arise.

Relationship Between Therapist and Client

Because REBT is a cognitive and directive behavioral process, a warm relationship between therapist and client is not required, but it may enhance the process for some. At the very least, a respectful relationship is recommended. As with the person-centered therapy of Rogers, REBT practitioners strive to unconditionally accept all clients and to teach them to unconditionally accept others and themselves. The therapist takes the mystery out of the therapeutic process, teaching clients about the cognitive hypothesis of disturbance and helping clients understand how they are continuing to sabotage themselves and what they can do to change. Insight alone does not typically lead to psychotherapeutic change, action is also required. The therapist frequently acknowledges any progress clients have made due to their own efforts. REBT practitioners accept their clients (and themselves!) as imperfect beings who can be helped through a variety of techniques including teaching, bibliotherapy, and behavior modification (A. Ellis & Ellis, 2011, 2014; D. Ellis, 2014).

Application: Therapeutic Techniques and Procedures

The Practice of Rational Emotive Behavior Therapy

Rational emotive behavior therapists are multimodal and integrative. REBT practitioners use a number of different modalities (cognitive, emotive, behavioral, and interpersonal) to dispel self-defeating cognitions and to teach people how to acquire a rational approach to living. Therapists are encouraged to be flexible and creative in their use of methods, making sure to tailor the techniques to the unique needs of each client (A. Ellis & Ellis, 2011; D. Ellis, 2014).

For a concrete illustration of how Dr. Ellis works with the client Ruth drawing from cognitive, emotive, and behavioral techniques, see *Case Approach to Counseling and Psychotherapy* (Corey, 2013, chap. 8). What follows is a brief summary of the major cognitive, emotive, and behavioral techniques Ellis describes (A. Ellis, 2004a; A. Ellis & Crawford, 2000; A. Ellis & Ellis, 2011).

Cognitive Methods REBT practitioners usually incorporate a persuasive LO3 cognitive methodology in the therapeutic process. They demonstrate to clients, often in a quick and direct manner, what it is that they are continuing to tell themselves. Then they teach clients how to challenge these self-statements so that they no longer believe them, encouraging them to acquire a philosophy based on facts. REBT relies heavily on thinking, disputing, debating, challenging, interpreting, explaining, and teaching. The most efficient way to bring about lasting emotional and behavioral change is for clients to change their way of thinking (A. Ellis & Ellis, 2011, 2014).

Here are some cognitive techniques available to the therapist.

- *Disputing irrational beliefs*. The most common cognitive method of REBT consists of the therapist actively disputing clients' irrational beliefs and teaching them how to do this challenging on their own. Clients dispute a particular "must," absolute "should," or "ought" until they no longer hold that irrational belief, or at least until it is diminished in strength. Here are some examples of questions or statements clients learn to tell themselves when they dispute their irrational ideas: "Why *must* people treat me fairly?" "How do I become a total flop if I don't succeed at important tasks I try?" "If I don't get the job I want, it may be disappointing, but I can certainly stand it." "If life doesn't always go the way I would like it to, it isn't *awful*, just inconvenient."
- *Doing cognitive homework*. REBT clients are expected to make lists of their problems, look for their absolutist beliefs, and dispute these beliefs. Clients are encouraged to record and think about how their beliefs contribute to their personal problems and are asked to work hard at uprooting these self-defeating cognitions. Homework assignments are a way of tracking down and attending to the "shoulds" and "musts" that are part of their internalized self-messages. In this way, clients gradually learn to lessen anxiety and to challenge basic irrational thinking. They often fill out the REBT Self-Help Form, which is reproduced in the *Student Manual for Theory and Practice of Counseling and Psychotherapy* (Corey, 2017). Their comments on this form can focus therapy sessions as they critically evaluate the disputation of their beliefs. Clients may be encouraged to put themselves in risk-taking situations that will allow them to challenge self-limiting beliefs. For example, a client with a talent for acting who is afraid to act in front of an audience because of fear of failure may be asked to take a small part in a stage play. Work in the therapy session can be designed so that out-of-session tasks are feasible and the client has the skills to complete these tasks. Making changes tends to be hard work. Doing work outside sessions is of real value in revising clients' thinking, feeling, and behaving.
- *Bibliotherapy*. REBT, and other CBT approaches, can utilize bibliotherapy as an adjunctive form of treatment. There are advantages of

bibliotherapy, such as cost-effectiveness, widespread availability, and the potential of reaching a broad spectrum of populations. Bibliotherapeutic approaches have empirical support for a range of clinical problems, including the treatment of depression and many anxiety disorders (Jacobs, 2008). Because therapy is seen as an educational process, clients are encouraged to read REBT self-help books such as *Rational Emotive Behavior Therapy: It Works for Me—It Can Work for You* (A. Ellis, 2004a) and other books by Ellis (1999, 2000, 2001a, 2001b, 2005, 2010; A. Ellis & Ellis, 2011).

- *Changing one's language.* REBT rests on the premise that imprecise language is one of the causes of distorted thinking processes. Clients learn that "musts," "oughts," and absolute "shoulds" can be replaced by *preferences.* Instead of saying "It would be absolutely awful if ..." they learn to say "It would be inconvenient if ..." Clients who use language patterns that reflect helplessness and self-condemnation can learn to employ new self-statements, which help them think and behave differently. As a consequence, they also begin to feel differently.
- *Psychoeducational methods.* REBT programs introduce clients to various educational materials such as books, DVDs, and articles. Therapists educate clients about the nature of their problems and how treatment is likely to proceed. They ask clients how particular concepts apply to them. Clients are more likely to cooperate with a treatment program if they understand how the therapy process works and if they understand why particular techniques are being used (Ledley, Marx, & Heimberg, 2010).

Emotive Techniques REBT practitioners use a variety of emotive procedures, including unconditional acceptance, rational emotive role playing, modeling, rational emotive imagery, and shame-attacking exercises. These emotive techniques tend to be vivid and evocative in nature, and their purpose is to dispute clients' irrational beliefs. These strategies are used both during the therapy sessions and as homework assignments in daily life. Their purpose is not simply to provide a cathartic experience but to help clients *change* some of their thoughts, emotions, and behaviors (A. Ellis, 2001b; A. Ellis & Ellis, 2011). Let's look at some of these evocative and emotive therapeutic techniques in more detail.

- *Rational emotive imagery.* This is a form of intense mental practice designed to establish new emotional patterns in place of disruptive ones by thinking in healthy ways (see A. Ellis, 2001a, 2001b). In **rational emotive imagery (REI)**, clients are asked to vividly imagine one of the worst things that might happen to them and to describe their disturbing feelings. Clients are shown how to train themselves to develop healthy emotions, and as their feelings about adversities change, they stand a better chance of changing their behavior in the situation. This technique can be usefully applied to interpersonal and other situations that are problematic for the individual. Clients who practice rational emotive imagery several times a week for a few weeks may reach the point where they no longer feel upset over these negative events (A. Ellis, 2001a; A. Ellis & Ellis, 2011; D. Ellis, 2014).

- *Humor*. Ellis contends that emotional disturbances often result from taking oneself too seriously. He wrote hundreds of "Rational Humorous Songs" (A. Ellis, 2005) and often led attendees at his workshops in singing them. One appealing aspect of REBT is that it fosters the development of a better sense of humor and helps put life into healthy perspective (A. Ellis 2004a, 2010). Humor has both cognitive and emotional benefits in bringing about change. Humor shows the absurdity of certain ideas that clients steadfastly maintain, and it teaches clients to laugh—not at themselves but at their self-defeating ways of thinking.
- *Role playing*. Role playing has emotive, cognitive, and behavioral components. The therapist may interrupt to show clients what they are telling themselves to create their disturbances and what they can do to change unhealthy feelings to healthy ones. Clients can rehearse certain roles to bring out what they feel in a situation. For example, Dawson may put off applying to a graduate school because he is afraid he won't be accepted. Just the thought of not being accepted to the school of his choice brings out intense feelings of shame for "being stupid." The focus is on working through underlying irrational beliefs related to his unpleasant feelings. Dawson role-plays an interview with the dean of graduate students, notes his anxiety and the specific beliefs leading to it, and challenges his conviction that he absolutely must be accepted and that not gaining such acceptance means that he is a stupid and incompetent person.
- *Shame-attacking exercises*. Ellis developed exercises to help people reduce shame and anxiety over behaving in certain ways. He asserts that we can stubbornly refuse to feel ashamed by telling ourselves that it is not catastrophic if someone thinks we are foolish. Practicing **shame-attacking exercises** can reduce, minimize, and prevent feelings of shame, guilt, anxiety, and depression (A. Ellis, 1999, 2000, 2001a, 2001b, 2005, 2010; A. Ellis & Ellis, 2011, 2014). The exercises are aimed at increasing self-acceptance and mature responsibility, as well as helping clients see that much of what they think of as being shameful has to do with the way they define reality for themselves. Clients may take the risk of doing something that they are ordinarily afraid to do because of what others might think. Through homework practice, clients eventually learn that they can choose not to let others' reactions or possible disapproval stop them from doing the things they would like to do. For example, clients may wear "loud" clothes designed to attract attention, sing loudly, ask a silly question at a lecture, or ask for a left-handed monkey wrench in a grocery store. By carrying out such assignments, clients are likely to find out that other people are not really that interested in their behavior. Note that these exercises do not involve illegal activities or acts that will be harmful to oneself, to others, or that will unduly alarm other people!

Behavioral Techniques REBT practitioners use most of the standard behavior therapy procedures, especially operant conditioning, self-management principles, systematic desensitization, relaxation techniques, and modeling. Behavioral homework assignments carried out in real-life situations are particularly important. These assignments are done systematically and are recorded and analyzed. Homework gives clients opportunities to practice new skills outside of the therapy session, which may be even more valuable for clients than work done during the therapy hour (Ledley et al., 2010). Doing homework may involve in-vivo desensitization (A. Ellis & Ellis, 2011) and live exposure in daily life situations. Clients actually do new and difficult things, and in this way they put their insights to use in the form of concrete action. Acting differently helps them incorporate functional beliefs.

Applications of REBT as a Brief Therapy

Ellis originally developed REBT to try to make psychotherapy more efficient than other systems of therapy. He maintained that the best and most effective therapy quickly teaches clients how to tackle present as well as future problems. REBT is well suited as a brief form of therapy, whether it is applied to individuals, groups, couples, or families. Clients learn self-therapy techniques that they can continue to apply through their own ongoing work and practice (A. Ellis & Ellis, 2011).

Application to Group Counseling

Cognitive behavior therapy (CBT) groups are among the most popular treatments in clinics and community agency settings. One of the most common CBT group approaches is based on REBT principles and techniques. REBT practitioners employ an active role in encouraging members to commit themselves to practicing what they are learning in the group sessions in everyday life. What goes on during the group is valuable, but therapists know that consistent work between group sessions and after a group ends is crucial. The group context provides members with tools they can use to become self-reliant and to accept themselves, and others, unconditionally as they encounter new problems in daily living.

In group therapy, members are taught how to apply REBT principles to one another. Ellis recommends that some clients experience group therapy as well as individual therapy. Group members (1) learn how their beliefs influence what they feel and what they do, (2) explore ways to change self-defeating thoughts in various concrete situations, and (3) learn to minimize symptoms through a profound change in their philosophy. Ellis and Ellis (2011, 2014) contend that group REBT is frequently the treatment of choice because it affords many opportunities to practice assertiveness skills, to take risks by practicing different behaviors, to challenge self-defeating thinking, to learn from the experiences of others, and to interact therapeutically and socially with each other in after-group sessions. All of the cognitive, emotive, and behavioral techniques described earlier are applicable to group counseling as are the techniques covered in Chapter 9 on behavior therapy. Behavioral homework and skills training are just two useful methods for a group format. For a more detailed discussion of REBT applied to group counseling, see Corey (2016, chap. 14).

Aaron T. Beck
Courtesy of Beck Institute for Cognitive Behavior Therapy, Bala Cynwyd, PA.

AARON TEMKIN BECK (b. 1921) was born in Providence, Rhode Island. His childhood, although happy, was interrupted by a life-threatening illness when he was 8 years old. As a consequence, he experienced blood injury fears, fear of suffocation, and anxiety about his health. Beck used his personal problems as a basis for understanding others and for developing his cognitive theory.

A graduate of Brown University and Yale School of Medicine, Beck initially was trained as a neurologist, but he switched to psychiatry during his residency. Beck attempted to validate Freud's theory of depression, but the results of his research did not support Freud's motivational model and the explanation of depression as "anger turned inward." Beck set out to develop a model for depression that fit with his empirical findings, and for many years Beck endured isolation from and rejection by most of his colleagues in the psychiatric community. Through his research, Beck developed a cognitive theory of depression, which represented a new and comprehensive conceptualization. He found the cognitions of depressed individuals were characterized by errors in interpretation that he called "cognitive distortions." For Beck, negative thoughts reflect underlying dysfunctional beliefs and assumptions. When these beliefs are triggered by situational events, a depressive pattern is put in motion. Beck believes clients can assume an active role in modifying their dysfunctional thinking and thereby gain relief from a range of psychiatric conditions. His continuous research in the areas of psychopathology and the utility of cognitive therapy eventually earned him a place of prominence in the scientific community in the United States. Beck is the founder of cognitive therapy (CT), one of the most influential and empirically validated approaches to psychotherapy. He has won nearly every national and international prize for his scientific contributions to psychotherapy and suicide research and was even short-listed for the Nobel Prize in medicine.

Beck joined the Department of Psychiatry of the University of Pennsylvania in 1954, where he currently holds the position of University Professor (Emeritus) of Psychiatry. Beck has successfully applied cognitive therapy to depression, generalized anxiety and panic disorders, suicide, alcoholism and drug abuse, eating disorders, marital and relationship problems, psychotic disorders, and personality disorders. He has developed assessment scales for depression, suicide risk, anxiety, self-concept, and personality.

He is the founder of the Beck Institute, which is a research and training center directed by one of his four children, Dr. Judith Beck. He has nine grandchildren and five great-grandchildren and has been married for more than 60 years. To his credit, Aaron Beck has focused on developing the cognitive therapy skills of tens of thousands of clinicians throughout the world. In turn, many of them have established their own cognitive therapy centers. Beck has a vision for the cognitive therapy community that is global, inclusive, collaborative, empowering, and benevolent. He continues to remain active in writing and research and has published 24 books and more than 600 articles and book chapters. For more on the life of Aaron T. Beck, see *Aaron T. Beck* (Weishaar, 1993) or "Aaron T. Beck: Mind, Man and Mentor" (Padesky, 2004).

Judith S. Beck
Courtesy of Beck Institute for Cognitive Behavior Therapy, Bala Cynwyd, PA.

JUDITH S. BECK (b. 1954) was born in Philadelphia, the second of four children. Both her parents were quite notable in their fields: her father, as "the father of cognitive therapy," and her mother, as the first female judge on the appellate court of the Commonwealth of Pennsylvania. From an early age, Beck wanted to be an educator, and she began her professional career teaching children with learning disabilities. Her ability to break down complex subjects into easily understandable ideas, so critical in the education of children with learning differences, is characteristic of all her work.

Beck later returned to graduate school, studied education and psychology, and completed a postdoctoral fellowship at the Center for Cognitive Behavior Therapy at the University of Pennsylvania. In 1994 she and her father opened the nonprofit Beck Institute for Cognitive Therapy in suburban Philadelphia, and she is currently president of the institute. A premier training organization, the institute is devoted to national and international training in cognitive therapy through workshop and supervision programs for students and faculty, deployed and returning military families, and health and mental health professionals at all levels.

Beck travels extensively in the United States and abroad, teaching and disseminating cognitive behavior therapy and assisting a wide variety of organizations in developing or strengthening their CT programs. She writes a number of CT-oriented blogs and edits "Cognitive Therapy Today," an e-newsletter. She is coauthor of the widely adopted self-report scales, the *Personality Belief Questionnaire* and the *Beck Youth Inventories II*, which screens children aged 7–18 for symptoms of depression, anxiety, disruptive behavior, self-concept, and anger.

Beck is Clinical Associate Professor at the University of Pennsylvania and was instrumental in founding the Academy of Cognitive Therapy, the "home" organization for cognitive therapists worldwide. She has written nearly a hundred articles and chapters on a variety of CT topics and authored several books on cognitive therapy, including *Cognitive Behavior Therapy: Basics and Beyond* (2011a), *Cognitive Therapy for Challenging Problems: What to Do When the Basics Don't Work* (2005), and the *Cognitive Therapy Worksheet Packet* (2011b), as well as trade books with a cognitive behavioral program for diet and maintenance. Judith Beck has been married for 34 years and has three adult children, one of whom is a social worker specializing in CT.

Aaron Beck's Cognitive Therapy

Introduction

Aaron T. Beck developed **cognitive therapy** (CT) about the same time that Ellis was developing REBT. They were not aware of each others' work and created their approaches independently. Ellis developed REBT based on philosophical tenets, whereas Beck's CT was based on empirical research (Padesky & Beck, 2003). Like REBT, CT emphasizes education and prevention but uses specific methods tailored to particular issues. The specificity of CT allows therapists to link assessment, conceptualization, and treatment strategies. LO4

Beck (A. Beck 1963, 1967) set out to create an evidence-based therapy for depression, and he tested each of his theoretical constructs with empirical studies and conducted controlled outcome studies to determine how CT's outcomes compared with existing psychotherapy and pharmacotherapy treatments for depression. Beck's careful empirical approach was eventually adopted by colleagues around the world. Evidence-supported CT approaches were developed for many disorders including depression, panic disorder, social anxiety, phobias, posttraumatic stress disorder, schizophrenia and other psychotic disorders, hypochondriasis, body dysmorphic disorder, eating disorders, insomnia, anger issues, stress, chronic pain and fatigue, and distress due to general medical problems such as cancer (Hofmann, Asnaani, Vonk, Sawyer, & Fang, 2012; White & Freeman, 2000).

Beck's original depression research revealed that depressed clients had a negative bias in their interpretation of certain life events, which resulted from active processes of cognitive distortion (A. Beck, 1967). This led Beck to believe that a therapy that helped depressed clients become aware of and change their negative thinking could be helpful. Unlike Ellis, Beck did not assert that negative thoughts were the sole cause of depression. Beck's research indicated that depression could result from negative thinking, but it could also be precipitated by genetic, neurobiological, or environmental changes. One of Beck's early contributions was to recognize that regardless of the cause of depression, once people became depressed, their thinking reflected what Beck referred to as the **negative cognitive triad**: negative views of the self (self-criticism),the world (pessimism), and the future (hopelessness). Beck believed this negative cognitive triad maintained depression, even when negative thoughts were not the original cause of an episode of depression (A. Beck 1967; A. Beck, Rush, Shaw, & Emery, 1979).

Cognitive therapy (CT) has a number of similarities to both rational emotive behavior therapy and behavior therapy. All of these therapies are active, directive, time-limited, present-centered, problem-oriented, collaborative, structured, and empirical. They include homework assignments and require clients to explicitly identify problems and the situations in which they occur (A. Beck & Weishaar, 2014). Similar to REBT and unlike behavior therapy, CT is based on the theoretical rationale that the way people feel and behave is influenced by how they perceive and place meaning on their experience. Three theoretical assumptions of CT are (1) that people's thought processes are accessible to introspection, (2) that people's beliefs have highly personal meanings, and (3) that people can discover these meanings themselves rather than being taught or having them interpreted by the therapist (Weishaar, 1993).

From the beginning Beck developed specific treatment protocols for each problem whereas Ellis might teach similar philosophical principles to people with anxiety, depression, or anger. Despite these differences, therapists who practice behavior therapy, REBT, and CT learn from each other, and considerable overlap exists in methods used by all three schools of therapy in contemporary clinical practice. The highest standard of practice today is to offer the best "evidence-based practice" regardless of its origins, so a therapist might use behavioral methods to treat phobias and cognitive methods to treat panic disorder because research has demonstrated these methods to be most effective in treating these problems. Many therapists refer to themselves as offering cognitive behavioral therapy regardless of whether their original training was primarily in behavior therapy, REBT, or CT.

A Generic Cognitive Model

Reflecting on 50 years of research and the various applications of cognitive therapy, Beck has proposed a **generic cognitive model** to describe principles that pertain to all CT applications from depression and anxiety treatments to therapies for a wide variety of other problems including psychosis and substance use (A. Beck & Haigh, 2014). By linking psychological difficulties with adaptive human responses, Beck believes the generic cognitive model "has the potential to be the only empirically supported general theory of psychopathology" (A. Beck & Haigh, 2014, p. 21). The generic cognitive model provides a comprehensive framework for understanding psychological distress, and some of its major principles are described here. Beck encouraged others to design research to investigate the components of his model in an effort to reach the best understanding possible of human cognition, behavior, and emotion. Let's look at some of the principles on which this model is based.

Psychological distress can be thought of as an exaggeration of normal adaptive human functioning. When people are functioning well, they experience many different emotions in response to life events and behave in ways that help them solve problems, achieve goals, and protect themselves from harm. It is normal to sometimes withdraw from relationships, avoid situations we don't feel prepared to handle, or worry about problems in the search of a solution. A psychological disorder begins when these normal emotions and behaviors become disproportionate to life events in degree or frequency. For example, when a person begins to worry most of the time, even about situations that most people take in stride, that person is showing signs of generalized anxiety disorder.

Faulty information processing is a prime cause of exaggerations in adaptive emotional and behavioral reactions. Our thinking is directly connected to our emotional reactions, behaviors, and motivations. When we think about things in erroneous or distorted ways, we experience exaggerated or distorted emotional and behavioral reactions as well. Beck identifies several common cognitive distortions:

- *Arbitrary inferences* are conclusions drawn without supporting evidence. This includes "catastrophizing," or thinking of the absolute worst scenario and outcomes for most situations. You might begin your first job as a counselor with the conviction that you will not be liked or valued. You are convinced that you fooled your professors and somehow just managed to get your degree, but now people will certainly see through you!
- *Selective abstraction* consists of forming conclusions based on an isolated detail of an event while ignoring other information. The significance of the total context is missed. As a counselor, you might measure your worth by your errors and weaknesses rather than by your successes.
- *Overgeneralization* is a process of holding extreme beliefs on the basis of a single incident and applying them inappropriately to dissimilar events or settings. If you have difficulty working with one adolescent, for example, you might conclude that you will not be effective counseling any adolescents. You might also conclude that you will not be effective working with *any* clients!
- *Magnification and minimization* consist of perceiving a case or situation in a greater or lesser light than it truly deserves. You might make this cognitive error by assuming that even minor mistakes in counseling a client could easily create a crisis for the individual and might result in psychological damage.
- *Personalization* is a tendency for individuals to relate external events to themselves, even when there is no basis for making this connection. If a client does not return for a second counseling session, you might be absolutely convinced that this absence is due to your terrible performance during the initial session. You might tell yourself, "This situation proves that I really let that client down, and now she may never seek help again."
- *Labeling and mislabeling* involve portraying one's identity on the basis of imperfections and mistakes made in the past and allowing them to define one's true identity. If you are not able to live up to all of a client's expectations, you might say to yourself, "I'm totally worthless and should turn my professional license in right away."

- *Dichotomous thinking* involves categorizing experiences in either-or extremes. With such polarized thinking, you might view yourself as either being the perfectly competent counselor (you always succeed with all clients) or as a total flop if you are not fully competent (there is no room for any mistakes).

Our beliefs play a major role in determining what type of psychological distress we will experience. Each emotional and behavioral disorder is accompanied by beliefs specific to that problem. Consider two students who apply to college and are not accepted to their first choice of school. One of the students becomes depressed, the other becomes anxious. Depression is accompanied by negative thoughts about oneself ("I've failed," "Nothing will work out for me," "I'll never get into medical school"). Anxious thoughts reflect overestimations of threat or danger ("Everyone will think less of me when they find out I wasn't admitted to that college") and underestimations of one's coping ("I won't know what to say to people about it") and underestimation of resources ("These other colleges won't prepare me well enough for medical school").

Central to cognitive therapy is the empirically supported observation that "changes in beliefs lead to changes in behaviors and emotions" (A. Beck & Haigh, 2014, p.14). If the students in the previous example can change the way they think about not being accepted to their first choice school, their depression and anxiety are likely to be lessened. The first student will undoubtedly feel less depressed once a more balanced view of the rejection letter is adopted ("More good students apply than can be admitted. My rejection does not mean I failed. I'm sure many students from my second choice school go on to attend medical school."). Similarly, the anxious student would benefit from new beliefs as well ("I can tell others that I am disappointed that I did not get into my first choice college. Some people might think less of me, but those who really care about me will understand that not everyone gets their first choice and they will be supportive.").

If beliefs are not modified, clinical conditions are likely to reoccur. Even without counseling or a change in beliefs, people often recover from feelings of depression or anxiety and return to their usual healthy functioning. However, these feelings may return in times of future stress or disappointment if their basic beliefs have not changed. In studies of the long-term effects of treatments for depression and anxiety disorders, cognitive therapy and other types of CBT therapies have the lowest rates of relapse (Hollon, Stewart, & Strunk, 2006). Many believe this is because these therapies lead to enduring changes in beliefs.

Basic Principles of Cognitive Therapy

Cognitive therapy (CT) perceives psychological problems as an exaggeration of adaptive responses resulting from commonplace cognitive distortions. Like REBT, CT is an insight-focused therapy with a strong psychoeducational component that emphasizes recognizing and changing unrealistic thoughts and maladaptive beliefs. Cognitive therapy is highly collaborative and involves designing specific learning experiences to help clients understand the links between their thoughts, behaviors, emotions, physical responses, and situations (Greenberger & Padesky, 2016). The goal of CT is to help clients learn practical skills that they can use to make changes in their thoughts, behaviors, and emotions and how to sustain these changes over time. **LO5**

In cognitive therapy, clients learn how to identify their dysfunctional thinking. Once clients identify cognitive distortions, they are taught to examine and weigh the evidence for and against them. This process of critically examining thoughts involves empirically testing them by looking for evidence, actively engaging in a Socratic dialogue with the therapist, carrying out homework assignments, doing behavioral experiments, gathering data on assumptions made, and forming alternative interpretations (Dattilio, 2000a; Freeman & Dattilio, 1994; Tompkins, 2004, 2006). From the start of treatment, clients learn to employ specific problem-solving and coping skills. Through a process of guided discovery, clients acquire insight about the connection between their thinking and the ways they act and feel.

Cognitive therapy is focused on present problems, regardless of a client's diagnosis. The past may be brought into therapy when the therapist considers it essential to understand how and when certain core dysfunctional beliefs originated and how these ideas have a current impact on the client's difficulties (Dattilio, 2002a). The goals of this brief therapy include providing symptom relief, assisting clients in resolving their most pressing problems, changing beliefs and behaviors that maintain problems, and teaching clients skills that serve as relapse prevention strategies.

Some Differences Between CT and REBT In both CT and REBT, reality testing is highly organized. Clients come to realize on an experiential level that they have misconstrued situations. Yet there are some important differences between these two approaches, especially with respect to therapeutic methods and style.

REBT is often highly directive, persuasive, and confrontational, and the teaching role of the therapist is emphasized. The therapist models rational thinking and helps clients to identify and dispute irrational beliefs. In contrast, CT uses Socratic dialogue, posing open-ended questions to clients with the aim of getting clients to reflect on personal issues and arrive at their own conclusions. CT places more emphasis on helping clients identify misconceptions for themselves rather than being taught. Through this reflective questioning process, the cognitive therapist collaborates with clients in testing the validity of their cognitions (a process called **collaborative empiricism**). Therapeutic change is the result of clients reevaluating faulty beliefs based on contradictory evidence that they have gathered.

There are also differences in how Ellis and Beck view faulty thinking. Through a process of rational disputation, Ellis works to persuade clients that certain of their beliefs are irrational and nonfunctional. Beck views his clients' distorted beliefs as being the result of cognitive errors rather than being driven solely by irrational beliefs. Beck asks his clients to conduct behavioral experiments to test the accuracy of their beliefs (Hollon & DiGiuseppe, 2011). Cognitive therapists view dysfunctional beliefs as being problematic when they are a distortion of the whole picture, or when they are too absolute, broad, and extreme (A. Beck & Weishaar, 2014). For Beck, people live by *rules* (underlying assumptions); they get into trouble when they label, interpret, and evaluate by a set of rules that are unrealistic or when they use the rules inappropriately or excessively. If clients decide they are living by rules that are likely to lead to misery, the therapist asks clients to consider and test out alternative rules. Although cognitive therapy operates within clients' frame of reference, the therapist continually asks clients to examine evidence for and against their belief system.

The Client–Therapist Relationship

The therapeutic relationship is basic to the application of cognitive therapy. Through his writings, it is clear that Beck believes effective therapists must combine empathy and sensitivity with technical competence (A. Beck, 1987). The core therapeutic conditions described by Rogers in his person-centered approach are viewed by cognitive therapists as being *necessary*, but *not sufficient*, to produce optimum therapeutic effect. A therapeutic alliance is a necessary first step in cognitive therapy, especially in counseling difficult-to-reach clients. Without a working alliance, techniques applied will not be effective (Dattilio & Hanna, 2012; Dienes et al., 2011). Therapists must have a cognitive conceptualization of cases, be creative and active, be able to engage clients through a process of Socratic questioning, and be knowledgeable and skilled in the use of cognitive and behavioral strategies aimed at guiding clients in significant self-discoveries that will lead to change (A. Beck & Weishaar, 2014).

Cognitive therapists are continuously active and deliberately interactive with clients, helping clients frame their conclusions in the form of testable hypotheses. The cognitive therapist functions as a catalyst and a guide who helps clients understand how their beliefs and attitudes influence the way they feel and act. Clients are expected to identify the distortions in their thinking, summarize important points in the session, and collaboratively devise homework assignments that they agree to carry out. Cognitive therapists emphasize the client's role in self-discovery. The assumption is that lasting changes in the client's thinking and behavior will be most likely to occur with the client's initiative, understanding, awareness, and effort (A. Beck & Weishaar, 2014; J. Beck, 2005, 2011a; J. Beck & Butler, 2005).

Cognitive therapists identify specific, measurable goals and move directly into the areas that are causing the most difficulty for clients (Dienes et al., 2011). Typically, a therapist will educate clients about the nature and course of their problem, about the process of cognitive therapy, and how thoughts influence their emotions and behaviors.. One way of educating clients is through bibliotherapy, in which clients complete readings that support and expand their understanding of cognitive therapy principles and skills. These readings are assigned as an adjunct to therapy and are designed to enhance the therapeutic process by providing an educational focus (Dattilio & Freeman, 2007; Jacobs, 2008). Self-help books such as *Mind Over Mood* (Greenberger & Padesky, 2016) also provide an educational focus.

Homework is often used as a part of cognitive therapy because practicing cognitive behavioral skills in real life facilitates more rapid and enduring gains (Dienes et al., 2011). The purpose of homework is not merely to teach clients new skills but also to enable them to test their beliefs and to try out different behaviors in daily-life situations. Homework is generally presented to clients as an experiment that serves to continue work on issues addressed in a therapy session (Dattilio, 2002b). Cognitive therapists realize that clients are more likely to complete homework if it is tailored to their needs, if they participate in designing the homework, if they begin the homework in the therapy session, and if they talk about potential problems in implementing the homework (J. Beck, 2005). Tompkins (2004, 2006) points out that there are clear advantages to the therapist and the client working in a collaborative manner in negotiating mutually agreeable homework tasks. One indicator of a good therapeutic alliance is whether homework is done and done well (Kazantzis, Dattilio, Cummins, & Clayton, 2014).

Applications of Cognitive Therapy

Cognitive therapy initially gained recognition as an approach to treating depression, but extensive research has been devoted to the study and treatment of many other psychiatric disorders. The popularity of cognitive therapy is due in part to the "strong empirical support for its theoretical framework and to the large number of outcome studies with clinical populations" (A. Beck & Weishaar, 2014, p. 260). Hundreds of research studies have confirmed the theoretical underpinnings of CT, and hundreds of outcome trials have established its efficacy for a wide range of psychiatric disorders, psychological problems, and medical conditions with psychological components (Hofmann et al., 2012).

Cognitive therapy has been successfully used to treat depression, each of the anxiety disorders, cannabis dependence, hypochondriasis, body dysmorphic disorder, eating disorders, anger, schizophrenia, insomnia, and chronic pain (Chambless & Peterman, 2006; Dattilio & Kendall, 2007; Hofmann et al., 2012; Riskind, 2006); suicidal behavior, borderline personality disorders, narcissistic personality disorders, and schizophrenic disorders (Dattilio & Freeman, 2007); personality disorders (Pretzer & Beck, 2006); substance abuse (Newman, 2006); medical illness (Dattilio & Castaldo, 2001); crisis intervention (Dattilio & Freeman, 2007); couples and families therapy (Dattilio, 1993, 1998, 2001, 2005, 2010; Dattilio & Padesky, 1990; Epstein, 2006); and child abusers, divorce counseling, skills training, and stress management (Dattilio, 1998; Granvold, 1994; Reinecke, Dattilio, & Freeman, 2002). With children and adolescents, CT has been shown to be effective in the treatment of depression and anxiety disorders and more effective than medications for these problems. Clearly, cognitive therapy programs have been designed for all ages and for a variety of client populations.

Moreover, the effects of CT for depression and anxiety disorders seem to be more enduring that the effects of other treatments, with the exception of behavior therapy, which sometimes matches CT in duration of positive outcome. People who get better using CT are less likely to relapse than those who improve with medication or most other psychotherapy approaches (Hollon et al., 2006). For an excellent resource on the clinical applications of cognitive therapy to a wide range of disorders and populations, see *Contemporary Cognitive Therapy* (Leahy, 2006a).

Applying Cognitive Techniques Beck and Weishaar (2014) describe both cognitive and behavioral methods that are part of the overall strategies used by cognitive therapists. Cognitive methods focus on identifying and examining a client's beliefs, exploring the origins of these beliefs, and modifying them if the evidence does not support these beliefs. Examples of behavioral techniques typically used by cognitive therapists include activity scheduling, behavioral experiments, skills training, role playing, behavioral rehearsal, and exposure therapy. Regardless of the nature of the specific problem, the cognitive therapist is mainly interested in applying procedures that will assist individuals in making alternative interpretations of events in their daily living and behaving in ways that move them closer to their goals and values.

Treatment Approaches The length and course of cognitive therapy varies greatly and is determined by the therapy protocols used for specific diagnoses. For example, cognitive therapy for depression generally lasts 16 to 20 sessions and begins with behavioral activation. Activity has an antidepressant effect, especially when the client engages in a mix of pleasurable, accomplished, and anti-avoidance activities. Clients rate their moods in relation to the activities they do throughout the day, and these observations are used as guides to find activities that provide a mood boost in subsequent weeks. As depression begins to lift, the therapist introduces additional skills such as **thought records**, which help clients identify negative **automatic thoughts** and test them. When evidence does not support the automatic thought, clients learn to generate alternative explanations that are less depressing. When evidence does support the problematic thought, clients are helped to create an **action plan** to solve the problem rather than ruminating on it (Greenberger & Padesky, 2016). Before the end of treatment, underlying assumptions that put clients at risk for relapse are examined such as perfectionistic assumptions ("If I make a mistake, then I am worthless"). These assumptions are tested with behavioral experiments. For example, a perfectionistic client may intentionally make a mistake doing a particular task and evaluate whether there is still some worth and value to the outcome.

In contrast, cognitive therapy for panic disorder generally lasts only 6 to 12 sessions and targets catastrophic beliefs about internal physical and mental sensations (Clark et al., 1999). Clients are helped to identify the sensations that trigger a panic attack and the catastrophic beliefs about these sensations. For example, a client may think, "My heart is racing (sensation). That means I am having a heart attack (catastrophic belief)." The therapist helps the client generate an alternative hypothesis to explain these feared sensations. For example, "A racing heart is not dangerous. It can be caused by exercise, anxiety, caffeine, and many other things. The heart is a muscle, and doctors recommend that you regularly raise your heart rate in exercise to keep it healthy." The therapist then guides the client to conduct a series of experiments in a session in which the client creates the sensation and weighs evidence in support of the catastrophic and alternative hypotheses. Once the client begins to believe the alternative hypotheses in these experiments, which later are also done outside of therapy, panic attacks are reduced or disappear.

Application to Family Therapy The cognitive behavioral approach focuses on cognitions, emotions, and behavior as they exert a mutual influence on one another within family relationships to cause dysfunction. Cognitive theory (A. Beck, 1976; A. Beck & Haigh, 2014) emphasizes **schema**, elsewhere defined as core beliefs, as key aspect of the therapeutic process. Therapists help families restructure distorted beliefs (or schema) in order to change dysfunctional behaviors. Some CT therapists place a strong emphasis on examining cognitions among individual family members as well as on what may be termed the "family schemata" (Dattilio, 1993, 1998, 2001, 2010). These jointly held beliefs about the family have formed as a result of years of interaction among family members. These schemata are influenced by the parents' family of origin and have a major impact on how each individual thinks, feels, and behaves in the family system (Dattilio, 2001, 2005, 2010).

For a concrete illustration of how Dr. Dattilio applies cognitive principles and works with family schemata, see his cognitive behavioral approach with Ruth in *Case Approach to Counseling and Psychotherapy* (Corey, 2013, chap. 8). For a discussion of myths and misconceptions of cognitive behavior family therapy, see Dattilio (2001); for a concise presentation on the cognitive behavioral model of family therapy, see Dattilio (2010). Also, for an expanded treatment of applications of cognitive behavioral approaches to working with couples and families, see Dattilio (1998).

Christine Padesky and Kathleen Mooney's Strengths-Based Cognitive Behavioral Therapy

Introduction

Strengths-based cognitive behavior therapy (SB-CBT) is a variant of Aaron Beck's cognitive therapy developed by Christine Padesky and her colleague Kathleen Mooney (Padesky & Mooney, 2012). All the principles and evidence-based treatments developed by Aaron Beck and his colleagues are incorporated in strengths-based CBT.

CHRISTINE A. PADESKY (b. 1953) was born and raised in the Midwest. As an undergraduate science major at Yale University, she took a psychology course and became fascinated with this field, which offered a link between her scientific and social change interests. While a PhD student in clinical psychology at the University of California, Los Angeles, Padesky and her graduate research adviser published an article on gender differences in depression symptoms that caught the attention of Aaron Beck. Beck and Padesky met and became friends, and he was her mentor throughout her career (see Padesky, 2004). In the 1980s she and Beck taught more than 20 workshops together in the United States and abroad.

Christine A. Padesky

At Beck's invitation, in 1983 Padesky opened one of the first Centers for Cognitive Therapy in the western United States (now located in Huntington Beach, California). She partnered in this venture with Kathleen Mooney, a creative CBT therapist dedicated to innovation and therapist education. Together they trained and hired staff for their clinic, which became a leading international training center. Padesky and Mooney developed many innovations in the practice of cognitive therapy including the use of constructive questions, the importance of identifying client imagery and metaphors for change, and an emphasis on client strengths. These innovations eventually formed the foundation of their therapy approach, known as strengths-based CBT (SB-CBT).

In 1995, Greenberger and Padesky (2016) first published *Mind Over Mood: Change How You Feel by Changing the Way You Think*, which became a popular self-help sensation. With sales of more than one million copies worldwide in 23 languages, Padesky's dream of teaching people skills to improve their own moods so they did not need to rely on experts was realized.

Padesky lectures and teaches workshops in the United States and abroad. She is a consultant to therapists and clinics worldwide and participates in a number of research programs evaluating strengths-based CBT. She was a featured presenter at the Evolution of Psychotherapy conference in 2013 and the Brief Therapy conference in 2014. In addition to *Mind Over Mood*, she has written four professional books and numerous articles and book chapters on a variety of CBT topics. She produces top-rated video demonstrations of CBT in action and has an extensive catalog of audio training programs for mental health professionals and graduate students in mental health fields.

As the name implies, one central addition of SB-CBT is an emphasis on identification and integration of client strengths at each phase of therapy. The main idea of **SB-CBT** is that active incorporation of client strengths encourages clients to engage more fully in therapy and often provides avenues for change that otherwise would be missed.

SB-CBT expands previous models of CBT to include methods that help people develop positive qualities. Their ideas developed in parallel with positive psychology, a research field that investigates happiness, resilience, altruism, and a host of positive emotions and behaviors (Lopez & Snyder, 2011). In a keynote address at an international conference, Padesky (2007) proposed that the next frontier in psychotherapy would be development of methods to enhance human experience and strengths instead of working solely to alleviate suffering. SB-CBT is a step in that direction.

Basic Principles of Strengths-Based CBT

LO6

Like cognitive therapy, SB-CBT is empirically based. This means that (1) therapists should be knowledgeable about evidence-based approaches pertaining to client issues discussed in therapy, (2) clients are asked to make observations and describe the details of their life experiences so what is developed in therapy is based in the real data of clients' lives, and (3) therapists and clients collaborate in testing beliefs and experimenting with new behaviors to see if they help achieve desired goals.

Strengths are integrated into each phase of treatment in SB-CBT beginning with the intake interview. After reasons for seeking therapy are described and explored, the SB-CBT therapist expresses an interest in positive aspects of the client's life: "Thank you for telling me about the reasons you came to therapy. Even though this is a tough time for you, I wonder if there are some things that are going well in your life or that bring you happiness, even now. If you are willing to tell me about some of those things, it will help me know you more as a whole person."

In *Collaborative Case Conceptualization: Working Effectively With Clients in CBT*, Kuyken, Padesky, and Dudley (2009) show how positive interests and strengths identified in early therapy sessions can provide a wealth of information to help therapist and client collaboratively integrate strengths into case conceptualization and treatment. For example, clients often discover that they use more resilient strategies when they encounter obstacles in areas of positive interest than they do in problem areas of their life. These strategies can be added to plans to deal positively with problem areas. A depressed client learning to be more active to boost mood will have an easier time engaging in activities that are part of a hobby or positive pastime than participating in activities that hold little interest for the client.

SB-CBT therapists help clients develop and construct new positive ways of interacting in the world. The SB-CBT model for building and strengthening personal resilience can be used on its own or integrated with another evidenced-based CBT treatment for a diagnostic disorder (Padesky & Mooney, 2012). For clients with chronic difficulties that have proven resistant to change, SB-CBT proposes that it is often easier to construct an entirely new way of doing things than to problem solve or modify a chronic way of doing things. When clients do not respond to standard treatments, SB-CBT therapists help clients co-create a "NEW Paradigm," which is their vision of how they would like to be and how they would like the difficult area of their life to be.

The Client–Therapist Relationship

As with Beck's cognitive therapy, SB-CBT therapists are collaborative, active, here-and-now focused, and client-centered. SB-CBT therapists are encouraging allies of their clients and need to be genuine, caring, and willing to engage with clients as full human beings in both struggles and successes. SB-CBT therapists do not take an "expert" stance but instead serve as curious assistants or guides to their clients' own discovery and growth.

SB-CBT practitioners ask clients for imagery and metaphors to describe their experiences, both positive and negative. More than words, imagery and metaphors capture and integrate the emotional, cognitive, physiological, and behavioral aspects of experience. In addition to deconstructing beliefs and problems, SB-CBT emphasizes the constructive use of Socratic questioning. The SB-CBT therapist asks constructive questions such as, "How would you like to be? "How would you like this part of your life or relationships to be?" When clients are stuck in recurring patterns, SB-CBT teaches them that we do things "for good reasons" and shows clients how even destructive behaviors (such as cutting oneself when distressed) are done for self-protective reasons and as attempts to cope ("If I cut myself, then I will feel some emotional relief.").

Applications of Strengths-Based CBT

Three current applications for SB-CBT are as (1) an add-on for classic CBT, (2) a four-step model to build resilience and other positive qualities, and (3) the NEW Paradigm for chronic difficulties and personality disorders. SB-CBT operates as an add-on to classic CBT when clients come to therapy with goals to reduce problematic moods (depression, anxiety, anger), behaviors (eating disorders, substance misuse) or other difficulties (psychoses, hypochondriasis) for which there are well-established and effective CBT protocols. In those cases, SB-CBT therapists help clients identify their strengths and rely on these whenever helpful to guide therapy choices.

The four-step model to build resilience provides a template for building positive qualities (Padesky & Mooney, 2012). Their four steps are (1) search, (2) construct, (3) apply, and (4) practice. Padesky and Mooney point out that there are usually just a few common pathways to a psychological disorder, but there are thousands of pathways to resilience. Rather than teach clients particular ways to be resilient, Padesky and Mooney suggest that therapists inquire about activities in clients' lives that are going well and that clients do on a regular basis. These everyday activities clients are motivated to do are *areas of strength*. This search for strengths is the first step in their model.

The second step is to discover what obstacles clients encounter while doing these activities and how they manage these obstacles. A central idea is that everybody encounters obstacles in any frequently practiced activity but we manage obstacles without even realizing that is what we are doing when we enjoy the activity. For example, Joseph loves to play video games. He uses a variety of strategies to manage obstacles as they occur within the game and from external causes (such as loss of power to his electronic device). Joseph's strategies include problem solving, seeking help from friends, reminding himself that "I've been stuck before and always found a way through," and music to keep up his energy. These strategies are written down as his Personal Model of Resilience (PMR).

The third step involves the therapist helping Joseph creatively consider how he can apply his PMR to remain resilient in a more problematic area of his life, such as dating. Joseph makes a plan for how to use these strategies to help him meet people he would like to date, ask them out, and solve various dating difficulties than have proven challenging for him in the past.

The fourth stage involves Joseph conducting a series of dating experiments while he practices maintaining a focus on resilience. A key to this stage of the therapy is that Joseph sets a goal to "be resilient in the face of challenges," not to succeed at dating. Because his goal is to "stay resilient" he has a better chance of experiencing his dates in a positive way. Even if he and his date don't get along, he can feel good about staying resilient. This can help Joseph feel motivated no matter what happens. Over time, his resilience will be expressed both in persistence (problem solving, getting help from friends) and in acceptance that not every date will turn out as he would like (but he can enjoy the music anyway).

The same principles can be used to build other positive qualities such as altruism, creativity, and courage. The key is to find everyday areas of the person's life where these qualities are already in evidence. For example, even a self-centered person may be very kind and concerned for a pet or certain friends. From these everyday experiences, the person can be helped to build a Personal Model of X (for example, altruism) and then consider how to apply and practice this positive quality in other life settings.

The final application of SB-CBT is the NEW Paradigm for chronic issues and personality disorders. This approach is more comprehensive and requires clients to vividly construct new ways to feel, think, and behave in their life. The four steps of this model are (1) Conceptualize the OLD System of operating and help clients understand they do things "for good reasons," (2) construct NEW systems of how clients would like to be, (3) strengthen the NEW using behavioral experiments to try on NEW ways of being and edit them as needed, and (4) relapse management. Therapists need significant training to practice the NEW Paradigm because it is essential that the therapist stay alert to identify when the OLD System interferes with client learning. The therapist must be able to help the client learn from every experience and process this learning through the NEW System, not the OLD.

DONALD MEICHENBAUM (b. 1940) was born in New York City (the Bronx) and learned early to be "street smart" and to be on the lookout for high-risk situations. He attended City College of New York and received his PhD in clinical psychology from the University of Illinois. At the University of Waterloo in Ontario, Canada, he conducted research on the development of cognitive behavior therapy (CBT). He is one of the founders of cognitive behavior therapy, and in a survey of clinicians he was voted one of the most influential therapists in the 20th century. He is the recipient of a Lifetime Achievement Award from the Clinical Division of the American Psychological Association for his work on suicide prevention. In 1995 Meichenbaum retired from the University of Waterloo to become the research director of the Melissa Institute for Violence Prevention, which is designed to "give science away" in order to reduce violence and to treat victims of violence.

Donald Meichenbaum

Meichenbaum attributes the origin of CBT to his mother, who had a knack for telling stories about her daily activities that were peppered with her thoughts, feelings, and a running commentary. This childhood experience contributed to Meichenbaum's psychotherapeutic approach of constructivist narrative therapy, in which clients tell their stories and describe what they did to "survive and cope." Meichenbaum's recent work with returning service members using iPod technology to bolster resilience is modeled on this approach. When therapy is successful, Meichenbaum ensures that clients take credit for the changes they have achieved. As he observes, "I am at my therapeutic best when the clients I see are one step ahead of me offering the observations or suggestions that I would otherwise offer" (Donald Meichenbaum, personal communication, October 21, 2010).

Meichenbaum has published extensively, including *Cognitive Behavior Therapy: An Integrative Approach* (1977), *Stress Inoculation Training* (1985), *Treatment of Individuals With Anger-Control Problems and Aggressive Behaviors* (2002), and *Roadmap to Resilience* (2012). He has lectured in every state and in all provinces in Canada as well as internationally. He was a featured presenter at the Evolution of Psychotherapy conference in 2013 and the Brief Therapy conference in 2014.

Donald Meichenbaum's Cognitive Behavior Modification

Introduction

Donald Meichenbaum's **cognitive behavior modification** (CBM) focuses on changing the client's self-talk. According to Meichenbaum (1977), self-statements affect a person's behavior in much the same way as statements made by another person. A basic premise of CBM is that clients, as a prerequisite to behavior change, must notice how they think, feel, and behave and the impact they have on others. For change to occur, clients need to interrupt the scripted nature of their behavior so that they can evaluate their behavior in various situations (Meichenbaum, 1993, 2007).

This approach shares with REBT and Beck's cognitive therapy the assumption that distressing emotions are often the result of maladaptive thoughts. REBT is more direct and confrontational in uncovering and disputing irrational thoughts, whereas Meichenbaum's *self-instructional training* focuses more on helping clients become aware of their self-talk and the stories they tell about themselves. Both REBT and CT focus on changing thinking processes, but Meichenbaum suggests that it may be easier and more effective to change our behavior rather than our thinking. Furthermore, our emotions and thinking are two sides of the same coin: the way we feel can affect our way of thinking, just as how we think can influence how we feel. The therapeutic process consists of teaching clients to make self-statements and training clients to modify the instructions they give to themselves so that they can cope more effectively with the problems they encounter. Cognitive restructuring plays a central role in Meichenbaum's (1977, 1993) self-instructional training. He describes cognitive structure as the organizing aspect of thinking, which monitors and directs the choice of thoughts through an "executive processor" that "holds the blueprints of thinking" that determines when to continue, interrupt, or change thinking. Together, therapist and client practice the self-instructions and the desirable behaviors in role-play situations that simulate problem situations in the client's daily life. The emphasis is on acquiring practical coping skills for problematic situations such as impulsive and aggressive behavior, anxiety in social situations, fear of taking tests, eating problems, and fear of public speaking.

How Behavior Changes

Meichenbaum (1977) proposes that "behavior change occurs through a sequence of mediating processes involving the interaction of inner speech, cognitive structures, and behaviors and their resultant outcomes" (p. 218). He describes a three-phase process of change in which those three aspects are interwoven and believes that focusing on only one aspect will probably prove insufficient. LO7

Phase 1: Self-observation. Clients learning how to observe their own behavior. When clients begin therapy, their internal dialogue is characterized by negative self-statements and imagery. A critical factor is their willingness and ability to *listen* to themselves. This process involves an increased sensitivity to their thoughts, feelings, actions, physiological reactions, and ways of reacting to others. If depressed clients hope to make constructive changes, for example, they must first realize that they are not "victims" of negative thoughts and feelings. Rather, they are actually contributing to their depression through the things they tell themselves. Although self-observation is necessary if change is to occur, it is not sufficient for change.

Phase 2: Starting a new internal dialogue. As a result of the early client–therapist contacts, clients learn to notice their maladaptive behaviors, and they begin to see opportunities for adaptive behavioral alternatives. If clients hope to change what they are telling themselves, they must initiate a new behavioral chain, one that is incompatible with their maladaptive behaviors. Clients learn that psychological distress is a function of the interdependence of cognitions, emotions, behaviors, and resultant consequences. In therapy, clients learn to change their internal dialogue, which serves as a guide to new behavior.

Phase 3: Learning new skills. Clients learn to interrupt the downward spiral of thinking, feeling, and behaving, and the therapist teaches clients more adaptive ways of coping using the resources they bring to therapy. Clients learn more effective coping skills, which are practiced in real-life situations. As they behave differently in situations, they typically get different reactions from others. The stability of what they learn is greatly influenced by what they say to themselves about their newly acquired behavior and its consequences.

Stress Inoculation Training

A particular application of a coping skills program is teaching clients stress management techniques by way of a strategy known as **stress inoculation training** (SIT). Using cognitive techniques, Meichenbaum (1985, 2007, 2008) has developed stress inoculation procedures that are a psychological and behavioral analog to immunization on a biological level. Individuals are given opportunities to deal with relatively mild stress stimuli in successful ways, and they gradually develop a tolerance for stronger stimuli. This training is based on the assumption that we can affect our ability to cope with stress by modifying our beliefs and self-statements about our performance in stressful situations. Meichenbaum's stress inoculation LO8 training is concerned with more than merely teaching people specific coping skills. His program is designed to prepare clients for intervention and motivate them to change, and it deals with issues such as resistance and relapse.

Stress inoculation training is a combination of information giving, Socratic discovery-oriented inquiry, cognitive restructuring, problem solving, relaxation training, behavioral rehearsals, self-monitoring, self-instruction, self-reinforcement, and modifying environmental situations (Meichenbaum, 2008). Collaborative goals are set that nurture hope, direct-action skills, and acceptance-based coping skills. These coping skills are designed to be applied to both present problems and future difficulties. Clients are assisted in generalizing what they have learned so they can use these skills in daily living, and relapse prevention strategies are taught. Meichenbaum (2008) describes stress inoculation training as a complex, multifaceted, cognitive behavioral intervention that is both a preventive and a treatment approach.

Clients can acquire more effective strategies in dealing with stressful situations by learning how to modify their cognitive "set," or core beliefs. The following procedures are designed to teach these coping skills:

- Expose clients to anxiety-provoking situations by means of role playing and imagery
- Require clients to evaluate their anxiety level
- Teach clients to become aware of the anxiety-provoking cognitions they experience in stressful situations
- Help clients examine these thoughts by reevaluating their self-statements
- Have clients note the level of anxiety following this reevaluation

The Phases of Stress Inoculation Training Meichenbaum (2007, 2008) has designed a three-stage model for stress inoculation training: (1) the conceptual-educational phase, (2) the skills acquisition and consolidation phase, and (3) the application and follow-through phase.

During the *conceptual-educational phase*, the primary focus is on creating a therapeutic alliance with clients. This is done by helping clients gain a better understanding of the nature of stress and reconceptualizing it in social-interactive terms. Initially, clients are provided with a conceptual framework in simple terms designed to educate them about ways of responding to a variety of stressful situations. They learn about the role cognitions and emotions play in creating and maintaining stress through didactic presentations, by curious questioning, and by a process of guided self-discovery. A collaborative relationship is created during this early phase, and together they rethink the stress concerns clients bring to understand the nature of the problem.

Clients often begin treatment feeling that they are victims of external circumstances, thoughts, feelings, and behaviors over which they have no control. As a way to understand the subjective world of clients, the therapist generally elicits stories that clients tell themselves. Training includes teaching clients to become aware of their own role in creating their stress and their life stories. They acquire this awareness by systematically observing the statements they make internally as well as by monitoring the maladaptive behaviors that flow from this inner dialogue. Such self-monitoring continues throughout all the phases. As is true in cognitive therapy, clients typically keep an open-ended diary in which they systematically monitor and record their specific thoughts, feelings, and behaviors. In teaching these coping skills, therapists strive to be flexible in their use of techniques and to be sensitive to the individual, cultural, and situational circumstances of their clients.

During the *skills acquisition and consolidation phase*, the focus is on giving clients a variety of behavioral and cognitive coping skills to apply to stressful situations. This phase involves direct actions, such as gathering information about their fears, learning specifically what situations bring about stress, arranging for ways to lessen the stress by doing something different, and learning methods of physical and psychological relaxation. The training involves cognitive coping; clients are taught that adaptive and maladaptive behaviors are linked to their inner dialogue. Through this training, clients acquire and rehearse a new set of self-statements. Meichenbaum (1986) provides some examples of coping statements that are rehearsed in this phase of SIT:

- "How can I prepare for a stressor?" ("What do I have to do? Can I develop a plan to deal with the stress?")
- "How can I confront and deal with what is stressing me?" ("What are some ways I can handle a stressor? How can I meet this challenge?")
- "How can I cope with feeling overwhelmed?" ("What can I do right now? How can I keep my fears in check?")
- "How can I make reinforcing self-statements?" ("How can I give myself credit?")

Clients also are exposed to various behavioral interventions, such as relaxation training, social skills training, time-management instruction, and self-instructional training. They are helped to make lifestyle changes by reevaluating priorities, developing support systems, and taking direct action to alter stressful situations. Through teaching, demonstration, and guided practice, clients learn the skills of progressive relaxation and practice them regularly to decrease arousal due to stress.

During the *application and follow-through phase*, the focus is on carefully arranging for transfer and maintenance of change from the therapeutic situation to everyday life. Clients practice their new self-statements and apply their new skills to everyday life. To consolidate the lessons learned in the training sessions, clients participate in a variety of activities, including imagery and behavior rehearsal, role playing, modeling, and graded in-vivo exposure. Once clients have become proficient in cognitive and behavioral coping skills, they practice behavioral assignments, which become increasingly demanding. They are asked to write down the homework assignments they are willing to complete. The outcomes of these assignments are carefully checked at subsequent meetings, and if clients do not follow through with them, the therapist and the client collaboratively consider the reasons for the failure.

Relapse prevention, which consists of procedures for dealing with the inevitable setbacks clients are likely to experience as they apply what they are learning to daily life, is taught at this stage (Marlatt & Donovan, 2005). Clients learn to view any lapses that occur as "learning opportunities" rather than as "catastrophic failures." Clients explore a variety of possible high-risk, stressful situations that they may reexperience. In a collaborative fashion with the therapist, and with other clients in a group, clients rehearse and practice applying the skills they have learned to maintain the gains they have made. Follow-up and booster sessions typically take place at 3-, 6-, and 12-month periods as an incentive for clients to continue practicing and refining their coping skills. SIT can be considered part of an ongoing stress management program that extends the benefits of training into the future.

Stress inoculation training has potentially useful applications for a wide variety of problems and clients and for both remediation and prevention. Clinical applications of SIT are individually tailored to specific target populations and include anger control, pain control, anxiety management, assertion training, improving creative thinking, treating depression, dealing with health problems, and preparing for surgery. Stress inoculation training has been employed with medical patients and with psychiatric patients. Meichenbaum (2007) contends that the flexibility of the SIT format has contributed to its robust effectiveness. SIT has been successfully used with children, adolescents, and adults who have anger problems, anxiety disorders, phobias, social incompetence, addictions, alcoholism, sexual dysfunctions, social withdrawal, or posttraumatic stress disorder (PTSD), including use with veterans who experience combat-related PTSD (Meichenbaum, 1993, 1994a, 1994b, 2007, 2008, 2012).

A Cognitive Narrative Approach to Cognitive Behavior Therapy

Meichenbaum (2015) has embraced a cognitive narrative perspective, which focuses on the plots, characters, and themes in the stories people tell about themselves and others regarding significant events in their lives. Therapists elicit stories from their clients that are explored in the therapy process. This approach begins with the assumption that there are multiple realities. One of the therapeutic tasks is to help clients appreciate how they construct their realities and how they author their own stories (see Chapter 13). Meichenbaum claims that we are all "story tellers" and that we should be aware of the stories we tell ourselves and others. For example, some clients might see themselves as "prisoners of the past" or as "stubborn victims." These phrases are not idle metaphors; they are the organizing schemas that color the ways individuals view themselves, their world, and their future. Therapists help clients appreciate how they construct reality and examine the implications and conclusions clients draw from their stories. Telling the "rest of the story"—what they did to survive and cope—bolsters clients' strengths and helps them develop resilient-engendering behaviors. In this way, clients can move from being "stubborn victims" to becoming "tenacious survivors" and perhaps "impressive thrivers." Meichenbaum (2012) works in a collaborative fashion with clients to develop the coping skills necessary to achieve these treatment goals. He uses a Socratic discovery-oriented approach and the art of questioning to assist clients in reaching their goals.

Meichenbaum (1997) uses these questions to evaluate the outcomes of therapy:

- Are clients now able to tell a new story about themselves and the world?
- Do clients now use more positive metaphors to describe themselves?
- Are clients able to predict high-risk situations and employ coping skills in dealing with emerging problems?
- Are clients able to take credit for the changes they have been able to bring about?

In successful therapy clients develop their own voices, take pride in what they have accomplished, and take ownership of the changes they are bringing about. In short, clients become their own therapists and take the therapist's voice with them.

Cognitive Behavior Therapy From a Multicultural Perspective

Strengths From a Diversity Perspective

Cognitive behavioral approaches have several strength in working with individuals from diverse cultural, ethnic, and racial backgrounds. If therapists understand the core values of their culturally diverse clients, they can help clients explore these values and gain a full awareness of their conflicting feelings. Then the client and the therapist can work together to modify selected beliefs and practices. Cognitive behavior therapy tends to be culturally sensitive because it uses the individual's belief system, or worldview, as part of the method of self-exploration. LO9

Because counselors with a cognitive behavioral orientation function as teachers, clients are actively involved in learning skills to deal with the problems of living. In speaking with colleagues who work with culturally diverse populations, I have learned that their clients tend to appreciate the emphasis on cognition and action, as well as the stress on relationship issues. The collaborative approach of CBT offers clients a structured therapy program, yet the therapist still makes every effort to enlist clients' active cooperation and participation. According to Spiegler (2013), because of its basic nature and the way CBT is practiced, it is inherently suited to treating diverse clients. Some of the factors that Spiegler identifies that makes CBT diversity effective include individualized treatment, focus on the external environment, active nature, emphasis on learning, reliance on empirical evidence, concern with present behavior, and brevity. A strength of CBT is integrating assessment of client beliefs, emotional responses, and behavioral choices throughout therapy, which communicates respect for clients' viewpoints regarding their progress.

Hays (2009) asserts there is an "almost perfect fit" between cognitive behavior therapy and multicultural therapy because these perspectives share common assumptions that make integration possible. Aspects that contribute to an integrative framework include the following:

- Interventions are tailored to the unique needs and strengths of the individual.
- Clients are empowered by learning specific skills they can apply in daily life (CBT) and by the emphasis on cultural influences that contribute to clients' uniqueness (multicultural therapy).
- Inner resources and strengths of clients are activated to bring about change.
- Clients make changes that minimize stressors, increase personal strengths and supports, and establish skills for dealing more effectively with their physical and social (cultural) environments.

Shortcomings From a Diversity Perspective

Exploring values and core beliefs plays an important role in all of the cognitive behavioral approaches, and it is crucial for therapists to have some understanding of the cultural background of clients and to be sensitive to their struggles. REBT therapists would do well to use caution in their choice of language and expression when confronting clients about their beliefs and behaviors. REBT suggests that the therapist's job is to help clients critically examine long-standing cultural values that result in dysfunctional emotions or behaviors, but a potential limitation of REBT is its negative view of dependency. Many cultures view interdependence as necessary to good mental health. Clients with long-cherished cultural values pertaining to interdependence may not respond favorably to forceful methods of persuasion toward independence. Skillful REBT practitioners carefully monitor their manner, style, and choice of words and communicate whenever possible in language that is congruent with the client's culture.

Hays (2009) suggests that therapists avoid challenging the core cultural beliefs of clients unless the client is clearly open to this. By emphasizing collaboration over confrontation, as the cognitive behavioral approaches do, the therapist can avoid seeming to be disrespectful. Hays recommends drawing on the client's culturally related strengths in developing helpful ways of thinking to replace unhelpful cognitions. For example, consider an Asian American client, Sung, from a culture that stresses values such as doing one's best, cooperation, interdependence, and working hard. Sung may feel that she is bringing shame to her family if she is going through a divorce, and she may feel guilt if she perceives that she is not living up to the expectations and standards set for her by her family and her community. Sung can be helped to consider how her cultural values of cooperation and interdependence may enable her family to support her during a difficult divorce. The rules for Sung are likely to be different than are the rules for a male member of her culture. The counselor could assist Sung in understanding and exploring how both her gender and her culture are factors to consider in her situation. If Sung is confronted too quickly on living by the expectations or rules of others, the results are likely to be counterproductive. Sung might even leave counseling if she feels that she is not being understood.

The emphasis of CBT on assertiveness, independence, verbal ability, rationality, cognition, and behavioral change may limit its use in cultures that value subtle communication over assertiveness, interdependence over personal independence, listening and observing over talking, and acceptance over behavior change (Hays, 2009). In CBT the focus is on the present, which can result in the therapist failing to recognize the role of the past in a client's development. Cognitive behavioral assessments involve the investigation of a client's *personal* history. If the therapist is unaware of a client's *cultural* beliefs, which are rooted in the past, the therapist may have difficulty interpreting the client's personal experiences accurately.

Another limitation of CBT from a multicultural perspective involves its individualistic orientation. An inexperienced therapist may overemphasize cognitive restructuring to the neglect of environmental interventions. Hays (2009) points out that these potential limitations do not preclude the integration of CBT and multicultural counseling. Instead, being aware of these limitations "presents opportunities for rethinking, refining, adapting and increasing the relevance and effectiveness of psychotherapy" (p. 356).

Cognitive Behavior Therapy Applied to the Case of Stan

From a cognitive behavioral perspective, I want Stan to critically evaluate and modify his self-defeating beliefs, which will likely result in Stan acquiring more effective behavior. As his therapist, I am both goal oriented and problem focused. From the initial session, I ask Stan to identify his problems and formulate specific goals and help him reconceptualize his problems in a way that will increase his chances of finding solutions.

I follow a clear structure for every session. The basic procedural sequence includes (1) preparing him by providing a cognitive rationale for treatment and demystifying treatment; (2) encouraging him to monitor the thoughts that accompany his distress; (3) implementing behavioral and cognitive techniques; (4) assisting him in identifying and examining some basic beliefs and ideas; (5) teaching him ways to examine his beliefs and assumptions by testing them in the real world; and (6) teaching him basic coping skills that will enable him to avoid relapsing into old patterns.

As a part of the structure of the therapy sessions, I ask Stan for a brief review of the week, elicit feedback from the previous session, review homework assignments, collaboratively create an agenda for the session, discuss topics on the agenda, and set new homework for the week. I encourage Stan to perform personal experiments and practice coping skills in daily life.

Stan tells me that he would like to work on his fear of women and would hope to feel far less intimidated by them. He reports that he feels threatened by most women, but especially by women he perceives as powerful. In working with Stan's fears, I proceed with four steps: educating him about his self-talk; having him monitor and evaluate his faulty beliefs; using cognitive and behavioral interventions; and collaboratively designing homework with Stan that will give him opportunities to practice new behaviors in daily life.

First, I educate him about the importance of examining his automatic thoughts, his self-talk, and the many "shoulds," "oughts," and "musts" he has accepted without questioning. Working with Stan as a collaborative partner in his therapy, I guide him in discovering some basic thoughts that influence what he tells himself and how he feels and acts. Here are some of his beliefs:

- "I always have to be strong, tough, and perfect."
- "I'm not a man if I show any signs of weakness."
- "If everyone didn't love me and approve of me, things would be catastrophic."
- "If a woman rejected me, I really would be reduced to a 'nothing.'"
- "If I fail, I am then a failure as a person."
- "I'm apologetic for my existence because I don't feel equal to others."

Second, I assist Stan in monitoring and evaluating the ways in which he keeps telling himself these self-defeating ideas. I assist him in clarifying specific problems and learning how to critically evaluate his thinking.

Therapist: You're not your father. I wonder why you continue telling yourself that you're just like him. Where is the evidence that your parents were right in their assessment of you? What is the evidence they were not right in their assessment of you? You say you're such a failure and that you feel inferior. Do your present activities support this? If you were not so hard on yourself, how might your life be different?

Third, once Stan more fully understands the nature of his cognitive distortions and his self-defeating beliefs, I draw on a variety of cognitive and behavioral techniques to help Stan learns to identify, evaluate, and respond to his beliefs. I rely heavily on cognitive techniques such as *Socratic questioning*, *guided discovery*, and *cognitive restructuring* to assist Stan in examining the evidence that seems to support or contradict his core beliefs. I work with Stan so he will view his basic beliefs and automatic thinking as hypotheses to be tested. In a way, he will become a personal scientist by checking out the validity of many of the conclusions and basic assumptions that contribute to his personal difficulties. By the use of guided discovery, Stan learns to evaluate the validity and functionality of his beliefs and conclusions. Stan can also profit from cognitive restructuring, which would entail observing his own behavior in various situations. For example, during the week he can take a particular situation that is problematic for him and pay attention to his automatic thoughts and internal dialogue: What is he telling himself as he approaches a difficult situation? As he learns to attend to his thoughts and behaviors, he may begin to see that what he tells himself has as much impact as others' statements about him. He also sees the connections between his thinking and his behavioral problems. With this awareness he is in an ideal place to begin to learn a new, more functional internal dialogue.

Fourth, I work collaboratively with him in creating specific homework assignments to help him deal with his fears. It is expected that Stan will learn new coping skills, which he can practice first in session and then in daily life situations. It is not enough for him to merely say new things to himself; Stan needs to apply his new cognitive and behavioral coping skills in various daily situations. At one point, for instance, I ask Stan to explore his fears of powerful women and his reasons for continuing to tell himself: "They expect me to be strong and perfect. If I'm not careful, they'll dominate me." His homework includes approaching a woman for a date. If he succeeds in getting the date, he can think about his catastrophic expectations of what might happen. What would be so terrible if she did not like him or if she refused the date? Stan tells himself over and over that he must be *approved of* and that if any woman rebuffs him the consequences are more than he can bear. With practice, he learns to label distortions and is able to automatically identify his negative thoughts and monitor his cognitive patterns. Through a variety of cognitive and behavioral strategies, he is able to acquire new information, change his basic beliefs, and implement new and more effective behavior.

Questions for Reflection

- My therapeutic style is characterized as an integrative form of cognitive behavioral therapy. I borrow concepts and techniques from the approaches of Ellis, Beck, and Meichenbaum. In your work with Stan, what specific concepts would you borrow from these approaches? What cognitive behavioral techniques would you use? What possible advantages do you see, if any, in applying an integrative cognitive behavioral approach in your work with Stan? Would there be any benefits in adding ideas from Padesky and Mooney's strengths-based CBT?
- What are some things you would most want to teach Stan about how cognitive behavior therapy works? How would you explain to him the therapeutic alliance and the collaborative therapeutic relationship?
- What are some of Stan's most prominent faulty beliefs that get in the way of his living fully? What cognitive and behavioral techniques might you use in helping him examine his beliefs?
- Stan lives by many "shoulds" and "oughts." His automatic thoughts seem to impede him from getting what he wants. What techniques would you use to encourage guided discovery on his part?
- What are some homework assignments that would be useful for Stan to carry out? How would you collaboratively design homework with Stan? How would you encourage him to develop action plans to test the validity of his thinking and his conclusions?

Visit CengageBrain.com or watch the DVD for *Theory and Practice of Counseling and Psychotherapy: The Case of Stan and Lecturettes*, Session 8 (cognitive behavior therapy), for a demonstration of my approach to counseling Stan from this perspective. This session focuses on exploring some of Stan's faulty beliefs through the use of role-reversal and cognitive restructuring techniques.

Cognitive Behavior Therapy Applied to the Case of Gwen*

Gwen comes in, takes a seat, and begins telling me about the upcoming office retreat that she has to attend. Gwen wants to be more accepted and connected but has gotten into a pattern of isolating herself and using excuses not to socialize with others.

Gwen: I am dreading spending eight hours out in the country with a bunch of people I don't really care to spent time with in the office! I know it's going to be horrible!

Therapist: Stop for a moment and pay attention to your thoughts around being with your colleagues. What evidence do you have to support your prediction about attending the retreat? [*Sensing a cognitive distortion*]

Gwen: I never interact with my coworkers, and I can't imagine that the retreat will be interesting. I feel anxious when I am around my coworkers. I do not feel that I am a part of their group. I feel judged and scrutinized by them.

Gwen's faulty assumptions and cognitive distortions fuel her anxiety. I want to help Gwen recognize these old irrational thoughts and learn that these thoughts have caused her anxiety. "Awfulizing" the upcoming social event leads to more anxiety and triggers her desire to isolate herself. If Gwen can become more self-aware, she will be able to actively dispute her faulty beliefs.

Therapist: You are telling yourself that you will have a horrible time at the retreat. You think your coworkers will judge you. What evidence do you have that they are judging you? Do you have any evidence that suggests one or several of your coworkers are not judging you? Imagine that you are holding a picture of the retreat and how you fit in at work. The frame is old and dusty. What would happen if you put a new frame on the picture? Can you reframe your thoughts about going to the retreat and interacting with your coworkers in a more positive way?

Gwen: Well, I don't have to say it will be horrible. I guess that thought makes me dread it. I truthfully don't know how it will go at all. Maybe I can tell myself to show up without judgment for a change and just see what happens. I get caught up in negative thinking sometimes.

Therapist: When you hear negative words in your mind or say them, allow yourself to cancel those thoughts. Dispute the negative statement, and replace it with a statement that supports how you want to feel and think about yourself. Tell me some of the cognitive distortions that keep you stuck in anxiety or negative feelings.

Gwen: I say to myself that the people at work are waiting for me to make a mistake, that I am different, and that they don't want to socialize with me. Actually, I haven't really tried to get to know them.

Therapist: What can you do differently in the workplace to foster relationships with your coworkers that might serve to reduce your anxiety?

Gwen: I guess I could say hello to my coworkers instead of walking through the office ignoring them. I really do want to create positive relationships in the office and not feel like an outsider.

Therapist: And how will you respond to those nagging thoughts that everyone is against you?

Gwen: I am beginning to realize that there is really no evidence to support feeling that I am being judged and scrutinized by my coworkers. Maybe I am quiet because I am afraid they will reject me, and so I reject them first.

Therapist: Let's agree on some homework for this week. When you are feeling judged and scrutinized, see if you can counter the assumptions you are making by looking at the facts.

Gwen: Maybe I could make a list of my assumptions and some of the negative thoughts that result from them. Then I could try to list some facts that counter those negative thoughts.

Therapist: I am glad you are willing to try to find some facts to work with. I think this will help you to be less anxious.

---

*Dr. Kellie Kirksey writes about her ways of thinking and practicing in a CBT framework and applying this model to Gwen.

Gwen: And I will try to be more friendly at work.

Therapist: Isolating yourself doesn't seem to be working, so let's see how you feel when you talk with your coworkers.

I give Gwen a journal to record her homework experiments and how doing a new behavior affects her anxiety level. I encourage her to develop awareness of the automatic thoughts that occur to her so she can become more adept at catching and disputing them. In our next session, we discuss her homework and evaluate the response it has had on her level of anxiety in the workplace.

Questions for Reflection

- What role, if any, does Gwen play in her experiences of isolation?
- How does the therapist intervene to assist Gwen in looking for evidence for her negative thinking?
- How would you encourage Gwen to complete her homework assignment?
- How would you respond if you knew that Gwen was being subjected to racism and rejection in the office? How would CBT help her in that case?
- What additional CBT technique might you use if you were counseling Gwen?

Summary and Evaluation

Summary

REBT has evolved into a comprehensive and integrative approach that emphasizes thinking, assessing, deciding, doing, and compassion. This approach is based on the premise of the interconnectedness of thinking, feeling, and behaving. Therapy can begin with clients' problematic behaviors and emotions, and clients can learn to dispute the thoughts that directly create them. To block any self-defeating beliefs that are reinforced by a process of self-indoctrination, REBT therapists employ active and directive techniques such as teaching, suggestion, persuasion, and homework assignments, and they encourage clients to substitute a rational belief system for an irrational one. Therapists demonstrate how and why dysfunctional beliefs lead to negative emotional and behavioral results. They teach clients how to dispute self-defeating beliefs and behaviors that might occur in the future. REBT emphasizes the benefit of taking action—doing something about the insights one gains in therapy. Change comes about mainly by practicing new behaviors that replace old and ineffective ones. Unconditional self-acceptance, unconditional other-acceptance, and unconditional life-acceptance are strongly encouraged. Rational emotive behavior therapists are typically eclectic in selecting therapeutic strategies. They have the latitude to develop their own personal style and to exercise creativity; they are not bound by fixed techniques for particular problems.

Cognitive therapists also practice from an integrative stance, using many methods to help clients learn to identify links between thoughts, emotions, behaviors, physiology, and situations. Some defining characteristics of cognitive therapy are that the client is active and works as a partner with the therapist; the therapist is active and directive; the therapy is structured and psychoeducational; an agenda provides focus for each session; and therapy is time limited (Freeman & Freeman, 2016). The working alliance is given special importance in cognitive therapy as a way of forming a collaborative partnership. Although rapport in the client–therapist relationship is viewed as helpful by Beck, it is not considered sufficient for therapy success. In cognitive therapy, it is presumed that clients are helped by the skillful use of a range of cognitive and behavioral interventions and by therapists engaging clients' willingness to perform homework assignments between sessions. Therapists are expected to be able to conceptualize client problems in ways that link personal client experiences to the evidence-based treatments that are most likely to be successful.

All of the cognitive behavioral approaches stress the importance of links between cognitive processes, emotions, and behavior. It is assumed that how people *feel* and what they actually *do* is largely influenced by their subjective assessment and interpretation of situations. Because this appraisal of life situations is influenced by beliefs, attitudes, assumptions, and internal dialogue, such cognitions become a major focus of therapy.

Contributions of the Cognitive Behavioral Approaches

Most of the therapies discussed in this book can be considered "cognitive" **LO10** in a general sense because they have the aim of changing clients' subjective views of themselves and the world. The cognitive behavioral approaches have developed systematic and sophisticated forms of psychotherapy that focus on testing assumptions and beliefs and teaching clients the coping skills needed to deal with their problems. A basic principle of CBT is emotional and behavioral changes can be achieved by changing cognitions, just as cognitive change can be altered by actions and emotions (Freeman & Freeman, 2016).

Ellis's REBT and Beck's CT represent the most systematic applications of cognitive behavior therapy. Both REBT and CT are based on a wide range of cognitive behavioral techniques and follow a defined plan of action; they can often be relatively brief and structured treatments in keeping with the spirit of maximizing effectiveness and efficiency, cost effectiveness, and evidence-based practice (Hollon & DiGiuseppe, 2011). The psychoeducational aspect of CBT and REBT is a clear strength that can be applied to many clinical problems and used effectively in many settings with diverse client populations (A. Ellis & Ellis, 2011). The evidence basis in support of CBT therapies often makes them the "gold standard" by which therapy effectiveness is judged.

Ellis's REBT One of the strengths of REBT is the focus on teaching clients ways to carry on their own therapy without the direct intervention of a therapist. I particularly like the emphasis that REBT puts on supplementary and psychoeducational approaches such as listening to tapes, reading self-help books, keeping a record of what they are doing and thinking, and carrying out homework assignments. In this way clients can further the process of change in themselves without becoming excessively dependent on a therapist.

Beck's Cognitive Therapy Beck's key concepts share similarities with REBT but differ in being empirically rather than philosophically derived, the processes by which therapy proceeds, and the formulation and treatment for different disorders. Beck made pioneering efforts in the treatment of anxiety, phobias, and depression. Beck demonstrated that a structured therapy that is present centered and problem oriented can be very effective in treating depression and anxiety in a relatively short time. Today, empirically validated treatments for both anxiety and depression have revolutionized therapeutic practice; research has demonstrated the efficacy of cognitive therapy for a variety of problems (Leahy, 2002; Scher, Segal, & Ingram, 2006; Hofmann et al., 2012). Beck developed specific cognitive procedures to help depressive clients evaluate their assumptions and beliefs and to create a new cognitive perspective that can lead to optimism and changed behavior. Research demonstrates that the effects of cognitive therapy on depression and hopelessness are usually maintained for at least one year after treatment. Cognitive therapy has been applied to a wide range of clinical populations that Beck did not originally believe were appropriate for this model, including treatment for posttraumatic stress disorder, schizophrenia, delusional disorders, bipolar disorder, and various personality disorders (Hofmann et al., 2012). The credibility of the cognitive model grows out of the fact that many of its propositions have been empirically tested.

Padesky and Mooney's Strengths-Based CBT Beck's CT has been further expanded with Padesky and Mooney's strengths-based CBT approach. In addition to incorporating strengths at each phase of treatment, SB-CBT has successfully incorporated a wide range of modalities including imagery, metaphor, stories, and kinesthetic body experiences into the broad repertoire of CBT interventions. SB-CBT also provides models that extend CBT from evidence-based treatment of client problems to evidence-based models for developing positive qualities and client strengths. Instead of focusing solely on testing existing beliefs, SB-CBT offers systematic methods for helping clients construct new beliefs and behaviors that help realize their goals of "how they would like to be."

Meichenbaum's Cognitive Behavior Modification Meichenbaum's work in self-instruction and stress inoculation training has been applied successfully to a variety of client populations and specific problems. Of special note is his contribution to understanding how stress is largely self-induced through inner dialogue. Meichenbaum's integration of the cognitive narrative perspective is a key strength of his therapy style. He is able to combine elements of the postmodern interest in stories clients tell with assisting clients in changing their cognitions, feelings, and behaviors by drawing on a cognitive behavioral conceptual framework.

A contribution of all of the cognitive behavioral approaches is the emphasis on putting newly acquired insights into action. Homework assignments are well suited to enabling clients to practice new behaviors and assisting them in the process of learning more effective coping skills. It is important that collaboratively created homework be a natural outgrowth of what is taking place in the therapy session. Ellis's REBT, Beck's cognitive therapy, Padesky and Mooney's strengths-based CBT, and Meichenbaum's stress inoculation training all place special emphasis on practicing new skills both in therapy and in daily life, and homework is a key part of the learning process. Clients learn how to generalize coping skills to various problem situations and acquire relapse prevention strategies to ensure that their gains are consolidated.

A major contribution made by Ellis, the Becks, Padesky and Mooney, and Meichenbaum is the demystification of the therapy process. The cognitive behavioral approaches are based on an educational model that stresses a working alliance between therapist and client. The models encourage self-help, provide for continuous feedback from the client on how well treatment strategies are working, and provide a structure and direction to the therapy process that allows for evaluation of outcomes. Clients are active, informed, and responsible for the direction of therapy because they are partners in the enterprise.

Limitations and Criticisms of the Cognitive Behavioral Approaches

Some critics have charged that the cognitive behavioral approaches focus **LO11** only limited attention on the role of emotions in treatment. These therapies were originally developed to help people already experiencing extreme emotional arousal, and this perception may be an artifact of that fact. When clients are severely depressed or highly anxious, it is beneficial to focus less directly on these emotions per se and more on the balancing roles of belief and behavior. When CBT therapists work with clients who keep emotion at arms' length, they use imagery, role play, and emotional expression to elicit emotion and bring it into therapy. Although CBT therapists may not talk *about* emotion as frequently as some other therapies, CBT is almost always dealing directly *with* emotion and its consequences. Some potential limitations of the various CBT approaches follow.

Ellis's REBT I question the REBT assumption that exploring the past is ineffective in helping clients change faulty thinking and behavior. From my perspective, exploring past childhood experiences can have a great deal of therapeutic power if the discussion is connected to present functioning. In fact, Albert Ellis would (and Debbie Joffe Ellis continues to) listen to past childhood experiences in the initial session, or during early sessions. These stories can be valuable as sources of irrational beliefs still held by the client in the here and now. Attention would then very quickly move to exploring, disputing, and replacing these beliefs.

Another potential limitation involves the misuse of the therapist's power by imposing ideas of what constitutes rational thinking. Due to the active and directive nature of this approach, it is particularly important for practitioners to avoid imposing their own philosophy of life on their clients. The skillful REBT therapist clarifies the REBT definitions of rational versus irrational thoughts and healthy negative emotions versus unhealthy negative emotions (A. Ellis & Ellis, 2011).

Some clients may have trouble with a confrontational style of REBT, especially if a strong therapeutic alliance has not been established. It is well to underscore that REBT can be effective when practiced in a style different from Ellis's. Albert Ellis often expressed that therapists do not need to emulate his style to effectively incorporate REBT into their own repertoire of interventions. Debbie Joffe Ellis, who continues to teach and write about the "Ellis" REBT approach, enthusiastically encourages therapists to adhere to REBT tenets and principles in their own authentic manner and style (D. Ellis, 2014).

Beck's Cognitive Therapy Cognitive therapy has been criticized for focusing too much on the power of positive thinking; being too superficial and simplistic; denying the importance of the client's past; being too technique oriented; failing to use the therapeutic relationship; working only on eliminating symptoms, but failing to explore the underlying causes of difficulties; ignoring the role of unconscious factors; and neglecting the role of feelings (Freeman & Dattilio, 1992; Weishaar, 1993).

Although the cognitive therapist is straightforward and looks for simple rather than complex solutions, this does not imply that the practice of cognitive therapy is simple. Cognitive therapists do not pursue positive thinking but rather thinking based on actual experiences. Cognitive therapists do not believe the unconscious is difficult to access. With direct and guided questioning, clients can identify assumptions and beliefs that exist below awareness and also link these beliefs to behavioral patterns and emotional reactions. They also recognize that clients' current problems are often a product of earlier life experiences, and they may explore with clients the ways their past is presently influencing them.

Padesky and Mooney's Strengths-Based CBT The biggest criticism of strengths-based CBT is that the evidence base supporting the approach is still in its infancy. Some CBT therapists question whether the addition of client strengths adds anything to CBT's effectiveness. Studies currently under way in Europe and the United Kingdom are testing this hypothesis, especially to see whether a strengths and resilience focus increases the enduring effects of therapy. Further research is necessary to examine whether construction of new beliefs and behaviors is more effective than examining current beliefs and behaviors in the treatment of chronic problems.

Meichenbaum's Cognitive Behavior Modification Meichenbaum is very charismatic in his workshop presentations. Much of the success of his approach may be based on his level of caring and his creativity in implementing CBT interventions. Practitioners without his wit, energy, personal flair, and direct therapeutic style may not get the same results even though they follow his treatment protocol. This emphasizes the importance for each therapist to develop his or her own unique therapeutic style.

A potential limitation of any of the cognitive behavioral approaches is the therapist's level of personal development, training, knowledge, skill, perceptiveness, and ability to establish a therapeutic alliance. Although this is true of all therapeutic approaches, it is especially true for CBT practitioners because they tend to be active, highly structured, offer clients useful information, and teach life skills. Who the therapist is as a person is as important as knowledge and skills. Therapists teach their clients through what they model. Debbie Joffe Ellis (2014) encourages practitioners to strive to be mindful, to think about their thinking, and to do their best to practice what they preach. In so doing, they can be healthy models for their clients and others and experience greater authenticity and satisfaction in their own lives as well.

Self-Reflection and Discussion Questions

1. In most CBT models, the therapist functions in many ways as a teacher. How does a psychoeducational model fit with your way of practicing counseling?
2. Cognitive behavioral practitioners use a brief, active, directive, collaborative, present-focused, didactic, psychoeducational model of therapy

that relies on empirical validation of its concepts and techniques. What potential advantages do you see of this focus? Any disadvantages?

3. Ellis, Beck, Padesky, and Meichenbaum are all in the cognitive behavioral camp, yet they all have distinctive approaches to counseling. Which of these approaches are you most drawn to and why?
4. CBT provides for use of a wide range of techniques. What techniques might you apply to yourself? What techniques are you likely to incorporate in your work with clients?
5. The cognitive behavioral therapies are among the most popular with today's practitioners. What do you think accounts for the increased interest in CBT?

Where to Go From Here

In the *DVD for Integrative Counseling: The Case of Ruth and Lecturettes,* I work with Ruth from a cognitive behavioral perspective in a number of therapy sessions. In Sessions 6, 7, and 8, I demonstrate my way of working with Ruth from a cognitive, emotive, and behavioral focus. See also Session 9 ("Integrative Perspective"), which illustrates the interactive nature of working with Ruth on thinking, feeling, and doing levels.

Other Resources

DVDs relevant to this chapter offered by the American Psychological Association from their Systems of Psychotherapy Video Series include the following:

Beck, J. (2005). *Cognitive Therapy*

Ellis, D. J. (2014). *Rational Emotive Behavior Therapy*

Meichenbaum, D. (2007). *Cognitive Behavioral Therapy With Donald Meichenbaum*

Vernon, A. (2010). *Rational Emotive Behavior Therapy Over Time*

Dobson, K. S. (2010). *Cognitive Therapy Over Time*

Persons, J. (2006). *Cognitive-Behavior Therapy*

Dobson, K. S. (2008). *Cognitive-Behavioral Therapy for Perfectionism Over Time*

Dobson, K. S. (2011). *Cognitive-Behavioral Therapy Strategies*

Audio recordings of workshops and videos relevant to this chapter that illustrate CBT protocols and methods in practice are also offered by Padesky at www.padesky.com:

Padesky, C. A. (1993). *Cognitive Therapy for Panic Disorder*

Padesky, C. A. (1996).*Guided Discovery Using Socratic Dialogue*

Padesky, C. A. (1996). *Testing Automatic Thoughts With Thought Records*

Padesky, C. A. (1997). *Collaborative Case Conceptualization*

Padesky, C. A. (2003). *Constructing NEW Core Beliefs*

Padesky, C. A. (2004). *Constructing NEW Underlying Assumptions & Behavioral Experiments*

Padesky, C. A. (2008). *CBT for Social Anxiety*

Padesky, C. A. (2015). *A Four-Step Approach to Building Resilience*

Psychotherapy.net is a comprehensive resource for students and professionals that offers videos and interviews on cognitive behavior therapy. New video and editorial content is made available monthly. DVDs relevant to this chapter are available at www.psychotherapy.net.

For information about the work of Albert Ellis, and current presentations and REBT trainings, contact:

Debbie Joffe Ellis
www.debbiejoffeellis.com

Additional websites of interest on REBT:

www.ellisrebt.com
www.rebtnetwork.org

The *International Journal of Cognitive Therapy* provides information on theory, practice, and research in cognitive behavior therapy. For information about the journal, contact:

International Journal of Cognitive Therapy
www.guilford.com

Padesky and Mooney's *Center for Cognitive Therapy*, Huntington Beach, California, has separate websites for mental health professionals and for the public. At the website for mental health professionals, you can download pdf files of many of Padesky and Mooney's writings, visit Padesky's blog, and find recommendations for cognitive therapy books for both professionals and the public, audio and video training programs, workshops, consultations, and other cognitive therapy resources and information. The website for the public offers information about finding a CBT therapist, CBT articles of interest to the public, and links to the publishers of *Mind Over Mood* in more than 22 languages.

Center for Cognitive Therapy
www.padesky.com (for mental health professionals)
www.MindOverMood.com (for the public)

For more information about CBT workshops, supervision, a CBT blog, and newsletter, contact:

Beck Institute for Cognitive Behavior Therapy
www.beckinstitute.org

The "home" organization for cognitive therapists worldwide is the Academy of Cognitive Therapy, which Aaron T. Beck and Judith S. Beck were instrumental in founding. Links to certified cognitive therapists worldwide as well as links to research and professional books of interest to therapists are available at this website:

Academy of Cognitive Therapy
www.academyct.org

Donald Meichenbaum is research director of the Melissa Institute for Violence Prevention, a nonprofit organization designed to "give science away" in order to reduce violence and to treat victims of violence. The institute is dedicated to the study and prevention of violence through education, community service, research support, and consultation.

Melissa Institute for Violence Prevention
www.melissainstitute.org

Recommended Supplementary Readings

Rational Emotive Behavior Therapy (A. Ellis & Ellis, 2011) is a concise basic primer on REBT and is a good resource for updated information about the approach.

Albert Ellis Revisited (Carlson & Knaus, 2014) contains some of Ellis's most influential writings on a variety of subjects. This edited book includes commentaries by contributors for each of Ellis's articles.

Cognitive Therapy: Basics and Beyond (J. Beck, 2011a) is a main text in cognitive therapy that presents a comprehensive overview of the approach. An earlier edition of this book was translated into 20 languages.

Cognitive Therapy for Challenging Problems (J. Beck, 2005) is a comprehensive account of cognitive therapy procedures applied to clients who present a multiplicity of difficult behaviors. It covers the nuts and bolts of cognitive therapy with various populations and cites important research on cognitive therapy since its inception.

Mind Over Mood: Change How You Feel by Changing the Way You Think (Greenberger & Padesky, 2016) provides step-by-step worksheets to identify moods, solve problems, and test thoughts related to depression, anxiety, anger, guilt, and shame. This is a popular self-help workbook and a valuable tool for therapists and clients learning cognitive therapy skills.

Clinician's Guide to Mind Over Mood (Padesky & Greenberger, 1995) shows therapists how to integrate *Mind Over Mood* in therapy and use cognitive therapy treatment protocols for specific diagnoses. This succinct overview of cognitive therapy has troubleshooting guides, reviews cultural issues, and offers guidelines for individual, couples, and group therapy.

Collaborative Case Conceptualization: Working Effectively With Clients in CBT (Kuyken, Padesky, & Dudley, 2009) shows therapists how to collaboratively construct case conceptualizations with clients in session and use these to guide treatment planning. This book emphasizes using client strengths to build client resilience while targeting distress.

Choice Theory/ Reality Therapy

11

LEARNING OBJECTIVES

1. Identify the key figures associated with reality therapy.
2. Describe how choice theory is the theoretical underpinning of reality therapy.
3. Understand the concept and clinical implications of total behavior.
4. Examine the basic assumptions, unique characteristics, and goals of reality therapy.
5. Understand the role of therapist involvement in creating a counseling environment that is conducive to success.
6. Explain how the WDEP model is applied to practice.
7. Describe the application of reality therapy to group counseling.
8. Identify the strengths and shortcomings of reality therapy in a multicultural context.
9. Examine the contributions and limitations of the reality therapy approach.

WILLIAM GLASSER (1925–2013) was educated at Case Western Reserve University in Cleveland, Ohio. Initially a chemical engineer, he turned to psychology (MA, Clinical Psychology, 1948) and then to psychiatry, attending medical school (MD, 1953) with the intention of becoming a psychiatrist. By 1957 he had completed his psychiatric training at the Veterans Administration and UCLA in Los Angeles and in 1961 was board certified in psychiatry. Glasser was married to Naomi for 47 years, and she was very involved with the William Glasser Institute until her death in 1992. In 1995 Glasser married Carleen, who is an instructor at the institute and coauthor of several of his books.

Courtesy of The William Glasser Institute, Courtesy of Robert E. Wubbolding Chatsworth, CA

William Glasser

Very early Glasser rejected the Freudian model, partly due to his observation of psychoanalytically trained therapists who did not seem to be implementing Freudian principles. Rather, they tended to hold people responsible for their behavior. Early in his career, Glasser was a psychiatrist at the Ventura School, a prison and school for girls operated by the California Youth Authority. He became convinced that his psychoanalytic training was of limited utility in counseling these young people. From these observations, Glasser thought it best to talk to the sane part of clients, not their disturbed side. Glasser was also influenced by G. L. Harrington, a psychiatrist and mentor. Harrington believed in getting his patients involved in projects in the real world, and by the end of his residency Glasser began to put together ideas that would later be known as reality therapy.

In 1962 Glasser began to present public lectures on "reality psychiatry," but few psychiatrists were in the audience. Most of those attending were educators, social workers, counselors, and correctional workers, so Glasser changed the name of his system to "reality therapy," which became the title of his groundbreaking book published in 1965. Educators found the principles of reality therapy helpful, and he was asked to apply it to the classroom and the school as an organization. As a result of this experience, he wrote *Schools Without Failure* in 1968, which had a major impact on the administration of schools, the training of teachers, and the way learning is conducted in schools. Glasser took the position that schools needed to be structured in ways to help students achieve a *success identity* as opposed to a *failure identity*. He advocated for a curriculum geared to the lives of learners. Glasser made significant contributions through in-service workshops for teachers and administrators. Since the late 1960s, reality therapy has been further applied to education and to virtually all other human relationships, especially intimate relationships. Most recently, reality therapy has been applied to management and supervision, coaching, family therapy, and parenting. It is now taught and embedded on every continent except Antarctica.

Glasser became convinced that it was of paramount importance that clients accept personal responsibility for their behavior. By the early 1980s, Glasser was looking for a theory that could explain all his work. Glasser learned about *control theory* from William Powers, and he believed this theory had great potential. He spent the next 10 years expanding, revising, and clarifying what he was initially taught. By 1996 Glasser had become convinced that these revisions had so changed the theory that it was misleading to continue to call it control theory, and he changed the name to *choice theory* to reflect all that he had developed. The essence of reality therapy, now taught all over the world, is that we are all responsible for what we choose to do. We are internally motivated by current needs and wants, and we control our present behavioral choices.

ROBERT E. WUBBOLDING (b. 1936), born and raised in Cincinnati, Ohio, is the youngest of six children. He received his doctorate in counseling from the University of Cincinnati, is a member of several professional organizations, and has licenses as a counselor and as a psychologist. He taught high school history, worked as a high school and elementary school counselor, and served as a consultant to drug and alcohol abuse programs of the U.S. Army and Air Force. Wubbolding began a career in the Catholic priesthood but later "left the clergy freely and honorably." He is married to Sandra Trifilio, a former French teacher, who shares his passion for his work and is administrator of the Center for Reality Therapy and editor of his writings.

Courtesy of Robert E. Wubbolding

Robert E. Wubbolding

Wubbolding is now the director of the Center for Reality Therapy in Cincinnati and faculty associate at Johns Hopkins University. He is also professor emeritus of Xavier University, where he taught counselor education for 32 years. He loved teaching and viewed his students as being highly motivated, eager to learn, and experienced. One of his most meaningful experiences was teaching graduate students in the counseling department at Xavier University.

After completing his doctorate, Wubbolding attended training sessions representing a wide range of counseling approaches, yet he found reality therapy to be best suited to his interests. He attended many intensive training workshops conducted by William Glasser in Los Angeles, and in 1988 Glasser appointed him director of training for the William Glasser Institute.

Wubbolding served as visiting professor at the University of Southern California in their overseas programs in Japan, Korea, and Germany, thus fulfilling his lifelong desire to travel and to live in other countries. He has become an internationally known teacher, author, and practitioner of reality therapy and has introduced choice theory and reality therapy in Europe, Asia, and the Middle East. Among his specialties is adapting choice theory and reality therapy to various cultures and ethnic groups. He received the Gratitude Award (2009) for Initiating Reality Therapy in the United Kingdom and the Certificate of Reality Therapy Psychotherapist by the European Association for Psychotherapy (2009).

Wubbolding extended the theory and practice of reality therapy with his conceptualization of the WDEP system. He has written 14 books and more than 150 articles, essays, and chapters in textbooks as well as preparing more than 20 DVDs, some of which are referenced in this chapter. His religious commitment and his life of service to others are apparent in his work, and he continues his vocation of teacher, counselor, psychologist, and active member of his church.

Introduction

Reality therapists believe the underlying problem for most clients is the same: they are either involved in a present unsatisfying relationship or lack what could even be called a relationship. Many client problems are caused by their inability to connect, to get close to others, or to have a satisfying or successful relationship with at least one significant person in their life. The therapist guides clients toward a satisfying relationship and teaches them more effective ways of behaving. The more clients are able to connect with people, the greater chance they have to experience happiness. LO1

Few clients understand that their problem, which is unhappiness, results from the way they are choosing to behave. What they do know is that they feel a great deal of pain or that they are unhappy because they have been sent for counseling by someone with authority who is not satisfied with their behavior—typically a court official, a school administrator, an employer, a spouse, or a parent. Reality therapists recognize that clients choose their behaviors as a way to deal with the frustrations caused by unsatisfying relationships.

Glasser (2003) maintained that clients should not be labeled with a diagnosis except when it is necessary for insurance purposes. From Glasser's perspective, diagnoses are descriptions of the behaviors people choose in their attempt to deal with the pain and frustration that is endemic to their unsatisfying present relationships. Labeling these ineffective behaviors as mental illness is inaccurate. Glasser limits the term *mental illness* to conditions such as Alzheimer's disease, epilepsy, head trauma, and brain infections—conditions associated with tangible brain damage. Because these people are suffering from a brain abnormality, Glasser's view is that they should be treated primarily by neurologists. Wubbolding tempers these principles, advising counselors to follow standard practice and the standard of care regarding diagnosis and use of psychiatric medications.

Reality therapy is based on choice theory as it is explained in several of Glasser's (1998, 2001, 2003) books. (In this chapter, the discussion of Glasser's ideas pertains to these three books, unless otherwise specified.) **Choice theory** is the theoretical basis for reality therapy; it explains why and how we function. **Reality therapy** provides a delivery system for helping individuals take more effective control of their lives. If choice theory is the highway, reality therapy is the vehicle delivering the product (Wubbolding, 2011a). Therapy consists mainly of helping and sometimes teaching clients to make more effective choices as they deal with the people they need in their lives. It is essential for the therapist to establish a satisfying relationship with clients as a prerequisite for effective therapy. Once this relationship is developed, the skill of the therapist as listener and teacher assumes a central role.

Reality therapy has been used in a variety of settings. The approach is applicable to counseling, social work, education, crisis intervention, corrections and rehabilitation, institutional management, and community development. Reality therapy is popular in schools, state mental health hospitals, halfway houses, and alcohol and drug abuse centers. Many of the military clinics that treat substance abusers use reality therapy as their preferred therapeutic approach.

Visit CengageBrain.com or watch the DVD for the video program for Chapter 11, *Theory and Practice of Counseling and Psychotherapy: The Case of Stan and Lecturettes*. I suggest that you view the brief lecture for each chapter prior to reading the chapter.

Key Concepts

View of Human Nature

Choice theory posits that we are not born blank slates waiting to be *externally motivated* by forces in the world around us. Rather, we are born with five genetically encoded needs that drive us all our lives: *survival*, or self-preservation; *love and belonging; power*, or inner control; *freedom*, or independence; and *fun*, or enjoyment. Each of us has all five needs, but they vary in strength. For example, we all have a need for love and belonging, but some of us need more love than others. Choice theory is based on the premise that because we are by nature social creatures we need to both receive and give love. Glasser (2001, 2005) believes the need *to love and to belong* is the primary need because we need people to satisfy the other needs. It is also the most difficult need to satisfy because we must have a cooperative person to help us meet it. LO2

Our brain functions as a control system. It continually monitors our feelings to determine how well we are doing in our lifelong effort to satisfy these needs. Whenever we feel bad, one or more of these five needs is unsatisfied. Although we may not be aware of our needs, we know that we want to feel better. Driven by pain, we try to figure out how to feel better. Reality therapists teach clients choice theory, sometimes subtly and indirectly, so clients can identify unmet needs and try to satisfy them.

Choice theory teaches that we do not satisfy our needs directly. Beginning shortly after birth and continuing all our lives, we keep close track of anything we do that feels very good. We store information inside our minds and build a file of wants, called our **quality world**, which is at the core of our life. It is our personal Shangri-la—the world we would like to live in if we could. It is completely based on our wants and needs, but unlike the needs, which are general, it is very specific. The quality world consists of specific images of people, activities, events, beliefs, possessions, and situations that fulfill our needs (Wubbolding, 2000, 2011a). In our quality world we develop an inner **picture album** of specific wants as well as precise ways to satisfy these wants. We are attempting to behave in a way that gives us the most effective control over our lives. Some pictures may be blurred, and the therapist's role is to help the client clarify them. Pictures exist in priority for most people, yet clients may have difficulty identifying their priorities. Part of the process of reality therapy is assisting clients in prioritizing their wants and uncovering what is most important to them (Wubbolding, 2011a).

People we are closest to and most enjoy being with are the most important component of our quality world, and we most want to connect with these people. Those who enter therapy may have no one in their quality world or, more often, may have someone in their quality world whom they are unable to relate to in a satisfying way. For therapy to have a chance of success, a therapist must be the kind of person that clients would consider putting in their quality world. Getting into the clients' quality world is the art of therapy. It is from this relationship with the therapist that clients begin to learn how to get close to the people they need.

Choice Theory Explanation of Behavior

Choice theory explains that all we ever do from birth to death is behave, and, LO3 with some exceptions, everything we do is chosen or at least generated from within ourselves. Every total behavior is our best attempt to get what we want to satisfy our needs. **Total behavior** teaches that all behavior is made up of four inseparable but distinct components—*acting, thinking, feeling,* and *physiology*—that necessarily accompany all of our actions, thoughts, and feelings. Choice theory emphasizes thinking and acting, which makes this a general form of cognitive behavior therapy. The primary emphasis is on what the client is doing and how the doing component influences the other aspects of total behavior. Behavior is purposeful because it is designed to close the gap between what we want and what we perceive we are getting. Specific behaviors are always generated from this discrepancy. Our behaviors come from the inside, and thus we choose our destiny.

From Glasser's perspective, to speak of being depressed, having a headache, being angry, or being anxious implies passivity and lack of personal responsibility, and it is inaccurate. It is more accurate to think of these as parts of total behaviors and to use the verb forms *depressing, headaching, angering,* and *anxietying* to describe them. It is more accurate to think of people depressing or angering themselves rather than having the behaviors thrust upon them from the outside world. When people choose misery by developing a range of "paining" behaviors, it is because these are the best behaviors they are able to devise at the time, and these behaviors often get them what they want.

When a reality therapist starts teaching choice theory, the client will often protest and say, "I'm suffering, don't tell me I'm choosing to suffer like this." As painful as depressing is, the therapist explains that people do not choose pain and suffering directly; rather, it is an unchosen part of their total behavior. The behavior of the person is the best effort, ineffective as it is, to satisfy needs.

Robert Wubbolding (personal communication, April 4, 2015) has added a new idea to choice theory. He believes that behavior is a language and that we send messages by what we are doing. The purpose of behavior is to influence the world to get what we want. Therapists ask clients what messages they are sending to the world by way of their actions: "What message do you want others to get?" "What message are others getting whether or not you intended to send them?" By considering the messages clients send to others, counselors can help clients indirectly gain a greater appreciation of messages they unintentionally send to others.

Characteristics of Reality Therapy

LO4

The role of meaningful relationships in fostering emotional health is receiving increased attention in contemporary **reality therapy**, which quickly focuses on the unsatisfying relationship or the lack of a relationship. Clients may complain of not being able to keep a job, not doing well in school, or not having a meaningful relationship. When clients complain about how other people are causing them pain, reality therapists ask clients to consider how effective their choices are, especially as these choices affect their relationships with significant people in their lives. Choice theory teaches that talking about what clients cannot control is of minimal value; the emphasis is on what clients *can* control in their relationships. The basic axiom of choice theory, which is crucial for clients to understand, is that "the only person you can control is yourself."

Reality therapists spend little time listening to complaining, blaming, and criticizing, for these are the most ineffective behaviors in our behavioral repertoire. What do reality therapists focus on? Here are some underlying characteristics of reality therapy.

Emphasize Choice and Responsibility Reality therapists see clients as being responsible for their own choices as they have more control of their behavior than they often believe. This does not mean people should be blamed or punished, unless they break the law, but it does mean the therapist never loses sight of the fact that clients are responsible for what they do. Choice theory changes the focus of responsibility to choice and choosing.

Reality therapists deal with people "as if" they have choices. Therapists focus on those areas where clients have choice, for doing so gets them closer to the people they need. For example, being involved in meaningful activities, such as work, is a good way to gain the respect of other people, and work can help clients fulfill their need for power. It is very difficult for adults to feel good about themselves if they don't engage in some form of meaningful activity. As clients begin to feel good about themselves, it is less necessary for them to continue to choose ineffective and self-destructive behaviors.

Reject Transference Reality therapists strive to be themselves in their professional work. By being themselves, therapists can use the relationship to teach clients how to relate to others in their lives. Glasser contends that transference is a way that both therapist and client avoid being who they are and owning what they are doing right now. It is unrealistic for therapists to go along with the idea that they are anyone but themselves. Assume the client claims, "I see you as my father or mother and this is why I'm behaving the way I am." In such a situation a reality therapist is likely to say clearly and firmly, "I am not your mother, father, or anyone but myself." Wubbolding (personal communication, April 4, 2015) states that he discusses this issue with clients in a detailed manner.

Keep the Therapy in the Present Some clients come to counseling convinced that they must revisit the past if they are to be helped. Many therapeutic models teach that to function well in the present people must understand and revisit their past. Glasser (2001) disagrees with this assumption and contends that whatever mistakes were made in the past are not pertinent now. An axiom of choice theory is that the past may have contributed to a current problem but that the past is never the problem. To function effectively, people need to live and plan in the present and take steps to create a better future. We can only satisfy our needs in the present.

The reality therapist does not totally reject the past. If the client wants to talk about past successes or good relationships in the past, the therapist will listen because these may be repeated in the present. Reality therapists will devote only enough time to past failures to assure clients that they are not rejecting them. As soon as possible, therapists tell clients, "What has happened is over; it can't be changed. The more time we spend looking back, the more we avoid looking forward." Wubbolding states, "history is not destiny" (personal communication, April 4, 2015). Although the past has propelled us to the present, it does not have to determine our future. We are free to make choices, even though our external world limits our choices (Wubbolding, 2011b).

Avoid Focusing on Symptoms In traditional therapy a great deal of time is spent focusing on symptoms by asking clients how they feel and why they are obsessing. Focusing on the past "protects" clients from facing the reality of unsatisfying present relationships, and focusing on symptoms does the same thing. Whether people are depressing or paining, they tend to think that what they are experiencing is happening to them. They are reluctant to accept the reality that their suffering is due to the total behavior they are choosing. Their symptoms can be viewed as the body's way of warning them that the behavior they are choosing is not satisfying their basic needs. The reality therapist spends as little time as he or she can on the symptoms because they will last only as long as they are needed to deal with an unsatisfying relationship or the frustration of basic needs.

According to Glasser, if clients believe that the therapist wants to hear about their symptoms or spend time talking about the past, they are more than willing to comply. Engaging in long journeys into the past or exploring symptoms results in lengthy therapy. Glasser (2005) maintains that almost all symptoms are caused by a present unhappy relationship. By focusing on present problems, especially interpersonal concerns, therapy can generally be shortened considerably.

Challenge Traditional Views of Mental Illness Choice theory rejects the traditional notion that people with problematic physical and psychological symptoms are mentally ill. Wubbolding (personal communication, April 4, 2015) takes a firm stand on using the *DSM-5* in creative ways and adhering to standard practice, which includes diagnosing mental disorders. Glasser (2003), however, has warned people to be cautious of psychiatry, which can be hazardous to both one's physical and mental health. He criticizes the traditional psychiatric establishment for relying heavily on the *DSM-5* (American Psychiatric Association, 2013) for both diagnosis and treatment. Glasser (2003) challenges the traditionally accepted views of mental illness and treatment by the use of medication, especially the widespread use of psychiatric drugs that often results in negative side effects both physically and psychologically. Wubbolding (personal communication, April 4, 2015) emphasizes that reality therapy is a mental health system rather than a remediating system. He incorporates the Ericksonian principle that "people don't have problems, they have solutions that have not worked." By reframing diagnostic categories and negative behaviors, the counselor helps clients perceive their behaviors in a very different light, which facilitates the search for more effective solutions and choices.

The Therapeutic Process

Therapeutic Goals

A primary goal of contemporary reality therapy is to help clients get connected or reconnected with the people they have chosen to put in their quality world. In addition to fulfilling this need for love and belonging, a basic goal of reality therapy is to help clients learn better ways of fulfilling all of their needs, including achievement, power or inner control, freedom or independence, and fun. The basic human needs serve to focus treatment planning and setting both short- and long-term goals. Reality therapists assist clients in making more effective and responsible choices related to their wants and needs.

In many instances, clients come voluntarily for therapy, and these clients are the easiest to help. However, another goal entails working with an increasing number of involuntary clients who may actively resist the therapist and the therapy process. These individuals often engage in violent behavior, addictions, and other kinds of antisocial behaviors. It is essential for counselors to do whatever they can to connect with involuntary clients. If the counselor is unable to make a connection, there is no possibility of providing significant help. If the counselor *can* make a connection, the goal of teaching the client how to fulfill his or her needs can slowly begin.

Therapist's Function and Role

Therapy is often considered as a mentoring process in which the therapist **LO5** is the teacher and the client is the student. Reality therapists teach clients how to engage in self-evaluation, which is done by raising the question, "Is what you are

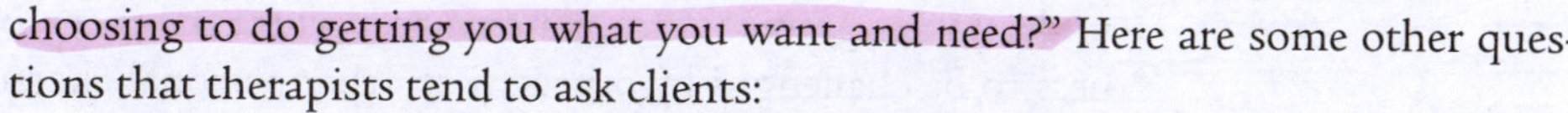

choosing to do getting you what you want and need?" Here are some other questions that therapists tend to ask clients:

- How would you most like to change your life?
- What do you want in your life that you are not getting?
- What would you have in your life if you were to change?
- What do you have to do now to make the changes happen?

The role of the reality therapist is not to make the evaluation for clients but to challenge clients to examine what they are doing. Reality therapists assist clients in evaluating their own behavioral direction, specific actions, wants, perceptions, level of commitment, possibilities for new directions, and action plans. Clients then decide what to change and formulate a plan to facilitate the desired changes. The outcome is better relationships, increased happiness, and a sense of inner control over their life (Wubbolding, 2011b).

It is the job of therapists to convey the idea that no matter how bad things are there is hope. If therapists are able to instill this sense of hope, clients feel that they are no longer alone and that change is possible. The therapist functions as an advocate, someone who is on the client's side. Together they creatively address a range of concerns and options.

Client's Experience in Therapy

Clients are not expected to backtrack into the past or get sidetracked into talking about symptoms. Neither will much time be spent talking about feelings separate from the acting and thinking that are part of the total behaviors over which clients have direct control. The emphasis is on actions. When clients change what they are doing, they often change how they are feeling and thinking.

Reality therapists will gently, but firmly challenge clients. They often ask clients questions such as these: "Is what you are choosing to do bringing you closer to the people you want to be closer to right now?" "Is what you are doing getting you closer to a new person if you are presently disconnected from everyone?" These questions are part of the self-evaluation process, which is the cornerstone of reality therapy.

Clients can expect to experience some urgency in therapy. Time is important, as each session may be the last. Clients should be able to say to themselves, "I can begin to use what we talked about today in my life. I am able to bring my present experiences to therapy as my problems are in the present, and my therapist will not let me escape from that fact."

Relationship Between Therapist and Client

Reality therapy emphasizes an understanding and supportive relationship, or therapeutic alliance, which is the foundation for effective outcomes. The therapist's skill in establishing a trusting relationship is critical. It is also important that the client perceives the therapist as being skilled and knowledgeable. Although the therapeutic relationship is paramount, it is not an end in itself, and it is not automatically curative or healing (Wubbolding, 2011a).

For involvement between the therapist and the client to occur, the counselor must have certain personal qualities, including warmth, sincerity, congruence, understanding, acceptance, concern, respect for the client, openness, and the willingness to be challenged by others. (For other personal characteristics, see Chapter 2.) Wubbolding (2011a, 2011b; 2015a) identifies specific ways for counselors to create a climate that leads to involvement with clients. Some of these ways entail using attending behavior, listening to clients, suspending judgment, doing the unexpected, using humor appropriately, being oneself as a counselor, engaging in facilitative self-disclosure, listening for metaphors in the client's mode of self-expression, listening for themes, summarizing and focusing, allowing consequences, allowing silence, and being an ethical practitioner. For therapeutic interventions to work effectively, a fair, firm, friendly, and trusting environment is necessary. Once involvement has been established, the counselor assists clients in gaining a deeper understanding of the consequences of their current behavior.

Application: Therapeutic Techniques and Procedures

The Practice of Reality Therapy

LO6

The practice of reality therapy can best be conceptualized as the *cycle of counseling* (Wubbolding, 2015a), which consists of two major components: (1) creating the counseling environment and (2) implementing specific procedures that lead to changes in behavior. The art of counseling is to weave these components together in ways that lead clients to evaluate their lives and decide to move in more effective directions.

How do these components blend in the counseling process? The cycle of counseling begins with creating a working relationship with clients and proceeds through an exploration of clients' wants, needs, and perceptions. Clients explore their total behavior and make their own evaluation of how effective they are in getting what they want. If clients decide to try new behavior, they make plans that will lead to change, and they commit themselves to those plans. The cycle of counseling includes following up on how well clients are doing and offering further consultation as needed.

The concepts of reality therapy may seem simple as they are presented here, but being able to translate these principles into therapeutic practice takes considerable skill and creativity (Wubbolding, 2007, 2011b). All certified reality therapy counselors are grounded in the same principles, but the manner in which these principles are applied varies depending on the counselor's style and personal characteristics. These principles are applied in a progressive manner, but they should not be thought of as discrete and rigid categories. The art of practicing reality therapy involves far more than following procedures in a step-by-step, cookbook fashion. With choice theory in the background of practice, the counselor tailors the counseling to what each client presents. Although the counselor is prepared to work in a way that is meaningful to the client, the move toward satisfying relationships remains in the foreground.

Wubbolding has played a major role in the development of reality therapy and has extended the practice of reality therapy through development of the WDEP system (Wubbolding, 2009). I especially value Wubbolding's contributions to teaching reality therapy and to conceptualizing therapeutic procedures. His ideas render choice theory practical and useable by counselors, and his system provides a basis for conceptualizing and applying the theory. The *Student Manual* that accompanies this textbook contains Wubbolding's (2015a) chart, which diagrams the WDEP model. It describes coaching, managing, supervising, and parenting and highlights issues and tasks to be accomplished throughout the cycle of counseling. The following sections are based on material from various sources (Glasser, 1992, 1998, 2001; Wubbolding, 1988, 1991, 2000, 2007, 2011a, 2011b, 2013, 2015a; 2015c; Wubbolding et al., 1998, 2004).

The Counseling Environment

The practice of reality therapy rests on the assumption that a supportive and challenging environment allows clients to begin making life changes. The therapeutic relationship is the foundation for effective practice; if this is lacking, there is little hope that the system can be successfully implemented. Counselors who hope to create a therapeutic alliance strive to avoid arguing, attacking, accusing, demeaning, blaming, bossing, criticizing, finding fault, coercing, encouraging excuses, holding grudges, instilling fear, or giving up easily (Wubbolding, 2011a, 2011b, 2015a). In a short period of time, clients generally begin to appreciate the caring, accepting, noncoercive choice theory environment. It is from this mildly confrontive yet always caring environment that clients learn to create the satisfying environment that leads to successful relationships. In this coercion-free atmosphere, clients feel free to be creative and to begin to try new behaviors.

Procedures That Lead to Change

Reality therapists operate on the assumption that we are motivated to change (1) when we are convinced that our present behavior is not meeting our needs and (2) when we believe we can choose other behaviors that will get us closer to what we want. Reality therapists begin by asking clients what they want from therapy. Therapists take the mystery and uncertainty out of the therapeutic process. They also inquire about the choices clients are making in their relationships.

In the first session a skilled therapist looks for and defines the wants of the client. The therapist also looks for a key unsatisfying present relationship—usually with a spouse, a child, a parent, or an employer. The therapist might ask, "Whose behavior can you control?" This question may need to be asked several times during the next few sessions to deal with the client's resistance to looking at his or her own behavior. The emphasis is on encouraging the client to focus on what he or she can control.

When clients begin to realize that they can control only their own behavior, therapy is under way. The rest of therapy focuses on how clients can make better choices. There are more choices available than clients realize, and the therapist explores these possible choices. Clients may be stuck in misery, blaming, and the past, but they can choose to change—even if the other person in the relationship does not change. Wubbolding (2011a) points out that clients can learn they are not at the mercy of others, are not victims, are capable of gaining a sense of inner control, and have a range of choices open to them. In short, clients in reality therapy often acquire a sense of hope for a better future.

Reality therapists explore the tenets of choice theory with clients, helping them identify basic needs, discovering their quality world, and, finally, helping clients understand that they are choosing the total behaviors that are their symptoms. In every instance when clients make a change, it is their choice. With the therapist's help, clients learn to make better choices than they did when they were on their own. Through choice theory, clients can acquire and maintain successful relationships.

The "WDEP" System

Wubbolding (2000, 2015a, 2015c) uses the acronym WDEP to describe key procedures in the practice of reality therapy. The WDEP system can be used to help clients explore their *wants*, possible things they can *do*, opportunities for *self-evaluation*, and design *plans* for improvement (Wubbolding, 2007, 2011a, 2011b, 2015b, 2015c). Grounded in choice theory, the WDEP system assists people in satisfying their basic needs. Each of the letters refers to a cluster of strategies: W = wants, needs, and perceptions; D = direction and doing; E = self-evaluation; and P = planning. These strategies are designed to promote change. Let's look at each one in more detail.

Wants (Exploring Wants, Needs, and Perceptions) Reality therapists assist clients in discovering their wants and hopes. All wants are related to the five basic needs. The key question asked is, "What do you want?" Through the therapist's skillful questioning, clients are assisted in defining what they want from the counseling process and from the world around them. It is useful for clients to define what they expect and want from the counselor and from themselves. Part of counseling consists of exploring the "picture album," or **quality world**, of clients and how their behavior is aimed at moving their perception of the external world closer to their inner world of wants.

Clients are given the opportunity to explore every facet of their lives, including what they want from their family, friends, and work. Furthermore, this exploration of wants, needs, and perceptions should continue throughout the counseling process as clients' pictures change.

Here are some useful questions to help clients pinpoint what they want:

- If you were the person that you wish you were, what kind of person would you be?
- What would your family be like if your wants and their wants matched?
- What would you be doing if you were living as you want to live?
- Do you really want to change your life?
- What is it you want that you don't seem to be getting from life?
- What do you think stops you from making the changes you would like?

Wubbolding and Brickell (2009) and Gerdes, Wubbolding, and Wubbolding (2012, p. 51) now include questions focused on perceptions:

- How do you look at the situation?
- Where do you see your control?

People have a great deal more control than they often perceive, and these questions help clients move from a sense of external control to a sense of internal control. This line of questioning sets the stage for applying other procedures in reality therapy. It is an art for counselors to know *what* questions to ask, *how* to ask them, and *when* to ask them. Relevant questions help clients gain insights and arrive at plans and solutions. Although well-timed, open-ended questions can help clients identify their counseling goals, excessive questioning can result in resistance and defensiveness. In this phase of counseling, clients begin to commit to making changes in their behavior.

Direction and Doing The focus on the present is characterized by the key question asked by the reality therapist: "What are you doing?" Even though problems may be rooted in the past, clients need to learn how to deal with them in the present by learning better ways of getting what they want. Problems must be solved either in the present or through a plan for the future. The therapist's challenge is to help clients make more need-satisfying choices.

Early in counseling it is essential to discuss with clients the overall direction of their lives, including where they are going and where their behavior is taking them. This exploration is preliminary to the subsequent evaluation of whether it is a desirable direction. The therapist holds a mirror before the client and asks, "What do you see for yourself now and in the future?" It often takes some time for this reflection to become clearer to clients so they can verbally express their perceptions.

Reality therapy focuses on gaining awareness of and changing current total behavior. To accomplish this, reality therapists focus on questions like these: "What are you doing now?" "What did you actually do yesterday?" "What did you want to do differently this past week?" "What stopped you from doing what you said you wanted to do?" "What will you do tomorrow?"

Listening to clients talk about feelings can be productive, but only if it is linked to what they are doing. When an emergency light on the car dashboard lights up, the driver is alerted that something is wrong and that immediate action is necessary to remedy a problem. In a similar way, when clients talk about problematic feelings, most reality therapists affirm and acknowledge these feelings. Rather than focusing mainly on these feelings, however, reality therapists encourage clients to take action by changing what they are doing and thinking. It is easier to change what we are doing and thinking than to change our feelings. From a choice theory perspective, discussions centering on feelings, without strongly relating them to what people are doing and thinking, are counterproductive.

Self-Evaluation **Self-evaluation** is the cornerstone of reality therapy procedures. "Conducting a searching and fearless self-evaluation is the royal road to behavioral change" (Wubbolding, 2015c, p. 860). Clients are asked to make the following self-evaluation: "Does your present behavior have a reasonable chance of getting you what you want now, and will it take you in the direction you want to go?" This evaluation involves the client examining behavioral direction, specific actions, wants, perceptions, new directions, and plans (Wubbolding, 2011b, 2015b). Wubbolding believes that clients often present a problem with a significant relationship, which is at the root of much of their dissatisfaction. The counselor can help clients evaluate their behavior by asking this question: "Is your current behavior bringing you closer to people important to you or is it driving you further apart?" Through skillful questioning, the counselor helps clients determine if what they are doing is helping them.

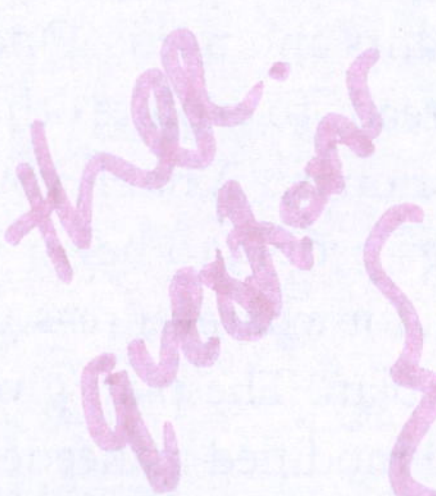

Artful questioning assists clients in evaluating their present behavior and the direction this is taking them. Wubbolding (2000, 2011a, 2015b) suggests questions like these:

- Is what you are doing helping or hurting you?
- Is what you are doing now what you want to be doing?
- Is your behavior working for you?
- Is there a healthy congruence between what you are doing and what you believe?
- Is what you are doing against the rules?
- Is what you want realistic or attainable?
- Does it help you to look at it that way?
- Is it really true that you have no control over your situation?
- How committed are you to the therapeutic process and to changing your life?
- After carefully examining what you want, does it appear to be in your best interests and in the best interest of others?

Asking clients to evaluate each component of their total behavior is a major task in reality therapy. It is the counselor's task to assist clients in evaluating the quality of their actions and to help them make responsible choices and devise effective plans.

Individuals will not change until they first decide that a change would be more advantageous. Without an honest self-assessment, it is unlikely that clients will change. Reality therapists are relentless in their efforts to help clients conduct explicit self-evaluations of each behavioral component. When therapists ask a depressing client if this behavior is helping in the long run, they introduce the idea of choice to the client. The process of evaluation of the doing, thinking, feeling, and physiological components of total behavior is within the scope of the client's responsibility.

Reality therapists may be directive with certain clients at the beginning of treatment to help clients recognize that some behaviors are not effective. In working with clients who are in crisis, for example, it is sometimes necessary to suggest straightforwardly what will work and what will not. Other clients, such as alcoholics and children of alcoholics, need direction early in the course of treatment, for they often do not have the thinking behaviors in their control system to be able to make consistent evaluations of when their lives are seriously out of effective control. These clients are likely to have blurred pictures and, at times, to be unaware of what they want or whether their wants are realistic. As they grow and continue to interact with the counselor, they learn to make evaluations with less and less help from the counselor (Wubbolding, 2011a; Wubbolding & Brickell, 2005).

Planning and Action Much of the significant work of the counseling process involves helping clients identify specific ways to fulfill their wants and needs. Once clients determine what they want to change, they are generally ready to explore other possible behaviors and formulate an action plan. The key question is, "What is your plan?" The process of creating and carrying out plans enables people to begin to gain effective control over their lives. If the plan does not work, for whatever reason, the counselor and client work together to devise a different plan. The plan gives the client a starting point, a toehold on life, but plans can be modified as needed.

Throughout this planning phase, the counselor continually urges the client to be willing to accept the consequences for his or her own choices and actions. Not only are plans discussed in light of how they can help the client personally, but plans are also designed in terms of how they are likely to affect others in the client's life.

Wubbolding (2000, 2007, 2011a, 2011b, 2013, 2015b) discusses the central role of planning and commitment. The culmination of the cycle of counseling rests with a plan of action. Although planning is important, it is effective only if the client has made a self-evaluation and determined that he or she wants to change a behavior. Wubbolding uses the acronym SAMIC to capture the essence of a good plan: simple, attainable, measurable, immediate, involved, controlled by the planner, committed to, and consistently done. Wubbolding contends that clients gain more effective control over their lives with plans that have the following characteristics:

- The plan is within the limits of the motivation and capacities of the client. Skillful counselors help clients identify plans that involve greater need-fulfilling payoffs. Clients may be asked, "What plans could you make now that would result in a more satisfying life?"
- Good plans are simple and easy to understand. They are realistically doable, positive rather than negative, dependent on the planner, specific, immediate, and repetitive. Although they need to be specific, concrete, and measurable, plans should be flexible and open to revision as clients gain a deeper understanding of the specific behaviors they want to change.
- The plan involves a positive course of action, and it is stated in terms of what the client is willing to do. Even small plans can help clients take significant steps toward their desired changes.
- Counselors encourage clients to develop plans that they can carry out independently of what others do. Plans that are contingent on others lead clients to sense that they are not steering their own ship but are at the mercy of the ocean.
- Effective plans are repetitive and, ideally, are performed daily.
- Plans are carried out as soon as possible. Counselors can ask the question, "What are you willing to do today to begin to change your life?"
- Plans involve process-centered activities. For example, clients may plan to do any of the following: apply for a job, write a letter to a friend, take a yoga class, substitute nutritious food for junk food, devote two hours a week to volunteer work, or take a vacation that they have been wanting.
- Before clients carry out their plan, it is a good idea for them to evaluate it with their therapist to determine whether it is realistic and attainable and whether it relates to what they need and want. After the plan has been carried out in real life, it is useful to evaluate it again and make any revisions that may be necessary.
- To help clients commit themselves to their plan, it is useful for them to firm it up in writing.

Resolutions and plans are empty unless there is a commitment to carry them out. It is up to clients to determine how to take their plans outside the restricted world of therapy and into the everyday world. Effective therapy can be the catalyst that leads to self-directed, responsible living.

Asking clients to determine what they want for themselves, to make a self-evaluation, and to follow through with action plans includes assisting them in determining how intensely they are willing to work to attain the changes they desire. Commitment is not an all-or-nothing matter; it exists in degrees. Wubbolding (2007, 2011a, 2011b) maintains that it is important for a therapist to ask about clients' level of commitment, or how much they are willing to work to bring about change. This communicates in an implicit way to clients that they have within them the power to take charge of their lives. It is essential that those clients who are reluctant to make a commitment be helped to express and explore their fears of failing. Clients are helped by a therapist who does not easily give up believing in their ability to make better choices, even if they are not always successful in completing their plans. In his workshops, Wubbolding often mentions this axiom of reality therapy: "To fail to plan is to plan to fail."

Application to Group Counseling

With the emphasis on connection and interpersonal relationships, reality therapy is well suited for various kinds of group counseling. Groups provide members with many opportunities for exploring ways to meet their needs through the relationships formed within the group. In particular, the WDEP system can be applied to helping group members satisfy their basic needs. If members talk about their past experiences or make excuses for their current behavior, the group leader redirects them to what they are presently doing. From the very beginning of a group, the members can be asked to take an honest look at what they are doing and to clarify whether their behavior is getting them what they say they want. Once group members get a clearer picture of what they have in their life now and what they want to be different, they can use the group as a place to explore alternative courses of behavior. LO7

This model lends itself to expecting the members to carry out homework assignments between the group meetings. However, it is the members, with the help of the leader, who evaluate their own behavior and decide whether they want to change some aspect of their life. Members also take the lead in deciding what kinds of homework tasks they will set for themselves as a way to achieve their goals. Group leaders often meet with resistance if they make poorly timed suggestions and plans for how the members should best live. To their credit, reality therapists continue asking the members to evaluate for themselves whether what they are doing is getting them what they want. If the members concede that what they are doing is not working for them, their resistance is much more likely to melt, and they tend to be more open to trying different behaviors.

Once the members make some changes, reality therapy provides the structure for them to formulate specific plans for action and to evaluate their level of success. Feedback from the members and the leader can help individuals design realistic and attainable plans. Considerable time is devoted during the group sessions for developing and implementing plans. If people do not carry out a plan, it is important to discuss with them what stopped them. Perhaps they set their goals unrealistically high, or perhaps there is a discrepancy between what they *say* they want to change and the steps they are willing to take to bring about change.

I also like reality therapy's insistence that change will not come by insight alone; rather, members have to begin doing something different once they determine that their behavior is not working for them. I am skeptical about the value of catharsis as a therapeutic vehicle unless the release of pent-up emotions is eventually put into some kind of cognitive framework and is followed up with an action plan. In the groups that I facilitate, group members are challenged to look at the futility of waiting for others to change. I ask members to assume that the significant people in their life may never change, which means that they will have to take a more active stance in shaping their own destiny. I appreciate the emphasis of reality therapy on teaching clients that the only life they can control is their own and the focus placed on helping group members change their own patterns of acting and thinking.

For a more detailed discussion of reality therapy in groups, see Corey (2016, chap. 15).

Choice Theory/Reality Therapy From a Multicultural Perspective

Strengths From a Diversity Perspective

The core principles of choice theory and reality therapy have much to offer in the area of multicultural counseling. In cross-cultural therapy it is essential that counselors respect the differences in worldview between themselves and their clients. Counselors demonstrate their respect for the cultural values of their clients by helping them explore how satisfying their current behavior is both to themselves and to others. Once clients make this assessment, they can formulate realistic plans that are consistent with their cultural values. It is a further sign of respect that the counselor refrains from deciding what specific behaviors should be changed. Through skillful questioning on the counselor's part, clients from diverse ethnic backgrounds can be helped to determine the degree to which they have become acculturated into the dominant society. Is it possible for them to find a balance, retaining their ethnic identity and values while integrating some of the values and practices of the dominant group? Again, the counselor does not determine this balance for clients, but works with them to arrive at their own answers. With this focus on thinking and acting rather than on exploring feelings, many clients are less likely to display resistance to counseling. LO8

Wubbolding (2007, 2011a, 2011b) asserts that the principles underlying choice theory are universal, which makes choice theory applicable to all people. We are all members of the same species and have the same genetic structure; therefore, relationships are the problem in all cultures. All of us have internal needs, we all make choices, and we all seek to influence the world around us. Putting the principles of choice theory into action demands creativity, sensitivity to cultures and individuals, and flexibility in implementing the procedures of reality therapy. Reality therapy principles and procedures need to be applied differently in various cultures and must be adapted to the psychological and developmental levels presented by individuals (Wubbolding, 2011b).

Based on the assumption that reality therapy must be modified to fit the cultural context of people other than North Americans, Wubbolding (2000, 2011a) and Wubbolding and colleagues (1998, 2004) have expanded the practice of reality therapy to multicultural situations. Wubbolding's experience in conducting reality therapy workshops in Japan, Taiwan, Hong Kong, Singapore, Korea, India, Kuwait, Morocco, Malta, Romania, Australia, Slovenia, Croatia, and countries in western Europe has taught him the difficulty of generalizing about other cultures. Growing out of these multicultural experiences, Wubbolding (2000) has adapted the cycle of counseling in working with Japanese clients. He points to some basic language differences between Japanese and Western cultures. North Americans are inclined to say what they mean and to be assertive. In Japanese culture, assertive language is not appropriate between a child and a parent or between an employee and a supervisor. Ways of communicating are more indirect. To ask some Japanese clients what they want may seem harsh and intrusive to them. Because of these style differences, adaptations may be needed to make the practice of reality therapy relevant to Japanese clients:

- The reality therapist's tendency to ask direct questions may need to be softened, with questions being raised more elaborately and indirectly. It may be a mistake to ask individualistic questions built around whether specific behaviors meet the client's need. Confrontation should be done only after carefully considering the context.
- There is no exact Japanese translation for the word "plan," nor is there an exact word for "accountability," yet both of these are key dimensions in the practice of reality therapy and are central to Japanese culture.
- In asking clients to make plans and commit to them, Western counselors do not settle for a response of "I'll try." Instead, they tend to push for an explicit pledge to follow through. In Japanese culture, however, the counselor is likely to accept "I'll try" as a firm commitment.

These are but a few illustrations of ways in which reality therapy might be adapted to non-Western clients. Even though all people have the same basic needs (survival, love and belonging, power, freedom, and fun), the way these needs are expressed depends largely on the cultural context. In working with culturally diverse clients, the therapist must allow latitude for a wide range of acceptable behaviors to satisfy these needs. As with other theories and the techniques that flow from them, flexibility is a foremost requirement.

A key strength of reality therapy is that it provides clients with tools to make the changes they desire. This is especially true during the planning phase, which is central to the process of reality therapy. The focus is on positive steps that can be taken, not on what cannot be done. Clients identify those problems that are causing them difficulty, and these problems become the targets for change. This type of specificity and the direction that is provided by an effective plan are certainly assets in working with diverse client groups. Reality therapy is an open system that allows for flexibility in application based on the needs of culturally diverse individuals.

Reality therapy needs to be used artfully and to be applied in different ways with a variety of clients. Many of its principles and concepts can be incorporated in a dynamic and personal way in the style of counselors, and there is a basis for integrating these concepts with most of the other therapeutic approaches covered in this book.

Shortcomings From a Diversity Perspective

One of the shortcomings of reality therapy in working with clients from certain ethnic groups is that it may not take fully into account some very real environmental forces that operate against them in their everyday lives. Counselors need to be broadly trained and be able to compensate for the limitation inherent in all counseling theories, Reality therapy gives only limited attention to helping people address environmental and social problems. Discrimination, racism, sexism, homophobia, heterosexism, ageism, negative attitudes toward disabilities, and other social injustices are unfortunate realities, and these forces do limit many individuals in getting what they want from life. It is important that therapists acknowledge that people do not choose to be the victims of various forms of discrimination and oppression. If therapists do not accept these environmental restrictions or are not interested in bringing about social justice as well as individual change, clients are likely to feel misunderstood. There is a danger that some reality therapists may overstress the ability of these clients to take charge of their lives and not pay enough attention to systemic and environmental factors that can limit the potential for choice.

Some reality therapists may make the mistake of too quickly or too forcefully stressing the ability of their clients to take charge of their lives. On this point, Wubbolding (2013) maintains that because of oppression and discrimination, some people have fewer choices available to them, yet they *do* have choices. Although focusing on choices clients do have is useful, I believe clients may need to talk about the ways their choices are restricted by environmental circumstances. Therapists would do well to consider how both they and their clients could take even small steps toward bringing about societal changes, as do feminist therapists (see Chapter 12).

Another shortcoming associated with reality therapy is that some clients are very reluctant to directly verbally express what they need. Their cultural values and norms may not reinforce them in assertively asking for what they want. In fact, they may be socialized to think more of what is good for the social group than of their individual wants. In working with people with these values, counselors must "soften" reality therapy somewhat. If reality therapy is to be used effectively with clients from other cultures, the procedures must be adapted to the life experiences and values of members from various cultures (Wubbolding, 2000, 2011a; Wubbolding et al., 2004).

Reality Therapy Applied to the Case of Stan

As a reality therapist, I am guided by the key concepts of choice theory to identify Stan's behavioral dynamics, to provide a direction for him to work toward, and to teach him about better alternatives for achieving what he wants. Stan has not been effective in getting what he needs—a satisfying relationship.

Stan has fallen into a victim role, blaming others, and looking backward instead of forward. Initially, he wants to tell me about the negative aspects of his life, which he does by dwelling on his major symptoms: depression, anxiety, inability to sleep, and other psychosomatic symptoms. I listen carefully to his concerns, but I hope he will come to realize that he has many options for *acting* differently. I operate on the premise that therapy will offer the opportunity to explore with Stan what he can build on—successes, productive times, goals, and hopes for the future.

After creating a relationship with Stan, I am able to show him that he does not have to be a victim of his past unless he chooses to be, and I assure him that he has rehashed his past miseries enough. As counseling progresses, Stan learns that even though most of his problems did indeed begin in childhood, there is little he can do now to undo his childhood. However, he can adopt a different perspective on his past experiences and the meaning they hold for him today. He eventually realizes that he has a great deal of control over what he can do for himself now.

I have Stan describe how his life would be different if he were symptom free. I am interested in knowing what he would be doing if he were meeting his needs for belonging, achievement, power, freedom, and fun. I explain to him that he has an ideal picture of what he wants his life to be, yet he does not possess effective behaviors for meeting his needs. I talk to him about all of his basic psychological needs and how this type of therapy will teach him to satisfy them in effective ways. I also explain that his *total behavior* is made up of acting, thinking, feeling, and physiology. Even though he says he hates feeling anxious most of the time, Stan learns that much of what he is doing and thinking is directly leading to his unwanted feelings and physiological reactions. When he complains of feeling depressed much of the time, anxious at night, and overcome by panic attacks, I let him know that I am more interested in what he is *doing* and *thinking* because these are the behavioral components that can be directly changed.

I help Stan understand that his *depressing* is the feeling part of his choice. Although he may think he has little control over how he feels, over his bodily sensations, and over his thoughts, I want him to understand that he can begin to take different action, which is likely to change his depressing experience. I frequently ask this question, "Is what you are choosing to do getting you what you want?" I lead Stan to begin to recognize that he does have *some*, indirect control over his feelings. This is best done after he has made some choices about doing something different from what he has been doing. At this point he is in a better place to see that the choice to take action has contributed to feeling better, which helps him realize that he has some power to change.

Stan tells me about the pictures in his head, a few of which are becoming a counselor, acting confident in meeting people, thinking of himself as a worthwhile person, and enjoying life. Through therapy he makes the evaluation that much of what he is doing is not getting him closer to these pictures or getting him what he wants. After he decides that he is willing to work on himself to be different, the majority of time in the sessions is devoted to making plans and discussing their implementation. We both focus on the specific steps he can take right now to begin the changes he would like.

As Stan continues to carry out plans in the real world, he gradually begins to experience success. When he does backslide, we talk about this and together help him fine tune his plan. I am not willing to give up on Stan even when he does not make major progress, and Stan lets me know that my support is a source of real inspiration for him to keep working on himself.

I teach Stan about choice theory and encourage him to do some reading that can stimulate his thinking about changes in his life. Stan brings some of what he is learning from his reading into his sessions, and eventually he is able to achieve some of his goals. The combination of working with a reality therapist, his reading, and his willingness to put what he is learning into practice by engaging in new behaviors in the world assist him in replacing ineffective choices with life-affirming choices. Stan comes to accept that he is the only person who can control his destiny.

Questions for Reflection

- If Stan complains of feeling depressed most of the time and wants you to "fix" him, how would you proceed?
- If Stan persists, telling you that his mood is getting the best of him and that he wants you to work with his physician in getting him on an antidepressant drug, what would you say or do?
- What are some of Stan's basic needs that are not being met? What action plans can you think of to help Stan find better ways of getting what he wants?
- Would you be inclined to do a checklist on alcoholism with Stan? Why or why not? If you determined that he was addicted to alcohol, would you insist that he attend a program such as Alcoholics Anonymous in conjunction with therapy with you? Why or why not?
- What interventions would you make to help Stan explore his total behavior?

Visit CengageBrain.com or watch the DVD *for Theory and Practice of Counseling and Psychotherapy: The Case of Stan and Lecturettes*, Session 9 (reality therapy), for a demonstration of my approach to counseling Stan from this perspective. This session deals with assisting Stan in forming an action plan.

Reality Therapy Applied to the Case of Gwen*

Gwen has lived for a long time believing therapy was for weak and crazy people, and certainly not for an African American woman of strong faith. Gwen has not been in therapy before, and I need to establish a climate of trust and respect so she feels it is safe to express her feelings. As we develop our working alliance, I help Gwen understand that she has already begun the change process by doing something different and coming in for therapy.

Therapist: Tell me what you want your life to be like? [*Inquiry about her quality world*]

Gwen: I want to feel appreciated and relaxed. I don't want work to be the most important aspect of my life. I want to feel strong and healthy in my body. I am tired of feeling achy and overwhelmed. I want to feel respected and loved by my family. I am tired of feeling like I have to do everything alone.

Therapist: Think back over this past week and tell me something you did to move yourself closer to the life you want.

Gwen: I took a beginner's yoga class, and it helped me relax. I didn't feel as achy the next day, so I signed up for an eight-week class. [*Gwen tries out a new behavior*]

Therapist: That's great. I am proud of you! You sound committed.

Gwen has gotten into the habit of letting life happen to her rather than taking the steering wheel and driving in the direction of her hopes and dreams. For real change to occur, Gwen must "do" something different. The yoga class is a good start for her plan.

Therapist: Now think about what you can do differently in another aspect of your life to move closer to your ideal scene.

Gwen: I feel like I am doing a lot already.

Therapist: You are doing a lot. Is that what you want to continue to do? [*A reality check*]

Gwen: I know I need to prioritize my life and put myself first. I know I take on too much. It's a bad habit, and it is wearing me out. [*Self-evaluation*]

Therapist: How well is taking on the role of a martyr working for you? [*No criticism is implied*]

Gwen: Not at all! I watched my grandmother wear herself out taking care of the entire family. I need to pull back.

I will not abandon Gwen if she does not meet her goals or if her plans are unsuccessful. I do challenge her in an empathic and supportive manner to discuss what she can do to get back on course. I stay committed to Gwen and help her make the small incremental changes that she desires.

Therapist: What are you willing to do differently this week that you can commit to?

Gwen: I can make sure I get more time for myself. I will definitely do the yoga at least twice a week to help me with my flexibility and stress management. I can set up Meals on Wheels for my mom. That could really free up some of my time.

Therapist: Those are good first steps. You are on your way to creating a healthy action plan for your life. Taking these steps can help relieve some of the anxiety you have been feeling. I will check in with you next week at the beginning of our session to see how well you carried out your plan.

Before she leaves, I encourage Gwen to consider reading a book I suggest. We will build on her action plan at the next session.

Therapist: Do you think you could find time to read a short book that is easy to read? [*I give her Wubbolding's book,* A Set of Directions for Putting and Keeping Yourself Together] This will give you some ideas on action steps you might want to take in other areas of your life. Start by picking just one or two of the activities that you think you can use.

Gwen: What other changes do you think I should make?

The success of our work together depends not only on my skill and ability to establish a relationship with Gwen but also on her willingness to take responsibility

*Dr. Kellie Kirksey writes about her ways of thinking and practicing using a reality therapy perspective and applying this model to Gwen.

for her behavior and her willingness to make alternative choices. I want to support Gwen as she discovers her own answers to that question. I refrain from telling her what to choose for her action plan. Her success must come from her own evaluation of what needs to shift in her life.

Therapist: This is your journey, and you know best what changes could be beneficial for you. Keep your hands on the steering wheel of your life and notice how you begin to feel once you get in the habit of saying, "yes" to your health and well-being. Take things slowly. There is no need to rush and make a lot of changes right away.

I hope Gwen will notice a difference in her anxiety level as she begins to implement her action plan. As she feels more comfortable with taking charge of her life, I believe that she will be able to tackle more significant changes, such as setting clear boundaries with her adult children. Gwen is beginning to venture down a new road. She is stepping up to a new level of personal responsibility and is moving away from being a passive victim of her life circumstances.

Questions for Reflection

- What interventions did the therapist make to help Gwen evaluate her current behavior?
- Assess the usefulness of this question in working with Gwen: "Is what you're doing helping you get what you want?"
- To what degree do you think Gwen is ready to make an action plan?
- How would you describe the interaction and the relationship between the therapist and Gwen.

Summary and Evaluation

Summary

LO9

The reality therapist functions as a teacher, a mentor, and a model, confronting clients in ways that will help them evaluate what they are doing and whether their behavior is fulfilling their basic needs without harming themselves or others. The heart of reality therapy is learning how to make better and more effective choices and gain more effective control. People take charge of their lives rather than being the victims of circumstances beyond their control. Practitioners of reality therapy focus on what clients are *able and willing to do in the present* to change their behavior. Practitioners teach clients how to make significant connections with others. Therapists continue to ask clients to evaluate the effectiveness of what they are choosing to do to determine if better choices are possible.

The practice of reality therapy weaves together two components, the counseling environment and specific procedures that lead to changes in behavior. This therapeutic process enables clients to move in the direction of getting what they want. The goals of reality therapy include behavioral change, better decision making, improved significant relationships, enhanced living, and more effective satisfaction of all the psychological needs.

Contributions of Choice Theory/Reality Therapy

Among the advantages of reality therapy are its relatively short-term focus and the fact that it deals with conscious behavioral problems. Insight and awareness are not enough; the client's self-evaluation, a plan of action, and a commitment to following through are the core of the therapeutic process. I like the focus on strongly encouraging clients to engage in self-evaluation, to decide if what they are doing is working or not, and to commit themselves to doing what is required to make changes they desire. The existential underpinnings of choice theory are a major strength of this approach, which accentuates taking responsibility for what we are doing. People are not viewed as being hopelessly and helplessly depressed. Instead, people are viewed as doing the best they can, or making the choices they hope will result in fulfilling their needs. With the emphasis on responsibility and choice, individuals can acquire a sense of self-direction and empowerment.

Too often counseling fails because therapists have an agenda for clients. The reality therapist helps clients conduct a searching inventory of what they are doing. If individuals determine that their present behavior is not working, they are then much more likely to consider acquiring a new behavioral repertoire. Many clients approach counseling with a great deal of skepticism. Reality therapy can be used effectively with individuals who manifest reluctance and ambivalence to change. For example, in working with people with addictions, reality therapy strategies can be used to help clients evaluate where their behavior is leading them and to provide clients with options to bring about positive changes in their behavior. Reality therapy has been effectively used in addiction treatment and recovery programs for more than 30 years (Wubbolding & Brickell, 2005). With these populations, it would be inappropriate to embark on long-term therapy that delves into unconscious dynamics and an intensive exploration of one's past. Addressing what clients are presently doing and asking clients to evaluate what they want to change fits well in various settings. Reality therapy is an effective, short-term approach, often requiring 10 sessions or less, that can enable people to make life changes without prolonged therapy.

Limitations and Criticisms of Choice Theory/Reality Therapy

From my perspective, one of the main limitations of reality therapy is that it does not give adequate emphasis to the role of the following aspects of the counseling process: the role of insight, the unconscious, the power of the past and the effect of traumatic experiences in early childhood, the therapeutic value of dreams, and the place of transference. Because reality therapy focuses almost exclusively on consciousness, it does not take into account factors such as repressed conflicts and the power of the unconscious in influencing how we think, feel, behave, and choose.

Dealing with dreams is not part of the reality therapist's repertoire. According to Glasser (2001), it is not therapeutically useful to explore dreams, an idea which I find limiting in this approach. For him, spending time discussing dreams can be a defense used to avoid talking about one's behavior and, thus, is time wasted. From my perspective, dreams are powerful tools in helping people recognize their internal conflicts. I believe that there is richness in dreams, which can be a shorthand message of clients' central struggles, wants, hopes, and visions of the future. Asking clients to recall, report, share, and relive their dreams in the here and now of the therapeutic session can help unblock them and can pave the way for clients to take a different course of action.

Similarly, I have a difficult time accepting Glasser's view of transference as a misleading concept, for I find that clients are able to learn that significant people in their lives have a present influence on how they perceive and react to others. To rule out an exploration of transference that distorts accurate perception of others seems narrow in my view.

I believe reality therapy is vulnerable to the practitioner who assumes the role of an expert in deciding for others how life should be lived and what constitutes responsible behavior. Wubbolding (2013) admits that reality therapy can lend itself to fixing problems and imposing a therapist's values on clients, especially by inexperienced or inadequately trained counselors. Wubbolding adds that it is not the therapist's role to evaluate the behavior of clients. Generally, clients need to engage in a process of courageous self-evaluation to determine how well certain behaviors are working and what changes they may want to make. It is critical that therapists monitor any tendency to judge clients' behavior, but instead to do all that is possible to get clients to make their own evaluation of their behavior.

Finally, reality therapy makes use of concrete language and simple concepts. This can erroneously be viewed as a simple approach that does not require a high level of competence. Because reality therapy is easily understood, it might appear to be easy to implement. However, the effective practice of reality therapy requires practice, supervision, and continuous learning (Wubbolding, 2007, 2011a). Competent reality therapists have a thorough understanding of choice theory and have mastered the art of applying reality therapy procedures to working with diverse clients with a range of clinical problems.

Self-Reflection and Discussion Questions

1. What do you think of reality therapy's focus on present behavior and lack of attention to past events?
2. How could you help your clients to make a self-evaluation to determine if what they are doing is working for them?
3. If you are working with involuntary clients, how could you use choice theory and reality therapy principles to increase their cooperation with the therapy program?
4. What potential do you see in combining reality therapy with some of the other therapies you have studied? Which theory would you most be inclined to integrate with reality therapy?
5. Think of a behavior you would like to change. What are some steps you would take in creating an action plan to get what you want?

Where to Go From Here

Visit CengageBrain.com or watch the DVD for *Integrative Counseling: The Case of Ruth and Lecturettes*, Session 8 (behavioral focus in counseling), to see how I attempt to assist Ruth in specifying concrete behaviors that she will target for change. In this session I am drawing heavily from principles of reality therapy in assisting Ruth to develop an action plan to make the changes she desires.

Free Podcasts for ACA Members

You can download ACA Podcasts (prerecorded interviews) at www.counseling.org; click on the Resource button and then the Podcast Series. For Chapter 11, Reality Therapy, look for these podcasts:

Podcast ACA088, "Reality Therapy, Choice Theory: What's the Difference?" by Dr. Robert Wubbolding.

Podcast ACA194, "William Glasser: A Retrospective and Why His Groundbreaking Work Will Continue to Matter in Professional Counseling," by Dr. Robert Wubbolding.

Other Resources

DVDs offered by the American Psychological Association that are relevant to this chapter include the following:

Wubbolding, R. (2007). *Reality Therapy*

Psychotherapy.net is a comprehensive resource for students and professionals that offers videos and interviews on demonstrating reality therapy working with addictions, adults, and children. New video and editorial content is made available monthly. DVDs relevant to this chapter are available at www.psychotherapy.net and include the following:

Wubbolding, R. (2000). *Reality Therapy* (Psychotherapy With the Experts Series)

Wubbolding, R. (2000). *Reality Therapy for Addictions* (Brief Therapy for Addictions Series)

Wubbolding, R. (2002). *Reality Therapy With Children* (Child Therapy With the Experts Series)

Wubbolding, R. (2014). *Choice Theory/Reality Therapy Demonstration: Couple Counseling "Elroy and Judy"* (Center for Reality Therapy)

The programs offered by William Glasser International are designed to teach the concepts of choice theory and the practice of reality therapy. More than 7,800 therapists have completed the training in reality therapy and choice theory. The institute offers a certification process, which starts with a three-day introductory course known as "basic training" in which participants are involved in discussions, demonstrations, and role playing. For those wishing to pursue more extensive training, the institute offers a five-part sequential course of study leading to certification in reality therapy, which includes basic training, a basic practicum, advanced training, an advanced practicum, and a certification week. This 18-month training program culminates in a Certificate of Completion. For complete information on this program, contact:

William Glasser International
www.wglasserinternational.org

The Center for Reality Therapy provides training in the principles of choice theory/reality therapy applied to counseling, coaching, classroom management, addictions, corrections, and families. Robert Wubbolding is a frequent presenter at state, national, and international conferences. The three-day workshops apply to certification in reality therapy.

Center for Reality Therapy
Robert E. Wubbolding, EdD, Director
www.realitytherapywub.com

The *International Journal of Choice Theory and Reality Therapy* (online journal) focuses on concepts of internal control psychology, with particular emphasis on research, development, and practical applications of choice theory and reality therapy principles in various settings. For more information about this journal, contact:

Tom Parish, PhD, Editor
Email: Parishts@gmail.com

Recommended Supplementary Readings

Counseling With Choice Theory: The New Reality Therapy (Glasser, 2001) represents the author's latest thinking about choice theory and develops the existential theme that we choose all of our total behaviors. Case examples demonstrate how choice theory principles can be applied in helping people establish better relationships.

Reality Therapy (Wubbolding, 2011a) updates and extends previous publications on choice theory and reality therapy. As a part of the APA theories of psychotherapy series, this is a well-written and comprehensive overview of reality therapy and choice theory.

Case Approach to Counseling and Psychotherapy (Corey, 2013) illustrates how prominent reality therapists Drs. William Glasser and Robert Wubbolding would counsel Ruth from their different perspectives of choice theory and reality therapy.

Feminist Therapy 12

Coauthored by Barbara Herlihy and Gerald Corey*

LEARNING OBJECTIVES

1. Identify the key figures and their contributions to the development of feminist therapy.
2. Examine the different forms of feminist therapy.
3. Differentiate between the six interrelated principles associated with feminist therapy.
4. Identify the therapeutic goals that guide feminist therapists in their work.
5. Understand the roles of gender and power in the therapeutic process.
6. Describe the importance of an egalitarian relationship and how collaboration works in the therapy process.
7. Identify standard feminist therapy procedures such as therapist self-disclosure, reframing, relabeling, gender-role analysis and intervention, power analysis and intervention, and social action.
8. Understand the value of empowerment as a basic strategy.
9. Describe the role of social action in therapy.
10. Examine the application of feminist principles to group work.
11. Understand the relationship between feminist therapy and multicultural therapy.
12. Identify the key contributions and main limitations of feminist therapy.

*I invited a colleague and friend, Barbara Herlihy, a professor of counselor education at the University of New Orleans, to coauthor this chapter. We have coauthored two books (Herlihy & Corey, 2015a, 2015b), which seems like a natural basis for collaboration on a project that we both consider valuable.

Some Contemporary Feminist Therapists

Feminist therapy does not have a single founder. Rather, it has been a collective effort by many. We have selected a few individuals who have made significant contributions to feminist therapy for inclusion here, recognizing full well that many other equally influential scholar-practitioners could have appeared in this space. Feminist therapy is truly founded on a theory of inclusion.

Jean Baker Miller / Carol Zerbe Enns / Oliva M. Espín / Laura S. Brown

JEAN BAKER MILLER (1928–2006) was a clinical professor of psychiatry at Boston University School of Medicine and director of the Jean Baker Miller Training Institute at the Stone Center, Wellesley College. She wrote *Toward a New Psychology of Women* (1986) and coauthored *The Healing Connection: How Women Form Relationships in Therapy and in Life* (Miller & Stiver, 1997) and *Women's Growth in Connection* (Jordan et al., 1991). Miller collaborated with diverse groups of scholars and colleagues on the development of relational-cultural theory. She made important contributions toward expanding this theory and exploring new applications to complex issues in psychotherapy and beyond, including issues of diversity, social action, and workplace change.

Courtesy, Jean Baker Miller Training Institute

Jean Baker Miller

CAROLYN ZERBE ENNS is Professor of Psychology and participant in the Women's Studies and Ethnic Studies programs at Cornell College in Mt. Vernon, Iowa. Enns became interested in feminist therapy while she was completing her PhD in Counseling Psychology at the University of California, Santa Barbara. She devotes much of her work to exploring the profound impact feminist theory has on the manner in which therapists implement therapeutic practices. Enns most recent efforts are directed toward articulating the importance of multicultural feminist therapy, exploring the practice of feminist therapy around the world (especially in Japan), and writing about multicultural feminist pedagogies. Two of her recent edited book projects reflect these priorities: *Oxford Handbook of Feminist Multicultural Counseling Psychology* (co-edited with Elizabeth Nutt Williams, 2013) and *Psychological Practice With Women: Guidelines, Diversity, Empowerment* (co-edited with Joy K. Rice and Roberta L. Nutt, 2015), which focuses on applying the APA (2007) Guidelines to diverse groups of women.

Courtesy of Carolyn Zerbe Enns

Carolyn Zerbe Enns

OLIVA M. ESPÍN is Professor Emerita in the Department of Women's Studies at San Diego State University and at the California School of Professional Psychology of Alliant International University. A native of Cuba, she did her undergraduate work in psychology at the Universidad de Costa Rica and received her PhD from the University of Florida, specializing in counseling and therapy with women from different cultures and in Latin American Studies. She is a pioneer in the theory and practice of feminist therapy with women from different cultural backgrounds and has done extensive research, teaching, and training on multicultural issues in psychology. Espín has published on psychotherapy with Latinas, women immigrants and refugees, the sexuality of Latinas, language in therapy with fluent bilinguals, and training clinicians to work with multicultural populations. Espín co-edited *Refugee Women and Their Mental Health: Shattered Societies, Shattered Lives* (Cole, Espín, & Rothblum, 1992)

Courtesy of Dr. Oliva Espín, Professor Emerita of Women's Studies, San Diego State University

Oliva M. Espín

and has written *Latina Healers: Lives of Power and Tradition* (1996), *Latina Realities: Essays on Healing, Migration, and Sexuality* (1997), and *Women Crossing Boundaries: A Psychology of Immigration and the Transformation of Sexuality* (1999), which is based on a study of women immigrants from all over the world.

LAURA S. BROWN is a founding member of the Feminist Therapy Institute, an organization dedicated to the support of advanced practice in feminist therapy, and a member of the theory workgroup at the National Conference on Education and Training in Feminist Practice. She has written several books considered core to feminist practice in psychotherapy and counseling, and *Subversive Dialogues: Theory in Feminist Therapy* (1994) is considered by many to be the foundation book addressing how theory informs practice in feminist therapy. Her most recent book is *Feminist Therapy* (2010). Brown has made particular contributions to thinking about ethics and boundaries and the complexities of ethical practice in small communities. Her current interests include feminist forensic psychology and the application of feminist principles to treatment of trauma survivors.

Courtesy of Dr. Laura S. Brown

Laura S. Brown

Introduction

The broad scope of feminist thought goes far beyond gender considerations. LO1 Multicultural and social justice issues are equally relevant to the therapeutic enterprise, and, as you will see, feminist counseling/therapy puts intersections of gender and other social identities, social location, and power at the core of the therapeutic process. **Feminist counseling** is built on the premise that it is essential to consider the social, cultural, and political context that contributes to a person's problems in order to understand that person. This perspective has significant implications for the development of counseling theory and for how practitioners intervene with diverse client populations.

Feminist psychotherapy is a philosophical orientation that lends itself to an integration of feminist, multicultural, and social justice concepts with a variety of psychotherapy approaches (Enns, Williams, & Fassinger, 2013). A central concept in feminist therapy is the importance of understanding and acknowledging psychological oppression and the constraints imposed by the sociopolitical status to which women, underrepresented, and marginalized individuals have been relegated. A **feminist perspective** offers a unique approach to understanding the roles that women and men with diverse social identities and experiences have been socialized to accept and to bringing this understanding into the therapeutic process. The socialization of women with multiple social identities inevitably affects their identity development, self-concept, goals and aspirations, and emotional well-being (Gilligan, 1982; King, 2013; Turner & Werner-Wilson, 2008). As Natalie Rogers (1995) has observed, socialization patterns tend to result in women giving away their power in relationships, often without being aware of it. Feminist counseling keeps knowledge about gender socialization, sexism, and related "isms" in mind in the work with all. For some women, ethnicity or race may be experienced as a more salient identity than gender; for others, identity and the oppression associated with gender may be fused with racism.

The majority of clients in counseling are women, and the majority of psychotherapy practitioners at the master's level are women. However, most theories that are traditionally taught—including all of the other theories in this book—were founded by White males from Western (American or European) cultures, with only Adler taking a pro-feminist stance in early theory development. The need for a theory that evolves from the thinking and experiencing of women seems self-evident. Theories are developed from the experiences of the "developer," and feminist theory is the first therapeutic theory to emerge from a collective effort by women to include the experiences of multiple voices.

Feminist therapists have challenged male-oriented assumptions regarding what constitutes a mentally healthy individual. Early feminist therapy efforts focused on valuing women's experiences, recognizing political realities, and understanding the unique issues facing women within a patriarchal system. Contemporary practice keeps the impact of gender socialization in the forefront when working with clients. Current feminist practice also emphasizes a diverse approach that includes an understanding of multiple oppressions, power, privilege, multicultural competence, social justice, and the oppression of all marginalized people (American Psychological Association, 2007; Enns & Byars-Winston, 2010). Feminists believe that gender cannot be considered apart from other identities related to race, ethnicity, socioeconomic class, age, and sexual orientation. Recent developments relevant to social justice in psychology have led to an integration of key themes of multiculturalism and feminism (Enns, Williams, & Fassinger, 2013). The contemporary version of feminist therapy and the multicultural and social justice perspectives to counseling practice have a great deal in common (Crethar, Torres Rivera, & Nash, 2008). All these approaches provide a systemic perspective based on understanding the social context of clients' lives and are aimed toward affecting social change as well as individual change.

Visit CengageBrain.com or watch the video program on Chapter 12, *Theory and Practice of Counseling and Psychotherapy: The Case of Stan and Lecturettes*. I suggest that you view the brief lecture for each chapter prior to reading the chapter.

History and Development

The history of feminist therapy is relatively brief. No single individual can be identified as the founder of this approach, reflecting a central theme of feminist collaboration. Feminist therapy was developed by several feminist therapists, all of whom shared the same vision—to improve mental health treatment for women (Evans & Miller, 2016). The beginnings of feminism (often referred to as the first wave) can be traced to the late 1800s, but the women's movement of the 1960s (the second wave) laid the foundation for the development of feminist therapy. In the 1960s women began uniting their voices to express their dissatisfaction with the limiting and confining nature of traditional female roles. Consciousness-raising groups, in which women came together to share their experiences and perceptions, helped individual women become aware that they were not alone. A sisterhood developed, and some of the services that evolved from women's collective desires to improve society included shelters for battered women, rape crisis centers, and women's health and reproductive health centers.

Believing that personal counseling was a legitimate means to effect change, feminist therapists viewed therapy as a partnership between equals and built mutuality and collaboration into the therapeutic process. They took the stance that therapy needed to move away from an intrapsychic perspective on psychopathology (in which the sources of a woman's unhappiness reside within her) to a focus on understanding the social, political, and cultural forces in society that damage, oppress, and constrain girls and women, as well as boys and men.

Gilligan's (1982) work on the development of a morality of care in women, and the work of Miller (1986) and the Stone Center scholars in developing the *self-in-relation* model (now called the "relational-cultural" model) were influential in the evolution of a feminist personality theory. New theories emerged that honored the relational and cooperative dimensions of women's experiencing (Enns, 1991, 2000, 2004). Feminist therapists began to formally examine the relationship of feminist theory to traditional psychotherapy systems, and integrations with various existing systems were proposed. Some counselors identified themselves as psychoanalytic feminist therapists or as Adlerian-feminist counselors, to mention just two possible integrations.

By the 1980s feminist group therapy had changed dramatically, becoming more diverse as it focused increasingly on specific problems and issues such as body image, abusive relationships, eating disorders, incest, and other forms of sexual abuse (Enns, 1993). The feminist philosophies that guided the practice of therapy also became more diverse.

The variety within feminist theories provides a range of different but overlapping perspectives from which to work (Enns & Sinacore, 2001). Brown (2010) defines feminist therapy as a postmodern, technically integrative approach that emphasizes the analysis of gender, power, and social location as strategies for facilitating change. Feminist therapists, both male and female, believe that understanding and confronting gender-role stereotypes and power are central to therapeutic practice and that addressing a client's problems requires adopting a sociocultural perspective: namely, understanding the impact of the society and culture in which a client lives.

Key Concepts

Constructs of Feminist Theory

LO2

Worell and Remer (2003) describe the constructs of feminist theory as being gender fair, flexible-multicultural, interactionist, and life-span-oriented. **Gender-fair approaches** explain differences in the behavior of women and men in terms of socialization processes rather than on the basis of our "innate" natures, thus avoiding dichotomized stereotypes in social roles and interpersonal behavior. A **flexible-multicultural perspective** uses concepts and strategies that apply equally to individuals and groups regardless of age, race, culture, gender, ability, class, or sexual orientation. The **interactionist** view contains concepts specific to the thinking, feeling, and behaving dimensions of human experience and accounts for contextual and environmental factors. A **life-span perspective** assumes that human development is a lifelong process and that personality and behavioral changes can occur at any time rather than being fixed during early childhood.

Feminist Perspective on Personality Development

Feminist therapists emphasize that societal gender-role expectations profoundly influence a person's identity from the moment of birth, or even prior to birth once the sex is identified, and become deeply ingrained in adult personality. Gilligan (1977) recognized that theories of moral development were based almost exclusively on research with White males. Gilligan was the first to recognize that male development was presented as the norm and that development of women, though different, was judged by male norms. As a result of her studies on women's moral and psychosocial development, Gilligan came to believe women's sense of self and morality is based in issues of responsibility and care for other people and is embedded in a cultural context. She posited that the concepts of connectedness and interdependence—virtually ignored in male-dominated developmental theories—are central to women's development.

Kaschak (1992) used the term *engendered lives* to describe her belief that gender is the organizing principle in people's lives. She has studied the role gender plays in shaping the identities of females and males and believes the masculine defines the feminine. In most cultures what is considered attractive in a female is defined by men in that culture. For instance, because men pay great attention to women's bodies in Western society, women's appearance is given tremendous importance. It is easy to see how this perspective gets reified in both eating disorders and various forms of depression. Men, as the dominant group, also define and determine the roles that women play. Because women occupy a subordinate position, to survive and thrive in society they must be able to interpret the needs and behaviors of the dominant group. To that end, women have developed "women's intuition" and have included in their gender schema an internalized belief that women are less important than men.

Females are raised in a culture grounded in sexism, and understanding and acknowledging internalized oppression is central in feminist work. Like all marginalized groups, women are bicultural. They share their own culture with other women and also have a deep understanding of the male culture that perpetuates patriarchy. Men, on the other hand, do not have to understand the culture of women in order to survive.

Feminist practitioners remind us that traditional gender stereotypes of women are still prevalent in cultures throughout the world. They teach their clients that uncritical acceptance of traditional roles can greatly restrict their range of freedom. Today many women and men are resisting being so narrowly defined. Women and men in therapy learn that, if they choose to, they can experience mutual behavioral characteristics such as accepting themselves as being interdependent, giving to others, being open to receiving, thinking and feeling, and being tender and strong. Rather than being cemented to a single behavioral style, women and men who reject traditional roles are saying that they are entitled to express the complex range of characteristics that are appropriate for different situations and that they are open to their vulnerability as human beings.

Relational-Cultural Theory

Most models of human growth and development emphasize a struggle toward independence and autonomy, but feminists recognize that many women are searching for a connectedness with others as well as possibilities for autonomy. In feminist therapy, women's relational qualities are seen as strengths and as pathways for healthy growth and development, instead of being identified as weaknesses or defects.

The founding scholars of **relational-cultural theory (RCT)** have elaborated on the vital role that relationships and connectedness with others play in the lives of women (Jordan, 2010; Jordan et al,, 1991; Miller, 1986, 1991; Miller et al., 1999; Miller & Stiver, 1997; Surrey, 1991; Trepal, 2010). These scholars suggest that a woman's sense of identity and self-concept develop in the context of relationships. They describe a process of relational movement in which women move through connections, disconnections, and enhanced transformative relationships throughout their lives (Comstock et al., 2008). Therapists emphasize the qualities of authenticity and transparency that contribute to the flow of the relationship; being empathically present with the suffering of the client is at the core of treatment (Surrey & Jordan, 2012). Therapists aim to lessen the suffering caused by disconnection and isolation, increase clients' capacity for relational resilience, develop mutual empathy and mutual empowerment, and foster social justice (Jordan, 2010). According to Jordan, through mutual empathy people find that they can bring more of themselves into relationships, and in this process they become more open to learning and change. Jordan notes that RCT is not about helping people adjust to conditions; rather, this therapy is about enhancing the client's desire for connection and building networks and community. Finding growth-fostering relationships leads to a greater sense of involvement in the world and in the well-being of others. Relational-cultural therapy practitioners emphasize mutual empathy and deep respect for the client, understand how disconnections affect the individual, and create a therapeutic relationship that is healing (Surrey & Jordan, 2012). For empathy to result in healing and decreased isolation, clients must be able to feel the therapist's empathic response. As you will see, many of the techniques of feminist therapy foster mutuality, equality, relational capacities, and growth in connection.

Principles of Feminist Therapy

A number of feminist writers have articulated the interrelated and overlapping core principles that form the foundation for the practice of feminist therapy: LO3

1. *The personal is political and critical consciousness.* This principle is based on the assumption that the personal or individual problems individuals bring to counseling originate in a political and social context. For females this is often a context of marginalization, oppression, subordination, and stereotyping. Acknowledgment of the political and societal impact on an individual's life is perhaps the most fundamental tenet that lies at the core of feminist therapy.
2. *Commitment to social change.* Feminist therapies aim not only for individual change but also for societal change. A distinctive feature of feminist therapy is the assumption that direct action for social change is one of the responsibilities of therapists. Counselors who work with women survivors of sexual violence also do social justice work to educate and transform the rape culture in which we live. It is important for clients who engage in the therapy process to recognize how some of their social identities may grant them unearned privileges and advantages as

well as to recognize how they have suffered from oppression as members of a subordinate group and that they can join with others to right these wrongs. Counselors cannot help clients recognize privilege and oppression if they do not understand how these identities have affected their own lives. The goal is to advance a different vision of societal organization that frees both women and men from the constraints imposed by gender-role and social class-related expectations. This vision of counseling, which moves away from the traditional focus on change from within the individual out into the realm of social activism and societal change, distinguishes feminist therapy from other historically accepted approaches.

3. *Women's and girls' voices and ways of knowing, as well as the voices of others who have experienced marginalization and oppression, are valued and their experiences are honored.* Traditional therapies operate on androcentric, heterosexist norms embedded in White middle-class heterosexual values and describe women and other marginalized individuals as deviant. Feminist therapists replace patriarchal and other forms of "objective truth" with feminist and social justice consciousness and encourage clients to use their personal experience as a touchstone for determining what is "reality." Shifting women's experiences from being ignored and devalued to being sought after and valued is strongly encouraged by feminist therapists (Evans & Miller, 2016). When women's voices are acknowledged as authoritative, invaluable sources of knowledge, women and other marginalized people can contribute to profound change in the body politic of society.
4. *The counseling relationship is egalitarian.* Attention to power is central in feminist therapy. The **egalitarian relationship**, which is marked by authenticity, mutuality, and respect, is at the core of feminist therapy (Pusateri & Headley, 2015). Feminist therapists recognize that there is a power imbalance in the therapeutic relationship, so they strive to shift power and privilege to the voices and experiences of clients and away from themselves. An open discussion of power and role differences in the therapeutic relationship helps clients to understand how power dynamics influence both counseling and other relationships and also invites a dialogue about ways to reduce power differentials (Enns, 2004; Evans & Miller, 2016).
5. *A focus on strengths and a reformulated definition of psychological distress.* Feminist therapy has a "conflicted and ambivalent relationship" with diagnostic labeling and the "disease model" of mental illness (Brown, 2010, p. 50). Psychological distress is reframed, not as disease but as a communication about unjust systems. When contextual variables are considered, symptoms can be reframed as survival strategies. Feminist therapists talk about problems in the context of living and coping skills rather than pathology (Enns, 2004; Worell & Remer, 2003). For example, a client who is a survivor of childhood sexual abuse may present with dissociation, which is understood as a way of coping in order to survive as a child.

6. *All types of oppression are recognized along with the connections among them.* Clients can best be understood in the context of their sociocultural environments. Feminist practitioners acknowledge that social and political inequities have a negative effect on *all* people. Feminist therapists work to help individuals make changes in their lives, but they also are committed to working toward social change that will liberate all members of society from stereotyping, marginalization, and oppression. Diverse sources of oppression, not simply gender, are identified and interactively explored as a basis for understanding the concerns that clients bring to therapy. Framing clients' issues within a cultural context leads to empowerment, which can be fully realized only through social change (Evans & Miller, 2016; Worell & Remer, 2003).

The Therapeutic Process

Therapeutic Goals

According to Enns (2004), goals of feminist therapy include empowerment, valuing and affirming diversity, striving for change rather than adjustment, equality, balancing independence and interdependence, social change, and self-nurturance. A key goal of feminist therapy is to assist individuals in viewing themselves as active agents on their own behalf and on behalf of others. At the individual level, feminist and other social justice therapists work to help individuals recognize, claim, and embrace their personal power. A related goal is to help individuals come together to strengthen collective power. Through empowerment, clients are able to free themselves from the constraints of their gender-role socialization and other internalized limitations and to challenge ongoing institutional oppression. LO4

According to Worell and Remer (2003), feminist therapists help clients:

- Become aware of their own gender-role socialization process
- Identify their internalized messages of oppression and replace them with more self-enhancing beliefs
- Understand how sexist and oppressive societal beliefs and practices influence them in negative ways
- Acquire skills to bring about change in the environment
- Restructure institutions to rid them of discriminatory practices
- Develop a wide range of behaviors that are freely chosen
- Evaluate the impact of social factors on their lives
- Develop a sense of personal and social power
- Recognize the power of relationships and connectedness
- Trust their own experience and their intuition

Feminist therapists aim to empower all people to create a world of equality that is reflected at individual, interpersonal, institutional, national, and global levels (Enns & Byars-Winston, 2010). Making oppression transparent is the first step, but the ultimate goal is to replace sexism and other forms of discrimination and oppression with empowerment for all marginalized groups (Brabeck & Brabeck, 2013; Worell & Remer, 2003). Feminist counseling strives for transformation for both the individual client and society as a whole.

Therapist's Function and Role

Many therapeutic orientations articulate a belief in a therapeutic milieu that is free of biased assumptions about women and other oppressed and marginalized groups. Therapeutic orientations and counseling theories, on the whole, assert that all clients should be treated with respect. The difference between these approaches and feminist therapy is that feminist therapy is based firmly in feminist philosophy that centralizes the sociocultural context of clients' mental health status.

Theories and techniques are based on the lives and experiences of individuals (lived experiences) as well as research supporting gender and other inequities (Evans, Kincade, & Seem, 2011). Feminist therapists have shared assumptions about therapy, but they come from diverse backgrounds and have various lived experiences that may affect how techniques are applied as well as how clients are conceptualized. In *Case Approach to Counseling and Psychotherapy* (Corey, 2013, chap. 10), three feminist therapists (Drs. Evans, Kincade, and Seem) team up to demonstrate a variety of feminist interventions in their work with Ruth. They also conceptualize the case of Ruth from a feminist therapy perspective.

Feminist practitioners have integrated feminism, multiculturalism, and other social justice perspectives into their approach to therapy and into their lives. Their actions and beliefs and their personal and professional lives are congruent. They are committed to monitoring their own biases and distortions, especially the social and cultural dimensions of women's experiences. Feminist and social justice therapists are also committed to understanding oppression in all its forms—including but not limited to sexism, racism, heterosexism—and they consider the impact of oppression and discrimination on psychological well-being. They value being emotionally present for their clients, being willing to share themselves during the therapy hour, modeling proactive behaviors, and being committed to their own consciousness-raising process (Evans, Kincade, Marbley & Seem, 2005).

Feminists share common ground with Adlerian therapists in their emphasis on social equality and social interest, and with existential therapists who emphasize therapy as a shared journey, one that is life changing for both client and therapist, and with their basic trust in the client's ability to move forward in a positive and constructive manner (Bitter, Robertson, Healey, & Cole, 2009). Feminist therapists believe the therapeutic relationship should be a nonhierarchical, person-to-person relationship, and they aim to empower clients to live according to their own values and to rely on an internal (rather than external or societal) locus of control in determining what is right for them. Like person-centered therapists, feminist therapists convey their genuineness and strive for mutual empathy between client and therapist. Unlike person-centered therapists, however, feminist therapists do not see the therapeutic relationship alone as being sufficient to produce change. Insight, introspection, and self-awareness are springboards to action.

Feminist therapists share with postmodern therapists (see Chapter 13) an emphasis on the politics and power relationships in the therapy process and a concern about power relations in the world in general. Both feminist and postmodern thought asserts that psychotherapists must not replicate societal power imbalances or foster dependency in the client. Rather, therapist and client take active and equal roles, working together to determine goals and procedures. A common denominator of both feminist and postmodern approaches is the avoidance of assuming a therapist role of all-knowing expert.

Client's Experience in Therapy

Clients are partners in the therapeutic process. It is important that clients **LO5** tell their stories and give voice to their experiencing. Clients determine what they want from therapy and are the experts on their own lives. A male client, for example, may choose to explore ways in which he has been both limited and privileged by his gender-role socialization. In the safe environment of the therapeutic sessions, he may be able to fully experience emotions of sadness, tenderness, uncertainty, and empathy. As he transfers these ways of being to daily living, he may find that relationships change in his family, his social world, and at work.

Feminist practitioners recognize that gender is only one identity and source of marginalization and oppression, and they value the complex ways in which multiple identities shape a person's concerns and preferences. Worell and Remer (2003) write that clients acquire a new way of looking at and responding to their world. They add that the shared journey of empowerment can be both frightening and exciting—for both client and therapist. Clients need to be prepared for major shifts in their way of viewing the world around them, changes in the way they perceive themselves, and transformed interpersonal relationships.

Relationship Between Therapist and Client

In feminist therapy, the very structure of the client–therapist relationship **LO6** models how to identify and use power responsibly. A defining theme of the client–counselor relationship is the inclusion of clients in both the assessment and the treatment process, keeping the therapeutic relationship as egalitarian as possible. Feminist therapists clearly state their values during the informed consent process to reduce the chance of value imposition. This allows clients to make a choice regarding whether or not to work with the therapist. It also is a step in demystifying the process.

As mentioned, although there is an inherent power differential in the therapy relationship, feminist therapists are aware of ways they might abuse their own power in the therapy relationship, such as by diagnosing unnecessarily, or without the client's knowledge and input, by interpreting or giving advice, by staying aloof behind an "expert" role, or by discounting the impact the power imbalance between therapist and client has on the relationship. They work to demystify the counseling relationship by sharing with the client their own perceptions about what is going on in the relationship, by conveying clearly that the client is the expert on her or his life, and by using appropriate self-disclosure.

Application: Therapeutic Techniques and Procedures

The Role of Assessment and Diagnosis

Feminist therapists have been sharply critical of past versions of the DSM classification system (*DSM-III* through *DSM-IV-TR*), as well as of the current *DSM-5* edition (Marecek & Gavey, 2013). This critique is based on research indicating that gender, culture, and race may influence assessment of clients' symptoms (e.g., Enns, 2000; Eriksen & Kress, 2005). To the degree that conceptualization and assessment are influenced by subtle forms of sexism, racism, ethnocentrism, heterosexism, ageism, or classism, it is extremely difficult to arrive at a meaningful conceptualization, assessment, or diagnosis. LO7

From the perspective of feminist therapy, diagnoses are based on the dominant culture's view of normalcy and therefore cannot account for cultural differences (Pusateri & Headley, 2015). Feminist therapists refer to distress rather than psychopathology (Brown, 2010), and they use diagnostic labels quite carefully, if at all. They believe diagnostic labels are severely limiting for these reasons: (1) they focus on the individual's symptoms and not the social factors that cause distress and dysfunctional behavior; (2) they are part of a system developed mainly within psychiatry, an institution that reinforces dominant cultural norms and may become an instrument of oppression; (3) they may reflect the inappropriate application of power in the therapeutic relationship; (4) they can lead to an overemphasis on individual solutions rather than social change; and (5) they have the potential to dehumanize the client through labeling.

Feminist therapists believe that external factors and contextual factors are as important as internal dynamics in understanding the client's presenting problems (Evans & Miller, 2016). The feminist approach emphasizes that many symptoms can be understood as coping or survival strategies rather than as evidence of pathology (Bitter, 2008; Worell & Remer, 2003). Due to the cultural and gender limitations of diagnoses, Eriksen and Kress (2005) encourage therapists "to be tentative in diagnosing those from diverse backgrounds, and to, as a part of a more egalitarian relationship, co-construct an understanding of the problem *with* the client, rather than imposing a diagnosis *on* the client" (p. 104). Reframing symptoms as resistance to oppression and as coping skills or strategies for survival and shifting the etiology of the problem to the environment avoids "blaming the victim" for her or his problems. Assessment is viewed as an ongoing process between client and therapist and is connected to treatment interventions. In the feminist therapy process, diagnosis of distress becomes secondary to identification and assessment of strengths, skills, and resources (Brown, 2010).

The emphasis of feminist therapy is on wellness rather than disease, resilience rather than deficits, and a celebration of diverse strengths (Brabeck & Brabeck, 2013). Diagnosis, when used, results from a shared dialogue between client and therapist. The counselor is careful to review with the client any implications of assigning a diagnosis so the client can make an informed choice, and discussion focuses on helping the client understand the role of socialization and culture in the etiology of these problems.

Techniques and Strategies

Feminist therapy does not prescribe any particular set of interventions and tailors interventions to clients' strengths with the goal of empowering clients while evoking their feminist consciousness (Brown, 2010). Nonetheless, they have developed several unique techniques and have borrowed others from traditional approaches. Particularly important are consciousness-raising techniques that help women differentiate between what they have been taught is socially acceptable or desirable and what is actually healthy for them. Some of the techniques described by Worell and Remer (2003), Enns (1993, 2004), Evans, Kincade, and Seem (2011) and Evans and Miller (2016) are discussed in this section, using the case example of Alma to illustrate how these techniques might be applied.

> Alma, age 22, comes to counseling reporting general anxiety about a new job she began a month ago. She states that she has struggled with depression off and on throughout her life because of bullying as a child and rejection from much of her family after coming out as a lesbian at age 14. Alma identifies as Dominican and continues to struggle with the loss of her place within her family of origin. She now believes coming out was a selfish mistake and is trying to make amends by keeping her feelings regarding her sexual and affectional orientation hidden. Due in part to past experiences, she is worried that if she comes out to her coworkers the company might find a reason to fire her. Alma says, "I would like to cut my hair short again because it is more manageable and I also prefer to wear what is considered to be more masculine clothing, but I am worried this will cause people at work to question my femininity. I really like my job, and I worked very hard to get it. I am afraid if I show them who I really am, they won't want me there anymore."

Empowerment At the heart of feminist strategies is the goal of empowering the client. Feminist therapists work in an egalitarian manner and use empowerment strategies that are tailored to each client (Brown, 2010; Evans et al,, 2011). Alma's therapist will pay careful attention to *informed consent* issues, discussing ways Alma can get the most from the therapy session, clarifying expectations, identifying goals, and working toward a contract that will guide the therapeutic process. **LO8**

Informed consent offers a place to begin a relationship that is egalitarian and collaborative. By explaining how therapy works and enlisting Alma as an active partner in the therapeutic venture, the therapy process is demystified and Alma becomes an equal participant. Alma will learn that she is in charge of the direction, length, and procedures of her therapy. Alma's therapist might ask her, "What is the most powerful thing you could do for yourself right now?" The intent of this question is to "interrupt the trance of powerlessness" by inviting Alma to notice how power is actually available to her (Brown, 2010, p. 35). Given Alma's cultural background, it may be particularly important to address power within the therapeutic relationship because Alma may view the therapist as an expert who holds the answers she is seeking.

Self-Disclosure Feminist therapists use therapeutic self-disclosure in the best interests of the client to equalize the client–therapist relationship, to provide modeling, to normalize women's collective experiences, to empower clients, and to establish informed consent. The counselor engages in self-disclosure only when it is judged to be therapeutically helpful to the client. For example, Alma's therapist may briefly disclose her own difficulties in relating to members of her family of origin, acknowledging that at times hiding information seems important in order to keep the peace. The counselor might share how she decides when and when not to be open about her personal life. The counselor could then discuss with Alma ways in which they have both experienced cultural and social pressures to conform to a hetero-normative ideal. Alma benefits from this modeling by a woman who does not meet society's expectations for female behavior and appearance but is comfortable with the image she has developed and how it has worked for her, not against her. The counselor's disclosure would happen over time, for it is crucial that the counselor does not overshadow the client's time to explore the concerns that bring her to therapy.

Self-disclosure goes beyond sharing information and experiences; it also involves the quality of presence the therapist brings to the therapeutic sessions. Effective therapist self-disclosure is grounded in authenticity and a sense of mutuality. The therapist explains to Alma the therapeutic interventions that are likely to be employed. Alma, as an informed consumer, will be involved in evaluating how well these strategies are working and the degree to which her personal goals in therapy are being met.

Gender-Role or Social Identity Analysis A hallmark of feminist therapy, gender-role analysis assists clients in identifying the impact that their own gender-role socialization has played in shaping their values, thoughts, and behaviors (Evans & Miller, 2016). Some feminist therapists prefer the term "social identity analysis" because it reflects the importance of assessing all relevant aspects of a client's identity, including multiple memberships in both socially disempowered and privileged groups. For example, Alma identifies as a female, a lesbian, and a Dominican—all marginalized identities within the dominant culture. Social identity and gender-role analysis begins with clients identifying the societal messages they received about how women and men should be and act as well as how these messages interact with other important aspects of identity (Remer, 2013). The therapist begins by asking Alma to identify messages she has received related to sexuality, race/ethnicity, and appearance from her culture, society, her peers, the media, and her family. The therapist talks about how body image expectations differ between females and males in our culture and how they may differ in other cultures. The therapist explains how expectations related to appearance could intersect with beliefs about what it means to be gay or straight in Alma's culture, family, and society as it relates to her working environment. As Alma identifies the messages playing in her head and the voices behind those messages, she is living with a mindfulness of her internalized oppression. Alma decides what messages she would prefer to have in her mind and keeps an open awareness when the discounting messages play in her head. The goal is for Alma to adopt realistic and affirming internal messages.

Gender-Role Intervention Using this technique, the therapist responds to Alma's concern by placing it in the context of society's role expectations for women. The aim is to provide Alma with insight into the ways social issues are affecting her. Alma's therapist responds to her statement with, "Our society really focuses on sometimes unrealistic beauty ideals with females. The media bombards girls and

women with the message that they must be thin, have long strai
attractive clothing. The message is so ingrained that many girls ar
self-esteem issues related to their appearance as early as elementary
being bullied or to fit in." By placing Alma's concern in the con
expectations, the therapist gives Alma insight into how these expectations have affected her psychological condition and have contributed to her feeling depressed and anxious about judgment from others. The therapist's statement also paves the way for Alma to think more positively about her unity with other women and even to think about how she might contribute as a role model for girls and young women in the future. Alma is increasing her awareness of the strong role media play in perpetuating oversexualized images of women and how those images affect her self-esteem. Alma may decide to begin a dialogue with other women to discuss ways to create significant change.

Power Analysis Power analysis refers to the range of methods aimed at helping clients understand how unequal access to power and resources can influence personal realities. Together therapists and clients analyze how various forms of power in the dominant and subordinate group limit self-definition and well-being (Enns, 2004; Pusateri & Headley, 2015). Alma will become aware of the power difference between women and men as well as the power differences associated with sexual orientation and ethnic status in our society. Specific issues related to Alma's cultural perspective also are explored. The power analysis may focus on helping Alma identify alternate kinds of power she may exercise and learn how to challenge the gender-role messages that prohibit the exercise of that kind of power. Alma choreographs the changes she wants to make in her life. Interventions are aimed at helping Alma learn to appreciate herself as she is, regain her self-confidence based on the personality attributes she possesses, and set goals that will be fulfilling to her within the context of her cultural values.

Bibliotherapy Nonfiction books, psychology and counseling textbooks, autobiographies, self-help books, educational videos, films, and even novels can all be used as bibliotherapy resources. Reading about feminist and multicultural perspectives on common issues in women's lives (incest, rape, domestic violence, and sexual harassment) may challenge a woman's tendency to blame herself for these problems (Remer, 2013). The therapist describes a number of books that address issues of relevance to Alma, and she selects one to read over the next few weeks. Providing Alma with reading material increases knowledge and decreases the power difference between Alma and her therapist. Reading can supplement what is learned in the therapy sessions, and Alma can enhance her therapy by exploring her reactions to what she is reading. For women with diverse social identities, books, biographies, and memoirs written by women with similar or related identities can provide concrete examples of empowerment and can facilitate growth.

Assertiveness Training By teaching and promoting assertive behavior, women become aware of their interpersonal rights, transcend stereotypical gender roles, change negative beliefs, and implement changes in their daily life. Alma may learn how sexism has contributed to keeping females passive. For example, a woman behaving in an assertive way is often labeled "aggressive," but similar behavior in a man may be viewed as "assertive." Therapist and client consider what is culturally appropriate, and the client decides when and how to be assertive, balancing the potential costs and benefits of assertiveness within the ecological context relevant to the client. The therapist helps Alma evaluate and anticipate the consequences of behaving assertively, which might range from criticism to actually getting what she wants.

Through learning and practicing assertive behaviors and communication, Alma may increase her own power, which will ameliorate her depression and anxiety. Alma learns that it is her right to ask for what she wants and needs in the workplace.

Reframing and Relabeling Like bibliotherapy, therapist self-disclosure, and assertiveness training, reframing is not unique to feminist therapy. However, reframing is applied uniquely in feminist therapy. **Reframing** includes a shift from placing the problem internally and "blaming the victim" to a consideration of social factors in the environment that contribute to a client's problem. Rather than dwelling exclusively on intrapsychic factors, the focus is on examining societal or political dimensions. Alma may come to understand that her depression and anxiety are linked to social pressures to behave within hetero-normative gender-role expectations and to develop an appearance that matches these culturally and societally prescribed ideals.

Relabeling is an intervention that changes the label or evaluation applied to some behavioral characteristic. Alma can change certain labels she has attached to herself, such as being inadequate or socially unwanted because she does not conform to ideals commonly associated with femininity. An example might be that Alma is encouraged to talk about herself as a strong and healthy woman rather than as being "selfish" or too "masculine."

Social Action Social action, or social activism, is an essential quality of **LO9** feminist counseling (Enns et al., 2013; Evans et al., 2011; Evans & Miller, 2016). As clients become more grounded in their understanding of feminism, therapists may suggest that clients become involved in activities such as volunteering at a rape crisis center, lobbying lawmakers, or providing community education about gender issues. Participating in such activities can empower clients and help them see the link between their personal experiences and the sociopolitical context in which they live. Alma might decide to join and participate in organizations that are working to change societal stereotypes about female beauty expectations for women or social groups that affirm people who identify with a variety of sexual and affectional orientations. Participating in social action can increase self-esteem and a sense of personal power.

Group Work Feminist therapists often encourage their clients to make the **LO10** transition from individual therapy to a group format such as joining a support group or a political action group as soon as this is realistic (Herlihy & McCollum, 2011). Although these groups are as diverse as the women who comprise them, they share a common denominator emphasizing support for the experience of women. The literature reveals that women who join these groups eventually realize that they are not alone and gain validation for their experiences by participating in the group. These groups can provide women with a social network, decrease feelings of isolation, create an environment that encourages sharing of experiences, and help women realize that they are not alone in their experiences (Eriksen & Kress, 2005). Groups provide a place where women are valued and affirmed and where they can share and begin to critically explore the messages they have internalized about their self-worth and their place in society. The self-disclosures of both the members and the leader foster deeper self-exploration, a sense of universality, and increased levels of cohesion. Members learn to use power effectively by providing support to one another, practicing behavioral skills, considering social/political actions, and by taking interpersonal risks in a safe setting (Enns, 2004). Through their group participation, women learn that their individual experiences are frequently rooted in problems within the system. Participation in a group experience can inspire women to take up some form of social action. Indeed, a form of homework can be to carry out what women are learning in the group to bring about changes in their lives outside of the group.

Alma and her therapist will likely discuss the possibility of Alma joining a women's support group, a gay-straight alliance, or another type of group as a part of the process of terminating individual therapy. Participating in a group can enhance Alma's sense of community. She will witness the journey of personal and collective transformation and growth as she adds to her group of supporters, encouragers, and teachers. Other women can provide her with nurturance and support, and Alma will have the chance to be significant to other women as they engage in their healing process.

The Role of Men in Feminist Therapy

Men can be feminist therapists, and feminist therapy can be practiced with male clients. It is an erroneous perception that feminist therapy is conducted only by women and for women, or that feminist therapy is anti-men because it is pro-women (Evans et al., 2011; Herlihy & McCollum, 2011). Although the original feminist therapists were all women, men have now joined their ranks. Male feminist therapists are willing to understand and "own" their male privilege, confront sexist behavior in themselves and others, redefine masculinity and femininity according to other than traditional values, work toward establishing egalitarian relationships, and actively engage in and support women's efforts to create a just society.

The principles and practices of feminist psychotherapy are useful in working with male clients, individuals from diverse racial and cultural backgrounds, and people who are committed to addressing social justice issues in counseling practice (Enns, 2004; Worell & Remer, 2003). Social mandates about masculinity such as restrictive emotionality, overvaluing power and control, the sexualization of emotion, and obsession with achievement can be limiting to males (Englar-Carlson, 2014).

Female counselors who work with male clients have an opportunity to create an accepting, authentic, and safe climate in which men can reflect on their needs, choices, past and present pain, and hopes for their future. By using relational-cultural theory, female counselors provide a forum for men to consider the contexts that helped shape them (Duffey & Haberstroh, 2014). Any presenting issue of male clients can be dealt with from a feminist perspective. For a comprehensive treatment of counseling men in specialized modalities and settings, intersections of identity, and specialized populations and concerns, see Englar-Carlson, Evans, and Duffey (2014).

Feminist Therapy From a Multicultural and Social Justice Perspective

Strengths From a Diversity Perspective

LO11

Of all the theoretical approaches to counseling and psychotherapy in this book, feminist therapy has the most in common with the multicultural and social justice perspectives. Historically, multicultural approaches evolved in response to societal oppression, discrimination, and marginalization faced by people of color. Over time, the multicultural perspective has made counseling more inclusive. Contemporary counselors who infuse their work with a multicultural perspective address a wide variety of inequities that limit full participation in society. The social justice perspective in counseling aims to empower the individual as well as to confront injustice and inequality in society.

Although multicultural, feminist, and social justice counseling have been viewed as disparate models, they have many common threads (Crethar et al., 2008). All three approaches emphasize the need to promote social, political, and environmental changes within the counseling context. Practitioners of all three perspectives strive to create an egalitarian relationship in which counselor and client co-construct the client's problems from a contextual perspective and collaborate in setting goals and choosing strategies. All three approaches reject the "disease model" of psychopathology; they view clients' problems as symptoms of their experiences of living in an unjust society rather than as having an intrapsychic origin.

Feminist therapy's primary tenet, "the personal is also the political," has been embraced by the multicultural and social justice perspectives. None of the perspectives rests solely on individual change; they all emphasize direct action for social change as a part of the role of therapists. Williams and Enns (2013) encourage therapists to become activists by making a commitment to social change: "Make the political personal—understand your own history and roots and work to own your own privilege. Perhaps most important, you should choose to do social justice work *for you*" (p. 488).

Culture encompasses the sociopolitical reality of people's lives, including how the privileged dominant group (in Western societies: males, Whites, Christians, heterosexuals, and the rich) treats those who are different from them. Feminist therapists believe psychotherapy is inextricably bound to culture, and, increasingly, they are being joined by thoughtful leaders in the field of counseling practice.

Culturally competent feminist therapists look for ways to work within the context of the client's culture by exploring consequences and alternatives. They appreciate the complexities involved in changing within one's culture, but do not view culture as sacrosanct (Worell & Remer, 2003). It is important to understand and respect diverse cultures, but most cultural contexts have both positive and toxic aspects, and the toxic aspects that oppress and marginalize groups of people need to be explored. Feminist therapists are committed to taking a critical look at cultural beliefs and practices that discriminate against, subordinate, and restrict the potential of groups of individuals.

Shortcomings From a Diversity Perspective

Feminist practitioners advocate for change in the social structure, especially in the areas of inequality, power in relationships, the right to self-determination, freedom to pursue a career outside or inside the home, and the right to an education. This agenda could pose some problems when working with women who do not share these beliefs. Remer (2013) acknowledges that if therapists do not fully understand and respect the cultural values of clients from diverse groups, they run the risk of imposing their own values. Remer claims "a potential danger inherent in feminist counseling is that counselors' values will too strongly influence clients or will conflict with clients' values" (p. 404).

Being aware of the cultural context is especially important when feminist therapists work with women from cultures that endorse culturally prescribed roles that keep women in a subservient place or that are grounded in patriarchy. Consider this scenario. You are a feminist therapist working with a Vietnamese woman who is struggling to find a way to be true to her culture and also to follow her own educational and career aspirations. Your client is a student in a helping profession who is being subjected to extreme pressure from her father to return home and take care of her family. Although she wants to complete a degree and eventually help others in the Vietnamese community, she feels a great deal of guilt when she considers "selfishly" pursuing her education when her family at home needs her.

In this complex situation, the therapist is challenged to work together with the client to find a path that enables her to consider her own individual goals without ignoring or devaluing her collectivistic cultural values. The therapist's job is not to take away her pain or struggle, or to choose for the client, but to be present in such a way that the client will truly be empowered to make significant decisions. The feminist counselor must remain aware that the price may be very high if this woman chooses to go against what is culturally expected of her, and that the client is the one to ultimately decide which path to follow. As can be seen from this example, to minimize this potential shortcoming of imposing cultural values on a client, it is essential that therapists understand how their own cultural perspectives are likely to influence their interventions with culturally diverse clients. A safeguard against value imposition is for feminist therapists to clearly present their values to clients early in the course of the counseling relationship so that clients can make an informed choice about continuing this relationship (Remer, 2013).

Feminist Therapy Applied to the Case of Stan

Stan's fear of women and his gender-role socialization experiences make him an excellent candidate to benefit from feminist therapy. A therapeutic relationship that is egalitarian will be a new kind of experience for Stan.

Stan has indicated that he is willing and even eager to change. Despite his low self-esteem and negative self-evaluations, he is able to identify some positive attributes. These include his determination, his ability to articulate his feelings, and his gift for working with children. Stan knows what he wants out of therapy and has clear goals: to stop drinking, to feel better about himself, to relate to women on an equal basis, and to learn to love and trust himself and others. Operating from a feminist orientation, I will build on these strengths.

In the first session I focus on establishing an egalitarian working relationship to help Stan begin to regain his personal power. It is important that the therapeutic relationship does not replicate other relationships Stan has had with significant figures in his life. I consciously work to demystify the therapeutic process and equalize the relationship, conveying to Stan that he is in charge of the direction of his therapy. I spend time explaining my view of the therapy process and how it works.

A gender-role analysis is conducted to help Stan become aware of the influence of gender-role expectations in the development of his problems. First, I ask him to identify gender-role messages he received while growing up from his parents, teachers, the media, faith community, and peers. In his autobiography Stan has written about some of the messages his parents gave him, and this provides a natural starting point for his analysis. He remembers his father calling him "dumb" and his mother saying, "Why can't you grow up and be a man?" Stan wrote about his mother "continually harping at" his father and telling Stan how she wished she hadn't had him. He describes his father as weak, passive, and mousy in relating to his mother and remembers that his father compared him unfavorably with his siblings. Stan internalized these messages, often crying himself to sleep and feeling very hopeless.

I ask Stan to identify the damaging self-statements he makes now that are based on these early experiences. As we review his writings, Stan sees how societal messages he received about what a man "should" be were reinforced by parental messages and have shaped his view of himself today. For example, he wrote that he feels sexually inadequate. It appears that he has introjected the societal notion that men should always initiate sex, be ready for sex, and be able to achieve and sustain an erection. Stan also sees that he has already identified and written about how he wants to change those messages, as exemplified in his statements that he wants to "feel equal with others" and not "feel apologetic" for his existence and develop a loving relationship with a woman. Stan begins to feel capable and empowered as I acknowledge the important work he has already done, even before he entered therapy.

I follow this gender-role analysis with a gender-role intervention to place Stan's concerns in the context of societal role expectations.

Therapist: Indeed, it is a burden to try to live up to society's notion of what it means to be a man, always having to be strong and tough. Sometimes real strength comes through our vulnerability. Those aspects of yourself that you would like to value—your ability to experience your feelings, being good with children—are qualities society tends to label as "'feminine."

Stan: [*replies wistfully*] Yeah, it would be a better world if women could be strong without being seen as domineering and if men could be sensitive and nurturing without being seen as weak.

Therapist: Are you sure that's not possible? Have you ever met a woman or a man who was like that?

Stan ponders for a minute and then with some animation describes the college professor who taught his Psychology of Adjustment class. Stan saw her as very accomplished and strong, but also as someone who empowered him by encouraging him to find his own voice through writing his autobiography. He also remembers a male counselor at the youth rehabilitation facility where he spent part of his adolescence as a man who was strong as well as sensitive and nurturing. I ask Stan if there are other people in his life now who might support his efforts to be more accepting and affirming of his androgyny.

As the first session draws to a close, I invite Stan to talk about what he learned from our time together. Stan says two things stand out for him. First, he is beginning to believe he doesn't need to keep blaming himself. He knows that many of the messages he has received from his parents and from society about what it means to be a man have been undesirable and one-dimensional. He acknowledges that he has been limited and constrained by his gender-role socialization. Second, he feels hopeful because there are alternatives to those parental and societal definitions—people he admires have been able to successfully combine "masculine" and "feminine" traits. If they can do it, so can he. I ask Stan whether he chooses to return for another session. When he answers in the affirmative, I give him W. S. Pollack's (1998) book *Real Boys* to read. I explain that this book descriptively captures the gender-role socialization that many boys experience.

Stan comes to the following session eager to talk about his homework assignment. He tells me that he gained some real insights into his own attitudes and beliefs by reading *Real Boys*. What Stan learned from reading this book leads to a further exploration of his relationship with his mother. He finds it helpful to understand his parents' behavior in the context of societal expectations and stereotypes rather than continuing to blame them. I help Stan to see how our culture tends to hold extreme positions about mothers—that they are either perfect or wicked—and that neither of these extremes is true. We talk briefly about what he has learned about mothers as saints or sinners. As Stan learns to reframe his relationship with his mother, he develops a more realistic picture of her. He comes to realize, too, that his father has been oppressed by his own socialization experiences and by an idealistic view of masculinity that he may have felt unable to achieve.

Stan continues to work at learning to value the nurturing and sensitive aspects of himself. He is learning to value the "feminine" as well as the "masculine" aspects of his personality. He continues to monitor and make changes in his self-talk about what it means to be a man. He is gaining awareness of these messages that come from current sources such as the media and friends, and each day he adds to his journal, noting how these messages are transmitted and the ways that he is challenging them.

Throughout our therapeutic relationship, we discuss with immediacy how we are communicating and relating to each other during the sessions. I am self-disclosing and treat Stan as an equal, continually acknowledging that he is the "expert" on his life.

Questions for Reflection

- What unique values do you see in working with Stan from a feminist perspective as opposed to working from the other therapeutic approaches you've studied thus far?
- If you were to continue working with Stan, what self-statements regarding his view of himself as a man might you focus on, and what alternatives might you offer?
- In what ways could you integrate cognitive behavior therapy with feminist therapy in Stan's case? What possibilities do you see for integrating Gestalt therapy methods with feminist therapy? What other therapies might you combine with a feminist approach?

Visit CengageBrain.com or watch the video program for *Theory and Practice of Counseling and Psychotherapy: The Case of Stan and Lecturettes*, Session 10 (feminist therapy), for a demonstration of my approach to counseling Stan from this perspective. This session deals with Stan's exploration of his gender-role identity and messages he has incorporated about being a man.

Feminist Therapy Applied to the Case of Gwen*

Powerlessness is the theme I hear from Gwen at the beginning of this session. She talks about her sadness in seeing her granddaughter going through the same things she experienced as a young girl. Gwen feels invisible and unappreciated. I want to help Gwen become aware of how gender-role socialization has influenced her and help her reclaim her personal power.

Gwen: I can't tell you how many times in one day I tell myself that I'm not worth anything.

Therapist: Give me an example of something that happens to you and the message you hear inside yourself.

Gwen: Well, in a meeting at work with the partners, I may make a suggestion about something we might do, but I'm ignored. Then Joe, this White guy, makes the same suggestion with just a little twist and the partners are all over it.

Therapist: So your voice is ignored, but the White man gets heard. What do you tell yourself?

Gwen: I get really angry! If I say something, I am accused of "always making it about race." Then I say to myself, "they are right because most of the time it is about race." I usually think, "here we go again!"

*Dr. Kellie Kirksey writes about her ways of thinking and practicing from a feminist therapy perspective and applying this model to Gwen.

Therapist: Even though you push back against their message, a part of you believes them—that you are making too big a deal out of your voice being ignored.

Gwen: No, I don't believe that. Some things are about being a woman of color and not being heard, and that's just how it is. Society ignores it, but it is real. When someone does not know what it's like to be invisible and unheard, they are privileged! This is an old, tired story for me.

Therapist: What did you learn growing up about the value of your voice and your value as a girl and a young woman?

Gwen: I learned that boys were valued more than girls. I received the message that being a girl meant you were not strong enough, not smart enough, and that you were required to be in the kitchen cleaning up after a meal.

I asked Gwen to write a gender-role analysis before our next session. In it she provides more information about the gender-role expectations in her home and in her community as she was growing up. Gwen also writes about telling an adult that her older cousin had touched her inappropriately. She was told to be quiet about the situation, and her sexual abuse was never spoken of again. Gwen learned early that her voice did not matter. In this session, I work toward validating her experiences and the value of her voice. I acknowledge her pain and let her know that society has perpetuated this unequal and devaluing view of women and girls globally.

Therapist: Gwen, I read your gender-role analysis thoroughly, and I really appreciate you trusting me with the information you shared.

Gwen: It was hard.

Therapist: I'm sure it was. I was especially struck with how early in your life you learned a lesson that too many girls learn—that your voice didn't count and that your body was not yours. I am so sorry that you had the experience of sexual abuse as a child [*It is important to name the reality of her experience and not side-step it*].

Gwen: I don't think I realized until this moment what a strong message was sent to me that day—the day I tried to share with my mother what had happened to me.

Therapist: What message did you receive?

Gwen: My mother said, "Are you sure that happened? I think you are making it up to get him in trouble!"

Therapist: In a culture where males are valued more than females and where males have much more power than females, the response you got from your mother is often given directly or indirectly to girls and women when they tell their truth about being abused.

Gwen: I thought my mother would believe me and would support me.

Therapist: You were and still are disappointed because your mother, a person you trusted, silenced you. And you're confused about why she, as a woman, would do this.

Gwen: Yes, I am.

Therapist: Keep in mind that your mother was raised in the same culture in which the men are raised. Women hear the same messages discounting females that the men hear.

Gwen: You know, at work I get more angry at the women than at the men. When I'm being discounted and being told that I'm too angry and using the "race card," I rage more at the women than I do at the men.

Therapist: What do you think that is about?

Gwen: Perhaps it is that I'm more disappointed in the women for not standing with me. Or perhaps, like my mother, I value the men more. It really hurts me to believe that might be true.

By placing Gwen's issue in a larger societal context, she begins to understand that her experiences resonate with the experiences of other women. It helps her to understand that she, too, might be working from a model of males being valued more than females. If she can get a clear understanding of this, she can move more easily to a place of truly believing in her own value.

Gwen is a professional woman with an MBA from a prestigious university. She has had to continuously negotiate minefields of racism, sexism, and multiple forms of inequality. Institutional racism perpetuates the oppression she has experienced and continues to experience, but she sees that using her voice might begin the process of healing her personal wounds from this societal injustice. I discuss with Gwen the potential risks of using her voice (becoming more outspoken) in her present professional environment.

Gwen: I'm really tired of feeling angry all the time, but I can tell you I'm also really tired of being treated as "less than."

Therapist: Tell me more about your experiences of being treated as less than.

Gwen: If I raise my voice or express frustration at work—even if I'm not angry—I am told that I'm too emotional and too angry. I really feel that I've been labeled "the angry black woman," and no matter how appropriate I am with my frustration or with my voice, it is always seen as "there goes that angry black woman again."

Therapist: So, people at work have written this story about you—angry black woman—and many things that you do are filtered through the lens of that story.

Gwen: Yes, that's right.

Therapist: Think about the times when you are appropriately speaking your mind and sharing your frustration. Tell me what words you use to describe yourself.

Gwen: [*pause*] Sometimes I am angry, and I have a right to be, but I would say that I am being passionate and assertive.

Therapist: I really like that! How might it be for you to make sure that you restate in your own head that message: "Gwen, you are being passionate and assertive." This is a way to define yourself.

Gwen: It is definitely something I would like to do.

Therapist: You have walked a path cluttered with micro-aggressions for over 50 years, sometimes experiencing these toxic messages multiple times a day. As a woman of color, you are bombarded with the messages from a culture that devalues people of color and women. We can draw on the strength of those who came before us. We are standing on the shoulders of those who fought for our rights as people of color and as women. We know there is injustice in the fabric of our society. What will you do to make changes that are important to you?

Gwen: [*Listening intently and reflecting on ways she has been slighted*] It feels good to talk about all this.

Therapist: You are an intelligent, passionate, creative, and strong woman. I'm wondering how you might use these parts of you to design your life to be more the way you want it to be.

Gwen: I'm not sure. I do know that I want to be more proactive in my community and more patient with my mother. I'm learning that I still hold resentments from my childhood, and I want to let that go.

Therapist: That sounds like a good place to start.

Gwen: I also want to make sure that I handle my voice and my frustration in the workplace appropriately. I want my voice to be heard. Perhaps I can assertively ask not to be interrupted when folks start to interrupt me. When someone else is getting credit for my idea, I will remind them that I had shared it earlier. I will ask why it wasn't heard when I presented it. I could do this calmly, but consistently.

Therapist: I think that is an excellent idea.

Gwen has been sitting on the curb of her life watching the traffic go by for far too long. She does not realize her own strength to create change. I share with Gwen some of my challenges with racism. My self-disclosure is intended to join with her in affirming that her experience of oppression is, in fact, valid. As Gwen hears that she is not alone and that she can begin to stand up and use her authentic voice, it is my hope that Gwen will realize she can join with others to make some change in society through conscious action.

I collaborate with Gwen in identifying her resources and deciding how she can make fuller use of them in daily life. I become an ally and supporter as she begins to create a plan of action for social and personal transformation.

Therapist: You have shared some of the ways that you want to be more visible in your work environment and more assertive in your daily living. You have also shared some ways that you plan on engaging with your mother differently. I'm wondering if there are any social groups you could become part of that would help you feel more connected and involved in the community? Do you know some other women who are also strong and with whom you could find and offer support?

Gwen: There is a women's group in my church that is made up of professional women. I've avoided being a part of it because I'm so busy and because I was afraid that I wouldn't fit in. There is one woman in the group I trust, and I think I will talk with her about ways I'm trying to restructure my life and see if she thinks the group would be a good fit for me.

Therapist: So, she would serve for a while like your mirror. She could reflect how she perceives you as you interact with these women.

Gwen: I wasn't thinking of it exactly in that way. It will just feel good to have someone in the group who I know and feel comfortable with.

As we continue our discussions in future sessions, my goal is to help Gwen reclaim her power, increase her self-esteem, and ultimately reach her full potential as a valuable and significant member of her community.

Questions for Reflection

- What reactions do you have to the therapist's interventions with Gwen?
- What differences do you see when working with Gwen from a feminist perspective rather than from other theoretical frameworks?
- What are your reactions to the therapist's self-disclosure?
- What are potential dangers for Gwen if she increasingly speaks her mind in professional settings?

Summary and Evaluation

Summary

Feminist therapy largely grew out of the recognition by women that the traditional models of therapy suffer from basic limitations due to the inherent bias of earlier White male theoreticians. Feminist therapy emphasizes these concepts: LO12

- Viewing problems in a sociopolitical and cultural context rather than on an individual level
- Recognizing that clients are experts on their own lives
- Striving to create a therapeutic relationship that is egalitarian through the process of self-disclosure and informed consent
- Demystifying the therapeutic process by including the client as much as possible in all phases of assessment and treatment, which increases client empowerment
- Viewing women's and other marginalized and oppressed group's experiences from a unique perspective
- Understanding that gender never exists in isolation from other aspects of identity
- Understanding and appreciating the lives and perspectives of diverse women and other marginalized and oppressed groups
- Challenging traditional ways of assessing the psychological health of women and other marginalized and oppressed groups
- Emphasizing the role of the therapist as advocate as well as facilitator
- Encouraging clients to get involved in social action to address oppressive aspects of the environment

The feminist approach is aimed at both personal and social change. The theoretical orientation is continually evolving and maturing. The major goal is to replace the current patriarchal system with feminist consciousness and thus create a society that values equality in relationships, values diversity, stresses interdependence rather than dependence, and encourages both women and men to define themselves rather than being defined by societal stereotypes.

Feminist practice tends to be diverse because it has been developed and expanded by multiple voices. As the feminist approach has matured, it has become more self-critical and varied. Feminist therapists and other therapists who infuse their work with multicultural and social justice perspectives share a number of basic assumptions and roles: they engage in appropriate self-disclosure; they make their values and beliefs explicit so that the therapy process is clearly understood; they establish egalitarian roles with clients; they work toward client empowerment; they emphasize the commonalities among women and other marginalized and oppressed groups while honoring their diverse life experiences; and they all have an agenda to bring about social change.

Feminist practitioners are committed to actively breaking down the hierarchy of power in the therapeutic relationship through the use of various interventions. Some of these strategies are unique to feminist therapy, such as gender-role analysis and intervention, power analysis, assuming a stance of advocate in challenging conventional attitudes toward appropriate roles for women, and encouraging clients to take social action. Other therapeutic strategies are borrowed from various therapy models, including bibliotherapy, assertiveness training, cognitive restructuring, reframing and relabeling, counselor self-disclosure, role playing, identifying and challenging untested beliefs, and journal writing. Feminist therapy principles and techniques can be applied to a range of therapeutic modalities such as individual therapy, couples counseling, family therapy, group counseling, and community intervention. Regardless of the specific techniques used, the overriding goals are client empowerment and social transformation.

Contributions of Feminist Therapy and Multicultural and Social Justice Perspectives

One of the major contributions feminist theorists and practitioners have made to the field of counseling and psychotherapy is paving the way for gender-sensitive practice and an awareness of the impact of the cultural context and multiple oppressions. By focusing attention on our attitudes and biases pertaining to gender and culture, feminist therapists have expanded the awareness of therapists of all theoretical orientations regarding how social justice issues may touch clients. A significant contribution of feminist therapy is the emphasis on social change, which can lead to a transformation in society. Feminist therapists have brought about significant theoretical and professional advances in counseling practice. Some of these contributions include power sharing with clients, cultural critiques of both assessment and treatment approaches, and the validation of women and their normative experiences. Feminist therapists have also made important contributions by questioning the androcentricity of traditional counseling theories and models of human development. Most theories place the cause of problems within individuals rather than with external circumstances and the environment. This has led to holding individuals fully responsible for their problems and not giving recognition to social and political realities that create problems. A key contribution feminist theorists and practitioners continue to make is reminding all of us that the proper focus of therapy includes addressing oppressive factors in society rather than expecting individuals to merely adapt to expected role behaviors. This emphasis on social justice issues has expanded the role of therapists to be advocates for clients. For a discussion of adaptations to traditional approaches to counseling women, see Enns (2003).

Another major contribution of the feminist movement is in the area of ethics in psychology and counseling practice (Brabeck & Brabeck, 2013). The unified feminist voice called attention to the extent and implications of child abuse, incest, rape, sexual harassment, and domestic violence. Feminists pointed out the consequences of failing to recognize and take action when children and women were victims of physical, sexual, and psychological abuse.

Feminist therapists demanded action in cases of sexual misconduct at a time when male therapists misused the trust placed in them by their female clients. Not too long ago the codes of ethics of all the major professional organizations were silent on the matter of therapist and client sexual liaisons. Now, virtually all of the professional codes of ethics prohibit sexual intimacies with current clients and with former clients for a specified time period. Furthermore, the professions agree that a sexual relationship cannot later be converted into a therapeutic relationship. Largely due to the efforts and input of women on ethics committees, the existing codes are explicit with respect to sexual harassment and sexual relationships with clients, students, and supervisees (Herlihy & Corey, 2015b).

Feminist theory has been applied to supervision, teaching, consultation, ethics, research, and theory building as well as to the practice of psychotherapy. Building community, providing authentic mutual empathic relationships, creating a sense of social awareness, and addressing social injustices are all significant strengths of this approach.

The principles and techniques of feminist therapy can be incorporated in many other contemporary therapy models and vice versa. Both feminist and Adlerian therapists view the therapeutic relationship as egalitarian. Both feminist and person-centered therapists agree on the importance of therapist authenticity, modeling, and self-disclosure; empowerment is the basic goal of both orientations. When it comes to making choices about one's destiny, existential and feminist therapists are speaking the same language—both emphasize choosing for oneself instead of living a life determined by societal dictates.

Although feminist therapists have been critical of psychoanalysis as a sexist orientation, a number of feminist therapists believe psychoanalysis can be an appropriate approach to helping women. Object-relations theory may help clients examine internalized object representations that are based on their relationships with their parents. Indeed, relational-cultural therapy has roots in object-relations theory. Psychodynamic approaches might include an examination of unconscious learning about women's roles through the mother–daughter relationship to provide insights into why gender roles are so deeply ingrained and difficult to change.

Cognitive behavioral therapies and feminist therapy are compatible in that they view the therapeutic relationship as a collaborative partnership, with the client being in charge of setting goals and selecting strategies for change. These approaches are committed to demystifying therapy, and both aim to help clients take charge of their own lives. Both the cognitive behavior therapist and the feminist therapist assume a range of information-giving and teaching functions so clients can become active partners in the therapy process. A feminist therapist could employ action-oriented strategies, such as assertiveness training and behavioral rehearsal, and suggest homework assignments for clients to practice in their everyday lives. A useful source for further discussion of feminist cognitive behavior therapy is Worell and Remer (2003).

Limitations and Criticisms of Feminist Counseling

Feminist therapists need to identify any sources of bias and work toward restructuring or eliminating biased aspects in any theories or techniques they employ. This is indeed a demanding endeavor, and it may involve the counselor's own therapeutic work and work with a consultant. It is possible for feminist therapists to unduly influence clients, especially those who lack a strong sense of their own values. Feminist therapists must remain aware of their own values pertaining to individual and social change and explicitly share these values with clients in an appropriate, timely, and respectful manner to reduce the risk of value imposition.

Feminist therapists call attention to clients' unexamined choices, and they must honor clients' choices as long as those choices are indeed informed. Once clients understand the impact of gender and cultural factors on their choices, the therapist must guard against providing specific directions for client growth. Feminist therapists are committed to helping clients weigh the costs and benefits of their current life choices but should not push clients too quickly toward changes they feel are beyond their reach. Lenore Walker (1994) raised this issue with regard to working with abused women. Although Walker focuses on the importance of asking questions that enable women to think through their situations in new ways and of helping women develop "safety plans," she emphasizes how critical it is to understand those factors in a woman's life that often pose difficulties for her in making changes.

Looking at contextual or environmental factors that contribute to a woman's problems and moving away from exploring the intrapsychic domain can be both a strength and a limitation. Instead of being blamed for her depression, the client is able to come to an understanding of external realities that are indeed oppressive and are contributing to her state of depression. A client can make some internal changes even in those circumstances where external realities may largely be contributing to her problems. Therapists must balance an exploration of the outer and inner worlds of the client if the client is to find a way to take action in her own life.

Factors that inhibit the growth of feminist therapy include training that is often offered only sporadically in a nonsystematic way (Brown, 2010) and the lack of quality control. No credentialing organization confers official status as a qualified feminist therapist, so formalized training and credentialing need to be addressed in the future. In addition, evidence-based research on the efficacy of feminist therapy is lacking, as is an understanding of feminist therapy as an integrative approach that can inform therapeutic practice for counselors of varied theoretical orientations. Feminist and most other social justice psychotherapies do integrate evidenced-based treatment approaches (e.g., CBT and trauma-focused interventions) within a social justice value system.

Self-Reflection and Discussion Questions

1. What key concepts or principles of feminist therapy could you incorporate in your counseling practice regardless of your theoretical orientation?
2. Feminist therapists engage in self-disclosure only when it is judged to be therapeutically helpful to the client. How could you assess the degree to which your personal disclosures are appropriate, timely, and helpful to your client?
3. Feminist therapy aims to include social change as well as individual change. How competent will you be in facilitating work with your clients in the area of social action?
4. This approach to therapy places value on exploring issues of power, privilege, oppression, and discrimination. Do you see yourself as being primarily interested in exploring these facets with your clients?
5. A number of feminist therapy techniques are described in this chapter. What one technique do you find particularly interesting? Why?

Where to Go From Here

The *DVD for Integrative Counseling: The Case of Ruth and Lecturettes* is especially useful as a demonstration of interventions I make with Ruth that illustrate some principles and procedures of feminist therapy. For example, in Session 1 ("Beginning of Counseling") I ask Ruth about her expectations and initiate the informed consent process. I attempt to engage Ruth as a collaborative partner in the therapeutic venture, and I teach her how counseling works. Clearly, Ruth is the expert on her own life, and my job is to assist her in attaining the goals we collaboratively identify as a focus of therapy. In Session 4 ("Understanding and Dealing With Diversity") Ruth brings up gender differences, and she also mentions our differences in religion, education, culture, and socialization. Ruth and I explore the degree to which she feels comfortable with me and trusts me.

Other Resources

DVDs offered by the American Psychological Association that are relevant to this chapter include the following:

Brown, L. S. (2009). *Feminist Therapy Over Time* (APA Psychotherapy Video Series)

Psychotherapy.net is a comprehensive resource for students and professionals that offers videos and interviews on feminist therapy. New video and editorial content is made available monthly. DVDs relevant to this chapter are available at www.psychotherapy.net and include the following:

Walker, L.(1994). *The Abused Woman: A Survivor Therapy Approach*

Walker, L. (1997). *Feminist Therapy* (Psychotherapy With the Experts Series)

The Jean Baker Miller Training Institute offers workshops, courses, professional training, publications, and ongoing projects that explore applications of the relational-cultural approach and integrate research, psychological theory, and social action. This relational-cultural model is based on the assumption that growth-fostering relationships and disconnections are constructed within specific cultural contexts.

Jean Baker Miller Training Institute
www.wellesley.edu/JBMTI/

The American Psychological Association has two divisions devoted to special interests in women's issues: Division 17 (Counseling Psychology's Section on Women) and Division 35 (Psychology of Women).

American Psychological Association
www.apa.org
Division 17: www.div17.org
Division 35: www.apa.org/divisons/div35

The Association for Women in Psychology (AWP) sponsors an annual conference dealing with feminist contributions to the understanding of life experiences of women. AWP is a scientific and educational feminist organization devoted to reevaluating and reformulating the role that psychology and mental health research generally play in women's lives.

Association for Women in Psychology
www.awpsych.org

The Psychology of Women Resource List, or POWR online, is cosponsored by APA Division 35, Society for the Psychology of Women, and the Association for Women in Psychology. This public electronic network facilitates discussion of current topics, research, teaching strategies, and practice issues among people interested in the discipline of psychology of women. Most people with computer access to Bitnet or the Internet can subscribe to POWR-L at no cost. To subscribe, send the command below via e-mail to:

LISTSERV@URIACC (Binet) or LISTSERV@URIACC.URI.EDU

Subscribe POWR-L Your name (Use first and last name)

The University of Kentucky offers a minor specialty area in counseling women and feminist therapy within the Counseling Psychology graduate programs. For information, contact Dr. Pam Remer:

University of Kentucky
Department of Educational and Counseling Psychology
www.uky.edu/Education/edphead.html

Texas Women's University offers a training program with emphasis in women's issues, gender issues, and family psychology. For information, contact:

Texas Women's University
www.twu.edu/as/psyphil/Counseling_Home.htm

Recommended Supplementary Readings

Feminist Perspectives in Therapy: Empowering Diverse Women (Worell & Remer, 2003) is an outstanding text that clearly outlines the foundations of empowerment in feminist therapy. The book covers a range of topics such as integrating feminist and multicultural perspectives on therapy, changing roles for women, feminist views of counseling practice, feminist transformation of counseling theories, and a feminist approach to assessment and diagnosis. There also are excellent chapters dealing with depression, surviving sexual assault, confronting abuse, choosing a career path, and lesbian and ethnic minority women.

Oxford Handbook of Feminist Multicultural Counseling Psychology (Enns & Williams, 2013) is a 26-chapter handbook that integrates feminist and multicultural scholarship and applies the perspective to a variety of women's diverse identities related to race/ethnicity, social class, disability, religion, culture, and so forth. Multiple chapters focus on the practice of feminist multicultural therapy, pedagogy, mentoring, and social advocacy.

Psychological Practice With Women: Guidelines, Diversity, Empowerment (Enns, Rice, & Nutt, 2015) discusses the assessment of women's social identities and diversity and features chapters that focus on psychotherapy with African American women; Latinas; Asian American and Pacific Islander women; Native women; lesbian, bisexual, and transgender women; women with disabilities; and women in transnational practice. Each chapter includes the application of the APA (2007) Guidelines through one or more case studies.

Feminist Therapy (Brown, 2010) provides an interesting perspective on the history of feminist therapy and speculates about future developments of the approach. Brown clearly explains key concepts of feminist theory and the therapeutic process.

Introduction to Feminist Therapy: Strategies for Social and Individual Change (Evans, Kincade, & Seem, 2011) emphasizes the practical applications of feminist theory to clinical practice. They provide useful information on social change and empowerment, the importance of establishing an egalitarian relationship, and intervention strategies when working with people from diverse cultural backgrounds.

Postmodern Approaches

13

LEARNING OBJECTIVES

1. Identify how the postmodern approaches differ from the modernist approaches.
2. Describe the historical roots of social constructionism.
3. Understand the collaborative language systems approach.
4. Examine the distinguishing features and key concepts of solution-focused brief therapy.
5. Identify the role of the therapeutic relationship in the solution-focused approach.
6. Describe the techniques often used by solution-focused brief therapists.
7. Understand the application of solution-focused therapy to group counseling.
8. Identify the distinguishing features and key concepts of narrative therapy.
9. Understand the role of the therapeutic relationship in narrative therapy.
10. Describe the techniques often used by narrative therapists.
11. Examine the application of narrative therapy to group counseling.
12. Identify the strengths and shortcomings of the postmodern approaches from a multicultural perspective.
13. Describe the contributions and limitations of the postmodern approaches.

Some Contemporary Founders of Postmodern Therapies

The postmodern approaches do not have a single founder. Rather, it has been a collective effort by many. I have highlighted two cofounders of solution-focused brief therapy and two cofounders of narrative therapy who have had a major impact on the development of these therapeutic approaches. These cofounders are introduced at the beginning of the sections on these therapies.

Introduction to Social Constructionism

Each of the models of counseling and psychotherapy we have studied so far **LO1** has its own version of "reality." The simultaneous existence of multiple and often conflicting "truths" has led to increasing skepticism that a singular, universal theory will one day explain human behavior and the systems in which we live. We have entered a postmodern world, and truth and reality are often now understood as representing points of view bounded by history and context rather than being objective, immutable facts.

Modernists believe in the ability to describe objective reality accurately and assume that it can be observed and systematically known through the scientific method. They further believe reality exists independent of any attempt to observe it. Modernists believe people seek therapy for a problem when they have deviated too far from some objective norm. For example, clients may think they are abnormally depressed when they experience sadness for longer than they think is normal. They might then seek help to return to "normal" behavior.

Postmodernists, in contrast, do not believe realities exist independent of observational processes and of the language systems within which they are described. **Social constructionism** is a psychological expression of this postmodern worldview; it values the client's reality without disputing whether it is accurate or rational (Gergen, 1991, 1999; Weishaar, 1993). To social constructionists, any understanding of reality is based on the use of language and is largely a function of the situations in which people live. Our knowledge about realities is socially constructed. A person is depressed when he or she adopts a definition of self as depressed. Without the cultural conditions that accept the concept of depression, talking about a person as depressed would mean nothing. Once a definition of self is adopted, it is hard to recognize behaviors counter to that definition; for example, it is hard for someone who is suffering from depression to acknowledge the value of a periodic good mood in his or her life.

In postmodern thinking, forms of language and the use of language in stories create meaning. There may be as many meanings as there are people to tell the stories, and each of these stories expresses a truth for the person telling it. Even science is not free from the influence of such processes of social construction. Every person involved in a situation has a perspective on the "reality" of that situation, but the range of truths is limited due to the effects of specific historical events and the language uses that dominate particular social contexts. In practice, therefore, the range of possible meanings is not infinite. When Kenneth Gergen (1985, 1991, 1999) and others began to emphasize the ways in which people make meaning in social relationships, the field of social constructionism was born.

In social constructionism the therapist disavows the role of expert, preferring a more collaborative or consultative stance. Clients are viewed as experts about their own lives. De Jong and Berg (2013) put this notion about the therapist's task well:

> We do not view ourselves as expert at scientifically assessing client problems and then intervening. Instead, we strive to be expert at exploring clients' frames of reference and identifying those perceptions that clients can use to create more satisfying lives. (p. 19)

The collaborative partnership in the therapeutic process is considered more important than assessment or technique. Understanding narratives and deconstructing language processes (discourses) are the focus for both understanding individuals and helping them construct desired change.

Social constructionist theory is grounded on the premise that knowledge is constructed through social processes. What we consider to be "truth" is a product of interactions between people in daily life. Thus there is not a single or "right" way to live one's life or to understand the world. Social constructionism explains how values are transmitted through language by the social milieu and suggests that individuals are constantly changing with the ebb and flow of the influences of family, culture, and society (Neukrug, 2016).

Visit CengageBrain.com or watch the DVD for the video program on Chapter 13, *Theory and Practice of Counseling and Psychotherapy: The Case of Stan and Lecturettes*. I suggest that you view the brief lecture for each chapter prior to reading the chapter.

Historical Glimpse of Social Constructionism

LO2

A mere hundred years ago, Freud, Adler, and Jung were part of a major paradigm shift that transformed psychology as well as philosophy, science, medicine, and even the arts. In the 21st century, postmodern constructions of alternative knowledge sources seem to be one of the paradigm shifts most likely to affect the field of psychotherapy. Postmodernist thought is influencing the development of many psychotherapy theories and contemporary psychotherapeutic practice. The creation of the self, which so dominated the modernist search for human essence and truth, is being replaced with the concept of socially *storied lives*. Diversity, multiple frameworks, and integration—collaboration of the knower with the known—are all part of this new social movement, which provides a wider range of perspectives in counseling practice. For some social constructionists, the process of "knowing" includes a distrust of the dominant cultural positions that permeate families and society today (White & Epston, 1990), particularly when the dominant culture exerts a destructive impact on the lives of those who live beyond the margins of what is generally considered normal. Change begins by deconstructing the power of cultural narratives and then proceeds to the co-construction of a new life of meaning.

Among the best-known postmodern perspectives on therapy practice are the collaborative language systems approach (Anderson & Goolishian, 1992), solution-focused brief therapy (de Shazer, 1985, 1988, 1991, 1994), solution-oriented therapy (Bertolino & O'Hanlon, 2002; O'Hanlon & Weiner-Davis, 2003), narrative therapy (White & Epston, 1990), and feminist therapy (Brown, 2010). The next section examines the collaborative language systems approach, but the heart of this chapter addresses two of the most significant postmodern approaches: solution-focused brief therapy and narrative therapy.

The Collaborative Language Systems Approach

LO3

When people seek therapy, they are often "stuck" in a dialogic system that has a unique language, meaning, and process related to "the problem." Therapy is another conversational system that becomes therapeutic through its "problem-organizing, problem-dissolving" nature (Anderson & Goolishian, 1992, p. 27). It is therapists' willingness to enter the therapeutic conversation from a "not-knowing" position that facilitates this caring relationship with the client. In the *not-knowing position*, therapists still retain all of the knowledge and personal, experiential capacities they have gained over years of living, but they allow themselves to enter the conversation with curiosity and with an intense interest in discovery. The aim here is to enter a client's world as fully as possible. Clients become the experts who are informing and sharing with the therapist the significant narratives of their lives. The not-knowing position is empathic and is most often characterized by questions that "come from an honest, continuous therapeutic posture of not understanding too quickly" (Anderson, 1993, p. 331).

Based on the referral or intake process, the therapist enters the session with some sense of what the client may wish to address. The questions the therapist asks are informed by the answers the client-expert has provided. The client's answers provide information that stimulates the interest of the therapist, still in a posture of inquiry, and another question proceeds from each answer given. The process is similar to the Socratic method without any preconceived idea about how or in which direction the development of the stories should go. The intent of the conversation is not to confront or challenge the narrative of the client but to facilitate the telling and retelling of the story until opportunities for new meaning and new stories develop: "Telling one's story is a representation of experience; it is constructing history in the present" (Anderson & Goolishian, 1992, p. 37). By staying with the story, the therapist–client conversation evolves into a dialogue of new meaning, constructing new narrative possibilities. This not-knowing position of the therapist has been infused as a key concept for both the solution-focused and the narrative therapeutic approaches.

INSOO KIM BERG (1935–2007) was a Korean-born American psychotherapist and a pioneer of solution-focused brief therapy (SFBT). In 1978 she and her husband, Steve de Shazer, cofounded the Brief Family Therapy Center in Milwaukee, Wisconsin. As a leader in the practice of SFBT, she provided workshops in the United States, Japan, South Korea, Australia, Denmark, England, and Germany. Berg published 10 groundbreaking books that elucidated the application of SFBT in a wide variety of clinical settings; among them are *Family Based Services: A Solution-Focused Approach* (1994), *Working With the Problem Drinker: A Solution-Focused Approach* (Berg & Miller, 1992), and *Interviewing for Solutions* (De Jong & Berg, 2013). Berg's colleagues described her as inspiring, humble, and passionate. She was committed to her work and rarely took time off, but she did enjoy a wide range of physical activities: stretching exercises, yoga, walking, and gardening.

Courtesy of Brief Family Therapy Center

Insoo Kim Berg

STEVE de SHAZER (1940–2005) was one of the pioneers of solution-focused brief therapy. For many years he was the director of research at the Brief Family Therapy Center in Milwaukee, where solution-focused brief therapy was developed. He wrote several books on SFBT, including *Keys to Solutions in Brief Therapy* (1985), *Clues: Investigating Solutions in Brief Therapy* (1988), *Putting Difference to Work* (1991), and *Words Were Originally Magic* (1994).

Courtesy of Brief Family Therapy Center

Steve de Shazer

De Shazer loved baseball, was a gourmet cook, and made time for long daily walks. Some of his leisure pursuits included reading philosophy tracts in the original German or French, listening to jazz, and perusing esoteric cookbooks. He was trained as a classical musician and played several instruments at a professional level. During his youth he made his living as a jazz saxophonist. He presented workshops, trained, and consulted widely in North America, Europe, Australia, and Asia. While on a teaching tour in Europe in 2005, de Shazer went to a hospital in Vienna for medical help; he died several hours after being admitted.

Solution-Focused Brief Therapy

Introduction

Solution-focused brief therapy (SFBT) is a future-focused, goal-oriented therapeutic approach to brief therapy developed initially by Steve de Shazer and Insoo Kim Berg at the Brief Family Therapy Center in Milwaukee in the early 1980s. SFBT emphasizes strengths and resiliencies of people by focusing on exceptions to their problems and their conceptualized solutions. SFBT is an optimistic, antideterministic, future-oriented approach based on the assumption that clients have the ability to change quickly and can create a problem-free language as they strive for a new reality (Neukrug, 2016).

Key Concepts

Unique Focus of SFBT The solution-focused philosophy rests on the assumption that people can become mired in unresolved past conflicts and blocked when they focus on past or present problems rather than on future solutions. Solution-focused brief therapy differs from traditional therapies by eschewing the past in favor of both the present and the future (Franklin, Trepper, Gingerich, & McCollum, 2012). Therapists focus on what is possible, and they have little or no interest in gaining an understanding of how the problem emerged. Behavior change is viewed as the most effective approach to assisting people in enhancing their lives. De Shazer (1988, 1991) suggests that it is not necessary to know the cause of a problem to solve it and that there is no necessary relationship between the causes of problems and their solutions. Assessing problems is not necessary for change to occur. If knowing and understanding problems are unimportant, so is searching for "right" or absolute solutions. Any person might consider multiple solutions, and what is right for one person may not be right for others. LO4

It is within the scope of SFBT practice to allow for some discussion of presenting problems to validate clients' experience and to let them describe their pain, struggles, and frustrations (Murphy, 2013, 2015). However, this brief exploration differs from the lengthy discourse into the history and causes of problems common to some other types of therapy. In solution-focused brief therapy, clients choose the goals they wish to accomplish; little attention is given to diagnosis, history taking, or exploring the emergence of the problem (O'Hanlon & Weiner-Davis, 2003).

Positive Orientation Solution-focused brief therapy is grounded on the optimistic assumption that people are healthy and competent and have the ability to construct solutions that can enhance their lives. An underlying assumption of SFBT is that we already have the ability to resolve the challenges life brings us, but at times we lose our sense of direction or our awareness of our competencies. Regardless of what shape clients are in when they enter therapy, solution-focused therapists believe clients are competent. The therapist's role is to help clients recognize the competencies they already possess and apply them toward solutions. The essence of therapy involves building on clients' hope and optimism by creating positive expectations that change is possible. Solution-focused brief therapy has parallels with **positive psychology**, which concentrates on what is right and what is working for people rather than dwelling on deficits, weaknesses, and problems (Murphy, 2015). By emphasizing positive dimensions, clients quickly become involved in resolving their problems, which makes this a very empowering approach.

Because clients often come to therapy in a "problem-oriented" state, even the few solutions they have considered are wrapped in the power of the problem orientation. Clients often have a story that is rooted in a deterministic view that what has happened in their past will certainly shape their future. Solution-focused practitioners counter this negative client presentation with optimistic conversations that highlight a belief in achievable and usable goals. Therapists can be instrumental in assisting clients in making a shift from a fixed problem state to a world with new possibilities. One of the goals of SFBT is to shift clients' perceptions by reframing what White and Epston (1990) refer to as clients' *problem-saturated stories* through the counselor's skillful use of language.

Looking for What Is Working The emphasis of SFBT is to focus on what is working in clients' lives, which stands in stark contrast to the traditional models of therapy that tend to be problem-focused. Individuals bring stories to therapy, some of which are used to justify the client's belief that life can't be changed or, worse, that life is moving them further and further away from their goals. Solution-focused brief therapists assist clients in paying attention to the exceptions to their problem patterns, or their instances of success. They promote hope by helping clients discover exceptions, or times when the problem is less intrusive in their life (Metcalf, 2001). SFBT focuses on finding out what people are doing that is working and then helping them apply this knowledge to eliminate problems in the shortest amount of time possible. Identifying what is working and encouraging clients to replicate these patterns is extremely important (Murphy, 2015). A key theme of SFBT is, When you know what is working, do more of it. If something is not working, try something different (Hoyt, 2015).

There are various ways to assist clients in thinking about what has worked for them. De Shazer (1991) prefers to engage clients in conversations that lead to progressive narratives whereby people create situations in which they can make steady gains toward their goals. De Shazer might say, "Tell me about times when you felt a little better and when things were going your way." It is in these stories of life worth living that the power of problems is deconstructed and new solutions are manifest and made possible.

Basic Assumptions Guiding Practice Walter and Peller (1992, 2000) think of solution-focused therapy as a model that explains how people change and how they can reach their goals rather than a model of the causes of problems. Here are some of their basic assumptions about solution-focused therapy:

- Individuals who come to therapy do have the capability of behaving effectively, even though this effectiveness may be temporarily blocked by negative cognitions. Problem-focused thinking prevents people from recognizing effective ways they have dealt with problems.
- There are advantages to a positive focus on solutions and on the future. If clients can reorient themselves in the direction of their strengths using solution-talk, there is a good chance therapy can be brief.
- There are exceptions to every problem, or times when the problem was absent. By talking about these exceptions, clients can get clues to effective solutions and can gain control over what had seemed to be an insurmountable personal difficulty. Rapid changes are possible when clients identify exceptions to their problems and begin to organize their thinking around these exceptions instead of around the problem.
- Clients often present only one side of themselves. Solution-focused therapists invite clients to examine another side of the story they are presenting.
- No problem is constant, and change is inevitable. What people need to do is become aware of any positive changes that are happening. Small changes pave the way for larger changes, and these changes are often all that is needed to resolve the problems clients bring to counseling (Guterman, 2013).
- Clients are doing their best to make change happen. Therapists should adopt a cooperative stance with clients rather than devising strategies to control resistive patterns. When therapists find ways to cooperate with people, resistance does not occur.
- Clients can be trusted in their intention to solve their problems. Therapists assume that clients want to change, can change, and will change under cooperative and empowering therapeutic conditions. There are no "right" solutions to specific problems that can be applied to all people. Each individual is unique and so, too, is each solution.

Characteristics of Brief Therapy The average length of therapy is three to eight sessions, with the most common length being only one session (Hoyt, 2015). The main goal of brief therapy is to help clients efficiently resolve problems and to move forward as quickly as possible. Some of the defining characteristics of brief therapy include the following (Hoyt, 2009, 2011, 2015):

- Rapid working alliance between therapist and client
- Clear specification of achievable treatment goals

- Clear division of responsibilities between client and therapist, with active client participation and a high level of therapist activity
- Emphasis on client's strengths, competencies, and adaptive capacities
- Expectation that change is possible and realistic and that improvement can occur in the immediate future
- Here-and-now orientation with a primary focus on current functioning in thinking, feeling, and behaving
- Specific, integrated, pragmatic, and eclectic techniques
- Periodic assessment of progress toward goals and outcomes
- Time sensitive, including making the most of each session and ending therapy as soon as possible

The core task is for SFBT practitioners to learn how to rapidly and systematically identify problems, create a collaborative relationship with clients, and intervene with a range of specific methods. Because most therapy is time-limited, therapists should learn to practice brief therapy well (Hoyt, 2011).

The Therapeutic Process

The therapeutic process rests on the foundation that clients are the experts on their own lives and often have a good sense of what has or has not worked in the past and what might work in the future. Solution-focused counseling assumes a collaborative approach with clients in contrast to the educative stance that is typically associated with most traditional models of therapy. If clients are involved in the therapeutic process from beginning to end, the chances are increased that therapy will be successful. In short, collaborative and cooperative relationships tend to be more effective than hierarchical relationships in therapy.

De Shazer (1991) believes clients can generally build solutions to their problems without any assessment of the nature of their problems. Given this framework, the structure of solution building differs greatly from traditional approaches to problem solving as can be seen in this brief description of the steps involved (De Jong & Berg, 2013):

1. Clients are given an opportunity to describe their problems. The therapist listens respectfully and carefully as clients answer the therapist's question, "How can I be useful to you?"
2. The therapist works with clients in developing well-formed goals as soon as possible. The question is posed, "What will be different in your life when your problems are solved?"
3. The therapist asks clients about those times when their problems were not present or when the problems were less severe. Clients are assisted in exploring these exceptions, with special emphasis on what they did to make these events happen.
4. At the end of each solution-building conversation, the therapist offers clients summary feedback, provides encouragement, and suggests what clients might observe or do before the next session to further solve their problem.

5. The therapist and clients evaluate the progress being made in reaching satisfactory solutions by using a rating scale. Clients are asked what needs to be done before they see their problem as being solved and also what their next step will be.

Therapeutic Goals SFBT reflects some basic notions about change, about interaction, and about reaching goals. The solution-focused therapist believes people have the ability to define meaningful personal goals and that they have the resources required to solve their problems. Goals are unique to each client and are constructed by the client to create a richer future (Prochaska & Norcross, 2014). A lack of clarity regarding client preferences, goals, and desired outcomes can result in a rift between therapist and client. During the early phase of therapy, it is important that clients be given the opportunity to express what they want from therapy and what concerns they are willing to explore. From the first contact with clients, the therapist strives to create a climate that will facilitate change and encourage clients to think in terms of a range of possibilities.

Solution-focused therapists concentrate on small, realistic, achievable changes that can lead to additional positive outcomes. Because success tends to build upon itself, modest goals are viewed as the beginning of change. The therapist looks for ways to amplify the client's movement in the desired direction as quickly as possible (Hoyt, 2015). Solution-focused therapists use questions such as these that presuppose change, posit multiple answers, and remain goal-directed and future-oriented: "What did you do, and what has changed since last time?" or "What did you notice that went better?" (Bubenzer & West, 1993).

Murphy (2015) emphasizes the importance of assisting clients in creating well-defined goals that are (1) stated positively in the client's language; (2) are action-oriented; (3) are structured in the here and now; (4) are attainable, concrete, specific, and measurable; and (5) are controlled by the client. Counselors should not too rigidly impose an agenda of getting precise goals before clients have a chance to express their concerns. Clients must feel that their concerns are heard and understood before they can formulate meaningful personal goals. In a therapist's zeal to be solution-focused, it is possible to get lost in the mechanics of therapy and not attend sufficiently to the interpersonal aspects. Therapists need to be mindful of not becoming overly technique driven at the expense of the therapeutic alliance.

Solution-oriented therapy offers several forms of goals: changing the *viewing* of a situation or a frame of reference, changing the *doing* of the problematic situation, and tapping client *strengths* and *resources* (O'Hanlon & Weiner-Davis, 2003). Therapists note the language they use, so they can increase their clients' hope and optimism and their openness to possibilities and change. Clients are encouraged to engage in change- or solution-talk, rather than problem-talk, on the assumption that what we talk about most will be what we produce. Talking about problems can produce ongoing problems. Talk about change can produce change.

Therapist's Function and Role Solution-focused practitioners believe that every client is motivated in the sense that he or she wants something as a consequence of meeting with a therapist (George, Iveson, & Ratner, 2015). Clients are much more likely to get involved in the therapeutic process if they believe they are determining the direction and purpose of the conversation. Much of what the therapeutic process is about involves clients' thinking about their future and what they want to be different in their lives. Consistent with the postmodern and social constructionist perspective, solution-focused brief therapists adopt a *not-knowing position* to put clients in the position of being the experts about their own lives. Therapists do not assume that by virtue of their expert frame of reference they know the significance of the client's actions and experiences (Anderson & Goolishian, 1992). This model casts the role and function of a therapist in quite a different light from traditionally oriented therapists who view themselves as experts in assessment and treatment. The therapist-as-expert is replaced by the client-as-expert, especially when it comes to what the client wants in life and in therapy. It is important that therapists actually believe that their clients are the true experts on their own lives. Although therapists have expertise in the process of change, clients are the experts on *what* they want changed. Clients will have their own ways of building their preferred futures, even if this is often not clear to them when they begin therapy. The therapist's task is to point clients in the direction of change without dictating what to change (George et al., 2015; Guterman, 2013).

Therapists strive to create a climate of mutual respect, dialogue, and affirmation in which clients experience the freedom to create, explore, and coauthor their evolving stories. A key therapeutic task consists of helping clients imagine how they would like life to be different and what it would take to make this transformation happen. One of the functions of the therapist is to ask questions and, based on the answers, generate further questions. Examples of some useful questions are "What do you hope to gain from coming here?" "If you were to make the changes you desire, how would that make a difference in your life?" and "What steps can you take now that will lead to these changes?"

The Therapeutic Relationship The quality of the relationship between **LO5** therapist and client is a determining factor in the outcomes of SFBT, so relationship building or engagement is a basic step in SFBT. The attitude of the therapist is crucial to the effectiveness of the therapeutic process. It is essential to create a sense of trust so clients will return for further sessions and will follow through on homework suggestions. The therapeutic process works best when clients become actively involved, when they experience a positive relationship with the therapist, and when counseling addresses what clients see as being important (Murphy, 2015). One way of creating an effective therapeutic partnership is for the therapist to show clients how they can use the strengths and resources they already have to construct solutions. Clients are encouraged to do something different and to be creative in thinking about ways to deal with their present and future concerns.

De Shazer (1988) has described three kinds of relationships that may develop between therapists and their clients:

1. *Customer:* the client and therapist jointly identify a problem and a solution to work toward. The client realizes that to attain his or her goals, personal effort will be required.
2. *Complainant:* the client describes a problem but is not able or willing to assume a role in constructing a solution, believing that a solution

is dependent on someone else's actions. In this situation, the client generally expects the therapist to change the other person to whom the client attributes the problem.

3. *Visitor:* the client comes to therapy because someone else (a spouse, parent, teacher, or probation officer) thinks the client has a problem. This client may not agree that he or she has a problem and may be unable to identify anything to explore in therapy.

De Jong and Berg (2013) recommend using caution so that therapists do not box clients into static identities. These three roles are only starting points for conversation. Rather than categorizing clients, therapists can reflect on the kinds of relationships that are developing between their clients and themselves. For example, clients who tend to place the cause of their problems on another person or persons in their lives (complainants) may be helped by skilled intervention to begin to see their own role in their problems and the necessity for taking active steps in creating solutions. How the therapist responds to different behaviors of clients has a lot to do with bringing about a shift in the relationship. In short, both complainants and visitors have the capacity for becoming customers.

Application: Therapeutic Techniques and Procedures

Some of the key techniques that solution-focused practitioners are likely to employ include looking for differences in doing, exception questions, scaling questions, and the miracle question. If these techniques are used in a routine way without developing a collaborative working alliance, they will not lead to effective results. Murphy (2015) reminds us that these solution-focused techniques should be used flexibly and tailored to the unique circumstances of each client. Therapy is best guided by the client's goals, perceptions, resources, and feedback. Therapy should not be determined by any absolutes or rigid standards outside the therapeutic relationship (namely, evidence-based treatments). LO6

Pretherapy Change Simply scheduling an appointment often sets positive change in motion. During the initial therapy session, it is common for solution-focused therapists to ask, "What have you done since you called for the appointment that has made a difference in your problem?" (de Shazer, 1985, 1988). By asking about such changes, the therapist can elicit, evoke, and amplify what clients have already done by way of making positive change. These changes cannot be attributed to the therapy process itself, so asking about them tends to encourage clients to rely less on their therapist and more on their own resources to accomplish their treatment goals.

Exception Questions SFBT is based on the notion that there were times in clients' lives when the problems they identify were not problematic. These times are called *exceptions* and represent *news of difference* (Bateson, 1972). Solution-focused therapists ask **exception questions** to direct clients to times when the problem did not exist, or when the problem was not as intense. **Exceptions** are those past experiences in a client's life when it would be reasonable to have expected the problem to occur, but somehow it did not (de Shazer, 1985; Murphy, 2015).

By helping clients identify and examine these exceptions, the chances are increased that they will work toward solutions (Guterman, 2013). Once identified by an individual, these instances of success can be useful in making further changes. This exploration reminds clients that problems are not all-powerful and have not existed forever; it also provides a field of opportunity for evoking resources, engaging strengths, and positing possible solutions. The therapist asks clients what has to happen for these exceptions to occur more often.

The Miracle Question Therapy goals are developed by using what de Shazer (1988) calls the **miracle question**, which is a main SFBT technique. The therapist asks, "If a miracle happened and the problem you have was solved overnight, how would you know it was solved, and what would be different?" Clients are then encouraged to enact "what would be different" in spite of perceived problems. If a client asserts that she wants to feel more confident and secure, the therapist might say: "Let yourself imagine that you leave the office today and that you are on track to acting more confidently and securely. What will you be *doing* differently?" This process of considering hypothetical solutions reflects O'Hanlon and Weiner-Davis's (2003) belief that changing the *doing* and *viewing* of the perceived problem changes the problem.

De Jong and Berg (2013) identify several reasons the miracle question is a useful technique. Asking clients to consider that a miracle takes place opens up a range of future possibilities. Clients are encouraged to allow themselves to dream as a way of identifying the kinds of changes they most want to see. This question has a future focus in that clients can begin to consider a different kind of life that is not dominated by a particular problem. This intervention shifts the emphasis from both past and current problems toward a more satisfying life in the future.

Scaling Questions Solution-focused therapists also use **scaling questions** when change in human experiences are not easily observed, such as feelings, moods, or communication, and to assist clients in noticing that they are not completely defeated by their problem (de Shazer & Berg, 1988). For example, a woman reporting feelings of panic or anxiety might be asked: "On a scale of zero to 10, with zero being how you felt when you first came to therapy and 10 being how you feel the day after your miracle occurs and your problem is gone, how would you rate your anxiety right now?" Even if the client has only moved away from zero to 1, she has improved. How did she do that? What does she need to do to move another number up the scale? Scaling questions enable clients to pay closer attention to what they are doing and how they can take steps that will lead to the changes they desire.

Formula First Session Task The **formula first session task** (FFST) is a form of homework a therapist might give clients to complete between their first and second sessions. The therapist might say: "Between now and the next time we meet, I would like you to observe, so that you can describe to me next time, what happens in your (family, life, marriage, relationship) that you want to continue to have happen" (de Shazer, 1985, p. 137). At the second session, clients can be asked what they observed and what they would like to have happen in the future. This kind of assignment offers clients hope that change is inevitable. It is not a matter of *if* change will occur, but *when* it will happen. According to de Shazer, this intervention tends to increase clients' optimism and hope about their present and future situation. The FFST technique emphasizes future solutions rather than past problems (Murphy, 2015).

Therapist Feedback to Clients Solution-focused practitioners generally take a break of 5 to 10 minutes toward the end of each session to compose a summary message for clients. During this break therapists formulate feedback that will be given to clients after the break. The summary might contain strengths the therapist has noticed about the client during the session, signs of hope and identifying exceptions to a problem, and a commentary on what the client is already doing that is useful in moving in a desired direction (George et al., 2015).

De Jong and Berg (2013) describe three basic parts to the structure of the summary feedback: compliments, a bridge, and suggesting a task. *Compliments* are genuine affirmations of what clients are already doing that is leading toward effective solutions. It is important that complimenting is not done in a routine or mechanical way, but in an encouraging manner that creates hope and conveys the expectation to clients that they can achieve their goals by drawing on their strengths and successes. Second, a *bridge* links the initial compliments to the suggested tasks that will be given. The bridge provides the rationale for the suggestions. The third aspect of feedback consists of *suggesting tasks* to clients, which can be considered as homework. Observational tasks ask clients to simply pay attention to some aspect of their lives. This self-monitoring process helps clients note the differences when things are better, especially what was different about the way they thought, felt, or behaved. Behavioral tasks require that clients actually do something the therapist believes would be useful to them in constructing solutions. De Jong and Berg (2013) stress that a therapist's feedback to clients addresses what they need to do more of and do differently in order to increase the chances of obtaining their goals.

Terminating From the very first solution-focused interview, the therapist is mindful of working toward termination. Once clients are able to construct a satisfactory solution, the therapeutic relationship can be terminated. The initial goal-formation question that a therapist often asks is, "What needs to be different in your life as a result of coming here for you to say that meeting with me was worthwhile?" Through the use of scaling questions, therapists can assist clients in monitoring their progress so clients can determine when they no longer need to come to therapy (De Jong & Berg, 2013). Establishing clear goals from the beginning of therapy lays the groundwork for effective termination (Murphy, 2015). Prior to ending therapy, therapists assist clients in identifying things they can do to continue the changes they have already made into the future. Clients can also be helped to identify hurdles or perceived barriers that could get in the way of maintaining the changes they have made.

Guterman (2013) maintains that the ultimate goal of solution-focused counseling is to end treatment. He adds, "If counselors are not proactive in making their treatment brief by design, then in many cases counseling will be brief by default" (p. 104). Because this model of therapy is brief, present-centered, and addresses specific complaints, it is very possible that clients will experience other developmental concerns at a later time. Clients can be invited to ask for additional sessions whenever they feel a need to get their life back on track or to update their story.

Dr. John Murphy puts many SFBT techniques into action as he illustrates assessment and treatment from a solution-focused brief therapy approach in the case of Ruth in *Case Approach to Counseling and Psychotherapy* (Corey, 2013, chap. 11).

Application to Group Counseling The solution-focused group practitioner LO7 believes that people are competent, and that given a climate where they can experience their competency, they are able to solve their own problems, enabling them to live a richer life. From the beginning, the group facilitator sets a tone of focusing on solutions (Metcalf, 1998) in which group members are given an opportunity to describe their problems briefly. A facilitator might begin a new group by requesting, "I would like each of you to introduce yourself. As you do, give us a brief idea as to why you are here and tell us what you would like for us to know about you." Facilitators help members to keep the problem external in conversations, which tends to be a relief because it gives members an opportunity to see themselves as less problem-saturated. It is the facilitator's role to create opportunities for the members to view themselves as being resourceful. Because SFBT is designed to be brief, the leader has the task of keeping group members on a solution track rather than a problem track, which helps members to move in a positive direction.

The group leader works with members in developing well-formed goals as soon as possible. Leaders concentrate on small, realistic, achievable changes that may lead to additional positive outcomes. Because success tends to build upon itself, modest goals are viewed as the beginning of change. Questions used to assist members in formulating clear goals might include "What will be different in your life when each of your problems is solved?" and "What will be going on in the future that will tell you and the rest of us in the group that things are better for you?" Sometimes members talk about what others will be doing or not doing and forget to pay attention to their own goals or behavior. At times such as this they can be asked, "And what about yourself? What will you be doing differently in that picture? As a result of your doing things differently, how would you imagine others responding to you?"

The facilitator asks members about times when their problems were not present or when the problems were less severe. The members are assisted in exploring these exceptions, and special emphasis is placed on what they did to make these events happen. The participants engage in identifying exceptions with each other. This improves the group process and promotes a solution focus, which can become quite powerful. Exceptions are real events that take place outside of the problem context. In individual counseling, only the therapist and the client are observers of competency. An advantage of group counseling is that the audience widens and more input is possible (Metcalf, 1998).

The art of questioning is a main intervention used in solution-focused groups. Questions are asked from a position of respect, genuine curiosity, sincere interest, and openness. Group leaders use questions such as these that presuppose change and remain goal-directed and future-oriented: "What did you do and what has changed since last time?" or "What did you notice that went better?" Other group members are encouraged to respond along with the group leader to promote group interaction. Facilitators may pose questions like these: "Someday, when the problems that brought you to this group are less problematic to you, what will you be doing?" "As each of you listened to others today, is there someone in our group who could be a source of encouragement for you to do something different?" The leader is attempting to help the members identify exceptions and begin to recognize personal resiliency and competency. Creating a group context in which the members are able to learn more about their personal abilities is key to members learning to resolve their own concerns.

Solution-focused group counseling offers a great deal of promise for practitioners who want a practical and time-effective approach to interventions in school settings. As a cooperative approach, SFBT shifts the focus from what's wrong in students' lives to what's working for them (Murphy, 2015; Sklare, 2005). Rather than being a cookbook of techniques for removing students' problems, this approach offers school counselors a collaborative framework aimed at achieving small, concrete changes that enable students to discover a more productive direction. This model has much to offer to school counselors who are responsible for serving large caseloads of students in a K–12 school system. For a more detailed discussion of SFBT in groups, see Corey (2016, chap. 16).

MICHAEL WHITE (1949–2008) was the cofounder, with David Epston, of the narrative therapy movement. He founded the Dulwich Centre in Adelaide, Australia, and his work with families and communities has attracted widespread international interest. Among his many books are *Narrative Means to Therapeutic Ends* (White & Epston, 1990), *Reauthoring Lives: Interviews and Essays* (1995), *Narrative of Therapists' Lives* (1997), and *Maps of Narrative Practice* (2007). Michael White died in April 2008 while visiting San Diego for a teaching workshop.

Courtesy of Cheryl White, Dulwich Centre, Adelaide, Australia

Michael White

DAVID EPSTON (b. 1944) is one of the developers of narrative therapy. He is a director of the Family Therapy Centre in Auckland, New Zealand. He is an international traveler, presenting lectures and workshops in Australia, Europe, and North America. He is a coauthor of *Narrative Means to Therapeutic Ends* (White & Epston, 1990) and *Playful Approaches to Serious Problems: Narrative Therapy With Children and Their Families* (Freeman, Epston, & Lobovits, 1997). He is well known for his work with persons affected by eating disorders and was a coauthor of *Biting the Hand That Starves You* (Maisel, Epston, & Borden, 2004).

Courtesy of David Epston

David Epston

Narrative Therapy

Introduction

Of all the social constructionists, Michael White and David Epston (1990) are best known for their use of narrative in therapy. According to White (1992), individuals construct the meaning of life in interpretive stories, which are then treated as "truth." Because of the power of dominant culture narratives, individuals tend to internalize the messages from these dominant discourses, which often work against the life opportunity of the individual.

Adopting a postmodern, narrative, social constructionist view sheds light on how power, knowledge, and "truth" are negotiated in families and other social and cultural contexts (Freedman & Combs, 1996). Narrative therapy is a strengths-based approach that emphasizes collaboration between client and therapist to help clients view themselves as empowered and living the way they want (Rice, 2015).

Key Concepts

The key concepts and therapeutic process sections are adapted from several different works, but primarily from these sources: Winslade and Monk (2007), Monk (1997), Winslade, Crocket, and Monk (1997), McKenzie and Monk (1997), and Freedman and Combs (1996). LO8

Focus of Narrative Therapy The narrative approach involves adopting a shift in focus from most traditional theories. Therapists are encouraged to establish a collaborative approach with a special interest in listening respectfully to clients' stories; to search for times in clients' lives when they were resourceful; to use questions as a way to engage clients and facilitate their exploration; to avoid diagnosing and labeling clients or accepting a totalizing description based on a problem; to assist clients in mapping the influence a problem has had on their lives; and to assist clients in separating themselves from the dominant stories they have internalized so that space can be opened for the creation of alternative life stories (Freedman & Combs, 1996).

The Role of Stories One of the theoretical underpinnings of narrative therapy is the notion that problems are manufactured in social, cultural, and political contexts. We live our lives by the stories we tell about ourselves and that others tell about us. Our stories shape reality in that they construct and constitute what we see, feel, and do. The stories we live by grow out of conversations in a social and cultural context. Change occurs by exploring how language is used to create and maintain problems (Rice, 2015). Therapy clients have vivid stories to recount. When stories are changed, not only is the person telling the story changed but the therapist who is privileged to be a part of this unfolding process is also changed (Monk, 1997).

Listening With an Open Mind All social constructionist theories emphasize listening to clients without judgment or blame, affirming and valuing them. Narrative practice goes further in deconstructing the systems of normalizing judgment that are found in medical, psychological, and educational discourse. *Normalizing judgment* is any kind of judgment that locates a person on a normal curve and is used to assess intelligence, mental health, or normal behavior. Because these kinds of judgments claim to be objective measures, they are difficult for individuals to resist and usually are internalized. Narrative therapists argue that suspending personal judgment is of little value if you participate in normalizing judgment. Deconstruction involves turning the tables and asking what clients think of the judgments they have been assigned. Narrative practitioners might be said to invite people to pass judgment on the judgments that have been working them over. Narrative therapists help clients modify their painful beliefs, values, and interpretations as clients create meaning and new possibilities from the stories they share. Therapists do not impose their value system, and interpretations flow from clients' stories rather than from a preconceived and ultimately imposed theory of importance and value.

Narrative therapists strive to listen to the problem-saturated story of the client without getting stuck. Therapists stay alert for details that give evidence of the client's competence in taking stands against oppressive problems. Winslade and Monk (2007) maintain that the therapist believes the client's abilities, talents, positive intentions, and life experiences can be the catalysts for new possibilities for action. The narrative therapist demonstrates faith that these inner resources and competencies can be identified, even when the client is having difficulty seeing them.

During the narrative conversation, attention is given to avoiding totalizing language, which reduces the complexity of the individual by assigning an all-embracing, single description to the essence of the person. Therapists begin to separate the person from the problem in their mind as they listen and respond (Winslade & Monk, 2007). This is called *double listening*.

The narrative perspective focuses on the capacity of humans for creative and imaginative thought, which is often found in their resistance to dominant discourse. Narrative practitioners do not assume that they know more about the lives of clients than their clients do. Clients are the primary interpreters of their own experiences. People are viewed as active agents who are able to derive meaning from their experiential world, and they are encouraged to join with others who might share in the development of a counter story.

The Therapeutic Process

This brief overview of the steps in the narrative therapeutic process illustrates the structure of the narrative approach (O'Hanlon, 1994, pp. 25–26):

- Collaborate with the client to come up with a mutually acceptable name for the problem.
- Personify the problem and attribute oppressive intentions and tactics to it.
- Investigate how the problem has been disrupting, dominating, or discouraging to the client.
- Invite the client to see his or her story from a different perspective by inquiring into alternative meanings for events.
- Discover moments when the client wasn't dominated or discouraged by the problem by searching for exceptions to the problem.
- Find historical evidence to bolster a new view of the client as competent enough to have stood up to, defeated, or escaped from the dominance

or oppression of the problem. (At this phase the person's identity and life story begin to be rewritten.)
- Ask the client to speculate about what kind of future could be expected from the strong, competent person who is emerging. As the client becomes free of problem-saturated stories of the past, he or she can envision and plan for a less problematic future.
- Find or create an audience for perceiving and supporting the new story. It is not enough to recite a counter story. The client needs to live the counter story outside of therapy. Because the person's problem initially developed in a social context, it is essential to involve the social environment in supporting the new life story that has emerged in the conversations with the therapist.

Winslade and Monk (2007) stress that narrative conversations do not follow the linear progression described here; it is better to think of these steps in terms of cyclical progression containing the following elements:

- Move problem stories toward externalized descriptions of problems
- Map the effects of a problem on the individual
- Invite the individual to evaluate the problem and its effects
- Listen to signs of strength and competence in an individual's problem-saturated stories
- Build a new story of competence and document these achievements

Therapy Goals A general goal of narrative therapy is to invite people to describe their experience in new and fresh language. In doing this, they open new vistas of what is possible. This new language enables clients to develop new meanings for problematic thoughts, feelings, and behaviors (Freedman & Combs, 1996). Narrative therapy almost always includes an awareness of the impact of various aspects of dominant culture on human life. Narrative practitioners seek to enlarge the perspective and facilitate the discovery or creation of new options that are unique to the people they see.

Therapist's Function and Role Narrative therapists are active facilitators. The concepts of care, interest, respectful curiosity, openness, empathy, contact, and even fascination are seen as a relational necessity. The not-knowing position, which allows therapists to follow, affirm, and be guided by the stories of their clients, creates participant-observer and process-facilitator roles for the therapist and integrates therapy with a postmodern view of human inquiry.

A main task of the therapist is to help clients construct a preferred story line. The narrative therapist adopts a stance characterized by respectful curiosity and works with clients to explore both the impact of the problem on them and what they are doing to reduce the effects of the problem (Winslade & Monk, 2007). One of the main functions of the therapist is to ask questions of clients and, based on the answers, to generate further questions.

White and Epston (1990) start with an exploration of the client in relation to the presenting problem. It is not uncommon for clients to present initial stories in which they and the problem are fused, as if one and the same. White uses questions aimed at separating the problem from the people affected by the problem. This shift in language begins the deconstruction of the original narrative in which the person and the problem were fused; now the problem is objectified as external to the client.

Like the solution-focused therapist, the narrative therapist assumes the client is the expert when it comes to what he or she wants in life. The narrative therapist tends to avoid using language that embodies diagnosis, assessment, treatment, and intervention. Functions such as diagnosis and assessment often grant priority to the practitioner's "truth" over clients' knowledge about their own lives. The narrative approach gives emphasis to understanding clients' lived experiences and de-emphasizes efforts to predict, interpret, and pathologize.

Monk (1997) emphasizes that narrative therapy will vary with each client because each person is unique. For Monk, narrative conversations are based on a way of being, and if narrative counseling "is seen as a formula or used as a recipe, clients will have the experience of having things done *to* them and feel left out of the conversation" (p. 24).

The Therapeutic Relationship Narrative therapists place great importance **LO9** on the values and ethical commitments a therapist brings to the therapy venture. Some of these attitudes include optimism and respect, curiosity and persistence, valuing the client's knowledge, and creating a special kind of relationship characterized by a real power-sharing dialogue (Winslade & Monk, 2007). Collaboration, compassion, reflection, and discovery characterize the therapeutic relationship. The strengths-based and future-focused nature of narrative therapy lends itself to a more collaborative relationship than problem-based approaches that emphasize the therapist as the expert in the relationship (Rice, 2015). If this relationship is to be truly collaborative, the therapist needs to be aware of how power manifests itself in his or her professional practice. This does not mean that the therapist does not have authority as a professional. He or she uses this authority, however, by treating clients as experts in their own lives.

Winslade, Crocket, and Monk (1997) describe this collaboration as coauthoring or sharing authority. Clients function as authors when they have the authority to speak on their own behalf. In the narrative approach, the therapist-as-expert is replaced by the client-as-expert. This notion challenges the stance of the therapist as being an all-wise and all-knowing expert.

Clients are often stuck in a pattern of living a problem-saturated story that does not work. When a client has a limited perception of his or her capacities due to being saturated in problem thinking, it is the job of the therapist to elicit other strength-related stories to modify the client's perception. The therapist assists the client in this pursuit by entering into a dialogue and asking questions in an effort to elicit the perspectives, resources, and unique experiences of the client. The past is history, but it sometimes provides a foundation for understanding and discovering news of differences or unique outcomes that will make a difference. The history of the problem often dominates understanding, but there is another history that narrative therapists argue should not be neglected. It is the history of the counter story to the problem story, which is constructed in conversation and becomes the foundation for a different future. The narrative therapist supplies the optimism and sometimes a process, but the client generates what is possible and contributes the movement that actualizes it.

Application: Therapeutic Techniques and Procedures

LO10

The effective application of narrative therapy is more dependent on therapists' attitudes or perspectives than on techniques. In the practice of narrative therapy, there is no recipe, no set agenda, and no formula that the therapist can follow to assure positive results (Drewery & Winslade, 1997). When externalizing questions are approached mainly as a technique, the intervention will be shallow, forced, and unlikely to produce significant therapeutic effects (Freedman & Combs, 1996; O'Hanlon, 1994).

Narrative therapists are in agreement with Carl Rogers on the importance of the therapist's way of being rather than being technique driven. A narrative approach to counseling is more than the application of skills; it is based on the therapist's personal characteristics that create a climate that encourages clients to see their stories from different perspectives. Narrative therapists emphasize their willingness to see beyond dominant cultural norms and to appreciate clients' differences. However, a series of "maps" of narrative conversational trajectories can help give structure and direction to a therapeutic conversation (White, 2007).

Questions . . . and More Questions The questions narrative therapists ask may seem embedded in a unique conversation, part of a dialogue about earlier dialogues, a discovery of unique events, or an exploration of dominant culture processes and imperatives. Whatever the purpose, the questions are often circular, or relational, and they seek to empower clients in new ways. To use Gregory Bateson's (1972) famous phrase, they are questions in search of a difference that will make a difference.

Narrative therapists use questions as a way to generate experience rather than to gather information. The aim of questioning is to progressively discover or construct the client's experience so that the client has a sense of a preferred direction. Questions are always asked from a position of respect, curiosity, and openness. Therapists ask questions from a not-knowing position, meaning that they do not pose questions that they think they already know the answers to.

Through the process of asking questions, therapists provide clients with an opportunity to explore various dimensions of their life situations. This questioning process helps bring out the unstated cultural assumptions that contribute to the original construction of the problem. The therapist is interested in finding out how the problems first became evident, and how they have affected clients' views of themselves (Monk, 1997). Narrative therapists attempt to engage people in deconstructing problem-saturated stories, identifying preferred directions, and creating alternative stories that support these preferred directions. For a more complete discussion of the use of questions in narrative therapy, see Madigan (2011).

Externalization and Deconstruction Narrative therapists believe it is not the person that is the problem, but the problem that is the problem (White, 1989). These problems often are products of the cultural world or of the power relations in which this world is located. Living life means relating to problems, not being fused with them. Narrative therapists help clients deconstruct these problematic stories by disassembling the taken-for-granted assumptions that are made about an event, which then opens alternative possibilities for living.

Externalization is one process for deconstructing the power of a narrative. This process separates the person from identification with the problem. When clients view themselves as "being" the problem, they are limited in the ways they can effectively deal with the problem. When clients experience the problem as being located outside of themselves, they create a relationship with the problem. For example, there is quite a difference between labeling someone an alcoholic and indicating that alcohol has invaded his or her life. Separating the problem from the individual facilitates hope and enables clients to take a stand against specific story lines, such as self-blame. By understanding the cultural invitations to blame oneself, clients can deconstruct this story line and generate a more positive, healing story.

The method used to separate the person from the problem is referred to as externalizing conversation, which opens up space for new stories to emerge. This method is particularly useful when people have internalized diagnoses and labels that have not been validating or empowering of the change process (Bertolino & O'Hanlon, 2002). **Externalizing conversations** counteract oppressive, problem-saturated stories and empower clients to feel competent to handle the problems they face. Two stages of structuring externalizing conversations are (1) to map the influence of the problem in the person's life, and (2) to map the influence of the person's life back on the problem (McKenzie & Monk, 1997).

Mapping the influence of the problem on the person generates a great deal of useful information and often results in people feeling less shamed and blamed. People feel listened to and understood when the problem's influences are explored in a systematic fashion. A common question is, "When did this problem first appear in your life?" When this mapping is done carefully, it lays the foundation for coauthoring a new story line for the client. Often clients feel outraged when they see for the first time how much the problem is affecting them. The job of the therapist is to assist clients in tracing the problem from when it originated to the present. Therapists may put a future twist on the problem by asking, "If the problem were to continue for a month (or any time period), what would this mean for you?" This question can motivate the client to join with the therapist in combating the impact of the problem's effects. Other useful questions are "To what extent has this problem influenced your life?" and "How deeply has this problem affected you?"

It is important to identify instances when the problem did not completely dominate a client's life. This kind of mapping can help the client who is disillusioned by the problem see some hope for a different kind of life. Therapists look for these "sparkling moments" as they engage in externalizing conversations with clients (White & Epston, 1990).

The case of Brandon illustrates an externalizing conversation. Brandon says that he gets angry far too much, especially when he feels that his wife is criticizing him unjustly: "I just flare! I pop off, get upset, fight back. Later, I wish I hadn't, but it's too late. I've messed up again." Questions about how his anger occurs, complete with specific examples and events, can help chart the influence of the problem. However, it is questions like the ones that follow that *externalize* the problem: "What is the mission of the anger, and how does it recruit you into this mission?" "How does the anger get you, and how does it trick you into letting it become so powerful?" "What does the anger require of you, and what happens to you when you meet its requirements?" "What cultural supports (in your family/community/world) have shaped the role that anger plays for you?"

Search for Unique Outcomes In the narrative approach, externalizing questions are followed by questions searching for unique outcomes. The therapist talks to the client about moments of choice or success regarding the problem. This is done by selecting for attention any experience that stands apart from the problem story, regardless of how insignificant it might seem to the client. The therapist may ask: "Was there ever a time in which anger wanted to take you over, and you resisted? What was that like for you? How did you do it?" These questions are aimed at highlighting moments when the problem has not occurred or when the problem has been dealt with successfully. Unique outcomes can often be found in the past or the present, but they can also be hypothesized for the future: "What form would standing up against your anger take?" Exploring questions such as these enables clients to see that change is possible. Linking a series of such unique outcomes together starts to form a counter story. It is within the account of unique outcomes that a gateway is provided for alternative versions of a person's life (White, 1992).

Following the description of a unique outcome, White (1992) suggests posing questions, both direct and indirect, that lead to the elaboration of preferred identity stories:

- What do you think this tells me about what you have wanted for your life and about what you have been trying for in your life?
- How do you think knowing this has affected my view of you as a person?
- Of all those people who have known you, who would be least surprised that you have been able to take this step in addressing your problem's influence in your life?
- What actions might you commit yourself to if you were to more fully embrace this knowledge of who you are? (p. 133)

The development of unique outcome stories into solution stories is facilitated by what Epston and White (1992) call "circulation questions":

- Now that you have reached this point in life, who else should know about it?
- I guess there are a number of people who have an outdated view of who you are as a person. What ideas do you have about updating these views?
- If other people seek therapy for the same reasons you did, can I share with them any of the important discoveries you have made? (p. 23)

These questions are not asked in a barrage-like manner. Questioning is an integral part of the context of the narrative conversation, and each question is sensitively attuned to the responses brought out by the previous question (White, 1992).

McKenzie and Monk (1997) suggest that therapists seek permission from the client before asking a series of questions. By letting a client know that they do not have answers to the questions they raise, therapists are putting the client in control of the therapeutic process. Asking permission of the client to use persistent questioning tends to minimize the risk of inadvertently pressuring the client.

Alternative Stories and Reauthoring Constructing counter stories goes hand in hand with deconstruction, and the narrative therapist listens for openings to counter stories. People can continually and actively reauthor their lives, and narrative therapists invite clients to author alternative stories through "unique outcomes"; these events could not be predicted from listening to the dominant problem-saturated story and are not included in any narrative about the person. The narrative therapist asks for openings: "Have you ever been able to escape the influence of the problem?" The therapist listens for clues to competence in the midst of a problematic story and builds a story of competence around it. Madigan (2011) suggests that a person's life story is probably much more interesting than the story being told. He maintains a therapist's main task is "to help people to remember, reclaim and reinvent a richer, thicker, and more meaningful alternative story" (p. 159).

A turning point in the narrative interview comes when clients make the choice of whether to continue to live by a problem-saturated story or to state a preference for an alternative story (Winslade & Monk, 2007). Through the use of unique possibility questions, the therapist moves the focus into the future. For example: "Given what you have learned about yourself, what is the next step you might take?" "When you are acting from your preferred identity, what actions will it lead you to do more of?" Such questions encourage people to reflect upon what they have presently achieved and what their next steps might be.

White and Epston's (1990) inquiry into unique outcomes is similar to the exception questions of solution-focused therapists. Both seek to build on the competence already present in the person. The development of alternative stories, or narratives, is an enactment of ultimate hope: Today is the first day of the rest of your life. Refer to *Case Approach to Counseling and Psychotherapy* (Corey, 2013, chap. 11) for two concrete examples of a narrative approach to working with Ruth from the perspectives of Dr. Gerald Monk and Dr. John Winslade.

Documenting the Evidence Narrative practitioners believe that new stories take hold only when there is an audience to appreciate and support them. Gaining an audience for the news that change is taking place needs to occur if alternative stories are to stay alive, and an appreciative audience to new developments is consciously sought.

One technique for consolidating the gains a client makes involves a therapist writing letters to the person. Narrative therapists have pioneered the development of therapeutic letter writing. These letters that the therapist writes provide a record of the session and may include an externalizing description of the problem and its influence on the client, as well as an account of the client's strengths and abilities that are identified in a session. Letters can be read again at different times, and the story that they are part of can be reinspired. The letter highlights the struggle the client has had with the problem and draws distinctions between the problem-saturated story and the developing new and preferred story (McKenzie & Monk, 1997).

Epston has developed a special facility for carrying on therapeutic dialogues between sessions through the use of letters (White & Epston, 1990). His letters may be long, chronicling the process of the interview and the agreements reached, or short, highlighting a meaning or understanding reached in the session and asking a question that has occurred to him since the end of the previous therapy visit.

Usually they include as many direct quotations from what the client said as possible. These letters are used to encourage clients, noting what they said about their own accomplishments in relation to handling problems or speculating on the meaning of their accomplishments for others in their community. Letters documenting the changes clients have achieved tend to strengthen the significance of the changes, both for the client and for others in the client's life.

Narrative letters reinforce the importance of carrying what is being learned in the therapy office into everyday life. The message conveyed is that participating fully in the world is more important than being in the therapy office. In an informal survey of the perceptions of the value of narrative letters by past clients, the average worth of a letter was equal to more than three individual sessions (Nylund & Thomas, 1994). This finding is consistent with McKenzie and Monk's (1997) statement: "Some narrative counselors have suggested that a well-composed letter following a therapy session or preceding another can be equal to about five regular sessions" (p. 113).

Application to Group Counseling Many of the techniques described **LO11** in this chapter can be applied to group counseling. Winslade and Monk (2007) claim that the narrative emphasis on creating an appreciative audience for new developments in an individual's life lends itself to group counseling. They state: "Groups provide a ready-made community of concern and many opportunities for the kind of interaction that opens possibilities for new ways of living. New identities can be rehearsed and tried out into a wider world" (p. 135). They give several examples of working in a narrative way with groups in schools: getting back on track in schoolwork; an adventure-based program; an anger management group; and a grief counseling group. For a detailed description of these narrative groups, see Winslade and Monk (2007, chap. 5).

Postmodern Approaches From a Multicultural Perspective

Strengths From a Diversity Perspective

Social constructionism is congruent with the philosophy of multicultur- **LO12** alism. One of the problems that culturally diverse clients often experience is the expectation that they should conform their lives to the truths and reality of the dominant society of which they are a part. With the emphasis on multiple realities and the assumption that what is perceived to be a truth is the product of social construction, the postmodern approaches are a good fit with diverse worldviews.

The social constructionist approach to therapy provides clients with a framework to think about their thinking and to determine the impact stories have on what they do. Clients are encouraged to explore how their realities are being constructed out of cultural discourse and the consequences that follow from such constructions. Within the framework of their cultural values and worldview, clients can explore their beliefs and provide their own reinterpretations of significant life events. The practitioner with a social constructionist perspective can guide clients in a manner that respects their underlying values. This dimension is especially important in those cases where counselors are from a different cultural background or do not share the same worldview as their clients.

Narrative therapy is grounded in a sociocultural context, which makes this approach especially relevant for counseling culturally diverse clients. Narrative therapists operate on the premise that problems are identified within social, cultural, political, and relational contexts rather than existing within individuals. They are very much concerned with considering the specifications of gender, ethnicity, race, disability, sexual orientation, social class, and spirituality and religion as therapeutic issues. Furthermore, therapy becomes a place to reauthor the social constructions and identity narratives that clients are finding problematic.

Narrative therapy is a relational and anti-individualistic practice. Michael White believes that to address a person's struggles in therapy without a relational and contextual understanding of his or her story is entirely absurd (as cited in Madigan, 2011). Narrative therapists concentrate on problem stories that dominate and subjugate at the personal, social, and cultural levels. The sociopolitical conceptualization of problems sheds light on those cultural notions and practices that produce dominant and oppressive narratives. From this orientation, practitioners take apart the cultural assumptions that are a part of a client's problem situation. People are able to come to an understanding of how oppressive social practices have affected them. This awareness can lead to a new perspective on dominant themes of oppression that have been such an integral part of a client's story, and with this cultural awareness new stories can be generated.

In their discussion of the multicultural influences on clients, Bertolino and O'Hanlon (2002) approach clients without a preconceived notion about their experience and learn from their clients about their experiential world. Bertolino and O'Hanlon practice multicultural curiosity by listening respectfully to their clients, who become their best teachers. Here are some questions these authors suggest as a way to more fully understand multicultural influences on a client:

- Tell me more about the influence that [some aspect of your culture] has played in your life.
- What can you share with me about your background that will enable me to more fully understand you?
- What challenges have you faced growing up in your culture?
- What, if anything, about your background has been difficult for you?
- How have you been able to draw on strengths and resources from your culture? What resources can you draw from in times of need?

Questions such as these can shed light on specific cultural influences that have been sources of support or that contributed to a client's problem.

Shortcomings From a Diversity Perspective

A potential shortcoming of the postmodern approaches pertains to the not-knowing stance the therapist assumes, along with the assumption of the client-as-expert. Individuals from many different cultural groups tend to elevate the professional as the expert who will offer direction and solutions for the person seeking help. If the therapist is telling the client, "I am not really an expert; you are the expert; I trust in your resources for you to find solutions to your problems," then this may engender lack of confidence in the therapist. To avoid this situation, the therapist using a solution-focused or a narrative orientation needs to convey to clients that he or she has expertise in the process of therapy but clients are the experts in knowing what they want in their lives. The postmodern approaches stress being transparent with clients and honoring their hopes and expectations in therapy. This emphasis creates a context for providing culturally responsive services.

Postmodern Approaches Applied to the Case of Stan

I operate from an integrative perspective by combining concepts and techniques from the solution-focused and narrative approaches. From this framework, I am philosophically opposed to assessment and diagnosis using the *DSM-5* model, and I do not begin therapy with a formal assessment. Instead, I engage Stan in collaborative conversations centered on change, competence, preferences, possibilities, and ideas for making changes in the future.

I begin my work with Stan by inviting him to tell me about the concerns that brought him to therapy and what he expects to accomplish in his sessions. I also provide Stan with a brief orientation of some of the basic ideas that guide my practice and describe my view of counseling as a collaborative partnership in which he is the senior partner. Stan is somewhat surprised by this because he expected that I was the person with the experience and expertise. He informs me that he has very little confidence in knowing how to proceed with his life, especially since he has "messed up" so often. I am aware that he has self-doubts when it comes to assuming the role of senior partner. However, I work to demystify the therapeutic process and establish a collaborative relationship, conveying to Stan that he is in charge of the direction his therapy will take. I also promise to explore the undermining effects of the self-doubts in his life and how he has managed to live life in spite of these.

Soon after this orientation to how therapy works, I inquire about some specific goals that Stan would like to reach through the therapy sessions. Stan gives clear signs that he is willing and eager to change. However, he adds that he has become convinced that he suffers from low self-esteem. As he tells me more about how self-doubts cripple him regularly and lead to a negative evaluation of himself as "messed up," I begin to externalize the idea of self-doubts and inquire into the history of their appearance in his life. I also carefully map the effects of self-doubts in his life. Then I start to focus Stan on looking for exceptions to the self-doubts. I pose an exception question (solution-focused therapy): "What is different about the contexts or times when you have not experienced self-doubts?" Stan is able to identify some positive characteristics: his courage, determination, and willingness to try new things in spite of his self-doubts, and his gift for working with children. Stan knows what he wants out of therapy and has clear goals: to achieve his educational goals, to enhance his belief in himself, to relate to women without fear, and to feel more joy instead of sadness and anxiety. I invite Stan to talk more about how he has managed to make the gains he has in spite of struggling with the problem of self-doubt.

I allow Stan to share his problem-saturated story, but I do not get stuck in this narrative. I invite Stan to think of his problems as external to the core of his selfhood. I help him to notice the cultural forces that have recruited him into a story of thinking less about himself. Even during the early sessions, I encourage Stan to separate his being from his problems by posing questions that externalize his problem.

Although Stan presents several problem areas that are of concern to him, I work with him on identifying one particular problem. Stan says he is depressed a great deal of the time, and he worries that his depression might someday overwhelm him. After listening to Stan's fears and concerns, I ask Stan the miracle question (solution-focused technique): "Let's suppose that a miracle were to happen while you are asleep tonight. When you wake up tomorrow, the problems you are mentioning are gone. What would be the signs to you that this miracle actually occurred and that your problems were solved? How would your life be different?" With this intervention, I am shifting the focus from talking about problems to talking about solutions. I explain to Stan that much of his therapy will deal with finding both present and future solutions rather than dwelling on past problems. Together we engage in a conversation that features change-talk rather than problem-talk.

To a great extent, Stan has linked his identity story with his problems, especially depression. He doesn't think of his problems as being separate from himself. I want Stan to realize that he personally is not his problem, but instead that the problem is the problem. When I ask Stan to give a name to his problem, he eventually comes up with "Disabling depression!" He then relates how his depression has kept him from functioning the way he would like in many areas of his life. I then use *externalizing questions* (narrative technique) as a way to separate Stan from his problem: "How long has depression gotten the best of you?" "What has depression cost you?" "What conclusions about yourself does it talk you into?" "What do you think of what it has been doing to mess up your life?" "Have there been times when you stood up to depression and did not let it win?" Of course, I briefly explain to him what I am doing by using externalizing language, lest he think this is a strange way to counsel. I talk more about the advantages of engaging in externalizing conversations. I also talk with Stan about the importance of mapping the effects of the problem on his life. This process involves exploring how long the problem has been around, the extent to which the problem has influenced various aspects of his life, and how deeply the problem continues to affect him.

As the sessions progress, there is a collaborative effort aimed at investigating how the problem has been a disrupting, dominating, and discouraging influence. Stan comes to view his story from a different perspective. I continue talking with Stan about those moments when he has not been dominated or discouraged by depression and anxiety and continue to search for exceptions to these problematic experiences. Stan and I participate in conversations about unique outcomes, or occasions when he has demonstrated courage and persistence in the face of discouraging events. Some of these "sparkling moments" include Stan's accomplishments in college, volunteer work with children, progress in curbing his tendencies to abuse alcohol, willingness to challenge his fears and make new acquaintances, talking back to self-defeating internal messages, accomplishments in securing employment, and his willingness to create a vision of a productive future.

With my help, Stan accumulates evidence from his past to bolster a new view of himself as competent enough to have escaped from the dominance of problematic stories. At this phase in his therapy, Stan makes a decision to create an alternative narrative. Several sessions are devoted to reauthoring Stan's story in ways that are lively, creative, and colorful. Along with the process of creating an alternative story, I explore with Stan the possibilities of recruiting an audience who will reinforce his positive changes. I ask, "Who do you know who would be least surprised to hear of your recent changes, and what would this person know about you that would lead to him or her not being so surprised?" Stan identifies one of his early teachers who served as a mentor to him and who believed in him when Stan had little belief in himself. Some therapy time is devoted to discussing how new stories take root only when there is an audience to appreciate them.

After five therapy sessions, Stan brings up the matter of termination. At the sixth and final session, I introduce scaling questions, asking Stan to rate his degree of improvement on a range of problems we explored in the past weeks. On a scale of zero to 10, Stan ranks how he saw himself prior to his first session and how he sees himself today on various specific dimensions (scaling technique). We also talked about Stan's goals for his future and what kinds of improvements he will need to make to attain what he wants. I then give Stan a letter I wrote summarizing both the problem story and its effects and also the counter story that we have been developing in therapy. In my narrative letter, I describe Stan's determination and cooperation in his own words and encourage him to circulate the news of the differences he has brought about in his life. I also ask some questions that invite him to develop the new story of identity more fully.

Questions for Reflection

- As Stan's therapist, I borrowed key concepts and techniques common to both solution-focused and narrative orientations. In your work with Stan, what specific concepts would you borrow from each of these approaches? What techniques would you draw from each of the approaches? What possible advantages do you see, if any, in applying an integration of solution-focused and narrative models in your work with Stan?

- What unique values, if any, do you see in working with Stan from a postmodern perspective as opposed to working with Stan from the other therapeutic approaches you've studied thus far?
- I asked many questions of Stan. List some additional questions you would be particularly interested in pursuing with Stan.
- In what ways could you integrate SFBT and narrative therapy with feminist therapy in Stan's case? What other therapies might you combine with the postmodern approaches? What other therapies would not combine so well with these postmodern therapies?
- At this point, you are very familiar with the themes in Stan's life. If you were to write a narrative letter that you would then give to Stan, what would you most want to include? What would you want to talk to him about regarding his future?

Visit CengageBrain.com or watch the DVD for the video program on *Theory and Practice of Counseling and Psychotherapy: The Case of Stan and Lecturettes*, Session 11 (SFBT) and Session 12 (narrative therapy), for a demonstration of my approach to counseling Stan from this perspective. Session 11 illustrates techniques such as identifying exceptions, the miracle question, and scaling. Session 12 focuses on Stan's work in creating a new story of his life.

Postmodern Approaches Applied to the Case of Gwen*

Solution-Focused Brief Therapy With Gwen

This session begins with Gwen expressing how overwhelmed she is with the number of assignments she has at work.

Gwen: I don't think I can handle the pressure of these new assignments.

Therapist: On a scale of zero to 10, where zero is no pressure and 10 is extreme pressure. Where would your feeling of pressure be on the scale?

Gwen: 8! I should have just kept quiet and not taken on any new projects. I always do this to myself. I wish I could start over and not take on so much. I am missing out on time with my family and friends because I have piled the work on so high! I don't know why I create so much work for myself. I know people at work can see that I am on the edge. I am not feeling good about anything I am doing these days. I know I'm ruining my reputation because I just can't get things done. I am missing in action in my own life.

Therapist: Tell me about some times when you did not feel this way. What were you doing when things were getting done that you are not doing now?

I encourage Gwen to think about some time when her stress was not so overwhelming and what she did to better manage her stress. This focus on discovering Gwen's strengths puts Gwen in the position of being the expert on her own life. I am confident that Gwen has the a capacity to find solutions to her challenges.

Gwen is so accustomed to her story of anxiety and feeling overwhelmed that it is difficult for her to shift gears and observe that she is doing several things well in her life. My interventions are aimed at assisting her in seeing herself as more than being highly anxious.

Therapist: In the midst of your busy life, you have remained committed to therapy. I find that very impressive given your schedule and the number of obligations you are juggling. I wonder what else might be going well in your life.

Gwen: I have been arriving at work on time, and that feels pretty good. Also, I took time for a swimming lesson even though I was stressed out about getting my projects done. I must say that I felt so much better afterward.

*Dr. Kellie Kirksey writes about her ways of thinking and practicing from a postmodern perspective, first using SFBT and then using narrative therapy, and applying these models to Gwen.

Therapist: If you had a magic wand and could solve your problem today, how would you know it was solved? [*The miracle question*]

Gwen: I would know it was solved if I did not have a stomach ache, did not triple book meetings, didn't have five projects due all at once, felt comfortable taking time for relaxation, had time to go out with friends, and didn't have stacks of paper around my house and office just waiting for me to handle it all.

Therapist: What would you be doing or feeling that would be different?

Gwen: I would be able to go home at a reasonable time at after work. I would feel more rested. I would have healthy and balanced meals, and I would have more quality time with my husband and children. At work, I would feel good about the projects I was finishing, and I would resist taking on too many projects at the same time.

The miracle question, or the magic wand question as I call it, is a way to assist Gwen in projecting into the future to the life she wants to experience. I emphasize that doing one thing differently could be a significant step in finding a solution.

Therapist: I invite you to rip up your canvas of anxiety and create a new portrait of calm in your life by doing one thing differently. What do you think you can change this week?

Gwen: I will begin my day with prayer and some stretching exercises to help me loosen up and to reduce my stress level. And I think it is time to resign from one of the committees I am on now.

Therapist: Those are great choices you are making. I look forward to hearing how you did when we meet next week.

I compliment Gwen on the progress she is making, and in our next session I will follow up on her homework. I hope Gwen will discover that the answers she is seeking reside within herself.

Questions for Reflection

- What interventions helped Gwen begin to think more about her resources and strengths than about her problems?
- What do you think of the application of the miracle question with Gwen? What steps did Gwen decide to take as a result of her answer?
- If you were counseling Gwen and she was unable to recall any time when the problem did not exist, how would you move forward with her?

Narrative Therapy With Gwen

Words have the power to heal and transform our lives. Words also have the power to keep us spiraling downward, accepting a negative story line that perpetuates feelings of depression, scarcity, fear, anxiety, self-loathing, and more. Our stories fuel our thoughts and behaviors, and we must make sure that these stories are not a source of negative programming that keeps us stuck. If Gwen is willing to keep a journal and write about her younger self, I think she will begin to reconstruct the story of her true self today.

Therapist: Words can become our medicine and our tool for transformation and healing. I would like you to use this journal to write about your story of loneliness. Try to identify when loneliness first appeared in your life. Let the words present themselves in whatever way they come.

Gwen: I think I could write volumes about feeling unimportant, invisible, and insignificant when I was a child.

Therapist: Before you begin writing, sit quietly for 5 minutes and connect to your younger self who first experienced these feelings of loneliness. Give that part of yourself a name and become a loving companion to that lonely little girl inside of you.

My goal is to help Gwen externalize the problem she is experiencing and move it outside of herself. As Gwen separates herself from her problem-saturated story, she can release the old patterns associated with the old story and literally rewrite her life to include peace, joy, and connection.

Gwen writes about staying in the house to avoid being called names by the kids on her street; being the odd child in the family and wanting to hide because she was different; waiting days for her dad to return home; hiding her precious items in a special box so they wouldn't get stolen when the house was broken into; being the only Black child in the Catholic Church and feeling like she was under a microscope; and how she began to stay busy to keep herself safe. I work with Gwen to help her view her stories through a lens of compassion, growth, and healing.

As Gwen began to reconstruct her story, she was able to see that her parents did the best they could. She looked at the entire cast of her narrative with deeper compassion and saw that through the challenges of her childhood she become a strong, creative, resilient woman. From a position of adult strength, Gwen began to sooth the lonely little girl that still resides in her heart. Through writing, Gwen could see that she was wounded but not broken. Narrative therapy helped Gwen come closer to a place of self-love and forgiveness, and her anxiety began to lessen as she released the repressed emotions that had kept her isolated and lonely. In her final session, Gwen and I developed a written "graduation speech" together in which we formalized the fact that she is no longer a child and has moved beyond her history.

Questions for Reflection

- What therapeutic purpose is served when the therapist helps Gwen separate herself from the problem?
- What value do you see in journal writing as a tool to assist Gwen in reconstructing her story?
- What is one other technique from narrative therapy that you would want to use with Gwen?
- How do you experience hearing about Gwen's stories of loneliness?

Summary and Evaluation

Summary

LO13

In social constructionist theory the therapist-as-expert is replaced by the client-as-expert. Although clients are viewed as experts on their own lives, they are often stuck in patterns that are not working well for them. Both solution-focused and narrative therapists enter into dialogues in an effort to elicit the perspectives, resources, and unique experiences of their clients. The therapeutic endeavor is a highly collaborative relationship in which the client is the senior partner. The qualities of the therapeutic relationship are at the heart of the effectiveness of both SFBT and narrative therapy. This has resulted in many therapists giving increased attention to creating a collaborative relationship with clients. Collaborative therapists adjust their approach to each client or group instead of requiring clients to adapt to their approach. Thus therapy may look very different for one client than for another.

The not-knowing position of the therapist has been infused as a key concept of both the solution-focused and narrative therapeutic approaches. The not-knowing position, which allows therapists to be curious about, affirm, and be guided by the stories of their clients, creates participant-observer and process-facilitator roles for the therapist and integrates therapy with a postmodern perspective of human inquiry.

Both solution-focused brief therapy and narrative therapy are based on the optimistic assumption that people are healthy, competent, resourceful, and possess the ability to construct solutions and alternative stories that can enhance their lives. In SFBT the therapeutic process provides a context whereby individuals focus on creating solutions rather than talking about their problems. Some common techniques include the use of miracle questions, exception questions, and scaling questions. In narrative therapy the therapeutic process attends to the sociocultural context wherein clients are assisted in separating themselves from their problems and are afforded the opportunity of authoring new stories.

Practitioners with solution-focused or narrative orientations tend to engage clients in conversations that lead to progressive narratives that help clients make steady gains toward their goals. Therapists often ask clients: "Tell me about times when your life was going the way you wanted it to." These conversations illustrate stories of life worth living. On the basis of these conversations, the power of problems is taken apart (deconstructed) and new directions and solutions are manifest and made possible.

Contributions of Postmodern Approaches

Social constructionism, SFBT, and narrative therapy are making many contributions to the field of psychotherapy. I especially value the optimistic orientation of these postmodern approaches that rest on the assumptions that people are competent and can be trusted to use their resources in creating better solutions and more life-affirming stories. Many postmodern practitioners and writers have found that clients are able to make significant moves toward building more satisfying lives in a relatively short period of time (Bertolino & O'Hanlon, 2002; De Jong & Berg, 2013; de Shazer, 1991; Freedman & Combs, 1996; Hoyt, 2009, 2015; Miller, Hubble, & Duncan, 1996; O'Hanlon & Weiner-Davis, 2003; Walter & Peller, 1992, 2000; Winslade & Monk, 2007).

To its credit, solution-focused therapy is a brief approach, of about five sessions, that seems to show promising results (de Shazer, 1991). SFBT tends to be very brief, even among the time-limited therapies. It should be noted that the brevity comes from the client being in charge of goal setting and determining which issues are of immediate concern. This differs from many other models in which the therapist determines the direction therapy should take.

I think the nonpathologizing stance characteristic of practitioners with a social constructionist, solution-focused, or narrative orientation is a major contribution to the counseling profession. Rather than dwelling on what is wrong with a person, these approaches view the client as being competent and resourceful. People cannot be reduced to a specific problem nor accurately labeled and identified with a disorder. Even practitioners who are expected to formulate a diagnosis can learn the value of a respectful way to relate to clients.

One particular area where the solution-focused approach shows promise is in group treatment with domestic violence offenders. Lee, Sebold, and Uken (2003) describe a cutting-edge treatment approach that seems to create effective, positive change in domestic violence offenders. This approach is dramatically different from traditional approaches in that there is virtually no emphasis on the presenting problem of domestic violence. The approach focuses on holding offenders accountable and responsible for building solutions rather than emphasizing their problems and deficits. The process described by Lee and colleagues is brief when measured against traditional program standards, lasting only eight sessions over a 10- to 12-week period. Lee, Sebold, and Uken report research that indicates a recidivism rate of 16.7% and completion rates of 92.9%. In contrast, more traditional approaches typically generate recidivism rates between 40 and 60% and completion rates of less than 50%.

A major strength of both solution-focused and narrative therapies is the use of questioning, which is the centerpiece of both approaches. Open-ended questions about the client's attitudes, thoughts, feeling, behaviors, and perceptions are one of the main interventions. Especially useful are future-oriented questions that get clients thinking about how they are likely to solve potential problems in the future. Questions can assist clients in developing their story and discovering better ways to deal with their concerns. Effective questioning can help individuals examine their story and find new ways to present it.

Limitation and Criticisms of Postmodern Approaches

To effectively practice solution-focused brief therapy, it is essential that therapists are skilled in brief interventions. Although it may appear that SFBT is simple and easy to implement, therapists practicing within this framework must be able to make assessments, assist clients in formulating specific goals, and effectively use a range of appropriate interventions. Some inexperienced or untrained therapists may be enamored by the variety of techniques: the miracle question, scaling questions, the exception question, and externalizing questions. But effective therapy is not simply a matter of relying on any of these interventions. The attitudes of the therapist and his or her ability to use questions that are reflective of genuine respectful interest are crucial to the therapeutic process.

McKenzie and Monk (1997) express their concerns over those counselors who attempt to employ narrative ideas in a mechanistic fashion. They caution that a risk in describing a map of a narrative orientation lies in the fact that some beginners will pay more attention to following the map than they will to following the lead of the client. In such situations, McKenzie and Monk are convinced that mechanically using techniques will not be effective. They add that although narrative therapy is based on some simple ideas, it is a mistake to assume that the practice is simple. Some solution-focused practitioners now acknowledge the problem of relying too much on a few techniques, and they are placing increased importance on the therapeutic relationship and the overall philosophy of the approach (Lipchik, 2002; Murphy, 2015).

Despite these limitations, the postmodern approaches have much to offer practitioners, regardless of their theoretical orientation. Many of the basic concepts and techniques of both solution-focused brief therapy and narrative therapy can be integrated into the other therapeutic orientations discussed in this book.

Self-Reflection and Discussion Questions

1. Both solution-focused brief therapy and narrative therapy emphasize viewing the client-as-expert, creating new stories, establishing a collaborative therapeutic relationship, discovering resources and strengths of the client, and separating the problem from the person. What are your thoughts about these ideas?
2. What key concept are you most drawn to in SFBT? In narrative therapy? What do you find of interest in this key concept?

3. A SFBT practitioner has many techniques to choose from in helping clients create their own solutions. Which of these techniques would you like to become skilled at using?
4. Narrative therapists talk about deconstructing a problem-saturated story and reauthoring a life-enhancing story. What do you think of this idea?
5. How do the postmodern approaches differ from some of the other theories you have studied thus far?

Where to Go From Here

Free Podcasts for ACA Members

You can download ACA Podcasts (prerecorded interviews) at www.counseling.org; click on the Resource button and then the Podcast Series. For Chapter 13, Postmodern Approaches, look for the following:

Interview with Dr. John Murphy on *Solution-Focused Counseling in Schools* (Podcast 5)

Lorraine Hedtke, L. & Winslade, J., *Remembering Lives, Conversations With the Dying and Bereaved*

Other Resources

Psychotherapy.net is a comprehensive resource for students and professionals that offers videos and interviews on the postmodern approaches. New video and editorial content is made available monthly. DVDs relevant to this chapter are available at www.psychotherapy.net and include the following:

Madigan, S. (2002). *Narrative Therapy With Children* (Child Therapy With the Experts)

Madigan, S. (1998). *Narrative Family Therapy* (Family Therapy With the Experts)

Murphy, J. (2002). *Solution-Focused Therapy With Children* (Child Therapy With the Experts)

If you are interested in keeping up to date with the developments in brief therapy, the *Journal of Brief Therapy* is a useful resource. It is devoted to developments, innovations, and research related to brief therapy with individuals, couples, families, and groups. The articles deal with brief therapy related to all theoretical approaches, but especially to social constructionism, solution-focused therapy, and narrative therapy. For subscription information, contact:

Springer Publishing Company
www.springerpub.com

Another useful journal is the *International Journal of Narrative Therapy and Community Work*. For more information, contact:

Dulwich Centre
http://dulwichcentre.com.au

Training in Solution-Focused Therapy Approaches

The Solution Focused Institute (SFI) at Texas Wesleyan University was founded in January 2009 in Fort Worth, Texas, to provide training to mental health practitioners and school teachers and counselors who want to implement a solution-focused approach in their work. The institute provides training on- and off-site in solution-focused therapy and offers supervision to individuals and groups. For information on SFI services, contact:

Solution Focused Institute
www.Solutionfocusedinstitute.com

Change-Focused Practice in Schools (CFPS) was initiated by John Murphy in 2005 to translate psychotherapy research into practical applications in schools and other settings. CFPS offers international training, supervision, and consultation on solution-focused/client-directed approaches to helping young people change in ways that honor their strengths, resources, and feedback. For more information, contact:

Department of Psychology & Counseling
University of Central Arkansas
www.drjohnmurphy.com

Training in Narrative Therapy

Evanston Family Therapy Institute
www.narrativetherapychicago.com/

Dulwich Centre
www.dulwichcentre.com.au/

Bay Area Family Therapy Training Associates
www.baftta.com

The Houston-Galveston Institute
www.talkhgi.com

Recommended Supplementary Readings

Interviewing for Solutions (De Jong & Berg, 2013) is a practical text aimed at teaching and learning solution-focused skills. It is written in a conversational and informal style and contains many examples to solidify learning.

Solution-Focused Counseling in Schools (Murphy, 2015) is a clearly written and practical book that offers efficient strategies for addressing a range of problems from preschool through high school. Numerous case examples illustrate the foundations, tasks, and techniques of solution-focused counseling. The book also describes how the principles of client-directed, outcome-informed practice can be integrated in solution-focused counseling.

Brief Psychotherapies: Principles and Practices (Hoyt, 2009) is an excellent resource for learning more about brief psychotherapy as it applies to many theoretical approaches.

Narrative Means to Therapeutic Ends (White & Epston, 1990) is the most widely known book on narrative therapy.

Maps of Narrative Practice (White, 2007) is Michael White's final book, which brings together much of his work over several decades in one accessible volume.

Narrative Therapy (Madigan, 2011) provides an updated discussion of the theory and therapeutic process of narrative therapy.

Narrative Counseling in Schools (Winslade & Monk, 2007) is a basic and easy-to-read guide to applying concepts and techniques of narrative therapy to school settings.

Family Systems Therapy 14

Coauthored by James Robert Bitter and Gerald Corey

LEARNING OBJECTIVES

1. Identify the key figures and major schools of family therapy.
2. Understand the commonalities among all models of family systems therapy.
3. Describe how family systems therapy is different from individual therapy.
4. Differentiate the key concepts and goals associated with each of the separate schools of family therapy.
5. Identify recent innovations in family therapy.
6. Understand the multilayered process of family therapy.
7. Describe the strengths and shortcomings of family systems therapy from a diversity perspective.
8. Identify the contributions and limitations of the family systems approaches.

Introduction

Although the seeds of a North American family therapy movement were **LO1** planted in the 1940s, it was during the 1950s that systemic family therapy began to take root (Becvar & Becvar, 2012). During the early years of its evolution, working with families was considered to be a revolutionary approach to treatment. In the 1960s and 1970s, psychodynamic, behavioral, and humanistic approaches (called the first, second, and third force, respectively) dominated counseling and psychotherapy. Today, the various approaches to family systems represent a paradigm shift that we might even call the "fourth force." Family systems therapy is represented by a variety of theories and approaches, all of which focus on the relational aspects of human problems.

The Family Systems Perspective

Perhaps the most difficult adjustment for counselors and therapists from **LO2** Western cultures is the adoption of a "systems" perspective. Our personal experience and Western culture often tell us that we are autonomous individuals, capable of free and independent choice. And yet we are born into families—and most of us live our entire lives attached to one form of family or another. Within these families, we discover who we are; we develop and change; and we give and receive the support we need for survival. We create, maintain, and live by often unspoken rules and routines that we hope will keep the family (and each of its members) functional.

A family systems perspective holds that individuals are best understood through assessing the interactions between and among family members. The development and behavior of one family member is inextricably interconnected with others in the family. Symptoms are often viewed as an expression of a set of habits and patterns within a family. It is revolutionary to conclude that the identified client's problem might be a symptom of how the system functions, not just a symptom of the individual's maladjustment, history, and psychosocial development. This perspective is grounded on the assumptions that a client's problematic behavior may (1) serve a function or purpose for the family; (2) be unintentionally maintained by family processes; (3) be a function of the family's inability to operate productively, especially during developmental transitions; or (4) be a symptom of dysfunctional patterns handed down across generations. All these assumptions challenge the more traditional intrapsychic frameworks for conceptualizing human problems and their formation.

The central principle agreed upon by family therapy practitioners, regardless of their particular approach, is that the client is connected to living systems. Attempts at change are best facilitated by working with and considering the family or set of relationships as a whole. Therefore, a treatment approach that comprehensively addresses the family as well as the "identified" client is required. Because a family is an interactional unit, it has its own set of unique traits. It is not possible to accurately assess an individual's concern without observing the interaction of the other family members, as well as the broader contexts in which the person and the family live.

Family therapy perspectives call for a conceptual shift from evaluating individuals to focusing on system dynamics, or how individuals within a system react to one another. Actions by any individual family member will influence all family members, and their reactions will have a reciprocal effect on the individual. When change occurs, a ripple effect flows throughout the family system. Effective changes support the family system and the new behaviors of the individual or family (Lambert, Carmichael, & Williams, 2016). Goldenberg and Goldenberg (2013) point to the need for therapists to view all behavior, including all symptoms expressed by the individual, within the context of the family and society. They add that a systems orientation does not preclude dealing with the dynamics within the individual, but that this approach broadens the traditional emphasis on individual internal dynamics.

Visit CengageBrain.com or watch the DVD for the video program on Chapter 14, *Theory and Practice of Counseling and Psychotherapy: The Case of Stan and Lecturettes*. I suggest that you view the brief lecture for each chapter prior to reading the chapter.

Differences Between Systemic and Individual Approaches

There are significant differences between individual therapeutic approaches and systemic approaches. A case may help to illustrate these differences. Ann, age 22, sees a counselor because she is suffering from a depression that has lasted for more than two years and has impaired her ability to maintain friendships and work productively. She wants to feel better, but she is pessimistic about her chances. How will a therapist choose to help her? **LO3**

Both the individual therapist and the systemic therapist are interested in Ann's current living situation and life experiences. Both discover that she is still living at home with her parents, who are in their 60s. They note that she has a very successful older sister, who is a prominent lawyer in the small town in which the two live. The therapists are impressed by Ann's loss of friends who have married and left town over the years while she stayed behind, often lonely and isolated. Finally, both therapists note that Ann's depression affects others as well as herself. It is here, however, that the similarities tend to end:

The individual therapist may:	*The systemic therapist may:*
Focus on obtaining an accurate diagnosis, perhaps using the *DSM-5* (American Psychiatric Association, 2013)	Explore the system for family process and rules, perhaps using a genogram
Begin therapy with Ann immediately	Invite Ann's mother, father, and sister into therapy with her
Focus on the causes, purposes, and cognitive, emotional, and behavioral processes involved in Ann's depression and coping	Focus on the family relationships within which the continuation of Ann's depression "makes sense"
Be concerned with Ann's individual experiences and perspectives	Be concerned with transgenerational meanings, rules, cultural, and gender perspectives within the system, and even the community and larger systems affecting the family
Intervene in ways designed to help Ann cope	Intervene in ways designed to help change Ann's context

Systemic therapists do not deny the importance of the individual in the family system, but they believe an individual's systemic affiliations and interactions have more power in the person's life than a single therapist could ever hope to have. By working with the whole family (or even community) system, the therapist has a chance to observe how individuals act within the system and participate in maintaining the status quo; how the system influences (and is influenced by) the individual; and what interventions might lead to changes that help the couple, family, or larger system as well as the individual expressing pain.

In Ann's case, her depression may have organic, genetic, or hormonal components. It may also involve cognitive, experiential, or behavioral patterns that interfere with effective coping. Even if her depression can be explained in this manner, however, the systemic therapist is very interested in how her depression affects others in the family and how it influences family processes. Her depression may signal both her own pain and the unexpressed pain of the family. Indeed, many family system approaches would investigate how the depression serves other family members; distracts from problems in the intimate relationships of others; or reflects her need to adjust to family rules, to cultural injunctions, or to processes influenced by gender or family life-cycle development. Rather than losing sight of the individual, family therapists understand the person as specifically embedded in larger systems.

Development of Family Systems Therapy

Family systems theory has evolved throughout the past 100 years, and today therapists creatively employ various perspectives when tailoring therapy to a particular family. Alfred Adler (1927) and Rudolf Dreikurs (1950, 1973) and their associates were the first known practitioners of family therapy, often using a model now called open-forum family counseling (Christensen, 2004). Adler introduced phenomenology to our understanding of the family system (or family constellation). Assessment is based on the subjective descriptions that family members use to define themselves and the interactions that occur in everyday life. It is within these interactions that Adlerians seek to discover the purposes and goals of behavior (Bitter, 2014; Bitter, Roberts, & Sonstegard, 2002). LO4

Take a moment and think about two different family experiences in your own life. When you were little, what descriptions would you have used for your parents? What do these descriptions tell you about what was important to you? Let's say that one's father is described as kind, generous, and childlike. The mother is described as beautiful, very hard working, and sacrificing. No adjective or description exists outside of the relationship. When the person says the father was *kind*, this means that the father was kind to the person as a child. When the mother is described as *very hard working,* the person is suggesting that access to mother was difficult to get. Still, mother's hard work has a purpose: she is *sacrificing* for the child. What else can we know from these descriptions? Father was *generous* and *childlike*: "he played with me." He may not have been very oriented toward discipline. Mother was *beautiful.* The message is that for women appearances are important.

Now, think about your current family situation, either your family of origin or a new family you have started. What descriptions would family members use to describe you? What does that tell you about your place or role in the family? Finally, think about a recent family interaction that was difficult for you. What goals or purposes did you have for your part of the interaction? What goals or purposes might have been involved for those interacting with you? You can generally discover the goal or purpose of behavior by looking at the consequence of that behavior in the responses of others: "What do people do when I act in one way or another?"

We now take a look at the most prominent models and what they have contributed to the evolution of family systems therapy.

MURRAY BOWEN (1913–1990) believed families could best be understood when analyzed from a three-generation perspective because patterns of interpersonal relationships connect family members across generations. Two of his objectives in therapy were to help family members develop a rational, nonreactive approach to living (called a differentiation of self) and to de-tangle family interactions that involved two people pulling a third person into the couple's problems and arguments (or triangulation).

Murray Bowen

Courtesy of The Bowen Center for the Study of the Family; photo by Andrea Schara

Bowen's observations led to his interest in patterns across multiple generations. He contended that problems manifested in one's current family will not significantly change until relationship patterns in one's family of origin are understood and directly challenged. His approach operates on the premise that a predictable pattern of interpersonal relationships connects the functioning of family members across generations. According to Kerr and Bowen (1988), the cause of an individual's problems can be understood only by viewing the role of the family as an emotional unit. Within the family unit, unresolved emotional reactivity to one's family must be addressed if one hopes to achieve a mature and unique personality. Emotional problems will be transmitted from generation to generation until unresolved emotional attachments are dealt with effectively. Change must occur with other family members and cannot be done by an individual in a counseling room.

Murray Bowen (1978) was one of the original developers of mainstream family therapy. His family systems theory, which is a theoretical and clinical model that evolved from psychoanalytic principles and practices, is sometimes referred to as **multigenerational family therapy**. The goal of this approach is to differentiate self within a system and to understand one's family of origin. Bowen and his associates implemented an innovative approach to schizophrenia at the National Institute of Mental Health where Bowen hospitalized entire families so that the family system could be the focus of therapy.

Bowen's emphasis on a multigenerational perspective laid a foundation for work by two of Bowen's most prominent colleagues, Betty Carter and Monica McGoldrick, who almost single-handedly initiated both a developmental and a multicultural perspective in family therapy. Indeed, McGoldrick's work includes the field's most important work on genograms (McGoldrick, Gerson, & Petry, 2008), family life cycle (McGoldrick, Carter, & Garcia-Preto, 2011), and gender (McGoldrick, Anderson, & Walsh, 1991).

VIRGINIA SATIR (1916–1988) developed conjoint family therapy, a **human validation process model** that emphasizes communication and emotional experiencing. Like Bowen, she used an intergenerational model, but she worked to bring family patterns to life in the present through sculpting and family reconstructions. Claiming that techniques were secondary to relationship, she concentrated on the personal relationship between therapist and family to achieve change. The core of Satir's model relied on the power of congruence to help family members communicate with emotional honesty. Her presence with people encouraged them to get in touch with what was significant within, to become more fully human, and to share the individual's best self with a significant other. Satir called this experience "making contact," and she believed that it extended the peace one had within to a peace between people and, eventually, to a peace among people.

At about the same time that Bowen was developing his approach, Virginia Satir (1983) began emphasizing family connection. Her therapeutic work had already led her to believe in the value of a strong, nurturing relationship based on interest and fascination with those in her care. Unlike Bowen, Satir could envision and sought to support the development of a nurturing triad: two people, for example parents, working for the well-being of another, perhaps a child. Satir thought of herself as a detective who sought out and listened for the reflections of self-esteem in the communication of her clients. She placed a strong emphasis on the importance of communication and metacommunication in family interactions, and the value of therapeutic validation in the process of change (Satir & Bitter, 2000). From Satir, family therapy gets it model for empathic listening, therapeutic presence, and nurturance (Satir, Banmen, Gerber, & Gomori, 1991).

Courtesy of The Virginia Satir Global Network

Virginia Satir

Structural-Strategic Family Therapy

The origins of **structural family therapy** can be traced to the early 1960s when Salvador Minuchin was conducting therapy, training, and research with delinquent boys from poor families at the Wiltwyck School in New York. Minuchin's (1974) central idea was that an individual's symptoms are best understood from the vantage point of interactional patterns, or sequences, within a family. He further stated that structural changes must occur in a family before an individual's symptoms can be reduced or eliminated. The goals of structural family therapy include (1) reducing symptoms of dysfunction and (2) bringing about structural change within the system by modifying the family's transactional rules and establishing more appropriate boundaries.

In the late 1960s, Jay Haley joined Minuchin at the Philadelphia Child Guidance Clinic. The work of Haley and Minuchin shared so many similarities in goals and process that many clinicians in the 1980s and 1990s began to question whether the two models were distinct schools of thought. Indeed, by the late 1970s, **structural-strategic approaches** were the most used models in family systems therapy. The interventions generated in these models became synonymous with a systems approach; they included joining, boundary setting, unbalancing, reframing, ordeals, paradoxical interventions, and enactments.

If you divided your family of origin into subsystems, who would be in the parental subsystem? The spousal subsystem? The sibling subsystem? What rules and boundaries were set around each subsystem? Were the boundaries ever crossed? By whom and with what result? What were common interactional sequences in your family? Who had the power in your family, and how was it exercised? Who was aligned with whom, and what did they use that alignment to achieve? These are just a few of the assessments structural-strategic therapists taught us to consider.

Recent Innovations in Family Therapy

LO5

In the last decade, *feminism, multiculturalism*, and *postmodern social constructionism* have all entered the family therapy field. These models are more collaborative, treating clients—individuals, couples, or families—as experts in their own lives. The therapeutic conversations start with the counselor in a "not-knowing" position in which clients are approached with curiosity and interest. The therapist is socially active and aids clients in taking a preferred stand in relation to the dominant culture that may be oppressing them. Therapy often incorporates "reflecting teams" and "definitional ceremonies" to bring multiple perspectives to the work (see West, Bubenzer, & Bitter, 1998).

Feminist, multicultural, and postmodern therapists are extremely aware of the power they have entering into already established systems, and they work to promote understanding through curiosity and interest rather than through formal assessments. Adopting a decentered position allows them to be part of the system without taking it over.

Postmodern approaches to family therapy, like narrative therapy, seek to reduce or eliminate the power and impact of the family therapist. Taken together, postmodern approaches represent a real paradigm shift in the field of family therapy.

This brief discussion of the various systemic viewpoints in family therapy provides a context for understanding the development of family therapy. For an in-depth treatment of the schools of family therapy, see *Theory and Practice of Family Therapy and Counseling* (Bitter, 2014) and the recommended readings at the end of the chapter.

A Multilayered Process of Family Therapy

LO6

Families are multilayered systems that both affect and are affected by the larger systems in which they are embedded. Families can be described in terms of their individual members and the various roles they play, the relationships between the members, and the sequential patterns of the interactions and the purposes these sequences serve. Both the members and the system can be assessed based on power, alignment, organization, structure, development, culture, and gender (Breunlin, Schwartz, & MacKune-Karrer, 1997). Even individuals can be considered from the perspective of an internal family system (Schwartz, 1995). In addition, nuclear families in a global community are often part of extended, if distant, families; multiple families make up a community; multiple communities make up both regions and cultures, which in turn constitute nations (or societies). The power of these macrosystems to influence family life—especially in the areas of gender and culture—is significant. Given our presuppositions about families and the larger systems in which families are embedded, a multilayered approach to family therapy is essential.

Several forms and structures have been proposed for integrative models of family counseling and therapy (e.g., Carlson, Sperry, & Lewis, 2005; Gladding, 2014; Hanna, 2007; Nichols, 2013). The integrative model we have chosen to present here allows for an enlarged integration of ideas from multiple models of family therapy. Similar to a piece of classical music, the process of family therapy, it seems to us, has movements. These movements can be described as separate experiences embedded in the larger flow of therapy. In this section we describe four general movements, each with different tasks: forming a relationship, conducting an assessment, hypothesizing and sharing meaning, and facilitating change. In rare instances, these four movements might occur within a single session; in most cases, however, each movement requires multiple sessions.

Forming a Relationship

Over the years, family systems therapists have used a wide range of metaphors to describe the role of the therapist and the therapeutic relationship. The emergence of feminist and postmodern models in therapy has moved the field of family therapy toward more egalitarian, collaborative, cooperative, co-constructing relationships (see T. Andersen, 1987, 1991; H. Anderson, 1993; Anderson & Goolishian, 1992; Epston & White, 1992; Luepnitz, 1988/2002).

The debate Carl Rogers (1980) first introduced to individual therapy in the 1940s has reemerged within family therapy in the form of these questions:

- What expertise does the therapist have in relation to the family, and how should that expertise be used?
- How directive should therapists be in relation to families, and what does that say about the uses of power in therapy?

We believe a multilayered approach to family therapy is best supported by a collaborative therapist–client relationship in which mutual respect, caring, empathy, and a genuine interest in others is primary. In addition, we believe directed actions and enactments are most useful when they are a joint venture of both the therapist and the family.

Therapists begin to form a relationship with clients from the moment of first contact. In most cases, we believe therapists should make their own appointments, answer initial questions clients may have, and give clients a sense of what to expect when they come for their first session. This is also a time when counselors can let families know their position on whether all members should be present. Some family therapists will work with any of those members of the family who wish to come; others will only see the family if everyone is a part of the therapy session.

From the moment of first face-to-face contact, good therapeutic relationships start with efforts at making contact with each person present (Satir & Bitter, 2000). Whether it is called *joining*, *engagement*, or simple *care and concern*, it is the therapist's responsibility to meet each person with openness and warmth. Generally, a focused interest on each family member helps to reduce the anxiety the family may be feeling.

Therapeutic process and structure are part of the therapist's job description. It is important for family members to introduce themselves and to express their concerns, but the therapist should not focus too tightly on content issues. Understanding family process is almost always facilitated by *how* questions. Questions that begin with *what*, *why*, *where*, or *when* tend to overemphasize content details (Gladding, 2014).

All change in human systems starts with understanding and accepting things just as they are (Satir & Baldwin, 1983). The family practitioner's skill in communicating that understanding and empathy through active listening lays the foundation for an effective working relationship. Those counselors and therapists who use validation and encouragement, who support family resilience, and who elicit cooperation experience the greatest amount of success in therapy.

Conducting an Assessment

The multiple layers we have noted provide numerous entry points for conducting family assessments, but beginning counselors and therapists will often find that more formal assessment procedures, such as genograms (McGoldrick et al., 2008), enable the family structure and stories to be presented in a clearer, more orderly manner. In some cases, formal tests and rating scales also can be useful (see, for example, Gottman, 1999).

Let's start with the process for co-constructing a genogram. Most family practitioners start with a map of the family that comes to therapy. The parents are listed with their name, age, and date of birth in either a rectangle (for men) or a circle (for women). If there are multiple relationships involved in the parental subsystem, they are generally indicated in chronological order with men listed on the left and women on the right.

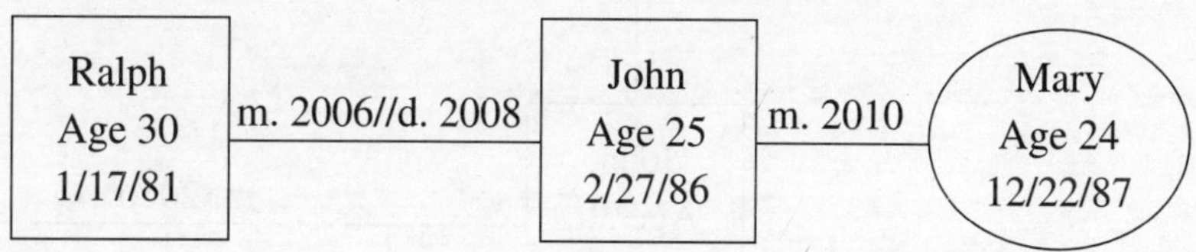

In the above genogram, Mary married Ralph when she was 20 and Ralph was 26; their marriage lasted about two years, and then they were divorced. In 2010, Mary and John were married. If John and Mary had decided to live together, but not commit to a formal marriage, the genogram would use a broken line (or dashes) to indicate an informal relationship, like this:

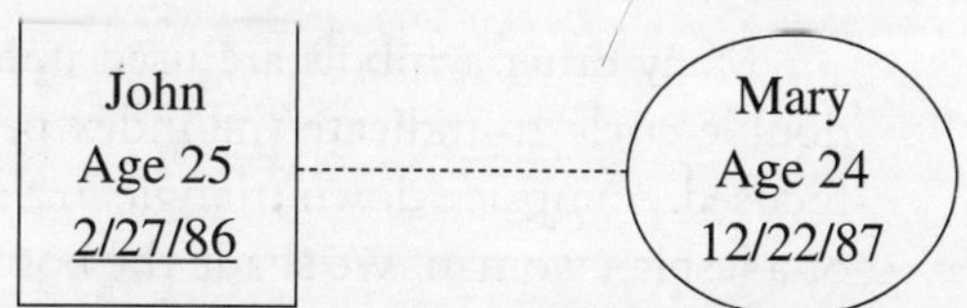

If Ralph had died instead of divorcing Mary, it would look like this:

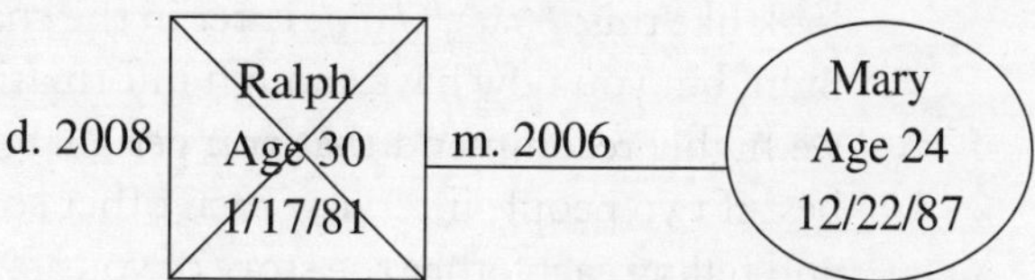

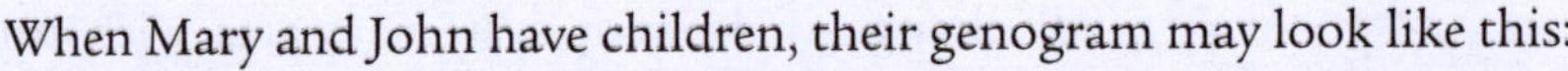
When Mary and John have children, their genogram may look like this:

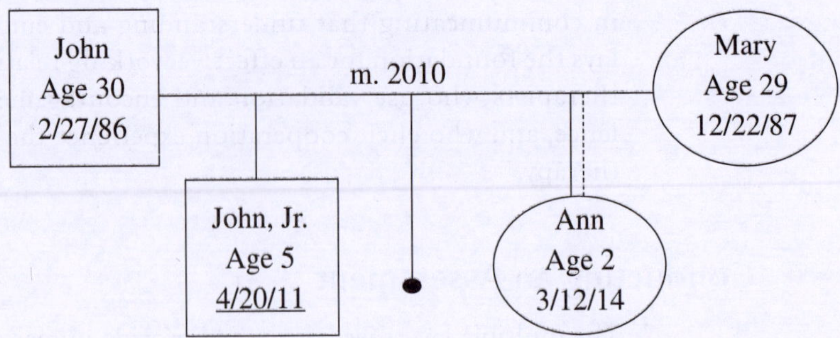

In the above genogram, it is now 2016, and John and Mary have been married for six years. When they had been married for one year, Mary gave birth to their first child, a boy that they named John Jr. A year later, Mary had a miscarriage, indicated by a black oval at the end of a child line. Two years ago, they adopted (indicated by a solid line next to a broken line) their daughter Ann. If we extend John and Mary's genogram to three generations and if we assume that both John and Mary were only children, the basic three generation family genogram would look like this:

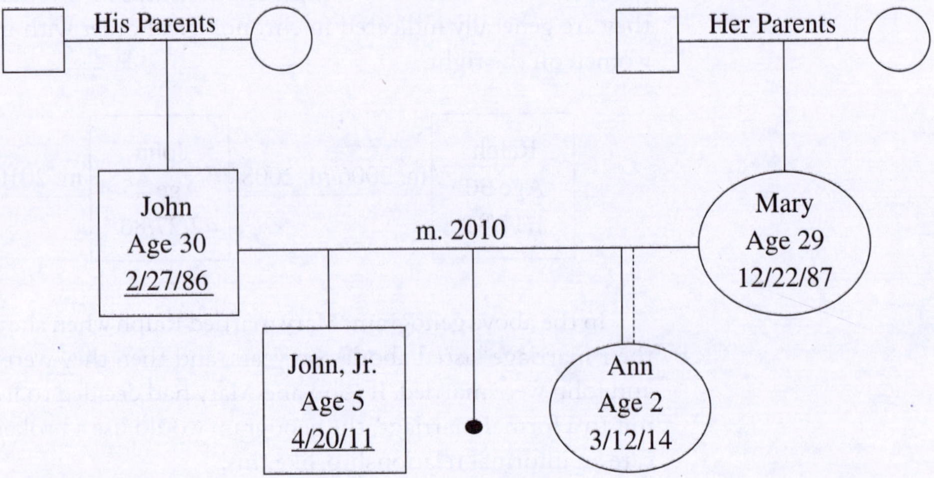

Many other symbols are used in a genogram, including a double square or a double circle to indicate the index person, or person on whom the genogram is focused. An upside down triangle in a square or circle is used to indicate a gay man or a lesbian woman. We shade the bottom half of a square or circle to indicate substance abuse. We use double parallel lines to indicate a strong relationship between two people and three parallel lines to indicate a fused or enmeshed relationship. A dotted line indicates a distant relationship, and conflict is indicated with lines that look like this: /\/\/\/\/\/\/. Later in the chapter we use a genogram in our work with Stan, but you now have enough information to construct your own genogram, and we highly recommend that you get a large piece of paper and get started. It works best if two people interview each other so that you are both drawing the genogram and telling each other the story of your family.

As the therapist listens to family members describe the story of their family, it may be difficult to know where to start with a family. Family members are often the best people to choose a focus. Family practitioners may use circular or relational questioning to get at the systemic issues presented in the family story that will provide meaning for the therapist and the family. For example, suppose Tammy is upsetting the family system by ignoring the curfew her parents have set for her. The therapist might ask: "What will happen if Tammy stays out past curfew and is picked up by the police? Who will be most upset by this?" Here is Tammy's father's reply:

> I will probably be the most upset on the outside. I tend to go off before I think, and then I regret it later. On the other hand, her mother may not show it immediately, but her hurt will stay with her longer, and then she will get mad at me for "letting Tammy off the hook." She will say that Tammy is manipulating me, but I just don't see why we should keep fighting about things. It doesn't do any good. We fight, and Tammy disappears. She wants to run with the big kids, some of whom are in college, over 18, and have no curfew.

From this father's response, the therapist can choose from a number of points of entry into the life of this family. The counselor might choose to work with the anger or guilt expressed by the members and present in their interactions. Sequential patterns were clearly articulated by the father when the family members are trying to resolve conflict and handle problems. His description also includes implied positions on the roles of men, women, and female children in families—as well as developmental issues related to Tammy wanting to be older than she is.

In the assessment process, it is helpful to inquire about family perspectives on issues inherent in each of these layers. In addition to the points of entry we have noted, here are some other questions that might be included in a more detailed assessment.

- What does each family member bring to the session?
- How does each person describe who he or she is?
- What are the goals of each family member? What goals does each family member have for the other people in the family?
- What routines support the daily living of each member of the family?
- Who makes decisions? How are conflicts resolved or problems handled?
- What parts are involved in the most common sequences in the family?
- What is a typical day like?
- Are the parents effective leaders of the family, and is the process of leadership balanced or imbalanced?
- How do the children respond to parental leadership? What are the children's goals in responding the way they do?
- Where is each person in the family in relation to personal biological, cognitive, emotional, and social development?
- Where is the family in the family life cycle, and how are they handling transitions?
- What cultures are in the family backgrounds of each of the family members?
- In what culture or region is the family currently living, and is immigration or migration a recent family experience?

- How do economics, education, ethnicity, religion, race, regional background, gender, sexual orientation, ableness, and age affect family processes—and how is the fit between the family practitioner and the family with regard to these aspects of family life?
- What effects has racism, patriarchy, or heterosexism had on this family and its members?
- What ideas in relation to gender need to be affirmed or challenged?
- Where is this family in the process of change?
- What resources (internal or external) need to be accessed?

Hypothesizing and Sharing Meaning

To hypothesize is to form a set of ideas about people, systems, and situations that focus meaning in a useful way. In family therapy, hypothesizing flows from the ideas and understandings generated in the assessment process. Two questions are germane to the form of hypothesizing one chooses to do: (1) How much faith do the therapist and the family have in the ideas they generate? (2) How much of an influence is the therapist willing to be in the lives of people and families?

Family counselors, like individual therapists, cannot avoid influencing the family and its members. But what kind of influence will the therapist bring to the session? Satir and Bitter (2000) suggest that family therapists cannot be in charge of the people, but they need to be in charge of the process; that is, they own the responsibility for how therapy is conducted. Feminists and social constructionists are, perhaps, the most expressive of their concerns about the misuse of power in therapy. They are joined by multiculturalists, person-centered therapists, Adlerians, and existentialists, to name a few, who have also witnessed the often unconscious imposition of "dominant culture" in therapy. In the early days of family therapy, the mostly male therapists often ignored the effects on family life of patriarchy, poverty, racism, cultural discrimination and marginalization, homo-prejudice, and other societal problems. At the strategic-structural end of the continuum, therapists were more likely to claim a certain expertise in systems work that allowed them to make direct interventions in the enactment of "needed" changes in the family. To counteract therapeutic abuses and what some perceived to be an ongoing misuse of power in therapy, some narrative therapists adopted a *decentered* position in relation to the family (White, 1997, 2007). Like person-centered therapists before them, decentered therapists seek to keep families and family members at the center of the therapeutic process.

It is important for families to be invited into respectful, essentially collaborative dialogues in therapeutic work. The different perspectives discovered in this work tend to coalesce into working hypotheses, and sharing these ideas provides the family with a window into the heart and mind of the therapist as well as themselves. Sharing hypotheses almost immediately invites and invokes feedback from various family members. And it is this feedback that enables the therapist and the family to develop a good fit with each other, which in turn tends to cement a working relationship.

The tentative hypothesizing and sharing process that Dreikurs (1950, 1997) developed is well designed for the kind of collaborative work envisioned here.

Dreikurs would use a passionate interest and curiosity to ask questions and gather together the subjective perspectives of family members. Indeed, he would honor the ideas that individuals brought to their joint understanding. When he had an idea that he wanted to share, he would often seek permission for his disclosure:

1. I have an idea I would like to share with you. Would you be willing to hear it?
2. Could it be that . . .

The value of this way of presenting hypotheses is that it invites families and family members to consider and to engage without giving up their right to discard anything that does not fit. When a suggested idea does not fit, the therapist is then clear about letting it go and letting the family redirect the conversation toward more useful conceptualizations.

Facilitating Change

Facilitating change is what happens when family therapy is viewed as a joint or collaborative process. Techniques are more important to models that see the therapist-as-expert and in charge of *making change happen*. Collaborative approaches require *planning*. "Planning can still include what family therapy has called *techniques* or *interventions*, but with the family's participation" (Breunlin et al., 1997, p. 292). Two of the most common forms for facilitation of change are enactments and assignment of tasks. Both of these processes work best when the family co-constructs them with the therapist—or at least accepts the rationale for their use.

Within the change process, the number of possible outcomes is only limited by the resources available internally and externally to the family. This does not mean, however, that the family practitioner is without a guide for preferred or desired outcomes. In general, the internal parts of family members function best when they are balanced (not polarized) and when the individual experiences personal parts as resources. Being able to think is usually more useful than emotional reactivity; being able to feel is better than not feeling; good contact with others is more rewarding than isolation or self-absorption; and taking reasonable risks in the service of growth and development is more beneficial than stagnation or a retreat into fear.

Further, knowing the goals and purposes for our behaviors, feelings, and interactions tends to give us choices about their use. And understanding the patterns we enact in face-to-face relationships, the ebbs and flows of life, or across generations provide multiple avenues for challenging patterns and the enactment of new possibilities.

Family Systems Therapy From a Multicultural Perspective

Strengths From a Diversity Perspective

One of the strengths of the systemic perspective in working from a multicultural framework is that many ethnic and cultural groups place great value on the extended family. If therapists are working with an individual from a cultural background that gives special value to including grandparents, aunts, and uncles **LO7** in the treatment, it is easy to see that family approaches have a distinct advantage over individual therapy. Family therapists can do some excellent networking with members of the extended family.

Within the field of family therapy, Monica McGoldrick has been the most influential leader in the development of both gender and cultural perspectives and frameworks in family practice (see McGoldrick et al., 1991, 2005; McGoldrick, & Hardy, 2008). In many ways, McGoldrick and her colleagues approach families like systems anthropologists. They see each family as a unique culture whose particular characteristics must be understood. Like larger cultural systems, families have a unique language that governs behavior, communication, and even how to feel about and experience life. Families have celebrations and rituals that mark transitions, protect them against outside interference, and connect them to their past as well as to a projected future.

Similarly, families cannot escape the sexism and patriarchy that are inherent in all cultures. The roles for men and women are prescribed in different societies, but in every culture women tend to come out on the short end more often than not. The roles that women as mothers play in the family, in the world of work, and in the community set the model for female children often for generations to come. Because family life is where the roles of women can be most limited, a consideration of gender issues in families is an essential framework for family therapy (McGoldrick et al., 1991). Perhaps the most difficult integration of all is figuring out how to honor different cultures in therapy without supporting marginalization or oppression of women. Toward this end, it is important to remember that there are feminist voices in every culture throughout the world.

Just as differentiation means coming to understand our family well enough to be a part of it—to belong—and also to separate and be our own person, understanding cultures allows therapists and families to appreciate diversity and to contextualize family experiences in relation to the larger cultures. Today, family therapists explore the individual culture of the family, the larger cultures to which the family members belong, and the host culture that dominates the family's life. They look for ways in which culture can both inform and modify family work. Interventions are no longer applied universally, regardless of the cultures involved: rather, they are adapted and even designed to join with the cultural systems.

Shortcomings From a Diversity Perspective

Given the multicultural focus and collaborative approach of family systems therapy, it is difficult to find shortcomings from a diversity perspective. This model of family therapy embraces attitudes, knowledge, and skills that are essential to a multicultural perspective. Perhaps the major concern for non-Western cultures would be with regard to the balance that this model advocates for the individual versus the collective. The process of differentiation occurs in most cultures, but it takes on a different shape due to cultural norms. For instance, a young person may become separate from her parents yet not move out of the house. When ethnic-minority families immigrate to North America, their children often adapt to a Western concept of differentiation. In such cases, the intergenerational process of therapy is appropriate if the therapist is sensitive to the family-of-origin's cultural roots. Although a multilayered approach addresses the notion of togetherness and individuality from a balanced perspective, many non-Western cultures would not embrace a theory that valued individuality above loyalty to family in any form. Nor would non-Western cultures have the same conceptualizations of time or even emotions. Therapists, regardless of their model of therapy, must find ways to enter the family's world and honor the traditions that support the family.

A possible shortcoming of the practice of family therapy involves practitioners who assume Western models of family are universal. Indeed, there are many cultural variations to family structure, processes, and communication. Family therapists are finding ways to broaden their views of individuation, appropriate gender roles, family life cycles, and extended families. Some family therapists focus primarily on the nuclear family, which is based on Western notions, and this could clearly be a shortcoming in working with clients in extended families.

Family Therapy Applied to the Case of Stan

In our work with Stan in this modality, we include examples of forming a relationship and joining, reading Stan's genogram, a multilayered assessment, reframing, boundary setting in therapy, and facilitating change. There are many useful models and ways to work with families; this discussion represents some possible ways to work with Stan from a multilayered perspective.

At an intake interview, a family therapist meets with Stan to explore his issues and concerns and to learn more about him and his life situation. As they talk, the therapist brings an intense interest and curiosity to the interview and wonders out loud about the familial roots of some of Stan's problems. It does not take much of an inquiry to learn that Stan is still very much engaged with his parents and siblings, no matter how difficult these relationships have been for him. This initial conversation involves the development of a genogram of Stan's family of origin (see Figure 14.1). This map will serve both Stan and the therapist as a guide to the people and the processes that influence Stan's life.

Stan's genogram is really a family picture, or map, of his family-of-origin system. In this genogram, we learn that Stan's grandparents tend to have lived fairly long lives. Stan's maternal grandparents are both alive. The shaded lower half of their square and circle indicates that each had some problem with alcohol. In the case of Tom, Stan reports that he was an admitted alcoholic who recommitted himself to Christ and found help through Alcoholics Anonymous. Stan's maternal grandmother always drank a little socially and with her husband, but she never considered herself to have a problem. In her later years, however, she seems to secretly use alcohol more and more, and it is a source of distress in her marriage. Stan also knows that Margie drinks a lot, because he has been drinking with his aunt for years. She is the one who gave him his first drink.

Angie, Stan's mother, married Frank Sr. after he had stopped drinking, also with the help of AA. He still goes to meetings. Angie is suspicious of all men around alcohol. She is especially upset with Stan and with Judy's husband, Matt, who "also drinks too much." The genogram makes it easy to see the pattern of alcohol problems in this family.

The jagged lines /\/\/\/\ between Frank Sr. and Angie indicate conflict in the relationship. The three solid lines ≡ between Frank Sr. and Frank Jr., and between Angie and Karl, indicate a very close or even fused relationship. The double lines ==== between Karl and Stan are used to note a close relationship only. As we will see, Karl actually looks up to Stan in this family. The dotted lines . . . . between Frank Sr. and Stan and between Frank Jr. and Stan indicate a distant or even disengaged relationship.

Because the family therapist believes that the whole family is involved in Stan's use of alcohol, she spends a good part of the first session exploring with Stan processes for asking his other family members to join him in therapy. Stan may have many difficulties, but at the moment his difficulty with alcohol is the primary focus.

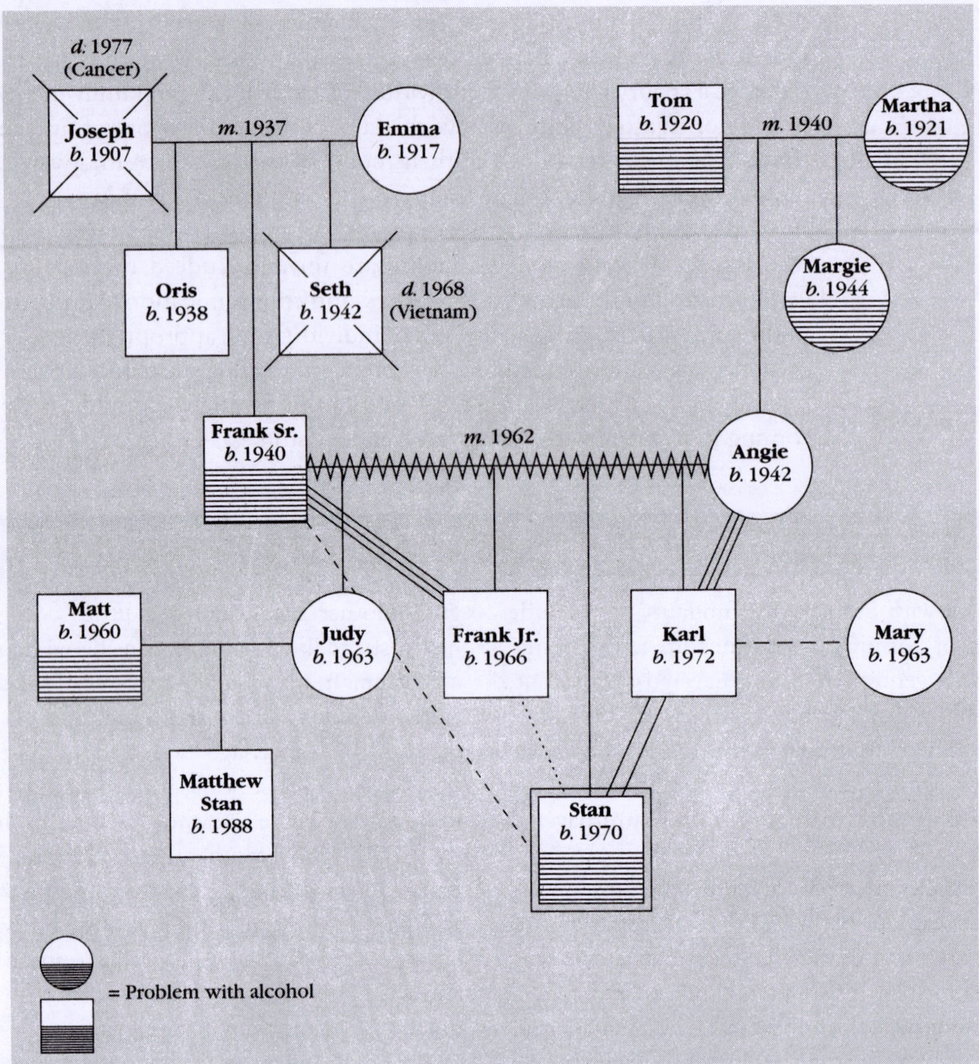

Figure 14.1 Three Generation Genogram of Stan's Family

Alcohol is a negative part of his life, and as such it has systemic meaning. It may have started out as a symptom of other problems, but now the alcohol is a problem in itself. From a systemic perspective, the questions are "How does this problem affect the family?" and "Is the family using this problem to serve some other purpose?"

In the first therapy session with the family, the therapist's main focus is in forming a relationship with each of the family members, but even here, a variety of approaches present themselves.

Therapist [*to Frank Sr.*]: I know coming here was an inconvenience for you, but I want you to know how appreciative I am that you came. Can you tell me what it's like for you to be here? [*Forming a relationship through joining*]

Frank Sr.: Well, I have to tell you that I don't like it much. [*Pause*] Things are a lot different today than they used to be. We didn't have counseling 20 years ago. I had a problem with drinking at one point, but I got over it. I just quit—on my own. That's what Stan needs to do. He just needs to stop.

Therapist: So I'm hearing that life is better for you without alcohol, and you would like Stan's life to be better too. [*Reframing*]

Frank Sr.: Yeah. I'd like his life to be better in a lot of different ways.

Therapist: Angie, what about you? What is it like for you to be here? [*Forming a relationship with each member*]

Angie: It's heartbreaking. It's always heartbreaking. He [*Referring to Frank Sr.*] makes it sound as if he just summoned up his own personal power and quit drinking through his own strength of character. That's a laugh. I threatened to leave him. That's what really happened. I was ready to get a divorce! And we're Catholics. We don't get divorced. [*Possible face-to-face sequence around family stress and coping*]

Therapist: So you've been through this before.

Angie: Oh my, yes. My father and mother drank. Dad still does. My sister won't admit it, but she drinks too much. She goes crazy with it. Judy's husband has a problem. I'm surrounded by alcoholics. I get so angry. I wish they would all just die or go away. [*Possible transgenerational family sequence: an entry point for exploring values, beliefs, and rules*]

Therapist: So this is something the whole family has been dealing with for a long time.

Angie: Not everyone. I don't drink. Frankie and Judy don't drink. And Karl doesn't seem to have a problem.

Therapist: Is that how the family gets divided: into those who drink and those who don't? [*Possible organization perspective*]

Judy: Drinking isn't the only problem we have. It's probably not even the most important.

Therapist: Say more about that.

Judy: Stan has always had it hard. I feel sorry for him. Frankie is clearly Dad's favorite [*Frank Sr. protests, saying he doesn't have favorites*], and things have always come easily for me. And Karl, he gets whatever he wants. He's Mom's favorite. Mom and Dad have fought a lot over the years. None of us have been that happy, but Stan seems to have the worst of it. [*Again, possible sequence and organization perspectives*]

Frank Jr.: As I remember it, Stan gave Dad and Mom a lot to fight about. He was always messing up in one way or another.

Therapist: Frankie, when your father was talking earlier, I sensed he had some disappointment about Stan too, but he also wanted to see things work out better for him. Is that true for you too? [*Reframing Frankie's comment, maintaining a focus on new possibilities and new relations that might be developed*]

Frank Jr.: Yes. I would like his life to be better.

The initial part of this counseling session has been devoted to meeting family members, listening intently to the multiple perspectives they present, and reframing Stan's problem into a family desire for a positive outcome. Although there is a long way to go, the seeds of change have already been planted. There is evidence in these early interactions that Stan's problem has a multigenerational context. If this context is explored, family sequences that support and maintain alcohol as a problem may be identified. It is possible to track these interactions and to work toward more congruent communications. Evolving relational, organizational, developmental sequences might be explored as a means of freeing family members for new possibilities in their life together. Among other possibilities still to be explored are perspectives related to gender and culture. If the therapist were just listening to Stan, only one point of view would be evident. In this family session, multiple perspectives and the entire interactive process become clear in a very short time.

As the family interview proceeds, a number of possibilities are presented for consideration. The therapist considers and may structure therapy around any or all of the following possibilities:

1. Stan's parents have not been a well-functioning leadership team for a long time, and both their spousal relationship and their parenting have suffered.
2. The adult siblings need a new opportunity to function together without the influence and distractions continually imposed by the parents.
3. Stan has been reduced to a single part (his alcoholic part), and his description and experience of himself needs to be enlarged—both for his own perspective and in the eyes of others.

A new place for Stan in the family, a better way of relating, and an ability to access "lost" parts of his internal system are all critical to winning his battle with alcohol. As therapy continues, it becomes clear that two separate relational-organization hypotheses must be explored. One is that the spousal relationship has been defined by the problem of alcohol too, and it has not evolved or developed in any kind of positive way over the years. Second, the transgenerational sequences have targeted Stan and assigned him to a fixed role that he has been expected to play that has blocked development past his middle to late adolescence, which was the period in which he started drinking.

Questions for Reflection

- What unique values do you see in working with Stan from a multilayered, systemic perspective as opposed to an individual therapy approach?
- What internal parts might Stan re-access as he continues in therapy? What parts of him might be polarized?
- Assuming that Stan was successful in getting at least some of his family members to another session, where would you begin? Would you get everyone involved in the sessions? If so, how would you do that?
- What are some specific ways to explore other perspectives with this family?
- What hypotheses are you developing, and how would you share them with the family?
- Are there systemic interventions that you would find hopeful in terms of facilitating change?

Family Therapy Applied to the Case of Gwen*

As a family therapist, I look at Gwen as the index person in the context of her family system. Gwen has a strong extended family system and kinship ties that go beyond blood relatives to close friends who are called aunts, uncles, and cousins. When Gwen begins to experience episodes of depression and feels overwhelmed, the entire family is affected. African American families often become enmeshed due to our collectivistic nature. The cultural theme most often expressed is that "when something happens to one of us, it happens to all of us." It has been challenging to get Gwen's entire family in for a session, but she has managed it. The extended family is a great strength in the African American community, and Gwen's family has provided her with a great deal of love and support. I want to validate these efforts and let the family know that they are already doing many things to support Gwen.

I invite everyone in, greeting each one individually. My first step with the family is to join with them by finding out how they feel about being in session.

Ron: [*Gwen's husband*] I rushed from work to be here, because, well, I want Gwen to feel better. I have to say I was not so sure about this when she first brought it up. I am not used to talking to strangers about my business, but I trust Gwen. I want what is best for her.

Therapist: Thanks Ron, I appreciate you being here. I know that you all have busy lives. But what is it that you want for yourself from these sessions?

Ron: Well, Gwen, she is an amazing woman, but ... when she has these episodes of depression, I feel helpless and nervous. I want to figure this thing out and get past it. I want my wife to feel better, and I want to help her however I can.

Therapist: I get the feeling that you would move heaven and earth to help your wife be happier than she is right now.

Ron: Yes, I certainly would.

Therapist: I appreciate that. And Lisa, what about you?

Lisa: [*the youngest daughter, age 26*] I want Mom to feel better, she is such a powerhouse. She helps everyone else, and then she crashes. I am a little nervous to be here. I don't want to find out that she is going through this because of something I did. She helps me out with my bills, and I know I could do more for her. I never help her with grandma, and I know that is just more work for her.

Therapist: Lisa, I am sure that is important for your mother to hear. But before I ask her to respond, I would like to hear from other family members.

*Dr. Kellie Kirksey writes about her ways of thinking and practicing from a family therapy perspective and applying this model to Gwen.

Brittany: [*the eldest daughter, age 29*] I have been really busy trying to get my career established. Mom has been helping me, and I really had no idea she was feeling overwhelmed and depressed. I am not sure I really understand what is happening. I love my mom, and I want to be here for her. She has always had these ups and downs. Is this any different? I love my mom, but she is so busy that I have given up on trying to keep up with her. So when I hear she wants to have a session, I am confused. Dad is so good with her. He keeps everything rolling when she is feeling down.

Therapist: I hear both your confusion and your willingness to be here for your mom. Gwen, what is this like for you?

Gwen: I am so thankful that I have such a loving family that is willing to come talk to a complete stranger so that I can get the help I need. Right now I am feeling overwhelmed with life, and I am tired of it. I am juggling so many things and feel like nothing is getting done. I know this has been going on for long time, but I am ready to find a better way of living. I know this pattern has not been easy for any of you, and I feel guilty over that too. I don't want to hide in bed anymore, like I remember my mom doing. I am not getting any younger, and I am so ready to show up in life in a healthier way.

Therapist: What would that look like?

Gwen: Well, I don't know for sure. I would be happy, I guess. I would not be worried about work or the family so much.

Therapist: And what would your family be doing if you were happier and healthier?

Gwen: I guess they would be happier too. It seems like if I am happy, then they are too.

Therapist: But how can you be happy and healthy with all these burdens hanging on you?

Gwen: I am hoping you can tell me.

Therapist: Would it be OK with you if I gave that a try?

Gwen: Yes, please.

Therapist: Here is what I think is almost always true. A super responsible person is always surrounded by people who will let her take charge and handle everything.

Gwen: What do you mean by that?

Therapist: It means, Gwen, that you have been in charge for a very long time, and you have forgotten how to ask for help. Maybe you never knew how to do that. But as long as you keep pushing forward, your family will let you.

Gwen's Mother: That's right there!

Ron: Wait a minute. I do everything I can to keep things moving! What else do you need?

Gwen: I don't know. I am just hearing that I need help.

Therapist: So that's the issue for this family. Mom is the only one that knows everything that needs to happen. She knows how to do everything, but she is overloaded. She doesn't know how to ask for help, and everyone else is hoping she won't because everyone is busy and overloaded. And, Gwen, even if you did ask for help from others, would you worry whether they were doing it right?

Brittany: Are you kidding? She would be supervising everything anyway.

Therapist: And how many of you would know how to mess it up just enough so that mom would take over again? [*pause while family members look at each other; some smile a bit; some hang their heads*] Wow. That brought everything to a standstill. Where do we go from here?

Ron: Maybe we need to go home and think about this. We definitely need to do something differently. I want to talk to your brother and let him know how much pressure your mom is under so he can start taking care of his own business. We better start by making a list of everything Gwen has been doing and see where we need to step up. [*pause*] And maybe Gwen needs to stay out of this part.

Therapist: Let's see where that goes.

We set a time for future sessions, and I let them know that coming in for therapy shows their commitment to Gwen and to each other as a family unit. I want them to know that I understand what it took for them to make it in the door and that their efforts are commendable.

Questions for Reflection

- What did you think of the way the therapist intervened to get family members connected in their first family therapy session?
- What do you imagine it would be like for you to be a participant in this family therapy session with this therapist?
- What value do you see for Gwen in having a family therapy session in addition to her individual therapy sessions?
- Beginning therapists are usually anxious about having so many people in the room because it can be confusing. How did the therapist in this case manage the session so that it did not become chaotic?

Summary and Evaluation

Summary

Let's first review the themes that unite the many approaches to family therapy, with particular emphasis on the multilayered approach. LO8

Basic Assumption If we hope to work therapeutically with an individual, it is critical to consider him or her within the family system. An individual's problematic behavior grows out of the interactional unit of the family as well as the larger community and societal systems.

Focus of Family Therapy Most of the family therapies tend to be brief because families who seek professional help typically want resolution of some problematic symptom. Changing the system can stimulate change quickly. In addition to being short-term, solution-focused, and action-oriented, family therapy tends to deal with present interactions. The main focus of family therapy is on here-and-now interactions in the family system. One way in which family therapy differs from many individual therapies is its emphasis on how current family relationships contribute to the development and maintenance of symptoms.

Role of Goals and Values Specific goals are determined by the practitioner's orientation or by a collaborative process between family and therapist. Global goals include using interventions that enable individuals and the family to change in ways that will reduce their distress. Tied to the question of what goals should guide a therapist's interventions is the question of the therapist's values. Family therapy is grounded on a set of values and theoretical assumptions. Ultimately, every intervention a therapist makes is an expression of a value judgment. It is critical for therapists, regardless of their theoretical orientation, to be aware of their values and monitor how these values influence their practice with families.

How Families Change An integrative approach to the practice of family therapy includes guiding principles that help the therapist organize goals, interactions, observations, and ways to promote change. Some perspectives of family systems therapy focus on perceptual and cognitive change, others deal mainly with changing feelings, and still other theories emphasize behavioral change. Regardless of the perspectives that a family therapist operates from, change needs to happen in relationships, not just within the individual.

Techniques of Family Therapy The intervention strategies therapists employ are best considered in conjunction with their personal characteristics. Bitter (2014), Goldenberg and Goldenberg (2013), and Nichols (2013) emphasize that techniques are tools for achieving therapeutic goals but that these intervention strategies do not make a family therapist. Personal characteristics such as respect for clients, compassion, empathy, and sensitivity are human qualities that influence the manner in which techniques are delivered. It is also essential to have a rationale for the techniques that are used, with some sense of the expected outcomes. Faced with meeting the demands of clinical practice, practitioners will need to be flexible in selecting intervention strategies. The central consideration is what is in the best interests of the family.

A multilayered approach to family therapy is more complex than models with a singular focus. At least initially, some of the confidence and clarity that might be gained from a single approach may be lost, but in time the flexibility to change directions is an asset. We have presented a structure for therapy that is useful across models. We have integrated a multilayered process of family therapy in assessment, hypothesizing, and facilitating change. This chapter has described a collaborative process for therapy in which both the family and the therapist share influence according to the needs of the situation.

Contributions of Family Systems Approaches

One of the key contributions of most systemic approaches is that neither the individual nor the family is blamed for a particular dysfunction. The family is empowered through the process of identifying and exploring internal, developmental, and purposeful interactional patterns. At the same time, a systems perspective recognizes that individuals and families are affected by external forces and systems, among them illness, shifting gender patterns, culture, and socioeconomic considerations. If change is to occur in families or with individuals, therapists must be aware of as many systems of influence as possible.

Most of the individual therapies considered in this textbook fail to give a primary focus to the systemic factors influencing the individual. Family therapy redefines the individual as a system embedded within many other systems, which brings an entirely different perspective to assessment and treatment. An advantage to this viewpoint is that an individual is not scapegoated as the "bad person" in the family. Rather than blaming either the "identified patient" or a family, the entire family has an opportunity (a) to examine the multiple perspectives and interactional patterns that characterize the unit and (b) to participate in finding solutions.

Limitations and Criticisms of Family Systems Approaches

In the early days of family therapy, therapists all too often got lost in their consideration of the "system." In adopting the language of systems, therapists began to describe and think of families as being made up of "dyads" and "triads"; as being "functional" or "dysfunctional," "stuck" or "unstuck," and "enmeshed" or "disengaged";

and as displaying "positive" and "negative" outcomes and "feedback loops." It was as if the family was a well-oiled machine or perhaps a computer that occasionally broke down. Just as it was easy to fix a machine without an emotional consideration of the parts involved, some therapists approached family systems work with little concern for the individuals as long as the "whole" of the family "functioned" better. Enactments, ordeals, and paradoxical interventions were often "done to" clients—sometimes even without their knowledge (see Haley, 1963, 1976, 1984; Minuchin & Fishman, 1981; Selvini Palazzolli, Boscolo, Cecchin, & Prata, 1978).

Feminists were perhaps the first, but not the only, group to lament the loss of a personal perspective within a systemic framework. As the field moves now toward an integration of individual and systemic frameworks, it is important to reinvest the language of therapy with human emotional terminology that honors the place real people have always held in families. It is our hope that this chapter gives you enough of an introduction to the diverse field of family therapy that you will want to learn more through reading as well as watching the many video currently available.

Self-Reflection and Discussion Questions

1. Several different approaches to family therapy are described in this chapter. Which of these approaches most interests you, and why?
2. How do you imagine it would be for you to be with your family as a participant in family therapy? What do you think you could learn about yourself from this experience?
3. What do you think you will need to learn and to experience before you will be able to effectively work with a family?
4. How do the family systems therapy approaches differ from other theories that you have studied thus far?
5. What are some major advantages of working with a family therapy perspective? Can you think of any disadvantages?

Where to Go From Here

You may want to consider joining the American Association for Marriage and Family Therapy, which has a student membership category. You must obtain an official application, including the names of at least two Clinical Members from whom the association can request official endorsements. You also need a statement signed by the coordinator or director of a graduate program in marital and family therapy in a regionally accredited educational institution, verifying your current enrollment. Student membership may be held until receipt of a qualifying graduate degree or for a maximum of five years. Members receive the *Journal of Marital and Family Therapy*, which is published four times a year, and a subscription to six issues yearly of *The Family Therapy Magazine*. For a copy of the AAMFT Code of Ethics, membership applications, and further information, contact:

American Association for Marriage and Family Therapy
www.aamft.org

The American Counseling Association has a division devoted to couples and family therapy called the International Association of Marriage and Family Counseling (IAMFC). This division publishes *The Family Journal* and *The Family Digest* and provides access to couples and family training and programs at the ACA convention. For more information, contact:

International Association of Marriage and Family Counseling
www.iamfconline.org/public/main.cfm

Recommended Supplementary Readings

Theory and Practice of Family Therapy and Counseling (Bitter, 2014) is a comprehensive textbook that seeks to develop personal and professional growth in family practitioners as well as orient the reader to the theories that make up the field of family therapy and counseling.

Family Therapy: History, Theory, and Practice (Gladding, 2014) is an overview of family therapy models and therapeutic interventions designed for counselors associated with ACA.

Family Therapy: An Overview (Goldenberg & Goldenberg, 2013) provides an excellent basic overview of these contemporary perspectives on family therapy.

Ethnicity and Family Therapy (McGoldrick, Giordano, & Garcia-Preto, 2005) is the seminal work on culture in family therapy. The authors review the importance of cultural considerations in relation to family therapy and provide chapters on the background, research, and therapy issues of more than 15 cultures.

Family Therapy: Concepts and Methods (Nichols, 2013) is an AAMFT-based text that covers seven of the major contemporary family systems models. The final chapter presents an integration of key themes among diverse approaches to family therapy.

An Integrative Perspective

15

LEARNING OBJECTIVES

1. Explain psychotherapy integration and why it is increasing in popularity.
2. Identify some specific advantages of psychotherapy integration.
3. Examine some of the main challenges of developing an integrative approach.
4. Discuss how multicultural issues can be addressed in counseling practice.
5. Discuss how spiritual and religious values can ethically and effectively be integrated into counseling practice.
6. Understand a basis for effectively drawing techniques from various theories.
7. Examine what research generally shows about the effectiveness of psychotherapy.
8. Describe feedback-informed treatment and explain how this is related to enhanced therapeutic outcomes.

Introduction

This chapter will help you think about areas of convergence and divergence among the 11 therapeutic systems covered in this book. Although these approaches all have some goals in common, they have many differences when it comes to the best route to achieve these goals. Some therapies call for an active and directive stance on the therapist's part, and others place value on clients being the active agent. Some therapies focus on experiencing *feelings*, others stress identifying *cognitive patterns*, and still others concentrate on actual *behavior*. The key task is to find ways to integrate certain features of each of these approaches so that you can work with clients on all three levels of human experience.

The field of psychotherapy is characterized by a diverse range of specialized models. With all this diversity, is there any hope that a practitioner can develop skills in all of the existing techniques? How does a student decide which theories are most relevant to practice? Looking for commonalities among the systems of psychotherapy is relatively new (Norcross & Beutler, 2014). Practitioners have been battling over the "best" way to bring about personality change dating back to the work of Freud. For decades, counselors resisted integration, often to the point of denying the validity of alternative theories and of ignoring effective methods from other theoretical schools. The early history of counseling is full of theoretical wars.

Since the early 1980s, psychotherapy integration has developed into a clearly delineated field. It is now an established and respected movement that is based on combining the best of differing orientations so that more complete theoretical models can be articulated and more efficient treatments developed (Goldfried, Pachankis, & Bell, 2005). The Society for the Exploration of Psychotherapy Integration, formed in 1983, is an international organization whose members are professionals working toward the development of therapeutic approaches that transcend single theoretical orientations. As the field of psychotherapy has matured, the concept of integration has emerged as a mainstay (Norcross & Beutler, 2014).

In this chapter I consider the advantages of developing an integrative perspective for counseling practice. I also present a framework to help you begin to integrate concepts and techniques from various approaches. As you read, start to formulate your own personal perspective for counseling. Look for ways to synthesize diverse elements from different theoretical perspectives. As much as possible, be alert to how these systems can function in harmony.

Visit CengageBrain.com or watch the DVD for the video program on Chapter 15, *Theory and Practice of Counseling and Psychotherapy: The Case of Stan and Lecturettes*. I suggest that you view the brief lecture for each chapter prior to reading the chapter.

The Movement Toward Psychotherapy Integration

A large number of therapists identify themselves as "eclectic," and this category covers a broad range of practice. At its worst, eclectic practice consists of haphazardly picking techniques without any overall theoretical rationale. This is known as **syncretism**, wherein the practitioner, lacking in knowledge and skill in selecting interventions, looks for anything that seems to work, often making little attempt to determine whether the therapeutic procedures are indeed effective. Such an uncritical and unsystematic combination of techniques is no better than a narrow and dogmatic orthodoxy. Pulling techniques from many sources without a sound rationale results in syncretistic confusion, which is detrimental to the successful treatment of clients (Corey, 2015; Neukrug, 2016; Norcross & Beutler, 2014).

Pathways Toward Psychotherapy Integration

Psychotherapy integration is best characterized by attempts to look beyond LO1 and across the confines of single-school approaches to see what can be learned from other perspectives and how clients can benefit from a variety of ways of conducting therapy. The majority of psychotherapists do not claim allegiance to a particular therapeutic school but prefer, instead, some form of integration (Norcross, 2005; Norcross & Beutler, 2014). In a 2007 survey, only 4.2% of respondents identified themselves as being aligned with one therapy model exclusively. The remaining 95.8% claimed to be *integrative*, meaning they combined a variety of methods or approaches in their counseling practice (*Psychotherapy Networker*, 2007). A panel of psychotherapy experts has predicted an increase in the popularity of integrative therapies in the next decade, particularly with regard to mindfulness, cognitive behavioral, multicultural, and integrative theories (Norcross, Pfund, & Prochaska, 2013).

The integrative approach is characterized by openness to various ways of integrating diverse theories and techniques, and there is a decided preference for the term *integrative* over *eclectic* (Norcross, Karpiak, & Lister, 2005). The ultimate goal of integration is to enhance the efficiency and applicability of psychotherapy. Norcross and Beutler (2014) and Stricker (2010) describe four of the most common pathways toward the integration of psychotherapies: technical integration, theoretical integration, assimilative integration, and common factors approach. All of these approaches to integration look beyond the restrictions of single approaches, but they do so in distinctive ways.

Technical integration aims at selecting the best treatment techniques for the individual and the problem. It tends to focus on differences, chooses from many approaches, and is a collection of techniques. This path calls for using techniques from different schools without necessarily subscribing to the theoretical positions that spawned them. For those who practice from the perspective of technical integration, there is no necessary connection between conceptual foundations and techniques. Therapists have a variety of tools in their toolkit to use with clients. One of the best-known forms of technical integration, which Lazarus (2008a) refers to as *technical eclecticism*, is the basis of *multimodal therapy*. Multimodal therapists borrow from many other therapeutic models, using techniques that have been demonstrated to be effective in dealing with specific clinical problems. Whenever feasible, multimodal therapists employ empirically supported techniques.

In contrast, **theoretical integration** refers to a conceptual or theoretical creation beyond a mere blending of techniques. This route has the goal of producing a conceptual framework that synthesizes the best aspects of two or more theoretical approaches under the assumption that the outcome will be richer than either theory alone. This approach emphasizes integrating the underlying theories of therapy along with techniques from each. Examples of this form of integration are *dialectical* *behavior therapy* (DBT) and *acceptance and commitment therapy* (ACT), both of which are described in Chapter 9.

Emotion-focused therapy (EFT), introduced in Chapter 7, is another form of theoretical integration. This approach is informed by the role of emotion in psychotherapeutic change. Greenberg (2011), a key figure in the development of EFT, conceptualizes the model as an empirically supported, integrative, experiential approach to treatment. Emotion-focused therapy is rooted in a person-centered philosophy, but it is integrative in that it synthesizes aspects of Gestalt therapy, experiential therapy, and existential therapy. Emotion-focused therapy blends the relational aspects of the person-centered approach with the active phenomenological awareness experiments of Gestalt therapy.

The **assimilative integration** approach is grounded in a particular school of psychotherapy, along with an openness to selectively incorporate practices from other therapeutic approaches. Assimilative integration combines the advantages of a single coherent theoretical system with the flexibility of a variety of interventions from multiple systems. An example of this form of integration is *mindfulness-based cognitive therapy* (MBCT), which integrates aspects of cognitive therapy and mindfulness-based stress reduction procedures. As you may recall from Chapter 9, MBCT is a comprehensive integration of the principles and skills of mindfulness that has been applied to the treatment of depression (Segal, Williams, & Teasdale, 2013).

The **common factors approach** searches for common elements across different theoretical systems. Despite many differences among the theories, a recognizable core of counseling practice is composed of nonspecific variables common to all therapies. Lambert (2011) concludes that common factors can be a basis for psychotherapy integration:

> The common factors explanation for the general equivalence of diverse therapeutic interventions has resulted in the dominance of integrative practice in routine care by implying that the dogmatic advocacy of a particular theoretical school is not supported by research. Research also suggests that *common factors* can become the focal point for integration of seemingly diverse therapy techniques. (p. 314)

Some of these common factors include empathic listening, support, warmth, developing a working alliance, opportunity for catharsis, practicing new behaviors, feedback, positive expectations of clients, working through one's own conflicts, understanding interpersonal and intrapersonal dynamics, change that occurs outside of the therapy office, client factors, therapist effects, and learning to be self-reflective about one's work (Norcross & Beutler, 2014; Prochaska & Norcross, 2014).These common factors are thought to be far more important in accounting for therapeutic outcomes than the unique factors that differentiate one theory from another. Specific treatment techniques make relatively little difference in outcome when compared with the value of common factors, especially the human elements (Elkins, 2016). Among the approaches to psychotherapy integration, the common factors approach has the strongest empirical support (Duncan, Miller, Wampold, & Hubble, 2010).

Of all of the common factors investigated in psychotherapy, none has received more attention and confirmation than a facilitative therapeutic relationship (Lambert, 2011). The importance of the therapeutic alliance is a well-established critical component of effective therapy. Research confirms that the client–therapist relationship is central to therapeutic change and is a significant predictor of both effectiveness and retention of therapy outcomes (Elkins, 2016; Miller, Hubble, & Seidel, 2015).

Advantages of Psychotherapy Integration

LO2

An integrative approach provides a general framework that enables practitioners to make sense of the many aspects of the therapy process and provides a map giving direction to what practitioners do and say (Corey, 2015). One reason for the movement toward psychotherapy integration is the recognition that no single theory is comprehensive enough to account for the complexities of human behavior, especially when the range of client types and their specific problems are taken into consideration. Because no one theory contains all the truth, and because no single set of counseling techniques is always effective in working with diverse client populations, integrative approaches hold promise for counseling practice. Norcross and Wampold (2011b) maintain that effective clinical practice requires a flexible and integrative perspective. Psychotherapy should be flexibly tailored to the unique needs and contexts of the individual client. Norcross and Wampold contend that using an identical therapy relationship style and treatment method for all clients is inappropriate and can be unethical.

The 11 systems discussed in this book have evolved in the direction of broadening their theoretical and practical bases and have become less restrictive in their focus. Many practitioners who claim allegiance to a particular system of therapy are expanding their theoretical outlook and developing a wider range of therapeutic techniques to fit a more diverse population of clients. There is a growing recognition that psychotherapy can be most effective when contributions from various approaches are integrated (Goldfried, Glass, & Arnkoff, 2011). Although to date the bulk of psychotherapy integration has been based on theoretical and clinical foundations, Goldfried and colleagues suggest that evidence-based practice will increasingly become the organizing force for integration. Empirical pragmatism, not theory, will be the integrative theme of the 21st century.

Practitioners who are open to an integrative perspective will find that several theories play a crucial role in their personal counseling approach. Each theory has its unique contributions and its own domain of expertise. By accepting that each theory has strengths and weaknesses and is, by definition, "different" from the others, practitioners have some basis to begin developing a theory that fits for them and their clients. It takes considerable time to learn the various theories in depth. It is not realistic for any of us to expect that we can integrate all the theories. Instead, integration of some aspects of some theories is a more realistic goal. Developing an integrative perspective is a lifelong endeavor that is refined with clinical experience, reflection, reading, and discourse with colleagues.

The Challenge of Developing an Integrative Perspective

LO3

A survey of approaches to counseling and psychotherapy reveals that no common philosophy unifies them. Many of the theories have different basic philosophies and views of human nature (Table 15.1). As the postmodern therapists

TABLE 15.1 The Basic Philosophies

Psychoanalytic therapy	Human beings are basically determined by psychic energy and by early experiences. Unconscious motives and conflicts are central in present behavior. Early development is of critical importance because later personality problems have their roots in repressed childhood conflicts.
Adlerian therapy	Humans are motivated by social interest, by striving toward goals, by inferiority and superiority, and by dealing with the tasks of life. Emphasis is on the individual's positive capacities to live in society cooperatively. People have the capacity to interpret, influence, and create events. Each person at an early age creates a unique style of life, which tends to remain relatively constant throughout life.
Existential therapy	The central focus is on the nature of the human condition, which includes a capacity for self-awareness, freedom of choice to decide one's fate, responsibility, anxiety, the search for meaning, being alone and being in relation with others, striving for authenticity, and facing living and dying.
Person-centered therapy	Positive view of people; we have an inclination toward becoming fully functioning. In the context of the therapeutic relationship, the client experiences feelings that were previously denied to awareness. The client moves toward increased awareness, spontaneity, trust in self, and inner-directedness.
Gestalt therapy	The person strives for wholeness and integration of thinking, feeling, and behaving. Some key concepts include contact with self and others, contact boundaries, and awareness. The view is nondeterministic in that the person is viewed as having the capacity to recognize how earlier influences are related to present difficulties. As an experiential approach, it is grounded in the here and now and emphasizes awareness, personal choice, and responsibility.
Behavior therapy	Behavior is the product of learning. We are both the product and the producer of the environment. Traditional behavior therapy is based on classical and operant principles. Contemporary behavior therapy has branched out in many directions, including mindfulness and acceptance approaches.
Cognitive behavior therapy	Individuals tend to incorporate faulty thinking, which leads to emotional and behavioral disturbances. Cognitions are the major determinants of how we feel and act. Therapy is primarily oriented toward cognition and behavior, and it stresses the role of thinking, deciding, questioning, doing, and redeciding. This is a psychoeducational model, which emphasizes therapy as a learning process, including acquiring and practicing new skills, learning new ways of thinking, and acquiring more effective ways of coping with problems.
Choice theory/ Reality therapy	Based on choice theory, this approach assumes that we need quality relationships to be happy. Psychological problems are the result of our resisting control by others or of our attempt to control others. Choice theory is an explanation of human nature and how to best achieve satisfying interpersonal relationships.
Feminist therapy	Feminists criticize many traditional theories to the degree that they are based on gender-biased concepts, such as being androcentric, gendercentric, ethnocentric, heterosexist, and intrapsychic. The constructs of feminist therapy include being gender fair, flexible, interactionist, and life-span-oriented. Gender and power are at the heart of feminist therapy. This is a systems approach that recognizes the cultural, social, and political factors that contribute to an individual's problems.
Postmodern approaches	Based on the premise that there are multiple realities and multiple truths, postmodern therapies reject the idea that reality is external and can be grasped. People create meaning in their lives through conversations with others. The postmodern approaches avoid pathologizing clients, take a dim view of diagnosis, avoid searching for underlying causes of problems, and place a high value on discovering clients' strengths and resources. Rather than talking about problems, the focus of therapy is on creating solutions in the present and the future.
Family systems therapy	The family is viewed from an interactive and systemic perspective. Clients are connected to a living system; a change in one part of the system will result in a change in other parts. The family provides the context for understanding how individuals function in relationship to others and how they behave. Treatment deals with the family unit. An individual's dysfunctional behavior grows out of the interactional unit of the family and out of larger systems as well.

remind us, our philosophical assumptions are important because they influence which "reality" we perceive, and they direct our attention to the variables that we are "set" to see. A word of caution, then: Beware of subscribing exclusively to any one view of human nature. Remain open and selectively incorporate a framework for counseling that is consistent with your own personality and belief system and that validates clients' belief systems as well.

Despite the divergences in the various theories, creative syntheses among some models are possible. For example, an existential orientation does not necessarily preclude using techniques drawn from behavior therapy or from some of the cognitive theories. Each point of view offers a perspective for helping clients in their search for self. I encourage you to study all the major theories and to remain open to what you might take from the various orientations as a basis for an integrative perspective that will guide your practice.

In developing a personal integrative perspective, it is important to be alert to the problem of attempting to mix theories with incompatible underlying assumptions. Examine the key concepts of various theories as you begin to think about integration (Table 15.2). By remaining theoretically consistent, but technically integrative, practitioners can spell out precisely the interventions they will employ with various clients, as well as the means by which they will select these procedures.

TABLE 15.2 Key Concepts

Psychoanalytic therapy	Normal personality development is based on successful resolution and integration of psychosexual stages of development. Faulty personality development is the result of inadequate resolution of some specific stage. Anxiety is a result of repression of basic conflicts. Unconscious processes are centrally related to current behavior.
Adlerian therapy	Key concepts include the unity of personality, the need to view people from their subjective perspective, and the importance of life goals that give direction to behavior. People are motivated by social interest and by finding goals to give life meaning. Other key concepts are striving for significance and superiority, developing a unique lifestyle, and understanding the family constellation. Therapy is a matter of providing encouragement and assisting clients in changing their cognitive perspective and behavior.
Existential therapy	Essentially an experiential approach to counseling rather than a firm theoretical model, it stresses core human conditions. Interest is on the present and on what one is becoming. The approach has a future orientation and stresses self-awareness before action.
Person-centered therapy	The client has the potential to become aware of problems and the means to resolve them. Faith is placed in the client's capacity for self-direction. Mental health is a congruence of ideal self and real self. Maladjustment is the result of a discrepancy between what one wants to be and what one is. In therapy attention is given to the present moment and on experiencing and expressing feelings.
Gestalt therapy	Emphasis is on the "what" and "how" of experiencing in the here and now to help clients accept all aspects of themselves. Key concepts include holism, figure-formation process, awareness, unfinished business and avoidance, contact, and energy.
Behavior therapy	Focus is on overt behavior, precision in specifying goals of treatment, development of specific treatment plans, and objective evaluation of therapy outcomes. Present behavior is given attention. Therapy is based on the principles of learning theory. Normal behavior is learned through reinforcement and imitation. Abnormal behavior is the result of faulty learning.

(continued)

TABLE 15.2 Key Concepts (continued)

Cognitive behavior therapy	Although psychological problems may be rooted in childhood, they are reinforced by present ways of thinking. A person's belief system and thinking is the primary cause of disorders. Internal dialogue plays a central role in one's behavior. Clients focus on examining faulty assumptions and misconceptions and on replacing these with effective beliefs.
Choice theory/ Reality therapy	The basic focus is on what clients are doing and how to get them to evaluate whether their present actions are working for them. People are mainly motivated to satisfy their needs, especially the need for significant relationships. The approach rejects the medical model, the notion of transference, the unconscious, and dwelling on one's past.
Feminist therapy	Core principles of feminist therapy are that the personal is political, therapists have a commitment to social change, women's voices and ways of knowing are valued and women's experiences are honored, the counseling relationship is egalitarian, therapy focuses on strengths and a reformulated definition of psychological distress, and all types of oppression are recognized.
Postmodern approaches	Therapy tends to be brief and addresses the present and the future. The person is not the problem; the problem is the problem. The emphasis is on externalizing the problem and looking for exceptions to the problem. Therapy consists of a collaborative dialogue in which the therapist and the client co-create solutions. By identifying instances when the problem did not exist, clients can create new meanings for themselves and fashion a new life story.
Family systems therapy	Focus is on communication patterns within a family, both verbal and nonverbal. Problems in relationships are likely to be passed on from generation to generation. Key concepts vary depending on specific orientation but include differentiation, triangles, power coalitions, family-of-origin dynamics, functional versus dysfunctional interaction patterns, and dealing with here-and-now interactions. The present is more important than exploring past experiences.

One of the challenges you will face as a counselor is to deliver therapeutic services in a brief, comprehensive, effective, and flexible way. Many of the theoretical orientations addressed in this book can be applied to brief forms of therapy. One of the driving forces of the psychotherapy integration movement has been the increase of brief therapies and the pressures to do more for a variety of client populations within the limitations of 6 to 20 sessions. Short-term and very-short-term therapies are increasing (Norcross et al., 2013). Time-limited brief therapy refers to a variety of time-sensitive, goal-directed, efficiency-oriented methods. These methods can be incorporated in any theoretical approach (Hoyt, 2015). Lambert (2011) believes the future direction of theory, practice, and training will see (1) the decline of single-theory practice and the growth of integrative therapies, and (2) the increase in short-term, time-limited, and group treatments that seem to be as effective as long-term individual treatments with many client populations.

An integrative perspective at its best entails a *systematic integration* of underlying principles and methods common to a range of therapeutic approaches. The strengths of systematic integration are based on its ability to be taught, replicated, and evaluated (Norcross & Beutler, 2014). To develop this kind of integration, you will eventually need to be thoroughly conversant with a number of theories, be open to the idea that these theories can be connected in some ways, and be willing to continually test your hypotheses to determine how well they are working. Neukrug (2016) reminds us that "the ability to assimilate techniques from varying theoretical perspectives takes knowledge, time, and finesse" (p. 139).

Integration of Multicultural Issues in Counseling

Multiculturalism is a reality that cannot be ignored by practitioners if they hope to meet the needs of diverse client groups. I believe current theories, to varying degrees, can and should be expanded to incorporate a multicultural dimension. I have consistently pointed out that if contemporary theories do not account for the cultural dimension, they will have limited applicability in working with diverse client populations. For some theories, this transition is easier than for others. LO4

Clients can be harmed if they are expected to fit all the specifications of a given theory, whether or not the values espoused by the theory are consistent with their own cultural values. Rather than stretching the client to fit the dimensions of a single theory, practitioners need to tailor their theory and practice to fit the unique needs of the client. This calls for counselors to possess knowledge of various cultures, to be aware of their own cultural heritage, and to have skills to assist a wide spectrum of clients in dealing with the realities of their culture. Psychotherapy integration stresses tailoring interventions to the individual client rather than to an overarching theory, making this approach particularly well suited to considering cultural factors and the unique perspective of each client. Comas-Diaz (2014) believes that cultural competence enables counselors to work effectively in most clinical settings. Practitioners demonstrate their cultural competence by becoming aware of their own and their clients' worldviews, and by being able to use culturally appropriate interventions to reflect their cultural beliefs, knowledge, and skills. This is a good time to review the discussion of the culturally skilled counselor in Chapter 2 and to consult Tables 15.7 and 15.8, which appear later in this chapter.

In your role as a counselor, you need to be able to assess the special needs of clients. The client's ethnicity and culture and the concerns that bring this person to counseling challenge you to develop flexibility in utilizing an array of therapeutic strategies. Some clients will need more direction and guidance; others will be hesitant to talk about themselves in personal ways, especially during the early phase of the counseling process. What you may see as resistance could be the client's response to years of cultural conditioning and respect for certain values and traditions. Basically, it comes down to your familiarity with a variety of theoretical approaches and your ability to employ and adapt your techniques to fit the person-in-the-environment. It is not enough to merely assist your clients in gaining insight, expressing suppressed emotions, or making certain behavioral changes. The challenge is to find practical strategies for adapting the techniques you have developed to enable clients to examine the impact their culture continues to have on their lives and to make decisions about what, if anything, they want to change.

Being an effective counselor involves reflecting on how your own culture influences you and your interventions in your counseling practice. This awareness is critical in becoming more sensitive to the cultural backgrounds of the clients who seek your help. Using an integrative perspective, therapists can encompass social, cultural, spiritual, and political dimensions in their work with clients.

Integration of Spirituality and Religion in Counseling

The counseling process can help clients gain insight into the ways their core beliefs and values are reflected in their behavior. Current interest in spiritual and religious beliefs has implications for how such beliefs might be incorporated in LO5 therapeutic relationships (Frame, 2003; Johnson, 2013; Young & Cashwell, 2011a). Survey data from members of both the American Psychological Association and the American Counseling Association indicate that spiritual and religious matters are therapeutically relevant, ethically appropriate, and potentially significant topics for the practice of counseling in secular settings (Delaney, Miller, & Bisono, 2007; Young, Wiggins-Frame, & Cashwell, 2007).

Worthington (2011) asserts that the increasing openness of therapists to clients' spiritual and religious concerns and interests has been fueled by the multicultural evolution. The emphasis on multiculturalism has empowered people to define themselves from a cultural perspective, which includes their spiritual, religious, and ethnic contexts. Johnson (2013) views spiritually informed therapy as a form of multicultural therapy. The first step is for the therapist to be sincerely interested in the client's spiritual beliefs and experiences and how he or she finds meaning in life. Johnson believes that a client-defined sense of spirituality can be a significant avenue for connecting with the client and can be an ally in the therapeutic change process. However, the emphasis is on what the client wants, not on the therapist's spiritual experiences or agenda for the client.

Clients who are experiencing a crisis situation may find a source of comfort, support, and strength in drawing upon their spiritual resources. For some clients spirituality entails embracing a religion, which can have many different meanings. Other clients value spirituality, yet do not have any ties to a formal religion. Whatever one's particular view of spirituality, it is a force that can help the individual to find a purpose (or purposes) for living. Spiritual or religious beliefs can be a major sustaining power that supports clients when all else fails. Other clients may be affected by depression and a sense of worthlessness due to guilt, anger, or sadness created by their unexamined acceptance of spiritual or religious dogma. Counselors must remain open and nonjudgmental in conversations about religion or spirituality. Furthermore, counselors cannot ignore a client's spiritual and religious perspectives if they want to practice in a culturally competent and ethical manner (Johnson, 2013; Young & Cashwell, 2011a, 2011b). It is essential for counselors to be aware of and understand their spiritual or religious attitudes, beliefs, values, and experiences if they expect to facilitate an exploration of these issues with clients.

Common Goals Spiritual values have a major part to play in human life and struggles. Exploring these values has a great deal to do with providing solutions for clients' struggles. Because spiritual and therapeutic paths converge in some ways, integration is possible, and dealing with a client's spirituality will often enhance the therapy process. Themes that have healing influences include loving, caring, learning to listen with compassion, challenging clients' basic life assumptions, accepting human imperfection, and going outside of self-oriented interests (social interest). Both a spiritual perspective and counseling can help people ponder questions of "Who am I?" and "What is the meaning of my life?" Pursuing these existential questions can foster healing.

Implications for Assessment and Treatment Traditionally, when clients come to a therapist with a problem, the therapist explores all the factors that contributed to the development of the problem. A background of involvement in religion can be part of a client's history, and thus it can be a part of the intake assessment and can be explored in counseling sessions. Frame (2003) presents many reasons for including spirituality in the assessment process: understanding clients' worldviews and the contexts in which they live, assisting clients in grappling with questions regarding the purpose of their lives and what they most value, exploring religion and spirituality as client resources, and uncovering religious and spiritual problems. This information will assist the therapist in choosing appropriate interventions. Young and Cashwell (2011a) maintain that counselors must assess whether clients' spiritual or religious beliefs may be exacerbating or helping clients' psychological problems.

Your Role as a Counselor It is critical that counselors not be judgmental when it comes to their clients' beliefs and that counselors create an inviting and safe climate for clients to explore their values and beliefs. There are many paths toward fulfilling spiritual needs, and it is not your role as a counselor to prescribe any particular pathway. By conducting a thorough assessment on a client's background, you will obtain many clues regarding personal themes for potential exploration. If you remain finely tuned to clients' stories and to the purpose for which they sought therapy, clients' concerns about spiritual or religious values, beliefs, and practices will surface. It is critical that you listen for how clients talk about existential concerns of meaning, values, mortality, and being in the world. Remain open to how your clients define, experience, and access whatever helps them stay connected to their core values and their inner wisdom (Johnson, 2013).

If you are to effectively serve diverse client populations, it is essential that you pay attention to your training and competence in addressing spiritual and religious concerns your clients bring to therapy. Ethically, it is important to monitor yourself for subtle ways that you might be inclined to influence clients to embrace a spiritual perspective or to give up certain religious beliefs that you think are no longer functional for them. It is important to keep in mind that clients, not therapists, should determine the specific values they want to retain, replace, or modify.

From my vantage point, the emphasis on spirituality will continue to be important in counseling practice, which makes it imperative that you prepare yourself to work competently with the spiritual and religious concerns that your clients bring up. For further reading on the topic of integrating spirituality and religion into counseling, I highly recommend *Integrating Spirituality and Religion into Counseling: A Guide to Competent Practice* (Cashwell & Young, 2011) and *Spirituality in Counseling and Psychotherapy: An Integrative Approach That Empowers Clients* (Johnson, 2013).

Issues Related to the Therapeutic Process

Therapeutic Goals

The goals of counseling are almost as diverse as are the theoretical approaches (Table 15.3). Some possible goals include the following:

- Restructuring the personality
- Uncovering the unconscious
- Creating social interest

TABLE 15.3 Goals of Therapy

Approach	Goals
Psychoanalytic therapy	To make the unconscious conscious. To reconstruct the basic personality. To assist clients in reliving earlier experiences and working through repressed conflicts. To achieve intellectual and emotional awareness.
Adlerian therapy	To challenge clients' basic premises and life goals. To offer encouragement so individuals can develop socially useful goals and increase social interest. To develop the client's sense of belonging.
Existential therapy	To help people see that they are free and to become aware of their possibilities. To challenge them to recognize that they are responsible for events that they formerly thought were happening to them. To identify factors that block freedom.
Person-centered therapy	To provide a safe climate conducive to clients' self-exploration. To help clients recognize blocks to growth and experience aspects of self that were formerly denied or distorted. To enable them to move toward openness, greater trust in self, willingness to be a process, and increased spontaneity and aliveness. To find meaning in life and to experience life fully. To become more self-directed.
Gestalt therapy	To assist clients in gaining awareness of moment-to-moment experiencing and to expand the capacity to make choices. To foster integration of the self.
Behavior therapy	To eliminate maladaptive behaviors and learn more effective behaviors. To identify factors that influence behavior and find out what can be done about problematic behavior. To encourage clients to take an active and collaborative role in clearly setting treatment goals and evaluating how well these goals are being met.
Cognitive behavior therapy	To teach clients to confront faulty beliefs with contradictory evidence that they gather and evaluate. To help clients seek out their faulty beliefs and minimize them. To become aware of automatic thoughts and to change them. To assist clients in identifying their inner strengths, and to explore the kind of life they would like to have.
Choice theory/ Reality therapy	To help people become more effective in meeting all of their psychological needs. To enable clients to get reconnected with the people they have chosen to put into their quality worlds and teach clients choice theory.
Feminist therapy	To bring about transformation both in the individual client and in society. To assist clients in recognizing, claiming, and using their personal power to free themselves from the limitations of gender-role socialization. To confront all forms of institutional policies that discriminate or oppress on any basis.
Postmodern approaches	To change the way clients view problems and what they can do about these concerns. To collaboratively establish specific, clear, concrete, realistic, and observable goals leading to increased positive change. To help clients create a self-identity grounded on competence and resourcefulness so they can resolve present and future concerns. To assist clients in viewing their lives in positive ways, rather than being problem saturated.
Family systems therapy	To help family members gain awareness of patterns of relationships that are not working well and to create new ways of interacting. To identify how a client's problematic behavior may serve a function or purpose for the family. To understand how dysfunctional patterns can be handed down across generations. To recognize how family rules can affect each family member. To understand how past family of origin experiences continue to have an impact on individuals.

- Finding meaning in life
- Curing an emotional disturbance
- Examining old decisions and making new ones
- Developing trust in oneself
- Becoming more self-actualizing

- Reducing maladaptive behavior and learning adaptive patterns
- Becoming grounded in the present moment
- Managing intense emotions such as anxiety
- Gaining more effective control of one's life
- Reauthoring the story of one's life

This diversity can be simplified by considering the degree of generality or specificity of goals. Goals exist on a continuum from specific, concrete, and short term on one end, to general, global, and long term on the other. The cognitive behavioral approaches stress the former; the relationship-oriented therapies tend to stress the latter. The goals at opposite ends of the continuum are not necessarily contradictory; it is a matter of how specifically they are defined.

Therapist's Function and Role

In working toward an integrative perspective, ask yourself these questions:

- How do the counselor's functions change depending on the stage of the counseling process?
- Does the therapist maintain a basic role, or does this role vary in accordance with the characteristics of the client?
- How does the counselor determine how active and directive to be?
- How is structuring handled as the course of therapy progresses?
- What is the optimum balance of responsibility in the client–therapist relationship?
- What is the most effective way to monitor the therapeutic alliance?
- What, when, and how much counselor self-disclosure is therapeutic?

As you saw through your study of the 11 therapeutic approaches, a central issue of each system is the degree to which the therapist exercises control over clients' behavior both during and outside the session. Cognitive behavior therapists and reality therapists, for example, operate within a present-centered, directive, didactic, structured, and psychoeducational context. As a collaborative endeavor, they frequently design homework assignments to assist clients in practicing new behavior outside therapy sessions. In contrast, person-centered therapists operate with a much looser and less defined structure. Solution-focused and narrative therapists view the client as the expert on his or her own life; they assist the client in reflection outside of the session that might result in self-directed change. Although they are active questioners, they are not prescriptive in their practice.

Structuring depends on the particular client and the specific circumstances he or she brings to the therapy situation. From my perspective, clear structure is most essential during the early phase of counseling because it encourages the client to talk about the problems that led to seeking therapy. In a collaborative way, it is useful for both counselor and client to make some initial assessment that can provide a focus for the therapy process. As soon as possible, the client should be given a significant share of the responsibility for deciding on the content and agenda of the sessions. From early in the therapy process the client can be empowered if the counselor expects the client to become an active participant in the process.

Client's Experience in Therapy

Most clients share some degree of suffering, pain, or at least discontent. There is a discrepancy between how they would like to be and how they are. Some individuals initiate therapy because they hope to cure a specific symptom or set of symptoms. They want to get rid of migraine headaches, free themselves of chronic anxiety attacks, lose weight, or get relief from depression. They may have conflicting feelings and reactions, may struggle with low self-esteem, or may have limited information and skills. Many seek to resolve conflicts in their close relationships. I believe people are increasingly entering therapy with existential problems. Their complaints often relate to the these existential issues: a sense of emptiness, meaninglessness in life, routine ways of living, unsatisfying personal relationships, anxiety over uncertainty, a lack of intense feelings, and a loss of their sense of self.

The initial expectation of many clients is that results will come quickly. They often have great hope for major changes in their life and rely on direction from the therapist. As therapy progresses, clients discover that they must be active in the process, selecting their own goals and working toward them, both in the sessions and in daily living. Some clients can benefit from recognizing and expressing pent-up feelings, others will need to examine their beliefs and thoughts, others will most need to begin behaving in different ways, and others will benefit from talking with you about their relationships with the significant people in their lives. Most clients will need to do some work in all three dimensions—feelings, thoughts, and behaviors—because these dimensions are interrelated.

In deciding what interventions are most likely to be helpful, it is important to take into account the client's cultural, ethnic, and socioeconomic background. Moreover, the focus of counseling may change as clients enter different phases in the counseling process. Although some clients initially feel a need to be listened to and allowed to express deep feelings, they can profit later from examining the thought patterns that are contributing to their psychological pain. A some point in therapy, it is essential that clients translate what they are learning about themselves into concrete action. The client's given situation in the environment provides a framework for selecting interventions that are most appropriate.

Relationship Between Therapist and Client

Most approaches share common ground in accepting the importance of the therapeutic relationship. The existential, person-centered, Gestalt, Adlerian, and postmodern views emphasize the personal relationship as *the* crucial determinant of treatment outcomes. Rational emotive behavior therapy, reality therapy, cognitive behavior therapy, cognitive therapy, and behavior therapy do not ignore the relationship factor but place less emphasis on the relationship and more emphasis on the effective use of techniques (Table 15.4).

Counseling is a personal matter that involves a personal relationship, and evidence indicates that honesty, sincerity, acceptance, understanding, and spontaneity are basic ingredients for successful outcomes. Therapists' degree of caring, their interest and ability in helping their clients, and their genuineness influence the

TABLE 15.4 The Therapeutic Relationship

Psychoanalytic therapy	The classical analyst remains anonymous, and clients develop projections toward him or her. The focus is on reducing the resistances that develop in working with transference and on establishing more rational control. Clients undergo long-term analysis, engage in free association to uncover conflicts, and gain insight by talking. The analyst makes interpretations to teach clients the meaning of current behavior as it relates to the past. In contemporary relational psychoanalytic therapy, the relationship is central and emphasis is given to here-and-now dimensions of this relationship.
Adlerian therapy	The emphasis is on joint responsibility, on mutually determining goals, on mutual trust and respect, and on equality. The focus is on identifying, exploring, and disclosing mistaken goals and faulty assumptions within the person's lifestyle.
Existential therapy	The therapist's main tasks are to accurately grasp clients' being in the world and to establish a personal and authentic encounter with them. The immediacy of the client–therapist relationship and the authenticity of the here-and-now encounter are stressed. Both client and therapist can be changed by the encounter.
Person-centered therapy	The relationship is of primary importance. The qualities of the therapist, including genuineness, warmth, accurate empathy, respect, and being nonjudgmental—and communication of these attitudes to clients—are stressed. Clients use this genuine relationship with the therapist to help them transfer what they learn to other relationships.
Gestalt therapy	Central importance is given to the *I/Thou* relationship and the quality of the therapist's presence. The therapist's attitudes and behavior count more than the techniques used. The therapist does not interpret for clients but assists them in developing the means to make their own interpretations. Clients identify and work on unfinished business from the past that interferes with current functioning.
Behavior therapy	The therapist is active and directive and functions as a teacher or mentor in helping clients learn more effective behavior. Clients must be active in the process and experiment with new behaviors. Although a quality client–therapist relationship is not viewed as sufficient to bring about change, it is considered essential for implementing behavioral procedures.
Cognitive behavior therapy	In REBT the therapist functions as a teacher and the client as a student. The therapist is highly directive and teaches clients an A-B-C model of changing their cognitions. In CT the focus is on a collaborative relationship. Using a Socratic dialogue, the therapist assists clients in identifying dysfunctional beliefs and discovering alternative rules for living. The therapist promotes corrective experiences that lead to learning new skills. Clients gain insight into their problems and then must actively practice changing self-defeating thinking and acting. In strengths-based CBT, active incorporation of client strengths encourages full engagement in therapy and often provides avenues for change that otherwise would be missed.
Choice theory/ Reality therapy	A fundamental task is for the therapist to create a good relationship with the client. Therapists are then able to engage clients in an evaluation of all of their relationships with respect to what they want and how effective they are in getting this. Therapists find out what clients want, ask what they are choosing to do, invite them to evaluate present behavior, help them make plans for change, and get them to make a commitment. The therapist is a client's advocate, as long as the client is willing to attempt to behave responsibly.
Feminist therapy	The therapeutic relationship is based on empowerment and egalitarianism. Therapists actively break down the hierarchy of power and reduce artificial barriers by engaging in appropriate self-disclosure and teaching clients about the therapy process. Therapists strive to create a collaborative relationship in which clients can become their own expert.

(continued)

TABLE 15.4 The Therapeutic Relationship (continued)

Postmodern approaches	Therapy is a collaborative partnership. Clients are viewed as the experts on their own life. Therapists use questioning dialogue to help clients free themselves from their problem-saturated stories and create new life-affirming stories. Solution-focused therapists assume an active role in guiding the client away from problem-talk and toward solution-talk. Clients are encouraged to explore their strengths and to create solutions that will lead to a richer future. Narrative therapists assist clients in externalizing problems and guide them in examining self-limiting stories and creating new and more liberating stories.
Family systems therapy	The family therapist functions as a teacher, coach, model, and consultant. The family learns ways to detect and solve problems that are keeping members stuck, and it learns about patterns that have been transmitted from generation to generation. Some approaches focus on the role of therapist as expert; others concentrate on intensifying what is going on in the here and now of the family session. All family therapists are concerned with the process of family interaction and teaching patterns of communication.

relationship. Therapists can become more effective by developing their personal qualities and their interpersonal abilities. Psychotherapy is primarily a human and relational endeavor that depends on the quality of the interpersonal connection between participants (Duncan, 2014; Elkins, 2016). Both client and therapist bring origins, culture, expectations, biases, defenses, and strengths to this relationship. How we create and nurture this powerful human relationship can be guided by the fruits of research (Norcross & Wampold, 2011a).

As you think about developing your personal counseling perspective, give consideration to the issue of the match between client and counselor. I certainly do not advocate changing your personality to fit your perception of what each client is expecting; it is important that you be *yourself* as you meet clients. You also need to consider the reality that you will probably not be able to work effectively with every client. Some clients will work better with counselors who have another type of personal and therapeutic style than yours. Be sensitive in assessing what your client needs, and use good judgment when determining the appropriateness of the match between you and a potential client.

Although you do not have to be like your clients or have experienced the same problems to be effective with them, it is critical that you be able to understand their world and respect them. Ask yourself how well prepared you are to counsel clients from a different cultural background. To what degree do you think you can successfully establish a therapeutic relationship with a client of a different race? Ethnic group? Gender? Age? Sexual orientation? Spiritual/religious orientation? Socioeconomic group? Do you see any potential barriers that would make it difficult for you to form a working relationship with certain clients? It is also important to consider the client's diagnosis, resistance level, treatment preferences, and stage of change. Therapeutic techniques and styles should be selected to fit the client's personal characteristics. Norcross and Beutler (2014) suggest that therapists create a new therapy for each client:

> We believe that the purpose of integrative psychotherapy is *not* to create a single or unitary treatment. Rather, we select different treatment methods according to the patient and the context. The result is a more efficient and efficacious therapy—and one that fits both the client and the clinician. (p. 502)

The Place of Techniques and Evaluation in Counseling

Drawing on Techniques From Various Approaches

Effective therapists incorporate a wide range of procedures in their therapeutic style. Much depends on the purpose of therapy, the setting, the personality and style of the therapist, the qualities of the particular client, and the problems selected for intervention. Regardless of the therapeutic model you may be working with, you must decide *what* relationship style to adopt; *what* techniques, procedures, or intervention methods to use; *when* to use them; and with *which* clients. Take time to review Table 15.5 on therapeutic techniques and Table 15.6 on applications for LO6

TABLE 15.5 Techniques of Therapy

Psychoanalytic therapy	The key techniques are interpretation, dream analysis, free association, analysis of resistance, analysis of transference, and countertransference. Techniques are designed to help clients gain access to their unconscious conflicts, which leads to insight and eventual assimilation of new material by the ego.
Adlerian therapy	Adlerians pay more attention to the subjective experiences of clients than to using techniques. Some techniques include gathering life-history data (family constellation, early recollections, personal priorities), sharing interpretations with clients, offering encouragement, and assisting clients in searching for new possibilities.
Existential therapy	Few techniques flow from this approach because it stresses understanding first and technique second. The therapist can borrow techniques from other approaches and incorporate them in an existential framework. Diagnosis, testing, and external measurements are not deemed important. Issues addressed are freedom and responsibility, isolation and relationships, meaning and meaninglessness, living and dying.
Person-centered therapy	This approach uses few techniques but stresses the attitudes of the therapist and a "way of being." Therapists strive for active listening, reflection of feelings, clarification, "being there" for the client, and focusing on the moment-to-moment experiencing of the client. This model does not include diagnostic testing, interpretation, taking a case history, or questioning or probing for information.
Gestalt therapy	A wide range of experiments are designed to intensify experiencing and to integrate conflicting feelings. Experiments are co-created by therapist and client through an *I/Thou* dialogue. Therapists have latitude to creatively invent their own experiments. Formal diagnosis and testing are not a required part of therapy.
Behavior therapy	The main techniques are reinforcement, shaping, modeling, systematic desensitization, relaxation methods, flooding, eye movement and desensitization reprocessing, cognitive restructuring, social skills training, self-management programs, mindfulness and acceptance methods, behavioral rehearsal, and coaching. Diagnosis or assessment is done at the outset to determine a treatment plan. Questions concentrate on "what," "how," and "when" (but not "why"). Contracts and homework assignments are also typically used.
Cognitive behavior therapy	Therapists use a variety of cognitive, emotive, and behavioral techniques; diverse methods are tailored to suit individual clients. This is an active, directive, time-limited, present-centered, psychoeducational, structured therapy. Some techniques include engaging in Socratic dialogue, collaborative empiricism, debating irrational beliefs, carrying out homework assignments, gathering data on assumptions one has made, keeping a record of activities, forming alternative interpretations, learning new coping skills, changing one's language and thinking patterns, role playing, imagery, confronting faulty beliefs, self-instructional training, and stress inoculation training.

(continued)

TABLE 15.5 Techniques of Therapy (continued)

Choice theory/ Reality therapy	This is an active, directive, and didactic therapy. Skillful questioning is a central technique used for the duration of the therapy process. Various techniques may be used to get clients to evaluate what they are presently doing to see if they are willing to change. If clients decide that their present behavior is not effective, they develop a specific plan for change and make a commitment to follow through.
Feminist therapy	Although techniques from traditional approaches are used, feminist practitioners tend to employ consciousness-raising techniques aimed at helping clients recognize the impact of gender-role socialization on their lives. Other techniques frequently used include gender-role analysis and intervention, power analysis and intervention, demystifying therapy, bibliotherapy, journal writing, therapist self-disclosure, assertiveness training, reframing and relabeling, cognitive restructuring, identifying and challenging untested beliefs, role playing, psychodramatic methods, group work, and social action.
Postmodern approaches	In solution-focused therapy the main technique involves change-talk, with emphasis on times in a client's life when the problem was not a problem. Other techniques include creative use of questioning, the miracle question, and scaling questions, which assist clients in developing alternative stories. In narrative therapy, specific techniques include listening to a client's problem-saturated story without getting stuck, externalizing and naming the problem, externalizing conversations, and discovering clues to competence. Narrative therapists often write letters to clients and assist them in finding an audience that will support their changes and new stories.
Family systems therapy	A variety of techniques may be used, depending on the particular theoretical orientation of the therapist. Some techniques include genograms, teaching, asking questions, joining the family, tracking sequences, family mapping, reframing, restructuring, enactments, and setting boundaries. Techniques may be experiential, cognitive, or behavioral in nature. Most are designed to bring about change in a short time.

TABLE 15.6 Applications of the Approaches

Psychoanalytic therapy	Candidates for analytic therapy include professionals who want to become therapists, people who have had intensive therapy and want to go further, and those who are in psychological pain. Analytic therapy is not recommended for self-centered and impulsive individuals or for people with psychotic disorders. Techniques can be applied to individual and group therapy.
Adlerian therapy	Because the approach is based on a growth model, it is applicable to such varied spheres of life as child guidance, parent–child counseling, marital and family therapy, individual counseling with all age groups, correctional and rehabilitation counseling, group counseling, substance abuse programs, and brief counseling. It is ideally suited to preventive care and alleviating a broad range of conditions that interfere with growth.
Existential therapy	This approach is especially suited to people facing a developmental crisis or a transition in life and for those with existential concerns (making choices, dealing with freedom and responsibility, coping with guilt and anxiety, making sense of life, and finding values) or those seeking personal enhancement. The approach can be applied to both individual and group counseling, and to couples and family therapy, crisis intervention, and community mental health work.
Person-centered therapy	Has wide applicability to individual and group counseling. It is especially well suited for the initial phases of crisis intervention work. Its principles have been applied to couples and family therapy, community programs, administration and management, and human relations training. It is a useful approach for teaching, parent–child relations, and for working with groups of people from diverse cultural backgrounds.

Gestalt therapy	Addresses a wide range of problems and populations: crisis intervention, treatment of a range of psychosomatic disorders, couples and family therapy, awareness training of mental health professionals, behavior problems in children, and teaching and learning. It is well suited to both individual and group counseling. The methods are powerful catalysts for opening up feelings and getting clients into contact with their present-centered experience.
Behavior therapy	A pragmatic approach based on empirical validation of results. Enjoys wide applicability to individual, group, couples, and family counseling. Some problems to which the approach is well suited are phobic disorders, depression, trauma, sexual disorders, children's behavioral disorders, stuttering, and prevention of cardiovascular disease. Beyond clinical practice, its principles are applied in fields such as pediatrics, stress management, behavioral medicine, education, and geriatrics.
Cognitive behavior therapy	Has been widely applied to treatment of depression, anxiety, relationship problems, stress management, skill training, substance abuse, assertion training, eating disorders, panic attacks, performance anxiety, and social phobias. CBT is especially useful for assisting people in modifying their cognitions. Many self-help approaches utilize its principles. CBT can be applied to a wide range of client populations with a variety of specific problems.
Choice theory/ Reality therapy	Geared to teaching people ways of using choice theory in everyday living to increase effective behaviors. It has been applied to individual counseling with a wide range of clients, group counseling, working with youthful law offenders, and couples and family therapy. In some instances it is well suited to brief therapy and crisis intervention.
Feminist therapy	Principles and techniques can be applied to a range of therapeutic modalities such as individual therapy, relationship counseling, family therapy, group counseling, and community intervention. The approach can be applied to both women and men with the goal of bringing about empowerment.
Postmodern approaches	Solution-focused therapy is well suited for people with adjustment disorders and for problems of anxiety and depression. Narrative therapy is now being used for a broad range of human difficulties including eating disorders, family distress, depression, and relationship concerns. These approaches can be applied to working with children, adolescents, adults, couples, families, and the community in a wide variety of settings. Both solution-focused and narrative approaches lend themselves to group counseling and to school counseling.
Family systems therapy	Useful for dealing with marital distress, problems of communicating among family members, power struggles, crisis situations in the family, helping individuals attain their potential, and enhancing the overall functioning of the family.

each approach. Pay careful attention to the focus of each type of therapy and how that focus might be useful in your practice.

It is critical to be aware of how clients' cultural backgrounds contribute to their perceptions of their problems. Each of the 11 therapeutic approaches has both strengths (Table 15.7) and limitations (Table 15.8) when applied to culturally diverse client populations. Although it is unwise to stereotype clients because of their cultural heritage, it is useful to assess the bearing cultural context has on their concerns. Some techniques may be contraindicated because of a client's socialization. The client's responsiveness (or lack of it) to certain techniques is a critical barometer in judging the effectiveness of these methods.

Effective counseling involves proficiency in a combination of cognitive, affective, and behavioral techniques. Such a combination is necessary to help clients *think* about their beliefs and assumptions, to experience on a *feeling* level their conflicts

TABLE 15.7 Contributions to Multicultural Counseling

Psychoanalytic therapy	Its focus on family dynamics is appropriate for working with many cultural groups. The therapist's formality appeals to clients who expect professional distance. Notion of ego defense is helpful in understanding inner dynamics and dealing with environmental stresses.
Adlerian therapy	Its focus on social interest, helping others, collectivism, pursuing meaning in life, importance of family, goal orientation, and belonging is congruent with the values of many cultures. Focus on person-in-the-environment allows for cultural factors to be explored.
Existential therapy	Focus is on understanding client's phenomenological world, including cultural background. This approach leads to empowerment in an oppressive society. Existential therapy can help clients examine their options for change within the context of their cultural realities. The existential approach is particularly suited to counseling diverse clients because of the philosophical foundation that emphasizes the human condition.
Person-centered therapy	Focus is on breaking cultural barriers and facilitating open dialogue among diverse cultural populations. Main strengths are respect for clients' values, active listening, welcoming of differences, nonjudgmental attitude, understanding, willingness to allow clients to determine what will be explored in sessions, and prizing cultural pluralism.
Gestalt therapy	Its focus on expressing oneself nonverbally is congruent with those cultures that look beyond words for messages. Provides many experiments in working with clients who have cultural injunctions against freely expressing feelings. Can help to overcome language barrier with bilingual clients. Focus on bodily expressions is a subtle way to help clients recognize their conflicts.
Behavior therapy	Focus on behavior, rather than on feelings, is compatible with many cultures. Strengths include a collaborative relationship between counselor and client in working toward mutually agreed-upon goals, continual assessment to determine if the techniques are suited to clients' unique situations, assisting clients in learning practical skills, an educational focus, and stress on self-management strategies.
Cognitive behavior therapy	Focus is on a collaborative approach that offers clients opportunities to express their areas of concern. The psychoeducational dimensions are often useful in exploring cultural conflicts and teaching new behavior. The emphasis on thinking (as opposed to identifying and expressing feelings) is likely to be acceptable to many clients. The focus on teaching and learning tends to avoid the stigma of mental illness. Clients are likely to value the active and directive stance of the therapist.
Choice theory/ Reality therapy	Focus is on clients making their own evaluation of behavior (including how they respond to their culture). Through personal assessment clients can determine the degree to which their needs and wants are being satisfied. They can find a balance between retaining their own ethnic identity and integrating some of the values and practices of the dominant society.
Feminist therapy	Focus is on both individual change and social transformation. A key contribution is that both the women's movement and the multicultural movement have called attention to the negative impact of discrimination and oppression for both women and men. Emphasizes the influence of expected cultural roles and explores client's satisfaction with and knowledge of these roles.
Postmodern approaches	Focus is on the social and cultural context of behavior. Stories that are being authored in the therapy office need to be anchored in the social world in which the client lives. Therapists do not make assumptions about people and honor each client's unique story and cultural background. Therapists take an active role in challenging social and cultural injustices that lead to oppression of certain groups. Therapy becomes a process of liberation from oppressive cultural values and enables clients to become active agents of their destinies.
Family systems therapy	Focus is on the family or community system. Many ethnic and cultural groups place value on the role of the extended family. Many family therapies deal with extended family members and with support systems. Networking is a part of the process, which is congruent with the values of many clients. There is a greater chance for individual change if other family members are supportive. This approach offers ways of working toward the health of the family unit and the welfare of each member.

TABLE 15.8 Limitations in Multicultural Counseling

Psychoanalytic therapy	Its focus on insight, intrapsychic dynamics, and long-term treatment is often not valued by clients who prefer to learn coping skills for dealing with pressing daily concerns. Internal focus is often in conflict with cultural values that stress an interpersonal and environmental focus.
Adlerian therapy	This approach's detailed interview about one's family background can conflict with cultures that have injunctions against disclosing family matters. Some clients may view the counselor as an authority who will provide answers to problems, which conflicts with the egalitarian, person-to-person spirit as a way to reduce social distance.
Existential therapy	Values of individuality, freedom, autonomy, and self-realization often conflict with cultural values of collectivism, respect for tradition, deference to authority, and interdependence. Some may be deterred by the absence of specific techniques. Others will expect more focus on surviving in their world.
Person-centered therapy	Some of the core values of this approach may not be congruent with the client's culture. Lack of counselor direction and structure are unacceptable for clients who are seeking help and immediate answers from a knowledgeable professional.
Gestalt therapy	Clients who have been culturally conditioned to be emotionally reserved may not embrace Gestalt experiments. Some may not see how "being aware of present experiencing" will lead to solving their problems.
Behavior therapy	Family members may not value clients' newly acquired assertive style, so clients must be taught how to cope with resistance by others. Counselors need to help clients assess the possible consequences of making behavioral changes.
Cognitive behavior therapy	Before too quickly attempting to change the beliefs and actions of clients, it is essential for the therapist to understand and respect their world. Some clients may have serious reservations about questioning their basic cultural values and beliefs. Clients could become dependent on the therapist choosing appropriate ways to solve problems.
Choice theory/ Reality therapy	This approach stresses taking charge of one's own life, yet some clients are more interested in changing their external environment. Counselors need to appreciate the role of discrimination and racism and help clients deal with social and political realities.
Feminist therapy	This model has been criticized for its bias toward the values of White, middle-class, heterosexual women, which are not applicable to many other groups of women nor to men. Therapists need to assess with their clients the price of making significant personal change, which may result in isolation from extended family as clients assume new roles and make life changes.
Postmodern approaches	Some clients come to therapy wanting to talk about their problems and may be put off by the insistence on talking about exceptions to their problems. Clients may view the therapist as an expert and be reluctant to view themselves as experts. Certain clients may doubt the helpfulness of a therapist who assumes a "not-knowing" position.
Family systems therapy	Family therapy rests on value assumptions that are not congruent with the values of clients from some cultures. Western concepts such as individuation, self-actualization, self-determination, independence, and self-expression may be foreign to some clients. In some cultures, admitting problems within the family is shameful. The value of "keeping problems within the family" may make it difficult to explore conflicts openly.

and struggles, and to translate their insights into *action* programs by behaving in new ways in day-to-day living. Table 15.9 outlines the contributions of various approaches, and Table 15.10 describes some of the limitations of the various therapeutic approaches. These tables will help you identify elements that you may want to incorporate in your own counseling perspective.

TABLE 15.9 Contributions of the Approaches

Psychoanalytic therapy	More than any other system, this approach has generated controversy as well as exploration and has stimulated further thinking and development of therapy. It has provided a detailed and comprehensive description of personality structure and functioning. It has brought into prominence factors such as the unconscious as a determinant of behavior and the role of trauma during the first six years of life. It has developed several techniques for tapping the unconscious and shed light on the dynamics of transference and countertransference, resistance, anxiety, and the mechanisms of ego defense.
Adlerian therapy	A key contribution is the influence that Adlerian concepts have had on other systems and the integration of these concepts into various contemporary therapies. This is one of the first approaches to therapy that was humanistic, unified, holistic, and goal-oriented and that put an emphasis on social and psychological factors.
Existential therapy	Its major contribution is recognition of the need for a subjective approach based on a complete view of the human condition. It calls attention to the need for a philosophical statement on what it means to be a person. Stress on the *I/Thou* relationship lessens the chances of dehumanizing therapy. It provides a perspective for understanding anxiety, guilt, freedom, death, isolation, and commitment.
Person-centered therapy	Clients take an active stance and assume responsibility for the direction of therapy. This unique approach has been subjected to empirical testing, and as a result both theory and methods have been modified. It is an open system. People without advanced training can benefit by translating the therapeutic conditions to both their personal and professional lives. Basic concepts are straightforward and easy to grasp and apply. It is a foundation for building a trusting relationship, applicable to all therapies.
Gestalt therapy	The emphasis on direct experiencing and doing rather than on merely talking about feelings provides a perspective on growth and enhancement, not merely a treatment of disorders. It uses clients' behavior as the basis for making them aware of their inner creative potential. The approach to dreams is a unique, creative tool to help clients discover basic conflicts. Therapy is viewed as an existential encounter; it is process-oriented, not technique-oriented. It recognizes nonverbal behavior as a key to understanding.
Behavior therapy	Emphasis is on assessment and evaluation techniques, thus providing a basis for accountable practice. Specific problems are identified, and clients are kept informed about progress toward their goals. The approach has demonstrated effectiveness in many areas of human functioning. The roles of the therapist as reinforcer, model, teacher, and consultant are explicit. The approach has undergone extensive expansion, and research literature abounds. No longer is it a mechanistic approach, for it now makes room for cognitive factors and encourages self-directed programs for behavioral change.
Cognitive behavior therapy	Major contributions include emphasis on a comprehensive therapeutic practice; numerous cognitive, emotive, and behavioral techniques; an openness to incorporating techniques from other approaches; and a methodology for challenging and changing faulty or negative thinking. Most forms can be integrated into other mainstream therapies. REBT makes full use of action-oriented homework, various psychoeducational methods, and keeping records of progress. CT is a structured therapy that has a good track record for treating depression and anxiety in a short time. Strengths-based CBT is a form of positive psychology that addresses the resources within the client for change.
Choice theory/ Reality therapy	This is a positive approach with an action orientation that relies on simple and clear concepts that are easily grasped in many helping professions. It can be used by teachers, nurses, ministers, educators, social workers, and counselors. Due to the direct methods, it appeals to many clients who are often seen as resistant to therapy. It is a short-term approach that can be applied to a diverse population, and it has been a significant force in challenging the medical model of therapy.

Feminist therapy	The feminist perspective is responsible for encouraging increasing numbers of women to question gender stereotypes and to reject limited views of what a woman is expected to be. It is paving the way for gender-sensitive practice and bringing attention to the gendered uses of power in relationships. The unified feminist voice brought attention to the extent and implications of child abuse, incest, rape, sexual harassment, and domestic violence. Feminist principles and interventions can be incorporated in other therapy approaches.
Postmodern approaches	The brevity of these approaches fit well with the limitations imposed by a managed care structure. The emphasis on client strengths and competence appeals to clients who want to create solutions and revise their life stories in a positive direction. Clients are not blamed for their problems but are helped to understand how they might relate in more satisfying ways to such problems. A strength of these approaches is the question format that invites clients to view themselves in new and more effective ways.
Family systems therapy	From a systemic perspective, neither the individual nor the family is blamed for a particular dysfunction. The family is empowered through the process of identifying and exploring interactional patterns. Working with an entire unit provides a new perspective on understanding and working through both individual problems and relationship concerns. By exploring one's family of origin, there are increased opportunities to resolve other conflicts in systems outside of the family

TABLE 15.10 Limitations of the Approaches

Psychoanalytic therapy	Requires lengthy training for therapists and much time and expense for clients. The model stresses biological and instinctual factors to the neglect of social, cultural, and interpersonal ones. Its methods are less applicable for solving specific daily life problems of clients and may not be appropriate for some ethnic and cultural groups. Many clients lack the degree of ego strength needed for regressive and reconstructive therapy. It may be inappropriate for certain counseling settings.
Adlerian therapy	Weak in terms of precision, testability, and empirical validity. Few attempts have been made to validate the basic concepts by scientific methods. Tends to oversimplify some complex human problems and is based heavily on common sense.
Existential therapy	Many basic concepts are fuzzy and ill-defined, making its general framework abstract at times. Lacks a systematic statement of principles and practices of therapy. Has limited applicability to lower functioning and nonverbal clients and to clients in extreme crisis who need direction.
Person-centered therapy	Possible danger from the therapist who remains passive and inactive, limiting responses to reflection. Many clients feel a need for greater direction, more structure, and more techniques. Clients in crisis may need more directive measures. Applied to individual counseling, some cultural groups will expect more counselor activity.
Gestalt therapy	Techniques lead to intense emotional expression; if these feelings are not explored and if cognitive work is not done, clients are likely to be left unfinished and will not have a sense of integration of their learning. Clients who have difficulty using imagination may not profit from certain experiments.
Behavior therapy	Major criticisms are that it may change behavior but not feelings; that it ignores the relational factors in therapy; that it does not provide insight; that it ignores historical causes of present behavior; that it involves control by the therapist; and that it is limited in its capacity to address certain aspects of the human condition.
Cognitive behavior therapy	Tends to play down emotions, does not focus on exploring the unconscious or underlying conflicts, de-emphasizes the value of insight, and sometimes does not give enough weight to the client's past. CBT might be too structured for some clients.

(continued)

TABLE 15.10 Limitations of the Approaches (continued)

Choice theory/ Reality therapy	Discounts the therapeutic value of exploration of the client's past, dreams, the unconscious, early childhood experiences, and transference. The approach is limited to less complex problems. It is a problem-solving therapy that tends to discourage exploration of deeper emotional issues.
Feminist therapy	A possible limitation is the potential for therapists to impose a new set of values on clients—such as striving for equality, power in relationships, defining oneself, freedom to pursue a career outside the home, and the right to an education. Therapists need to keep in mind that clients are their own best experts, which means it is up to them to decide which values to live by.
Postmodern approaches	There is little empirical validation of the effectiveness of therapy outcomes. Some critics contend that these approaches endorse cheerleading and an overly positive perspective. Some are critical of the stance taken by most postmodern therapists regarding assessment and diagnosis, and also react negatively to the "not-knowing" stance of the therapist. Because some of the solution-focused and narrative therapy techniques are relatively easy to learn, practitioners may use these interventions in a mechanical way or implement these techniques without a sound rationale.
Family systems therapy	Limitations include problems in being able to involve all the members of a family in the therapy. Some family members may be resistant to changing the structure of the system. Therapists' self-knowledge and willingness to work on their own family-of-origin issues is crucial, for the potential for countertransference is high. It is essential that the therapist be well trained, receive quality supervision, and be competent in assessing and treating individuals in a family context.

Evaluating the Effectiveness of Counseling and Therapy

LO7 Mental health providers must be accountable and be able to demonstrate the efficacy of their services. In the era of managed care, it is essential for practitioners to demonstrate the degree to which their interventions are both clinically sound and cost-effective. Does therapy make a significant difference? Are people substantially better after therapy than they were without it? Can therapy actually be more harmful than helpful?

Evaluating how well psychotherapy works is far from simple. Therapeutic systems are applied by practitioners who have unique individual characteristics, and clients themselves have much to do with therapeutic outcomes. For example, effects resulting from unexpected and uncontrollable events in the client's social environment can lessen the impact of gains made in psychotherapy. Moreover, practitioners who adhere to the same approach are likely to use techniques in various ways and to relate to clients in diverse fashions, functioning differently with different clients and in different clinical settings.

How effective is psychotherapy? A meta-analysis of psychotherapy outcome literature conducted by Smith, Glass, and Miller (1980) concluded that psychotherapy was highly effective and that all psychotherapeutic approaches worked about equally well. Prochaska and Norcross (2014) note that controlled outcome research consistently supports the effectiveness of psychotherapy. They point out that more than 5,000 individual studies and 500 meta-analyses have been conducted on the effectiveness of psychotherapy; these studies demonstrate that well-developed therapy interventions have meaningful, positive effects on the intended outcome variables. In short, not only does psychotherapy work, but research demonstrates that therapy is remarkably effective. Psychotherapy is an efficacious approach to helping people who experience psychological distress improve their functioning (Miller et al., 2015).

A summary of the research data shows little or no difference in outcome between specific therapeutic approaches (Miller et al., 2015). Lambert's (2011) review of psychotherapy research makes it clear that the similarities rather than the differences among models account for the effectiveness of psychotherapy. Interpersonal, social, and affective factors common across therapeutic orientations are the primary determinants of effectiveness (Elkins, 2016).

Although it is clear that therapy works, there are no simple explanations of how it works. Research indicates that a variety of treatments are equally effective—when administered by therapists who believe in them and when they are accepted by the client. Wampold (2010) concludes that "there is little evidence that the specific ingredients of any treatment are responsible for the benefits of therapy" (p. 71).

The various therapy approaches and techniques work equally well because they share the most important ingredient accounting for change—the client. Data point to the conclusion that the engine of change is the client (Bohart & Tallman, 2010; Bohart & Wade, 2013), and we can most productively direct our efforts toward ways of employing the client in the process of change.

Feedback-Informed Treatment

LO8

Listening to client feedback about the therapy process is of the utmost importance. **Feedback-informed treatment (FIT)** is designed to evaluate and to improve the quality and effectiveness of counseling services. FIT is an evidence-based practice that monitors client change and identifies modifications needed to enhance the therapeutic endeavor (Miller et al., 2015). FIT involves consistently obtaining feedback from clients regarding the therapeutic relationship and their clinical progress, which is then used to tailor therapy to their unique needs. If therapists learn to listen to clients' feedback throughout the therapeutic process, clients can become full and equal participants in all aspects of their therapy (Miller et al., 2015).

Monitoring outcome and adjusting accordingly on the basis of feedback from the client must become routine practice. The client's theory of change can be used as a basis for determining which approach, by whom, can be most effective for this person, with his or her specific problem, under this particular set of circumstances. This approach to practice requires continuous active client input, which is the most significant predictor of change in therapy (Hubble, Duncan, Miller, & Wampold, 2010).

Duncan (2014) believes that systematic client feedback should be integrated into all psychotherapeutic approaches because of its proven effectiveness in helping clients monitor and improve their therapy experience. Scott Miller and his associates at the International Center for Clinical Excellence (ICCE) developed two 4-item instruments to measure client progress and to rate the quality of the therapeutic relationship. These rating instruments are brief, well-validated, client-rated scales. The **Outcome Rating Scale (ORS)** assesses the client's therapeutic progress through ratings of a client's personal experience of well-being in his or her individual, interpersonal, and social functioning. The **Session Rating Scale (SRS)** measures a client's perception of the quality of the therapeutic relationship, which includes the relational bond with the therapist, the perceived collaboration around specific tasks in therapy, and agreement on goals, methods, and client preferences (Miller et al., 2015).

Feedback from clients regarding the therapeutic alliance and outcomes increases the effect of treatment, cuts dropout rates in half, and decreases the risk of deterioration (Miller, 2011). Using client feedback, therapists can adjust and accommodate to maximize beneficial outcomes for clients. In essence, Duncan, Miller, and Sparks (2004) are arguing for *practice-based evidence* rather than evidence-based practice: "Becoming outcome informed not only amplifies the client's voice but offers the most viable, research-tested method to improve clinical effectiveness" (p. 16). Client strengths and perceptions are the foundation of therapy work. Systematic and consistent assessment of the client's perceptions of progress allows the therapist to customize the therapy to the individual needs and characteristics of each client. Ongoing client feedback provides practitioners with a simple, practical, and meaningful method for documenting the usefulness of treatment.

An Integrative Approach Applied to the Case of Stan

In this section, I describe how I would integrate concepts and techniques from the 11 theoretical perspectives in counseling Stan on the levels of *thinking, feeling,* and *doing.* I indicate what aspects from the various theories I would draw on in working with Stan at the various stages of his therapy. As you read the Questions for Reflection at the end of this section, think about how you would work with Stan from your own integrative perspective.

Clarifying the Therapeutic Relationship

In establishing the therapeutic relationship, I am influenced by the person-centered, existential, Gestalt, feminist, postmodern, and Adlerian approaches. I ask myself these questions: "To what degree am I able to listen to and hear Stan in a nonjudgmental way? Am I able to respect and care for him? Do I have the capacity to enter his subjective world without losing my own identity? Am I able to share with him my own thoughts and reactions as they pertain to our relationship?" I invite Stan's questions about this therapeutic relationship. One goal is to demystify the therapy process; another is to get some focus for the direction of our sessions by developing clear goals for the therapy.

Clarifying the Goals of Therapy

With respect to setting goals, precision and clarity are essential. Once we have identified some goals, Stan can begin to observe and measure his own behavior, both in the sessions and in his daily life. This self-monitoring is a vital step in any effort to bring about change. I will be asking for Stan's feedback throughout the therapeutic process and will use his feedback as a basis for making modifications in our therapeutic alliance.

Throughout our time together, I ask Stan to decide time and again what he wants from his therapy and to assess the degree to which our work together is helping him meet his goals. It is important that Stan provide the direction in which he wants to travel on his journey. Once I have a clear sense of the specific ways Stan wants to change how he is thinking, feeling, and acting, I am likely to take an active role in co-creating experiments with Stan that he can do both in the therapy sessions and on his own away from our sessions.

Working With Stan's Past, Present, and Future

Dealing With the Past In my integrative approach, I tend to give weight to understanding, exploring, and working with Stan's early history and to connect his past with what he is doing today. My view is that themes running through our life can become evident if we come to terms with significant experiences in our childhood. I favor the Gestalt approach of asking Stan to bring into the here and now those people in his life with whom he feels unfinished. A variety of role-playing techniques in which Stan addresses significant others through symbolic work in our sessions will bring Stan's past intensely to life in the present moment of our sessions.

Dealing With the Present Being interested in Stan's past does not mean that we get lost in history or that we dwell on reliving traumatic situations. By paying attention to what is going on in the here and now during the counseling session, I get significant clues about what is unfinished from Stan's past. He and I can direct attention to his immediate feelings as well as to his thoughts and actions. It seems essential to me that we work with all three dimensions–what he is thinking, what he is actually doing, and how his thoughts and behaviors affect his feeling states.

Dealing With the Future If Stan decides that his present behavior is not getting him what he wants, he is in a good position to think ahead about the changes he would like to make and what he can do now to actualize his aspirations. The present-oriented behavioral focus of reality therapy is a good reference point for getting Stan to dream about what he would like to say about his life five years hence. Connecting present behavior with future plans is an excellent way to help Stan formulate a concrete plan of action, which can give him a way to create his future.

Identifying and Exploring Feelings

The authenticity of my relationship with Stan encourages him to begin to identify and share with me a range of feelings. Our open and trusting relationship is not sufficient to change Stan's personality and behavior, however, and I continue to use my knowledge, skills, and experiences to help Stan clarify his own thoughts. Stan is the best expert on his own life, and I assist him in coming to value the ways in which he is the expert in the therapeutic endeavor as well.

I draw heavily on Gestalt experiments to help Stan express and explore his feelings. Eventually, I ask him to avoid merely talking about situations and about feelings. Rather, I encourage him to bring whatever reactions he is having into the present. For instance, if I notice tears in his eyes, I may direct him to "be his tears now." By putting words to his tears, he avoids abstract intellectualization about all the reasons he is sad or tense. Before he can change his feelings, Stan must allow himself to *fully experience* them. The experiential therapies provide valuable tools for guiding him to the expression of his feelings.

The Thinking Dimension in Therapy

Once Stan has experienced some intense feelings and perhaps released pent-up feelings, some cognitive work is essential. To bring in this cognitive dimension, I focus Stan's attention on messages he incorporated as a child and on the decisions he made. I get him to think about the reason he made certain early decisions. Finally, I challenge Stan to look at these decisions about life, about himself, and about others and to make necessary revisions that can lead him to creating a life of his own choosing.

The cognitive behavioral therapies have a range of cognitive techniques that can help Stan recognize connections between his cognitions and his behaviors. Over a number of sessions we work on specific beliefs. My role is to promote corrective experiences that will lead to changes in his thinking. Eventually, our goal is some cognitive restructuring work by which Stan can learn new ways to think, new things to tell himself, and new assumptions about life. I have given Stan a number of homework assignments aimed at helping him identify a range of feelings and thoughts that may be problematic for him. This provides a basis for change in his behavior.

Doing: Another Essential Component of Therapy

Feeling and thinking are not a complete therapy process. *Doing* is a way of bringing these feelings and thoughts together by applying them to real-life situations in various action programs. I ask Stan to think of as many ways as possible of actually bringing into his daily living the new learning he is acquiring in our sessions. Homework assignments (preferably ones that Stan gives himself) are an excellent way for Stan to become an active agent in his therapy. He must *do* something himself for change to occur. The degree to which he will change is directly proportional to his willingness to experiment. Thus, each week we discuss his progress toward meeting his goals, and we review how well he is completing his assignments, as well as how his action plan is working.

Moving Toward Termination of Therapy

Termination of therapy is as important as the initial phase, for now the key task is to put into practice what he has learned in the sessions by applying new skills and attitudes to daily social situations without professional assistance. When Stan brings up a desire to "go it alone," we talk about his readiness to end therapy and his reasons for thinking about termination. I also share with him my perceptions of the directions I have seen him take. This is a good time to talk about where he can go from here. We spend time developing an action plan and talking about how he can best maintain his new learning.

In a behavioral spirit, evaluating the process and outcomes of therapy seems essential. This evaluation can take the form of devoting some time to discussing Stan's specific changes in therapy. A few questions for focus are: "What stands out the most for you, Stan? What did you learn that you consider the most valuable? How did you learn these lessons? What can you do now to keep practicing new behaviors? What will you do if you experience a setback?" We explore potential difficulties he expects to face when he no longer comes to weekly counseling sessions. At this point, I introduce some relapse prevention strategies to help Stan cope constructively with future problems. By addressing potential problems and stumbling blocks that he might have to deal with, Stan is less likely to become discouraged if he experiences any setbacks. If any relapses do occur, we talk about seeing these as "learning opportunities" rather than as signs that he has failed. I let Stan know that his termination of formal therapy does not mean that he cannot return for a visit or session when he considers it appropriate.

Commentary on the Thinking, Feeling, and Doing Perspective

Although the steps I described with Stan may appear relatively structured and even simple, actually working with clients is more complex and less predictable. If you are practicing from an integrative perspective, it would be a mistake to assume that it is best to always begin working with what clients are thinking (or feeling or doing). Effective counseling begins where the client is, not where a theory indicates a client should be.

In summary, depending on what clients need at the moment, I may focus initially on what they are thinking and how this is affecting them, or I may focus on how they feel, or I may choose to direct them to pay attention to what they are doing. If Stan can change his thoughts, I believe he is likely to change some of his behaviors and his feelings. If he changes his feelings, he might well begin to think and act differently. If he changes certain behaviors, he may begin thinking and feeling differently. Because these facets of human experience are interrelated, one route generally leads to the other dimensions.

A person-centered focus respects the wisdom within the client and uses it as a lead for where to go next. As counselors, a mistake we can make is getting too far ahead of our clients by thinking, "What should I do next?" By staying with our clients and asking them what they want, they will tell us which direction to take either directly or indirectly. We can learn to pay attention to our own reactions to our clients and to our own energy. By doing so we can engage in a therapeutic connection that is helpful for both parties in the relationship.

Questions for Reflection

- What themes in Stan's life do you find most significant, and how might you draw on these themes during the initial phase of counseling?
- What specific concepts from the various theoretical orientations would you be most inclined to utilize in your work with Stan?
- Identify some key techniques from the various therapies that you are most likely to employ in your therapy with Stan.
- How would you develop experiments for Stan to carry out both inside and outside the therapy sessions?
- Knowing what you do about Stan, what do you imagine it would be like to be his therapist? What problems, if any, might you expect to encounter in your counseling relationship with him?

Visit CengageBrain.com or watch the DVD for the video program on *Theory and Practice of Counseling and Psychotherapy: The Case of Stan and Lecturettes*, Session 13 (an integrative approach), for a demonstration of my approach to counseling Stan from this perspective. This session deals with termination and takes an integrative view of Stan's work.

An Integrative Approach Applied to the Case of Gwen*

There are multiple pathways to health and well-being, and I believe Gwen can benefit from a variety of counseling theories and holistic practices. The integrative approach embraces an attitude that affirms the intrinsic value of each individual. It is a unifying approach that attends to the person at the affective, behavioral, cognitive, and physiological levels of functioning. It also addresses the spiritual dimension of a client's life.

As an integrative therapist and a woman of color, I am willing to share my experiences with Gwen when it is therapeutically appropriate. I want Gwen to know that I respect her life experiences, struggles, strengths, unique qualities, and personal reality. I see Gwen as an intelligent African American woman with great depth and wisdom. Utilizing an integrative approach with Gwen allows me to take into account the many views of the change process that are available to assist her at this time in her life.

In my initial interview with Gwen, I let her know that I am not a purist in my approach to therapy and that I will draw from different counseling theories to create a treatment approach that is tailored to her needs. I begin establishing a therapeutic alliance with Gwen by drawing heavily from a client-centered orientation It is important for me to extend unconditional positive regard in the midst of acknowledging the suffering and anxiety Gwen is experiencing in her day-to-day life. I want Gwen to know that she is the expert on her life and that she is in charge of our work together. I will introduce ideas and techniques, and I let Gwen know that she is free to say what does not work for her in our sessions.

When Gwen and I began our therapeutic journey together, I was very interested in learning about her family history. I encouraged Gwen to create a genogram that depicted three generations and indicated educational levels, health issues, relationship patterns, and religious orientation. This approach was borrowed from family therapy and assisted us in seeing family patterns that have given her strength and support (her spirituality), as well as patterns that have caused challenges for her (taking on family members' problems). Through exploring her family history, Gwen begins to slowly recognize she has taken on characteristics that don't necessarily belong to her. Generational transmission—passing down traits, habits, and values from one generation to the next—has predisposed Gwen to be a rescuer like many of her female relatives. She explores some of the old automatic negative thoughts that were passed on from other generations that keep her feeling overwhelmed. One of Gwen's faulty beliefs is that "If I don't do it, no one else will." This particular cognitive distortion keeps her is a spiral of doing everything without reaching out to others for assistance or support. Her belief that no one else can assist her has caused fatigue and frustration. Through cognitive behavior therapy, Gwen becomes more aware of the thoughts she is thinking and how they affect how she feels about herself.

Using an integrative format allows me to incorporate everything Gwen brings to therapy as a route to her own healing process. Gwen shared with me early in our sessions that her relationship with God was a source of great strength in her life. I acknowledge and respect Gwen's spiritual values, and I pay attention to how her spirituality can be a significant part of her treatment and healing. Spirituality became a central part of our therapy sessions because Gwen made it clear that her spiritual beliefs were a vital resource for her.

I asked Gwen to talk about what was most helpful about the way she worshiped. Gwen replied, "I enjoy reading the scriptures. It helps me to see that I am not alone and that my problems are not new. There are messages that I can reflect on in scripture. Reading the Bible gives me comfort in my spirit." We explore the existential questions around the meaning in life and talk about suffering, anxiety, and death. Gwen struggles with fears for her son's life, and she feels great sadness as her mother's health declines. Gwen's spirituality is becoming her anchor and support as she wrestles with these realities of life.

Bringing in the dimension of spirituality reconnects Gwen to a daily practice of reading scripture in the morning and listening to praise music on the way

*Dr. Kellie Kirksey writes about her ways of thinking and practicing from an integrative perspective and applying this model to Gwen.

to the office. Gwen notices that her mood is not as negative when she engages in her daily spiritual practice. She hadn't realized that she had stopped engaging in activities that kept her focused and uplifted. The stress of taking care of her mother and juggling work and family life created an imbalance that perpetuated faulty cognitions and behaviors.

In our early sessions Gwen engaged in automatic negative thinking and made statements such as "I am never going to feel healthy again." "My children never want to spend time with me." "I will always feel isolated." Examining Gwen's cognitive distortions and assisting her in noticing and challenging them helped her to become increasingly aware of how these thought patterns cause her distress.

I introduced Gwen to a simple 5-minute meditation practice aimed at both calming her mind of anxious thoughts and increasing her ability to focus. I suggested to Gwen that during these brief meditations she could notice her thoughts without judgment. This simple mindfulness practice is likely to have a cumulative impact on her ability to relax and gain more inner resilience. With continued practice, Gwen discovers that she is not simply her thoughts, that she can be the observer of those thoughts, and that she can watch them flow by rather than letting them control her behavior and mood.

I typically begin and end each session with a brief assessment by Gwen about the session. I depend on regular feedback to make the process truly collaborative and to ensure that Gwen's therapeutic needs are being met. My first question for Gwen is always: "How would you like to best use the time we have together?" My job is to be fully present so that I can effectively integrate therapeutic approaches that will assist Gwen on her journey of transformation as she returns to a state of optimal functioning and balance.

I make no assumptions and ask Gwen if she is willing to work with what naturally arises as the therapy progresses. If she does not give an affirmative answer, then our direction of therapy needs to be modified. I explain that my techniques are aimed at meeting Gwen's goals and healing her needs. This statement seems to increase Gwen's comfort level, and she is more willing to try new ways of being in a session.

To decrease Gwen's symptoms of depression and anxiety, I introduce her to a process I call "transformative movement and reflection." I teach Gwen a variety of techniques, range from subtle to dynamic, that come from global healing practices such as yoga, tai chi, drumming, and yogic pranayama, to mention a few. These activities increase mindfulness and present moment awareness and help Gwen release tension and stress from her body and mind. The movement practices also assist in healthy emotional expression. Gwen is not very interested in drumming, but listening to music and moving is relaxing for her while in session and at home. Gwen begins to see that she has resources and tools that she can use in moments of stress in her daily life. My goal is to introduce Gwen to multiple tools to heal on the levels of mind, body, and spirit. I am sensitive to Gwen's personal goals from the moment she walks into my office, and I remain open to the possibilities that lie ahead of us until the very end.

Questions for Reflection

- What ideas and techniques shared in this piece belong to each theoretical approach?
- How comfortable are you in introducing nontraditional therapeutic techniques?
- Based on who you are, what theories seem to be the most natural for you to utilize from an integrative theoretical approach when working with Gwen?

Summary

Creating an integrative stance is truly a challenge. Therapists cannot simply pick bits and pieces from theories in a random and fragmented manner. In forming an integrated perspective, it is important to ask: Which theories provide a basis for understanding the *cognitive* dimensions? What about the *feeling* aspects? And how about the *behavioral* dimension? Most of the 11 therapeutic orientations discussed here focus primarily on one of these dimensions of human experience. Although the other dimensions are not necessarily ignored, they are often given short shrift.

Developing an integrated theoretical perspective requires an accurate, in-depth knowledge of the various theories. Without such knowledge, you cannot formulate a true synthesis. Simply put, you cannot integrate what you do not know (Norcross & Beutler, 2014). A central message of this book has been to remain open to each theory, to do further reading, and to reflect on how the key concepts of each approach fit your personality. Building your personalized orientation to counseling, which is based on what you consider to be the best features of several theories, is a long-term venture.

In addition to considering your own personality, think about what concepts and techniques work best with a range of clients. It requires knowledge, skill, art, and experience to be able to determine what techniques are suitable for particular problems. It is also an art to know when and how to use a particular therapeutic intervention. Although reflecting on your personal preferences is important, I hope that you balance your preferences with evidence from the research studies. Developing a personal approach to counseling practice does not imply that anything goes. Indeed, in this era of managed care and evidence-based practice, your personal preferences will not likely be the sole determinant of your psychotherapy practice. In counseling clients with certain clinical problems (such as depression and generalized anxiety), specific techniques have demonstrated their effectiveness. For instance, behavior therapy, cognitive behavior therapy, cognitive therapy, mindfulness-based cognitive therapy, and short-term psychodynamic therapy have repeatedly proved successful in treating depression. Your use of techniques must be grounded on solid theoretical constructs. Ethical practice implies that you employ efficacious procedures in dealing with clients and their problems, and that you are able to provide a theoretical rationale for the interventions you make in your clinical work.

This is a good time to review what you have learned about counseling theory and practice. Identify a particular theory that you might adopt as a foundation for establishing your counseling perspective. Consider from which therapies you would be most inclined to draw (1) underlying assumptions, (2) major concepts, (3) therapeutic goals, (4) therapeutic relationship, and (5) techniques and procedures. Also, consider the major applications of each of the therapies as well as their basic limitations and major contributions. The tables presented in this chapter are designed to assist you in conceptualizing your view of the counseling process.

Concluding Comments

At the beginning of the introductory course in counseling, my students typically express two reactions: "How will I ever be able to learn all these theories, and how can I see the differences among them?" and "How can I make sense out of all this information?" By the end of the course, these students are often surprised by how much work they have done *and* by how much they have learned. Although an introductory survey course will not turn you into accomplished counselors, it generally provides the basis for selecting from among the many models to which you are exposed.

At this point you may be able to begin putting the theories together in some meaningful way for yourself. This book will have served its central purpose if it has encouraged you to read further and to expand your knowledge of the theories that most caught your interest. I hope you have seen something of value that you can use from each of the approaches described. You will not be in a position to conceptualize a completely developed integrative perspective after your first course in counseling theory, but you now have the tools to *begin* the process of integration. With additional study and practical experience, you will be able to expand and refine your emerging personal philosophy of counseling.

Finally, the book will have been put to good use if it has stimulated you to think about the ways in which your philosophy of life, your values, your life experiences, and the person you are becoming are vitally related to the caliber of counselor you can become and to the impact you can have on those who establish a relationship with you personally and professionally. This book and your course may have raised questions for you regarding your decision to become a counselor. Seek out at least one of your professors and explore any questions you may have.

Self-Reflection and Discussion Questions

1. What are the four major approaches to psychotherapy integration? How can these routes to integration be useful for you in designing your perspective on counseling?
2. In feedback-informed treatment, clients provide reactions to their experience of the session and to the therapist. How open do you imagine you would be to hearing honest feedback from your clients about you as a therapist and about the interventions you are making? Do you see yourself as being able to engage in a discussion with your clients regarding both their positive and negative reactions to a session?
3. In developing your integrative approach to counseling, what factors would you most consider?
4. What importance do you place on research that seeks to identify what makes psychotherapy work?
5. If you had to select one theory that would serve as your primary theory, which theory would you select and why?

Where to Go From Here

In the *DVD for Integrative Counseling: The Case of Ruth and Lecturettes* (Session 9, "An Integrative Perspective") you will view my ways of working with Ruth by drawing on techniques from various theoretical models. I demonstrate how the foundation of my integrative approach rests on existential therapy. In this session I am drawing heavily from principles of the action-oriented therapies.

Other Resources

The International Center for Clinical Excellence (ICCE) is a worldwide web-based community of practitioners, health care managers, administrators, educators, policymakers, and researchers dedicated to promoting excellence in behavioral health care services. This online community facilitates sharing best practices and innovative ideas specifically designed to improve behavioral health care practice and enable practitioners and managers to achieve their personal best as helping professionals. The ORS and the SRS rating scales described in the text can be downloaded for free at the website.

The ICCE manuals on feedback-informed treatment (FIT) consist of a series of six guides covering the most important information for practitioners and agencies implementing FIT as a part of routine care. The manuals cover the following content areas:

Manual 1. What Works in Therapy: A Primer

Manual 2. Feedback-Informed Clinical Work: The Basics

Manual 3. Feedback-Informed Supervision

Manual 4. Documenting Change: A Primer on Measurement, Analysis, and Reporting

Manual 5. Feedback-Informed Clinical Work: Specific Populations and Service Settings

Manual 6. Implementing Feedback-Informed Work in Agencies and Systems of Care

The goal for the series is to provide practitioners with a thorough grounding in the knowledge and skills associated with outstanding clinical performance. These manuals are a useful resource for clinicians who want to learn to practice FIT. For more information about ICCE and the resources available, contact:

The International Center for Clinical Excellence
www.centerforclinicalexcellence.com

Scott D. Miller's website has additional information on workshops on clinical excellence:

Scott D. Miller
www.scottdmiller.com

Recommended Supplementary Readings

Psychotherapy Integration (Stricker, 2010) is a concise presentation that deals with the theory, therapeutic process, evaluation, and future developments of integrative approaches.

The Human Element of Psychotherapy: A Nonmedical Model of Emotional Healing (Elkins, 2016) develops the thesis that psychotherapy is decidedly a relational, not a medical, endeavor. This book summarizes research supporting the notion that the quality of the interpersonal connection between client and therapist is what determines effectiveness, not the therapist's theory or techniques.

Handbook of Psychotherapy Integration (Norcross & Goldfried, 2005) is an excellent resource for conceptual and historical perspectives on therapy integration. This edited volume gives a comprehensive overview of the major current approaches, such as theoretical integration and technical eclecticism.

The Sage Encyclopedia of Theory in Counseling and Psychotherapy (Neukrug, 2015) is an comprehensive collection of short articles on the spectrum of approaches and techniques for counseling.

The Art of Integrative Counseling (Corey, 2013a) is designed to assist students in developing their own integrative approach to counseling. This book is complemented by the *DVD for Integrative Counseling: The Case of Ruth and Lecturettes* (Corey, 2013c).

Case Approach to Counseling and Psychotherapy (Corey, 2013b) illustrates each of the 11 contemporary theories by applying them to the single case of Ruth. I also demonstrate my integrative approach in counseling Ruth in the final chapter. This book also is designed to fit well with the *DVD for Integrative Counseling: The Case of Ruth and Lecturettes* (Corey, 2013c).

Integrating Spirituality and Religion into Counseling: A Guide to Competent Practice (Cashwell & Young, 2011) offers a concrete perspective on how to provide counseling in an ethical manner, consistent with a client's spiritual beliefs and practices. The authors help practitioners develop a respectful stance that honors the client's worldview and works within this framework in a collaborative fashion to achieve the client's goals.

References and Suggested Readings

*Books and articles marked with an asterisk are suggested for further study.

Part 1

Basic Issues in Counseling Practice

American Counseling Association. (2014). *ACA code of ethics.* Alexandria, VA: Author.

American Psychiatric Association. (2013). *Diagnostic and statistical manual of mental disorders* (5th ed.). Washington, DC: Author.

American Psychological Association. (2010). *Ethical principles of psychologists and code of conduct* (2002, Amended June 1, 2010). Retrieved from http://www.apa.org/ethics/code/index.aspx.

***American Psychological Association Presidential Task Force on Evidence-Based Practice.** (2006). Evidence-based practice in psychology. *American Psychologist, 61,* 271–285.

Arredondo, P., Toporek, R., Brown, S., Jones, J., Locke, D., Sanchez, J., & Stadler, H. (1996). Operationalization of multicultural counseling competencies. *Journal of Multicultural Counseling and Development, 24*(1), 42–78.

***Barnett, J. E., & Johnson, W. B.** (2008). *Ethics desk reference for psychologists.* Washington, DC: American Psychological Association.

***Barnett, J. E., & Johnson, W. B.** (2015). *Ethics desk reference for counselors* (2nd ed.). Alexandria, VA: American Counseling Association.

***Chung, R. C-Y., & Bemak, F.** (2012). *Social justice counseling: The next step beyond multiculturalism.* Thousand Oaks, CA: Sage.

Codes of Ethics for the Helping Professions (5th ed.). (2015). Boston, MA: Cengage Learning.

***Corey, G.** (2010). *Creating your professional path: Lessons from my journey* Alexandria, VA: American Counseling Association.

***Corey, G.** (2013a). *The art of integrative counseling* (3rd ed.). Belmont, CA: Brooks/Cole, Cengage Learning.

***Corey, G.** (2013b). *Case approach to counseling and psychotherapy* (8th ed.). Belmont, CA: Brooks/Cole, Cengage Learning.

***Corey, G.** (2013c). *DVD for Theory and Practice of Counseling and Psychotherapy: The case of Stan and lecturettes.* Belmont, CA: Brooks/Cole, Cengage Learning.

***Corey, G.** (2017). *Student manual for theory and practice of counseling and psychotherapy* (10th ed.). Boston, MA: Cengage Learning.

***Corey, G., & Corey, M.** (2014). *I never knew I had a choice* (10th ed.). Belmont, CA: Cengage Learning.

***Corey, G., Corey, M., Corey, C., & Callanan, P.** (2015). *Issues and ethics in the helping professions* (9th ed.). Boston, MA: Cengage Learning.

***Corey, G., Corey, M., & Haynes, R.** (2015). *Ethics in action: DVD and workbook* (3rd ed.). Boston, MA: Cengage Learning.

***Corey, G., & Haynes, R.** (2013). *DVD for integrative counseling: The case of Ruth and lecturettes.* Belmont, CA: Cengage Learning.

***Corey, M., & Corey, G.** (2016). *Becoming a helper* (7th ed.). Boston, MA: Cengage Learning.

Cukrowicz, K. C., White, B. A., Reitzel, L. R., Burns, A. B., Driscoll, K. A., Kemper, T. S., & Joiner, T. E. (2005). Improved treatment outcome associated with the shift to empirically supported treatments in a graduate training clinic. *Professional Psychology: Research and Practice, 36*(3), 330–337.

***Dailey, S. F., Gill, C. S., Karl, S. L., & Minton, C. A. B.** (2014). *DSM-5 learning companion for counselors.* Alexandria, VA: American Counseling Association.

Deegear, J., & Lawson, D. M. (2003). The utility of empirically supported treatments. *Professional Psychology: Research and Practice, 34*(3), 271–277.

***Duncan, B. L., Miller, S. D., Wampold, B. E., & Hubble, M. A.** (Eds.). (2010). *The heart and soul of change: Delivering what works in therapy* (2nd ed.). Washington, DC: American Psychological Association.

Edwards, J. A., Dattilio, F. M., & Bromley, D. B. (2004). Developing evidence-based practice: The role of case-based research. *Professional Psychology: Research and Practice, 35*(6), 589–597.

***Elkins, D. N.** (2009). *Humanistic psychology: A clinical manifesto.* Colorado Springs, CO: University of the Rockies Press.

***Elkins, D. N.** (2016). *The human elements of psychotherapy: A nonmedical model of emotional healing.* Washington, DC: American Psychological Association.

***Geller, J. D., Norcross, J. C., & Orlinsky, D. E.** (Eds.). (2005a). *The psychotherapist's own psychotherapy: Patient and clinician perspectives.* New York: Oxford University Press.

***Geller, J. D., Norcross, J. C., & Orlinsky, D. E.** (2005b). The question of personal therapy: Introduction and prospectus. In J. D. Geller, J. C. Norcross, & D. E. Orlinsky (Eds.), *The psychotherapist's own psychotherapy: Patient and clinician perspectives* (pp. 3–11). New York: Oxford University Press.

Gold, S. H., & Hilsenroth, M. J. (2009). Effects of graduate clinicians' personal therapy on therapeutic alliance. *Clinical Psychology and Psychotherapy, 16*(3), 159–171.

Gutheil, T. G., & Brodsky, A. (2008). *Preventing boundary violations in clinical practice.* New York: Guilford Press.

***Herlihy, B., & Corey, G.** (2015a). *ACA ethical standards casebook* (7th ed.). Alexandria, VA: American Counseling Association.

***Herlihy, B., & Corey, G.** (2015b). *Boundary issues in counseling: Multiple roles and responsibilities* (3rd ed.). Alexandria, VA: American Counseling Association.

Herlihy, B., & Corey, G. (2015c). Confidentiality. In B. Herlihy & G. Corey, *ACA ethical standards casebook* (7th ed., pp. 169–182). Alexandria, VA: American Counseling Association.

Herlihy, B., & Corey, G. (2015d). Managing value conflicts. In B. Herlihy & G. Corey, *ACA ethical standards casebook* (7th ed., pp. 193–204). Alexandria, VA: American Counseling Association.

Herlihy, B., Hermann, M. A., & Greden, L. R. (2014). Legal and ethical implications of using religious beliefs as the basis for refusing to counsel certain clients. *Journal of Counseling & Development 92*(2), 148–153.

Jencius, M. (2015). Technology, social media, and online counseling. In B. Herlihy & G. Corey (Eds.), *ACA ethical standards casebook* (7th ed., pp. 245–258). Alexandria, VA: American Counseling Association.

Kaplan, D. M. (2014). Ethical implications of a critical legal case for the counseling profession: *Ward v. Wilbanks. Journal of Counseling & Development 92*(2), 142–146.

Kaplan, D. M. (2016). Raising the bar: New concepts in the 2014 ACA code of ethics. In I. Marini & M. A. Stebnicki (Eds.), *The Professional Counselor's Desk Reference* (2nd ed., pp. 37–42). New York: Springer.

Kocet, M. M., & Herlihy, B. J. (2014). Addressing value-based conflicts within the counseling relationship: A decision-making model. *Journal of Counseling & Development, 92*(2), 180–186.

*__Kottler, J. A., Englar-Carlson, M., & Carlson, J.__ (Eds.). (2013). *Helping beyond the 50-minute hour: Therapists involved in meaningful social action.* New York: Routledge (Taylor & Francis).

*__Knapp, S. J., & VandeCreek, L.__ (2006). *Practical ethics for psychologists: A positive approach.* Washington, DC: American Psychological Association.

Lambert, M. J. (2011). Psychotherapy research and its achievements. In J. C. Norcross, G. R. Vandenbos, & D. K. Freedheim (Eds.), *History of psychotherapy* (2nd ed., pp. 299–332). Washington, DC: American Psychological Association.

Lazarus, A. A., & Zur, O. (2002). *Dual relationships and psychotherapy.* New York: Springer.

*__Lee, C. C.__ (Ed.). (2013). *Multicultural issues in counseling: New approaches to diversity* (4th ed.). Alexandria, VA: American Counseling Association.

Lee, C. C. (2015). Social justice and counseling across cultures. In B. Helihy & G. Corey, *ACA ethical standards casebook* (7th ed., pp. 155–168). Alexandria, VA: American Counseling Association.

Lee, C. C., & Park, D. (2013). A conceptual framework for counseling across cultures. In C. C. Lee (Ed.), *Multicultural issues in counseling: New approaches to diversity* (4th ed., pp. 3–12). Alexandria, VA: American Counseling Association.

*__Nagy, T. F.__ (2011). *Essential ethics for psychologists: A primer for understanding and mastering core issues.* Washington, DC: American Psychological Association.

*__Norcross, J. C.__ (2005). The psychotherapist's own psychotherapy: Educating and developing psychologists. *American Psychologist, 60*(8), 840–850.

*__Norcross, J. C.__ (Ed.). (2011). *Psychotherapy relationships that work: Evidence-based responsiveness* (2nd ed.). New York: Oxford University Press.

Norcross, J. C., Beutler, L. E., & Levant, R. F. (2006). *Evidence-based practices in mental health: Debate and dialogue on the fundamental questions.* Washington, DC: American Psychological Association.

*__Norcross, J. C., & Guy, J. D.__ (2007). *Leaving it at the office: A guide to psychotherapist self-care.* New York: Guilford Press.

*__Norcross, J. C., Hogan, T. P., & Koocher, G. P.__ (2008). *Clinician's guide to evidence-based practices.* New York: Oxford University Press.

Norcross, J. C., & Lambert, M. J. (2011). Evidence-based therapy relationships. In J. C. Norcross (Ed.), *Psychotherapy relationships that work: Evidence-based responsiveness* (2nd ed., pp. 3–21). New York: Oxford University Press.

Norcross, J. C., & Wampold, B. E. (2011). Evidence-based therapy relationships: Research conclusions and clinical practices. In J. C. Norcross (Ed.), *Psychotherapy relationships that work: Evidence-based responsiveness* (2nd ed., pp. 423–430). New York: Oxford University Press.

Orlinsky, D. E., Norcross, J. C., Ronnestad, M. H., & Wiseman, H. (2005). Outcomes and impacts of the psychotherapists' own psychotherapy. In J. D. Geller, J. C. Norcross, & D. E. Orlinsky (Eds.), *The psychotherapist's own psychotherapy: Patient and clinician perspectives* (pp. 214–230). New York: Oxford University Press.

Ratts, M. J., & Pedersen, P. B. (2014). *Counseling for multiculturalism and social justice: Integration, theory, and application.* Alexandria, VA: American Counseling Association.

*__Remley, T. P., & Herlihy, B.__ (2016). *Ethical, legal, and professional issues in counseling* (5th ed.). Upper Saddle River, NJ: Merrill/Prentice-Hall.

*__Schank, J. A., & Skovholt, T. M.__ (2006). *Ethical practice in small communities: Challenges and rewards for psychologists.* Washington, DC: American Psychological Association.

*__Skovholt, T. M., & Jennings, L.__ (2004). *Master therapists: Exploring expertise in therapy and counseling.* Boston: Pearson Education.

*__Sperry, L., & Carlson, J.__ (2011). *How master therapists work: Exploring change from the first through the last session and beyond.* New York: Routledge (Taylor & Francis).

Spotts-De Lazzer, A. (2012). Facebook for therapists: Friend or unfriend? *The Therapist, 24*(5), 19–23.

*__Stebnicki, M. A.__ (2008). *Empathy fatigue: Healing the mind, body, and spirit of professional counselors.* New York: Springer.

Sue, D. W., Arredondo, P., & McDavis, R. J. (1992). Multicultural counseling competencies and standards. A call to the profession. *Journal of Counseling and Development, 70*(4), 477–486.

*__Sue, D. W., & Sue, D.__ (2013). *Counseling the culturally diverse: Theory and practice* (6th ed.). New York: Wiley.

Van Brunt, B. (2015). *Harm to others: The assessment and treatment of dangerousness.* Alexandria, VA: American Counseling Association.

Wampold, B. E. (2001). *The great psychotherapy debate: Models, methods, and findings.* Hillsdale, NJ: Erlbaum.

*__Wheeler, N., & Bertram, B.__ (2015). *The counselor and the law: A guide to legal and ethical practice* (7th ed.). Alexandria, VA: American Counseling Association.

*__Yalom, I. D.__ (1997). *Lying on the couch: A novel.* New York: Perennial.

*__Yalom, I. D.__ (2003). *The gift of therapy: An open letter to a new generation of therapists and their patients.* New York: HarperCollins (Perennial).

*__Zur, O.__ (2007). *Boundaries in psychotherapy: Ethical and clinical explorations.* Washington, DC: American Psychological Association.

Chapter 4

Psychoanalytic Therapy

Barber, J. P., Muran, J. C., McCarthy, K. S., & Keefe, J. R. (2013). Research on dynamic therapies. In M. J. Lambert (Ed.), *Bergin and Garfield's handbook of psychotherapy and behavior change* (6th ed., pp. 443–494). Hoboken, NJ: Wiley.

Clarkin, J., Yeomans, F., & Kernberg, O. (2006). *Psychotherapy for borderline personality: Focusing on object relations.* Washington DC: Psychiatric Press.

*__Corey, G.__ (2013). *Case approach to counseling and psychotherapy* (8th ed.). Belmont, CA: Brooks/Cole, Cengage Learning.

Corey, G. (2016). *Theory and practice of group counseling* (9th ed.). Boston, MA: Cengage Learning.

*__Curtis, R. C., & Hirsch, I.__ (2011). Relational psychoanalytic psychotherapy. In S. B. Messer & A. S. Gurman (Eds.), *Essential psychotherapies: Theory and practice* (3rd ed., pp. 72–104). New York: Guilford Press.

Enns, C. Z. (1993). Twenty years of feminist counseling and therapy: From naming biases to implementing multifaceted practice. *The Counseling Psychologist, 21*(1), 3–87.

***Erikson, E. H.** (1963). *Childhood and society* (2nd ed.). New York: Norton.

Freud, S. (1949). *An outline of psychoanalysis.* New York: Norton.

***Freud, S.** (1955). *The interpretation of dreams.* London: Hogarth Press.

***Gabbard, G.** (2005). *Psychodynamic psychiatry in clinical practice* (4th ed.). Washington, DC: American Psychiatric Press.

***Harris, A. S.** (1996). *Living with paradox: An introduction to Jungian psychology.* Belmont, CA: Brooks/Cole, Cengage Learning.

Hayes, J. A. (2004). Therapist know thyself: Recent research on countertransference. *Psychotherapy Bulletin, 39*(4), 6–12.

Hayes, J. A., Gelso, C. J., & Hummel, A. M. (2011). Management of countertransference. In J. C. Norcross (Ed.), *Psychotherapy relationships that work: Evidence-based responsiveness* (2nd ed., pp. 239–258). New York: Oxford University Press.

***Hedges, L. E.** (1983). *Listening perspectives in psychotherapy.* New York: Aronson.

***Jung, C. G.** (1961). *Memories, dreams, reflections.* New York: Vintage.

Kernberg, O. F. (1975). *Borderline conditions and pathological narcissism.* New York: Aronson.

Kernberg, O. F. (1976). *Object-relations theory and clinical psychoanalysis.* New York: Aronson.

Kernberg, O. F. (1997). Convergences and divergences in contemporary psychoanalytic technique and psychoanalytic psychotherapy. In J. K. Zeig (Ed.), *The evolution of psychotherapy: The third conference* (pp. 3–22). New York: Brunner/Mazel.

Kernberg, O. F., Yeomans, F. E., Clarkin, J. F., & Levy, K. N. (2008). Transference focused psychotherapy: Overview and update. *International Journal of Psychoanalysis, 89*, 601–620.

Klein, M. (1975). *The psychoanalysis of children.* New York: Dell.

Kohut, H. (1971). *The analysis of self.* New York: International Universities Press.

Kohut, H. (1977). *Restoration of the self.* New York: International Universities Press.

Kohut, H. (1984). *How does psychoanalysis cure?* Chicago: University of Chicago Press.

Levenson, H. (2010). *Brief dynamic therapy.* Washington, DC: American Psychological Association.

Linehan, M. M. (1993a). *Cognitive-behavioral treatment of borderline personality disorder.* New York: Guilford Press.

Linehan, M. M. (1993b). *Skills training manual for treating borderline personality disorder.* New York: Guilford Press.

Linehan, M. M. (2015). *DBT skills training manual* (2nd ed.). New York: Guilford Press.

***Luborsky, E. B., O'Reilly-Landry, M., & Arlow, J. A.** (2011). Psychoanalysis. In R. J. Corsini & D. Wedding (Eds.), *Current psychotherapies* (9th ed., pp. 15–66). Belmont, CA: Brooks/Cole, Cengage Learning.

Mahler, M. S. (1968). *On human symbiosis or the vicissitudes of individuation.* New York: International Universities Press.

Masterson, J. F. (1976). *Psychotherapy of the borderline adult: A developmental approach.* New York: Brunner/Mazel.

***McWilliams, N.** (2014). Psychodynamic therapy. In L. S. Greenberg, N. McWilliams, & A. Wenzel, *Exploring three approaches to psychotherapy* (pp. 71–127). Washington, DC: American Psychological Association.

McWilliams, N. (2016). Psychoanalysis. In I. Marini & M. A. Stebnicki (Eds.), *The professional counselor's desk reference* (2nd ed., pp. 183–190). New York: Springer.

Messer, S. B., & Gurman, A. S. (2011). *Essential psychotherapies: Theory and practice* (3rd ed.). New York: Guilford Press.

Messer, S. B., & Warren, C. S. (2001). Brief psychodynamic therapy. In R. J. Corsini (Ed.), *Handbook of innovative therapies* (2nd ed., pp. 67–85). New York: Wiley.

Mitchell, S. A. (1988). *Relational concepts in psychoanalysis: An integration.* Cambridge, MA: Harvard University Press.

***Mitchell, S. A.** (2000). *Relationality: From attachment to intersubjectivity.* Hillsdale, NJ: Analytic Press.

Mitchell, S. A., & Black, M. J. (1995). *Freud and beyond: A history of modern psychoanalytic thought.* New York: Basic Books.

Prochaska, J. O., & Norcross, J. C. (2014). *Systems of psychotherapy: A transtheoretical analysis* (8th ed.). San Francisco, CA: Cengage Learning.

***Rutan, J. S., Stone, W. N., & Shay, J. J.** (2014). *Psychodynamic group psychotherapy* (5th ed.). New York: Guilford Press.

***Safran, J. D., & Kriss, A.** (2014). Psychoanalytic psychotherapies. In D. Wedding & R. J. Corsini (Eds.), *Current psychotherapies* (10th ed., pp. 19–54). Belmont, CA: Brooks/Cole, Cengage Learning.

Schore, A. N. (2012). *The science of the art of psychotherapy.* New York: Norton.

Schore, A. N. (2014). The right brain is dominant in psychotherapy. *Psychotherapy, 51*, 388–397.

***Schultz, D. P., & Schultz, S. E.** (2013). *Theories of personality* (10th ed.). San Francisco, CA: Wadsworth, Cengage Learning.

Sharf, R. S. (2016). *Theories of psychotherapy and counseling: Concepts and cases* (6th ed.). Boston, MA: Cengage Learning.

***St. Clair, M.** (with Wigren, J.). (2004). *Object relations and self psychology: An introduction* (4th ed.). Belmont, CA: Brooks/Cole, Cengage Learning.

Stern, D. N. (1985). *The interpersonal world of the infant: A view from psychoanalysis and developmental psychology.* New York: Basic Books.

Strupp, H. H. (1992). The future of psychodynamic psychotherapy. *Psychotherapy, 29*(l), 21–27.

Wolitzky, D. L. (2011a). Contemporary Freudian psychoanalytic psychotherapy. In S. B. Messer & A. S. Gurman (Eds.), *Essential psychotherapies: Theory and practice* (3rd ed., pp. 33–71). New York: Guilford Press.

Wolitzky, D. L. (2011b). Psychoanalytic theories in psychotherapy. In J. C. Norcross, G. R. Vandenbos, & D. K. Freedheim (Eds.), *History of psychotherapy* (2nd ed., pp. 65–100). Washington, DC: American Psychological Association.

Yalom, I. D. (2003). *The gift of therapy: An open letter to a new generation of therapists and their patients.* New York: HarperCollins (Perennial).

Chapter 5

Adlerian Therapy

Adler, A. (1958). *What life should mean to you.* New York: Capricorn. (Original work published 1931)

Adler, A. (1959). *Understanding human nature.* New York: Premier Books. (Original work published 1927)

Adler, A. (1964). *Social interest. A challenge to mankind.* New York: Capricorn. (Original work published 1938)

Adler, A. (1969). *The practice and theory of Individual Psychology.* Totowa, NJ: Littlefield, Adams, and Company. (2nd rev. ed. published 1929)

American Psychiatric Association. (2013). *Diagnostic and statistical manual of mental disorders.* (5th ed.). Washington, DC: Author.

Ansbacher, H. L. (1974). Goal-oriented individual psychology: Alfred Adler's theory. In A. Burton (Ed.), *Operational theories of personality* (pp. 99–142). New York: Brunner/Mazel.

***Ansbacher, H. L.** (1979). The increasing recognition of Adler. In. H. L. Ansbacher & R. R. Ansbacher (Eds.), *Superiority and social interest. Alfred Adler, A collection of his later writings* (3rd rev. ed., pp. 3–20). New York: Norton.

***Ansbacher, H. L.** (1992). Alfred Adler's concepts of community feeling and social interest and the relevance of community feeling for old age. *Individual Psychology, 48*(4), 402–412.

***Ansbacher, H. L., & Ansbacher, R. R.** (Eds.). (1964). *The individual psychology of Alfred Adler.* New York: Harper & Row/Torchbooks. (Original work published 1956)

***Ansbacher, H. L., & Ansbacher, R. R.** (Eds.). (1979). *Superiority and social interest. Alfred Adler, A collection of his later writings* (3rd rev. ed.). New York: Norton.

Arciniega, G. M., & Newlon, B. J. (2003). Counseling and psychotherapy: Multicultural considerations. In D. Capuzzi & D. F. Gross (Eds.), *Counseling and psychotherapy: Theories and interventions* (3rd ed., pp. 417–441). Upper Saddle River, NJ: Merrill/Prentice-Hall.

Bitter, J. R. (2007). Am I an Adlerian? *Journal of Individual Psychology, 63*(1), 3–31.

Bitter, J. R. (2008). Reconsidering narcissism: An Adlerian-feminist response to the articles in the special section of the *Journal of Individual Psychology*, volume 63, number 2. *Journal of Individual Psychology, 64*(3), 270–279.

Bitter, J. R. (2012). On the essence and origin of character: An introduction. In J. Carlson & M. P. Maniacci (Eds.), *Alfred Adler revisited* (pp. 89–95). New York: Routledge (Taylor & Francis).

Bitter, J. R. (2014). *Theory and practice of family therapy and counseling* (2nd ed.). Belmont, CA: Brooks/Cole, Cengage Learning.

***Bitter, J. R., Christensen, O. C., Hawes, C., & Nicoll, W. G.** (1998). Adlerian brief therapy with individuals, couples, and families. *Directions in Clinical and Counseling Psychology, 8*(8), 95–111.

***Bitter, J. R., & Nicoll, W. G.** (2000). Adlerian brief therapy with individuals: Process and practice. *Journal of Individual Psychology, 56*(1), 31–44.

***Bitter, J. R., & Nicoll, W. G.** (2004). Relational strategies: Two approaches to Adlerian brief therapy. *Journal of Individual Psychology, 60*(1), 42–66.

Bitter, J. R., Robertson, P. E., Healey, A., & Cole, L. (2009). Reclaiming a pro-feminist orientation in Adlerian therapy. *Journal of Individual Psychology, 65*(1), 13–33.

Carlson, J., & Johnson, J. (2016). Adlerian therapy. In I. Marini & M. A. Stebnicki (Eds.), *The professional counselor's desk reference* (2nd ed., pp. 225–228). New York: Springer.

***Carlson, J., & Maniacci M.** (2012). *Alfred Adler revisited.* New York: Routledge.

***Carlson, J., Watts, R. E., & Maniacci, M.** (2006). *Adlerian therapy: Theory and practice.* Washington DC: American Psychological Association.

***Carlson, J. D., & Englar-Carlson, M.** (2013). Adlerian therapy. In J. Frew & M. Spiegler (Eds.), *Contemporary psychotherapies for a diverse world* (pp. 87–130). New York: Routledge (Taylor & Francis Group).

***Carlson, J. M., & Carlson, J. D.** (2000). The application of Adlerian psychotherapy with Asian-American clients. *Journal of Individual Psychology, 56*(2), 214–225.

Clark, A. (2002). *Early recollections: Theory and practice in counseling and psychotherapy.* New York: Brunner Routledge.

Clark, A. (2007). *Empathy in counseling and psychotherapy: Perspectives and practice.* Mahwah, NJ: Lawrence Earlbaum.

Clark, A. (2012). Significance of early recollections. In J. Carlson & M. P. Maniacci (Eds.), *Alfred Adler revisited* (pp. 303–306). New York: Routledge (Taylor & Francis).

***Corey, G.** (2013). *Case approach to counseling and psychotherapy* (8th ed.). Belmont, CA: Brooks/Cole, Cengage Learning.

***Corey, G.** (2016). *Theory and practice of group counseling* (9th ed.). Boston, MA: Cengage Learning.

Dinkmeyer, D., Jr., & Sperry, L. (2000). *Counseling and psychotherapy: An integrated Individual Psychology approach* (3rd ed.). Upper Saddle River, NJ: Merrill/Prentice-Hall.

***Disque, J. G., & Bitter, J. R.** (1998). Integrating narrative therapy with Adlerian lifestyle assessment: A case study. *Journal of Individual Psychology, 54*(4), 431–450.

Dreikurs, R. (1953). *Fundamentals of Adlerian psychology.* Chicago: Alfred Adler Institute.

Dreikurs, R. (1967). *Psychodynamics, psychotherapy, and counseling. Collected papers.* Chicago: Alfred Adler Institute.

Dreikurs, R. (1968). *Psychology in the classroom* (2nd ed.). New York: Harper & Row.

Dreikurs, R. (1969). Group psychotherapy from the point of view of Adlerian psychology. In H. M. Ruitenbeck (Ed.), *Group therapy today: Styles, methods, and techniques* (pp. 37–48). New York: Aldine-Atherton. (Original work published 1957)

Dreikurs, R. (1997). Holistic medicine. *Individual Psychology, 53*(2), 127–205.

Hayes, D. (2013). *Assessment in counseling: A guide to the use of psychological assessment procedures* (5th ed.). Alexandria, VA: American Counseling Association.

Hoffman, E. (1996). *The drive for self: Alfred Adler and the founding of Individual Psychology.* Reading, MA: Addison-Wesley.

Hoyt, M. F. (2015). Brief therapy. In E. Neukrug (Ed.), *The Sage encyclopedia of theory in counseling and psychotherapy,* (Vol. 1, pp. 144–147). Thousand Oaks, CA: Sage.

Kefir, N. (1981). Impasse/priority therapy. In R. J. Corsini (Ed.), *Handbook of innovative psychotherapies* (pp. 401–415). New York: Wiley.

Maniacci, M. P. (2012). An introduction to Alfred Adler. In J. Carlson & M. P. Maniacci (Eds.), *Alfred Adler revisited* (pp. 1–10). New York: Routledge (Taylor & Francis).

Maniacci, M. P., Sackett-Maniacci, L., & Mosak, H. H. (2014). Adlerian psychotherapy. In D. Wedding & R. J. Corsini (Eds.), *Current psychotherapies* (10th ed., pp. 55–94). Belmont, CA: Cengage Learning.

Milliren, A. P., & Clemmer, F. (2006). Introduction to Adlerian psychology: Basic principles and methodology. In S. Slavik & J. Carlson (Eds.), *Readings in the theory and practice of Individual Psychology* (pp. 17–43). New York: Routledge (Taylor & Francis).

Milliren, A. P., Evans, T. D., & Newbauer, J. F. (2007). Adlerian theory.

In D. Capuzzi & D. R. Gross (Eds.), *Counseling and psychotherapy: Theories and interventions* (4th ed., pp. 123–163). Upper Saddle River, NJ: Merrill Prentice-Hall.

***Mosak, H. H., & Di Pietro, R.** (2006). *Early recollections: Interpretative method and application.* New York: Routledge.

Mosak, H. H., & Shulman, B. H. (1988). *Lifestyle inventory.* Muncie, IN: Accelerated Development.

Mozdzierz, G. J., Peluso, P. R., & Lisiecki, J. (2009). *Principles of counseling and psychotherapy: Learning the essential domains and non-linear thinking of master practitioners.* New York: Routledge.

***Powers, R. L., & Griffith, J.** (2012a). *The key to psychotherapy: Understanding the self-created individual.* Port Townsend, WA: Adlerian Psychology Associates.

Powers, R. L., & Griffith, J. (2012b). *IPCW: The individual psychology client workbook with supplements.* Port Townsend, WA: Adlerian Psychology Associates. (Original work published 1986)

Schultz, D., & Schultz, S. E. (2013). *Theories of personality* (10th ed.). San Francisco, CA: Wadsworth, Cengage Learning.

Sherman, R., & Dinkmeyer, D. (1987). *Systems of family therapy. An Adlerian integration.* New York: Brunner/Mazel.

Shulman, B. H., & Mosak, H. H. (1988). *Manual for life style assessment.* Muncie, IN: Accelerated Development.

***Sonstegard, M. A., & Bitter, J. R. (with Pelonis, P.).** (2004). *Adlerian group counseling and therapy: Step-by-step.* New York: Brunner/Routledge (Taylor & Francis).

***Sonstegard, M. A., Bitter, J. R., Pelonis-Peneros, P. P., & Nicoll, W. G.** (2001). Adlerian group psychotherapy: A brief therapy approach. *Directions in Clinical and Counseling Psychology, 11*(2), 11–12.

Sperry, L., Carlson, J. D., Sauerheber, J. D., & Sperry, J. (2014). *Psychopathology and psychotherapy: DSM 5 case conceptualization and treatment* (3rd ed.). New York: Routledge.

***Sweeney, T. J.** (2009). *Adlerian counseling and psychotherapy: A practitioner's approach* (5th ed.). New York: Routledge (Taylor & Francis).

Terner, J., & Pew, W. L. (1978). *The courage to be imperfect: The life and work of Rudolf Dreikurs.* New York: Hawthorn.

Vaihinger, H. (1965). *The philosophy of "as if."* London: Routledge & Kegan Paul.

Watts, R. E. (2012). On the origin of the striving for superiority and of social interest. In J. Carlson & M. P. Maniacci (Eds.), *Alfred Adler revisited* (pp. 41–47). New York: Routledge (Taylor & Francis).

Watts, R. E. (2015). Adlerian therapy. In E. Neukrug (Ed.), *The Sage encyclopedia of theory in counseling and psychotherapy,* (Vol. 1, pp. 30–35). Thousand Oaks, CA: Sage.

Chapter 6

Existential Therapy

Binswanger, L. (1975). *Being-in-the-world: Selected papers of Ludwig Binswanger.* London: Souvenir Press.

Bohart, A. C., & Wade, A. G. (2013). The client in psychotherapy. In M. J. Lambert (Ed.), *Bergin and Garfield's handbook of psychotherapy and behavior change (*6th ed., pp. 219–257). Hoboken, NJ: Wiley.

Boss, M. (1963). *Daseinanalysis and psychoanalysis.* New York: Basic Books.

Buber, M. (1970). *I and thou* (W. Kaufmann, Trans.). New York: Scribner's.

***Bugental, J. F. T.** (1987). *The art of the psychotherapist.* New York: Norton.

Bugental, J. F. T. (1997). There is a fundamental division in how psychotherapy is conceived. In J. K. Zeig (Ed.), *The evolution of psychotherapy: The third conference* (pp. 185–196). New York: Brunner/Mazel.

***Bugental, J. F. T.** (1999). *Psychotherapy isn't what you think: Bringing the psychotherapeutic engagement into the living moment.* Phoenix, AZ: Zeig, Tucker.

Bugental, J. F. T., & Bracke, P. E. (1992). The future of existential-humanistic psychotherapy. *Psychotherapy, 29*(1), 28–33.

***Cooper, M.** (2003). *Existential therapies.* London: Sage.

***Corey, G.** (2013). *Case approach to counseling and psychotherapy* (8th ed.). Belmont, CA: Brooks/Cole, Cengage Learning.

Corey, G. (2016). *Theory and practice of group counseling* (9th ed.). Boston, MA: Cengage Learning.

***Corey, G., & Corey, M.** (2014). *I never knew I had a choice* (10th ed.). Belmont, CA: Brooks/Cole, Cengage Learning.

Dattilio, F. M. (2002, January-February). Cognitive-behaviorism comes of age: Grounding symptomatic treatment in an existential approach. *The Psychotherapy Networker, 26*(1), 75–78.

***Deurzen, E. van.** (2002). Existential therapy. In W. Dryden (Ed.), *Handbook of individual therapy* (4th ed., pp. 179–208). London: Sage.

Deurzen, E. van. (2009). *Psychotherapy and the quest for happiness.* London: Sage.

***Deurzen, E. van.** (2010). *Everyday mysteries: A handbook of existential psychotherapy* (2nd ed.). London: Routledge.

***Deurzen, E. van.** (2012). *Existential counselling and psychotherapy in practice* (3rd ed.). London: Sage.

Deurzen, E. van. (2014). Becoming an existential therapist. *Existential Analysis: Journal of the Society for Existential Analysis, 25*(1), 6–16.

***Deurzen, E. van, & Adams, M.** (2011). *Skills in existential counselling and psychotherapy.* London: Sage.

***Deurzen, E. van, & Iacovou, S.** (Eds.). (2013). *Existential perspectives on relationship therapy.* London: Palgrave, Macmillan.

Elkins, D. N. (2007). Empirically supported treatments: The deconstruction of a myth. *Journal of Humanistic Psychology, 47,* 474–500.

***Elkins, D. N.** (2009). *Humanistic psychology: A clinical manifesto.* Colorado Springs, CO: University of the Rockies Press.

Elkins, D. N. (2012). Toward a common focus in psychotherapy research. *Psychotherapy, 49*(4), 450–454.

***Elkins, D. N.** (2016). *The human elements of psychotherapy: A nonmedical model of emotional healing.* Washington, DC: American Psychological Association.

Farha, B. (1994). Ontological awareness: An existential/cosmological epistemology. *The Person-Centered Periodical, 1*(1), 15–29.

***Frankl, V.** (1963). *Man's search for meaning.* Boston: Beacon.

***Frankl, V.** (1978). *The unheard cry for meaning.* New York: Simon & Schuster (Touchstone).

Gould, W. B. (1993). *Viktor E. Frankl: Life with meaning.* Pacific Grove, CA: Brooks/Cole.

Heidegger, M. (1962). *Being and time.* New York: Harper & Row.

Leszcz, M. (2015). Existential group psychotherapy. In E. Neukrug (Ed.), *The Sage encyclopedia of theory in counseling and psychotherapy,* (Vol. 1, pp. 365–368). Thousand Oaks, CA: Sage.

May, R. (1950). *The meaning of anxiety.* New York: Ronald Press.

***May, R.** (1953). *Man's search for himself.* New York: Dell.

May, R. (1958). The origins and significance of the existential movement in psychology. In R. May, E. Angel, & H. R. Ellenberger (Eds.), *Existence: A new dimension in psychiatry and psychology*. New York: Basic Books.

***May, R.** (Ed.). (1961). *Existential psychology*. New York: Random House.

May, R. (1969). *Love and will*. New York: Norton.

May, R. (1975). *The courage to create*. New York: Norton.

May, R. (1981). *Freedom and destiny*. New York: Norton.

***May, R.** (1983). *The discovery of being: Writings in existential psychology*. New York: Norton.

May, R., Angel, E., & Ellenberger, H. F. (Eds.). (1958). *Existence: A new dimension in psychiatry and psychology*. New York: Basic Books.

Rubin, S., & Lichtanski, K. (2015). Existential therapy. In E. Neukrug (Ed.), *The Sage encyclopedia of theory in counseling and psychotherapy*, (Vol. 1, pp. 368–373). Thousand Oaks, CA: Sage.

Russell, J. M. (1978). Sartre, therapy, and expanding the concept of responsibility. *American Journal of Psychoanalysis, 38*, 259–269.

***Russell, J. M.** (2007). Existential psychotherapy. In A. B. Rochlen (Ed.), *Applying counseling theories: An online case-based approach* (pp. 107–125). Upper Saddle River, NJ: Pearson Prentice-Hall.

Sartre, J. P. (1971). *Being and nothingness*. New York: Bantam Books.

***Schneider, K. J.** (Ed.). (2008). *Existential-integrative psychotherapy: Guideposts to the core of practice*. New York: Routledge.

***Schneider, K. J.** (2011). Existential-humanistic psychotherapies. In S. B. Messer & A. S. Gurman, (Eds.), *Essential psychotherapies: Theory and practice* (3rd ed., pp. 261–294). New York: Guilford Press.

***Schneider, K. J., & Krug, O. T.** (2010). *Existential-humanistic therapy*. Washington, DC: American Psychological Association.

Sharf, R. S. (2016). *Theories of psychotherapy and counseling: Concepts and cases* (6th ed.). Boston, MA: Cengage Learning.

***Sharp, J. G., & Bugental, J. F. T.** (2001). Existential-humanistic psychotherapy. In R. J. Corsini (Ed.), *Handbook of innovative therapies* (2nd ed., pp. 206–217). New York: Wiley.

Tillich, P. (1952). *The courage to be*. New Haven, CT: Yale University Press.

***Vontress, C. E.** (2013). Existential therapy. In J. Frew & M. D. Spiegler (Eds.), *Contemporary psychotherapies for a diverse world* (pp. 131–164). Routledge (Taylor & Francis).

***Vontress, C. E., Johnson, J. A., & Epp, L. R.** (1999). *Cross-cultural counseling: A casebook*. Alexandria, VA: American Counseling Association.

***Walsh, R. A., & McElwain, B.** (2002). Existential psychotherapies. In D. J. Cain & J. Seeman (Eds.), *Humanistic psychotherapies: Handbook of research and practice* (pp. 253–278). Washington, DC: American Psychological Association.

***Yalom, I. D.** (1980). *Existential psychotherapy*. New York: Basic Books.

***Yalom, I. D.** (1987). *Love's executioner: And other tales of psychotherapy*. New York: Harper Perennial.

Yalom, I. D. (1992). *When Nietzche wept*. New York: Basic Books.

***Yalom, I. D.** (1997). *Lying on the couch: A novel*. New York: Harper Perennial.

***Yalom, I. D.** (2000). *Momma and the meaning of life: Tales of psychotherapy*. New York: Harper Perennial.

***Yalom, I. D.** (2003). *The gift of therapy: An open letter to a new generation of therapists and their patients*. New York: HarperCollins (Perennial).

Yalom, I. D. (2005a). *The Schopenhauer cure: A novel*. New York: HarperCollins.

***Yalom, I. D. (with Leszcz, M.).** (2005b). *The theory and practice of group psychotherapy* (5th ed.). New York: Basic Books. (Original work published 1970)

***Yalom, I. D.** (2008). *Staring at the sun: Overcoming the terror of death*. San Francisco: Jossey-Bass.

***Yalom, I. D., & Josselson, R.** (2014). Existential psychotherapy. In D. Wedding & R. Corsini (Eds.), *Current psychotherapies* (10th ed., pp. 265–298). Belmont, CA: Brooks/Cole, Cengage Learning.

Chapter 7

Person-Centered Therapy

***Arkowitz, H., & Miller, W. R.** (2008). Learning, applying, and extending motivational interviewing. In H. Arkowitiz, H. A. Westra, W. R. Miller, & S. Rollnick (Eds.), *Motivational interviewing in the treatment of psychological disorders* (pp. 1–25). New York: Guilford Press.

Arkowitz, H., & Westra, H. A. (2009). Introduction to the special series on motivational interviewing and psychotherapy. *Journal of Clinical Psychology, 65*(11), 1149–1155.

***Bohart, A. C., & Tallman, K.** (1999). *How clients make therapy work: The process of active self-healing*. Washington, DC: American Psychological Association.

***Bohart, A. C., & Tallman, K.** (2010). Clients: The neglected common factor in psychotherapy. In B. L. Duncan, S. D. Miller, B. E. Wampold, & M. A. Hubble (Eds.), *The heart and soul of change: Delivering what works in therapy* (2nd ed., pp. 83–111). Washington, DC: American Psychological Association.

Bohart, A. C., & Wade, A. G. (2013). The client in psychotherapy. In M. J. Lambert (Ed.), *Bergin and Garfield's handbook of psychotherapy and behavior change* (6th ed., pp. 219–257). Hoboken, NJ: Wiley.

Bohart, A. C., & Watson, J. C. (2011). Person-centered psychotherapy and related experiential approaches. In S. B. Messer & A. S. Gurman (Eds.), *Essential psychotherapies: Theory and practice* (3rd ed., pp. 223–260). New York: Guilford Press.

***Bozarth, J. D., Zimring, F. M., & Tausch, R.** (2002). Client-centered therapy: The evolution of a revolution. In D. J. Cain & J. Seeman (Eds.), *Humanistic psychotherapies: Handbook of research and practice* (pp. 147–188). Washington, DC: American Psychological Association.

***Cain, D. J.** (2002a). Defining characteristics, history, and evolution of humanistic psychotherapies. In D. J. Cain & J. Seeman (Eds.), *Humanistic psychotherapies: Handbook of research and practice* (pp. 3–54). Washington, DC: American Psychological Association.

Cain, D. J. (2002b). Preface. In D. J. Cain & J. Seeman (Eds.), *Humanistic psychotherapies: Handbook of research and practice* (pp. xix–xxvi). Washington, DC: American Psychological Association.

***Cain, D. J.** (2010). *Person-centered psychotherapies*. Washington, DC: American Psychological Association.

***Cain, D. J.** (2013). Person-centered therapy. In J. Frew & M. D. Spiegler (Eds.), *Contemporary psychotherapies for a diverse world* (pp. 165–213). New York: Routledge (Taylor & Francis).

***Cain, D. J., & Seeman, J.** (Eds.). (2002). *Humanistic psychotherapies: Handbook of research and practice*. Washington, DC: American Psychological Association.

Clark, A. J. (2010). Empathy: An integral model in the counseling process. *Journal of Counseling & Development, 88*(3), 348–356.

Corbett, G. (2016). Motivational interviewing. In I. Marini & M. A. Stebnicki (Eds.), *The professional counselor's desk reference* (2nd ed., pp. 235–240). New York: Springer.

Corey, G. (2013). *Case approach to counseling and psychotherapy* (8th ed.). Belmont, CA: Brooks/Cole, Cengage Learning.

Corey, G. (2016). *Theory and practice of group counseling* (9th ed.). Boston, MA: Cengage Learning.

Dean, L. M. (2015). Motivational interviewing. In E. Neukrug (Ed.), *The Sage encyclopedia of theory in counseling and psychotherapy*, (Vol. 2, pp. 668–672). Thousand Oaks, CA: Sage.

*__Duncan, B. L., Miller, S. D., Wampold, B. E., & Hubble, M. A.__ (Eds.). (2010). *The heart and soul of change* (2nd ed.). Washington, DC: American Psychological Association.

*__Elkins, D. N.__ (2009). *Humanistic psychology: A clinical manifesto*. Colorado Springs, CO: University of the Rockies Press.

Elkins, D. N. (2012). Toward a common focus in psychotherapy research. *Psychotherapy, 49*(4), 450–454.

*__Elkins, D. N.__ (2016). *The human elements of psychotherapy: A nonmedical model of emotional healing*. Washington, DC: American Psychological Association.

Elliott, R., Bohart, A. C., Watson, J. C., & Greenberg, L. S. (2011). Empathy. In J. C. Norcross (Ed.), *Psychotherapy relationships that work: Evidence-based responsiveness* (2nd ed., pp. 132–152). New York: Oxford University Press.

Farber, B. A., & Doolin, E. M. (2011). Positive regard and affirmation. In J. C. Norcross (Ed.), *Psychotherapy relationships that work: Evidence-based responsiveness* (2nd ed., pp. 168–186). New York: Oxford University Press.

*__Greenberg, L. S.__ (2011). *Emotion-focused therapy*. Washington, DC: American Psychological Association.

*__Greenberg, L. S.__ (2014). Emotion-focused therapy. In L. S. Greenberg, N. McWilliams, & A. Wenzel, *Exploring three approaches to psychotherapy* (pp. 15–69). Washington, DC: American Psychological Association.

*__Kirschenbaum, H.__ (2009). *The life and work of Carl Rogers*. Alexandria, VA: American Counseling Association.

Kolden, G. G., Klein, M. H., Wang, C., & Austin, S. B. (2011). Congruence/genuineness. In J. C. Norcross (Ed.), *Psychotherapy relationships that work: Evidence-based responsiveness* (2nd ed., pp. 187–202). New York: Oxford University Press.

Levensky, E. R., Kersh, B. C., Cavasos, L. L., & Brooks, J. A. (2008). Motivational interviewing. In W. O'Donohue & J. E. Fisher (Eds.), *Cognitive behavior therapy: Applying empirically supported techniques in your practice* (2nd ed., pp. 357–366). Hoboken, NJ: Wiley.

Maslow, A. (1968). *Toward a psychology of being*. New York: Van Nostrand Reinhold.

Maslow, A. (1970). *Motivation and personality* (2nd ed.). New York: Harper & Row.

Maslow, A. (1971). *The farther reaches of human nature*. New York: Viking.

McDonald, A. R. (2015). Emotion-focused therapy. In E. Neukrug (Ed.), *The Sage encyclopedia of theory in counseling and psychotherapy*, (Vol. 1, pp. 341–344). Thousand Oaks, CA: Sage.

*__Miller, W. R., & Rollnick, S.__ (2013). *Motivational interviewing: Preparing people for change* (3rd ed.). New York: Guilford Press.

*__Norcross, J. C.__ (2010). The therapeutic relationship. In B. L. Duncan, S. D. Miller, B. E. Wampold, & M. A. Hubble (Eds.), *The heart and soul of change: Delivering what works in therapy* (2nd ed., pp. 113–141). Washington, DC: American Psychological Association.

*__Norcross, J. C., Hogan, T. P., & Koocher, G. P.__ (2008). *Clinician's guide to evidence-based practices*. New York: Oxford University Press.

Norcross, J. C., Krebs, P. M., & Prochaska, J. O. (2011). Stages of change. In J. C. Norcross (Ed.), *Psychotherapy relationships that work: Evidence-based responsiveness* (2nd ed., pp. 279–300). New York. Oxford University Press.

Patterson, C. H. (1995). A universal system of psychotherapy. *The Person-Centered Journal, 2*(1), 54–62.

Prochaska, J., & Norcross, J. (2014). *Systems of psychotherapy: A transtheoretical analysis* (8th ed.). Belmont, CA: Cengage Learning.

Rogers, C. (1942). *Counseling and psychotherapy: Newer concepts in practice*. Boston: Houghton Mifflin.

Rogers, C. (1951). *Client-centered therapy*. Boston: Houghton Mifflin.

Rogers, C. (1957). The necessary and sufficient conditions of therapeutic personality change. *Journal of Consulting Psychology, 21*, 95–103.

*__Rogers, C.__ (1961). *On becoming a person*. Boston: Houghton Mifflin.

Rogers, C. (1967). The conditions of change from a client-centered viewpoint. In B. Berenson & R. Carkhuff (Eds.), *Sources of gain in counseling and psychotherapy*. New York: Holt, Rinehart & Winston.

Rogers, C. (1970). *Carl Rogers on encounter groups*. New York: Harper & Row.

Rogers, C. (1977). *Carl Rogers on personal power: Inner strength and its revolutionary impact*. New York: Delacorte Press.

*__Rogers, C.__ (1980). *A way of being*. Boston: Houghton Mifflin.

Rogers, C. (1986a). Carl Rogers on the development of the person-centered approach. *Person-Centered Review, 1*(3), 257–259.

Rogers, C. (1986b). Client-centered therapy. In I. L. Kutash & A. Wolf (Eds.), *Psychotherapists casebook* (pp. 197–208). San Francisco: Jossey-Bass.

Rogers, C. R. (1987a). Rogers, Kohut, and Erickson: A personal perspective on some similarities and differences. In J. K. Zeig (Ed.), *The evolution of psychotherapy* (pp. 179–187). New York: Brunner/Mazel.

Rogers, C. R. (1987b). Steps toward world peace, 1948–1986: Tension reduction in theory and practice. *Counseling and Values, 32*(1), 12–16.

*__Rogers, C. R., & Freiberg, H. J.__ (1994). *Freedom to learn* (3rd ed.). Upper Saddle River, NJ: Prentice-Hall.

Rogers, C. R., Lyon, H., & Tausch, R. (2014). *On becoming an effective teacher: Person-centered teaching, psychology, philosophy and dialogues with Carl R. Rogers and Harold Lyon*. New York: Routledge (Taylor & Francis).

*__Rogers, C. R., & Russell, D. E.__ (2002). *Carl Rogers: The quiet revolutionary*. Roseville, CA: Penmarin Books.

*__Rogers, N.__ (1993). *The creative connection: Expressive arts as healing*. Palo Alto, CA: Science & Behavior Books.

Rogers, N. (2002). *Carl Rogers: A Daughter's Tribute* (CD ROM). Mingarden Media, Inc. www.nrogers.com

*__Rogers, N.__ (2011). *The creative connection for groups: Person-centered expressive arts for healing and social change*. Palo Alto, CA: Science and Behavior Books.

*__Schneider, K. J., & Krug, O. T.__ (2010). *Existential-humanistic therapy*. Washington, DC: American Psychological Association.

*Watson, J. C.** (2002). Re-visioning empathy. In D. J. Cain & J. Seeman (Eds.), *Humanistic psychotherapies: Handbook of research and practice* (pp. 445–471). Washington, DC: American Psychological Association.

Watson, J. C., Goldman, R. N., & Greenberg, L. S. (2011). Humanistic and experiential theories in psychotherapy. In J. C. Norcross, G. R. Vandenbos, & D. K. Freedheim (Eds.), *History of psychotherapy* (2nd ed., pp. 141–172). Washington, DC: American Psychological Association.

Zimring, F. M., & Raskin, N. J. (1992). Carl Rogers and client/person-centered therapy. In D. K. Freedheim (Ed.), *History of psychotherapy: A century of change* (pp. 629–656). Washington, DC: American Psychological Association.

Chapter 8
Gestalt Therapy

*Barber, P.** (2006). *Becoming a practitioner researcher: A Gestalt approach to holistic inquiry.* London: Middlesex University Press.

Beisser, A. R. (1970). The paradoxical theory of change. In J. Fagan & I. L. Shepherd (Eds.), *Gestalt therapy now* (pp. 77–80). New York: Harper & Row (Colophon).

*Bowman, C.** (2005). The history and development of Gestalt therapy. In A. Woldt & S. Toman (Eds.), *Gestalt therapy: History, theory, and practice* (pp. 3–20). Thousand Oaks, CA: Sage.

Breshgold, E. (1989). Resistance in Gestalt therapy: An historical theoretical perspective. *The Gestalt Journal, 12*(2), 73–102.

*Brown, J. R.** (2007). Gestalt therapy. In A. B. Rochlen (Ed.), *Applying counseling theories: An online case-based approach* (pp. 127–141). Upper Saddle River, NJ: Pearson Prentice-Hall.

*Brownell, P.** (2008). *Handbook for theory, research and practice in Gestalt therapy.* Newcastle, UK: Cambridge Scholar Publishing.

Brownell, P. (2016). Gestalt therapy. In I. Marini & M. A. Stebnicki (Eds.), *The professional counselor's desk reference* (2nd ed., pp. 241–245). New York: Springer.

Clarkson, P., & Mackewn, J. (1993). *Fritz Perls.* Newbury Park, CA: Sage.

Conyne, R. K. (2015). Gestalt group therapy. In E. Neukrug (Ed.), *The Sage encyclopedia of theory in counseling and psychotherapy,* (Vol. 1, pp. 452–456). Thousand Oaks, CA: Sage.

*Corey, G.** (2013). *Case approach to counseling and psychotherapy* (8th ed.). Belmont, CA: Brooks/Cole, Cengage Learning.

Corey, G. (2016). *Theory and practice of group counseling* (9th ed.). Boston, MA: Cengage Learning.

Elliott, R., Watson, J. C., Goldman, R. N., & Greenberg, L. S. (2004). *Learning emotion-focused therapy: A process-experiential approach to change.* Washington, DC: American Psychological Association.

*Feder. B.** (2006). *Gestalt group therapy: A practical guide.* New Orleans: Gestalt Institute Press.

*Feder, B., & Frew, J.** (Eds.). (2008). *Beyond the hot seat revisited: Gestalt approaches to group.* New Orleans: Gestalt Institute Press.

Fernbacher, S., & Plummer, D. (2005). Cultural influences and considerations in Gestalt therapy. In A. Woldt & S. Toman (Eds.), *Gestalt therapy: History, theory, and practice* (pp. 117–132). Thousand Oaks, CA: Sage.

Frew, J. E. (1986). The functions and patterns of occurrence of individual contact styles during the development phase of the Gestalt group. *The Gestalt Journal, 9*(l), 55–70.

Frew, J. E. (1997). A Gestalt therapy theory application to the practice of group leadership. *Gestalt Review, 1*(2), 131–149.

*Frew, J.** (2013). Gestalt therapy. In J. Frew & M. D. Spiegler (Eds.), *Contemporary psychotherapies for a diverse world* (pp. 215–257). New York: Routledge (Taylor & Francis).

GANZ. (2013, April). *Gestalt Australia and New Zealand code of ethics.* Fairfield, Victoria, Australia: Author.

*Greenberg, L. S.** (2011). *Emotion-focused therapy.* Washington, DC: American Psychological Association.

*Greenberg, L. S.** (2014). Emotion-focused therapy. In L. S. Greenberg, N. McWilliams, & A. Wenzel, *Exploring three approaches to psychotherapy* (pp. 15–69). Washington, DC: American Psychological Association.

*Greenberg, L. S., McWilliams, N., & Wenzel, A.** (2014). *Exploring three approaches to psychotherapy.* Washington, DC: American Psychological Association.

Jacobs, L. (1989). Dialogue in Gestalt theory and therapy. *The Gestalt Journal, 12*(1), 25–67.

*Latner, J.** (1986). *The Gestalt therapy book.* Highland, NY: Center for Gestalt Development.

Levitsky, A., & Perls, F. (1970). The rules and games of Gestalt therapy. In J. Fagan & I. Shepherd (Eds.), *Gestalt therapy now* (pp. 140–149). New York: Harper & Row (Colophon).

Maurer, R. (2005). Gestalt approaches with organizations and large systems. In A. Woldt & S. Toman (Eds.), *Gestalt therapy: History, theory, and practice.* (pp. 237–256). Thousand Oaks, CA: Sage.

Melnick, J., & Nevis, S. (2005). Gestalt therapy methodology. In A. Woldt & S. Toman (Eds.), *Gestalt therapy: History, theory, and practice.* (pp. 101–116). Thousand Oaks, CA: Sage.

Passons, W. R. (1975). *Gestalt approaches in counseling.* New York: Holt, Rinehart & Winston.

*Perls, F.** (1969a). *Gestalt therapy verbatim.* Moab, UT: Real People Press.

Perls, F. (1969b). *In and out of the garbage pail.* Moab, UT: Real People Press.

Perls, F., Hefferline, R., & Goodman, R. (1951). *Gestalt therapy: Excitement and growth in the human personality.* New York: Dell.

Perls, L. (1976). Comments on new directions. In E. W. L. Smith (Ed.), *The growing edge of Gestalt therapy* (pp. 221–226). New York: Brunner/Mazel.

Polster, E. (1987a). Escape from the present: Transition and storyline. In J. K. Zeig (Ed.), *The evolution of psychotherapy* (pp. 326–340). New York: Brunner/Mazel.

*Polster, E.** (1987b). *Every person's life is worth a novel: How to cut through emotional pain and discover the fascinating core of life.* New York: Norton.

*Polster, E.** (1995). *A population of selves: A therapeutic exploration of personality diversity.* San Francisco: Jossey-Bass.

Polster, E. (2006). *Uncommon ground.* Phoenix, AZ: Zeig, Tucker, and Theissen.

*Polster, E., & Polster, M.** (1973). *Gestalt therapy integrated: Contours of theory and practice.* New York: Brunner/Mazel.

Polster, E., & Polster, M. (1976). Therapy without resistance: Gestalt therapy. In A. Burton (Ed.), *What makes behavior change possible?* (pp. 259–277). New York: Brunner/Mazel.

*Polster, E., & Polster, M.** (1999). *From the radical center: The heart of Gestalt therapy.* Cambridge, MA: Gestalt Institute of Cleveland Press.

Polster, M. (1987). Gestalt therapy: Evolution and application. In J. K. Zeig (Ed.), *The evolution of psychotherapy* (pp. 312–325). New York: Brunner/Mazel.

Polster, M. (1992). *Eve's daughters: The forbidden heroism of women*. San Francisco, CA: Jossey-Bass.

Polster, M., & Polster, E. (1990). Gestalt therapy. In J. K. Zeig & W. M. Munion (Eds.), *What is psychotherapy? Contemporary perspectives* (pp. 103–107). San Francisco: Jossey-Bass.

Resnick, R. W. (2015). Gestalt therapy. In E. Neukrug (Ed.), *The Sage encyclopedia of theory in counseling and psychotherapy*, (Vol. 1, pp. 456–461). Thousand Oaks, CA: Sage.

***Strumpfel, U., & Goldman, R.** (2002). Contacting Gestalt therapy. In D. J. Cain & J. Seeman (Eds.), *Humanistic psychotherapies: Handbook of research and practice* (pp. 189–219). Washington, DC: American Psychological Association.

Watson, J. C., Goldman, R. N., & Greenberg, L. S. (2011). Humanistic and experiential theories in psychotherapy. In J. C. Norcross, G. R. Vandenbos, & D. K. Freedheim (Eds.), *History of psychotherapy* (2nd ed., pp. 141–172). Washington, DC: American Psychological Association.

***Wheeler, G., & Axelsson, L. S.** (2015). *Gestalt therapy.* Washington, DC: American Psychological Association.

***Woldt, A., & Toman, S.** (Eds.). (2005). *Gestalt therapy: History, theory, and practice.* Thousand Oaks, CA: Sage.

***Yontef, G. M.** (1993). *Awareness, dialogue and process: Essays on Gestalt therapy.* Highland, NY: Gestalt Journal Press.

***Yontef, G.** (1995). Gestalt therapy. In A. S. Gurman & S. B. Messer (Eds.), *Essential psychotherapies: Theory and practice* (pp. 261–303). New York: Guilford Press.

Yontef, G. (1999). Awareness, dialogue and process: Preface to the 1998 German edition. *The Gestalt Journal, 22*(1), 9–20.

***Yontef, G. M.** (2005). Gestalt therapy theory of change. In A. Woldt & S. Toman (Eds.), *Gestalt therapy: History, theory, and practice* (pp. 81–100). Thousand Oaks, CA: Sage.

***Yontef, G., & Jacobs, L.** (2014). Gestalt therapy. In D. Wedding & R. J. Corsini (Eds.), *Current psychotherapies* (10th ed., pp. 299–338). Belmont, CA: Cengage Learning.

***Yontef, G., & Schulz, F.** (2013). *Dialogic relationship and creative techniques: Are they on the same team?* Los Angeles, CA: Pacific Gestalt Institute.

Zahm, S. (1998). Therapist self-disclosure in the practice of Gestalt therapy. *The Gestalt Journal, 21,* 21–52.

***Zinker, J.** (1978). *Creative process in Gestalt therapy.* New York: Random House (Vintage).

Chapter 9
Behavior Therapy

***Alberti, R. E., & Emmons, M. L.** (2008). *Your perfect right: A guide to assertive behavior* (9th ed.). Atascadero, CA: Impact.

Antony, M. M. (2014). Behavior therapy. In D. Wedding & R. J. Corsini (Eds.), *Current psychotherapies* (10th ed., pp. 193–229). Belmont, CA: Brooks/Cole, Cengage Learning.

***Antony, M. M., & Roemer, L.** (2011a). *Behavior therapy*. Washington, DC: American Psychological Association.

Antony, M. M., & Roemer, L. (2011b). Behavior therapy: Traditional approaches. In S. B. Messer & A. S. Gurman (Eds.), *Essential psychotherapies: Theory and practice* (3rd ed., pp. 107–142). New York: Guilford Press.

Bandura, A. (1969). *Principles of behavior modification.* New York: Holt, Rinehart & Winston.

Bandura, A. (Ed.). (1971a). *Psychological modeling: Conflicting theories.* Chicago: Aldine-Atherton.

Bandura, A. (1971b). Psychotherapy based upon modeling principles. In A. E. Bergin & S. L. Garfield (Eds.), *Handbook of psychotherapy and behavior change.* New York: Wiley.

Bandura, A. (1977). *Social learning theory.* Englewood Cliffs, NJ: Prentice-Hall.

Bandura, A. (1982). Self-efficacy mechanisms in human agency. *American Psychologist, 37,* 122–147.

Bandura, A. (1986). *Social foundations of thought and action: A social cognitive theory.* Englewood Cliffs, NJ: Prentice-Hall.

***Bandura, A.** (1997). *Self-efficacy: The exercise of self-control.* New York: Freeman.

Bandura, A., & Walters, R. H. (1963). *Social learning and personality development.* New York: Holt, Rinehart & Winston.

Batten, S. V., & Ciarrochi, J. V. (2015). Acceptance and commitment therapy. In E. Neukrug (Ed.), *The Sage encyclopedia of theory in counseling and psychotherapy*, (Vol. 1, pp. 7–10). Thousand Oaks, CA: Sage.

***Beck, A. T.** (1976). *Cognitive therapy and emotional disorders.* New York: New American Library.

***Beck, A. T., & Weishaar, M. E.** (2014). Cognitive therapy. In D. Wedding & R. J. Corsini (Eds.), *Current psychotherapies* (10th ed., pp. 231–264). Belmont, CA: Brooks/Cole, Cengage Learning.

***Beck, J. S.** (2011). *Cognitive behavior therapy: Basics and beyond* (2nd ed.). New York: Guilford Press.

***Corey, G.** (2013). *Case approach to counseling and psychotherapy* (8th ed.). Belmont, CA: Brooks/Cole, Cengage Learning.

***Corey, G.** (2016). *Theory and practice of group counseling* (9th ed.). Boston, MA: Cengage Learning.

***Corey, G.** (2017). *Student manual for theory and practice of counseling and psychotherapy* (10th ed.). Boston, MA: Cengage Learning.

***Cormier, S., Nurius, P. S., & Osborn, C.** (2013). *Interviewing and change strategies for helpers* (7th ed.). Belmont, CA: Brooks/Cole, Cengage Learning.

Dimidjian, S., & Linehan, M. M. (2008). Mindfulness practice. In W. O'Donohue & J. E. Fisher (Eds.), *Cognitive behavior therapy: Applying empirically supported techniques in your practice* (2nd ed., pp. 327–336). Hoboken, NJ: Wiley.

Dobson, K. S. (2012). *Cognitive therapy*. Washington, DC: American Psychological Association.

Ferguson, K. E., & Sgambati, R. E. (2008). Relaxation. In W. O'Donohue & J. E. Fisher (Eds.), *Cognitive behavior therapy: Applying empirically supported techniques in your practice* (2nd ed., pp. 434–444). Hoboken, NJ: Wiley.

***Fishman, D. B., Rego, S. A., & Muller, K. L.** (2011). Behavioral theories in psychotherapy. In J. C. Norcross, G. R. Vandenbos, & D. K. Freedheim (Eds.), *History of psychotherapy* (2nd ed., pp. 101–140). Washington, DC: American Psychological Association.

Follette, W. C., & Callaghan, G. M. (2011). Behavior therapy: Functional-contextual approaches. In S. B. Messer & A. S. Gurman, (Eds.), *Essential psychotherapies: Theory and practice* (3rd ed., pp.184–220). New York: Guilford Press.

Germer, C. K. (2012). Cultivating compassion in psychotherapy. In C. K. Germer & R. D. Siegel (Eds.), *Wisdom and compassion in psychotherapy: Deepening mindfulness in clinical practice* (pp. 93–110). New York: Guilford Press.

Germer, C. K. (2013). Mindfulness: What is it? What does it matter? In C. K. Germer, R. D. Siegel, & P. R. Fulton (Eds.), *Mindfulness and psychotherapy* (pp. 3-35). New York: Guilford Press.

***Germer, C. K., & Siegel, R. D.** (Eds.). (2012). *Wisdom and compassion in psychotherapy: Deepening mindfulness in clinical practice*. New York: Guilford Press.

***Germer, C. K., Siegel, R. D., & Fulton, P. R.** (Eds.). (2013). *Mindfulness and psychotherapy* (2nd ed.). New York: Guilford Press.

Hammond, C. F. (2015). Mindfulness-based cognitive therapy. In E. Neukrug (Ed.), *The Sage encyclopedia of theory in counseling and psychotherapy*, (Vol. 2, pp. 656–658). Thousand Oaks, CA: Sage.

Hayes, S. C. (2004). Acceptance and commitment therapy and the new behavior therapies: Mindfulness, acceptance, and relationship. In S. C. Hayes, V. M. Follette, & M. M. Linehan (Eds.), *Mindfulness and acceptance: Expanding the cognitive-behavioral tradition* (pp. 1–29). New York: Guilford Press.

***Hayes, S. C., Follette, V. M., & Linehan, M. M.** (Eds.). (2004). *Mindfulness and acceptance: Expanding the cognitive-behavioral tradition*. New York: Guilford Press.

***Hayes, S. C., Strosahl, K. D., & Houts, A.** (Eds.). (2005). *A practical guide to acceptance and commitment therapy*. New York: Springer.

***Hayes, S. C., Strosahl, K. D., & Wilson, K. G.** (Eds.). (2011). *Acceptance and commitment therapy: The process and practice of mindful change* (2nd ed.). New York: Guilford Press.

Hazlett-Stevens, H., & Craske, M. G. (2008). Live (in vivo) exposure. In W. O'Donohue & J. E. Fisher (Eds.), *Cognitive behavior therapy: Applying empirically supported techniques in your practice* (2nd ed., pp. 309-316). Hoboken, NJ: Wiley.

Head, L. S., & Gross, A. M. (2008). Systematic desensitization. In W. O'Donohue & J. E. Fisher (Eds.), *Cognitive behavior therapy: Applying empirically supported techniques in your practice* (2nd ed., pp. 542–549). Hoboken, NJ: Wiley.

***Herbert, J. D., & Forman, E. M.** (2011). *Acceptance and mindfulness in cognitive behavior therapy: Understanding and applying the new therapies*. Hoboken, NJ: Wiley.

***Hollon, S. D., & Beck, A. T.** (2013). Cognitive and cognitive-behavioral therapies. In M. J. Lambert (Ed.), *Bergin and Garfield's handbook of psychotherapy and behavior change* (6th ed., pp. 393–492). Hoboken, NJ: Wiley.

Hollon, S. D., & DiGiuseppe, R. (2011). Cognitive theories in psychotherapy. In J. C. Norcross, G. R. Vandenbos, & D. K. Freedheim (Eds.), *History of psychotherapy* (2nd ed., pp. 203-242). Washington, DC: American Psychological Association.

Jacobson, E. (1938). *Progressive relaxation*. Chicago: University of Chicago Press.

***Kabat-Zinn, J.** (1990). *Full catastrophe living: Using the wisdom of your body and mind to face stress, pain, and illness*. New York: Dell.

***Kabat-Zinn, J.** (1994). *Wherever you go there you are: Mindfulness meditation in everyday life*. New York: Hyperion.

Kabat-Zinn, J. (2003). Mindfulness-based interventions in context: Past, present and future. *Clinical Psychology: Science and Practice, 10*(2), 144–156.

Kress, V. E., & Henry, J. S. (2015). Behavioral group therapy. In E. Neukrug (Ed.), *The Sage encyclopedia of theory in counseling and psychotherapy*, (Vol. 1, pp. 105–108). Thousand Oaks, CA: Sage.

Kuo, J. R., & Fitzpatrick, S. (2015). Dialectical behavior therapy. In E. Neukrug (Ed.), *The Sage encyclopedia of theory in counseling and psychotherapy*, (Vol. 1, pp. 292–297). Thousand Oaks, CA: Sage.

Lazarus, A. A. (1989). *The practice of multimodal therapy*. Baltimore: Johns Hopkins University Press.

***Lazarus, A. A.** (1997). *Brief but comprehensive psychotherapy: The multimodal way*. New York: Springer.

***Lazarus, A. A.** (2005). Multimodal therapy. In J. C. Norcross & M. R. Goldfried (Eds.), *Handbook of psychotherapy integration* (2nd ed., pp. 105–120). New York: Oxford University Press.

Lazarus, A. A. (2008a). Multimodal behavior therapy. In W. O'Donohue & J. E. Fisher (Eds.), *Cognitive behavior therapy: Applying empirically supported techniques in your practice* (2nd ed., pp. 342–346). Hoboken, NJ: Wiley.

Lazarus, A. A. (2008b). Technical eclecticism and multimodal therapy. In J. L. Lebow (Ed.), *Twenty-first century psychotherapies* (pp. 424–452). Hoboken, NJ: Wiley.

Lazarus, C. N., & Lazarus, A. A. (2015). Multimodal therapy. In E. Neukrug (Ed.), *The Sage encyclopedia of theory in counseling and psychotherapy*, (Vol. 2, pp. 677–682). Thousand Oaks, CA: Sage.

***Ledley, D. R., Marx, B. P., & Heimberg, R. G.** (2010). *Making cognitive-behavioral therapy work: Clinical processes for new practitioners* (2nd ed.). New York: Guilford Press.

Linehan, M. M. (1993a). *Cognitive-behavioral treatment of borderline personality disorder*. New York: Guilford Press.

Linehan, M. M. (1993b). *Skills training manual for treating borderline personality disorder*. New York: Guilford Press.

Linehan, M. M. (2015). *DBT skills training manual* (2nd ed.). New York: Guilford Press.

Martell, C. R. (2007). Behavioral therapy. In A. B. Rochlen (Ed.), *Applying counseling theories: An online case-based approach* (pp. 143–156). Upper Saddle River, NJ: Pearson Prentice-Hall.

***Miller, W. R., & Rollnick, S.** (2013). *Motivational interviewing: Helping people change* (3rd ed.). New York: Guilford Press.

***Miltenberger, R. G.** (2012). *Behavior modification: Principles and procedures* (5th ed.). Belmont, CA: Brooks/Cole, Cengage Learning.

Morgan, S. P. (2013). Practical ethics. In C. K. Germer, R. D. Siegel, & P. R. Fulton (Eds.), *Mindfulness and psychotherapy* (pp. 112–129). New York: Guilford Press.

Morgan, W. D., Morgan, S. T., & Germer, C. K. (2013). Cultivating attention and compassion. In C. K. Germer, R. D. Siegel, & P. R. Fulton (Eds.), *Mindfulness and psychotherapy* (pp. 76–93). New York: Guilford Press.

Neff, K. D. (2012). The science of self-compassion. In C. K. Germer & R. D. Siegel (Eds.), *Wisdom and compassion in psychotherapy: Deepening mindfulness in clinical practice* (pp. 79–92). New York: Guilford Press.

***Norcross, J. C., Pfund, R. A., & Prochaska, J. O.** (2013). Psychotherapy in 2022: A Delphi poll on its future. *Professional Psychology: Research and Practice, 44*(5), 363–370.

Nye, R. D. (2000). *Three psychologies: Perspectives from Freud, Skinner, and Rogers* (6th ed.). Belmont, CA: Brooks/Cole, Cengage Learning.

***O'Donohue, W., & Fisher, J. E.** (Eds.). (2012). *Core principles for practice*. Hoboken, NJ: Wiley.

Panjares, F. (2004). *Albert Bandura: Biographical sketch*. Retrieved from http://des.emory.edu/mfp/bandurabio.html.

Paul, G. L. (1967). Outcome research in psychotherapy. *Journal of Consulting Psychology, 31*, 109–188.

*Pollak, S. M., Pedulla, T., & Siegel, R. D. (2014). *Sitting together: Essential skills for mindfulness-based psychotherapy*. New York: Guilford Press.

Prochaska, J. O., & Norcross, J. C. (2014). *Systems of psychotherapy: A transtheoretical analysis* (8th ed.). Belmont, CA: Cengage Learning.

*Robins, C. J., & Rosenthal, M. Z. (2011). Dialectical behavior therapy. In J. D. Hebert & E. M. Forman (Eds.), *Acceptance and mindfulness in cognitive behavior therapy: Understanding and applying the new therapies* (pp. 164–209). Hoboken, NJ: Wiley.

*Roemer, L., & Orsillio, S. M. (2009). *Mindfulness and acceptance-based behavioral therapies in practice*. New York: Guilford Press.

*Salmon, P. G., Sephton, S. E., & Dreeben, S. J. (2011). Mindfulness-based stress reduction. In J. D. Hebert & E. M. Forman (Eds.), *Acceptance and mindfulness in cognitive behavior therapy: Understanding and applying the new therapies* (pp.132–163). Hoboken, NJ: Wiley.

*Segal, Z. V., Williams, J. M. G., & Teasdale, J. D. (2013). *Mindfulness-based cognitive therapy for depression* (2nd ed.). New York: Guilford Press.

Segrin, C. (2008). Social skills training. In W. O'Donohue & J. E. Fisher (Eds.), *Cognitive behavior therapy: Applying empirically supported techniques in your practice* (2nd ed., pp. 502–509). Hoboken, NJ: Wiley.

*Shapiro, F. (2001). *Eye movement desensitization and reprocessing: Basic principles, protocols, and procedures* (2nd ed.). New York: Guilford Press.

Shapiro, F. (2002a). *EMDR as an integrative psychotherapy approach*. Washington, DC: American Psychological Association.

Shapiro, F. (2002b). EMDR twelve years after its introduction: Past and future research. *Journal of Clinical Psychology, 58*, 1–22.

Shapiro, F., & Solomon, R. (2015). Eye movement desensitization and reprocessing therapy. In E. Neukrug (Ed.), *The Sage encyclopedia of theory in counseling and psychotherapy*, (Vol. 1, pp. 388–394). Thousand Oaks, CA: Sage.

*Siegel, R. D. (2010). *The mindfulness solution: Everyday practices for everyday problems*. New York: Guilford Press.

Seigel, R. D. (2012). The wise psychotherapist. In C. K. Germer & R. D. Siegel (Eds.), *Wisdom and compassion in psychotherapy: Deepening mindfulness in clinical practice* (pp. 138–153). New York: Guilford Press.

Siegel, R. D., & Germer, C. K. (2012). Wisdom and compassion: Two wings of a bird. In C. K. Germer & R. D. Siegel (Eds.), *Wisdom and compassion in psychotherapy: Deepening mindfulness in clinical practice* (pp. 7–34). New York: Guilford Press.

Skinner, B. F. (1948). *Walden II*. New York: Macmillan.

Skinner, B. F. (1953). *Science and human behavior*. New York: Macmillan.

Skinner, B. F. (1971). *Beyond freedom and dignity*. New York: Knopf.

*Spiegler, M. D. (2016). *Contemporary behavior therapy* (6th ed.). Boston, MA: Cengage Learning.

Tanaka-Matsumi, J., Higginbotham, H. N., & Chang, R. (2002). Cognitive-behavioral approaches to counseling across cultures: A functional analytic approach for clinical applications. In P. B. Pedersen, J. G. Draguns, W. J. Lonner, & J. E. Trimble (Eds.), *Counseling across cultures* (5th ed., pp. 337–379). Thousand Oaks, CA: Sage.

Twohig, M. P., & Dehlin, J. P. (2012). Skills training. In W. O'Donohue & J. E. Fisher (Eds.), *Cognitive behavior therapy: Core principles for practice* (pp. 37–73). Hoboken, NJ: Wiley.

Vujanovic, A. A., Niles, B., Pietrefesa, A., Schmertz, S. K., & Potter, C. M. (2011). Mindfulness in the treatment of posttraumatic stress disorder among military veterans. *Professional Psychology: Research and Practice, 42*(1), 24–31.

*Watson, D. L., & Tharp, R. G. (2014). *Self-directed behavior: Self-modification for personal adjustment* (10th ed.). Belmont, CA: Wadsworth, Cengage Learning.

*Wilson, G. T. (2011). Behavior therapy. In R. Corsini & D. Wedding (Eds.), *Current psychotherapies* (9th ed., pp. 235–275). Belmont, CA: Brooks/Cole, Cengage Learning.

Wolpe, J. (1990). *The practice of behavior therapy* (4th ed.). Elmsford, NY: Pergamon Press.

Worthington, E. L., Jr. (2011). Integration of spirituality and religion into psychotherapy. In J. C. Norcross, G. R. Vandenbos, & D. K. Freedheim (Eds.), *History of psychotherapy* (2nd ed., pp. 533–544). Washington, DC: American Psychological Association.

Chapter 10

Cognitive Behavior Therapy

Beck, A. T. (1963). Thinking and depression: Idiosyncratic content and cognitive distortions. *Archives of General Psychiatry, 9*, 324–333.

Beck, A. T. (1967). *Depression: Clinical, experimental, and theoretical aspects*. New York: Harper & Row. (Republished as *Depression: Causes and treatment*. Philadelphia: University of Pennsylvania Press, 1972)

*Beck, A. T. (1976). *Cognitive therapy and emotional disorders*. New York: International Universities Press.

Beck, A. T. (1987). Cognitive therapy. In J. K. Zeig (Ed.), *The evolution of psychotherapy* (pp. 149–178). New York: Brunner/Mazel.

Beck, A. T., & Haigh, E. A. P. (2014). Advances in cognitive theory and therapy: The generic cognitive model. *Annual Review of Clinical Psychology, 10*, 1–24.

*Beck, A. T., Rush, A., Shaw, B., & Emery, G. (1979). *Cognitive therapy of depression*. New York: Guilford Press.

*Beck, A. T., & Weishaar, M. E. (2014). Cognitive therapy. In D. Wedding & R. J. Corsini (Eds.), *Current psychotherapies* (10th ed., pp. 231–264). Belmont, CA: Brooks/Cole, Cengage Learning.

*Beck, J. S. (2005). *Cognitive therapy for challenging problems: What to do when the basics don't work*. New York: Guilford Press.

*Beck, J. S. (2011a). *Cognitive behavior therapy: Basics and beyond* (2nd ed.). New York: Guilford Press.

*Beck, J. S. (2011b). *Cognitive therapy worksheet packet* (Rev.). Bala Cynwyd, PA: Beck Institute for Cognitive Therapy.

Beck, J. S., & Butler, A. C. (2005). Treating psychotherapists with cognitive therapy. In J. D. Geller, J. C. Norcross, & D. E. Orlinsky (Eds.), *The psychotherapist's own psychotherapy: Patient and clinician perspectives* (pp. 254–264). New York: Oxford University Press.

*Carlson, J., & Knaus, W. (2014). *Albert Ellis revisited*. New York: Routledge (Taylor & Francis).

Chambless, D. L., & Peterman, M. (2006). Evidence on cognitive-behavioral therapy for generalized anxiety disorder and panic disorder. In R. L. Leahy (Ed.), *Contemporary cognitive therapy: Theory, research, and practice* (pp. 86–115). New York: Guilford Press.

Clark, D. M., Salkovskis, P. M., Hackmann, A., Wells, A., Ludgate, J., & Gelder, M. (1999). Brief cognitive therapy for panic disorder: A randomized controlled trial. *Journal of Consulting and Clinical Psychology, 67*, 583–589.

***Corey, G.** (2013). *Case approach to counseling and psychotherapy* (8th ed.). Belmont, CA: Brooks/Cole, Cengage Learning.

***Corey, G.** (2016). *Theory and practice of group counseling* (9th ed.). Boston, MA: Cengage Learning.

Corey, G. (2017). *Student manual for theory and practice of counseling and psychotherapy* (10th ed.). Boston, MA: Cengage Learning.

***Dattilio, F. M.** (1993). Cognitive techniques with couples and families. *The Family Journal, 1*(1), 51–65.

***Dattilio, F. M.** (Ed.). (1998). *Case studies in couple and family therapy: Systemic and cognitive perspectives.* New York: Guilford Press.

Dattilio, F. M. (2000a). Cognitive-behavioral strategies. In J. Carlson & L. Sperry (Eds.), *Brief therapy with individuals and couples* (pp. 33–70). Phoenix, AZ: Zeig, Tucker & Theisen.

Dattilio, F. M. (2000b). Families in crisis. In F. M. Dattilio & A. Freeman (Eds.), *Cognitive-behavioral strategies in crisis intervention* (2nd ed., pp. 316–338). New York: Guilford Press.

Dattilio, F. M. (2001). Cognitive-behavior family therapy: Contemporary myths and misconceptions. *Contemporary Family Therapy, 23*(1), 3–18.

Dattilio, F. M. (2002a, January–February). Cognitive-behaviorism comes of age: Grounding symptomatic treatment in an existential approach. *The Psychotherapy Networker, 26*(1), 75–78.

Dattilio, F. M. (2002b). Homework assignments in couple and family therapy. *Journal of Clinical Psychology, 58*(5), 535–547.

Dattilio, F. M. (2005). Restructuring family schemas: A cognitive-behavioral perspective. *Journal of Marital and Family Therapy, 31*(1), 15–30.

Dattilio, F. M. (2010). *Cognitive-behavior therapy with couples and families: A comprehensive guide for clinicians.* New York: Guilford Press.

Dattilio, F. M., & Castaldo, J. E. (2001). Differentiating symptoms of anxiety from relapse of Guillain-Barre-syndrome. *Harvard Review of Psychiatry, 9*(5), 260–265.

***Dattilio, F. M., & Freeman, A.** (Eds.). (2007). *Cognitive-behavioral strategies in crisis intervention* (3rd ed.). New York: Guilford Press.

Dattilio, F. M., & Hanna, M. A. (2012). Collaboration in cognitive-behavior therapy. *Journal of Clinical Psychology, 68*(2), 146–158.

Dattilio, F. M., & Kendall, P. C. (2007). Panic disorder. In F. M. Dattilio & A. Freeman (Eds.), *Cognitive-behavioral strategies in crisis intervention* (3rd ed., pp. 59–83). New York: Guilford Press.

***Dattilio, F. M., & Padesky, C. A.** (1990). *Cognitive therapy with couples.* Sarasota, FL: Professional Resources Exchange.

Dienes, K. A., Torres-Harding, S., Reinecke, M. A., Freeman, A., & Sauer, A. (2011). Cognitive therapy. In S. B. Messer & A. S. Gurman (Eds.), *Essential psychotherapies: Theory and practice* (3rd ed., pp. 143–183). New York: Guilford Press.

Dobson, K. S. (2012). *Cognitive therapy.* Washington, DC: American Psychological Association.

***Ellis, A.** (1994). *Reason and emotion in psychotherapy revised.* New York: Kensington.

***Ellis, A.** (1996). *Better, deeper, and more enduring brief therapy: The rational emotive behavior therapy approach.* New York: Brunner/Mazel.

***Ellis, A.** (1997). The evolution of Albert Ellis and rational emotive behavior therapy. In J. K. Zeig (Ed.), *The evolution of psychotherapy: The third conference* (pp. 69–82). New York: Brunner/Mazel.

***Ellis, A.** (1999). *How to make yourself happy and remarkably less disturbable.* Atascadero, CA: Impact.

***Ellis, A.** (2000). *How to control your anxiety before it controls you.* New York: Citadel Press.

***Ellis, A.** (2001a). *Feeling better, getting better, and staying better.* Atascadero, CA: Impact.

***Ellis, A.** (2001b). *Overcoming destructive beliefs, feelings, and behaviors.* Amherst, NY: Prometheus Books.

***Ellis, A.** (2002). *Overcoming resistance: A rational emotive behavior therapy integrated approach* (2nd ed.). New York: Springer.

***Ellis, A.** (2004a). *Rational emotive behavior therapy: It works for me—It can work for you.* Amherst, NY: Prometheus.

***Ellis, A.** (2004b). *The road to tolerance: The philosophy of rational emotive behavior therapy.* Amherst, NY: Prometheus.

***Ellis, A.** (2005). *The myth of self-esteem.* Amherst, NY: Prometheus Books.

Ellis, A. (2008). Cognitive restructuring of the disputing of irrational beliefs. In W. O'Donohue & J. E. Fisher (Eds.), *Cognitive behavior therapy: Applying empirically supported techniques in your practice* (2nd ed., pp. 91–95). Hoboken, NJ: Wiley.

Ellis, A. (2010). *All out! An autobiography.* Amherst, NY: Prometheus Books.

***Ellis, A., & Blau, S.** (Eds.). (1998). *The Albert Ellis reader.* New York: Kensington.

***Ellis, A., & Crawford, T.** (2000). *Making intimate connections: Seven guidelines for great relationships and better communication.* Atascadero, CA: Impact.

***Ellis, A., & Ellis, D. J.** (2011). *Rational emotive behavior therapy.* Washington, DC: American Psychological Association.

***Ellis, A., & Ellis, D. J.** (2014). Rational emotive behavior therapy. In D. Wedding & R. J. Corsini (Eds.), *Current psychotherapies* (10th ed., pp. 151–191). Belmont, CA: Brooks/Cole, Cengage Learning.

Ellis, A., & Harper, R. A. (1997). *A guide to rational living* (3rd ed.). North Hollywood, CA: Melvin Powers (Wilshire Books).

***Ellis, D. J.** (2014) *Rational Emotive Behavior Therapy* [DVD]. Washington, DC: American Psychological Association.

Epstein, N. B. (2006). Cognitive-behavioral therapy with couples: Theoretical and empirical status. In R. L. Leahy (Ed.), *Contemporary cognitive therapy: Theory, research, and practice* (pp. 367–388). New York: Guilford Press.

Freeman, A., & Dattilio, R. M. (Eds.). (1992). *Comprehensive casebook of cognitive therapy.* New York: Plenum Press.

Freeman, A., & Dattilio, R. M. (1994). Cognitive therapy. In J. L. Ronch, W. Van Ornum, & N. C. Stilwell (Eds.), *The counseling sourcebook: A practical reference on contemporary issues* (pp. 60–71). New York: Continuum Press.

Freeman, A., & Freeman, S. E. M. (2016). Basics of cognitive behavior therapy. In I. Marini & M. A. Stebnicki (Eds.), *The professional counselor's desk reference* (2nd ed., pp. 191–196). New York: Springer.

***Gilbert, P., & Leahy, R. L.** (2009). *The therapeutic relationship in the cognitive behavioral psychotherapies.* New York: Routledge (Taylor & Francis).

Granvold, D. K. (Ed.). (1994). *Cognitive and behavioral treatment: Method and applications.* Pacific Grove, CA: Brooks/Cole.

*Greenberger, D., & Padesky, C. A. (2016). *Mind over mood: Change how you feel by changing the way you think* (2nd ed.). New York: Guilford Press.

Hays, P. A. (2009). Integrating evidence-based practice, cognitive-behavior therapy, and multicultural therapy: Ten steps for culturally competent practice. *Professional Psychology: Research and Practice, 40*(4), 354–360.

Hofmann, S. G., Asnaani, A., Vonk, I. J. J., Sawyer, A. T., & Fang, A. (2012). The efficacy of cognitive behavioral therapy: A review of meta-analyses. *Cognitive Therapy and Research, 36*, 427–440.

Hollon, S. D., & DiGiuseppe, R. (2011). Cognitive theories in psychotherapy. In J. C. Norcross, G. R. Vandenbos, & D. K. Freedheim (Eds.), *History of psychotherapy* (2nd ed., pp. 203–242). Washington, DC: American Psychological Association.

Hollon, S. D., Stewart, M. O., & Strunk, D. (2006). Enduring effects for cognitive behavior therapy in the treatment of depression and anxiety, *Annual Review of Psychology, 57*, 285–315.

Horney, K. (1950). *Neurosis and human growth*. New York: Norton.

Jacobs, N. N. (2008). Bibliotherapy utilizing CBT. In W. O'Donohue & J. E. Fisher (Eds.), *Cognitive behavior therapy: Applying empirically supported techniques in your practice* (2nd ed., pp. 60–67). Hoboken, NJ: Wiley.

Kazantzis, N., Dattilio, F. M., Cummins, A., & Clayton, X. (2014). Homework assignments and self-monitoring. In S. Hoffman & D. J. A. Dozois (Eds.), *Cognitive behavioral therapy: A complete reference guide, Volume I: CBT general strategies* (pp. 311–330). Hoboken, NJ: Wiley.

*Kazantzis, N., Deane, F. P., Ronan, K. R., & L'Abate, L. (2005). *Using homework assignments in cognitive behavior therapy*. New York: Routledge (Taylor & Francis).

*Kuyken, W., Padesky, C.A., & Dudley, R. (2009). *Collaborative case conceptualization: Working effectively with clients in CBT*. New York: Guilford Press.

Leahy, R. L. (2002). Cognitive therapy: Current problems and future directions. In R. L. Leahy & E. T. Dowd (Eds.), *Clinical advances in cognitive psychotherapy: Theory and application* (pp. 418–434). New York: Springer.

*Leahy, R. L. (Ed.). (2006a). *Contemporary cognitive therapy: Theory, research, and practice*. New York: Guilford Press.

*Leahy, R. L. (Ed.). (2006b). *Roadblocks in cognitive-behavioral therapy*. New York: Guilford Press.

*Ledley, D. R., Marx, B. P., & Heimberg, R. G. (2010). *Making cognitive-behavioral therapy work: Clinical processes for new practitioners* (2nd ed.). New York: Guilford Press.

Lopez, S. J., & Snyder, C. R. (Eds.). (2011). *The Oxford handbook of positive psychology*. New York: Oxford University Press.

Marlatt, G., & Donovan, D. M. (Eds.). (2005). *Relapse prevention: Maintenance strategies in the treatment of addictive behaviors* (2nd ed.). New York: Guilford Press.

*Meichenbaum, D. (1977). *Cognitive behavior modification: An integrative approach*. New York: Plenum Press.

*Meichenbaum, D. (1985). *Stress inoculation training*. New York: Pergamon Press.

Meichenbaum, D. (1986). Cognitive behavior modification. In F. H. Kanfer & A. P. Goldstein (Eds.), *Helping people change: A textbook of methods* (pp. 346–380). New York: Pergamon Press.

Meichenbaum, D. (1993). Stress inoculation training: A 20 year update. In P. M. Lehrer & R. L. Woolfolk (Eds.), *Principles and practice of stress management* (2nd ed., pp. 373–406). New York: Guilford Press.

Meichenbaum, D. (1994a). *A clinical handbook/practical therapist manual: For assessing and treating adults with post-traumatic stress disorder (PTSD)*. Waterloo, Ontario, Canada: Institute Press.

Meichenbaum, D. (1994b). *Treating adults with PTSD*. Clearwater, FL: Institute Press.

Meichenbaum, D. (1997). The evolution of a cognitive-behavior therapist. In J. K. Zeig (Ed.), *The evolution of psychotherapy: The third conference* (pp. 96–104). New York: Brunner/Mazel.

Meichenbaum, D. (2002). *Treatment of individuals with anger-control problems and aggressive behaviors: A clinical handbook*. Clearwater, FL: Institute Press.

Meichenbaum, D. (2007). Stress inoculation training: A preventive and treatment approach. In P. M. Lehrer, R. L. Woolfolk, & W. Sime (Eds.), *Principles and practices of stress management* (3rd ed., pp. 497–518). New York: Guilford Press.

*Meichenbaum, D. (2008). Stress inoculation training. In W. O'Donohue & J. E. Fisher (Eds.), *Cognitive behavior therapy: Applying empirically supported techniques in your practice* (2nd ed., pp. 529–532). Hoboken, NJ: Wiley.

*Meichenbaum, D. (2012). *Roadmap to resilience: A guide for military, trauma victims and their families*. Clearwater, FL: Institute Press.

Meichenbaum, D. (2015). Donald Meichenbaum. In E. Neukrug (Ed.), *The Sage encyclopedia of theory in counseling and psychotherapy*, (Vol. 2, pp. 641–642). Thousand Oaks, CA: Sage.

Newman, C. (2006). Substance abuse. In R. L. Leahy (Ed.), *Contemporary cognitive therapy: Theory, research, and practice* (pp. 206–227). New York: Guilford Press.

Padesky, C. A. (2004). Aaron T. Beck: Man, mind and mentor. In R. Leahy (Ed.), *Contemporary cognitive therapy: Theory, research and practice* (pp. 3–24). New York: Guilford Press.

Padesky, C. A. (2007, July). *The next frontier: Building positive qualities with CBT*. Invited keynote address at the World Congress of Behavioural and Cognitive Therapies, Barcelona, Spain.

Padesky, C. A., & Beck, A.T. (2003). Science and philosophy: Comparison of cognitive therapy (CT) and rational emotive behavior therapy (REBT). *Journal of Cognitive Psychotherapy: An International Quarterly, 17*, 211–224.

*Padesky, C. A., & Greenberger, D. (1995). *Clinician's guide to mind over mood*. New York: Guilford Press.

Padesky, C. A., & Mooney, K. A. (2012). Strengths-based cognitive-behavioural therapy: A four-step model to build resilience. *Clinical Psychology & Psychotherapy, 19*(4), 283–290.

Pretzer, J., & Beck, J. (2006). Cognitive therapy of personality disorders. In R. L. Leahy (Ed.), *Contemporary cognitive therapy: Theory, research, and practice* (pp. 299–318). New York: Guilford Press.

Reinecke, M., Dattilio, F. M., & Freeman, A. (Eds.). (2002). *Casebook of cognitive behavior therapy with children and adolescents* (2nd ed.). New York: Guilford Press.

Riskind, J. H. (2006). Cognitive theory and research on generalized anxiety disorder. In R. L. Leahy (Ed.), *Contemporary cognitive therapy: Theory, research, and practice* (pp. 62–85). New York: Guilford Press.

*Roemer, L., & Orsillio, S. M. (2010). *Mindfulness and acceptance-based behavioral therapies in practice*. New York: Guilford Press.

Scher, C. D., Segal, Z. V., & Ingram, R. E. (2006). Beck's theory of depression: Origins, empirical status, and future directions for cognitive vulnerability. In R. L. Leahy (Ed.), *Contemporary cognitive therapy: Theory, research, and practice* (pp. 27–61). New York: Guilford Press.

Spiegler, M. D. (2013). Behavior therapy II: Cognitive-behavioral therapy. In J. Frew & M. D. Spiegler (Eds.), *Contemporary psychotherapies for a diverse world* (Rev. ed., pp. 301–337). New York: Routledge (Taylor & Francis).

***Spiegler, M. D.** (2016). *Contemporary behavior therapy* (6th ed.). Boston, MA: Cengage Learning.

Tompkins, M. A. (2004). *Using homework in psychotherapy: Strategies, guidelines, and forms.* New York: Guilford Press.

Tompkins, M. A. (2006). Effective homework. In R. L. Leahy (Ed.), *Roadblocks in cognitive-behavioral therapy* (pp. 49–66). New York: Guilford Press.

Weishaar, M. E. (1993). *Aaron T. Beck.* London: Sage.

***White, J. R., & Freeman, A.** (Eds.). (2000). *Cognitive-behavioral group therapy for specific problems and populations.* Washington, DC: American Psychological Association.

Chapter 11

Choice Theory/Reality Therapy

American Psychiatric Association. (2013). *Diagnostic and statistical manual of mental disorders* (5th ed.). Washington, DC: Author.

***Corey, G.** (2013). *Case approach to counseling and psychotherapy* (8th ed.). Belmont, CA: Brooks/Cole, Cengage Learning.

Corey, G. (2016). *Theory and practice of group counseling* (9th ed.). Boston, MA: Cengage Learning.

Gerdes, P., Wubbolding, S., & Wubbolding, R. (2012). Expanding the practical use of the perceptual system. *International Journal of Choice Theory and Reality Therapy, 32*(1), 16–19.

Glasser, W. (1965). *Reality therapy: A new approach to psychiatry.* New York: Harper & Row.

Glasser, W. (1968). *Schools without failure.* New York: Harper & Row.

Glasser, W. (1992). Reality therapy. *New York State Journal for Counseling and Development, 7*(l), 5–13.

***Glasser, W.** (1998). *Choice theory: A new psychology of personal freedom.* New York: HarperCollins.

***Glasser, W.** (2001). *Counseling with choice theory: The new reality therapy.* New York: HarperCollins.

Glasser, W. (2003). *Warning: Psychiatry can be hazardous to your mental health.* New York: HarperCollins.

Glasser, W. (2005). *Defining mental health as a public health issue: A new leadership role for the helping and teaching professions.* Chatsworth, CA: William Glasser Institute.

***Wubbolding, R. E.** (1988). *Using reality therapy.* New York: Harper & Row (Perennial Library).

***Wubbolding, R. E.** (1991). *Understanding reality therapy.* New York: Harper & Row (Perennial Library).

***Wubbolding, R. E.** (2000). *Reality therapy for the 21st century.* Philadelphia, PA: Brunner-Routledge.

Wubbolding, R. E. (2007). Reality therapy. In A. B. Rochlen (Ed.), *Applying counseling theories: An online case-based approach* (pp. 193–207). Upper Saddle River, NJ: Pearson Prentice-Hall.

Wubbolding, R. E. (2009). Headline or footnote? Mainstream or backwater? Cutting edge or trailing edge? Included or excluded from the professional world? *International Journal of Reality Therapy, 29*(1), 26–29.

***Wubbolding, R. E.** (2011a). *Reality therapy.* Washington, DC: American Psychological Association.

***Wubbolding, R. E.** (2011b). Reality therapy/choice theory. In D. Capuzzi & D. R. Gross (Eds.), *Counseling and psychotherapy: Theories and interventions* (5th ed., pp. 263–285). Alexandria, VA: American Counseling Association.

Wubbolding, R. E. (2013). Reality therapy. In J. Frew & M. D. Spiegler (Eds.), *Contemporary psychotherapies for a diverse world* (pp. 339–372). New York: Routledge (Taylor & Francis).

Wubbolding, R. E. (2015a). *Cycle of psychotherapy, counseling, coaching, managing and supervising* (chart, 18th revision). Cincinnati, OH: Center for Reality Therapy.

Wubbolding, R. E. (2015b). *Reality therapy training manual* (16th rev.). Cincinnati OH: Center for Reality Therapy.

Wubbolding, R. E. (2015c). Reality therapy. In E. Neukrug (Ed.), *The Sage encyclopedia of theory in counseling and psychotherapy,* (Vol. 2, pp. 856–860). Thousand Oaks, CA: Sage.

***Wubbolding, R. E., & Brickell, J.** (2001). *A set of directions for putting and keeping yourself together.* Minneapolis, MN: Educational Media Corporation.

Wubbolding, R. E., & Brickell, J. (2005). Reality therapy in recovery. *Directions in Addiction Treatment and Prevention, 9*(1), 1–10. New York: The Hatherleigh Company.

Wubbolding, R. E., & Brickell, J. (2009). Perception: The orphaned component of choice theory. *International Journal of Reality Therapy, 28*(2), 50–54.

Wubbolding, R. E., & Colleagues. (1998). Multicultural awareness: Implications for reality therapy and choice theory. *International Journal of Reality Therapy, 17*(2), 4–6.

Wubbolding, R. E., Brickell, J., Imhof, L., Kim, R., Lojk, L., & Al-Rashidi, B. (2004). Reality therapy: A global perspective. *International Journal for the Advancement of Counselling, 26*(3), 219–228.

Chapter 12

Feminist Therapy

American Psychiatric Association. (2013). *Diagnostic and statistical manual of mental disorders* (5th ed.). Washington, DC: Author.

American Psychological Association. (2007). Guidelines for psychological practice with girls and women. *American Psychologist, 62,* 949–979.

Belenky, M., Clinchy, B., Goldberger, N., & Tarule, J. (1997). *Women's ways of knowing: The development of self, voice, and mind* (10th anniv. ed.). New York: HarperCollins. (Original work published 1987)

Bitter, J. R. (2008). Reconsidering narcissism: An Adlerian-feminist response to the articles in the special section of the *Journal of Individual Psychology. Journal of Individual Psychology, 64*(3), 270–279.

Bitter, J. R., Robertson, P. E., Healey, A., & Cole, L. (2009). Reclaiming a profeminist orientation in Adlerian therapy. *Journal of Individual Psychology, 65*(1), 13–33.

***Brabeck, M. M., & Brabeck, K. M.** (2013). Feminist and multicultural ethics in counseling psychology. In C. Z. Enns & E. N. Williams (Eds.), *The Oxford handbook of feminist multicultural counseling psychology* (pp. 27–44). New York: Oxford.

*Brown, L. S. (1994). *Subversive dialogues: Theory in feminist therapy.* New York: Basic Books.

*Brown, L. S. (2010). *Feminist therapy.* Washington, DC: American Psychological Association.

Cole, E., Espín, O. M., & Rothblum, E. D. (1992). *Refugee women and their mental health: Shattered societies, shattered lives.* Binghamton, NY: Haworth Press.

Comstock, D. L., Hammer, T. R., Strentzsch, J., Cannon, K., Parsons, J., & Salazar, G. (2008). Relational-cultural theory: A framework for bridging relational, multicultural, and social justice competencies. *Journal of Counseling & Development, 86,* 279–287.

*Corey, G. (2013). *Case approach to counseling and psychotherapy* (8th ed.). Belmont, CA: Brooks/Cole, Cengage Learning.

Crethar, H. C., Torres Rivera, E., & Nash, S. (2008). In search of common threads: Linking multicultural, feminist, and social justice counseling paradigms. *Journal of Counseling & Development, 86,* 269–278.

Duffey, T., & Haberstroh, S. (2014). Female counselors working with male clients using relational-cultural theory. In M. Englar-Carlson, M. P. Evans, & T. Duffey, *A counselor's guide to working with men* (pp. 307–323). Alexandria, VA: American Counseling Association.

Englar-Carlson, M. (2014). Introduction: A primer on counseling men. In M. Englar-Carlson, M. P. Evans, & T. Duffey, *A counselor's guide to working with men* (pp. 1–31). Alexandria, VA: American Counseling Association.

Englar-Carlson, M., Evans, M. P., & Duffey, T. (2014). *A counselor's guide to working with men.* Alexandria, VA: American Counseling Association.

Enns, C. Z. (1991). The "new" relationship models of women's identity: A review and critique for counselors. *Journal of Counseling & Development, 69,* 209–217.

Enns, C. Z. (1993). Twenty years of feminist counseling and therapy: From naming biases to implementing multifaceted practice. *The Counseling Psychologist, 21*(1), 3–87.

Enns, C. Z. (2000). Gender issues in counseling. In S. D. Brown & R. W. Lent (Eds.), *Handbook of counseling psychology* (3rd ed., pp. 601–638). New York: Wiley.

Enns, C. Z. (2003). Contemporary adaptations of traditional approaches to the counseling of women. In M. Kopala & M. Keitel (Eds.), *Handbook of counseling women* (pp. 1–21). Thousand Oaks, CA: Sage.

*Enns, C. Z. (2004). *Feminist theories and feminist psychotherapies: Origins, themes, and diversity* (2nd ed.). New York: Haworth.

Enns, C. Z., & Byars-Winston, A. (2010). Multicultural feminist therapy. In H. Landrine & N. F. Russo (Eds.), *Handbook of diversity in feminist psychology* (pp. 367–388). New York: Springer.

*Enns, C. Z., Rice, J. K., & Nutt, R. L. (Eds.). (2015). *Psychological practice with women: Guidelines, diversity, empowerment.* Washington, DC: American Psychological Association.

Enns, C. Z., & Sinacore, A. L. (2001). Feminist theories. In J. Worell (Ed.), *Encyclopedia of gender* (Vol. 1, pp. 469–480). San Diego, CA: Academic Press.

*Enns, C. Z., & Williams, E. N. (Eds.). (2013). The *Oxford handbook of feminist multicultural counseling psychology.* New York: Oxford.

*Enns, C. Z., Williams, E. N., & Fassinger, R. E. (2013). Feminist multicultural psychology: Evolution, change, and challenge. In C. Z. Enns & E. N. Williams (Eds.), *The Oxford handbook of feminist multicultural counseling psychology* (pp. 3–26). New York: Oxford.

*Eriksen, K., & Kress, V. E. (2005). *Beyond the DSM story: Ethical quandaries, challenges, and best practices.* Thousand Oaks, CA: Sage.

Espín, O. M. (1996). *Latina healers: Lives of power and tradition.* Encino, CA: Floricanto Press.

Espín, O. M. (1997). *Latina realities: Essays on healing, migration, and sexuality.* Boulder, CO: Westview Press.

Espín, O. M. (1999). *Women crossing boundaries: A psychology of immigration and the transformation of sexuality.* New York: Routledge.

Evans, K. M., Kincade, E. A., Marbley, A. F., & Seem, S. R. (2005). Feminism and feminist therapy: Lessons from the past and hopes for the future. *Journal of Counseling & Development, 83*(3), 269–277.

*Evans, K. M., Kincade, E. A., & Seem, S. R. (2011). *Introduction to feminist therapy: Strategies for social and individual change.* Thousand Oaks, CA: Sage.

Evans, K. M., & Miller, M. (2016). Feminist therapy. In I. Marini & M. A. Stebnicki (Eds.), *The professional counselor's desk reference* (2nd ed., pp. 247–251). New York: Springer.

Gilligan, C. (1977). In a different voice: Women's conception of self and morality. *Harvard Educational Review, 47,* 481–517.

*Gilligan, C. (1982). *In a different voice.* Cambridge, MA: Harvard University Press.

*Hays, P. A. (2008). *Addressing cultural complexities in practice* (2nd ed.). Washington DC: American Psychological Association.

Herlihy, B., & Corey, G. (2015a). *ACA ethical standards casebook* (7th ed.). Alexandria, VA: American Counseling Association.

Herlihy, B., & Corey, G. (2015b). *Boundary issues in counseling: Multiple roles and responsibilities* (3rd ed.). Alexandria, VA: American Counseling Association.

*Herlihy, B., & McCollum, V. J. (2011). Feminist theory. In D. Capuzzi & D. R. Gross (Eds.), *Counseling and psychotherapy: Theories and interventions* (5th ed., pp. 313–333). Alexandria, VA: American Counseling Association.

*Jordan, J. V. (2010). *Relational-cultural therapy.* Washington, DC: American Psychological Association.

Jordan, J. V., Kaplan, A. G., Miller, J. B., Stiver, I. P., & Surrey, J. L. (Eds.). (1991). *Women's growth in connection: Writings from the Stone Center.* New York: Guilford Press.

Kaschak, E. (1992). *Engendered lives.* New York: Basic Books.

King, A. R (2013). Mixed messages: How primary agents of socialization influence adolescent females who identify as multiracial-bisexual. *Journal of LGBT Youth, 10*(4), 308–327. doi:10.1080/19361653.2013.825198

Marecek, J., & Gavey, N. (2013). *DSM-5* and beyond: A critical feminist engagement with psychodiagnosis. *Feminism & Psychology, 23*(1), 3–9. doi:10.1177/0959353512467962

Miller, J. B. (1986). *Toward a new psychology of women* (2nd ed.). Boston: Beacon.

Miller, J. B. (1991). The development of women's sense of self. In J. V. Jordan, A. G. Kaplan, J. B. Miller, I. P. Stiver, & J. L. Surrey (Eds.), *Women's growth in connection* (pp. 11–26). New York: Guilford Press.

Miller, J. B., Jordon, J., Stiver, I. P., Walker, M., Surrey, J., & Eldridge, N. S. (1999). *Therapists' authenticity* (Work in progress no. 82). Wellesley, MA: Stone Center Working Paper Series.

*Miller, J. B., & Stiver, I. P. (1997). *The healing connection: How women form relationships in therapy and in life.* Boston: Beacon Press.

Pleck, J. H. (1995). The gender role strain paradigm: An update. In R. R. Levant & W. S. Pollack (Eds.), *A new psychology of men* (pp. 11–32). New York: Basic Books.

Pollack, W. S. (1998). *Real boys.* New York: Henry Holt.

Pusateri, C. G., & Headley, J. A. (2015). Feminist therapy. In E. Neukrug (Ed.), *The Sage encyclopedia of theory in counseling and psychotherapy*, (Vol. 1, pp. 414–418). Thousand Oaks, CA: Sage.

***Remer, P.** (2013). Feminist therapy. In J. Frew & M. D. Spiegler (Eds.), *Contemporary psychotherapies for a diverse world* (pp. 373–414). New York: Routledge (Taylor & Francis).

***Rogers, N.** (1995). *Emerging woman: A decade of midlife transitions.* Manchester, England: PCCS Books.

Surrey, J. L. (1991). The "self-in-relation": A theory of women's development. In J. V. Jordan, A. G. Kaplan, J. B. Miller, I. P. Stiver, & J. L. Surrey (Eds.), *Women's growth in connection* (pp. 51–66). New York: Guilford Press.

Surrey, J., & Jordan, J. V. (2012). The wisdom of connection. In C. K. Germer & R. D. Siegel (Eds.), *Wisdom and compassion in psychotherapy: Deepening mindfulness in clinical practice* (pp. 163–175). New York: Guilford Press.

Trepal, H. (2010). Exploring self-injury through a relational-cultural lens. *Journal of Counseling & Development, 88*(4), 492–499.

Turner, L. C., & Werner-Wilson, R. J. (2008). Phenomenological experiences of girls in a single-sex day treatment group. *Journal of Feminist Family Therapy, 20*(3), 220–250.

Walker, L. (1994). *Abused women and survivor therapy: A practical guide for the psychotherapist.* Washington, DC: American Psychological Association.

Williams, E. N., & Enns, C. Z. (2013). Making the political personal. In C. Z. Enns & E. N. Williams (Eds.), *The Oxford handbook of feminist multicultural counseling psychology* (pp. 485–489). New York: Oxford.

***Worell, J., & Remer, P.** (2003). *Feminist perspectives in therapy: Empowering diverse women* (2nd ed.). New York: Wiley.

Chapter 13

Postmodern Approaches

Anderson, H. (1993). On a roller coaster: A collaborative language system approach to therapy. In S. Friedman (Ed.), *The new language of change* (pp. 324–344). New York: Guilford Press.

***Anderson, H., & Goolishian, H.** (1992). The client is the expert: A not-knowing approach to therapy. In S. McNamee & K. J. Gergen (Eds.), *Therapy as social construction* (pp. 25–39). Newbury Park, CA: Sage.

Bateson, G. (1972). *Steps to an ecology of mind.* New York: Ballantine.

Berg, I. K. (1994). *Family based services: A solution-focused approach.* New York: Norton.

Berg, I. K., & Miller, S. D. (1992). *Working with the problem drinker: A solution-focused approach.* New York: Norton.

***Bertolino, B., & O'Hanlon, B.** (2002). *Collaborative, competency-based counseling and therapy.* Boston: Allyn & Bacon.

***Brown, L. S.** (2010). *Feminist therapy.* Washington, DC: American Psychological Association.

Bubenzer, D. L., & West, J. D. (1993). William Hudson O'Hanlon: On seeking possibilities and solutions in therapy. *The Family Journal: Counseling and Therapy for Couples and Families, 1*(4), 365–379.

Corey, G. (2013). *Case approach to counseling and psychotherapy* (8th ed.). Belmont, CA: Brooks/Cole, Cengage Learning.

Corey, G. (2016). *Theory and practice of group counseling* (9th ed.). Boston, MA: Cengage Learning.

***De Jong, P., & Berg, I. K.** (2013). *Interviewing for solutions* (4th ed.). Belmont, CA: Brooks/Cole, Cengage Learning.

***De Shazer, S.** (1985). *Keys to solutions in brief therapy.* New York: Norton.

***De Shazer, S.** (1988). *Clues: Investigating solutions in brief therapy.* New York: Norton.

***De Shazer, S.** (1991). *Putting difference to work.* New York: Norton.

***De Shazer, S.** (1994). *Words were originally magic.* New York: Norton.

De Shazer, S., & Berg, I. (1988). Doing therapy: A post-structural revision. *Journal of Marital and Family Therapy, 18,* 71–81.

***De Shazer, S., & Dolan, Y. M.** (with Korman, H., Trepper, T., McCullom, E., & Berg, I. K.). (2007). *More than miracles: The state of the art of solution-focused brief therapy.* New York: Haworth Press.

Drewery, W., & Winslade, J. (1997). The theoretical story of narrative therapy. In G. Monk, J. Winslade, K. Crocket, & D. Epston (Eds.), *Narrative therapy in practice: The archaeology of hope* (pp. 32–52). San Francisco: Jossey-Bass.

Epston, D., & White, M. (1992). Consulting your consultants: The documentation of alternative knowledges. In *Experience, contradiction, narrative and imagination: Selected papers of David Epston and Michael White, 1989–1991* (pp. 11–26). Adelaide, South Australia: Dulwich Centre.

Franklin, C., Trepper, T. S., Gingerich, W. J., & McCollum, E. E. (Eds.). (2012). *Solution-focused brief therapy: Research, practice, and training.* New York: Oxford University Press.

***Freedman, J., & Combs, G.** (1996). *Narrative therapy: The social construction of preferred realities.* New York: Norton.

Freedman, J., Epston, D., & Lobovits, D. (1997). *Playful approaches to serious problems: Narrative therapy with children and their families.* New York: Norton.

George, E., Iveson, C., & Ratner, H. (2015). Solution-focused brief therapy. In E. Neukrug (Ed.), *The Sage encyclopedia of theory in counseling and psychotherapy*, (Vol. 2, pp. 946–950). Thousand Oaks, CA: Sage.

Gergen, K. (1985). The social constructionist movement in modern psychology. *American Psychologist, 40,* 266–275.

Gergen, K. (1991). *The saturated self.* New York: Basic Books.

Gergen, K. (1999). *An invitation to social construction.* Thousand Oaks, CA: Sage.

***Gingerich, W. J., & Peterson, L. T.** (2013). Effectiveness of solution-focused brief therapy: A systematic qualitative review of controlled outcome studies. *Research on Social Work Practice, 23*(3), 266–283.

***Guterman, J. T.** (2013). *Mastering the art of solution-focused counseling* (2nd ed.). Alexandria, VA: American Counseling Association.

Hoyt, M. F. (2009). *Brief psychotherapies: Principles and practices.* Phoenix, AZ: Zeig, Tucker & Theisen, Inc.

Hoyt, M. F. (2011). Brief psychotherapies. In S. B. Messer & A. S. Gurman (Eds.), *Essential psychotherapies: Theory and practice* (3rd ed., pp. 387–425). New York: Guilford Press.

Hoyt, M. F. (2015). Brief therapy. In E. Neukrug (Ed.), *The Sage encyclopedia of theory in counseling and psychotherapy*, (Vol. 1, pp. 144–147). Thousand Oaks, CA: Sage.

Lee, M. Y., Sebold, J., & Uken, A. (2003). *Solution-focused treatment of domestic violence offenders: Accountability for change.* New York: Oxford University Press.

Lipchik, E. (2002). *Beyond technique in solution-focused therapy: Working with emotion and the therapeutic relationship.* New York: Guilford Press.

***Madigan, S.** (2011). *Narrative therapy.* Washington, DC: American Psychological Association.

Maisel, R., Epston, D., & Borden, A. (2004). *Biting the hand that starves you: Inspiring resistance to anorexia/bulimia.* New York: Norton.

McKenzie, W., & Monk, G. (1997). Learning and teaching narrative ideas. In G. Monk, J. Winslade, K. Crocket, & D. Epston (Eds.), *Narrative therapy in practice: The archaeology of hope* (pp. 82–117). San Francisco: Jossey-Bass.

***Metcalf, L.** (1998). *Solution-focused group therapy: Ideas for groups in private practice, schools, agencies and treatment programs.* New York: The Free Press.

Metcalf, L. (2001). Solution focused therapy. In R. J. Corsini (Ed.), *Handbook of innovative therapy* (2nd ed., pp. 647–659). New York: Wiley.

Miller, S. D., Hubble, M. A., & Duncan, B. L. (Eds.). (1996). *Handbook of solution-focused brief therapy.* San Francisco: Jossey-Bass.

Monk, G. (1997). How narrative therapy works. In G. Monk, J. Winslade, K. Crocket, & D. Epston (Eds.), *Narrative therapy in practice: The archaeology of hope* (pp. 3–31). San Francisco: Jossey-Bass.

***Monk, G., Winslade, J., Crocket, K., & Epston, D.** (Eds.). (1997). *Narrative therapy in practice: The archaeology of hope.* San Francisco: Jossey-Bass.

***Murphy, J. J.** (2013). *Conducting student-driven interviews: Practical strategies for increasing student involvement and addressing behavior problems.* New York: Routledge.

***Murphy, J.** (2015). *Solution-focused counseling in schools* (3rd ed.). Alexandria, VA: American Counseling Association.

Neukrug, E. (2016). *The world of the counselor: An introduction to the counseling profession* (5th ed.). Boston, MA: Cengage Learning.

Nylund, D., & Thomas, J. (1994). The economics of narrative. *The Family Therapy Networker, 18*(6), 38–39.

O'Hanlon, W. H. (1994). The third wave: The promise of narrative. *The Family Therapy Networker, 18*(6), 19–26, 28–29.

O'Hanlon, W. H. (1999). *Do one thing different.* New York: HarperCollins.

***O'Hanlon, W. H., & Weiner-Davis, M.** (2003). *In search of solutions: A new direction in psychotherapy* (Rev. ed.). New York: Norton.

Prochaska, J. O., & Norcross, J. C. (2014). *Systems of psychotherapy: A transtheoretical analysis* (8th ed.). Belmont, CA: Brooks/Cole, Cengage Learning.

Rice, R. (2015). Narrative therapy. In E. Neukrug (Ed.), *The Sage encyclopedia of theory in counseling and psychotherapy*, (Vol. 2, pp. 695–700). Thousand Oaks, CA: Sage.

***Sklare, G. B.** (2005). *Brief counseling that works: A solution-focused approach for school counselors and administrators* (2nd ed.). Thousand Oaks, CA: Corwin Press.

***Walter, J. L., & Peller, J. E.** (1992). *Becoming solution-focused in brief therapy.* New York: Brunner/Mazel.

***Walter, J. L., & Peller, J. E.** (1996). Rethinking our assumptions: Assuming anew in a postmodern world. In S. D. Miller, M. A. Hubble, & B. L. Duncan (Eds.), *Handbook of solution-focused brief therapy* (pp. 9–26). San Francisco: Jossey-Bass.

***Walter, J. L., & Peller, J. E.** (2000). *Recreating brief therapy: Preferences and possibilities.* New York: Norton.

Weiner-Davis, M., De Shazer, S., & Gingerich, W. (1987). Using pre-treatment change to construct a therapeutic solution. *Journal of Marital and Family Therapy, 13*(4), 359–363.

Weishaar, M. E. (1993). *Aaron T. Beck.* London: Sage.

White, M. (1989). The externalizing of the problem in the reauthoring of lives and relationships. In *Selected Papers, Dulwich Centre Newsletter.* Adelaide, South Australia: Dulwich Centre.

White, M. (1992). Deconstruction and therapy. In *Experience, contradiction, narrative, and imagination: Selected papers of David Epston and Michael White, 1989–1991* (pp. 109–151). Adelaide, South Australia: Dulwich Centre.

White, M. (1995). *Reauthoring lives: Interviews and essays.* Adelaide, South Australia: Dulwich Centre.

White, M. (1997). *Narrative of therapists' lives.* Adelaide, South Australia: Dulwich Centre.

***White, M.** (2007). *Maps of narrative practice.* New York: Norton.

***White, M., & Epston, D.** (1990). *Narrative means to therapeutic ends.* New York: Norton.

***Winslade, J., Crocket, K., & Monk, G.** (1997). The therapeutic relationship. In G. Monk, J. Winslade, K. Crocket, & D. Epston (Eds.), *Narrative therapy in practice: The archaeology of hope* (pp. 53–81), San Francisco: Jossey-Bass.

***Winslade, J., & Monk, G.** (2007). *Narrative counseling in schools* (2nd ed.). Thousand Oaks, CA: Corwin Press (Sage).

Chapter 14

Family Systems Theory

Adler, A. (1927). *Understanding human nature* (W. B. Wolfe, Trans.). New York: Fawcett.

American Psychiatric Association. (2013). *Diagnostic and statistical manual of mental disorders* (5th ed.). Washington, DC: Author.

Andersen, T. (1987). The reflecting team: Dialogue and metadialogue in clinical work. *Family Process, 26*(4), 415–428.

***Andersen, T.** (1991). *The reflecting team: Dialogues and dialogues about the dialogues.* New York: Norton.

Anderson, H. (1993). On a roller coaster: A collaborative language system approach to therapy. In S. Friedman (Ed.), *The new language of change* (pp. 324–344). New York: Guilford Press.

***Anderson, H., & Goolishian, H.** (1992). The client is the expert: A not-knowing approach to therapy. In S. McNamee & K. J. Gergen (Eds.), *Therapy as social construction* (pp. 25–39). Newbury Park, CA: Sage.

***Becvar, D. S., & Becvar, R. J.** (2012). *Family therapy: A systemic integration* (8th ed.). Boston, MA: Allyn & Bacon (Pearson).

Bitter, J. R. (2009). The mistaken notions of adults with children. *Journal of Individual Psychology, 65*(4), 135–155.

***Bitter, J. R.** (2014). *Theory and practice of family therapy and counseling* (2nd ed.) Belmont, CA: Brooks/Cole, Cengage Learning.

Bitter, J. R., Roberts, A., & Sonstegard, M. A. (2002). Adlerian family therapy. In J. Carlson & D. Kjos (Eds.), *Theories and strategies of family therapy* (pp. 41–79). Boston: Allyn & Bacon.

***Bowen, M.** (1978). *Family therapy in clinical practice.* New York: Jason Aronson.

***Breunlin, D. C., Schwartz, R. C., & Mackune-Karrer, B.** (1997). *Metaframeworks: Transcending the models of family therapy* (Rev. ed.). San Francisco: Jossey-Bass.

*Carlson, J., Sperry, L., & Lewis, J. A. (2005). *Family therapy techniques: Integrating and tailoring treatment.* Belmont, CA: Brooks/Cole, Cengage Learning.

*Christensen, O. C. (Ed.). (2004). *Adlerian family counseling* (3rd ed.). Minneapolis, MN: Educational Media Corp. (Original work published 1983)

De Shazer, S. (1985). *Keys to solutions in brief therapy.* New York: Norton.

Doherty, W. J., & McDaniel, S. H. (2010). *Family therapy.* Washington, DC: American Psychological Association.

Dreikurs, R. (1950). The immediate purpose of children's misbehavior, its recognition and correction. *Internationale Zeitschrift fur Individual-psychologie, 19,* 70–87.

Dreikurs, R. (1973). Counseling for family adjustment. In R. Dreikurs, *Psychodynamics, psychotherapy, and counseling* (Rev. ed.). Chicago: Alfred Adler Institute. (Original work published 1949)

Dreikers, R. (1997). Holistic medicine. *Individual Psychology, 53*(2), 127–205.

Epston, D., & White, M. (1992). Consulting your consultants: The documentation of alternative knowledges. In *Experience, contradiction, narrative and imagination: Selected papers of David Epston and Michael White, 1989–1991* (pp. 11–26). Adelaide, South Australia: Dulwich Centre.

*Gladding, S. T. (2014). *Family therapy: History, theory, and practice* (6th ed.). Upper Saddle River, NJ: Merrill/Prentice-Hall.

*Goldenberg, H., & Goldenberg, I. (2013). *Family therapy: An overview* (8th ed.). Belmont, CA: Brooks/Cole, Cengage Learning.

Gottman, J. M. (1999). *The marriage clinic: A scientifically based marital therapy.* New York: Norton.

Haley, J. (1963). *Strategies of psychotherapy.* New York: Grune & Stratton.

Haley, J. (1976). *Problem-solving therapy: New strategies for effective family therapy.* San Francisco: Jossey-Bass.

Haley, J. (1984). *Ordeal therapy.* San Francisco: Jossey-Bass.

*Haley, J., & Richeport-Haley, M. (2003). *The art of strategic therapy.* New York: Brunner Routledge.

*Hanna, S. M. (2007). *The practice of family therapy: Key elements across models* (4th ed.). Belmont, CA: Brooks/Cole, Cengage Learning.

*Kerr, M. E., & Bowen, M. (1988). *Family evaluation: An approach based on Bowen theory.* New York: Norton.

Lambert, S. F., Carmichael, A., & Williams, L. (2016). Guidelines in counseling families. In I. Marini & M. A. Stebnicki (Eds.), *The professional counselor's desk reference* (2nd ed., pp. 351–356). New York: Springer.

*Luepnitz, D. A. (2002). *The family interpreted: Feminist theory in clinical practice.* New York: Basic Books. (Original work published 1988)

*Madanes, C. (1981). *Strategic family therapy.* San Francisco: Jossey-Bass.

*McGoldrick, M., Anderson, C., & Walsh, F. (1991). *Women in families: A framework for family therapy.* New York: Norton.

*McGoldrick, M., Carter, B., & Garcia-Preto, N. (Ed.). (2011). *The expanded family life cycle: Individual, family and social perspectives* (4th ed.). Boston: Allyn & Bacon (Pearson).

*McGoldrick, M., Gerson, R., & Petry, S. (2008). *Genograms: Assessment and intervention* (3rd ed.). New York: Norton.

*McGoldrick, M., Giordano, J., & Garcia-Preto, N. (Eds.). (2005). *Ethnicity and family therapy* (3rd ed.). New York: Guilford Press.

*McGoldrick, M., & Hardy, K. V. (2008). *Revisioning family therapy: Race, culture, and gender in clinical practice* (2nd ed.). New York: Guilford Press.

*Minuchin, S. (1974). *Families and family therapy.* Cambridge, MA: Harvard University Press.

*Minuchin, S., & Fishman, H. C. (1981). *Family therapy techniques.* Cambridge, MA: Harvard University Press.

*Nichols, M. P. (2013). *The essentials of family therapy* (6th ed.). Boston, MA: Pearson.

*Nichols, M. P. (with Schwartz, R. C.). (2013). *Family therapy: Concepts and methods* (10th ed.). Upper Saddle River, NJ: Prentice-Hall.

Richeport-Haley, M., & Carlson, J. (2010). *Jay Haley revisited.* New York: Routledge Books.

Rogers, C. R. (1980). *A way of being.* Boston: Houghton Mifflin.

*Satir, V. (1983). *Conjoint family therapy* (3rd ed.). Palo Alto, CA: Science and Behavior Books.

Satir, V. (1988). *The new peoplemaking.* Palo Alto, CA: Science and Behavior Books.

Satir, V., & Baldwin, M. (1983). *Satir: Step-by-step.* Palo Alto, CA: Science and Behavior Books.

*Satir, V. M., Banmen, J., Gerber, J., & Gomori, M. (1991). *The Satir model: Family therapy and beyond.* Palo Alto, CA: Science and Behavior Books.

Satir, V. M., & Bitter, J. R. (2000). The therapist and family therapy: Satir's human validation process model. In A. M. Horne (Ed.), *Family counseling and therapy* (3rd ed., pp. 62–101). Itasca, IL: F. E. Peacock.

Schwartz, R. (1995). *Internal family systems therapy.* New York: Guilford Press.

Selvini Palazzoli, M., Boscolo, L., Cecchin, F. G., & Prata, G. (1978). *Paradox and counterparadox.* Northvale, NJ: Aronson.

West, J. D., Bubenzer, D. L., & Bitter, J. R. (Eds.). (1998). *Social construction in couple and family counseling.* Alexandria, VA: ACA/IAMFC.

White, M. (1997). *Narratives of therapists' lives.* Adelaide, South Australia: Dulwich Centre.

*White, M. (2007). *Maps of narrative practice.* New York: Norton.

*White, M., & Epston, D. (1990). *Narrative means to therapeutic ends.* New York: Norton. (Original title *Linguistic means to therapeutic ends*)

Wilcoxon, S. A., Remley, T. P., & Gladding, S. T. (2012). *Ethical, legal, and professional issues in the practice of marriage and family therapy* (5th ed.). Upper Saddle River, NJ: Merrill/ Prentice-Hall (Pearson).

Chapter 15

An Integrative Perspective

*Bohart, A. C., & Tallman, K. (2010). Clients: The neglected common factor in psychotherapy. In B. L. Duncan, S. D. Miller, B. E. Wampold, & M. A. Hubble (Eds.), *The heart and soul of change: Delivering what works in therapy* (2nd ed., pp. 83–111). Washington, DC: American Psychological Association.

Bohart, A. C., & Wade, A. G. (2013). The client in psychotherapy. In M. J. Lambert (Ed.), *Bergin and Garfield's handbook of psychotherapy and behavior change* (6th ed., pp. 219–257). Hoboken, NJ: Wiley.

*Cashwell, C. S., & Young, J. S. (2011). *Integrating spirituality and religion into counseling: A guide to competent practice* (2nd ed.). Alexandria, VA: American Counseling Association.

Comas-Diaz, L. (2014). Multicultural theories of psychotherapy. In D. Wedding & R. J. Corsini (Eds.), *Current psychotherapies*

(10th ed., pp. 533-567). Belmont, CA: Brooks/Cole, Cengage Learning.

***Corey, G.** (2013a). *The art of integrative counseling* (3rd ed.). Belmont, CA: Brooks/Cole, Cengage Learning.

***Corey, G.** (2013b). *Case approach to counseling and psychotherapy* (8th ed.). Belmont, CA: Brooks/Cole, Cengage Learning.

***Corey, G.** (with Haynes, R.). (2013c). *DVD for integrative counseling: The case of Ruth and lecturettes.* Belmont, CA: Brooks/Cole, Cengage Learning.

Corey, G. (2015). Eclecticism. In E. Neukrug (Ed.), *The Sage encyclopedia of theory in counseling and psychotherapy* (Vol. 1, pp. 307-310). Thousand Oaks, CA: Sage.

Delaney, H. D., Miller, W. R., & Bisono, A. M. (2007). Religiosity and spirituality among psychologists: A survey of clinician members of the American Psychological Association. *Professional Psychology: Research and Practice, 38*(5), 538-546.

Duncan, B. (2014). *On becoming a better therapist: Evidence based practice one client at a time* (2nd ed.). Washington, DC: American Psychological Association.

***Duncan, B. L., Miller, S. D., & Sparks, J. A.** (2004). *The heroic client: A revolutionary way to improve effectiveness through client-directed, outcome-informed therapy.* San Francisco: Jossey-Bass.

***Duncan, B. L., Miller, S. D., Wampold, B. E., & Hubble, M. A.** (Eds.). (2010). *The heart and soul of change: Delivering what works in therapy* (2nd ed.). Washington DC: American Psychological Association.

***Elkins, D. N.** (2016). *The human elements of psychotherapy: A nonmedical model of emotional healing.* Washington, DC: American Psychological Association.

***Frame, M. W.** (2003). *Integrating religion and spirituality into counseling: A comprehensive approach.* Belmont, CA: Brooks/Cole, Cengage Learning.

***Goldried, M. R., Glass, C. R., & Arnkoff, D. B.** (2011). Integrative approaches to psychotherapy. In J. C. Norcross, G. R. Vandenbos, & D. K. Freedheim (Eds.), *History of psychotherapy* (2nd ed., pp. 269-296). Washington, DC: American Psychological Association.

Goldfried, M. R., Pachankis, J. E., & Bell, A. C. (2005). A history of psychotherapy integration. In J. C. Norcross & M. R. Goldfried (Eds.), *Handbook of psychotherapy integration* (2nd ed., pp. 24-60). New York: Oxford University Press.

***Greenberg, L. S.** (2011). *Emotion-focused therapy.* Washington, DC: American Psychological Association.

Hoyt, M. F. (2015). Brief therapy. In E. Neukrug (Ed.), *The Sage encyclopedia of theory in counseling and psychotherapy* (Vol. 1, pp. 144-147). Thousand Oaks, CA: Sage.

***Hubble, M. A., Duncan, B. L., Miller, S. D., & Wampold, B. E.** (2010). Introduction. In B. L. Duncan, S. D. Miller, B. E. Wampold, & M. A. Hubble (Eds.), *The heart and soul of change: Delivering what works in therapy* (2nd ed., pp. 23-46). Washington DC: American Psychological Association.

Johnson, R. (2013). *Spirituality in counseling and psychotherapy: An integrative approach that empowers clients.* Hoboken, NJ: Wiley.

Lambert, M. J. (2011). Psychotherapy research and its achievements. In J. C. Norcross, G. R. Vandenbos, & D. K. Freedheim (Eds.), *History of psychotherapy* (2nd ed., pp. 299-332). Washington, DC: American Psychological Association.

Lazarus, A. A. (2008a). Multimodal behavior therapy. In W. O'Donohue & J. E. Fisher (Eds.), *Cognitive behavior therapy: Applying empirically supported techniques in your practice* (2nd ed., pp. 342-346). Hoboken, NJ: Wiley.

Lazarus, A. A. (2008b). Technical eclecticism and multimodal therapy. In J. L. Lebow (Ed.), *Twenty-first century psychotherapies* (pp. 424-452). Hoboken, NJ: Wiley.

Miller, S. D. (2011). *Psychometrics of the ORS and SRS. Results from RCTs and meta-analyses of Routine Outcome Monitoring & Feedback. The available evidence.* http://www. slideshare.net/scottdmiller/measures-and-feedback-january-2011.

Miller, S. D., Hubble, M. A., & Seidel, J. (2015). Feedback-informed treatment. In E. Neukrug (Ed.), *The Sage encyclopedia of theory in counseling and psychotherapy* (Vol. 1, pp. 401-403). Thousand Oaks, CA: Sage.

Neukrug, E. (Ed.). (2015). *The Sage encyclopedia of theory in counseling and psychotherapy* (Vols. 1 & 2). Thousand Oaks, CA: Sage.

Neukrug, E. (2016). *The world of the counselor: An introduction to the counseling profession* (5th ed.). Boston, MA: Cengage Learning.

Norcross, J. C. (2005). A primer on psychotherapy integration. In J. C. Norcross & M. R. Goldfried (Eds.), *Handbook of psychotherapy integration* (2nd, ed., pp. 3-23). New York: Oxford University Press.

***Norcross, J. C.** (2011). (Ed.). *Psychotherapy relationships that work: Evidence-based responsiveness* (2nd ed.). New York: Oxford University Press.

***Norcross, J. C., & Beutler, L. E.** (2014). Integrative psychotherapies. In D. Wedding & R. J. Corsini (Eds.), *Current psychotherapies* (10th ed., pp. 499-532). Belmont, CA: Brooks/Cole, Cengage Learning.

***Norcross, J. C., & Goldfried, M. R.** (Eds.). (2005). *Handbook of psychotherapy integration* (2nd ed.). New York: Oxford University Press.

Norcross, J. C., Karpiak, C. P., & Lister, K. M. (2005). What's an integrationist? A study of self-identified integrative and (occasionally) eclectic psychologists. *Journal of Clinical Psychology, 61,* 1587-1594.

Norcross, J. C., Krebs, P. M., & Prochaska, J. O. (2011). Stages of change. In J. C. Norcross (Ed.), *Psychotherapy relationships that work: Evidence-based responsiveness* (2nd ed., pp. 279-300). New York: Oxford University Press.

Norcross, J. C., & Lambert, M. J. (2011). Evidence-based therapy relationships. In J. C. Norcross (Ed.), *Psychotherapy relationships that work: Evidence-based responsiveness* (2nd ed., pp. 3-21). New York: Oxford University Press.

Norcross, J. C., Pfund, R. A., & Prochaska, J. O. (2013). Psychotherapy in 2022: A Delphi poll on its future. *Professional Psychology: Research and Practice, 44*(5), 363-370.

Norcross, J. C., & Wampold, B. E. (2011a). Evidence-based therapy relationships: Research conclusions and clinical practices. In J. C. Norcross (Ed.), *Psychotherapy relationships that work: Evidence-based responsiveness* (2nd ed., pp. 423-430). New York: Oxford University Press.

Norcross, J. C., & Wampold, J. C. (2011b). What works for whom: Tailoring psychotherapy to the person. *Journal of Clinical Psychology, 67*(2), 127-132.

***Prochaska, J. O., & Norcross, J. C.** (2014). *Systems of psychotherapy: A transtheoretical analysis* (8th ed.). Belmont, CA: Brooks/Cole, Cengage Learning.

Psychotherapy Networker. (2007). The top 10: The most influential therapists of the past quarter-century. *Psychotherapy Networker, 31*(2), 24-37.

*__Segal, Z. V., Williams, J. M. G., & Teasdale, J. D.__ (2013). *Mindfulness-based cognitive therapy for depression* (2nd ed.). New York: Guilford Press.

Smith, M. L., Glass, G. V., & Miller, T. I. (1980). *The benefits of psychotherapy.* Baltimore: Johns Hopkins University Press.

Stricker, G. (2010). *Psychotherapy integration.* Washington, DC: American Psychological Association.

*__Wampold, B. E.__ (2001). *The great psychotherapy debate: Models, methods, and findings.* Hillsdale, NJ: Erlbaum.

Wampold, B. E. (2010). The research evidence for the common factors models: A historical situated perspective. In B. L. Duncan, S. D. Miller, B. E. Wampold, & M. A. Hubble (Eds.), *The heart and soul of change: Delivering what works in therapy* (2nd ed., pp. 49–81). Washington DC: American Psychological Association.

Worthington, E. L., Jr. (2011). Integration of spirituality and religion into psychotherapy. In J. C. Norcross, G. R. Vandenbos, & D. K. Freedheim (Eds.), *History of psychotherapy* (2nd ed., pp. 533–544). Washington, DC: American Psychological Association.

Young, J. S., & Cashwell, C. S. (2011a). Integrating spirituality and religion into counseling: An introduction. In C. S. Cashwell & J. S. Young (Eds.), *Integrating spirituality and religion into counseling: A guide to competent practice* (2nd ed., pp. 1–24). Alexandria, VA: American Counseling Association.

Young, J. S., & Cashwell, C. S. (2011b). Where do we go from here? In C. S. Cashwell & J. S. Young (Eds.), *Integrating spirituality and religion into counseling: A guide to competent practice* (2nd ed., pp. 279–289). Alexandria, VA: American Counseling Association.

Young, J. S., Wiggins-Frame, M., & Cashwell, C. S. (2007). Spirituality and counselor competence: A national survey of American Counseling Association members. *Journal of Counseling and Development, 85*(1), 47–52.

Name Index

Subject Index